The founding of a just relation of the white and dark races is not our problem alone. It is described as the most important business of this century. It is a world problem...Aggression against one race is aggression against all...there is no quarrel with the settlers: the objection is to the *system* – analogous to slavery – by which the natives are deprived of their livelihood with their hunting-grounds, thus compelled to work for the settlers and then prevented from selling their labour.

Mary Bennett,
The Australian Aboriginal as a Human Being, 1930

I think the country at large needs training in just ideas...

Mary Bennett to William Grayden, 23 April 1959

JUST RELATIONS

The Story of Mary Bennett's Crusade for Aboriginal Rights

Alison Holland

U W
A P
SCHOLARLY

First published in 2015 by
UWA Publishing
Crawley, Western Australia 6009
www.uwap.uwa.edu.au

THE UNIVERSITY OF
WESTERN
AUSTRALIA

National Library of Australia Cataloguing-in-Publication entry

Holland, Alison, author.

Just relations : the story of Mary Bennett's crusade for
Aboriginal rights / Alison Holland.

ISBN: 9781742586878 (paperback)

Bennett, M. M. (Mary Montgomerie)

Women civil rights workers—Australia—Biography.

Aboriginal Australians—Legal status, laws, etc.—History.

323.092

Typeset in Bembo by J&M Typesetting
Printed by Lightning Source

For Rob

CONTENTS

ACKNOWLEDGEMENTS

As in any project of this kind I have accumulated many debts on the way to bringing it to fruition. I particularly want to thank all those people I interviewed many years ago now, some of whom are no longer with us, in an attempt to trace Mary Bennett's impact on the post-war Aboriginal rights movement. Included are key members of the Council for Aboriginal Rights in Victoria; Shirley Andrews, Barry Christophers, Henry Wardlaw and Pauline Pickford, who worked so hard to keep the memory of Bennett alive and preserve her papers from destruction by the state. Other activists who generously shared their memories of Bennett were Faith Bandler, Alick Jackomos, Len Fox, Mona Brand, Alistair Campbell and Jack and Jean Horner. I would also like to thank Rosemary Duguid and Nancy Barnes, who generously shared their thoughts and memories of Charles Duguid, one of Mary's confidantes and friends.

Also incredibly generous was Dorita Thomson, wife of Donald Thomson, who posted correspondence to me between Donald and his friend Edith Ransom, an active feminist from his home state of Tasmania, which provided a deeply personal insight into his sense of desperation about Aboriginal policy on the eve of World War II. This correspondence graphically illustrated his hopes for a new-style of native administration in Australia in the late 1930s and his subsequent feeling of bitterness about the directions taken by the policymakers of the day.

There have been many librarians and archivists around the country and in England who have helped me track down papers and archives relevant to Bennett's story. I would like to thank, in particular, Clare Brown from Rhodes House Library in Oxford, Lindy Allen from the Museum of Victoria and Kate Butler from the Hull History Centre in England. Kate undertook research, from a distance, in the final stages of the book as I tried to track down whether Bennett's bequest to the Mission to Seafarers eventuated. The women of the Melbourne branch of the Woman's Christian Temperance Union were also extremely helpful, accommodating and prompt in responding to my research queries. A very special thank you, too, to Kaylene Heard whose last-minute, long-distance research for me was critical in the final stages of the book and for helping me to unravel the final years of Bennett's life.

I would like to thank Elizabeth Roberts, Mary Bennett's niece, who was the only surviving relative I was able to trace. I am also grateful to Rob Douglas, who shared what he knew of his father Wilf Douglas' relationship with Bennett and particularly his role, as benefactor of her papers, in the tussle over them after her death.

There are many colleagues that I would like to thank for their interest in and input to this project over the years. Intellectually, I am indebted to the handful of scholars who have occupied similar terrain and from whose research I have learnt much: C. D. Rowley, Raymond Evans, Henry Reynolds, Bain Attwood, Russell McGregor, Tim Rowse, Geoffrey Grey, Rani Kerin, Fiona Paisley, Lisa Ford, Anna Haebich, Catherine Bishop and Peter Biskup. Their collective works have been very important to my sense of early to mid–twentieth century Aboriginal affairs. Pat Jacobs' biography of A. O. Neville was also immensely helpful as I tried to map the battle between him and Bennett. I would also like to thank Valerie Munt, with whom I had a wonderful exchange about Jessie Street in the final stages of writing the book.

I was also fortunate to have a brief conversation with Professor Geoffrey Bolton in the final phases of writing the book. He pointed me in the direction of a file held in the Noel Butlin archives in Canberra that he and Jim Gibney had collated on Bennett in the preparation of their Australian Dictionary of Biography entry on her in the late 1970s. In this correspondence was a letter from Geoff in which he queried the value of such an undertaking because of the scattered nature of the material. He also wondered whether her career was important enough to warrant inclusion in the national dictionary. I found the entry he and Jim wrote most useful. I hope he finds my book, produced from the scattered material, validation of his decision, and mine, to push on with her.

There is also a handful of feminist historians in Australia and beyond whose work and/or whose interest and encouragement of me has been important, including Ann McGrath, Lyndall Ryan, Marilyn Lake, Victoria Haskins, Fiona Probyn-Rapsey, Ann Curthoys, Margaret Jacobs, Heather Radi, Peggy Pascoe, Susan Pedersen, Antoinette Burton, Lisa Featherstone, Anne O'Brien, Angela Woollacott, Pat Grimshaw and Barbara Brookes. I have to thank Sue Taffe, in particular, for her words of encouragement and enthusiasm about my work on Bennett. I am eternally grateful to Rae Frances and Bruce Scates who, many years ago, gave me somewhere to stay on my first trip to Western Australia. Thanks, also, to Kate Auty for sharing her thoughts with me about Bennett and the legacies of Aboriginal affairs in the west.

Special thanks to Jill Roe for appointing me to Macquarie University to teach Aboriginal History in the first place and a huge thanks to Mary Spongberg whose mentorship and unending support has meant an enormous amount to me over the years. While I benefited from discussion of draft chapters in my departmental research reading group, special thanks go to Margaret Sampson, Mark Hearn and Julia Miller for reading and commenting on drafts. I am grateful to the Faculty of Arts at Macquarie University for a subsidy which supported the book's publication.

A huge thank you to Terri-ann White, Director of UWA Publishing, for finally agreeing to take the book on. By the time Terri-ann sent confirmation of a contract I had sent the book proposal to a number of publishers over a two year period. A key concern was length. Terri-ann was also concerned about its scholarly nature. As she put it, 'scholarly is the crisis end of publishing'. I want to particularly thank Sam Trafford, the editor, whom I never met. We communicated in a strictly business-like way, between commas, references and 'check this and that'. If I do meet Sam I will give her a big hug, along with Terri-ann, of course.

The love and support of my family has underwritten this project – and me – from beginning to end. This has provided a much needed port in the storm for myself and my children, for which we are blessed. To Louis and Rose, treasures of my heart, when you read this perhaps it will help you understand my distractions, lapses and irritating commitment to the task from time to time. I hope it explains my particular interest in Aboriginal history and why I couldn't just 'forget about the book' despite your amazing selves and your occasional pleas. Rest assured your hugs and love fuelled every page.

Lastly, to Rob. I know you believe in actions speaking louder than words but you know that I love words! A mere 'thank you' seems totally inadequate for your endless patience, tolerance and belief. Suffice to say that your optimism and encouragement, as well as your long-term support, has been critical to the book's completion.

ABBREVIATIONS AND ACRONYMS

AAAA	Australian Aboriginal Amelioration Association
AAL	Australian Aborigines' League
AFA	Aborigines' Friends Association
AFWV	Australian Federation of Women Voters
ALP	Australian Labor Party
ALRC	Australian Law Reform Commission
Anti-Slavery Society	
	Anti-Slavery and Aborigines' Protection Society
APA	Aborigines' Progressive Association
APL	Aborigines' Protection League
APNR	Association for the Protection of Native Races
ASIO	Australian Security Intelligence Organisation
BCL	British Commonwealth League
CAR	Council for Aboriginal Rights
CDNR	Committee for the Defence of Native Rights
FCAA	Federal Council for Aboriginal Advancement
ILO	International Labour Organization
IWD	International Women's League
League for Aboriginal Women	
	League for the Protection and Advancement of Aboriginal and Half-Caste Women
Sub-Commission for Minorities	
	Sub-Commission for the Prevention of Discrimination and the Protection of Minorities (UN)
The 1937 Canberra conference	
	Initial Conference of Commonwealth and State Aboriginal Authorities, 21–23 April, 1937
UAM	United Aborigines' Mission
UN	United Nations
UNESCO	United Nations Educational, Scientific and Cultural Organisation
WCTU	Woman's Christian Temperance Union
Women's International League	
	Women's International League for Peace and Freedom
WNPA	Woman's Non-Party Association

NOTE ON TERMINOLOGY

The Dalleburra

Other names and dialect names: Yirandali, Dalebura, Dal-leyburra, Irendely, Pooroga, Yerrundulli, Yerrunthully
Location: Flinders River, Hughenden, Lammermoor, Landsborough Creek, Torrens Creek, Tower Hill Creek, Winton[1]

Critical to Mary Bennett's story is the group of Aboriginal people on whose country her father settled in the early 1860s in Queensland's north. Bennett's father named the tribe the Dalleburra and, as the above reference attests, it has been recorded thus ever since as a world language. It represents Robert Christison's translation of what he heard when he first made contact, catching 'at a word here and there', as Bennett put it.[2] She described Dalleburra country as on Tower Hill Creek at the head of the Thomson River and between Hughenden and Muttaburra. Bennett's family also recorded the group as Yirandali. Dalleburra was one of the four tribes which comprised the Yirandali language group.

Whereas Yirandali features on David Horton's Indigenous language map, Dalleburra does not. There is a group to the south of Yirandali identified as Dharawala. This group is associated with the Barcoo River and their country is around present-day Blackall, a couple of hundred kilometres to the south of Muttaburra. Not only are Dalleburra and Dharawala similar sounding, they appear to occupy similar country. The key river in the Lammermoor tablelands is the Thomson, which meets the Barcoo in the south. Both rivers share the same tributaries – the Torrens, Landsborough and Towerhill creeks – all of which Bennett mentions as significant to the Dalleburra. Notably, none of the language groups which Bennett identifies as surrounding the Dalleburra – the Quippenburra in the north, the Muttaburra in the south, the Munggoobra in the east and the Goamulgo in the west – are represented on Horton's map.

The Wongutha and Wongkai

Wongutha or Wongatha is the language of the large group of Aboriginal people of the northeastern goldfields in Western Australia. Their tribal boundary borders the regions of Coolgardie, southeast Wiluna and the western half of the Great Victoria Desert. Some of the people on

Mt Margaret Mission referred to themselves as 'Wongi' or 'Wangai'. Bennett used 'Wangkai' or 'Wongkai' to refer to the goldfields people among whom she worked after World War II. This included the desert people from the Warburton Ranges.

Commonly Used Words and Phrases

Throughout this book there are words and phrases used which relate to outmoded and offensive racialising discourses of the past. The two most frequently used are full-blood and half-caste. These terms relate to the connection between blood and race which, by the twentieth century, had preoccupied western thought for hundreds of years. They were readily adopted in Australia from the 1830s and were subsequently enshrined in legislation controlling Aborigines; however, they had particular resonance in the racial imaginary of the first half of the twentieth century. The connection between blood and race was greatly facilitated by the creation of a biochemical race index following World War I. This was thought to provide a scientific means of racially classifying people by blood type. This was particularly useful in Australia where scientists and administrators looked to science to solve the 'Aboriginal problem'. In the blood tests carried out amongst Aboriginal populations in the 1920s, scientists thought they'd found an empirical base for their view that the 'pure' race of full-blood Aboriginal people was dying out and being replaced by an allegedly inferior population of half-castes, or Aborigines of mixed descent.[3]

I also use the word native. It is notable that the etymology of this word, like full-blood and half-caste, is closely related to the era of European colonial and imperial expansion. It is used in this book as individuals used it at the time, as both a noun and an adjective. As an adjective it meant 'innate, produced by birth' from the fourteenth century and, from the fifteenth, 'born in a particular place'. As a noun it was applied by European powers to the original inhabitants of non-European lands from the seventeenth century.[4] In Australia it was still being used, in both senses, to refer to Aboriginal people until World War II. Afterwards it was still deployed in a bureaucratic setting. Legislation continued to define natives, and some administrators became native commissioners, following precedent elsewhere in the empire. It is testament to the power and hold of such concepts that even those, like Bennett, who fought against such essentialising terms still had recourse to use them.

Closely related to these words are the phrases 'Aboriginal problem' and 'native question'. Critical to the book is the recovery of a discourse about this problem/question. The phrases were used interchangeably, particularly from the late nineteenth century, to describe a problem the British inherited in colonising lands occupied and owned by indigenous peoples. Closely related to the notion of the white man's burden, the Aboriginal problem/native question generated much heated debate in England and Australia about 'what to do with the blacks', as Mary Bennett put it. In the nineteenth century it was described as 'the greatest moral difficulty of colonization'.[5] In tracing Bennett's and others' efforts to find a solution to this problem, this book charts the changing responses to and dynamics of this question from the late 1920s to the 1960s.

As the foregoing suggests, this book is not the biography of a key twentieth-century humanitarian alone. It is also a study of ideas about race, racial difference, racial destinies, racial discrimination and concepts of racial justice. Recourse to the language used to discuss and think about these ideas in the past has therefore been unavoidable. My inclination was to place quotation marks around the words and phrases wherever they appear in the text because I feared that their constant iteration normalised them. I wanted to demonstrate how contingent they were. However, they occur so frequently in the text that, in the interests of stylistic consistency and fluency, I decided not to do so. I apologise for any offence they may cause and want to emphasise that in using them I don't endorse the connotations of race they embody. As key imaginary significations of European colonial powers, we are still living with their institutional effects.

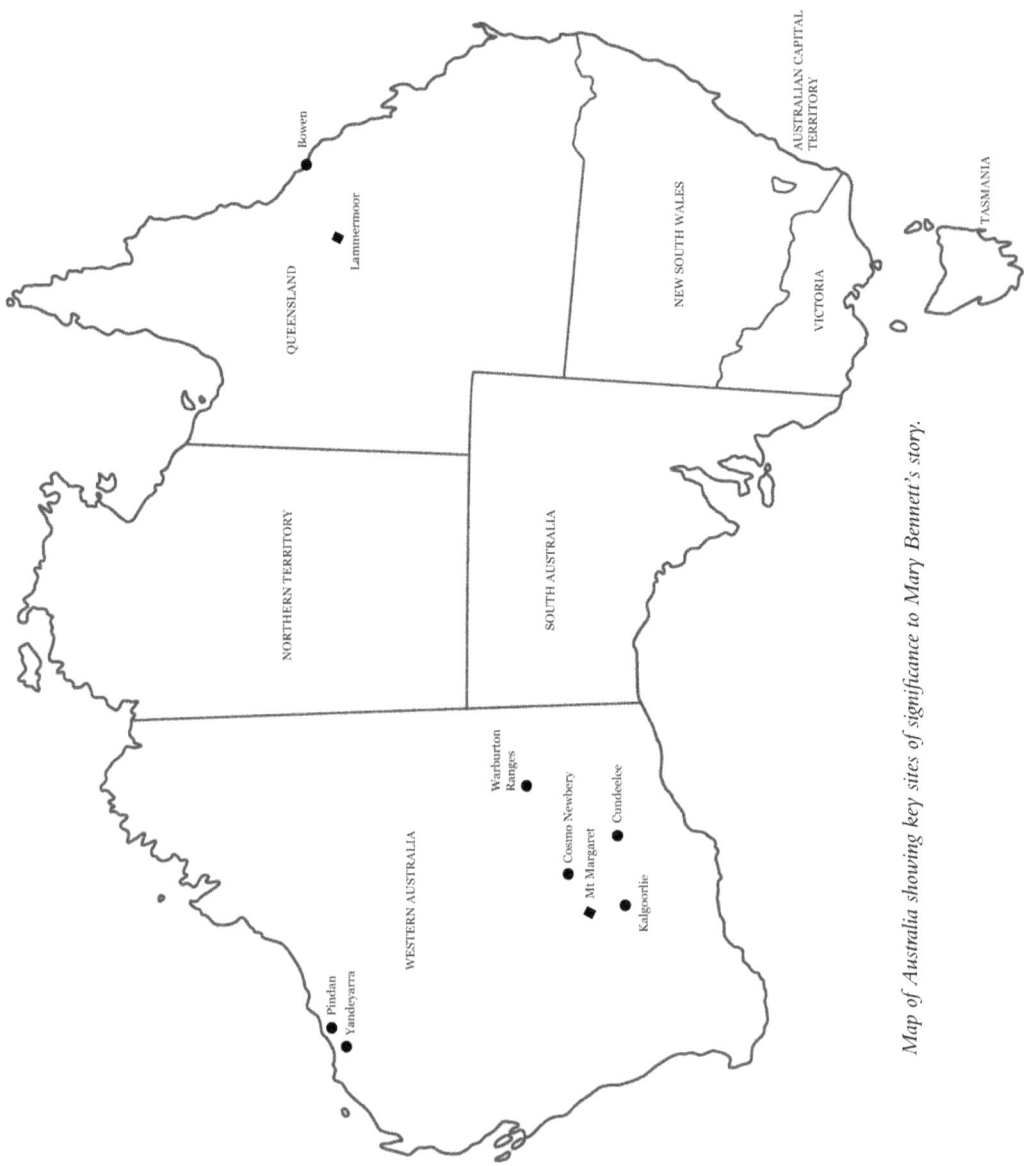

Map of Australia showing key sites of significance to Mary Bennett's story.

PROLOGUE

On 6 October 1961, Mary Bennett, leading advocate for Aboriginal human rights, died in Kalgoorlie hospital aged eighty. At that moment, a close friend of hers, Ada Bromham, was sitting at her kitchen table sorting through her papers, which she described as lining two rooms of the small home from the floor to three-quarters of the way up the walls. She had finished sorting through them when she received the news of Mary's death. Less than an hour later, Bromham heard a knock on the front door. On opening it two suited men representing the Western Australian Crown Law department, carrying large suitcases, barged past her into the house and scooped up as much as they were able, including what she had set aside for herself on the table, leaving only the Hansards.

A battle ensued between the state, Bromham and the Council for Aboriginal Rights, a Victorian-based Aboriginal rights organisation which Bromham was involved with and Bennett had been in close contact and communication with over the previous decade. By the time of her death she had amassed at least 40 years' evidence in defence of Aboriginal human rights. To her friends in the council Bromham exclaimed, 'you could not imagine such a huge collection of material unless [you] had seen it'. In a carefully orchestrated exchange, the state eventually returned the papers to Bromham. Packing them in boxes, she sent them by rail to Melbourne where they were collected by Dr Barry Christophers, then president of the council, who stored them in the garage of his surgery. Just weeks later they were stolen. When Christophers informed the police, no action was taken.

Mary Montgomerie Bennett (1881–1961) – 'Mimi', as she was known to her family – was the eldest daughter of Robert Christison, a Scottish immigrant to Australia who established a pastoral empire – Lammermoor – on Queensland's northern frontier in the 1860s. As her mother disliked living there, Bennett spent most of her life in England. She nonetheless experienced concentrated periods of time on Lammermoor where, when in Australia, the family would return from their southern residences for the winter. After marrying a merchant sea captain, Charles Douglas Bennett, in 1914 she settled in Hertfordshire. When he died, in 1927, she threw herself into the Aboriginal cause, gaining a reputation as a champion of the Aborigines.

In 1930 Bennett returned to Australia to take up the cause on the ground, becoming the first full-time teacher to Aboriginal children in the Great Victoria Desert of Western Australia. It was there that she launched a sustained and scathing critique of the administration of Aborigines in Australia generally and Western Australia in particular. This culminated in a full-scale row with A. O. Neville, the leading Aboriginal affairs bureaucrat in that state. Following a short period of reprieve in London between 1941 and 1950, she returned to Australia to continue her crusade, eventually settling in Kalgoorlie. Two of her closest Aboriginal friends were with her when she died: her ex-pupils Sadie Corner and Gladys Vincent. They later recorded how the Wongutha came from everywhere to attend her funeral, even the camp folk.

Her legacy was being rewritten at the moment of her death as her death notice in the *Kalgoorlie Miner* simply stated:

> Woman Who Worked For Natives Dies
> Mrs M M Bennett Well-Known
> For Assistance to Aborigines

> ...An urge to do something for other people saw her return to Australia where she settled down to devoting her life to the welfare of natives. One of her finest gestures was the donating of a hospital to the Mt Margaret Mission. Mrs Bennett was often seen around Kalgoorlie courthouse where she gave assistance to natives charged with offences.[1]

Welfare worker and philanthropist she certainly was, but she was also one of Australia's leading mid–twentieth century human-rights advocates.

Prologue

This book started with my efforts to retrieve Bennett's papers. I never found a single collection. Rather I found threads in archives around Australia and England, particularly in the papers of fellow humanitarians and advocates for Aboriginal rights. These threads and the tussle over her papers revealed an important part of her story. Bennett's articulation of the need for humane intervention in the lives of Aboriginal people was not hers alone but one she shared with others across the middle years of the twentieth century. Hers had particular resonance for the Australian state, however.

Just Relations is my attempt to pull these threads together. Part biography, it should more rightly be understood as the history of an idea or set of ideas about what constituted justice for Aboriginal people and just relations between Aborigines and non-Aborigines in Australia, which was central to Mary Bennett's life work.

INTRODUCTION

This book gives new meaning to the phrase 'long overdue'. To many in the Australian historical profession Mary Bennett is well known. There is a history prize in her name, and several historians have written about aspects of her life and career. As one of the latter, I had never envisaged writing her biography. What drew me to her were her ideas and her advocacy, and what her story could tell us about mid–twentieth century humanitarian endeavour around what had long been framed the Aboriginal problem in Australia. This was partly conditioned by the moment of our meeting, which was my stumbling upon a communication between Ada Bromham and Jessie Street concerning the removal of her papers. Who was this woman and why and in what context did this happen? In the course of writing this book, I've come to see that her biography and her humanitarianism are meshed: it is impossible to understand her story – her crusade – without understanding her biography and vice versa.

I began this book in earnest while on a six-month period of study leave in 2012 which offered me precious time to bring together my thoughts about the relevance of Mary Bennett and her life's work. I didn't have to look far. Indeed, the fraught politics of Aboriginal affairs in the late twentieth, and early twenty-first centuries resonated with the same about eighty years earlier in which Mary Bennett was a key protagonist. The discourse was remarkably similar, including the interjections of humanitarians like her. The cacophony of claims and counter-claims about the rights and wrongs of the past, about land, citizenship, the position of Aboriginal women and children, the statistics around Indigenous health, mortality and education, the high rates of incarceration, Aboriginal economies, Aboriginal futures and discrimination were as relevant then as they continue to be today. In particular, the conflicted politics around the federal government's Intervention in the

Northern Territory in 2007, and the issues that gave rise to it, led me to rethink the significance of Mary Bennett's life work.

She began active involvement in Aboriginal affairs in Australia with the publication of her book, *The Australian Aboriginal as a Human Being*, in 1930. Described at the time as a 'whole-hearted indictment of the Federal Government's treatment of the problem of the Aborigines', it was her response to the 1928 Bleakley Report, a federal government investigation into the condition, status and treatment of Aborigines in the centre and the north.[1] In it she argued that there was still time, in the context of the late 1920s, for an 'honourable settlement' to be made with the Aborigines in that region. Intervention was urgently needed to stem the flow of depopulation in an area which had the largest Aboriginal population of any region in Australia, and to save them from extinction. Land, education, food and medical attention was urgent. Intervention was needed to put a stop to the slave-like conditions in which Aboriginal people laboured. Intervention was needed to stop legal injustice, the abuse of women and children, and the racial violence which characterised that frontier. Intervention was needed to solve a problem we had created, repay our debts, honour our obligations and make restitution.

This burden was not Australia's alone, however. For Bennett the brutality of white settlement in Australia mirrored the processes of colonialism elsewhere. Dispossession was backed by race hate and discrimination wherever empires were made. Yet, the interwar period delivered some hope of redress. She was deeply impressed and influenced by the politics and rhetoric of the hour, particularly the ethics of care of imperial humanitarianism and its message of native peoples as a sacred trust of civilisation. The great hope for Australian Aborigines, according to this logic, was that Australians had an opportunity to make amends for the past. 'To give justice to the remnant of our Aboriginal tribes is the greatest and most urgent of all our duties', she said.[2] Describing the League of Nations as a mechanism for creating a 'larger society where aggression against one race was aggression against all', she defined the Aboriginal problem as a world problem, warning that the founding of a just relationship between black and white was the most important business of the twentieth century.[3] As we left the twentieth century and the founding of a just relationship, particularly in the north, continued to elude us, her story seemed more pertinent than ever.

In large part, this book locates Mary Bennett's life story in her humanitarianism. It privileges the second half of her life, from the mid-1920s to her death in 1961, which she spent tirelessly fighting for Aboriginal human rights as she defined them. She literally died fighting that cause. Her humanitarian crusade is meaningless, however, without an appreciation of her familial context and background. She was the privileged daughter of one of the most successful pastoralists of the nineteenth-century Australian frontier, described in the press of the day as a colonial millionaire.[4] Her father, Robert Christison, owned huge swathes of land in north Queensland which carried an enormous amount of cattle and delivered her family great comfort and wealth, including an immense English estate to which the family retired in the early years of the twentieth century.[5] Her ability to speak on Aboriginal issues at all was, quite literally, built on her father's dispossession of them. As her hand-drawn map adorning the back cover of her biography of him suggests, this was not Christison's country. It was the Dalleburra's. Her life and her life's work had purpose and meaning as a result of this fact.

Indeed, it is possible to interpret her tireless work on behalf of Aboriginal people in Australia as her own personal quest to alleviate the

Map of the Lammermoor Tableland and Surrounding Country - Dalleburra Country - as it appeared on the inside back cover of Christison of Lammermoor, *in 1927. This was hand-drawn, probably by Bennett herself. Note Lammermoor is positioned in the middle of a chain of waterholes on Towerhill Creek. Papers of MM Bennett, 1837-1928, UQFL202, Box 1, Fryer Library, University of Queensland Library.*

burden of guilt – even shame – of her privilege. This was made more pressing by her slow realisation of the humanity of Aboriginal people as against the inhumanities of her own class and society. It seems that she had an awakening around the middle years of her life which jolted her out of the safety and security of her own upbringing. This is epitomised in a comment she made to her very close friend, Ada Bromham, a month before she died: 'I grew up a shocking imperialist but not so shocking as to accept their blasphemies'.[6]

When she wrote of Aboriginal people as generous, intelligent, resourceful and compassionate, this was as a mirror to her own society. Their communal living, their cooperation, their strict morality and law, and their dedication to family contrasted sharply with the competition, war, selfishness and dislocation of her own world as she saw it and 'the very nasty civilized cut-throat way of doing things'.[7] Aboriginal people's lack of material things was compensated by a deep spirituality. When she said, in *The Australian Aboriginal as a Human Being*, that there was still time to co-operate with Aboriginal people in the Northern Territory, she saw this as an opportunity for 'us' as much as them, for 'civilisation will not be whole without them'.[8] We had much to learn from them, they were our allies and 'a spirit force which we lost at our own peril'.[9]

Her taking up the Aboriginal cause in earnest, moreover, was compensation for her own loss. Between 1915 and 1927 she lost her father, mother and husband. She also lost Wyma, the Aboriginal nursemaid who helped raise her as a young child when, at critical periods of her youth, she stayed at Lammermoor. Her father's death, in 1915, had a profound effect on the family. It was not just the loss of the patriarch who held the family together and gave it shape and force, it was the loss of family fortunes as a result of the war. While her mother returned to Australia with her sister not long after, Mary stayed on in England having married Charles Douglas Bennett just a year before her father's death. Charles was a mariner in the Royal Navy who had been an acquaintance of her father's since the early 1900s. While he appeared to be the cause of some rift in the family, his support of Mary, in her decision to take up the Aboriginal cause, was in marked contrast to the rest of her family who tried to steer her away from it. This rift was never repaired, and the Aboriginal cause filled the gap for the rest of her life while maintaining a connection to her adored father, who had himself desired to set the record straight on the humanity of Aboriginal people.

Yet, to reconstruct Bennett's life-long commitment to Aboriginal rights solely as the product of her own psychological quest would be to miss an important opportunity to tell a story which is deeply rooted in the Australian historical landscape. Bennett's inheritance and the burden which came with it was symptomatic of the inheritance British settlers gained when they dispossessed the Aborigines all over Australia. Hers is therefore an important story of Australian history, at once personal and private and public and political. On the one hand, it is a story she shares with a number of similarly placed daughters and wives of the nineteenth-century frontier, whose personal interactions with Aboriginal people at formative stages of their lives created deep memories shaped by their fathers' and husbands' pioneering.[10] On the other hand, it is the story of one person's attempts to bring that legacy to account, to have the Aboriginal problem raised as a national and imperial responsibility, to have Australia face its racist past. It is the story of the demand for Aboriginal human rights and their recognition – as compensation – in all policy formulations. The fact is that everything Bennett campaigned on – from Aboriginal human rights (including women's rights), to the high levels of Aboriginal incarceration, to the appalling health and educational standards of Aboriginal people, to equal wages and the Trust Fund system, to the fallout from the testing of atomic weapons after the war and, most importantly, her undying abhorrence of Aboriginal child removal – has subsequently come up for redress.

There is also the state's seizure of her papers at the moment of her death. In the epilogue I chart this moment more carefully. The swiftness of this action was an incredible act of intervention and we must ask why it happened. The question is simply whether the action was a tacit recognition of the veracity of some or all of her claims which, by the late 1950s, had become extraordinarily searing about the policy landscape. While critique of the system of mixed-descent child removal had characterised her efforts before World War II, her most radical claim after it was the genocide of full-descent Aborigines. It is thus important to measure the personal crusade, with all its deeply psychological underpinnings, against the political responses to the same.

It is also because of the removal and loss of her private papers that this story is not about Bennett alone. The fact that I was able to reconstruct it was because her humanitarianism was largely a discursive exercise. She left a paper trail of protest and resistance in a wider context of protest and resistance which is an important part of Australian social and political history. The reconstruction of her efforts as presented in this book is via her extensive archive of letters to like-minded people and organisations and to politicians and bureaucrats around the world. The connections she made, both physically and ideologically, in the cause of her crusade are, therefore, an important part of her story.

Hence, while parts of Bennett's biography are important, the book is as much the reconstruction of a discursive defence, fragments of which were found in the collections of other humanitarians, their organisations and networks. It is a history of an idea or set of ideas about what constituted justice for Aborigines which took shape in Bennett's mind and on her pages and which, in turn, helped shape a broader rights agenda. While unfolding her life and her life's work is central, woven through it are important strands of a story larger than her. It is also about those with whom she connected, as friends and foes, as well as key aspects of a broader humanitarian landscape. In the very least her battle with the Australian state is suggestive of a deeply relevant, as yet untold, story of Australian social and political history.

Indeed, her efforts to found a 'just relation' between Aboriginal and non-Aboriginal people provides an opportunity to explore the role of critique and reform in the processes of colonialism as they were enacted in Australia.[11] Her decision to return to Australia to 'serve the people who had made her childhood happy' was, in part, conditioned by concern on the ground where a small, but growing, network of humanitarians were mobilising to the Aboriginal cause.[12] Their concern with Aboriginal dispossession and depopulation led to a critique of contemporary conditions.[13] The important point about that critique was that it emphasised a *legacy* of colonialism. 'It is impossible', Bennett wrote, 'to take the whole of other peoples' countries without injuring them'.[14] The other building block was ownership of the problem. Aborigines were dying out not because they were unfit to survive, she said, but because 'we' were unfit to be trustees.[15]

In the context of the times this was a radical proposition. It related to her undying view that Britain and Australia were complicit in Aboriginal dispossession. Australian history was rooted in colonialism and must answer to and be responsible for this fact. To overlook it or turn a blind eye represented a grave dereliction of duty. Yet, this was not a view widely endorsed or understood, least of all by the Australian state. In the post-Mabo landscape it is easy to forget that until 1992 the official version of British sovereignty was that they had discovered and then peacefully settled a land belonging to primitive peoples who had underutilised it. Accordingly, there was no question to answer or problem to solve. Successive Australian governments deflected humanitarian criticism suggesting that, as British subjects / Australian citizens, Aboriginal people were under special laws as protective measures. In this way British sovereignty was indivisible and humane. *Terra nullius* hardly applied. However, it is generally recognised that, as a *legal* justification for British sovereignty, *terra nullius* made Australia exceptional in the history of British colonialism.[16]

Unlike the signing of treaties with Indigenous peoples in other parts of its empire (which ultimately conceded the fact of prior ownership), Britain did not recognise any such rights for Australian Aborigines.[17] Yet, discussion of Australia's so-called exceptionalism has elided an important concomitant of the process. The non-recognition of Aboriginal rights obscured the *fact* of colonialism on Australian soil. Colonisers could indulge in the belief that, while part of the British Empire, we had no empire ourselves. There were colonies but there was no colonialism.[18] Australia was not held under mandate and no treaties were necessary; therefore the question or problem, if there was one, remained here. There could be no external relevance to the issue. Australian governments were not required to engage with any of the discourses emanating from within the empire about this question.

For Bennett, it was primarily because this issue was not Australia's alone that a solution should be found. By recognising the broader imperial – and world – parameters of the question she was effectively breaking Australia's isolationism which, on this question, was ultimately an act of political pragmatism. In truth, those involved in the administration and governance of Aborigines, as with all other policies around race, had long been attuned to precedents elsewhere within the empire and beyond. When the colour problem was considered to be the most burning issue of the day at the end of the nineteenth century, there was a transnational circulation of emotions, ideas, people and racial knowledge that animated white men's countries.[19]

In fact, the Aboriginal problem or native question had occupied European empires long before the so-called colour problem was articulated. It was, according to McNab, 'the greatest moral difficulty of colonization'.[20] In Britain, it was elevated to a national discourse in the context of the granting of self-government to its colonies. From the humanitarian perspective the Aboriginal problem revolved around what this meant for native populations therein. It was about the duty and right policy of colonists and colonial governments towards the native inhabitants of these regions.[21] From the early nineteenth century there was understood to be a reasonably limited suite of possibilities. As the academic, civil servant and historian Herman Merivale put it in 1841, there were three alternatives for the ultimate destiny of native peoples: extermination, insulation (reservations) and amalgamation (gradual union leading to assimilation).[22]

Looked at in this way, the various policies enacted by Australian governments – protection, assimilation, self-determination, reconciliation – belong to this much longer tradition. They were/are responses to the perennial empire-wide coloniser question of 'what to do with the Blacks', as Bennett put it.[23] The Protection legislation which was enacted in the Australian colonies from the second half of the nineteenth century was the governments' response to a problem that was becoming particularly acute on the frontiers of settlement. While genuflecting to imperial humanitarian discourses of justice and humane treatment, compensation and land for native inhabitants, Protection was also about the *containment* of the problem and the humanitarians who exposed it.

Indeed, Protection legislation in Australia was preceded by what could only be described as a crisis of governance on this question. This was true of the southern colonies of Tasmania and Victoria where patterns of settlement represented a rapid and violent takeover of land. But it was perhaps even more obvious in the Western Australian and Queensland colonies, particularly in the northern regions, where law enforcement failed, corruption was rife and governments colluded or conspired to protect settler interests. Symptomatic of this were intense political battles between pastoralists and humanitarians, particularly in the far northwest and northeast, which showed deep suspicion at best and outright hatred at worst.[24] Though a localised expression of what was happening elsewhere in the empire, the Protection legislation was not about identifying and settling native interests. While a response to settler hunger for land and humanitarian critiques, and to prevent the charge of slavery, Protection was a means of governments taking ownership and control of the problem.[25]

It was not long into the new century before the problem reared itself again. World War I marked a turning point on this question both here and in Britain. It represented a line of demarcation with the past. In Britain, this was conditioned by the changing face of colonial policy in Africa and Britain's pivotal role in the League of Nations, where native peoples were identified as a sacred trust of civilisation who were to be treated fairly, justly and humanely. Australian critics and reformers had always been part of a broader transnational circulation of ideas and people on this question. After the war a network of groups evolved across the southern states to call for better management of the problem and an enlightened administration.

Highlighting Australia's mandatory responsibilities under the League of Nations, they questioned the contradictions between Australia's external and internal policies on this question. They formed lobbies, study groups, protection societies and networks.[26] Comprising Christian humanists, missionaries, women reformers and scientists, these groups saw their task as the reform of government policy and the education of public opinion. They also had a specific set of demands which revolved around reforming laws, practices and governance. While Protection *was* government policy, these groups were lobbying for an alternative, more professional form of protection. They were, as Bennett styled them, 'the growing number of enlightened humane Australians' who felt 'that the contemporary position of Aborigines was unworthy of a great nation'.[27]

While Bennett's ideas gained traction in this context, few humanitarians in Australia mirrored her knowledge, commitment or zealotry. Few were in a position to make the Aboriginal cause their life's work. In 1930, the year her landmark book was published, Bennett arrived in Australia from her home in London, aged forty-nine, to undertake this work. Her husband had died three years earlier and she was childless and of independent means. A dedicated Christian, she was also a supporter of the Labour Party in Britain and had been exposed to the rise and fall of the radical critique of imperial policy there. She was schooled in the principles of imperial humanitarianism. Faith in its central tenets, particularly benevolent trusteeship, was what connected her promotion of indirect rule for Aboriginal administration in Australia in the interwar years and the International Labour Organization's Convention 107 for the same in the post-war years. Spawned from her own colonial experience of the Australian frontier and of Aborigines, Bennett dedicated the rest of her life to what she defined as the Aboriginal cause: their justice, freedom and humanity.

If Bennett was unique, she was not alone. In her study of Charles Duguid, a friend of Bennett's and fellow Aboriginal rights campaigner, historian Rani Kerin argues that his exceptionalism among reformers was his capacity to implement solutions to the problem. A medical doctor, a family man and a leading member of the Presbyterian church, Duguid's respectability goes some way in explaining his success.[28] In contrast, Bennett's capacity to affect change in this way was limited, despite her respectability. She was female, widowed, had no family (was not a mother) and, while Christian and working on a mission, she saw her task as an educator and remained, in large part, self-funded in this work. Where Duguid was respected and could get the ear of governments, Bennett was reviled. They attempted to silence her.

However, Bennett's ideas continued to influence a developing rights discourse. Shaping much of what he saw as vital to Aboriginal interests, Duguid was strongly influenced by her.[29] In the late 1930s her critique of absorption, the government policy designed to biologically infuse Aboriginal people of mixed descent into the majority population, helped shape and propel a left-wing and feminist critique of the same.[30] Her knowledge and ideas helped to maintain British humanitarian interest in Australian conditions through the early to middle part of the twentieth century. Furthermore, in the 1950s and, 60s, Bennett's writings continued to fuel a critique of government policy, particularly her 1930 book, which became something of a bible among younger activists who styled her their 'spiritual mother'.[31]

Kerin suggests that what worked for Duguid was his moderation. On the whole, he was not radical. The same cannot be said of Bennett, whose radicalism, by contrast, was not necessarily what made her exceptional. If she was exceptional it was because she managed to combine both moderation and radicalism. Her active involvement in the native question in Australia coincided with a time in British colonial policy where the fundamental question was, in Bernard Porter's words, 'what was and what should be the position of tropical countries and peoples in relation to the industrial civilization of the West'.[32] In the context of the late 1920s, Bennett sided with the reformist ideals of interwar British humanitarianism which were enshrined in the ideals of indirect rule: 'systematic use of the customary institutions of the people as agencies of local rule'.[33] When compared with the long-standing policy positions on this question, identified by Merivale earlier, indirect rule was a provocative, albeit conservative and self-serving, new solution.[34]

We might say that Bennett was radical in applying this approach to Australian conditions in the first place. Very few humanitarians in Australia sought to do the same and those who did were strongly influenced by her. None of the lobby groups of the interwar period, save the Aboriginal Protection League in Adelaide, actively promoted indirect rule. Governments certainly didn't, even at the time of considering how to populate and develop the tropical north in the interwar years.[35] The humanitarians constituted a 'body of disaffection' in the way that British critics and reformers did at this time.[36] They felt that settlement and development in Australia had raised disturbing questions about the status of Aboriginal people. Yet, while critical of government policies, they were not anti-colonial. On the whole, as in Britain, they promoted reform of the system rather than its abolition. As in Britain, they were interested in the question of how to govern a native population justly and humanely.[37]

What made Bennett's approach radical was that embedded in it was an anti-colonial *critique* which stemmed from some of the more radical antecedents of indirect rule. As Porter points out, indirect rule may have been a pragmatic colonial policy but it had been anticipated by the critical theories of empire promoted by the left in the 1880s and '90s.[38] Important to these was an economic theory of imperialism which equated colonial expansion with capitalist exploitation. Such a view saw socialist politicians such as Edmund Dene Morel link the loss of land (peasant proprietorship) with the loss of freedom of contract (labour) in places like the Congo.

Morel's campaign against slavery in the Congo Free State had a profound impact on Bennett. Part of Morel's success was his ability to use the British press to publicise the atrocities of Leopold's rule.[39] As part of his reading public, Bennett absorbed the sensational politics around his demands for reform in the Congo at an important stage in her life. Even if she was not, at that point, deeply engaged with the Aboriginal question, there is no doubt that it formed an important impression on her developing consciousness. She later quoted Morel and had read his polemical tract, *Black Man's Burden* (1920). Furthermore, like Morel, she later used the press to publicise her views and, like him, her dogged pursuit of justice for Aborigines earned her a reputation in government circles, as the rapid removal of her papers after her death suggests. This was a remarkable moment. In a questionable exercise of power, the state stepped in to confiscate the personal papers of a citizen. Bennett had died. Were they attempting to bury her legacy too?

It was in an attempt to recover her papers that the threads of her advocacy, as they appear in this book, became apparent. Those threads give some clues as to why the state acted in this way. In the post World War II era, the economic aspects of Bennett's critique, along with its anti-racism, came into their own. They found a more receptive audience in developments within the Aboriginal rights movement, where questions of land and labour were increasingly taking a more prominent place and where justice and freedom for Aboriginal people were being understood in economic terms. Along with the growing global decolonisation movement, the fractious politics around American civil rights and anti-Apartheid movements in Africa, and the intensification of the Cold War, the espousal of Aboriginal freedom and rights was regarded with suspicion.

The state's intervention is salutary in another way, too. Over recent years there has been a strong critique of rights-based discourses, particularly those concerned with human rights, in government circles, within academia and in a range of other forums, in Australia and elsewhere.[40] Mary Bennett's story exposes something which is often sacrificed in these critiques. Not only do they elide important parts of the history, they also work to obscure the battles and tensions which advocacy of rights have exposed. They obscure the different responses to the question. On the one hand, Bennett was no more committed to the advocacy of Aboriginal rights than the state was to shutting her up. On the other hand, humanitarian efforts around the Aboriginal question were not only the preserve of her and those who shared her views. All humanitarians and reformers were driven by a conception (their own) of what was right and good for Aboriginal people but there were significant differences in ideas and methods. As in approaches to the native question elsewhere, divisions emerged over its solution.[41]

One of the most marked divisions was between those who worked for reform within government and administrative ranks and those, like Bennett, who critiqued it from the outside. This is important because humanitarianism was an outgrowth of and justification for imperialism;[42] however, it also manifested as opposition to colonial sentiments and actions, often simultaneously.[43] While it is important to deconstruct the power which underpins noble enterprises, as Michael Barnett suggests, it is also important to consider how humanitarians have rethought the ethics of care.[44] In recovering Bennett's papers I found a network of reformers who clearly felt marginal, defensive and part of an oppositional movement. Bennett's sending of a large parcel of letters to Charles Duguid was an example of her maintaining links with a fellow traveller in an otherwise hostile environment. Letters between reformers fashioned a discursive circuit of alliance and protest. They were compilations of information, facts and evidence, as well as elucidations of policy, reform and care. They were chains of trust and friendship, support and defence in the cause.

Under the weight of new imperial, postcolonial and transnational histories, there has been a growing interest in humanitarian history in Australia. Most of this work has focused on the nineteenth century, not least because this was a period of intense scrutiny by the colonial office into conditions in Australia and throughout the empire, sparked by the House of Commons Select Committee On Aborigines (1835–37). With this moment as a focus a handful of historians have begun to unpick the social, political and cultural investments and transnational meanings of humanitarianism in the nineteenth century.[45] Recent explorations on anti-slavery and its legacies are opening the lens still further, exploring the trajectory of anti-slavery critique from the late nineteenth century to the present.[46] Paisley explicitly focuses on Bennett's work on conditions of Aboriginal labour in the 1930s, particularly slavery and forced labour, to draw attention to the international dimensions of the Aboriginal question in the interwar years.[47]

This is a valuable interjection because it takes Bennett's work as a humanitarian seriously. Important for the story told here is Paisley's suggestion concerning the potential link between humanitarian critique and major shifts in government policy. The story told in this book – Bennett's story – is suggestive of a history of humanitarian critique and containment. In this sense humanitarian critique was a double-edged sword: it both raised concern in the public sphere and provided a space for governments to take control of the problem and steer it in the direction it wanted to go while looking reformist and responsive.

This is what happened in 1937 when government bureaucrats agreed that future policy would rest on the absorption of the mixed-descent community. This was in direct response to at least two decades of humanitarian critique, in which Bennett's interjections were among the most critical of all, as well as concerted Aboriginal resistance in the north and the south. However, the mid-century policy shift from protection to absorption represented a profound contraction of Bennett's and the broader humanitarian community's concerns and demands. It was a bureaucratic response to a humanitarian crisis but, in focusing on a solution to the half-caste problem, it failed to recognise what for those like Bennett was at the heart of the crisis: the position of the remaining full-bloods and the urgent need to prevent their extinction. The recovery of Bennett's defence of Aboriginal rights in this book uncovers a powerful humanitarian angst across the middle years of the century concerning the fate of the full-bloods who, at least up to the end of World War II, constituted the majority Aboriginal population. Despite this fact, the demographic evidence showed a slow decrease from the 1920s, when the full-bloods constituted 82.3 per cent of the total Aboriginal population, to 1944, when they constituted 66.2 per cent.[48]

The ideal of saving the race propelled Bennett's crusade and it was what provided the important link between her and the South Australian Aborigines' League, with whom she maintained a connection until her death. Bennett's story thus allows us to consider the meanings, investments and outcomes of humanitarian interjection on this issue. Part of this is recovering a history of such, but the abrupt removal of Bennett's papers also forces us to consider the relationship between governments and humanitarians acting outside governments which, in their twentieth-century guise, represented something new in the policy framework.

In his history of humanitarianism Michael Barnett asks that we decouple humanitarianism and human rights. He notes that while there are similarities, they are not synonymous:

Human rights relies on a discourse of rights, humanitarianism a discourse of needs. Human rights focuses on legal discourse and frameworks, whereas humanitarianism shifts attention to moral codes and sentiments. Human rights typically focuses on the long term goal of eliminating the causes of suffering, humanitarianism on the urgent goal of keeping people alive.[49]

According to this definition, this book is about human rights. In recovering Bennett's advocacy it tracks a campaign which drew on a discourse of rights, utilised legal frameworks and focused on the long term goal of eliminating the causes of Aboriginal suffering. Bennett was a human rights activist in Kenneth Cmiel's terms because she made claims across borders in the name of basic rights.[50] The chronology of this book, from the 1920s, when the possibility of Aboriginal human rights was first mooted, to the 1960s, when an attempt was made to have the Aboriginal question raised before the United Nations, charts this human rights history. These developments largely framed Bennett's activist career from the publication of her first human rights treatise in 1930 to her last four years before her death.

The book also tracks a discourse of needs, moral codes and sentiments and the urgent goal of keeping people alive (in saving Aboriginal people from extinction). In this sense, then, Bennett's story demonstrates the close connection between the rise of humanitarianism as a political project and the rise of human rights. Yet, Barnett is instructive. He stresses the need to consider humanitarianism as a morally complicated creature, a 'flawed hero defined by the passions, politics and power of its times even as it tries to rise above them'.[51] Indeed, despite her efforts to rise above them, the power and politics of her time not only shaped her efforts but practically buried her. In her story is reflected the heated contestation over Aboriginal people throughout the twentieth century.

Bennett's story is suggestive of Barnett's qualification. On the one hand, she spoke from the coloniser side, from a position of power, privilege and authority even if, as a leading public humanitarian critic, her power was circumscribed. Her work among missionaries meant that she was necessarily embedded in colonising practices and discourses and her deep appreciation of Aboriginal humanity elided – in part and when it suited – that which was central to: Aborigines' own cultural and social distinctiveness. The people who made her childhood happy were not the Wongutha and Wongkai of the eastern goldfields of Western Australia, with whom she ended up working so closely and who helped define her reform agenda, but the Dalleburra in north Queensland, the people of the grasslands rather than the desert. Nor did the former ask for her help or intervention – initially – despite doing so eventually.

Yet, while she might be construed as someone who used her privilege to speak *for* Aboriginal people, she spent much of her life trying to give voice and representation to them and they gravitated to her for the same. She reflected on how close alliances with Aboriginal people and their lived conditions generated empathy with their plight:

> The realization that our natives need complete emancipation and representation comes but slowly even to those few who are spend-ing their lives with them teaching and preaching and nursing and helping them in other ways, but the realization comes as one experiences WITH them the suffering which they are made to endure by the cruel discrimination of the various Aboriginal Acts and Ordinances and the often irresponsible officers who administer them.[52] [Bennett's emphasis]

Thus, following Barnett, one reading of Bennett's advocacy of Aboriginal human rights might be that, as the statement above attests, she saw the Aboriginal problem as her own. Yet, if her crusade was an act of atonement, much of it was similar to the demands of Aboriginal activists themselves. And it was remarkably prescient. She might have been a product of her time but she advocated things which have only recently been understood as important to Aboriginal well-being. There is nothing, for example, in the United Nations Declaration of the Rights of Indigenous Peoples (2007) that she would not have agreed with or, at some stage, articulated.[53] Parts of it she had argued for since the 1930s including, importantly, the rights and protection of Aboriginal women and children. Indeed, many of Bennett's ideas resonate with those emanating from some Aboriginal spokespeople and leaders today.[54]

By using the contours of Bennett's biography, this book will build on the picture of individual activist lives begun by Reynolds, Rowse, Haskins, Marcus, Kerin, Lake and Paisley with a view to considering what the individual story tells us about the humanitarian project in twentieth-century Australia more generally.[55] In particular, recovery of her story helps to historicise human rights in Australia, a task which has become more urgent in recent times. Not only have some Aboriginal spokespeople and other commentators demanded that policy be framed in a human rights context, the Australian government has faced questioning at the United Nations about its Indigenous policies.[56] Furthermore, the National Human Rights Action Plan, commissioned by the Labor federal government in 2010, recognised that 'lasting improvements in human rights ultimately depend on the government and the people of a particular country demanding to take action to bring about positive change'.[57] The recovery of Bennett's attempts to bring about positive change is therefore timely and of national significance.

1

CONTEXTUALISING DISSENT
Humanitarians and the Aboriginal Problem

> The white colonists of Australia have contracted a huge debt; they
> are under a moral obligation of no less magnitude than that of
> making some reparation for the filching of a whole vast continent
> from its real owners. This is a plain statement made without any
> sentimental bias.[1]

In 1927, on the occasion of the inaugural opening of the Commonwealth
Parliament in the new national capital, Canberra, David Jackson MP
made a speech about the 'obligation the nation owed to the Aboriginal
races of Australia'. The Aborigines, he said, were a vanishing race because
of dispossession, disease and deliberate killing. Ninety per cent of inter-
racial conflict in the north was due to the high level of immorality,
including the taking of black women, which was fuelled by the supply of
liquor and resulted in the spread of disease. Referring to the comparable
fate of the North American Indian, he also likened Australia's treatment of
Aborigines to the treatment of the indigenous population of the Belgian
Congo. Calling for a resolution to the problem and compensation for
past mistreatment, his solution was a large number of segregated areas on
unalienated country where 'the blacks' could be gradually educated to
work the country. Those Aborigines who had had contact with European
civilisation should also have areas of land set aside for pastoral and rural
pursuits. In language not unlike today's he concluded that, for the supply
of rations, the government should expect a return in the form of the
employment of Aborigines in useful works.[2]

This was a succinct statement of progressivist thinking on the
Aboriginal problem in the late 1920s. From the beginning of the twentieth century there had been a growing unease about the status and
condition of Aboriginal people in Australia. The sources of this unease

were dispossession, governance, past wrongs, ongoing inter-racial tension exacerbated by white men's sexual interactions with Aboriginal women, and depopulation. The notion of national obligation echoed the wider interest in the welfare and administrative treatment of the Aborigines, which represented 'the bulk of thinking Australians', according to Frederic Wood Jones, a leading scientist. This translated to the view that something must be done, not only for the Aborigines, but to save Australia's reputation abroad. It must be based on knowledge and must be done as soon as possible.[3]

There were several reasons for this upsurge of humanitarian concern by the late 1920s, both internal and external to Australia: progressivism and modernism, World War I and, in particular, attitudes towards the 'colour problem' at its close, an awareness of historical injustices and the influence of interwar British imperial humanitarianism. The local humanitarian movement developed considerable momentum in the interwar period and represented a significant challenge for policymakers. Indeed, by the eve of World War II, the government bureaucrats involved in Aboriginal affairs developed a resolution for the Aboriginal problem partly in response to over two decades of concerted humanitarian agitation.

The movement was also pivotal to Mary Bennett's decision to return to Australia in 1930 to support, in her terms, this 'merciful minority'.[4] Of particular importance for her future endeavours in Australia were the resolutions of the Aborigines' Protection League (APL) in South Australia, which, unlike all other humanitarian groups of this period, actively modelled its agenda on British humanitarian ideals. Changes and developments in British colonial policy in the interwar period were vital to the APL and to Bennett, who was the group's London representative. It was her enthusiasm for both that encouraged her Australian sojourn.

I

The year 1927 marked an important moment in the history of humanitarian intervention on behalf of Aboriginal people in Australia. Months before Jackson requested a parliamentary committee to consider the issue, a large deputation of humanitarians, including churchmen, missionaries, scientists, academics and feminists, approached the Federal Minister for Home and Territories demanding a royal commission to inquire into the status and condition of Aborigines said to be dying out as a result of

European civilisation. This followed the publication of a report of the royal commission investigating the Forrest River massacre (Onmalmeri massacre) in the Kimberley the year before. Several Aboriginal people were killed in a punitive raid and key white police offenders were let off in what were regarded as suspect judicial processes. Brutal details of the massacre, such as the burning of Aboriginal bodies, were particularly disturbing. The report confirmed the humanitarians' worst fears. It found a conspiracy of silence throughout the region and charged the settlers and police with deliberately lying and hiding important witnesses.

In the same year, Constance Cooke, as president of the Women's Non-Party Association and a member of the APL, raised the position of Aboriginal women and girls before the British Commonwealth League, an empire-wide network of feminists working to secure equality between men and women in the British Commonwealth.[5] Cooke warned that the survival or extermination of the Aboriginal race ultimately depended on the fate of Aboriginal women, pointing to the spread of venereal disease 'introduced by the white man' as the cause of their rapid decline.[6] By the end of that year she had formed part of a small deputation representing the London-based Anti-Slavery and Aborigines' Protection Society to the Australian High Commissioner in London, along with Professor Wood Jones. Their primary purpose was to push for an inland reservation for the Australian Aborigines as had been done for the native American Indians. They presented him with a petition, which had been sent to the Australian federal government in October that year, for the creation of a Model Aboriginal State in Central Australia to allay the rapid deterioration and decline of the Aboriginal population.[7]

The humanitarian efforts of the late 1920s were directed to saving the Aborigines from perceived imminent death. This was part of a revived Christian humanist perspective which challenged the hitherto dominant belief that Aborigines were doomed to extinction.[8] Indeed, the notion of inevitable extinction was critiqued as a smokescreen which amounted to doing nothing.[9] The critique was underpinned by a dissenting scientific voice which could be traced to the first decades of the twentieth century. Up until then, scientific discourse had been dominated by the belief in extinction, connected as it was to Darwinian ideas about race and progress. Evolutionary anthropology espoused the view that the rapid decline of the Aboriginal population over a century was the result of Aborigines' innate primitiveness and barbarism and, therefore, incapacity to advance or be civilised. Obeying the 'natural law' of progress, Aboriginal extinction was considered an inevitability.[10]

According to Wood Jones this translated into a common belief that 'it were best that they should die out and with their death we should forget the wrongs done to them'.[11] While the idea of a doomed race persisted well into the twentieth century, by the 1920s and 1930s an alternative vision had emerged. Humanitarians espoused the view that the fate of the Aborigines was not due to the workings of an immutable natural law, but was the product of ill-informed man-made laws, policies and practices which had worked to the detriment of Aboriginal survival. The new functionalist school of social anthropology emphasised a complex, highly organised yet finely balanced culture, based on land ownership, upon which the advent of the white man was described as 'the dropping of a stone into the midst of some delicate mechanism'.[12] Dispossession, traceable through history, was understood to be at the centre of the problem, the contaminating effects of the white man's drink, drugs and disease having exacerbated it. As the demoralisation of Aboriginal culture was understood to be the corollary of white settlement, segregation on inviolable reserves was the call of many.

On one reading the humanitarian challenge was radical. It was time, so they collectively said, to stop, take stock and alter our practices. Such interjection presupposed the question: if Aborigines were not to die out, what was their future to be? As the appeals of Jackson, Wood Jones and Cooke suggest, what drove the desire for reform was a sense that Aboriginal people had a place in the nation and that there was still time to make amends for the past. If we thought carefully about the problem, applied the most enlightened principles to it and put commitment and funding into its solution, we might yet save the Aborigines – and ourselves, in the eyes of the world. A line was drawn between the contemporary moment and the past. The future needed to avoid all the old rules of engagement – dispossession, punitive killing, sexual exploitation, maladministration and legal injustice.

This concern with the status and fate of Australian Aborigines was mirrored in a revived public interest in all things Aboriginal. As the anthropologist A. P. Elkin observed, Aboriginal matters became a subject of almost daily record in news items, in comments, in articles and in leaders in the press by the 1930s.[13] This rediscovery splintered off in many directions. The newspapers reveal a curious mix of issues and concerns: interest in a dying race; sketches of old Aboriginal characters, depicted as the 'last of his/her tribe'; a fascination for settler reminiscence and tales from the frontier and vignettes of Aboriginal people, personalities and incidents. Excerpts of anthropological knowledge of aspects of culture and origins, and descriptions of Aboriginal material culture, sat alongside details of census figures concerning population size. Editorials on 'what to do with the blacks' were accompanied by excerpts demanding that something be done to prevent their extinction.

Clearly, by the interwar years, there was a widespread anxiety about the Aboriginal presence in the nation. On the one hand, stories of the last Aborigines and tales from the frontier reminded colonisers of their own advance. National progress was built on the ashes of a less advanced race. But, against the backdrop of the rising humanitarianism, they might also been seen as a developing consciousness that we were witnessing the death of an interesting and noble culture, a culture born in this place and, thus, ultimately relevant to our own long-term survival. Certainly, the rise of humanitarian sentiment in the interwar period contains all the features of Michael Barnett's explanation for outbursts of compassion. There was an ethical awakening produced by a crisis of faith and a corresponding process of atonement. A sin (and corresponding suffering) had been committed in which non-Aboriginal Australia was implicated and which demanded a response.[14] Barnett argues that these processes are caused by cataclysmic events, and the cataclysmic events that seemed to sharpen the pang of conscience were a series of frontier massacres in the late 1920s to early 1930s, the acknowledgement of the violence of dispossession and its outcome, and World War I.

Indeed, World War I had a profound effect on the ideas and attitudes of the west to native populations, particularly in colonial outposts. It sharpened governments' desire to more adequately administer them, particularly Britain, which was at the peak of its imperial power. According to the British anthropologist George Lane-Fox Pitt-Rivers, the war and the peace settlement at its close did much to renew interest in the native races of empire. He argued that these world events led men to question the unchallenged assumptions in their own civilisations, prompting them to regard with real concern and a desire to understand civilisations unlike their own.[15] He admitted that the 'native problem' was as much about the 'recalcitrant' and 'irreconcilable' members of the black races – those who had not been exterminated or successfully pacified – as with their dying relations.[16] Writing about depopulation in the Pacific in the late 1920s, Pitt-Rivers stated the chief problem as the failure of western civilisation to stabilise relations between a subject and a ruling race. In this context, problems associated with racial conflict were conceived of as a new threat to a fragile world order and therefore required new vigilance.

Humanitarians saw racial conflict as a new threat, too, but tended to be more concerned about its impact on the subject races themselves. One of the marked features of the surge of humanitarianism in Australia that followed the war was a strong condemnation of white civilisation and its contaminating effects on a once-virile population, of man-made laws, of governments and, for women reformers and feminists, of the lingering 'customs and prejudices of the patriarchal age'.[17] While Pitt-Rivers surmised that the native problem in Australia was of minute concern to the European population because the Aborigines were rapidly following the road to extinction, the humanitarians argued that the decline of the Aboriginal population after a century of white occupancy was the principal problem.

Concerns over Aboriginal depopulation were part of the wider modernist anxiety over racial degeneration (of the white race) at this time.[18] For those concerned with Aboriginal degeneration a firmer sense of the scale of depopulation was required. Russell McGregor has shown how the concept of inevitable Aboriginal demise was not underpinned by any hard empirical evidence.[19] By the 1920s, however, statistical information concerning Aboriginal populations was more frequently sought. Although not counted in the national census, a census was conducted in 1924 with the help of state statisticians, protectors and police. This led to the mapping of estimated Aboriginal distribution (and decline) from 1788 to 1927, which was published for the first time in the Commonwealth Year Book of 1930. For the humanitarians this was graphic evidence of the scale of the problem. It revealed that the full-blood Aboriginal population had gone from an estimated 300,000 in 1788 to 60,000 in 1927. At the same time a half-caste community had grown, numbering approximately 16,800. While a variety of social reformers sought solutions for the degeneration of the white race, some humanitarians focused on the black, particularly the remaining full-blood Aborigines in the centre and north. It was those so-called uncontaminated Aborigines who, it was thought, might yet be saved.

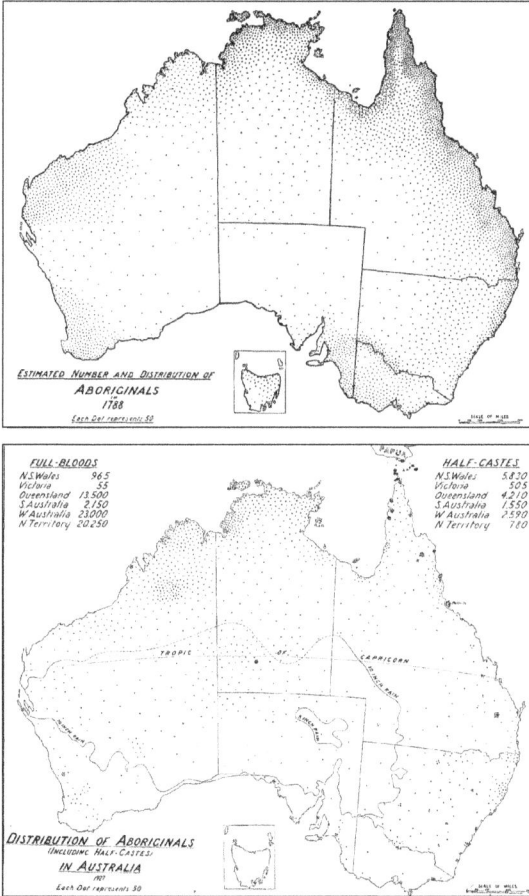

The 'Aboriginal Problem'. Estimated Aboriginal Population Distribution 1788 and 1927.

Although Aboriginal people were not counted in the national census, a conference of statisticians in 1925 called for annual surveys to ascertain approximate numbers and their participation in the workforce. These maps, published in the Commonwealth Year Book for the first time in 1930, compared estimated Aboriginal population distribution between 1788 and 1927. They not only demonstrated high levels of depopulation but rising numbers of half-castes. It was at this stage that the rough estimate of 60,000 remaining full-bloods was arrived at.

Along with degeneration, the focus on the so-called uncontaminated Aborigine demonstrates how humanitarian thinking was racialist, too.

Wood Jones argued that sympathy for Aborigines would come via anthropological knowledge of his 'race, racial principles, racial prejudices and racial proclivities'.[20] The fixation on the remaining full-blooded remnant was about preserving and protecting a distinct *race*. As Wood Jones said: 'continued racial life and adoption of the white man's ways are incompatible for the native'.[21] There was no mention of how, if at all, the white man's contact with Aborigines would result in modifications to *his* racial life or affect the white race. For people like Wood Jones, the Aboriginal race had a purity and vulnerability which the white race (a contaminated and contaminating influence) appeared not to have. It was why special care was needed if extinction was to be avoided. This purity related to its being native to the land. As Wood Jones commented

> we may safely say that no physical racial contacts have ever deprived the Australian native of the right to claim that his is a pure race – a race as pure as any that exists in the world today. And moreover he has the right to claim that all the diversities of his languages, of his culture and ceremonies, were begot in the wide environment of Australia since that far distant day when he arrived here as the first Australian colonist.[22]

Saving the Aborigines from extinction was, therefore, part of the early twentieth-century environmentalism evident in the rise of the conservation movement, the concern over rapidly disappearing habitats and the need for protection of vulnerable species of flora and fauna. It was part of the preservationist instinct characteristic of Australian responses to the environment in the period 1880–1930.[23]

Indeed, there appears to be a degree of overlap between the demand for greater protection for Australian wildlife and greater protection for Aborigines at the beginning of the twentieth century. The people who were interested in preserving the national estate were very often those who were demanding a better system of care and protection for Aborigines. Professor Wood Jones (1879–1954) is one such example. A trained anatomist and academic, he was fascinated by the evolution of mankind and was also a keen naturalist. One enticement for accepting academic positions in Australia, from his prestigious teaching posts in London, was the time it afforded him to study native fauna, a pastime in which he indulged in regular field excursions inland and to the islands. From these he developed a scientific and humanitarian interest in the Aborigines. In the mid-1920s, around the time he published a book on the mammals of South Australia, Wood Jones founded the Anthropological Society of South Australia.[24]

Baldwin Spencer (1860–1929) is another example. Appointed the first Chair of Biology at Melbourne University in 1886, he developed a major research centre into the Australian biota. An avid naturalist, he was president of the Field Naturalist Club in Victoria and was prominent in the Australasian Association for the Advancement of Science. In the early 1900s he was among those who sought support from Prime Minister Alfred Deakin on national uniform laws for bird protection.[25] Later, as Chief Protector of Aborigines in the Northern Territory, he recommended greater protections for Aborigines.[26]

As conservationists, Spencer and Wood Jones were leading Australian progressives. In their history of the Australian environmental movement, Hutton and Connors have argued for the inclusion of early twentieth-century conservationism in the broader progressivism of the era.[27] Based on the efficacy of science, utilitarianism and the drive for national efficiency, progressivism underpinned a raft of social reforms and institutional arrangements from urban reform to the establishment of national parks and forestry departments around the turn of the century. Symptomatic of these developments was the interest of scientific societies, such as the Linnean Society, and various bird and animal protection groups pushing for a national system of protection to circumvent state laws which failed to adequately protect native wildlife.[28] Similarly, humanitarians concerned with Aboriginal survival were deeply critical of the ability of state laws to adequately protect Aborigines. They believed that the problem needed a national focus – that the Commonwealth needed to intervene to arrest Aboriginal decline and provide an example to the states of best practice. As Wood Jones' comments suggest, they also saw science as playing a key role.

And it did. The Australasian Association for the Advancement of Science played a pivotal role in creating the Association for the Protection of Native Races (APNR). As the first national lobby group for Aborigines, it was the institutional embodiment of progressivist thinking on the Aboriginal problem. Among its members were Andrew Fisher, the then prime minister, and other distinguished members of parliament, including Alfred Deakin. Precipitated by the transference of control of the Northern

Territory from the South Australian to the federal government in 1911, the association was established as a co-operative humanitarian watchdog to protect native races in Australasia and Polynesia from 'oppression and outrage', to mitigate the 'injurious effects of the sordid practices of reckless and lawless men in the pursuit of various enterprises'.[29] Consisting of representatives from church, state, the professions, industry and trade, it sought, in its terms, the protection of native rights, including respect, the suppression of the 'gross interferences' in their racial and domestic rights, enjoyment of traditions, personal freedom and recognition of their human rights. As the Aboriginal problem was a national one, adequately protecting Aborigines would be of national benefit.

While the desire to preserve and protect Aborigines was important, the scheme developed by the Australasian Association for the Advancement of Science for the future of Aborigines became a blueprint for reform which lasted in the Australian reform imaginary until the 1967 referendum. At the heart of securing a future for Aborigines, according to the association, was an adequate national system of care for all surviving Aborigines. This was because 'the wider the area from which the governing power is derived, and the larger the task set, the more statesmanlike and continuous the policy is likely to be'.[30] This would take the form of a permanent native commission with legislative backing and would consist of representatives of state and federal governments. It was also recommended that the system of reserves be widely extended in the northern parts of the continent with training of Aborigines in pastoral pursuits, mechanical arts, carpentry and, eventually, agriculture. The association felt that in this way, 'for the first time in Australian history' the Aboriginal question would be treated as a whole and more systematically and scientifically, that the financial burden would be more evenly distributed, that a national sense of sympathy and pity would be created and that a valuable labour asset would be preserved. Furthermore, it would bring the treatment of Australian Aborigines in line with that practised by the governments of New Zealand, North America and South Africa, which had made their indigenous populations a national responsibility.[31]

As this suggests, an underlying assumption of the Aboriginal reform movement was that the Australian government had not taken the question of the Aborigines seriously enough. If not laissez-faire, governments were apathetic. Yet, by the early years of the twentieth century there was a vast administrative system in place, via which Aboriginal lives were said to be protected. Having evolved colony by colony from the middle of the nineteenth century, Protection was a reactive rather than proactive measure which was shaped by the peculiarities of each colony: the pace and timing of settlement, the level of internecine strife, the environment and climate, the level and style of contact, the economic needs of settlers and the level of Aboriginal resistance. In the first instance Protection represented a legislative response. Specific laws stipulated the removal of Aborigines to reserves and government settlements and the distribution of relief and rations. They also regulated Aboriginal movements, relationships, modes of living and working, sexual and family relationships, habitation, punishment for transgression and general management. The legislation also established a bureaucratic machinery consisting of a relevant government minister, a leading bureaucrat known as a Chief Protector, a board of Protection and then a wide network of police protection on the ground. To this system of management and surveillance were added further tiers of regulation. Aboriginal lives were further circumscribed by a labyrinth of additional laws and regulations, such as the Dog Act, the Liquor Act and the Firearms Act.[32]

Protection was also preceded by crises of governance on the question in each of the colonies as governments, settlers and humanitarians squabbled over the Aborigines. In Victoria, Protection legislation was enacted following the orchestrated failure of the first Aboriginal protectorate.[33] Although in existence for a decade, it was subjected to unrelenting pressure from settlers, who, frustrated by humanitarian efforts, were anxious to develop the fertile land on which the protectorate was based.[34] In Queensland the conflict centred around the activities of the native police, a paramilitary police force sent in to protect the settlers from the 'depredations' of the blacks.[35] In Western Australia the battles focused on the inter-racial conflicts over dispossession and the cattle-killing that ensued, as well as the harsh treatment of Aboriginal workers (including children) and prisoners, including the use of neck chains and an array of penal sanctions.[36] This was exacerbated by the pastoralist being his own recruiter. In the absence of a native police force, he took matters into his own hands, relying heavily on the local police.

The way in which Protection legislation came about in Western Australia demonstrates how fraught the business of protecting Aborigines was. The 1905 legislation was not the first but was the most comprehensive Protection legislation for that state. It followed the Roth Royal Commission, which had been appointed in 1904 against the backdrop of historic and ongoing charges of slavery in the pastoral industry, both here and in England. Indeed, it was the culmination of over 20 years of humanitarian angst over conditions in the northwest of the state. In the mid-1880s Reverend J. B. Gribble and ex-convict stockman David Carley protested the widespread abuse of Aborigines across the north of Western Australia. In his controversial book documenting it, Gribble described kidnapping, rape, murder and an oppressive labour system.[37] He referred to settler prejudice and the brutal treatment of Aboriginal prisoners. Such exposure led to a very nasty conflict between local settlers and Gribble, but it was largely via the publicity it generated that local control of Aboriginal affairs was withheld by Britain when the colony achieved self-government in 1890.[38] While this was repealed in 1898, continuing critiques of the system resulted in the appointment of Roth to inquire into the treatment of Aborigines.

Intended to vindicate the state, the Roth report ultimately vindicated Gribble. Suppressed at the time, it documented widespread abuse of Aboriginal women and men, as labourers, 'concubines' and prisoners. It detailed an 'industry' of indiscriminate arrests of large numbers of Aborigines on charges of cattle killing, facilitated by the payment of sustenance money to police officers. It also highlighted the non-regulation and ill-treatment of native labour and prostitution of Aboriginal women across the north.[39] Despite his criticisms of the administration and the police department, the new Aborigines Protection Act of 1905, which was modelled on the Queensland Protection Act of 1897,[40] failed to implement Roth's chief recommendations – the creation of hunting reserves, a minimum cash wage and an independent field organisation to watch and report on the handling of prisoners. Other reforms, particularly in relation to police practices and prisoner management, which were largely targeted to the handling of 'cattle-killers', were short-lived.[41] Yet, like its Queensland counterpart, the 1905 act remained the state's main administrative scaffolding well into the twentieth century.

Thus, by the early 1900s, state governments had assumed the right to determine and define the terms of Aboriginal protection, and the humanitarians had been contained. The new century was ushered in without significant reserves, without wages and with little legal protection, justice or equality for Aborigines. Aboriginal women remained vulnerable and the new nation was born with a compact that wrote the Aborigines out of the national population all together. In the 1901 Constitution of the new nation, Aborigines were neither to be counted in the national census nor come under federal control anywhere except the Northern Territory. In fact, in the first decades of the twentieth century most states increased their level of surveillance of Aboriginal lives, amending the Protection legislation to strengthen and extend their bureaucratic controls, including over Aboriginal children. By the 1930s the Protection regimes were exercising total control over Aboriginal lives. While there was some protection of Aboriginal women and workers, particularly in the Queensland and Western Australian legislation, the gap between theory and practice remained. Aborigines remained trapped in the net of state-based authorities and laws, thus negating any notion of national honour or obligation.

II

This historical overview gives some texture to the resurgent humanitarianism in the early decades of the twentieth century. Protection, as governments enacted it, was hardly the fulfilment of humanitarian ideals. From colonial times, these had been influenced by imperial humanitarianism which, by the 1900s, was deeply concerned by the effects of imperialism in the hothouse atmosphere of British expansion in Africa. Anxiety over the conflict between tropical development on the one hand and native welfare on the other led groups like the Anti-Slavery and Aborigines' Protection Society to advocate fairness and protection for native peoples. This would be achieved by the suppression of slavery and punitive expeditions, protecting natives from the 'evils' of liquor, the delivery of justice and the protection of native rights to land, cultural practice and equality.[42] These were the ideals of the APNR, which had been affiliated to the Anti-Slavery and Aborigines' Protection Society from its inception in 1911. The language used by the group, such as protecting Aborigines from 'oppression and outrage', and mitigating the effect of 'lawless men in the pursuit of various enterprises', is lifted straight from the late nineteenth-century anti-colonial critique of people such as E. D. Morel and J. A. Hobson, as are the radical claims of Aboriginal rights to land, culture and humanity.[43] Demanding native rights was a means of combating the rapaciousness of the new imperialism in Africa and settler greed in Australia.

Despite its promising start, the progress of the APNR, particularly in relation to Aboriginal affairs, stalled. World War I had something to do with this, but so too did the focus of the group. As Andrew Markus has shown, although Aborigines were an early priority, the focus of the association into the 1920s was conditions in Papua, New Guinea and Melanesia. This focus must not have been too exacting either because, by 1925, the association ceased to function.[44] Nevertheless, it was Aboriginal affairs and particularly conditions on the northern frontiers that led to its resuscitation in the late 1920s. As inaugural member and honorary secretary of the group, William Morley, secretary to the London Missionary Society, reactivated it in light of the Onmalmeri massacre in the Kimberley in 1926. Markus describes Morley as working, almost singularly, to keep the APNR afloat and improve conditions for Aborigines. While a conservative congregational minister he was no moderate, arousing public opinion on the Aboriginal question and alienating senior officials with his demands for the extension of reserves and reforms in the administration of justice. Indeed, Markus paints the figure of a man driven to his deathbed, if not in the cause alone, in tireless campaigning in the face of governmental distrust and intransigence.

By the mid-1920s Morley was not alone. As with the APNR, the Onmalmeri massacre did much to galvanise and formalise humanitarian concern. Massacres exposed problems in the administration of law and justice, particularly in remote communities in the north. They also provided a catalyst for simmering humanitarian angst concerning Protection itself. Onmalmeri was part of a string of frontier conflicts, including the Coniston massacre in central Australia in 1928 and the Caledon Bay affair in 1933 in Arnhem Land, which focused attention on inter-racial tension in these areas. For governments, these were graphic illustrations of the colour problem in their midst. For humanitarians, they were an illustration of the poor treatment of Aborigines by settlers and police. They were a grave indictment on the administration of justice. Of particular concern was what appeared to be indiscriminate shootings and dispersals of Aboriginal tribes as punitive measures for the 'offence' of cattle spearing. The policy of police protection was targeted as open to fraud and abuse. Critics maintained that justice could not be realised when the local protector was also, simultaneously, the prosecutor. Nor could white police officials be unbiased when it came to differences between local white settlers and Aborigines.

The interwar humanitarians thus took up where their nineteenth-century counterparts left off, but there was a noticeable shift of emphasis. As in Britain, the radical critique of the late nineteenth century gave way to conservative reform in the interwar period.[45] In Britain this related to the changing face of colonial policy. In Australia it related less to changing colonial policy and more to residual unease with native administration in general and Protection in particular. It was a modernist concern that we, as a nation, had not overcome the worst excesses of the past. Violence and injustice in the north suggested a continuation of frontier morays unacceptable to a civilised nation. By the 1930s there was a string of southern-based lobby groups monitoring policy and promoting reform. While aims and objectives varied from group to group and emphasis was placed in different areas, they shared a number of key concerns, including: the need to prevent further encroachment on Aboriginal reserves; the prevalence of disease among Aboriginal communities; the need for reforms in the systems of law and justice including police protection; the sexual exploitation of Aboriginal women; and the necessity for a scientifically informed administration.

This last demand reflects the connection between developments in Australia and those in Britain, where there was a lively interwar interest in modernising colonial governance. This was fuelled by Britain's extended imperial power and inheritance of the colour problem following World War I. It was also fuelled by Britain's leadership at the League of Nations, which produced the first international statement on the rights of native peoples. The league defined the native question as the various difficulties associated with western civilisation's assumption of control over the destinies of 'backward, dark-skinned races', the problem of subject races living under European tutelage and the associated clash of cultures. While inter-racial conflict was of concern, so too was indigenous depopulation, which appeared to be conditioned by contact with European races and to coincide with the disintegration of the former's culture. Described as one of the most urgent problems of the twentieth century, its solution, according to the league, lay in the 'strong and advanced races' protecting the 'weak and less advanced races'. Defining native races as 'a sacred trust of civilisation', Articles 22 and 23 of the league's Covenant required they be given fair and humane conditions of labour, just treatment, a voice in their own government *and* land.[46]

The notion of a sacred trust was key to so-called enlightened thinking on this question, and science, particularly anthropology, would underwrite it. This notion had been at the core of British propaganda justifying its imperial mission from the start.[47] In developing tropical lands, the empire was simultaneously entrusted with the care of the people of these lands. Critics of imperial policy had long reminded empire-makers of this fact.[48] In the context of the further imperial encroachments in the late nineteenth century, particularly in west Africa, colonial policy became yet another flashpoint of concern. It was in this context that anthropology moved from the margins to the centre, helping to shape a new approach to the moral dilemma of imperialism in Africa. People such as the explorer, traveller and anthropologist Mary Kingsley argued that assimilation of the African would not work because of the fundamental difference between African and European cultures. While civilising the native was worth pursuing, this should not be along European lines. Rather, it should be preceded by empirical study and encouragement of their own cultures.[49] Policy should be premised on cultural relativism and preservation. The African should develop on his own lines.[50]

This method of administration was dubbed scientific humanism because it promoted the view that to treat indigenous people humanely required an appreciation of the workings of their culture. As Barnett has argued, this was a step towards a rights–oriented humanitarianism.[51] It certainly inspired an Afrocentric critique of colonial policy into the interwar period.[52] People such as Edmund Dene Morel, socialist politician, took up Kingsley's ideas in his savage critique of imperial practices in west Africa and particularly in the Belgian Congo. There, imperial development via plantation agriculture had resulted in rapid loss of African territory, rapacious exploitation of resources and the sweeping aside of African culture in the name of civilisation. Morel argued that King Leopold's dictatorship of the region had robbed the African of his ability to develop on his own lines. The key causes of the Congo atrocities – monopoly and land alienation – had, in turn, facilitated forced labour. Such conditions constituted a de facto servitude, or slavery in disguise. For Morel, development of the African in economic terms meant freedom of contract and ownership of land and its resources. Following Kingsley, he promoted a doctrine of preservation of African culture and development of it on the African's own terms.[53]

The situation in the Congo pushed the native question to the forefront of imperial policy and forced people to think about the problems of tropical government.[54] For the likes of Kingsley and Morel, preservation of native culture was preferable to acculturation, which they saw as demoralisation. These were ideas born out of the new imperialism of the *fin de siècle*. They were idealistic and ultimately unsuitable to the changed conditions of the interwar years where the key concern had become Britain's east African dependencies, acquired at the end of World War I. Problems there were different from those in west Africa and demanded different solutions.[55] In particular, racial conflict festered as Africans demanded equality and European settlers more land and power. According to Robert Maxon, this saw the loss and reassertion of imperial initiative in Kenya, culminating in the Devonshire Declaration of 1923.[56] A reassertion of the notion of trust, it made African interests paramount over those of the European minority, arguing that where immigrant interests conflicted with those of African tribes, the latter would prevail. It defined a new notion of trusteeship as the protection and advancement of African populations. In an effort to keep both greedy settlers and anxious humanitarians at bay, trusteeship was capable of neither being shared nor delegated by governments.[57]

The ideal of African paramountcy was an expression of that other great imperial initiative in Africa, indirect rule, popularised in the first decades of the twentieth century by Lord Lugard, colonial governor of Nigeria (1912–19).[58] In 1922 Lugard reasserted the principle of the sacred trust in his *Dual Mandate*. The mandate held that civilised peoples had an obligation both to develop the resources of 'backward' areas and to protect their indigenous inhabitants.[59] Lugard described indirect rule as 'co-operative devolution'.[60] It consisted of administering colonial populations through native agencies – the systematic use of the customary institutions of the people as agencies of local rule.[61] According to Dr Lucy Mair, lecturer in colonial administration at the London School of Economics and a contemporary of Lugard's, the basic aim of the policy was preservation of native institutions on the one hand and development of them on the other.[62] The latter was targeted at enabling the participation of African society, in its own right, in the life of the modern world. For it to work properly, according to Mair, it required a deep understanding of African culture, its structure and the inter-relationship of its parts.

While indirect rule was maintained for east Africa, it was modified. Preservationism was now linked to the idea of gradual indigenous development. This was supported by changes in anthropological thinking and, in particular, a shift away from the old evolutionary paradigm towards functionalism or social anthropology. The work of Bronislaw Malinowski laid important foundations for this shift because he was interested in the question of culture contact. Such an approach was perfect for east African problems because the British encountered a people already in the throws of change. What made Malinowski's approach useful, according to Mair, was his interpretation of culture as a mechanism of cooperation for the satisfaction of human needs in which every element was linked with and conditioned by the rest. At the very least it assumed that instead of the unilateral imposition of an allegedly superior civilisation over an inferior one, with the potential loss of the latter, the colonial enterprise represented the juxtaposition of two distinct civilisations and therefore required more subtle handling.

As Porter puts it, the direction of indirect rule moved from an attempt to preserve the customs and practices of native races, in the style of Kingsley, to promote their progressive adaptation to modern conditions.[63] While this represented a level of African autonomy, it was less about sovereignty than about native advancement and development, an ideal with a long lineage in anthropological discourse. As McGregor has shown, even as the paradigm shifted, old evolutionary ideals concerning human progress through stages prevailed.[64] Such thinking stretched back to Herbert Spencer and Charles Darwin, who argued that the fate of native races rested on one of only two possible outcomes: extinction or parallel development. Yet by the 1920s the scientific pendulum had swung. Because of its professed capacity to interrogate the workings of native societies, functionalism was an important scientific support for the cause of indirect rule and empire itself.

By the interwar period, indirect rule had become the apotheosis of British imperial policy, widely advertised as a humane solution to the problem of colonial governance.[65] With the resuscitation of anti-slavery rhetoric and practice at the same time, particularly around the centenary of the abolition of slavery in 1933, the two merged to underwrite a renewed justification of imperialism that was simultaneously a rehearsal of British libertarian history and values. Wise and careful protection of native interests was part of this romanticised rendering of imperial purpose. The native question was at the centre of an extraordinary moveable cultural, political and intellectual feast, which was evident in both a wide circulation of ideas, debates, discussions, conferences and a nostalgic celebration of empire itself.[66] For the most part, empire-makers believed their own rhetoric. As John Cell has shown, despite indirect rule's failure, even at the time, a generation of colonial officials and liberal-minded people believed that it was the basis of progressive policy. The reason for this, he suggests, was because of the widespread disillusion with western civilisation. By contrast, native civilisation had attributes worth retaining.[67]

We have seen how the call for Aboriginal reform in Australia was stimulated after World War I by the same disillusion. It is necessary to understand interwar humanitarianism in Australia against the backdrop of this wider imperial setting, despite its apparent remoteness from Australian conditions, problems and developments. The ideas and contexts of imperial humanitarianism leached into and influenced humanitarianism on the ground. Nowhere was this clearer than in the unanimous demand for a centralised national system of administration backed by scientific knowledge. To the original template of a commission of native affairs promoted at the beginning of the century by the Australasian Association for the Advancement of Science were added scientific experts. These experts, presided over by a permanent commissioner, would replace the existing state-based systems of administration and the labyrinth of laws accompanying them. The new national body would be outside parliament, have adequate funding and consist of sympathetic men *and* women, trained social anthropologists, as well as Aboriginal representatives dedicated to administering a national Aboriginal agenda. They would be intimate with and sympathetic to Aboriginal needs, and would make inquiries and advise the prime minister on the native question.

The fact that humanitarians were considered important to the administration of Aborigines also reflects the influence of imperial humanitarianism. The historian Fiona Paisley has shown how Australian conditions were increasingly brought into the orbit of interwar imperial humanitarian concern, too, and how there were critics with Australian experience who, from the early 1900s, continued to fan the flame sparked by Gribble and others.[68] While only ever a relatively small group, they appealed to a powerful, established network working for the Aboriginal cause both in and outside parliament, including older prestigious groups like the Anti-Slavery and Aborigines' Protection Society and younger ones such as the League for Coloured Peoples, established by the Jamaican evangelist Harold Moody in 1931. The Anti-Slavery Society had long had parliamentary representation and, by the interwar period, had consultative status with the League of Nations. By the 1930s the work of the society was given renewed legitimacy and vigour by the League of Nations and International Labour Organization. While still interested in the abolition of native labour systems 'analogous to slavery', and the maintenance of justice for Aboriginal and native races, its principle objective became the prevention of any taint of slavery creeping into the administrations of the British dominions.

By the 1920s the society was suggesting an appeal on the Aboriginal question to either the Judicial Committee of the Privy Council or the League of Nations. Indeed, it expressed the hope that the local lobby groups would form a national coalition to facilitate these aims and regularly published reports, ideas and correspondence in its quarterly journal, *Anti-Slavery Reporter and Aborigines' Friend*. By 1932 it had established a 'Sub-committee on Australian Aborigines' and had begun a correspondence with the federal government which was to steadily into the 1960s. In it the society argued for a more humane and enlightened treatment of Aborigines, more in harmony with the ideas of the twentieth century and the principles of human rights enunciated by international forums. Also important was the Royal Anthropological Institute in London which, as a centre of learning and discussion on colonial administrations, was similarly concerned with the practical problems of administration in the colonies and dominions of the British Empire. The institute's quarterly journal, *Man*, provided an important forum for the publication of anthropological and other scientific findings and works on Australian Aborigines. General British interest in Australian Aborigines was reflected in the increased coverage of conditions and policies in the London press and by public bodies such as the Royal Empire Society and the British Commonwealth League throughout the 1930s.

III

The existence of humanitarian groups in Australia reflected Australia's involvement in this modernising project of empire. Their interjections from the periphery were part of this wider network of concern, debate and movement around the empire on this question, modified to Australian conditions. As the humanitarians defined it, the native question in Australia was not about the administration of a 'trust'. Rather it was about the inheritance of a debt. The problem was how to repay it. Humanitarians could help solve this problem because they could translate the latest, enlightened ideas on the issue to Australian audiences and policy-makers. Most of the scientific community interested in reforming policy and in a position to influence policymakers, such as Wood Jones and Spencer, had been trained in key British academic institutions around the late nineteenth and early twentieth centuries. They maintained links to the scientific and academic community in London, were exposed to British culture and discourse on the matter, exchanged information and published in the leading British journals. They were aware of developments elsewhere and, with their knowledge of Aborigines, participated in the cross-fertilisation of ideas about race, humankind, bodies, society, culture and environment which penetrated all corners of the academic fraternity at this time.[69]

As this suggests, the culture of interwar imperialism, particularly its self-projection as the source of enlightened colonial governance, provided an important fillip to humanitarians in Australia. This belief permeated Australian culture, too. Britain was enlightenment and refuge for disaffected reformers. In 1926, for example, Wood Jones argued that, in comparison to the empire's altruism in relation to native administration, Australia was retrograde.[70] In 1932, the prominent humanitarian and feminist Edith Jones declared that she hoped that what was said and heard in England 'will stir our kin in Australia to more enthusiasm for the Aboriginal cause'.[71] Feminist writers have shown how travel to and from England in the interwar period was an important part of women's citizenship and freedom.[72] In a similar vein, such travel provided an important support base for advocates of Aboriginal reform. The cause of reform was also influenced by the broader political changes in the relationship between Britain and Australia. In 1919 the latter became a dominion of the British Empire. This process opened up and invigorated a sense of national purpose. Would-be reformers and leaders were anxious to be good partners in the empire but also to be more independent, and were desiring to prove their mettle on the world stage.[73]

All reformers in Australia, including Aboriginal activists, were aware of this broader milieu. Paisley has shown how the Aboriginal activist Anthony Martin Fernando, so important to Bennett's crusade, defined the Aboriginal problem as a problem of the empire at large.[74] Similarly, other activists and critics understood Australian conditions as a version of developments elsewhere in the empire and they drew comparisons. Indeed, when David Jackson issued his plea in the Commonwealth Parliament in 1927, he noted how King Leopold, dictatorial ruler of the Congo Free State, deflected criticism of his own regime in the early 1900s by pointing to conditions in Western Australia and the findings of the Roth Royal Commission.[75] Together with the developments in the League of Nations, imperial humanitarianism emboldened local humanitarians to act and to speak. They used it as leverage to call Australia's record to account, particularly in relation to Australia's contradictory policies internally and externally: its administration of Aborigines on the one hand, and its administration of mandated territories of Papua and New Guinea on the other. While only a handful of reformers from Australia were affiliated to the Anti-Slavery and Aborigines' Protection Society, all were aware of its presence as an external watchdog and ally in the cause.

Yet, none of the local humanitarian groups promoted Lugard-style indirect rule for Australia, except the APL in South Australia, of which Wood Jones and Cooke were members. With a focus on Aboriginal communities in the north and propelled by a belief that they might yet be saved from extinction, the humanitarian lobby saw its task as creating a public conscience on the issue. While most conceded the fact of dispossession, few advocated the return of land. Many promoted inviolable reserves but none made it the centre of all else in the way the APL did. Few acknowledged Aboriginal *rights* to land, much less advocated a form of self-determination. Most advocated an alternative form of Protection. In calling for a form of indirect rule in Australia, the APL stood for an entirely different system of governance, one that was based on scientific humanism and ensured Aboriginal authority. The group's singularity was the result of a combination of factors: its proximity to Aboriginal populations in the centre and north; scholarly penetration of the region by Adelaide's scientific and academic fraternity; and early involvement in the creation of a large central Aboriginal reserve in which formative links were made with individuals such as Mary Bennett and groups such as the Anti-Slavery and Aborigines' Protection Society and the Royal Anthropological Institute.[76]

The federal government's assumption of control of the Northern Territory in 1911 did not allay the concerns about Aboriginal populations in the centre and north that had been gathering apace among Adelaide's humanitarian community. In 1910, for example, Dr William Ramsay-Smith, head of the Department of Public Health in Adelaide, argued that Aboriginal extinction was not inevitable and a solution could be found if it were really desired. At around the same time, the curator of mammals at the South Australian Museum, Hedley Herbert Finlayson, maintained that white settlement in the centre was only possible because of the black man's cooperation.[77] He spoke of a debt to the Aborigines which should be discharged by the entire white community. Zoologist Professor Harvey Johnston stated that the Aboriginal problem was a question of whether we were going to sacrifice the raising of a few thousand cattle, or the Aborigines, who had been dispossessed of their territories. Similarly, Dr Herbert Basedow was deeply concerned about the prevalence of disease among the inland tribes. Totally opposing the idea of the inevitability of decline, he argued instead that introduced diseases, such as syphilis and tuberculosis, had caused the greatest havoc among them.

Basedow's disaffection with the federal government was instrumental to the group's formation. This was largely the result of his extremely short stint as the first Chief Protector of the Northern Territory under the terms of the federal Aboriginals Ordinance (1911). The controversy he generated in his 45 days in the post was partly temperamental.[78] However, it was also underpinned by differences of view about policy and the way forward in a region still dominated by Aboriginal people, many of whom had had little or no contact with non-Aboriginal society. Basedow saw land and the preservation of Indigenous culture as critical to the long-term survival of Aboriginal people. A number of years after his resignation he undertook a medical relief tour to report on the prevalence of disease among Aborigines in the north and centre. On his return he pressed for a hinterland reservation to avert the danger of what he saw as complete extermination of some tribes. By then his ideas and concerns found a receptive ear in J. C. Genders, an elderly man of Adelaide's establishment who, deeply frustrated with existing humanitarian and governmental measures for Aborigines, established the Aborigines' Protection League in 1925 with Basedow its inaugural president.

Basedow's recommendations for policy conformed to the ideals of interwar imperial humanitarianism in terms of land (reserves), governance and labour. The establishment of carefully selected reserves of between 260 and 2,600 square kilometres were key. These would be for each tribe and would be self-supporting, 'if not a source of revenue', via trades such as horse and cattle breeding, and rabbit and dingo trapping. He stipulated that change was to be introduced to Aboriginal people through indigenous channels and that forms of indigenous authority and social and cultural practice were not to be interfered with unless they affected the general health and well-being of the communities.[79] Zogbaum has also pointed to Basedow's interest in the retention of Aboriginal languages.[80] The emphasis was on self-support. Reserves would have male and female instructors of craft, trade and other occupations, as well as native attendants and teachers. Inspectors would be appointed to exclusively defend and protect native interests and rights. His ideas around Aboriginal employment, which included freedom of contract and workers' compensation, demonstrated the connection being made in British humanitarian ranks between questions of land and labour and, in particular, a concern to prevent a form of de facto servitude in dispossessed territories.[81] Indeed, the Anti-Slavery and Aborigines' Protection Society based its notion of land trusts for Australian Aborigines, submitted to Australian governments in 1936, on Basedow's foundational work.[82]

In making Basedow inaugural president of the APL, Genders was recognising the worth of his ideas, which had never been taken seriously by the government. While Kevin Blackburn argues that Genders' own policy ideas were taken almost entirely from developments for the Maori in New Zealand, Basedow's ideas and influence are nonetheless evident in the Model Aboriginal State which became the *sine qua non* of the APL's recommendations in the late 1920s.[83] The suggestion was that an area of land be handed back to the Aboriginal custodians to manage by themselves, according to their own cultural and political structures. It would be voluntary, have representation in the Commonwealth Parliament and be managed by an Aboriginal tribunal. If successful, it would provide the prototype for similar native states in other parts of Australia. As Blackburn argues, the inspiration for the idea came from examples of self-government of Indian tribes in North America and, more particularly, the Maori who, by the second half of the nineteenth century, had achieved considerable political, economic and cultural autonomy.

Michael Roe has described this development as symptomatic of the times.[84] Indeed, David Jackson's appeal in parliament occurred on the same day as the petition for the Model Aboriginal State was first discussed there. It has been described as segregationist, but Genders subsequently rejected segregation as not giving the Aborigines the 'place in the sun' they deserved.[85] Blackburn argues that the Model Aboriginal State was primarily about governance. Certainly, Genders believed that their own territories under their own government would deliver better prospects for Aborigines than any form of white protection.[86] In the words of the Model State Manifesto, the strongest argument for the movement was the need for a change in policy to methods that avoided any further neglect or repeated past errors. It was about avoiding the haphazard and unregulated contact of old.

The Model Aboriginal State was thus a succinct statement of interwar humanitarian aims, with all the hallmarks of humanitarian angst in Australia and humanitarian solutions in England and elsewhere. It was driven by a concern with depopulation, dispossession, historic wrongs and poor administration. But it was clearly influenced by the discourse of imperial humanitarianism. According to Roe, one way of understanding the appeal for Aboriginal independence at the time was via the heated debate in England over Indian self-rule.[87] Equally important were aspects of indirect rule, particularly an emphasis on native rights and preservationism. The native tribunal would be run according to native laws and customs, with the exception of those declared to be 'cruel', and Aborigines would be assisted to accommodate their methods to new conditions, if they desired.

This notion of future development further demonstrates the link to the principles of indirect rule. The Model State would be an industrial reserve where Aboriginal people would be given some practical training and, with the help of sympathetic white residents in the form of agricultural teachers, medical officers and missionaries, voluntarily 'work out their own salvation' by slowly evolving from the hunting to the pastoral stage of culture. As H. K. Fry suggested, the idea of productive reserves for indigenous people underscored the British push for land rights in the post-abolition era.[88] He suggested that it related to a persistent British attitude that administration should be directed to the 'good' of these people. As we have seen, what constituted good had changed by the 1930s. To preservation of culture was added gradual development. Preservation *and* development became the new catchcry.

Indeed, it was precisely these ideas that Genders subsequently cited as the justification for his Model State. Genders revisited his proposal 10 years on in a defence of his position in *The NSW Honorary Magistrate*, a journal he published on behalf of the Justices Association of South Australia.[89] He justified it in retrospect as a policy of indirect rule, citing the work of Mair. In her *Native Policies for Africa*, Mair outlined the different forms of native administration by imperial powers. These were the 'white man's country' policy, where native interests were subservient to the dominant European population; the policy of assimilation as practised by the French, Belgian and Portuguese colonies, where native advancement was predicated on tribal detachment; and, lastly, the policy of indirect rule.[90] Genders argued that Australia fell into the first category. He preferred indirect rule, stating:

> When we have learnt not to discriminate between the colour of the skin (a very far cry) and when under [the] policy of 'Indirect Rule' the Australian Aborigine has achieved national pride with his own Government, Chiefs, etc, has his own universities, colleges, and Oxford or Cambridge men (like India), then it will be time enough to talk of assimilation.[91]

Like Mair, Genders went on to suggest that indirect rule was a more sympathetic form of colonial administration because it did not supplant indigenous systems with foreign ones in the way assimilation did. Such a system was based on discrimination. Under indirect rule, if and when Europeanisation occurred, it would be based on and would support and enhance native culture and authority in changed circumstances.

IV

Genders also cited a treatise titled 'A Native Policy for Australia' as being critical to his and the APL's sense of the problem and its solution. It was written by Mary Bennett on behalf of the APL and was strongly influenced by developments on the ground in London concerning the native question.[92] Bennett was not only on the periphery of the imperial humanitarian set, she also had Australian experience, having spent time on her father's pastoral run in northwest Queensland as a child, befriended by the local Aboriginal people, the Dalleburra. By the late 1920s she had emerged as someone who could provide knowledge and expertise on Australian conditions in the heart of the empire. She had made regular contributions on the Aborigines' question in Australia to *The Manchester Guardian*. She joined the Anti-Slavery and Aborigines' Protection Society in London at the suggestion of her friend, Edith Jones, who had similarly experienced Australian conditions. In 1927 she met Constance Cooke and Frederic Wood Jones when they took the message of the Model State to the Australian High Commissioner in London and to the British Commonwealth League. Bennett became the London-based representative of the APL and advocated the Model Aboriginal State in her biography of her father, which was published in that same year.

According to Bennett, a native policy for Australia rested on the need to discover and apply principles of a just relationship between a 'white', 'immigrant' and 'invading' race and a subject Aboriginal race. It was primarily a question of legal justice, an inquiry into the rights of Aborigines as British subjects and citizens of the Commonwealth to equality before the law. The aim was to end discrimination, for 'no nation can remain free that tolerates discrimination'. It was a moral issue, 'to remove abuse and the disparity in status which bred abuse'. Developments in the empire were pointing to three particularly important issues in the resolution of the native question: land, labour and a voice in their own concerns. While adequate areas of land should be reserved in perpetuity for native use, Aborigines should not be exploited as cheap labour, for 'to force them to labour for aliens by depriving them of their own resources is a system analogous to slavery'.[93]

Bennett argued that the question was bound up with how to bridge the gap between a communal civilisation and a competitive one. She suggested two possible modes of governance. The first was direct rule, which she said equated to white dominance and governing by regulations and was indistinguishable from assimilation. This, she argued, destroyed indigenous institutions and deprived the community of natural leaders.

It resulted in loss of interest in life by the governed and a 'slave mortality indistinguishable from extermination', and was the policy pursued by Australian governments. On the other hand, indirect rule allowed Aboriginal people to maintain their economies and adapt to the new within their own traditions, under their own leaders and with a form of government they could understand.

The Model State, as understood by Genders, conformed to the ideas Bennett outlined. However, despite his sense of urgency and the momentum he gathered around the proposal, he and it were not taken very seriously. This was not least because it was rejected as unrealistic and unworkable in an inquiry into the centre and north by Commissioner Bleakley, whose appointment represented the federal government's response to the growing humanitarian angst over the region.[94] It had also been subjected to intense ridicule and misrepresentation.[95] The story of the Model Aboriginal State is nevertheless illustrative of the divergence of views that was beginning to be seen by the end of the 1920s between governments and some humanitarian groups about the nature of the Aboriginal problem and its solution.

One of the key drivers of humanitarianism in the interwar period was the concern about racial and cultural loss as a result of dispossession which contemporary policies appeared to replicate. These smacked of racial superiority which humanitarians considered both erroneous and unfounded. The Aboriginal problem as they defined it (the white man's drink, drugs and disease) was demonstration alone of the fallacy of white superiority. About six months after launching the petition to Parliament calling for a Model State, Genders, Wood Jones, Cooke and other members of Adelaide's scientific and humanitarian community launched the 'Save the Aborigines Movement', an indication that they saw the Model State as an alternative to Aboriginal extinction.

Governments were moving in the direction of leaving full-blood people alone primarily because it meant no intervention at all, particularly no development. This was partly because the real Aboriginal problem, as far as governments were concerned, was the rise of the half-castes. It was a question of how to maintain the purity of the white race in the face of apparently increased and ongoing miscegenation between white and black, particularly in frontier regions with promise and potential for white settlement but still in their developmental infancy. It would be fair to say that, in the interwar years, the half-caste problem became a national obsession.[96]

According to the racialised thinking of the day, half-castes represented an anomalous, unregulated and unlegislated presence in the body politic. Indeed, the humanitarian lobby came to recognise two distinct problems: the remaining full-descent communities in the centre and north, and the growing mixed-descent or half-caste communities, mostly in the south. Most humanitarians believed that the problem of miscegenation could be solved with more adequate, modernised protection. By maintaining systems of tribal governance, for example, the Model State would regulate, if not eradicate, the problem, according to Genders. However, the original problem – the notion of preserving the race from extinction – remained a powerful underlying, enduring and, as this book will demonstrate, recurring refrain.

Both governments and humanitarians, therefore, saw the question as one of racial survival. This was the hour of eugenics.[97] It has been widely recognised how some Australian governments deployed a eugenic solution on the eve of World War II to solve the Aboriginal problem.[98] This would see mixed-descent communities biologically absorbed into the white majority to eradicate the 'colour problem' altogether. For their part, and completely against this grain, some humanitarians demanded a eugenic solution of their own. What mattered was the purity of the black. When, in their Model State proposal, the APL suggested removal of Aborigines on the fringes of settlement, they were alluding to what was widely believed to be the fragility of the black race in contact with the contaminating white race. This notion of preserving the purity of the black race underpinned the demand for inviolable reserves. Purity related to indigeneity, race *and* culture. Humanitarianism in the interwar period was replete with discovery and admiration of the black man's culture and civilisation which, when compared to the white, was noble, sophisticated and environmentally adept. Wood Jones' *Australia's Vanishing Race* (1934), a lecture series and radio broadcast speaking to the problem of depopulation and the need for administrative change, was a soliloquy to such.[99]

Preserving the race might lead to the call for absolute segregation, of which Wood Jones was the strongest proponent, but it might also lead to a better *relationship* between white and black in the future, a means of reconciling the two civilisations, recognising the interests of both 'immigrant invaders' and 'black subjects'. The appeal of indirect rule in the interwar period was the notion of preserving a race/culture/people while introducing change slowly. In promoting the Model State the APL was not advocating segregation in the way its critics, including some Aboriginal critics, understood at the time. It was propelled by an awareness of the inevitability of change and new conditions for Aborigines, but it wanted this to proceed differently from the past. As the APL saw it, the Model State was a means of regrouping and redefining an Aboriginal future in Aboriginal terms. It gave a communal civilisation time to adapt to a competitive one while utilising its own resources. It proferred the prospect of future development (economic, social and political) and a place in the nation, but not at the expense of the Aborigine's own culture.

Whereas the importance of indirect rule in the empire was as a philosophy justifying the British colonial order in tropical Africa, for the minority who advocated it in Australia, far removed from the practical implementation of policy or from direct power or the empire itself, it fused a modernist, progressivist and humanitarian platform for the recognition of Aboriginal rights to land, culture and humanity.[100] Above all, it was an *ideal*, or the APL's interpretation of an ideal, worth pursuing.

DEFINING A REFORM AGENDA
Mary Bennett and the Humanitarian Moment

> Protectors who cannot protect, regulations that are not enforced,
> political expediencies, are not going to save them. Only the grace
> of God can open the eyes of Australians to what they are doing
> and inspire them to reverse their practice…justice may be done
> before it is too late.[1]

Bennett's pamphlet 'A Native Policy for Australia' was an expression of progressive thinking in the heart of empire about the native question. In June 1929 she confirmed her sense of excitement about this moment in the empire in a letter to the editor of *Queensland Country Life,* from her home in Hertfordshire, England. In it she painted a picture of an empire deeply engaged in questions of native policy and administration and situated herself as a more-than-interested bystander. Because of her Australian experience she had been asked to speak to the British Commonwealth League (BCL) on the topic of 'Australian Administration and the Aborigines'. Admitting the difficulty of the task, she nevertheless set herself to work on what she saw as a matter of moulding public opinion on an important national subject. This interest in native policies was not in criticism of Australia, she said, but part of a new moment in the empire. The subject was in the air as a result of the Hilton Young Report on Kenya, the South African elections, the Simon inquiry in India and conferences of the League of Nations. It was simply the desire to know how matters were tackled elsewhere. However, she foresaw a growing experience of external interest in native policies in Australia and thought it best to be prepared in order to support 'all workers for humane conditions'.[2]

Bennett thus encapsulated the new humanitarian moment in the British Empire. The reports on Africa, India and the League of Nations, as well as the broader public engagement with the same, spoke to a wide interest in colonial policy and tropical governance for its own sake in the early decades of the twentieth century. As Sinha has shown, such interest also came at a transitional moment in empire, complicating and expanding the humanitarian frame.[3] Porter tells us that this frame shifted from the anti-imperialism of the late nineteenth-century radical critique of empire to more moderate questions concerning constructive colonial policy and native rights by the interwar years.[4] Whereas the former had focused on imperialism's domestic effects, the latter pushed the native question to the forefront of the radical case. Central to it were questions about native labour and land tenure. Natives lost their land, the critics said, to become a cheap labour supply for the colonists. A handful of reformers were particularly concerned that, under these circumstances, a de facto servitude, or slave conditions in disguise, had replaced the de jure slavery of old.[5]

Bennett's demands for the reform of Australian Aboriginal policy must be seen as part of this imperial milieu, particularly its reformism, evangelism and anti-slavery rhetoric. Like reformers all over the empire, hers was a Christian agenda for change which utilised the humanitarian moment to demand salvation and justice for Aboriginal people. As her invitation to speak indicates, she was embedded in this culture of empire which, by the interwar period, had expanded opportunities for women like herself to contribute to the discussion on imperial matters, including native administration.[6] The report she went on to present to the BCL demonstrates how intimately acquainted she was with Australian policies and practices and how she saw canvassing them as conforming to the spirit of the times. Energised by the moment, she saw it as an opportunity to launch her own campaign for humane conditions for Australian Aboriginal people. Hers would represent the Australian episode of this wider empire story.

I

By the time Bennett delivered her paper to the BCL in June 1929 she already had a reputation among London's reforming set as a champion of the Aborigines because of her regular newspaper contributions in their defence.[7] Her joining of the Anti-Slavery and Aborigines' Protection Society in 1927 coincided with the publication of her first book, *Christison of Lammermoor*, a biography of her father, in which she devoted considerable space to the Aboriginal problem in Australia. In that same year her 'Notes on the Dalleburra' compiled, in part, from her father's ethnographic notes and detailing the customs and culture of the Aboriginal people on whose land he settled in 1863, was published in the journal of the Royal Anthropological Institute.[8] Through her humanitarian connections she had also met Anthony Martin Fernando, an outspoken Aboriginal activist then living in England who travelled the world to publicise injustices to Australian Aborigines.[9] By the late 1920s he was regularly seen picketing Australia House, toy skeletons adorning his coat with placards proclaiming, 'this is all Australia has left of my people'.[10]

Fernando's was a complex, fascinating and tragic tale of protest and performance on the world stage.[11] Bennett's meeting him in 1929 appears to have been an epiphanic moment which fuelled her own crusade. Indeed, she subsequently described a gentle, self-educated, Christian man with an acute sense of injustice. She visited him in a prison cell at the Old Bailey where he was awaiting trial for an incident involving a racial taunt in which he had threatened his tormentor with a gun. By that stage he had attracted a great deal of curiosity and attention, particularly from among the humanitarian set in London, largely because of his articulateness and defiance. Rather than being cowed and defeated, he used the courtroom to accuse Britain and Australia of engineering Aboriginal demise through dispossession, starvation, neglect and racism. Nor did he expect justice from the British legal system which, he argued, was deeply implicated in these processes.

In her biography of Fernando, Fiona Paisley shows how this was a profound moment in the empire. A black man in such rage was clearly a spectacle which unnerved his onlookers and keepers, who looked for signs of insanity in his rants. Yet, when Bennett finally met him she was impressed by his sanity, his gentleness of demeanour and his intelligence. She was moved by his sense of desperation and passion, which had driven him into exile. She was equally affected by his accusations of cant and hypocrisy to her 'genuine concern'. His story of cultural and familial loss, including separation from his mother, would provide a key vignette in *The Australian Aboriginal as a Human Being*, which she was writing at the time. Fernando's story opened chapter six, which was dedicated to the 'Aboriginal Woman in the Federal Territories'. It started with a quote from Fernando: 'I was taken from my tribe before I was old enough to remember my mother but the thought of my mother is the guiding star of my life'.[12]

Bennett then relates how it was Fernando's witnessing a murder of an Aborigine by whites in Peak Hill, Western Australia, and his inability to give evidence in the subsequent trial, that led to his leaving Australia and travelling the world, protesting that 'the law of England has outlawed us' and calling for justice for his race. The memory of his people's suffering, according to Bennett, fuelled his constant travels, as did the 'imagination' of his mother. Bennett uses his story to question what happened to his mother and to explore the position of Aboriginal women and girls in the north and centre of Australia, a theme which was to dominate her reform agenda before World War II.

By 1929, then, Bennett was already a seasoned reformer. She was part of a bigger empire-wide conversation between concerned advocates and politicians about native conditions in colonised areas which effectively dated to at least a century before. Her paper to the BCL was a shortened version of key parts of *The Australian Aboriginal as a Human Being*, which was published in 1930. Both were focused on the position of Aborigines in the federal territories, rather than the states, because she believed that the problem was extremely urgent there and that an 'honourable settlement' with the Aborigines in those areas was still possible. The book also built on her earlier works, being an extended study of her more generalised comments in *Christison* concerning the nature of the Aboriginal problem. All had an impressive depth of research, demonstrating meticulousness in the compilation of the facts. They revealed that she had been a student of Australian history for some time. Indeed, she fancied herself an historian, telling editor, Mr Lees, in her letter that newspapers were 'an extraordinarily valuable record for the historian', where day-to-day happenings were recorded and 'sidelights make history real'.[13] History was central to her articulation of the Aboriginal problem because, as she described it, relations between Aborigines and settlers in Australia had a 'deadly continuity'.[14]

In both books she cites a variety of historical sources, including an extensive range of Australian periodicals, newspapers, histories and settler reminiscence from the earliest days of European settlement, and an enormous amount of evidence from commissions of inquiry in Australia, protectors' reports and parliamentary debate on the native question both in Australia and in England. She quoted extensively from accounts of exploration such as those of Eyre, Sturt and Sir Thomas Mitchell. Indeed, by the time she settled in Australia in 1930 she had a considerable discursive armoury with which to mount her case. She also had the contacts, having met and being in correspondence with leading members of Australia's humanitarian fraternity. As the London representative of the South Australian Aborigines' Protection League, she promoted and requested support for their solutions in all her works.

Bennett's books and papers to this point also demonstrate how completely steeped she was in the latest thinking and propaganda about colonial policy in the empire which she saw as relevant to Australian conditions. Looking at her works collectively we might say she was a student of British colonial policy. Her bibliographies listed several important works, including the 1837 House of Commons Report on Aborigines and Lord Durham's 1839 *Report on the Affairs of British North America*. Other references were R. L. Buell's *The Native Problem in Africa* (1928), Sir Frederick Lugard's *The Dual Mandate in British Tropical Africa* (1922), Belgian reports on the Congo, E. D. Morel's *The Black Man's Burden* (1920), a 'Memorandum on Administration of Justice in South Africa with Special Reference to the Native Population' (1928), C. F. Andrews' *Indentured Indians in Fiji* (1918), as well as League of Nations and International Labour Office propaganda, and the Report of the Hilton Young Commission. Reading her works one gets a sense of her excitement about the contemporary moment, the sense of urgency, the sense of opportunity. Here was a moment in which Australia could divest itself of its past and move forward with the world in what, by the interwar years, had been identified as the most important business of the twentieth century: 'to discover and apply the principles of just relations of the white and dark races'.[15]

That recent developments in British colonial policy and practice pointed the way forward for Bennett is hardly surprising. As Hyam suggests, this was a generation that was swimming in discursive pronouncements about trusteeship, particularly as it played out in central and east Africa.[16] According to a Fabian Society pamphlet on 'Imperial Trusteeship', between 1900 and 1929 there had been at least 200 reports and parliamentary papers on east Africa alone.[17] This was a time when principles of native paramountcy and indirect rule were promoted as models of humane colonial governance in providing the means to reconcile the interests of both settlers and natives. Progressivist thinking posited that where the former could develop the land and resources of the country, the latter required protection and advancement under benign British rule. Where there was conflict between the two, the interests of the Africans should prevail. These principles had been recognised for east Africa under the terms of the Devonshire Declaration (1923) and restated in the Hilton Young Report published in January 1929.[18]

The Hilton Young Commission was particularly relevant to Bennett. Its establishment and its recommendations represent a hallmark of the imperial humanitarian agenda. The report that resulted was a classic statement of humane aspiration and thought on the native question. The commission was appointed by Lord Amery in 1927 to investigate the desirability of closer union in east Africa. An ideal held dear by white settlers, closer union referred to the potential creation of a white dominion, a federation of Kenya, Uganda and Tanganika in which conservatives like Amery, who became colonial secretary in 1925, imagined white settlers responsible trustees of the Africans. A supporter of closer union, Sir Edward Hilton Young was appointed chair and was required to investigate the possibility. However, mounting criticism of continued white settler encroachments on African lands, apparently condoned by the administration, saw the conservative Hilton Young outvoted.

Closer union was rejected in his report in favour of emphasising the need to safeguard native interests. While restating the notion that trusteeship could not be delegated, it recommended that the first charge on any territory was the 'paramountcy of native interests', interpreted as the 'creation and preservation of a field for the full development of native life'.[19] The report considered native interests under five headings: land, economic development, labour, education, and political and administrative institutions.[20] The reservation of adequate areas of land for native use and the creation of conditions for the full development of native life, including assistance to develop their own territories, was key. Furthermore, the inquiry introduced an entirely new concept in suggesting that 'what the immigrant communities may justly claim is partnership not control'.[21]

The report was considered something of a watershed in colonial administration at the time. The east and central African dependencies had been acquired by Britain in the peace settlement following World War I. In terms of geography, climate and population, Britain inherited a very different native problem than in west Africa, which it had colonised from the late eighteenth century. In east Africa the issue was, in Lugard's terms, the problem of comparatively small white communities in tropical environments where there was a preponderant black population rapidly acquiring self-consciousness.[22] In his review of the commission's report the anthropologist Malinowski argued that the problem was complicated by the white settler with his needs and aspirations.[23] He went on to suggest that the government had modified Lugard's Dual Policy as a result, recognising native interests as paramount, but encouraging white settlement and protecting its interests in so far as they did not conflict with those of the native races. Nonetheless, it was widely understood that the principle of recognising the advancement of native interests as an end in itself would lead to considerable variation and interpretation in practice. The significance of the report, so it was said, was in laying down a native policy that was consistent in its main principles but which could be adapted to local conditions and groups.[24]

Bennett looked to apply the commission's chief recommendations to Australian conditions. It was the inspiration for her 'Native Policy' and it may well have been why she decided to focus on the problem in the centre and north, as conditions there were very similar to those in east Africa. There was a small white minority that was dependent on a preponderant black population, an Asiatic presence and a tropical climate.[25] As in east Africa there had been a great deal of discussion about the long-term viability of white settlement in the region.[26] There was an appreciation that this could only occur in the long term via the continued use of Aboriginal labour. There was also increasing encroachment on native lands and growing evidence of native hostility in the region. For Bennett, the Hilton Young Report provided a framework for a native policy that could deliver a different outcome for black and white in the region. As she wrote in her 'Native Policy', 'this exhaustive inquiry formulated the basis of a policy which would at once be just to the native and favourable to the whites'.[27] She cherry-picked from it, focusing on those parts she thought most relevant to Australia.

II

One part of the report which Bennett emphasised was that section which stipulated the importance of the quality of the early settlers in colonial territories. It was almost as important to colonial governments, according to the commissioners, as the quality of its own officials in establishing just relations between immigrant and native populations.[28] That Bennett instinctively understood this was evident in her first book, *Christison of Lammermoor,* which was largely testament to the difference a quality settler – her father – could make. Described by Professor Ernest Scott, history professor at the University of Melbourne, as the best Australian biography he had ever read, the book was part history of colonial Queensland, part biography of her father and part polemic for the better treatment of the Aborigines.[29] She shows how the question of 'what to do with the blacks' was a discourse of frontier settlement which largely revolved around how to rid them from the landscape. In three chapters titled 'What to do with the Blacks', she turns this everyday settler question into a much more serious one in which recognition of settler practice and legal and historical precedent are critical to the response.

Mary Bennett

Bennett's father, Robert Christison, established his property, Lammermoor, in the centre of Dalleburra country, an Aboriginal tribe of between 300 and 500 people who occupied the tableland and plains some 300 miles west of Bowen.[30] He reached their country in the early 1860s at the height of inter-racial tension in the region, where settlers described the blacks as 'bad' and, with government support, resorted to the native police to remove them. As history has shown, the native police were a brutal (and brutalising) force of Aboriginal decimation on the Queensland frontier.[31] Bennett's biography casually mentions massacres, conducted by the force and by local settlers, as part of the landscape her father traversed. She describes settlers nearby who, having good relations with the local Aborigines, were nonetheless powerless to prevent the native police from wreaking havoc upon them. Bennett wrote that entrenched settler antagonism to 'the blacks' overran any appreciation of their position or the cause of their hostility.

Bennett constructs Christison as the first white man in their country with a desire to deal justly with the Aborigines, arguing that he pursued a different approach to most. Chasing down one of the tribe, he used him as an emissary to send the message back to the Dalleburra of his friendly intentions. Bennett tells how the captured man related to her some 30 years later how he had formed a charter with Christison at that point. Christison had named him 'Barney' while he had named Christison 'Munggra', which Bennett surmised derived from 'mung-er', meaning 'to hear, to understand, to know'.[32] According to Bennett, Barney decided to stay near the property and work for Christison, to which Christison agreed, saying: 'You and me sit down two fellow messmates. Country belonging to you; sheep belonging to me'.[33] Bennett relates how Christison referred to his policy of 'letting the blacks in at all hazards' as the only workable one given that the homestead waterhole was a meeting-place of the tribes. But it was an extremely difficult undertaking as the massacres of the early 1860s and particularly the Wills massacre in 1861, after which reinforcements of native police were brought in, had produced fear and distrust among the 'far back' tribes and a determination on the part of the white-settler population to keep them out.

It has been argued that the policy of letting in the Aborigines led to the exploitation of their labour, including child labour.[34] Indeed, the Dalleburra became an important and long-term source of labour contributing to the success of the Lammermoor enterprise. However, Bennett uses her father's letting in of the Dalleburra as a trope for his exceptionalism and the possibility of an alternative approach on the frontier. One interpretation was that his letting the Dalleburra in was about his benevolent protection of them. Bennett paints a picture of a man determined to protect the group from the incursions of the native police at all costs. She claims that, in doing so, he was potentially making them an easier target as, to the native police, 'one black scapegoat served as well as another, and unresisting ones best of all'.[35]

Barney, 'The Faithful Dalleburra', whom Christison made a compact with in the 1860s, © Trustees of the British Museum.

Clearly, he was also protecting his labour supply but he understood that in order to do so he had to build trust. In this sense he went against the grain. As Bennett describes it, in the context of the mid to late 1860s Queensland frontier, letting in was ridiculed as naïve, particularly after the Wills massacre.[36] In that instance Wills and his party, some nineteen in all, had been subjected to a surprise attack and clubbed to death. In the aftermath, Wills' apparent friendliness and concern not to interfere with the local Aborigines was understood to have caused his downfall. Thereafter, letting in was scoffed at as placing unwarranted trust in the enemy. Thus, in Bennett's formulation, Christison's charter with the Dalleburra and his policy of letting them in was about establishing a relationship between the two which rested on a reciprocal understanding: he and his people would not harm the Dalleburra but they must not harm him or his.

It seemed to work. For another 40 years or so members of the Dalleburra stayed on Lammermoor, working and living in the huts Christison built for them in the station precinct. While it is certainly true that he displayed all the features of paternalism characteristic of the period – the Dalleburra were his 'faithfuls' – he also had a genuine interest in their culture and was moved by what he characterised as their loyalty to him. Indeed, Bennett's 'Notes on the Dalleburra' are substantially taken from notes Christison compiled for a study he intended to write. Bennett tells how his Dalleburra dictionary appeared in E. M. Curr's *The*

Australian Race (1886) and some of his observations were incorporated into A. W. Howitt's *Native Tribes of South-East Australia* (1904), two key works of nineteenth-century ethnography. Her detailed 'Notes' are testament to a keen and genuine appreciation of Dalleburra culture and a trust between parties. Christison also remained true to his word. Following the strain of the great drought at the end of the century, aged sixty, he sold Lammermoor, making the rights of the Dalleburra to their country a condition of purchase. As the stock and station owner recorded, Christison was very clear and adamant: 'I wish to find a purchaser who will treat my blacks well, for they have been loyal to me since 1864. I will send an annual contribution. And he (the potential buyer) won't haggle'.[37]

When Bennett returned to Lammermoor with her father in 1910 to sell the property, in her late twenties, she seemed genuinely moved by her nursemaid Wyma's old age and feebleness. One of the last vignettes in *Christison of Lammermoor* is the story of Wyma's protection of an Aboriginal woman, Jenny-Lin, from a nearby township. She had had a casual sexual relationship with a white man which Bennett described as fuelled by alcohol. A fight had ensued between Jenny-Lin's husband, Charley, and the white man. While the former was imprisoned, the latter was taken to hospital. Jenny-Lin then helped Charley escape and, with the help of the Lammermoor Aborigines, the pair evaded capture for some weeks. Upon recapture, Charley was imprisoned again and Jenny-Lin was taken to the women at Lammermoor. While recounting the story Bennett is clearly troubled by its injustice and asks: 'did the magistrate punish the rascally white people who had broken the law by supplying liquor to an aboriginal? Did he release the man whose crime was defending his much-persecuted wife? Not a bit'.[38]

It would seem that in telling the story when she did, Bennett was taking an opportunity to remind Australians of the significant contribution Aboriginal people made to pastoralism, a fact which has since been well documented. She also wanted to record the dark side of Queensland's settlement, reminding Australians that violence and massacre had characterised that frontier. She wanted to show that there was an alternative and that, with care and benevolence, Aboriginal people responded positively. They were hard working, generous, kind and respectful. White settlers were indebted to them for their aid in exploring and occupying the land.

Bennett had herself benefited from such generosity. Although born in England, she experienced Lammermoor at formative times of her childhood, between the ages of two and six and, intermittently, between the ages of twelve and about eighteen when, during her mother's sojourns to Australia, the family would retire to Lammermoor for the winter. Some of the Aboriginal workers would accompany them when they went south. Furthermore, in these formative years Bennett and her siblings were taught by a German governess and by an Aboriginal nurse. They were Wyma's 'pamboonas' whom she loved and spoilt.

Wyma, Booloodea Timullinya, Mary Bennett's nursemaid, from a photograph originally taken at Lammermoor by her mother in 1886, © Trustees of the British Museum.

The feeling was reciprocal. Not long after Wyma died in June 1926, Bennett contributed a moving tribute to her which was published in the *Townsville Daily Bulletin*. Born some time in the mid-1850s, her name was Booloodea Timullinya and she was one of three wives of Warmboomooloo, a ko-bee-berry or head-man.[39] Bennett describes Wyma's amazing resourcefulness as the youngest wife, her food-gathering skills, and her athleticism as she plunged into waterholes to gather water-lilies for Bennett and her siblings and climbed trees to gather honey. When Warmboomooloo died she married Freddy, a Kanaka stockman on Christison's station. She worked as a parlourmaid in Christison's house at first and was then 'promoted' to nursemaid – a job, Bennett said, she was never happier doing as her own children had died in infancy. Bennett described her with great admiration as having a brilliant intellect, great courage and kindness. Wyma was also generous. When Bennett grew up and became interested in Aboriginal handicrafts, Wyma would leave something on her dressing-table after cleaning her room – a quartz knife, a headband or a grass necklace. On the day of Wyma's death, Bennett was writing her a letter from her home in Hertfordshire, something she did every year since last seeing Wyma in 1910.

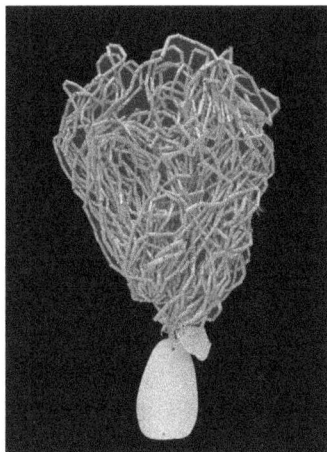

Grass necklace made by Wyma like the one she gave Bennett. It was donated to the British Museum by Robert Christison in 1901, © Trustees of the British Museum.

We see some of this emotional attachment in *Christison of Lammermoor*, too. Yet, historian Mark Cryle has questioned Bennett's sentimentalism, particularly her portrayal of Christison. Critiquing the book as a selective telling of family history, he maintains that Bennett excludes Christison's legacy of often violent mastery over the Dalleburra as he undertook to build a pastoral empire. This included not only dubious methods of recruitment but also harsh punishments and what Cryle suspects was his collusion with the native police on occasion. Cryle also points to Bennett's silence about Jane Gordon, the small half-caste child taken by Bennett's mother back to England to raise as an English child at the turn of the century. A combination of the cold weather and her mother's inability to cope saw the girl returned to Australia some two years later, aged only about four, and institutionalised on Fraser Island, 'to face the hellhole that was Bogimbah'.[40]

Cryle thus points to a more complex story of inter-racial contact. He suggests that Bennett's story is implicated in the violence it seeks to critique and points to the paradox at the heart of Christison's benevolence.

Certainly, Robert Christison had a reputation in Australia to protect. He was a powerful figure in colonial Queensland – a wealthy grazier who occupied an immense amount of territory.[41] He was a pioneer whose own personal story of exploration in the north intersected with the great nineteenth-century stories of Burke and Wills, and William Landsborough. Once on the land, he was a pioneer in other ways too. His attempts to deal with tick and rabbit infestations, his endless pioneering efforts at water conservation and his attempts to establish a chair of tropical agriculture at the University of Queensland are examples. While not a politician, he moved in political circles, contributed lectures and speeches, and wrote pamphlets on leading issues and questions of the day, from railways and the development of the colony, to a federated Australia, tropical life and the kindliness and intelligence of the 'blacks' and their shameful treatment by the whites. Among his circle of friends were the premier of Queensland, Thomas McIlwraith, Bishop Stanton of northern Queensland and Sir Horace Tozer, Agent-General for Queensland. Features on Lammermoor regularly appeared in *Dalgety's Review* and the *Pastoral Review*.[42] He was the patron of the Townsville Pastoral, Agricultural and Industrial Association and the Charters Towers Pastoral and Mining Association.[43]

Bennett paints her father as a leading pioneer in the sense of having to overcome many trials in the process of initiating new and important projects. He laboured, often against great odds, in the cause of the colony. Nowhere was this clearer than his efforts at being the first Australian to build a meat-freezing works in north Queensland to export meat to the British market and cut down on waste:

> But for Christison there would have been no freezing works in North Queensland in the Eighties. It was he who saw the need for freezing works; who tried to rouse colonists to join in the enterprise; who in London put forward Queensland as the great cattle-growing country; who collected and sifted information, and worked out the whole scheme; who impelled the Board of Directors to action and persuaded his fellow-colonists to second the undertaking. Why should the enterprise not succeed?[44]

Bennett then goes on to describe the problems her father had to confront in making this dream a reality, including his own health and the well-being of his family. He established the Australian Company which bought Poole Island, near Bowen, for the purpose. The company spent 20,000 pounds erecting buildings, stockyards, a jetty and punts, as well as purchasing machinery, horses and labour. It was described at one stage as the 'best establishment in Australia'.[45] However, a combination of factors, from unsuitable timber, scarce labour and cyclones to the wrong machinery and personnel, and timidity on the part of the company's British backers, conspired to see the enterprise collapse. Bennett shows how, far from denting his energy, her father saw Poole Island as opening the way for other such ventures.

That Robert Christison and his family were regarded as one of the more important families in Queensland is evident in the pages of the various daily and weekly newspapers in the colony since their arrival in the early 1860s. His affairs, both in relation to his activities as a squatter – his buying, selling, breeding and showing of cattle – and his various connections to the leading lights of the Queensland establishment, were regularly recorded. Births, deaths and burials associated with Lammermoor were all noted, as was his and his wife's movements when in Australia between Lammermoor and their southern residences. Their socialising was recorded in the gossip columns of the day. The presentation of Mary and her younger sister Helen at the court of King George was cause for comment, including what they wore for the occasion. The engagements of Helen and of Mary's brother, Robert (Roy) also featured, as did Mary's marriage. There were features on the station and the Lammermoor Hills and regular stories of Christison's pioneering days and his contributions to Queensland's history. His purchase of Burwell Park, a country estate in South Lincolnshire, following his retirement was referenced with one article declaring him to be part of the growing 'snobocracy' of Britain.

Bennett's writing to Mr Lees with news from London was therefore no accident. It demonstrated how intimately connected she and her family still were to affairs in Queensland. Christison would become part of an expatriate community in London which hankered for news from Australia and vice versa. Some of the reports of Christison's or his family affairs in the Queensland press came direct from the *British Australasian*, the British newspaper of the Australasian expatriate community in London, which acted as a social glue for settlers and sojourners alike.[46] In this context Christison's story was a bridge across the imperial divide. If telling it was an act of redemption for Bennett, perhaps it was also a redemptive tale for both the empire and the colony. As Bennett's story shows, Aboriginal affairs had been and continued to be one of the myriad threads on which this relationship was built. Yet the thread was tenuous and knotty, bound by tales of abandonment, mistrust, dispossession, frontier violence and police brutality, nowhere more so than in Queensland. In this sense, Christison's story carried moral cache. It was exemplar and escape.

It helps, therefore, to think about *Christison of Lammermoor* as an historical source, to think about the silences Cryle points to and the book itself in the context of Bennett's wider story. This was her first book and it launched her defence of the Aboriginal cause, providing crucial evidence of her credentials. It was written a decade after her father's death and published in the same year as the death of her husband, to whom it is dedicated. In some ways, the alleged silences are a function of the text. As Cryle admits, Bennett's romanticisation of her father fitted a standard of heroic masculine accomplishment in settler reminiscences of the period. But the text also leaves room for ambiguity. She writes it in the third person so that there is a more formal, objectified rendering of character and, in this context, it is difficult to know how to read her tone at times. Nowhere is this clearer than in her construction of her parents and herself, the privileged settlers who benefited from Dalleburra land and loyalty. In parts of the story Christison *is* implicated in both passive and active modes of violence to the Dalleburra. However, the focus of the book is undoubtedly the reciprocal tale of loyalty and friendship between Christison and the Dalleburra which underwrote his 'rule' and, ultimately, Bennett's own story of duty and restitution.

The connection between Christison and the Dalleburra also underwrote the disconnection in his family life. Bennett paints a picture of a beleaguered pioneer who fought the land, other settlers, police, stock, drought, banks, governments and even an uncooperative wife. Bennett's mother, Mary, Christison's second wife, did not feel comfortable at Lammermoor: 'she had never imagined the heat would be so trying, or that the parched land could look so dusty and shabby and tired; she thought she would die if she spent another summer in the north'.[47] As a result, the early years of Bennett's life were spent between homes in

England and Australia as her mother worked out where she wanted to settle. While in Australia, they had residences in the south, at Stanthorpe, Tenterfield and Tasmania. From 1908, they also had a permanent home in England. For Bennett this meant periods of time with her siblings either in England or Australia with their mother, grandmother, aunts and carers and/or Wyma. Just as the Dalleburra had been loyal to her father, they filled important gaps in Bennett's childhood. Bennett paints a picture of her mother as flighty, inconsistent and spoilt by Christison. There is a sense in which her mother is a distant figure in her life. Some of this was reflected in Bennett. She describes Mimi – herself – as spoilt, precious, self-absorbed and snobbish.

Robert Christison, 1912

Mary Christison, OM79-21, Robert Christison Papers, MM Bennett Collection,
John Oxley Library, State Library of Queensland.

Bennett told Anthony Martin Fernando that, like him, she never knew her mother. This was not because she was removed from her but because 'she was taken from me and I've always been sad that I did not know her'.[48] It is difficult to know what she meant by this. She had lived at Burwell Park with her parents until her marriage, aged thirty-three, to mariner Charles Douglas Bennett in 1914. At that point she moved to Hertfordshire. But the family fortunes had also changed after World War I. Before it, they were among the upper class in England. Burwell Park was luxurious, described as an 'immense estate'. They had a butler, a footman, a chauffeur and the girls had their own maids. They learned French, dance and piano and they travelled the continent. After the fashion of her mother, who was an accomplished artist, Bennett attended the Royal Academy of Arts as a young woman. Later, Bennett and her sister married into the establishment – Mary to a captain of the Royal Navy and Helen to a decorated soldier and wealthy Queensland grazier.

All this changed with the war, Christison losing many of his investments in Europe. He died in 1915 and, after the war, Burwell Park was sold. Helen returned to Australia in 1920 to marry and live at Bolivia in the northern tablelands of New South Wales, taking their mother, who lived in Australia for just two more years before her death and burial at Tenterfield in 1922. What happened in the period from Bennett's marriage to 1922? In what sense was Bennett's mother taken from her? There had been some sort of rift in the family over Bennett's marriage just a year before her father's death. Did her reflection about her mother refer, in some way, to this? Did it refer to her mother being taken to Australia by her sister? Had God taken her mother from her? Whatever it meant, it revealed a gulf in Bennett's life which would only have been exacerbated by her alienation from her family.

On Bennett's death in 1961 her sister, Helen Roberts, claimed to have attempted contact with her since 1923 to no avail. According to Helen, Mary lost everything once her husband died in 1927. It was after this that she received 'the call' to undertake mission work. Helen characterised this as stubborn resolve. It was a renunciation of everything that her sister was and it involved her turning her back on it all. As Helen recalled:

At the end of the war Burwell Park was sold, I came back to NSW to marry and live in the bush and our mother came with me.

> Then Captain Bennett died and everything had gone from my
> sister. Then she got her call. You will see now why she cut out all
> connection with her family and friends. We would all have tried
> to keep her from her resolve. She could only think of us as part of
> a world she wished to give up.[49]

For Helen, Bennett's alienation and exile – her mission – had the effect
of obscuring her origins: 'my sister gave up more than the average person
when she took up mission work'. As she reiterated, Bennett was not only
one of landed gentry but also of distinguished and deeply religious Scottish
pedigree, which included her father's uncle, Sir Robert Christison. He was
a highly esteemed member of the Scottish medical fraternity, a leading
toxicologist and physician to Queen Victoria in Scotland. He was also
the son of Alexander Christison, Bennett's great grandfather, who was
Professor of Humanity at Edinburgh High School between 1806–1820.[50]

Certainly these aspects of her biography were obscured in the course
of her future life as a campaigner for Aboriginal rights, although she
was widely known as having come from a wealthy pioneering family.
As Helen mused at the moment of her death, 'she was so unpreten-
tious I don't suppose anyone in WA knew her origin'. Without her own
explanation for the rupture with her family, it is difficult to know why
Bennett felt that her mother was *taken* from her, but it is interesting
that she felt she never knew her. It is also revealing that Helen casts her
sister's mission as something she would have tried to stop her from doing.
She clearly saw it as beneath their station. Yet her assessment might be
suggestive. Was Bennett's life, following the death of her mother and
then her husband, a conscious rejection or critique of her upbringing
and her past? Just years before her death she claimed that when her husband
died, she did too. Unlike her family, he had encouraged and supported her
efforts to publicise the Aboriginal condition and now she was all alone
in the cause. Certainly, she ended her days in relative obscurity, in a tiny
rented house in Kalgoorlie where she lived rather ascetically while sharing
her wealth with Aboriginal people in need and her closest friends.

It is revealing that Bennett's first foray into active social work, following the death of her husband, was not the Aborigines but the slums
of east London. Like many of her middle-class and aristocratic British
compatriots, Bennett was not unusual in renouncing the comforts of her

life to 'go slumming' among the poor. This was a cultural phenomenon in late nineteenth- and twentieth-century Britain, which saw leaders of church and state travelling to the slums to get first-hand experience of poverty to help formulate solutions to the pressing social problems of the day. It was propelled by a critique of aristocratic privilege and it often freed the participants from the conventions (and constraints) of that privilege.[51]

As it turned out Bennett's foray into slumming was short-lived. Her meeting with Fernando, a representative of the urban poor, proved an important turning point and segue. If his Aboriginality marked him out in those spaces, it spoke directly to Bennett in terms of her past as well as her present and her future. His resentful charges of hypocrisy to her were just the fuel at a time of great loss, grief and need in her own life. His unsettling accusation that 'if you are not working with the Aborigines you are working against them' was a truth which resonated at a time of profound personal readjustment and awakening.[52] Indeed, the force of his character resonated with Bennett's new-found understanding of the Aborigines as a people, as did his accusations of Aboriginal demise. His depiction of England as the land of 'cultivated savagery' resonated with her own critique of European civilisation and her despondency about the same. His claim that 'the natives of Australia must be looked upon as human beings' may well have been the inspiration for the title of *The Australian Aboriginal as a Human Being*.

Furthermore, the connection between her slumming and her taking up of the Aboriginal cause was the contemporary understanding of social problems. The native question or Aboriginal problem was a pre-eminent concern of a variety of social reformers in these years. In this sense the colonial periphery replaced the slum as the locus of concern. The fact that Bennett had undertaken what Koven would describe as 'casual slumming' is important. He argues that it was this kind of activity which merged into more sustained attempts not just to grapple with the costs of poverty in individual lives but also to formulate systemic critiques of social and economic injustices.[53] In this context it is not surprising to see Bennett's slumming morph into a full-scale and sustained critique of the poverty and social and economic injustices of Aboriginal people in Australia. By the time she met Fernando she had already formulated both a social and economic critique of Aboriginal conditions and a set of possible solutions. She used her biography of her father as a platform to publicise the same and, as the second half of this chapter will show, she would develop these ideas still further in *The Australian Aboriginal as a Human Being*, published just three years later. In this sense what, for her sister, was Bennett's unfortunate descent, was for Bennett herself an opportunity.

Her sister was therefore right when she mentioned Mary's renunciation of her origins. If the Aboriginal cause enabled her to critique her own privilege, was it also her means out of the physical, emotional and intellectual constraints of her class and upbringing, including its guilt and collusion in colonialism? The latter hovers around the contours of *Christison of Lammermoor*. A powerful theme underpinning the story of Christison's life is the steadfast loyalty and companionship of the Dalleburra. In Bennett's hands, the Dalleburra are representative of a civilisation which is diametrically opposite to her own, and it was this contrast between a competitive and communal civilisation which undergirded her advocacy from beginning to end. It is this contrast which she is toying with in her biography of her father while, at the same time, cordoning him from the worst excesses of a competitive civilisation which Aboriginal dispossession ultimately represented.

If her own family was symbolic of the ills of a competitive civilisation, much could be learned from the family in Aboriginal culture. With little material comforts, in Bennett's eyes, Aboriginal family nevertheless demonstrated the true meaning of the term. As she would reflect much later in her life:

> it is doubtful if there is a race in the world that feels as warmly, or appreciates as fully the value of the various members of the group, one to the other, as they do. For just as the branches are part of the tree, so aboriginal society is blood relative and your own family and thus life, to a very real degree, is a road along which the aborigine discovers other wider circles of his own loved relatives. This wonderful fact changes even the meaning of words, so for white people, words like mother, father, brother, sister and are made of silver – but for aborigines they are made of gold.[54]

If Helen Roberts' version of Bennett's familial alienation doesn't quite square with Bennett's own version of maternal loss, it is suggestive in terms of her portrayal of the Dalleburra in *Christison*. Their story of family love and loyalty clearly contrasted with Bennett's own, at least for her. Where Christison had been abandoned by his wife (as Bennett constructs it in the book), the Dalleburra stayed by his side. Mary Christison's leaving Australia and her husband on a regular basis to return to England was in stark contrast to Wyma who, given the choice to return with Christison's wife and children back to England, chose to stay close to her husband. In this context the Dalleburra became, quite literally, Christison's own family while in Australia, while he was their firm but steady, and loving, father figure – their 'beloved master'.[55]

Group of Dalleburra men and women. The men's bodies are painted and they are wearing personal ornaments, headgear and loin cloths, © Trustees of the British Museum.

This picture of her father suggests that the book might be read as a defence of him as much as a biography of pioneer and place. In this sense the silences are telling. In terms of Bennett's subsequent critique, Christison's story, and by implication her own, would not have been without fault. As she would admit just four years after the book's publication, 'I grew up in squatterdom and most of my friends are squatters, so I know their case through and through but this does not blind me to the fact that a party to a case ought not to be judge in his own cause'.[56] There is telling evidence of this in the book. There are examples of Christison's autocracy: his 'wallopings for naughty blacks', his refusal to allow a woman back on the station after she had drifted to the town and taken to drink, and his removal of a child of the 'station blacks' to a home on the coast. Warmboomooloo also received a whipping for orchestrating the theft of one of his sheep.

It is difficult to interpret Bennett's tone as she narrates these moments. They appear to be as much about the forbearance of the Dalleburra with the foolish white people as they are about Christison. As she wrote of herself, 'I used to abuse "blackfellows" to her [Wyma], not realizing that she was black and she only beamed on me indulgently'.[57] In Bennett's dedication to Wyma, Christison symbolises white civilisation's wastefulness. Referring to the large bonfire he constructs to burn the ram Warmboomooloo stole, so that 'they could not profit from their theft', she observes: 'Only the wasteful white man announces himself by a big blaze, ignorant of cooling, disregarding signals, careless of the danger of fire to the bush and its denizens'.[58]

A group of Dalleburra men and women who lived and worked on Lammermoor.
This was one of a series of photographs donated to the British Museum by
Mary Bennett in 1927. It is highly likely that she annotated the images with the
names of the individuals, © Trustees of the British Museum.

The loss of the Aborigines' means of subsistence through dispossession, and their starvation, would become central planks in her subsequent critique, as were the conditions of dependence which their dispossession sanctioned. Furthermore, Christison may well have provided purpose-built accommodation for the Dalleburra and allowed them to go walkabout, but he paid them in kind like all other squatters. Along with his virulent anti-unionism this would not have aligned with Bennett's support for

Labor, which she voted all her life. She went on to compare payment in kind to the truck system of 'fodder-and-harness-payment which enslaved and depopulated'.[59]

As this book will show, two of the key issues which dominated Bennett's critique till her death were Aboriginal child removal, particularly girls into domestic service, and the economic dependence and lack of wages of Aboriginal workers. Jane Gordon's story (alluded to earlier in the chapter) may have fuelled Bennett's implacable opposition to Aboriginal child removal and family breakdown for the rest of her life. It may well have formed part of her consciousness of the slave-like condition of Aboriginal people, as her mother adopted the child in 1898 after she'd been offered for sale for a pound. Jane's story, as reconstructed by Mark Cryle, reminds us of the arbitrary power of white masters and mistresses in colonial settings. Mary Christison may have adopted the child but, finding her a strain once back home in England, Robert Christison arranged for her return to Australia to relieve his wife of the 'burden'.[60] Jane's natal alienation and utter powerlessness remind us of the connection between settlement and the slavery of Aboriginal people.[61] The dispossession of the Dalleburra and their exploitation as workers on Lammemoor was emblematic of the connection being made between questions of land and labour and slavery in disguise by critics of empire in the first decades of the twentieth century.

Similarly, the dispossession and lack of economic independence on Lammermoor, despite, or perhaps because of, their loyalty to Christison, may well have formed part of her subsequent critique of the slavery of Aboriginal workers and her steadfast commitment to wage justice for them. Her life long campaign for equal wages for Aboriginal workers might be read as compensation for her father's complicity in this process.

Indeed, the theme of slavery would dominate Bennett's life work on behalf of Aboriginal people. Their economic dispossession was central to what she understood as the many other problems they faced. It is notable that, in *Christison*, she refrains from any form of extended critique of their conditions of labour in the way that she would in everything she subsequently wrote. Yet, her depiction of the Dalleburra, including photographic portraits she includes in the book, is reminiscent of the iconography associated with slavery. Presumably their slave-like status was alleviated by Christison's benevolence. Family folklore had it that the

Dalleburra and other Aborigines in the vicinity referred to Lammermoor as Canada, the mythic land of freedom for thousands of enslaved African Americans, made famous by Harriet Beecher Stowe's fictional account in *Uncle Tom's Cabin*.[62] This begs many questions, not least of which is what the Aboriginal people knew of Stowe's story. Was it simply an apocryphal family account, a selective rendering of family history or pure fantasy? Certainly, Stowe was never far from Bennett's mind as she pursued her mission.

If Lammermoor was regarded, figuratively, as Canada, it relieved her father of complicity. It also gave *Christison of Lammermoor* didactic purpose. There were benevolent paternal figures in Stowe's story, such as Augustine St Clare who buys Tom from his slave trader and takes him back to his home in New Orleans, eventually agreeing to free him. In telling Christison's story Bennett was paying homage to a father she loved deeply and admired. It was part eulogy which, in drawing out the positive aspects of his life, might contribute to the contemporary debates about Aboriginal futures. The moving depiction of loyalty and friendship between the Dalleburra and Christison had lessons for all. Christison may have been a dispossessing squatter but his relationship provided an example of an alternative approach to policy and practice and the rewards of such for both sides. This moral was partly directed to relations between black and white but it was also directed to white civilisation itself, which Bennett and her family epitomised.

In this context the story of Jenny-Lin was a further example of the loyalty, resourcefulness and compassion of a communally minded people. Bennett (described as 'the stupid white woman') had blustered in, with all her refinement, and demanded that Wyma remove Jenny-Lin from her hut. Wyma refused, counselling sensitivity.[63] While Bennett was repulsed by Jenny-Lin's half-caste child, Wyma sought to embrace and shelter it. Jenny-Lin and Charley evaded capture because of the loyalty and sustenance of the Lammermoor people. Their downfall was 'low whites' and the inequality of the law. The inference was that Aboriginal people were not dying out through any fault of their own but because of what had been imposed on them by an alien, hostile and inequitable system. In her 'Notes on the Dalleburra' Bennett details how her father believed that it was syphilis (the cause of Barney's death) and alcohol that had caused their speedy extinction. The reason she compiled them, so she maintained, was to document a once virile and healthy people, with a fascinating and complex culture, who were now at the point of extinction.

Looked at in this way, *Christison of Lammermoor* was far more than a biography of her father. It was a story of and for the times. It was published at a moment of heightened humanitarian angst about the condition and treatment of Australian Aborigines against the backdrop of the empire's interest in the native question. This had deeply personal resonance for Bennett but it was also deeply political. In the same year that she published *Christison*, her article on the Dalleburra appeared in the *Royal Anthropological Journal of Great Britain and Ireland*. This was an account of the Dalleburra, their country, culture and language as her father had documented it with a view to writing an ethnography. Her next book would also pursue her father's legacy by drawing heavily on the discourse of imperial humanitarianism to politicise Aboriginal people's humanity and the contemporary policies that denied it.

Christison had intended to write such a book himself. Among his notes was one which detailed his responses to a number of writers' representations of the 'Australian blacks as the lowest on the scale of humanity'. He was particularly concerned about the words of Anthony Trollope, the novelist and tourist to the Australian colonies in the nineteenth century. He noted Trollope's view that the Aborigines were repugnant and must go. Trollope wrote, 'that he [the Aborigine] should perish without unnecessary suffering should be the aim of all who are concerned in the matter'. Christison responded, 'Can Mr Trollope advocate annihilation and does he wish his countrymen in Australia to practice it now and here?' He then commented that the reason for compiling his notes was to write a book that would 'vindicate a character but little understood and very much misrepresented'.[64]

By interspersing Christison's story with her own polemic about the condition of Aborigines, Bennett was thus taking up her father's unfulfilled ambition. His twin concerns of imminent annihilation and colonial prejudice were, by the interwar period, more relevant to the position of Aborigines than ever. Two of the chapters in *Christison* explicitly addressed the contemporary debate about the Aboriginal problem. Bennett complained that Aborigines were debarred a 'true and fair trial by jury', as their evidence was inadmissible in a court of law, and they had never been recognised as having any legal rights to their tribal lands.[65] The 'problem', she said, was related to law, land and history, which the contemporary system of reserves and protection did little to solve. She used her book, instead, as a platform to garner support for the Model Aboriginal State being promoted by many 'high-minded Australians' as providing a more viable solution.[66]

III

From 1927, when *Christison* was published, to 1929, when she wrote 'A Native Policy for Australia' and presented her paper to the BCL, Bennett's thinking on this question developed considerably. The context of interwar imperial humanitarianism was important, as was her exposure to and meeting with Fernando, whose critique of Australian law and police corruption matched her own. But conditions on the ground in Australia were also critical. In particular, it was the Coniston massacre in central Australia in 1928 which galvanised local humanitarian concern and action and cemented her place in it. Correspondence between Bennett and her APL colleagues was stepped up as a result of this incident, which saw a large number of Aborigines killed in a punitive response to the murder of a white dingo shooter, Frederick Brookes. At the heart of humanitarian concern in this case was the operation of the law, particularly following an inquiry into the event wherein the police charged with the retaliatory murders of Aboriginal people were found to be justified. They were not only exonerated but reinstated.

This case was a perfect illustration, for Bennett and other humanitarians, of the discriminatory treatment of Aborigines in the federal territories of Australia. It formed a key part of the BCL paper and an entire chapter in *The Australian Aboriginal as a Human Being*. It demonstrated the consequences of ignoring Aboriginal interests in land which, in this case, was exacerbated by environmental conditions and competition for resources. When the massacre occurred, central Australia was in a state of drought. As a consequence, the small outback waterholes had dried up and the 'wild natives' came in to the river frontages, which were occupied by white settlers, and speared their goats and cattle which 'had taken the place of native game'.[67] Many were imprisoned in neck chains as a result. Furthermore, Aborigines who had been encouraged by settlers as homestead hangers-on, for employment, were now chased away. In this volatile mix the white dingo shooter may well have been a target. Dingos were used by Aborigines for hunting but they were destructive to sheep. Bennett argued that, as a result of a reward for dingo scalps, some men, styled 'doggers', made a living by shooting and poisoning them.[68] Ultimately, Bennett explained the massacre as the result of competition between opposing interests exacerbated by an 'evil' policy:

> The competition between opposing interests became more acute, while settlers tried to save the cattle which should pay their rents and natives tried to find food to save their families, until our evil policy came to fruition in murder. A dingo-shooter named Brookes was killed by natives, and a general indiscriminate massacre of natives by a police party followed – Aboriginals killed by a Protector of Aboriginals![69]

The question of police protection had been at the core of humanitarian angst for some time. The Coniston massacre illustrated the problem as it was a constable of police, a Protector of Aborigines, who sanctioned the punitive expedition against them.

Apart from the issue of police protection, the case also demonstrated the many other legal and administrative inequities Aborigines faced. There was no inquiry into the murder of Brookes. Instead the police protector held a number of 'wild natives' as prisoners (in neck chains) and charged two with the murder, despite the lack of evidence. Nor was there any investigation or inquest into the murder of the thirty or so Aborigines who were killed in the subsequent reprisal. While Aboriginal evidence was inadmissible, under section 58 of the Northern Territory Ordinance the magistrate could permit any person to address them on behalf of the Aboriginal. Yet, a humanitarian request for legal aid for the Aborigines was denied. Instead the government appointed a board of inquiry which consisted of a police magistrate, an inspector of police and the Commissioner of Police in Alice Springs. Worse still, the board found that there had been no provocation for the Aboriginal men's hostility to white men in the region.

Bennett argued that the only way this could be believed was by ignoring the testimony of Annie Lock, a missionary who had been working among Aborigines in central Australia for some 26 years.[70] In her evidence before the inquiry into the affair, Lock had stated that part of the hostility of Aboriginal men to the white men of the region was the appropriation of their women, the refusal to release them and the threats of violence to Aboriginal men who demanded their wives.[71] In subsequent correspondence to Bennett, Lock described a heightened state of tension in outback regions as a result:

> The greatest trouble is that the white men seem to delight to get the young girls from ten years up and will even come and ask for them and offer money, tobacco and all sorts of things to the women for the girls...I am not the least surprised at the trouble with these outback stations. The natives say the white men round them up like bullocks and take young girls away, keep them one week and sometimes send them back...and it makes them furious. They say, 'Why don't the white men leave the black girls alone? We no touch white girls and women.'[72]

Disregarding her evidence, the board of inquiry into the massacre asserted a complete lack of provocation, instead accusing Lock of causing inter-racial tension by being a 'woman missionary living amongst naked blacks' and thereby 'lowering respect for whites'.[73]

Bennett had been concerned about wronged Aboriginal husbands for some time. She had had first-hand experience of inter-racial unrest on the frontier and, as the case of Jenny-Lin and Charley demonstrated, an appreciation of how Aboriginal men were provoked. In describing the 'war of extermination' on the Palmer goldfields in north Queensland in *Christison*, she argued that the punishment of Aboriginal men for the 'crime' of defending their wives was partly responsible for increased racial tension on the frontiers of settlement. She subsequently complained to the secretary of the Anti-Slavery and Aborigines' Protection Society that, as Aboriginal evidence was frequently not taken, it could not be said that the white man had not 'broken tribal law' by stealing black men's womenfolk:

> This injury, which the blacks are not allowed to resist, and depriv-ing the blacks of water and land whereby they may live, are the true causes of cattle spearing and the very rare murder of white men.

This is perfectly well known to the Commonwealth Government who, presumably, feel bound to support their tenants and agents.[74]

By the time of the Coniston massacre, Bennett had formed a close working relationship with the Anti-Slavery and Aborigines' Protection Society, providing something of a link between them and the South Australian humanitarians. In bringing the central Australian murders to their notice she hoped that the society would conduct a conference on Aboriginal conditions, including discussion of the Model Aboriginal State proposal, along similar lines to that which she had attended on the East Africa Commission report. In a letter to Travers Buxton, the honorary secretary, she asked that in the society's representation to Australian governments they request three things: the removal of the control of the natives from the police; the institution of the practice in New Guinea whereby a native is not punished until he has been tried and convicted in exactly the same way as the white man; and the specification of particular waterholes to which the Aborigines may have undisturbed access.[75]

It was this notion of access to resources and land which underwrote her support for the Model Aboriginal State. Like Genders, Bennett was seeking fundamental change to the 'old, evil system', as she put it, in Australia.[76] In her paper to the BCL she referred to the Bleakley Report, commissioned by the federal government as a result of humanitarian agitation for reform in the north in 1927. While not supporting the Model State as such, many of his recommendations nonetheless supported the humanitarian critique. For Bennett, Bleakley had proposed many good things – compulsory education for Aboriginal children, a scale of wages for permanent workers, extended reserves and more adequate protection for Aboriginal women and girls. The shortcomings of the report related to his being an official and therefore a member of the establishment, his retention of police protection and his focus on the detribalised and half-caste Aborigines in the centre and north. In what was to become a constant refrain, Bennett argued that this focus left the position of the thousands of 'uncontaminated' Aborigines and their long-term survival unaddressed.[77]

Similarly, *The Australian Aboriginal as a Human Being* was a call for a different approach in the centre and north where Bennett and the APL thought there was still time to make a change in policy and practice. She wrote:

> As yet, [the] wild natives [there] still own their tribal lands and live a corporate life under the intricate tribal organisation which they have evolved. When we take away their land, and take away their status by relegating them in law to the same category as imbeciles, and break up their family life, we destroy the conditions which every race requires for surviving.[78]

One of her key critiques of the Australian system was how, in the process of creating wealth for the settlers, it had smashed the family life of the tribes which she saw as a central building block of their communal civilisation. A policy which worked to keep groups intact in their own territories, under their own leaders, protected from external influences and where they could develop in their own time, was therefore more humane. This was because it recognised land ownership as the basis of Aboriginal culture, which was, according to Bennett, the first principle of fuller knowledge and sounder administration.[79]

Bennett's ideas about the way forward in Australia were thus symptomatic of the progressivist critique of colonial policy promoted by the left in England at the time. This included a commitment to native paramountcy, interpreted as the protection of African land rights; an end to forced labour; the development of health and education services; and the gradual extension of self-government.[80] Furthermore, in promoting a more humane trusteeship for Australia, Bennett was advocating all the key elements of indirect rule, which included notions of cultural preservation and advancement, as well as native paramountcy, native interests in land and self-governance. Indirect rule was preferable to the 'fatal course of domination' or 'direct rule' which, she said, entailed a 'slave mortality' on Aboriginal people.[81] The following quote, while lengthy, is useful as a distillation of her interpretation of the central tenets of indirect rule:

> If the Aboriginals are not to be destroyed, they should not be dispossessed nor subjected to a system that is alien to them, but they should be secured in the possession of their tribal territories

and encouraged to adapt to new needs all that is best in their traditions under their own leaders, under the form of government that they can understand, the direction of their day to day affairs by the tribal council of their own choosing. The "Government Resident" settling in the most favourable spot, would be at first, an observer, and gaining their confidence he would become a helper, while the Aboriginals would retain their initiative and their responsibilities to the family and tribe, the duties which kindle and keep alive interest in life. There would be an end of the unpaid labour and destitution, of doles and "indigent camps", and end of parting people from their homeland, and end of parting parents and children, an end of the soulless institutionalism which we force on them when we deprive them of the wholesome human relationships which draw up humanity as light draws up plants. They would evolve gradually in their own way through the pastoral and agricultural stages of culture; and we should have the satisfaction of knowing that, though late, we have tried to do justice.[82]

The notion of gradual change through stages shows how embedded the enlightenment view of human progress still was and how it nicely justified a continuing colonial/imperial presence. It was also in keeping with the dictates of scientific humanism as they were enumerated in the interwar period: an anthropologically informed policy which worked to both preserve and advance native culture. Furthermore, that Aboriginal people could and would adapt to pastoralism and agriculture had been evidenced, not only on Bennett's father's pastoral property, but also in the Bleakley Report, which identified Aboriginal labour in the Northern Territory pastoral industry as indispensable to Australia's wealth.[83]

It was their indispensability as workers which made their near enslavement all the more problematic.[84] Bennett's constant reiteration of the slavery motif further demonstrates her links to the British humanitarian framework. As I suggested at the beginning of this chapter, a key concern for British humanitarians at this time was in preventing forms of de facto servitude from creeping into British colonial territories. Bennett's economic critique strongly resonated with parts of E. D. Morel's critique of conditions in the Belgian Congo with which she was familiar. Central to her critique – until her death – was the view that because of their dispossession and their lack of rights Aboriginal people lived, if not in slavery, in conditions very close to it:

> It pays white men to dispossess the natives of their land wholesale, because the Government permits them to impress the natives as labour without paying them. The compulsion is starvation and dispossession reinforced by violence.[85]

Slavery was never far from Bennett's mind when she was thinking about Aboriginal people's condition. This had much to do with the way in which the interwar years in Britain saw the rehearsal and celebration of Britain's part in the anti-slavery story.

While she also used terms like 'helotry' and 'peonage', Bennett ultimately defined the Aboriginal condition, particularly in parts of Western Australia and the federal territories, as a system 'analogous to' or 'akin to' slavery, rather than slavery outright. This was strategic as it signalled to the British humanitarian fraternity that its concern to eradicate any *taint* of slavery in the British dominions had relevance to Australia. In *The Australian Aboriginal as a Human Being* she argued that Aborigines were under a system analogous to slavery because they had no representation in parliament and no voice in their own concerns; they did not own land or exercise guardianship of their children. Nor could they sell their labour or control their wages.[86] She cited the permit system of employment in the Northern Territory as a practice open to abuse. Under this system, for the cost of 10 shillings, a settler bought a permit to employ any number of Aborigines from the local police protector. Bennett complained that because it was unregulated and unsupervised, there were huge discrepancies in practice from employer to employer. Where permanent workers were paid at the stipulated wage of 5 shillings, a percentage was banked into a trust account, the worker receiving only a percentage of his/her wage, which was rarely paid outside the towns.[87]

Furthermore, Bennett defined the non-payment of wages by pastoralists as a system of forced labour. Aborigines were not given the chance to become productive economic units or useful members of society, she argued, because they were deprived of their hunting grounds and allotted inadequate reserves and 'waterless wastes' which forced them into acceptance of unequal conditions. To add weight to her argument she drew on the Anti-Slavery and Aborigines' Protection Society's conclusion that the power to compel natives to accept any kind of employment offered by the department, wherever that employment was and regardless of the amount of wages offered or of the family separations involved, was forced labour.

In *The Australian Aboriginal as a Human Being* she cited Bleakley's reference to the fact that women sent into service in Darwin frequently left a husband behind in their homeland as further evidence of forced labour, arguing that there could be no freedom of contract in a country where such coercion was legal. Such a practice contravened Article 5 of the Slavery Convention which stipulated that compulsory or forced labour for other than public purposes shall only be of an exceptional character and 'shall not involve the removal of labourers from their usual place of residence'.[88] By ratifying the convention in 1927 Bennett argued that the Australian government had agreed to abolish forced labour wherever it still existed.

As this suggests, she utilised the new international environment to call Australia to account for its practices of near-slavery and forced labour which were ultimately related to its colonialism. While Australia was breaking the Slavery Convention, conditions of Aboriginal labour also contravened Article 23 of the League of Nations Covenant which stipulated fair and humane conditions of labour for men, women and children, as well as the preamble to the International Labour Organization, which stipulated that universal peace must be based on social justice which required the working out of equitable conditions of labour.[89] Quoting the Hilton Young Report, she argued that such conditions of labour underlined the importance of the setting aside of adequate areas of land, 'not merely to afford them the bare possibility of existence, but to provide them with an opportunity to improve their standard of living according to their capacity', which would help check their exploitation by giving them free choice. If the Aboriginal person wanted to leave the reserve to work for wages elsewhere it could be a voluntary decision, not because they were forced as the only means of earning a living. She even suggested that such reserves could take the place of trade unions, 'and help the native to maintain a proper standard of wages for his labour by providing him with protection against being forced to bargain at a disadvantage'.[90]

Underlining Aboriginal people's *humanity* in the title of her 1930 book was therefore a deliberate strategy to counter what she saw as a negative view of Aboriginality justifying their enslavement. Not only had Australia ignored its 'home native policy' in the pursuit of 'material desires' and subordinated the interest of the Aborigines to those of white men, it had debased Aboriginal people as savage, primitive, worthless.[91] They were an underclass, 'landless helots', thought of only as cheap labour, not as people in their own right.[92] Critical to her defence was the resurrection of Aboriginal humanity which, as she described it, resided in their complex, intricate and law-bound culture, their 'free and spontaneous intertribal associations suited to peace', 'their duty of sharing and their responsibility to family and tribe', 'their sophisticated marriage code', their environmental astuteness and ingenuity, and their many acts of kindness, generosity, endurance, bravery and compassion to both their own kind and to British settlers and explorers.

This was not merely a romanticised vision of the noble savage. It was about resurrecting the humanity of the people. In his history of humanitarianism, Barnett identifies a rights-based humanitarianism as developing after World War I. Characteristic of this was a form of cultural relativism which saw indigenous cultures as worthy of respect in their own right.[93] Mary Kingsley and E. D. Morel promoted it in west Africa and, along with a handful of other humanitarians, Bennett promoted it in Australia.[94] Her thick description of the beauty, richness and resourcefulness of Aboriginal culture was a counter to the predominant view of their primitivity. One of her key arguments in *The Australian Aboriginal* was a defence against the view that Aboriginal people had not advanced into a pastoral stage of civilisation and were therefore unalterably backward. On the first page of the book she wrote:

> But there are no indigenous animals that can be domesticated, and there are no indigenous plants that men can cultivate for food. You cannot 'herd' kangaroos nor plough with them. You cannot, in fertile eastern Queensland, bring on bunya pine seedlings to give you a crop of nuts in your lifetime, nor, in Central Australia, cultivate nardoo with a five-inch rainfall of doubtful occurrence. Under these limitations it was impossible for people to be pastoralists, agriculturalists or city-builders, but it is a mistake to assume that they did not make the best of their surroundings, or that they are not able to learn all that we can. It was the tyranny of

circumstance that made them hunters for their living in 'the most inhospitable continent in the world'.[95]

Bennett argued that the belief that Aboriginal people were backward, lacking intelligence and the capacity to advance was used to deny them equality and rights:

> All through history the dominant race has resented the subject race having any community life, and in spite of the League of Nations this bitter persecutionary feeling against the race, that has been dispossessed, triumphs and nowhere more than in Australia.[96]

Far from a Darwinian struggle between a superior and inferior race, for Bennett the contemporary moment witnessed the meeting of distinct cultures and civilisations with possibilities for both. Her argument was that Aborigines had a communal democracy from which a competitive civilisation had much to learn. The Aboriginal problem thus represented an opportunity, 'for co-operating with them is a Divine commission carrying blessings for them and for us'.[97] In the federal territories of the Commonwealth of Australia there was still time for cooperation rather than competition, but it required the government recognising that dispossession and control of one race by another was opposed to freedom and justice and that the only way to safeguard Aborigines was in tribal territories where they could 'work out their own salvation'.[98]

Bennett thus saw the Aboriginal predicament in Australia as part of an old discriminatory order which was being challenged by the new international edicts of the day. As she wrote in 'A Native Policy', the scope of the problem was about legal rights and equality and an end to discrimination. The question, as she defined it, was the right of Aborigines as British subjects and citizens of the Commonwealth to equality before the law. She identified the legal disparity between Aboriginal and non-Aboriginal as 'overwhelming':

> The employer cannot protect native women and female children from abuse by white men; and to deprive the natives of their women is to extinguish a tribe in a few years. The smashing of their family life takes away all the desire to live.[99]

Central to an honourable native policy was a moral obligation to remove abuses and the disparity in status which bred such abuse. The League of Nations provided a framework which stipulated land and the maintenance of Aboriginal law and custom where they did not conflict with human rights, and a voice in their own government. Her solutions to the problem were taken almost directly from the recommendations of the Hilton Young Report and other works promoting indirect rule and trusteeship. The principles of a just relationship between an 'immigrant, dominating white race' and a 'subject race' in Australia related to land, labour and a voice in their own concerns.[100] It also related to good statesmanship. As she said, to use Aborigines as cheap labour and debar them from the wealth 'their land' produced would give colour to the old fallacy 'that democracy cannot govern an Empire, that colonies cannot colonise and the rest'.[101]

IV

In her paper to the BCL Bennett asked that Australian women help to change an 'old evil system' for a humane and equitable one by going to the fringes of settlement and examining conditions on the spot. This notion of first-hand experience was very much in the vein of the slummers in fin de siècle England. Swapping the slum for the Australian frontier and acting on her own advice, she left England in the following year to examine Australian conditions first-hand. Before doing so she relinquished her own Dalleburra collection to the British Museum – photographs, implements, ornaments and weapons – which she requested be added to that of her father's, the 'Christison Collection', donated to the museum around 1900. The donations of these objects and photographs represented the completion of Christison's biography. They not only helped to tell the story of the Dalleburra – a material and photographic archive of the people – but they were deeply connected to Christison. That she understood this was evident in her simultaneous sending of duplicates to the Royal Scottish Museum and glass negatives of the images to the State Library of Queensland. To the University of Queensland library she sent the notes she had gathered in the preparation of *Christison*. These places traced the arc of his life and impact. Relinquishing them in this way was an act of renunciation and of rebirth. It both severed her link to her father and cemented it.

In this context, the three works she completed by 1930 before her 'return' to Australia in that year – 'Notes on the Dalleburra', *Christison*

87

of Lammermoor and *The Australian Aboriginal as a Human Being* – must be understood as a trilogy of works which not only defined her entry into the politics of Aboriginal reform but gave her credibility and purpose. She was completing a task begun by her father. In painting a picture of him as an incredibly hard-working pioneer, she claimed that he was far too busy with Lammermoor and Queensland affairs to undertake the task of defending the Aborigines in the way he'd hoped. The same could not be said of her. Indeed, Christison's very success, made possible by the faithful Dalleburra, underwrote the comfort and ease of her own life. In taking up the Aborigines' cause she was keeping faith with her father and with the Dalleburra, as they had kept faith with him. She was fulfilling a responsibility that came with her privilege and fulfilling Christison's legacy.

Despite her original intention to continue her research in central and South Australia among her friends in the Aborigines' Protection League, she arrived in Western Australia at the end of 1930. With the help of Perth's Christian and feminist community she made contact with missionaries in the north. These provided a base while she undertook a survey of conditions in the very heart of the troubled 'slave zone' of the northwest. She visited pastoral stations and missions in the Kimberley as well as some missions and reserves in the south, before returning briefly to Perth. During her year-long investigation she sharpened her critique of Aboriginal policy in Australia and her ideas for reform, noting a general hostility to any attempts at improving things for the Aborigines, and a willingness to let them 'die out'.[102] She later confided to her friend and colleague, Charles Duguid, that she had never experienced anything so awful as her year in the Kimberley.[103] Her experience directed her attention, even more forcefully, to the position of Aboriginal women, which was to remain a key focus up to World War II.

In December 1931 Bennett delivered a lengthy lecture to the peak feminist body in the state, the Women's Service Guilds, in which she outlined what she regarded as the foundation of a sound native policy for Australia. It was a succinct statement of imperial humanitarianism applied to local conditions. She spoke at length about the 'first-class native administration' of Kunmunya, the Presbyterian mission run by the Reverend J. R. B. Love in the northwest of the state, likening it to that of Lord Lugard's administration in Nigeria. Using it as a model, she asked that Australian women lobby for five principal reforms. Describing Reverend

Love's aim to conserve the 'good' in native culture while enabling the Aborigines to acquire what they needed from 'ours', her first reform was that policy be based on the ideal of indirect rule, which she defined as creating conditions for the eradication of undesirable customs while encouraging the admirable elements of Aboriginal culture.

She was quite clear about the 'good' and 'bad' in Aboriginal culture. Much of the paper to the feminists outlined the good. This, she said, was evident in their co-operative civilisation based on the family as the key social unit and a system of 'highly organized reciprocal obligations'. The result was a commendable sense of solidarity where there were no orphans. They had an acute knowledge of their country, which had its 'associations with a mythical ancestry just as important to them as the Arthurian myths are to us', a wonderfully rich cultural tradition of song and dance and beautiful expressive languages. On the other hand, she rarely itemised the so-called 'bad' in Aboriginal culture. As the following chapters will show, the 'bad' was mostly associated with what she understood as the violation of women's human rights. This was evident in certain cultural practices but it was also evident in their system of polygamy and its basis in gerontocracy. Even then, colonialism brought about conditions which exposed and exacerbated the 'bad' at the same time as providing an avenue for reform.

In this context, it is not surprising that Bennett singled out the right of all women to the 'sanctity of their persons' as the most important reform of all. Arguing that Aboriginal and half-caste women had neither human rights nor protection and describing their abuse by white men as 'the custom of the country', she called on women to reject complicity in this culture: 'It is bad, bad enough that white men should hold pagan ideas about native women — it is too horrible that white women should come to acquiesce'.[104]

Her determination to concentrate on the status of Aboriginal women was because she saw it as more realisable in the short term. In a letter to leading Western Australian feminist Bessie Rischbieth in 1931, she admitted that it was the economic position of Aborigines that was her primary concern. 'I really believe', she said, 'I desire payment of natives beyond everything else…but I don't think we ought to allow the present abuse of women to go on until we can get wages'.[105] It was also about capitalising on the growing feminist and humanitarian concern with the position of the women of the native races of empire. She had been privy to the efforts of British feminists in raising the status of Indian women and had witnessed the furore in England generated by Katherine Mayo's controversial propagandist tract *Mother India* in 1927, which, among other things, depicted the physical devastation that early marriage and motherhood imposed on Indian women. She characterised the subsequent passing of the Child Marriage Restraint Act in 1929 as a new era in the womanhood of India and applauded the moment as a British campaign for freedom.[106]

As the following chapter will show, Bennett drew considerable strength from this moment in the empire to draw attention to what she saw as the enslavement of Aboriginal women. Just as British feminists had defined the Indian woman as a special white woman's burden, Bennett saw the Aboriginal woman in the same terms, as her injunction to feminists in *The Australian Aboriginal as a Human Being* revealed:

> Faced with the suffering of our fellow women, with the suffering of children—is it beyond a woman's wit to find a way of helping them? A way to back up the work of women for them? Or is feminism a failure? Are we passing by on the other side?[107]

Burton has shown how British women's interventions on behalf of Indian women underpinned a feminism profoundly influenced by the imperial assumptions of the day.[108] Using the slavery motif Bennett was drawing on a deeply embedded British preoccupation with the same, which was greatly revivified and celebrated in the interwar years. What was interesting about this period was that it also revived British feminist interest in the enslaved black woman which, as Midgley has shown, had been central to their involvement in the anti-slavery cause in the first half of the nineteenth century but which had dissipated by the late 1860s with the growing awareness of their own subordination.[109] By the 1930s, as 'advanced' women, British feminists now had a special responsibility to share their light.

Bennett capitalised on this momentum to turn Australian attention to the position of Aboriginal women. Importantly, she had developed a close working relationship with two key Australian feminists who were themselves deeply engaged in the Aboriginal question. Edith Jones, wife of the missionary Reverend John Jones, was both a prominent Australian feminist and Aboriginal rights activist. She had worked with her husband on a mission on Bathurst Island and, by the 1930s, was living in England and working closely on the Aboriginal question with the Anti-Slavery and Aborigines' Protection Society.[110] As we've seen, Bennett had also met and was in correspondence with Constance Cooke, who was not only part of the Save the Aborigines Movement in Adelaide and the APL, but had delivered a paper on Aboriginal women to the BCL which Bennett had attended and applauded. In taking up the question with more determination she was thus supporting these workers for humane conditions while becoming one herself.

By the early 1930s she was able to do this from her base in Western Australia. She would later cite the death of her old nurse, Wyma, and the dispersal of her 'old playmates', the Dalleburra, as reasons for settling on the other side of the continent.[111] She had feminist and missionary connections in Western Australia and, in the course of her research, that state had loomed large for its historic mistreatment of Aboriginal people. Much of the inspiration of her critique of Aboriginal policy had come from the controversial findings of the Roth Royal Commission in that state in 1904–05. It had also been from that state that Fernando had fled to publicise his own discriminatory treatment at the hands of the criminal justice system and the condition of his people to the world.

During her year-long investigation along the Western Australian coast she visited several missions, including Kunmunya, Forrest River and Gnowangerup. At the conclusion of her journey she sought the permission of A. O. Neville, Chief Protector in that state, to go to Mt Margaret on the eastern goldfields. Arriving in April 1932, intending to stay for only a short period, she brought her own spinning wheels and two looms specially ordered from Sweden to introduce spinning to the Aboriginal women on the mission. From there she would send samples of her students' work to 'friends of the Aborigines' around Australia, in order to demonstrate Aboriginal people's intelligence and capacity for citizenship. She would correspond with fellow sympathisers and continue to accrue evidence, her personal campaign becoming more intense as she witnessed the result of Aboriginal policy in Western Australia first-hand.

3

FREEING WOMEN
Righting the Wrongs Done to Aboriginal Women

In the first year of this century, Australia led the world in the enfranchisement of women: yet during the whole of the past century, while the white woman has advanced in status in Australia, the position of the Aboriginal woman has gone from bad to worse...Would it not be worth meetings, processions and deputations in all the cities of Australia to awaken the governments to the determination of women to secure their share in the righting of the wrongs of the Australian native women, probably the most wronged in the British Empire?[1]

A noticeable feature of imperial trusteeship in the interwar period was its maternalism. The feminisation of imperial policy underpinned a new kind of empire after World War I.[2] One aspect of this was the efforts of British women to liberate non-western women from practices they considered antithetical to their freedom. They played a role via parliament, the League of Nations and leadership in the British Commonwealth League (BCL). Important to these developments was white middle-class British women's sense of themselves as free modern citizens, members of advanced races with a responsibility to protect and advance their 'less advanced sisters'. Such interventions were given a fillip by the revitalisation of the anti-slavery cause in these years. In this context, British feminists stepped up their campaigns to free women whom they considered to be enslaved by entrenched but outmoded patriarchal systems: indenture in Hong Kong, indigenous marital practices in Africa and India, and clitoridectomy in Kenya. Such campaigns reached a climax in 1933, the year of the Centenary of the Abolition of Slavery. By the mid-1930s the League of Nations was promoting the progressive abolition of 'domestic slavery' and 'marriage bondage' as the basis of a common native policy for the future.[3] Included in slavery and bondage was polygamy and its associated practice of infant betrothal. By 1935 the BCL requested empire women to promote the idea that 'whatever her race, a woman was not a chattel to be sold to a polygamist or anyone else', and the International Alliance of Women called on governments to abolish polygamy by law.[4]

Bennett's mobilisation on behalf of Aboriginal women was caught up in this moment. It represents the Australian chapter of this wider empire story. Together with Edith Jones and Constance Cooke, she brought the position of Aboriginal women to the centre of the debate about the Aboriginal problem and its solution in the interwar period, and indigenous domestic relations was at the heart of her concern. Emboldened by the international community's focus on the issue of slavery, they mounted a publicity campaign to expose slavery in Australia and liberate Aboriginal women from it. This reached a crescendo in 1933 when, following her British sisters, Jones called for the freeing of native women from conditions which, by restricting the liberty of their persons, constituted forms of slavery as recognised by the League of Nations. In that same year, Bennett's paper on the 'Aboriginal Mother' was read at the British Commonwealth League. Penned from her base in Western Australia it was a powerful early twentieth-century indictment of Australia's system of Aboriginal child removal and family breakup. It was a succinct statement of her view that what became of Aboriginal mothers was at the centre of the fate of the race as a whole.

Before the interwar years colonial administrations had not been overly burdened by the position of native women within the empire. That they were forced to turn their attentions to it by the 1920s was largely due to the rise of western feminism in these years. One of the key aims of the BCL upon its establishment in 1925 was 'to secure for the women of less forward races within the British Commonwealth the fullest preparation for freedom, while safeguarding them from the operation of custom or law which degraded them as human beings'. As well, British women MPs actively took interest in the colonial question. Here was a moment when white women attempted to make a difference, as they defined it, in the lives of native women. While couched as a cause of liberation it was legitimatised as a project of modernity: their own, and the projected futures of their native sisters. Australian women had a particular role to play, being world leaders in the cause of their own suffrage. British feminists, who lagged behind, were eager for Australian women's views and contributions on this and other questions.

This was an important opportunity for Australian feminists who, in the context of the changing world order following World War I, had an expanded sense of their own citizenship at home and abroad. Following dominionhood, Australian women were attending conferences like those of the League of Nations and the BCL not as affiliates of British women's organisations, but as Australian nationals and empire women in their own right. In taking up the cause of Aboriginal women, Australian feminists were thus flexing their citizenship muscles and, with their intimate knowledge and experience of Aboriginal conditions, Jones, Bennett and Cooke were important to this project.

It was largely via their efforts that the Aboriginal woman in Australia was included in discussions about the status of the native women of the empire. Furthermore, their formulations about Aboriginal women's slavery helped to fortify feminist interventions in Australia. By the early 1930s state feminist groups, like the Women's Service Guilds (WSG) in Western Australia and the Women's Non-Party Association in South Australia (WNPA), developed a specific plank on Aboriginal welfare in their reform agendas for the first time. They facilitated Bennett's work and adopted her ideas for reform. Thus, for a brief period the Aboriginal woman was at the centre of the debate. If Australia could solve the problem of her, it could solve the problem itself.

In this chapter I track the contexts, the issues and the investments of this moment to chart what righting the wrongs done to Aboriginal women in interwar Australia amounted to and to identify Bennett's contribution. The charges of slavery dovetailed with a crucial period in Aboriginal policy terms when, along with other western democracies, Australian governments were increasingly defining the Aboriginal problem as primarily one of race and colour. The slavery moment was a critical incident disrupting government aims and forcing the gendered dimensions of the question into the public arena. Read in conjunction with chapter four, this is a case study of how theories of Aboriginal women's freedom collided with the practice of race politics in interwar Australia.

I

By the time David Jackson MP pointed out the vulnerable position of Aboriginal women in the centre and north in the Commonwealth Parliament in 1927, the question of their status and position had been a growing feminist concern. Jackson's revelation that 90 per cent of inter-racial trouble in the north was the taking of Aboriginal women by white men had been implicitly acknowledged in 1911 by the Association for the Protection of Native Races, which aimed to suppress the 'gross interfer-ences' in the 'domestic rights' of Aborigines. At the time of its inception the APNR established a women's committee, of which Edith Jones was a member.[5] While it does not appear to have lasted long, its main sphere of activity was in the association's attempts, in 1918, to improve the conditions of indentured Indian labour in Fiji. The women's committee was successful in securing greater medical protection and attention for indentured women.[6] However, feminists were not yet concerned about the position of Aboriginal women in their midst. Indeed, Australian feminist suffrage campaigns were notable for their exclusion of Aboriginal women.[7]

Feminists became more committed to the 'problem' of Aboriginal women in the context of the interwar humanitarian upsurge. Their interventions at this time reflected the changing national and imperial relationship wherein, with their new-found citizenship, they were required to demonstrate their advanced race privilege and responsibility in seeking greater protection and advancement for their less forward sisters. In turn, this reflected interwar imperial humanitarianism in which British women were prominent. Of particular relevance was the BCL established after World War I. As a branch of the International Woman's Suffrage Alliance, British women thus signalled their determination to lead the world in matters affecting the empire.[8]

With consultative status in the League of Nations and close working ties with the Anti-Slavery and Aborigines' Protection Society, determina-tions at the BCL were a sensitive barometer of imperial humanitarian angst and feminist concern. Across the 1930s the BCL convened conferences on matters affecting women's lives, such as citizenship, marriage, educa-tion and work. Among the Australian contributions were those of Mary Bennett, who consistently presented papers on how these issues affected Aboriginal women too. The BCL expressed an early concern about native women, establishing a Less Forward Races Committee and convening a conference on the theme in 1927.

Constance Cooke presented a paper at this conference on Australian Aboriginal women. That she was the Australian feminists' representative was no coincidence. By the late 1920s Cooke was firmly ensconced in the vibrant reforming community emanating from South Australia, being vice-president of Genders' Aborigines' Protection League and a member of the Save the Aborigines Movement. While in London for her paper to the BCL she formed part of a deputation to the Australian ambassador, with Frederic Wood Jones, as representatives of the Anti-Slavery and Aborigines' Protection Society. Cooke had been particularly influenced by Herbert Basedow, who argued that disease (principally syphilis) had caused the greatest havoc among Aborigines. In referring to the 'ubiquitous concubinage' of Aboriginal women in the 'back blocks', he also emphasised the gendered parameters of what, for him, was a biomedical problem: 'civilization', he said, 'affected Aborigines like a canker'.[9]

This had particular resonance for non-Aboriginal women and, as president of the WNPA in Adelaide, Cooke had begun to apply her feminist mind to the question. Following a visit to central Australia in 1926, she added 'furtherance of the welfare of aboriginal women and children' to the plank of the WNPA. She had made a special study, informed by anthropological thinking, of the social, economic and political position of Aboriginal women. In 1927, due in large part to her lobbying, the South Australian government proclaimed a prohibited area for Aborigines 5 miles either side of the northsouth railway line during its construction. This was driven by the widespread view that contact led to demoralisation, but it was also driven by Cooke's feminism as the target was the protection of Aboriginal women from contact with male settlers and itinerant workers. This was certainly the tenor of her paper to the BCL, wherein she described Aboriginal women as 'fair game', 'the prey of viciously disposed white men' and that the murder of white men by Aboriginal men in the Northern Territory was justified by this 'unwritten law'.[10] She further maintained that venereal disease was causing their rapid decline. In condemning the home for mixed-descent children in Alice Springs, she argued that it had been the fate of the older girls, left in the home at night, that had precipitated her organisation's concern in the matter.

Indeed, by the 1920s, a debate was circulating around the fate of Aboriginal and mixed-descent women and children in the centre and north which focused on the question of their protection and futures. This exposed the growing tensions between the old guard, in positions of power and control in Aboriginal affairs, and the new humanitarian voices. The former, mostly male police officers, civil servants and missionaries, sought to defend their turf against a noisy minority from the south who were clamouring for change. As the mixed-descent community grew, and mindful of the high levels of venereal disease accompanying miscegenation, the federal government was looking to extend its control. As Haskins has suggested, the 1918 Aboriginals Ordinance (NT) was targeted at securing greater control over the mixed-descent girls and young women who were being sent to work as domestics in white households in Adelaide, as well as extending the government's guardianship of these women.[11]

At around the same time and into the early 1920s there was an emerging critique of their situation stimulated, in part, by two damning reports of the Bungalow, the makeshift home established for the mixed-descent children of central Australia by the local protector in 1914. The home for Aboriginal and mixed-descent girls in Darwin was equally of concern, it being located in the town and acting as a reservoir of cheap labour for the townsfolk. While these 'compounds' may have reflected an effort to contain the problem of the mixed-descent child and mother, the growing discourse of concern about them, what to do with them and where to place them indicated that it was far from successful.

By the mid-1920s there was a series of interlocking claims about their situation, demonstrating a range of anxieties and conflicting attitudes about what should be done. In particular, despite legislation empowering the Chief Protector as legal guardian and custodian of all Aboriginal children in the Northern Territory, there was a growing feminist and humanitarian representation of them as 'fatherless' and 'rootless' which exposed the otherwise 'quiet' frontier practice of miscegenation, now construed as settler contamination. The very existence of mixed-descent children epitomised a system in crisis for humanitarians and feminists fixated on the racial dynamics of the problem. For this reason, the presence of venereal disease in these communities was also of concern. In a searching exploration of this moment, Haskins depicts a tense political landscape which underscored a powerplay between competing interests, with the girls' sexuality providing the ignition.[12] How to adequately protect them from white male sexual predation in both urban and remote settings, and prevent the growth of half-castes altogether, became the key issue for many reformers. While the government saw domestic service as a strategy of dispersal and disposal of the problem, those more intimately involved became embroiled in a battle over what protection should mean and how it should be executed.

The debate over the fate of Aboriginal women and girls in the centre and north in the late 1920s was therefore a flashpoint – an indicator of the intersecting gendered and racial anxieties gathering around the Aboriginal problem. As Cooke described it, the Bungalow was a thoroughfare, next to a hotel with no windows or fences.[13] It was, therefore, symbolic of the problem as Cooke and the APL defined it. Aboriginal people, their land, their women, their culture, were constantly violated. Cooke told the BCL that while there were some admirable laws in the Northern Territory which might protect Aboriginal women, the problem was that they were not enforced, the evidence for which was the growing half-caste community there. Symptomatic of the racial and gendered anxieties of this moment was the conflict between Cooke and Reverend J. H. Sexton, the powerful secretary of the Aborigines' Friends Association (AFA) which, prior to the APL, had been the pre-eminent humanitarian group in the state and, arguably, in Australia. Both Cooke and her colleague Ida McKay, former resident of Alice Springs, were lobbying the AFA for a woman visitor for the Aboriginal domestic servants in Adelaide, a reform rejected by Sexton. It was largely as a result of his intransigence on this matter that Cooke decided to join the APL instead, where Genders was promoting Aboriginal women's protection through land and self-determination.

The cause of Aboriginal women's protection had the effect of cementing important alliances between women, too. It was against the backdrop of her disagreement with Sexton that Cooke began a correspondence with Mary Bennett, whom she had met in London in 1927 at the BCL. Bennett's biography of her father, as well as her 'Notes on the Dalleburra', were published in that year and although she was yet to meet Anthony Martin Fernando, whose story of maternal loss impressed the invidious position of Aboriginal women on her, she already had strong views on the subject. With a keen sense of the history of contact in Australia, Bennett identified Aboriginal women's position as central to a history of discrimination. As she wrote in *Christison*, to a colonial governor's proclamation in defence of Aboriginal women in 1837 came cries of 'mawkish sentimentality'.[14] The book had numerous examples of the use of 'black women' by white frontiersmen. She wrote how they took the Aborigines' hunting grounds and their daughters, sisters and wives, 'at will and unchecked'.[15] She detailed a history of venereal disease and its attendant effects on the Aboriginal population. She also documented the contaminating effects of the towns where Aboriginal girls were degraded by 'mean whites' and Christison's view that it was only by their staying at his station that he could defend them from molestation.[16]

The massacres of the late 1920s in the centre and north confirmed both Bennett's and Cooke's view that the exploitation of Aboriginal women was a key source of inter-racial conflict. Provoked Aboriginal men and victimised women were at the bottom of the Kimberley and Coniston massacres in 1926 and 1928. This had been confirmed by Annie Lock with whom both Cooke and Bennett had been in correspondence. Lock detailed the extent of white men's abuse of Aboriginal women and how she had been wrongly maligned by settlers and police, describing 'great battles' with both and pointing to the complicity of local policemen in the 'traffic' in native women. In *The Australian Aboriginal as a Human Being*, Bennett argued that the fact that the Coniston massacre occurred at the same time as Bleakley was undertaking his investigation demonstrated how reckless and blunted settlers and police had become. Lock claimed that while she had always had the greatest respect from Aboriginal men, they looked down upon white men living with their women, stating that 'it is only the white men's guns that protect them or more would be killed'.[17]

While the Coniston massacre should be seen as the result of a volatile mix of issues, including the presence and interventions of Lock herself, Bennett's, Cooke's and Jones' anxiety about the position of women was given further weight following the publication of the Bleakley Report. As an eye-witness account of black–white relations on the frontiers, he confirmed their worst fears – irresponsible white men, drunken orgies, prostitution, illegitimate half-castes, insufficient food, native dependency, trafficking in alcohol and opium, control of natives by station managers and police, evasion of laws relating to the harbouring of single native women by unmarried men and a general policy of laissez-faire.[18] He also revealed the vital role of Aboriginal women in the economic development of the north, revealing how miscegenation was an essential ingredient of frontier conditions where there was an absence of white women. But it was also the direct outcome of the semi-starvation of Aboriginal communities which led Aboriginal women to supplement their family's meagre resources by trading in prostitution. He argued that this was hardly avoidable as all public roads led through the stations and the nearby Aboriginal camps. He referred to 'motor car loads of men' from bush townships or construction camps bent on 'ginsprees', 'causing trouble on stations, even one hundred miles distant'. One man had apparently boasted to him of having a 'fresh lubra' every week.[19]

Bleakley's inquiry was not the first to identify the sexual exploitation and trading of Aboriginal women across the frontier with its attendant problems of alcohol and drug abuse and the demoralisation of communities. Reports of a similar nature had been circulating from the early colonial period. They continue to do so today. Contemporary reports such as *Little Children are Sacred* which, among other things, identified a sex trade between Aboriginal and non-Aboriginal men in the north, including the transporting of young girls to Darwin for the purposes of prostitution, must be seen as part of a very long continuum.[20] In 1837, for example, Saxe Bannister advised the Select Committee on Aborigines to end transportation to Australia in order to stop the 'evil' inflicted on Aborigines caused by the absence of domestic ties for the transportees.[21] In 1904 the Roth Inquiry in Western Australia linked the 'depravity' of the Aborigines to the supply of liquor for 'dishonest purposes'.[22] It referred to the universal prostitution of Aboriginal women across the northwest and highlighted the complicity of the police in this process.

II

Despite its prevalence and its relevance to the national story, the history of Aboriginal and non-Aboriginal sexual interaction is yet to be told in full. From a body of work detailing important aspects of it, as well as new histories and approaches in the study of empire, we can say that it is impossible to tell the history of black–white interaction without it.[23] We can also say that it is a complex and complicated story. It involves all the possibilities of intimate human contact across a spectrum from love, emotional connectedness and desire, to co-dependence, fear, secrecy, shame, pain, grief, loss, coercion, abduction, rape, violence, enslavement and probably even hate. It is a story heavily documented by cross-cultural misunderstanding. Non-Aboriginal men saw Aboriginal women as readily available. Indeed, even officials and administrators saw colonisation of native women as part of colonisation itself, as one admitted in relation to the Northern Territory in 1935:

> It is true that many men up here have lived with gins in the far outback, but as a high official said here today, 'In Tahiti, in Java, in India, in Fiji, in Samoa, and in Tonga white men have lived with native women, and there has not been the fuss caused by such mésalliance as is caused by every busybody who comes in the territory'.[24]

The flipside of this process was that the traditional system of wife lending for ceremonial and reciprocal purposes was consistently abused. Non-regulation or policing suited a male frontier where an 'economy of sex' saw women and children traded for alcohol, opium and other goods between Indigenous, European and non-European men.[25] For some Aboriginal people this provided a space where they might survive and adapt, which some managed to do better than others. Yet, these processes compromised Aboriginal communities.[26]

While part of a long tradition exposing this deep subterranean history of inter-racial sexual interdependency, the Bleakley Report coincided with a key moment of Australian modernity when feminist and humanitarian voices were demanding a revised system of protection. In 1927, just as Bleakley's investigation in the north was commissioned, the BCL identified the 'wandering members of the British race' who 'lived without ties' or 'fellowship' and 'in a dangerous loneliness' as posing the greatest danger to relations between the races.[27] Cooke subsequently claimed that this had particular reverberations for Australia where it was a 'well known fact' that the men who faced the hardships of the outback were seldom accompanied by wives.[28] At the same time, John Harris, parliamentary secretary of the Anti-Slavery and Aborigines' Protection Society, argued that the relationship between native women and white men was the gravest feature of the colonial question.[29] The theme of the BCL conference that year was the 'Social and Industrial Condition of Women of Other Than

British Race Governed Under the British Flag'. Aboriginal women, along with Chinese women in Hong Kong, native women in South Africa and New Guinea, and women in India, were defined as living under systems of servitude, either through indenture and/or via indigenous customs which made them the property of their fathers and husbands.

This demonstrated the connection being made between slavery and indigenous women's status in the empire. Pedersen has elaborated the context within which this development took place.[30] Important were the debates over *mui tsai* (bonded female domestic servants, including children) in China and Hong Kong, child marriage in India and clitoridectomy in Kenya. In each case prominent British feminists and humanitarians played key roles in the context of a changed political landscape, which saw an incumbent Labour Party dedicated to the principles of trusteeship, the League of Nations adopting a Slavery Convention in 1926, and the establishment of an expert commission to abolish all forms of slavery in 1932. Also important was the infusion of women MPs interested in the question of colonial policy in the British Parliament, many of whom took part in a parliamentary debate on colonial policy in relation to 'coloured races' and established a Committee for the Protection of Coloured Women. In 1927 the publication of Katherine Mayo's controversial exposé of Hindu marital and sexual practices, particularly as they affected women and girls, became an important flashpoint for feminist mobilisation.[31]

The imperial context was also deeply significant to the Aboriginal problem in Australia as women reformers were defining it. It was against this backdrop that Cooke informed the international feminist community about the position and status of Aboriginal women in Australia. At meetings of the BCL and Pan Pacific Women's conferences she outlined the slave-like status of Aboriginal women. Describing the Aboriginal woman as the 'burden bearer' of tribal life, she maintained that she was the greatest sufferer of dispossession. Her thesis was that while Aboriginal men were relegated by this process to the position of serfs, Aboriginal women's subservience to their men meant that they more easily became the prey of white male settlers. With contact, the 'strict native morality' was undermined and the Aboriginal man became 'demoralised enough to barter her even for a bottle of drink'. While their marriage laws were designed to maintain the physical and moral welfare of the race, women were subjected to 'cruel and revolting practices' in connection with marital rights. She maintained that it was women's 'chattel status' which rendered native women powerless in the face of white intrusion.[32]

Jones reiterated Cooke's claims three years later at an important conference of the BCL on 'domestic slavery'. On a theme to which she would later return, and clearly influenced by the Bleakley Report, Jones raised the 'hopeless' outlook of the Aborigines in the north and centre of Australia where, apart from on mission stations, she said, they were rapidly dying out. She argued that the real problem was the stealing of Aboriginal women and the supplying of alcohol to facilitate those thefts. Echoing David Jackson she said that this accounted for 'ninety percent of the trouble with the blacks'. She added that because of their starvation Aboriginal women were frequently traded by their men for tobacco and whiskey, and concluded:

> if a woman, white or black, has not the control of her body, she is a slave. Some of these black women are slaves, their bodies are not subject to their own discretion if they are traded by their men for tobacco and whiskey.[33]

Still in London at the time, Bennett also contributed to this conference. Emphasising the economic basis of her critique, she argued that Australia was breaking the Slavery Convention in three ways: employers were using forced labour on private property, they were refusing to pay wages to working natives and they were removing natives from their tribes and families to work in Darwin. Native women were also placed at the disposal of white men and it was all the result of the dispossession and consequent starvation of Aborigines in Australia.[34] When asked by a conference participant why this had not been addressed by the International Labour Office (ILO) instead, Bennett replied that she wanted women to take the question up as the chairman of the ILO had informed her that 'starvation and dispossession' did not constitute forced labour, despite her argument concerning the condition of dependence and lack of choice which resulted from dispossession.

On one reading, Bennett's response seemed out of sync with the general tenor of the discussion. The conference was dominated by topics like bride price, *mui tsai*, clitoridectomy and vice (prostitution) regulation. Leading the discussion and resolutions was Nina Boyle, who was attempting to have indigenous practices such as arranged marriages and bride price recognised as slavery under the terms of the League of Nations. A prominent feminist, journalist and welfare worker, Boyle was a member of the Women's Freedom League, a splinter group of the radical Women's Social and Political Union. By the 1930s she turned her attentions to the position of the women of native races, being strongly supported by the St Joan's Social and Political Alliance, an international Catholic women's organisation prominent in the BCL and concerned about the position of native women in Africa and throughout the world. At the conference Boyle argued that the Slavery Convention provided, for the first time, a working international definition of slavery as 'the status of a person over whom all or any of the powers attaching to the right of ownership are exercised', which opened the way for the progressive abolition of such customs as infant betrothal, polygamy, bride price and purchase of girls by dowry.[35]

Boyle identified the cause of native women 'enslaved by custom' as a distinctively feminist issue because she believed that, if left to men, native women would remain bound by custom. Furthermore, it was not an issue that the Anti-Slavery and Aborigines' Protection Society was prepared to take up. Perhaps there was something in Boyle's claims about male bias. As Pedersen has shown, there was a long-standing administrative preference for non-interference in domestic and familial cultural practices. Boyle argued that with the revival of interest in the whole question of slavery from the late 1920s, the focus had been on those forms which affected men, such as forced labour and slave trading. It was, therefore, up to women to 'do for our sex what man has done for his—set them free from personal possession that they may dispose of their bodies themselves'.[36] Boyle was thus seeking sex equality in the application of the Slavery Convention. Accordingly, the conference resolved that those forms of slavery which subjected the women of native races to customs that made them the property of their fathers and then their husbands be abolished in accordance with the convention.

Boyle's views about the potential sex discrimination in the application of the convention had been acknowledged. At the BCL conference in 1927 John Harris confirmed as much, arguing that anti-slavery work on native women's behalf was hampered by British administrators' recognition of the 'delicacy of interference'.[37] Quoting Lugard's *Dual Mandate*, he maintained that the difficulty resided in the fact that native women nearly always represented an asset of a varying and disposable value to their communities. Under indirect rule administrators were loathe to intervene in traditional marital relations. Pedersen argues that Lugard believed that the ongoing practice of bride price signified not slavery but dutiful and stable families.[38] According to historian H. F. Morris, district officers in Africa might condemn certain traditional practices but when it came to the family they preferred to leave it to customary law.[39] He argues that it remained a critical point of tension between missionaries and administrators and that the interventions of the St Joan's Alliance were not welcomed by administrators already under siege on the question of indigenous marriages in Africa.

Yet, under the weight of new directions in anthropology, some feminists, like Cooke and Jones, argued that native women's position and status was exacerbated by culture contact. Implicit in Boyle's understanding of the native woman's position were the problems associated with culture clash, too. She repudiated the argument of non-interference and rejected the claim that it was impossible to change tribal law.[40] Her argument was that if conditions affecting (native) men's lives had changed or were changing with the rapid spread of westernisation, so must the conditions affecting women.[41]

On this point she was tapping into a more widespread feminist concern. In 1928, for example, the Pan Pacific Union urged its members to study inter-racial relationships, particularly indigenous people governed by a dominant race. The International Woman Suffrage Alliance requested that the Australian Federation of Women Voters encourage women graduates to undertake as a subject of their university theses the study of the position of native women in Australia and under the mandatory territories of the Commonwealth.[42] At the BCL conference in 1931 on the theme of 'Preliminary Clash of Cultures', Jones moved that empire women request of their governments to make the condition of native women under their rule a priority, arguing that the introduction of western influences into tribal life had serious repercussions on the status of women.[43]

III

This was an important moment because no government had ever made the position and status of Aboriginal women under its rule a priority in Australia. The notable exception was Governor Bourke, whom Bennett singled out for comment. In 1837 he threatened the cancellation of depasturing licences of white men found guilty of detaining Aboriginal women by force. They would be prosecuted as illegal occupiers of Crown lands.[44] He was unusual in linking the position of Aboriginal women to the occupation of land, but was not exceptional. There was a colonial practice of issuing land grants to Aboriginal women who married white men in South Australia, for example. However, as Foster and Paul have shown, this was less about preventing their sexual exploitation than about supposedly civilising them.[45] Certainly, governments had not had to and did not worry themselves about the position of Aboriginal women in their own cultures. Despite repercussions on indigenous women as a result of contact and western influences, and periodic interjections about their vulnerability, no government was prepared to face the gendered, much less sexual, dimensions of this question even as they were becoming increasingly nervous about its racial ones.

Until Protection legislation at the turn of the century there were no specific legal enactments targeting Aboriginal women, and even indirect regulations were patchy and rarely enforced. As many historians have documented, there was a widespread unwillingness to prosecute white men.[46] 'Coloured' men (mostly Japanese and Chinese) were different, often targeted as the principal cause of the problem. Some of the early Protection legislation in the north was targeted at prohibiting the employment of Aboriginal women on pearling luggers predominantly manned by non-European men. Some specifically targeted their sexual interaction. For example, the 1905 Aborigines Act (WA) prohibited Aboriginal women under sixteen to be within 2 miles of any creek or inlet used by pearlers between sunset and sunrise. To missionary claims, in the 1930s, of Japanese fishermen buying the sexual services of Aboriginal women from Bathurst Island, the federal government set up a control post and sent a patrol boat.[47] This was largely because the Japanese had, by then, become a security threat. As Frances has pointed out, the measures were only partially successful in preventing the prostitution of the women.[48]

By the end of the nineteenth century, amid cries of the economic and sexual slavery of Aboriginal people, Protection legislation was enacted, in part, to address concerns about the exploitation of Aboriginal women. This generally took the form of regulating conditions of labour, removal to missions and reserves (including their mixed-descent progeny), the declaration of non-native areas and, according to Chesterman and Galligan, an approach which blamed the victim.[49] In parts of Australia, attempts to contain venereal disease led to the removal, incarceration and compulsory examination of all Aboriginal suspects. It was only in Western Australia, following the controversial Roth Report in 1904 which documented the exploitation of Aboriginal women, including their sale in parts of the north, that legislation specifically targeting inter-racial sex was promulgated. Section 43 of the Aborigines Act made cohabitation between Aboriginal women and non-Aboriginal men illegal.

This gesture reflected the widespread sexual morality of the west which, at the time, saw miscegenation as immoral.[50] Criminalising sex, restricting individual liberty and making it difficult for potentially loving unions, this did nothing to prevent abusive situations for Aboriginal women. After Protection legislation Aboriginal women's position was arguably worse than it had ever been as they were now subjected to constant surveillance, regulation, child removal, intra- as well as inter-racial violence and sexual exploitation. According to Haskins, the paradox of protection was demonstrated in New South Wales, where the Aborigines' Protection Board did nothing to stem the high illegitimate birth rate or the pattern of sexual exploitation of young Aboriginal domestic servants.[51]

By the late 1920s, where there was official concern about the position of Aboriginal women it was indirectly via a desire to solve the problem of the half-caste and 'coloured' population. Looking to take greater control of the problem, administrators saw separation and removal, domestic service of the girls and family dispersal as the way forward. By giving the Chief Protector and/or Board of Protection custody, care and supervision of Aboriginal people and, increasingly, guardianship of all Aboriginal and mixed-descent children, legislation enshrined the principle of white male patriarchal rule and control as the norm. The only administrator understood to be actively addressing the situation of Aboriginal women was Neville in Western Australia, whose interest was part of a longer-term strategy to gain control of the problem of the half-caste in that state. Believing that it threatened white Australia with problems of health, education and promiscuity, he was looking to a eugenic solution in the future. As part of this he lobbied the feminists to assist in his efforts to amend Section 43 of the Aborigines Act. His claim was that the emphasis on cohabitation in the act precluded him from intervening in cases of casual sexual intercourse between Aboriginal women and non-Aboriginal men and that it referred only to full-blood women, thus ignoring the exploitation of mixed-descent women who were increasingly the focus of his (and their) concern.

To Bleakley's exposé of Aboriginal women's exploitation in 1929, the federal government amended the Aboriginals Ordinance in 1933 such that, in addition to a fine or imprisonment for the white man found to be in 'illicit relations' with Aboriginal women, the latter could now be imprisoned for soliciting.[52] This is a perfect example of the punitive nature of Protection. The legislation was not designed to police the non-Aboriginal community in their interactions with Aboriginal people in the way humanitarians were hoping. It was not designed to prevent infringements on Aboriginal life and liberty. Rather the responsibility was on Aboriginal people to comply with the voluminous restrictions on their lives. As the humanitarians argued, even restrictions on entering Aboriginal reserves were constantly violated for the purposes of mining, prospecting, dogging and big game hunting. When it came to mixed-descent children, the focus was on the mother of those children rather than the father, notwithstanding the key role of white paternity in schemes to 'breed out the colour'.[53] Even in instances where fathers were required to pay maintenance, the burden of proof lay with anyone *other* than the mother.[54] Bennett argued at the time that this had the effect of silencing the woman from ever 'giving evidence against her oppressor'.[55] Thus, Protection meant that Aboriginal people, rather than non-Aboriginal people, were targeted for infringement, non-compliance and punishment.

By the 1930s governments anxious about the 'colour problem' were conceiving of inter-racial sex, largely via their control of Aboriginal marriages, as the solution. This necessarily entailed the manipulation and channelling of their sexuality but it was a delicate issue. As Pascoe has shown, the view of inter-racial sex and marriage as unnatural underpinned the invention of the term miscegenation in the first place, as did the idea of white supremacy.[56] On the other hand, the offspring of such unions had long been perceived as signs of racial degeneracy, and half-caste and/or 'coloured' women perceived as sexually promiscuous, immoral and incapable of effective mothering.[57] These very anxieties underpinned the universal concern about the so-called half-caste problem in Australia. Yet, it was by re-focusing on the problem as one of child welfare on the one hand and changing scientific and humanitarian explanations regarding half-castes on the other, that government plans were implemented. Indeed, this focus was echoed around the empire, where British feminists everywhere argued for stronger interventions and rescue of mixed-descent children, a concern replicated by feminists in Australia, who increasingly prioritised it. Concern with the mixed-descent child was also part of a wider international shift in thinking about illegitimacy wherein state guardianship of the children was understood as a panacea for the problem.[58]

Furthermore, promoting inter-racial sex, via intermarriage, became more acceptable in a scientific environment where Aboriginal people were declared to be related to 'us'. The way administrators overcame the difficulty of making miscegenation the basis of policy was the 'scientific' discovery of Aboriginal–Caucasian relatedness.[59] In what amounted to an inverted racism Australians told themselves that, as Cooke put it, 'Aborigines were quite distinct from the negro, they were our distant forefathers and where their blood mingled with ours we were dominant'.[60] While focusing on the mixed-descent child, widely understood as being in the custody of the state, the position of the mothers slipped from view and the fact of controlled miscegenation became less relevant. Inter-racial marriage as policy became not an early celebrated moment of tolerance and acceptance but a covert operation, shrouded in silence and secrecy.

This demonstrates the complex interwoven and often competing layers underpinning investment in the Aboriginal problem. While Neville used the 'science' to implement a biological solution (selective breeding), humanitarians used it as a progressivist injunction for Aboriginal salvation.[61] 'They' were one of 'us' after all, and therefore deserved a better fate. Indeed, it was leading humanitarian Herbert Basedow's anthropology that changed perceptions of half-castes.[62] On a Caucasian evolutionary scale where Aborigines were at the start and Europeans at the finish, half-castes were literally halfway. With early intervention, rather than having them drop back 'to the degradation of the Aboriginal', policymakers could keep them on an ascendant track by removing them to government institutions and out into the community. By and large feminists agreed with this. Even Cooke claimed that it was better that, once removed, the lighter skinned children at Alice Springs be taken over by the State Children's Department and fostered out in 'good homes'. To critics who argued the un-Christian nature of this proposal, she argued that, in the case of the children at Alice Springs, removal had already been undertaken by the Commonwealth Government. She argued that the Woman's Non-Party Association believed that 'a certain amount of grading was better for all'.[63]

While it seemed that Cooke was having a penny each way, this was not unusual. A distinguishing feature of feminist and humanitarian mobilisation was a curious mix of genuine sympathy, race and class-based thinking, western morality, political discourse and reformist intentions which sometimes appeared (and were) contradictory. To be fair, like many humanitarians, Cooke's understanding of the Aboriginal problem was splintered between reforms targeting the full-blood remnant and those targeting half-castes. As a promoter of the Model State her ideal was to prevent the growth of half-castes in the first place. On the other hand, the other dominant feminist group interested in this question, the Women's Service Guilds, were not necessarily interested in the full-blood remnant at all, focusing almost entirely on the 'menacing problem' of the half-caste.[64]

From the late 1920s the Women's Service Guilds had been working with Neville on securing changes to the Protection legislation in Western Australia. Concerned by the health ramifications of the problem, they wanted to empower him to have any half-caste suffering from venereal disease hospitalised. When he complained of the high level of pregnancy in 'coloured' girls sent out to service, they requested that his guardianship of them be extended from 16 to 21 years of age. When they asked his advice on the question of marriages between 'half-castes' and whites, they appeared unperturbed by his response that absorption of the blacks by the whites was inevitable, natural and logical.[65]

Yet, from the early 1930s, they also worked closely with Bennett and, as a result, the thrust of their policy recommendations were influenced by her deep concern about the position of Aboriginal women as wives and mothers. She had long since identified this as one of near enslavement created by the contact of two different civilisations. At the conference on domestic slavery in London in 1930, her concentration on forced labour was not in an effort to emphasise the slavery of Aboriginal men only. Rather it was demonstrating her acute appreciation of the fact that Aboriginal women's fate was linked to that of their men. Once in Australia she argued that lack of food (via dispossession) or wages (due to forced labour) led to the practice of the men selling the bodies of their wives to white men in order to obtain food for the livelihood and maintenance of their families.[66] Bennett characterised the native 'patriarchal system', 'like other man-made systems', as unjust on women and children but exhibiting many good elements in their 'wild, "uncontaminated" state'.[67] The main problem, according to Bennett, was the perpetuation and exploitation of this system once Aboriginal communities came into contact with whites.

IV

Once in Australia, from her base on the Mt Margaret Mission, Bennett unleashed her own anti-slavery campaign where the focus was not the Aboriginal worker or forced labour but the Aboriginal woman. The boldness of her claims, just one year after arriving in Australia, demonstrates how developments in the empire provided her with the ammunition. In focusing on Aboriginal domestic relations she was capitalising on the momentum around native women's rights in the heart of empire and in particular, the domestic slavery of native women as promoted by Boyle and other British feminists. Furthermore, her claims were seemingly validated by developments in the League of Nations, wherein native women's status, and particularly forms of domestic slavery, were being raised for the first time in the interwar period.

Bennett was also strongly encouraged to focus on the slave-like status of Aboriginal women through her association with Rod and Mysie Schenk, the missionaries running Mt Margaret Mission, where she lived and worked. Indeed, it was from the mission that she obtained the evidence she required to make her otherwise controversial allegations. But it was also her mission experience that led her to focus, in particular, on polygamy as a source of women's enslavement in the context of culture contact. When Rod Schenk moved from New South Wales to Western Australia in the early 1920s to cater to the physical and spiritual welfare of the Aborigines on the eastern goldfields, he was initially appalled by their condition. In an account of the mission's history, Mysie Schenk points out that he was primarily concerned with their starvation and malnutrition, which rendered them particularly vulnerable. As missionaries they were concerned with the ongoing practice of polygamy among the goldfields people, believing that it was the basis of women's subjection as well as causing much intra-tribal conflict.

Indeed, it was primarily via the promotion of Christian monogamous marriages that missionaries believed they could affect a change in the lives of Aboriginal women. According to Wyllie, while ethnologists and sociologists held differing views about the status of indigenous women under polygamy, the Christian church understood the system as sinful, contrary to Christian morality and harmful to indigenous women.[68] If underpinning it was sexual behaviour and practices which they labelled immoral, so was an almost puerile condescension of the very cultures they were claiming to protect. Christian churches and missionaries were not interested in the knowledge gleaned about the role of sex and marriage within indigenous cultures. Identifying a system they characterised as hard on women, they saw missionary work as a means of introducing new, 'positive' influences into Aboriginal women's existence and promoting monogamy was a key part of this. The Schenks were certainly carriers of these views. However, they were also concerned that polygamy and its associated practices opened the way for Aboriginal women's exploitation by white men. Rod Schenk noted how Aboriginal men procured the necessities of life by selling their youngest wives to white men with the result that 'teenagers in white men's camps were commonplace'.[69]

Before her stay at the mission Bennett had been less concerned about Aboriginal women's position within their own cultures. In 'Notes on the Dalleburra', she listed infant betrothal as an important part of their 'regular marriage system designed to meet a tribal sense of morality', an example of which were the consequences for the man who tried to take away the betrothed of another. This carried over to non-Aboriginal men whom, she said, broke tribal law by taking Aboriginal men's wives. In *The Australian Aboriginal as a Human Being* she quoted from Sir Baldwin Spencer's *Wanderings in Wild Australia*, in which he argued that in their 'primitive state, uncontaminated by whites', women were generally on an equal footing with men.[70] Bennett concluded that the life and treatment of the women in their own societies was, in fact, far preferable to that of the women in England's slums.[71]

Yet, by 1932, her critique had become more nuanced as she sought to expose Aboriginal women's and girls' vulnerability, caught between two patriarchal cultures – what she termed a 'double bondage', where polygamy provided the link. Even a short stay at Mt Margaret would have confirmed this, for the Schenks not only had evidence of young girls in white men's camps; they maintained they also had evidence of young girls seeking their freedom from the polygamous system and Aboriginal husbands jealously guarding their marital practices and rights. Mysie Schenk established a room for the women and girls on the mission where she taught them raffia work, the sale of which provided them with an income. She characterised her first recruits as trailblazers who braved their husband's wrath, a response which might even be caused by the washing of their hair, a practice she insisted on:

> Mysie got used to the sight of the men walking up and down the dry creek bed, rattling spears in anger and shouting abuse at the women. Mercifully, she did not understand what they were talking about. The women undeterred, crept round to Schenk's back verandah to wash their hair out of sight of the men. Bungin, king of the Linden tribe, was especially incensed. He came from Linden specially to keep his eye on things and kept shouting at the women that they were growing their hair for tribal purposes and should not wash it. But Mysie knew none of this. It was just as well, because the battle continued for months, and even years.[72]

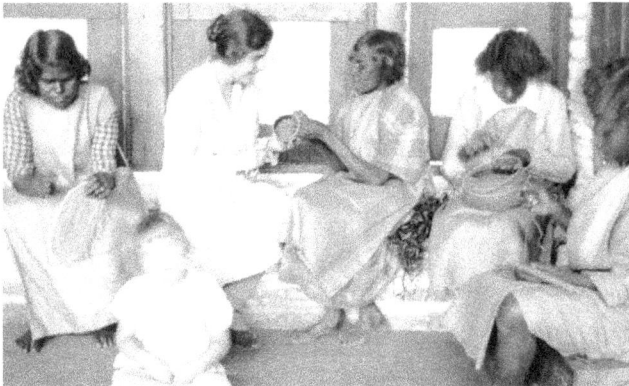

Mysie Schenk teaching Tarburry to make a raffia basket in the new raffia room, Mt Margaret, State Library of Western Australia.

The Schenks interpreted some of the old men's hostility to the mission as evidence of entrenched patriarchal practices. In their schema, it was almost always the men of the tribes who were 'polygamous', not the women. They were particularly concerned about polygamy as it was based on infant betrothal. This added a particular urgency to their critique of polygamy which, in their terms, almost became a pejorative term for young girls' sexual repression and abuse. As the US historian Margaret Jacobs has argued, in this way, Aboriginal people's sexuality was pathologised.[73] As Mysie Schenk reported it, the polygamous system saw girls as young as five given to men 40 years or older. She wrote that, from then on, she belonged to this man who might already have one or two wives. While he could take her to his camp at any time, at twelve or fourteen the girl became lawfully married to him as an extra wife. Writing an open letter to all Christian women she asked that they pray for Aboriginal women under 'men's law':

> She described the betrothal system and asked special prayer for the three eldest girls in the Graham Homes: Doris, Mona and Cissie – all betrothed to old men. She described the plight of the Christian girl who did not want to be a second or third wife but was caught in a system over which she was powerless. For generations these laws have been enforced, and the men make the women obey at the point of a spear. A woman cannot refuse to be lent, neither can she divorce herself from her husband and the other wives...[74]

Mysie represented the homes on the mission, where children received food and education, as one of the greatest threats to the polygamous system. Certainly one of the reasons for establishing them was to separate the girls from the old men of the tribes. There is little wonder that they were resented. Not only did the Schenks justify it as liberatory, it was understood as an important humanitarian intervention and a means of preserving the race. As representatives of the Christian church they maintained that polygamy contributed to racial decline because the old men monopolised the young women; it was associated with initiatory practices such as subincision, which could prevent conception and the young girls were frequently repulsed by the union. Once the woman was 'sold' to white men, disease exacerbated the problem.

Girls from the Graham Homes at Mt Margaret, 1934.
Back (left to right): Dimple, Queenie, Nina, Doolkie;
Centre: Gladys, Violet, Katie;
Front: Jean and Ningarlie.
Mary Bennett used these images to provide graphic illustration of the
young girls who were betrothed at birth according to Wongutha custom,
State Library of Western Australia, 009737d.

Bennett was also concerned about what was collectively understood as the property status of Aboriginal women. While the Schenks were doing battle with the old men, she turned her feminist lens on the practices of white frontiersmen. With her own experience in the north and against the backdrop of developments within the empire, she developed a nuanced argument about Aboriginal women's status which rested neither on their position within their own cultures or their exploitation in white society. Rather, their vulnerability was the combination of both in the context of dispossession. In May 1932, a month into her stay at the mission, her allegations of slavery, initially appearing in the Australian Board of Missions Review, were printed in *The West Australian*, the leading daily in the state. In it she argued that white men manipulated tribal custom for their own ends, capitalising on the property status of Aboriginal women and commercialising the practice of polygamy for personal gain:

> The destruction of the natives is caused by the white settlers dispossessing them of their land and by the settlers commercialising for their own advantage the native patriarchal system which...has the defects of other man-made systems in that it is unjust to the women and children, treating them as property. Commercialised

115

it is wholly evil…In the North-West white men barter with the old native men for the unpaid labour of the young men and for the old men's surplus property in wives "and a British and (supposedly) Christian public takes up the catchword and rivets the fetters of 'white slavery' on black women".[75]

Bennett argued that white men were primarily to blame because although Aborigines had lost their land to sheep and cattle stations and their culture had been destroyed, there had been a 'recrudescence' of polygamy for the purposes of prostitution.[76] This suggests that a target of her concern was the way polygamy was used to legitimise ongoing exploitation of Aboriginal women, including half-caste women, even when the conditions within which it normally operated were no longer.

The first marriage for two girls from the Graham Home, Mt Margaret, 1932, State Library of Western Australia, 09799d.

Her argument that polygamy stopped with dispossession and was revived under pressures of white contact was typically nuanced. Whether polygamy had ever completely died out is debateable, as is the related claim that Aboriginal culture had been destroyed. Bennett's claims, in fact, suggest that it is more likely that polygamy was utilised in the process of adaptation and survival. Indeed, the experience at Mt Margaret, a 'settled district for 40 years', was the *hold* of custom rather than its destruction or revival. As Bennett claimed, 'not one of the girls was "set free" there without a battle'.[77] This was demonstrated by the relatively slow adoption of monogamy on the mission. The first Christian marriages occurred there in 1932, some 11 years after the establishment of the mission. While this was regarded as a watershed, it did not open the floodgates. How typical this was is difficult to tell.

In fact, there are a number conflicting interpretations of the adoption of monogamy by Aboriginal people. These appear to correlate with the high degree of regional variability on this issue.[78] In her study of central and northern Australia, Diane Bell argued that economic changes in hunter-gatherer societies were more important than Christian ideology in the take-up of monogamy. As polygamy was integral to land tenure, dispossession provided the climate within which monogamy became the norm. On the other hand, Scanlon and the Berndts have suggested that where monogamy was adopted Christian ideology played a role – that Aboriginal people accepted the arguments put to them about the advantages of the system. In contradiction to this, Peggy Brock's study shows that although the United Aborigines' Mission succeeded in converting many of the people of Nepabuna in South Australia to Christianity, this did not extend to tribal marriages which, until the 1950s, were performed in the traditional manner.[79]

On the other hand, Christine Choo's study of mission marriages in the Kimberley between 1900 and 1950 confirms some of the Schenks' and Bennett's claims. She maintains that extramarital sexual relations, elopement and wife-stealing were rife in Aboriginal communities largely because of the impossibility, under gerontocratic rule, for young people to marry. While not all women were passive in these arrangements, Choo argues most became the focus of fights between men and many suffered violence, including death. While there was fear among the women about the possible impact of tribally 'wrong' unions, there was a willingness in some to partake. Choo maintains that, for the women involved, these marriages were generally happy affairs that resulted in security and safety and that, in accepting the mission way, these women were not necessarily relinquishing their tribal ways. At the same time, among her informants tribal marriages were not without criticism. Reflecting on the violence associated with polygamy, one of Choo's female Aboriginal informants admitted 'womans was like a slavegirl'.[80] Bennett also argued that some Aboriginal girls found protection at the mission rather than undergo introcision around puberty.[81]

However, Choo also acknowledges that mission intervention in tribal arrangements exacerbated Aboriginal women's vulnerability.[82] Mysie Schenk's account revealed how the missionary presence caused conflict within Aboriginal domestic lives on the Western Australian goldfields. It may well have exacerbated intra-tribal violence, too. Both the Schenks and Bennett consistently railed against the violence that they witnessed on the goldfields: men and men, women and women, and men and women. As Mysie put it, 'there was never a day without a fight'.[83] The Schenks didn't at first understand that there were two groups of Aboriginal people who came and went from the mission in its early phases. They saw them as one big group but came to understand that they were, in fact, two warring factions. Mt Margaret was the buffer between the two. In this context Mysie represented her husband's interventions as necessary, if risky, peacemaking. The many examples of women and men being nursed back to health at the mission by Mysie and Bennett suggest that they saw their intervention as necessary for a people already demoralised. They were defending women's human rights as they defined them. This was about breaking down a conservative male prerogative and tradition. As they said, each wedding was a 'tussle' and the women had to brave their husbands to begin work on the mission.[84]

Bennett argued that Aboriginal women in many of the settled districts of Western Australia were already vulnerable and that mission intervention was necessary in the context of contact and transition. What made her claims particularly sensational was her targeting of white men. Unlike Cooke, Bennett argued that it was not just 'low white men' who engaged in the 'traffic' in native women but the average, ordinary, man, the overwhelming majority of white men, including police protectors.[85] She alluded to 'a male confederacy' consisting of pastoralists, police and settlers who, benefiting from tribal law, would argue non-interference. She claimed that they protected the system in order to exploit it and the few who were not guilty of it condoned it in others. Above all, she believed it encapsulated the male double standard, arguing that while they defended the native man's right of ownership of many wives, they didn't defend his right of ownership of country, concluding that, 'Upholding the British law of land ownership is all right, but on a moral issue to emancipate the native women, they say, "Don't exercise British law"'.[86] Underlying her critique of white men and her accusation that they manipulated the

Aboriginal system was her sense that they abused their power and created conditions of dependence. Just as Aboriginal men lacked choice in selling their labour and had been forced into conditions of economic dependence, so had Aboriginal women.

Perhaps the most controversial aspect of her allegations was her argument that it was the white settlers' acceptance and protection of Aboriginal polygamy in the 'settled districts' which was the chief cause of the growing number of half-castes.[87] Bennett said she was not concerned about polygamy among the bush people. Rather, she was concerned with its lingering in towns such as Wiluna, Meekatharra, Peak Hill, Roebourne and Broome, where young Aboriginal people were growing up around a white community. She argued that the discountenance of polygamy and allowing Aboriginal women to 'invoke the protection of the law of the land' would result in fewer half-castes as 'there would be no plurality of wives to barter'. It would also result in young men obtaining young wives as it would stop the system of infant betrothal upon which polygamy rested. She pointed to the recent legislation in India on child marriage and concern over infant betrothal as an important precedent in the empire and one that Australia should follow, arguing that 'it is time that Australian women knew that it is countenanced in their own white settlements'.

Pointing to this precedent reveals just how imbued Bennett was with imperial ideas. She characterised the Child Marriage Restraint Act in India as a British attempt to free the women of subject races. Such a view simultaneously demonstrated her liberatory politics and her race-bound thinking for, as Sinha has shown, the debates over child marriage in India were as much about Indian nationalism as they were about the humane intervention of the colonial state.[88] But it also helps to explain her otherwise extraordinary claims. On one level her demand that polygamy be abolished seemed to expose a contradiction in her logic. The abolition of polygamy would surely have constituted a restriction on the liberty of the subject and potentially negatively impacted on the culture she otherwise admired. Abolishing polygamy by government edict would constitute a form of direct rule, which she so abhorred. Furthermore, she was cynical of government attempts to legislate Aboriginal women's protection, describing the changes to the Northern Territory Aboriginals Ordinance in 1933 as a 'window-dressing exercise' never adequately policed.[89] She surely knew that a law forbidding polygamy would not necessarily stop the practice.

Bennett was otherwise very careful about the claims she was making, believing that evidence was crucial. So, how do we explain her sensational and seemingly naïve demands and allegations? Her reference to British efforts in India provides some possible clues. Throughout this time there is a sense that Bennett was acting as interlocutor for Aboriginal women themselves. The inference was that these women were seeking their freedom and, as their spokesperson, she was the conduit for *their* cause. In 1932 in *The West Australian* she said: 'I have intimate knowledge of young native women far from happy under this system of polygamy and infant betrothal'. She also argued that if Aboriginal women were able to appeal to white man's law, 'under which many wish to live', the old men would be forced to submit. She said they were 'unwilling to go to the old men' and they suffered in silence because of an inability to make themselves understood and because they were victimised by the police. Her work was littered with vignettes of Aboriginal girls trapped by a system of 'patriarchal oligarchy' – women forced, frightened and harassed into acceptance of their fates under tribal law, who nonetheless wanted their 'freedom'.[90] Many of these came from Mt Margaret.

Whether this is right and Aboriginal women did appeal to Bennett is impossible to know, as is Aboriginal women's view of their domestic relationships. As Sinha's work suggests, one arrives at a different interpretation of these contestations when read from the perspective of the colonised. Were Aboriginal women seeking their freedom, as Bennett put it? If so, what did this mean in their terms? On the other hand, there is no reason to suppose that Bennett was making this up. Choo's work validates some of her claims and there were examples of Aboriginal women from the north and the south demanding freedom of choice in marriage as part of their campaigns for civil rights in these years.

Mysie Schenk's account of Mt Margaret suggests that some women were looking to obtain partners of choice there, too. They also used the mission as a place of refuge. Her account of the mission provides a number of examples where women and girls attempted to flout traditional marriages, often using the mission as a means of doing so. Desiring a younger man was one such instance, sending their children to the homes on the mission another. Given the fact that the number of girls in the mission homes increased almost threefold between 1928 and 1931, perhaps this was one method mothers used to steer their daughters away from traditional marital practices. Alternatively, Choo's work suggests that the women may not have seen monogamy as a separation from their own cultures. In this sense the mission may have been a buffer between two opposing cultural systems as much as warring tribes.

If this was the case, it is consistent with Bennett's own view. In her terms the abolition of polygamy would not, and should not, spell the end of Aboriginality. Rather it would merely eradicate the bad in the culture. In her terms, there was still much good to be preserved. Her sensational references to polygamy and infant betrothal were also about exposing violence in Aboriginal communities which was most frequently targeted at women. However, she wanted to counter the view that the banning of polygamy would lead to greater violence, an argument Neville used against her. Like the Schenks, she argued that polygamy was the cause of most of the fights and vendettas in the groups:

> The prevention of polygamy among these natives by the authorities would not cause any more trouble and bloodshed than is caused by its continuance. Many times an older wife has been beaten unmercifully because of her jealousy when a new wife has been brought in. Then again, the older wife will unmercifully beat the younger wife, or vice versa, in a fit of jealousy. In 99 cases out of 100 this happens. I can safely say that 90 per cent of the camp fights are caused for these domestic reasons and behind it all is polygamy.[91]

For Bennett the violence in Aboriginal communities was the result of their patriarchal structures, which were hard on women. She maintained that the prohibition of polygamy would stop a number of abuses against women, such as 'vicarious' killing and injury, wife lending as social obligation, wife exchange, wife barter to white men, initiation mutilations, witchcraft rituals and child marriage. She also pointed to a kind of double standard when it came to non-interference, claiming 'the death rate would be one per cent of that caused by dispossession and the punitive expeditions that followed the native's spearing of cattle for food'.[92] The Schenks also believed that abolishing polygamy would actually help to prevent race decline.

Yet, there were even more important reasons, for Bennett, why polygamy 'in the settled districts' should be banned and monogamy and free choice promoted instead. She believed that it would give Aboriginal women greater legal protection. Her otherwise astonishing claim for state intervention to ban polygamy was not just because 'we' were implicated but also because, while *recognised*, tribal marriages were not *legal* according to the laws of the state. This meant that white men who had casual sex with Aboriginal women or girls who were the wives or betrothed of Aboriginal men were immune from any consequences.[93] This was what she meant by their manipulation of tribal custom. Her inference was that because monogamy was the legally sanctioned marital code of the land, it made illicit sexual relations, if not more difficult, open to scrutiny and punishment in a way that Aboriginal polygamous arrangements were not.

Furthermore, with the Chief Protector the legal guardian of any offspring of such unions, Aboriginal women were doubly victimised as they were unable to claim their children as their own. One of her principal concerns was the 'smashing of family life', whether it be through removal and non-payment of workers, the taking of children or the victimisation of women. As it was, she argued that the 'system' rested on a western perception of Aboriginal women's alleged immorality. Her writings and protests were full of examples of girls and women with an 'instinctive passion for purity and innate desire for chastity' and freedom who, while in a transitional stage between white and black culture, were victimised and demoralised by the 'economy of sex'.[94] Monogamy would give the women freedom of choice and freedom to extricate themselves from abusive situations. They would have recourse to legal protection and have guardianship of their children. With land, food, education, medicine and citizenship, families could then be kept intact.

This concern with the smashing of family life would have been made more obvious to Bennett by her contact with the mission. One of the worst features of life on the goldfields in Western Australia, as Rod Schenk saw it, was the often violent removal of people to Moore River government settlement. Equally remarkable were the strategies of the people to withstand this onslaught, including escape and return to the goldfields and the blackening of half-caste children's faces to avoid being targeted. Being concerned with the physical as well as the moral condition of the people, the Schenks were appalled by the demoralised state of the communities.

The presence of Aboriginal girls in white men's camps was part of this demoralisation, for it created conditions of vulnerability as the offspring were targeted for removal and institutionalisation. The Schenks considered that the promotion of settled monogamous lives would be the foundation of self-supporting communities. Equally important was food, education and paid work.

Sadie Corner (child) as she arrived in her mother's arms at Mt Margaret in 1934, after escaping the police roundup of children for Moore River, State Library of Western Australia, 009997d.

Worrying about polygamy and encouraging legally recognised marriages within Aboriginal communities was totally antithetical to government aims in Western Australia, however. These were based on the removal of mixed-descent children to institutions, forcibly if need be; the sending of girls into domestic service; the encouragement of marriages between Aboriginal women and white men; the separation of full-bloods; and the denial of any rights of the mother to her children. Policies rested on the skilful manipulation of tribal custom. Neville recognised the 'evils attendant upon a plurality of wives', but argued that there was little 'we' could do as 'we' were not responsible.[95] On the other hand, he used custom as a justification for the removal of the half-castes:

> The removal of half-caste children is a necessity for so many reasons that it seems almost futile to mention them…The Department is not prepared to see its half-caste wards assigned to native husbands

already in possession of a wife. It considers they deserve a better fate.[96]

For Neville, Bennett's dredging up slavery was particularly provocative because it rehearsed a set of very old critiques which governments, particularly in Western Australia, had long since dispensed with under the guise of Protection.

V

Yet, by the 1930s, allegations of slavery abounded both inside and outside Australia. In 1932 public allegations by anthropologist Ralph Piddington confirmed Bennett's reports of slavery on pastoral stations in the northwest, along with the traffic in Aboriginal women and the collusion of settlers and police.[97] Western Australian feminists had also received a first-hand report of Aboriginal women's 'enslavement' to Asian and European men from a white woman living in Broome.[98]

Furthermore, Bennett's slavery allegations and her public protestations concerning Aboriginal women's marital fate coincided with the ongoing public allegations of a trade in Aboriginal women between polygamous Tiwi men and Japanese fishermen made by Father Gsell, a Catholic missionary on Bathurst Island.[99] Both coincided with the growing national and British feminist interest in the marital status of indigenous women across the empire. Regarded as among some of the most advanced white women in the world in the interwar period, Australian feminists not only wanted to contribute to these discussions but wanted to be seen to contribute. Bennett's deep knowledge and study of the question, along with Cooke's and Jones', was therefore important.

In 1932 Bennett's key ideas for the reform of Aboriginal policy, including the abolition of polygamy, were adopted by the Australian Federation of Women Voters (AFWV). This was largely the result of Bennett's close working relationship with the Women's Service Guilds in Western Australia and, in particular, Bessie Rischbieth, who was prominent in the guilds and the national feminist body. The latter's 'Call to the Women of Australia to Demand an Honourable Native Policy', published in 1932, earmarked the 'native and half-caste question' as the most urgent national problem of the day. Their ideas for a constructive national policy were a replica of both humanitarian and feminist concerns.

They repeated all of Bennett's reforms, including keeping the admirable elements of Aboriginal culture while dispensing with the undesirable parts, adequate territories for Aboriginal development, education for both Aboriginal and half-caste children, married police protectors, and human rights and protection for Aboriginal women from 'irresponsible white men'. This would involve the changes to Section 43 of the Aborigines Act in Western Australia that they were already requesting, and the ability of Aboriginal and half-caste women to 'free themselves' from the 'polygamy and prostitution of the commercialised patriarchal system' and, invoking legal protection, 'exercise free will in the choice of a husband rather than be handed over to claimants as property'.[100]

In that same year the AFWV took its program to the British Commonwealth League conference, the theme of which was 'Marriage from the Imperial Standpoint'. This was a fascinating moment as it was the first time the league explicitly considered inter-racial marriages and the status of women in them. The position of Aboriginal women and children in Australia was part of a broader discussion on native women's marital status both within their own cultures and in inter-racial unions throughout the empire. The resolutions of the AFWV were given prominence and were discussed at length. Talks by R. M. Fleming of the Royal Anthropological Institute and Dr Harold Moody of the League of Coloured People promoted the inevitability of inter-racial marriage in the modern world as well as its acceptability in racial terms. The conference was also an occasion where Nina Boyle and the league as a whole reiterated her resolutions on the abolition of slavery and all customs and abuses akin to slavery within the British Empire, in particular, 'the maintenance and protection of marriage customs which sanction the sale, purchase and other arbitrary disposals of the persons of women and the exercise over them of the "Rights of Ownership within His Majesty's Dominions".' In this context there was even the sense that inter-racial marriage be considered a means of improving indigenous women's status overall.

Thus, while Bennett's interventions were amazing and, in Australia, outrageous, they were not isolated. They struck a chord. If she was pragmatic in using the moment to expose exploitative conditions she was, nevertheless, bolstered by significant momentum. Nowhere was this clearer than in the determinations of the League of Nations on this question, which Bennett followed and was much heartened by. In particular, it was the report of Mary Jamieson-Williams, the AFWV alternate delegate to the league in 1933, that provided a further fillip to her cause. While evidence from South Africa dominated the discussion, Jamieson-Williams demonstrated the relevance of the forum's determinations for Aboriginal women in Australia by citing the recent Caledon Bay affair in Arnhem Land. In this case a punitive expedition was mooted for the murder of a white policeman following his investigations of the murders of Japanese fishermen by Aborigines in 1932. Jamieson-Williams pointed out that the real tragedy of the event was that the men of the tribes who had bartered their women for goods in return, notably tobacco, had not received the price of their women's bodies as agreed. The murder of the Japanese was therefore an act of revenge for the 'wrongful' appropriation of their women.[101]

Titled 'The League of Nations and a Problem for the Future—The Native Woman', her report demonstrates the concern gathering about the position of native women around the empire, which was being defined in the context of a demand for a common native policy throughout the empire. Those involved in colonial policy in Britain were looking for consistency in the administration of what was identified as the outstanding problem of the twentieth century – white settlement of tropical territories. Jamieson-Williams identified three areas of the league's work which might apply to the position of native women: mandates, traffic in women and children, and slavery. At the forum she argued that any policy aimed to train and educate the men of native tribes in mandated territories must also apply to the women. At the same time, she maintained that having dropped the 'white' from its banner, the traffic in women and children committee might now consider tribal customs and traditions which, if followed by the white race, would be considered traffic. Among these were the trading of daughters and female relatives under the 'semblance of marriage' to different men. Jamieson-Williams wrote that this was equivalent to the practice of the *souteneur*, the man who lived off the earnings of the immorality of women:

> When women are held in compulsion for sex purposes only, and their freedom restricted, it does not change the condition of Traffic, that there is a form of native marriage to support such compulsion.[102]

126

Jamieson-Williams reported that the League of Nations was promoting the breaking down of all forms of 'domestic slavery' and 'marriage bondage' as the direction of a common native policy. It was argued that in the process of 'assimilating Western white civilisation', the indigenous mind be enlightened as to the 'true value of human freedom' as it related to women. While all white workers in native territories should also adopt an enlightened attitude and policy to native women, the administration should aim to progressively abolish all customs that bordered on slavery, including the purchase, sale and barter of women and children which, 'under the semblance of marriage commit a woman to unwilling prostitution, degrade and cause suffering to children and deny women and children human rights'. Jamieson-Williams concluded by suggesting that the women of Australia should be abreast of this and 'be prepared to follow in the line of British advocates of the past in their outspoken utterances in the League and the world at large'.[103]

In this context, Bennett's interventions in Australia seemed much less controversial. She lost no time in capitalising on it; the opportunity to do so came in that same year. Coinciding with the centenary of the abolition of slavery in 1933, this was a significant moment in the empire, when it paused to reflect on its role in the liberation of enslaved people and to reinstate its central aims and purposes. This mood was reflected in Australia, too, where people like Cooke and William Morley organised activities such as sermons to town hall gatherings, addresses to schools, broadcasts and press publicity. At the time, Jones penned a paper titled 'The Australian Aborigine Woman: Is She a Slave?'. In it she pointed to the anomalous position of Aboriginal women as British subjects, claiming that their wills and their bodies were not their own. Calling for the outlawing of polygamy, she asked 'free' British women to consider whether Aboriginal women were free or enslaved:

> Does not the practice of wife lending by Aboriginal husbands to white men without the wife's consent constitute a breach of the moral law against slavery if not the written law of the British Empire? Can we truly meet the year 1933 with a clean slate in the British Dominions?[104]

She called on women to rouse 'a great wave of sympathy' all over Australia for the freeing of their native sisters from conditions which, by restricting the liberty of their persons, constituted a form of slavery as recognised by the League of Nations.

It was also in this context that Bennett's paper titled 'The Aboriginal Mother in Western Australia' was read at the BCL. The conference was dedicated to the slavery theme, and Bennett's paper coincided with the second day which focused on 'The Mother of Today Within the British Commonwealth'. It rehearsed all her key ideas and arguments already in the public domain, providing examples of the widespread prostitution of the women because of dispossession and starvation, the collusion of the police and the discrimination faced by women in relation to guardianship, healthcare and education for their children. While pointing to the property status of the women in their own societies, she identified 'contact with civilization' as making their situation much worse. Starvation, dispossession and prostitution turned their property status into merchandise.[105]

The paper also rehearsed her suggestions for reform. 'Good missions', like Kunmunya in the north and Mt Margaret on the eastern goldfields, were self-supporting communities which discouraged the 'bad' in Aboriginal culture and facilitated the 'good'. The solution to starvation and dispossession was more reserves throughout the state where communities could live and grow their own food in their own territories rather than being transported, often hundreds of miles away, for,

> Aboriginals are deeply attached to their own country, and should not be transported. It would be as reasonable to attempt to solve the problem of the English slums by snatching the children from their mothers and transporting them to a settlement in Teneriffe or Turkey. So vast are the distances in Western Australia.[106]

The vulnerability of Aboriginal mothers was further demonstrated by their being hunted by police to remove their half-caste children to remote government settlements. The 'agony of fear' the mothers experienced was then reflected in the children, who were intimidated and stunted. Land, and rights, such as medical services, wages and citizenship, were required, as was education, which she defined as fundamental to all other rights.

Bennett's conclusions were reinforced by Lady Simon, the patroness of the Anti-Slavery and Aborigines' Protection Society, who stressed the link between individual human rights and the anti-slavery cause, pointing to the property status of people under slavery and arguing that, under such a system, parents may even lose the custody of their children. Summing up, Reverend John Jones, husband of Edith, emphasised the virtual slave status of Aboriginal women and girls, maintaining that 'black men claimed them and white men used and abused them'.[107] It was resolved that women draw the attention of their governments to 'conditions akin to slavery' in any territory under British rule.

Does Australia Maltreat Aborigines?

POLYGAMY IS THE PRINCIPAL TROUBLE

Full Text of Mrs. Bennett's Paper

GIRLS MUST SUBMIT TO DEGRADING MUTILATION

COMMENTS in overseas newspapers have created wide interest in Australia's treatment of her aboriginal population. Some of these charges are: —

Aboriginal girls are bespoken in their infancy—sometimes before their birth—by the older men, who take them for their wives when they reach the age of ten. The older men usually have other wives already. Thus the property status causes women and children to suffer the evils of infant betrothal, child marriage and polygamy.

Polygamy causes most of the fights and vendettas of an otherwise singularly peaceful and unresentful people. Polygamy is encouraged by white settlers and protected by the administration.

These strong statements are taken from a paper read by Mrs. M. M. Bennett, at present at Mt. Margaret Mission Station, before the British Commonwealth League in London last week.

Mrs. Bennett has forwarded a copy of her paper exclusively to "The Daily News." In our issue of Tuesday last the Minister in charge of the Aborigines Department replied, at length, to the published summary of Mrs. Bennett's charges.

The paper sent to the British Commonwealth League sets out that the study of the aboriginal mother falls into two parts—one dealing with the aboriginal mother living a wild life, uncontaminated by whites, and the other with the aboriginal mother in touch with civilisation.

The chief characteristics of aboriginal women are affectionate responsiveness and great persistence in their work, whether in the age-old quest for food or in new industries, introduced into the missions, such as weaving.

The primitive culture of the aborigines built up the duty of everyone to his kin. Kin and duties were specified arbitrarily by the older men of the tribe. All power was vested in these older men. Their rule is hard on women.

PARTICULAR WORK

Here is very particular work to be done for women by women's societies: The work of preventing exploitation of witchcraft and mutilation by students of anthropology in their hunt for copy. I know cases and can give particulars. One [...] good mission's policy is to counter evil practices by showing a better way—not to meet violence with violence.

At Kunmunya, in the north of Western Australia, witchcraft is being voluntarily abandoned. People are finding happy security and new dignity and Mr. Love can encourage all that is good in their native culture without fear that it will revive evil. He told me that things which he discourages are polygamy, witchcraft and infanticide.

FIGHTING SUPERSTITION

The influence of Christian teaching in overcoming superstition was strikingly revealed in an incident which occurred at Kunmunya Presbyterian Mission station last Christmas. "To understand what happened," said Mr. Love, "I must tell you that when a black man dies it is the custom to put him on a platform of branches and then to place on the ground, surrounding the platform, a number of large stones.

"Each stone is given a man's name. Next day any old man come and examine the stones. Should any stone be stain- [...] the stones. Should any stone be stained with blood it means that the man whose name the stone bears is supposed to have caused the death of the men on the platform by evil magic and that man will be killed by relatives of the dead.

"Of course, what happens, actually is that during the night the wicked old medicine man steals out, cuts his arm and pours the blood on the stone of one man whom he hates.

"To return to Christmas Day. The dead man had been laid on the platform and covered with boughs. Several men then at once began to clear away leaves and grass from around the platform, making ready to place the stones, which were to be used to spy out the one who had caused the death.

"Sitting by was Woodoomnoia, an elderly man, who was in my catechumen's class, preparing for baptism on the following Sunday. He has been one of my regular translation team of helpers and one of the most useful men to me. As the clearing of the ground was begun Woodoomnoia spoke in a quiet level voice, 'We will put no stones.' No stones were placed and so no unfortunate [...]

WHITES' TREATMENT OF ABORIGINES

Urgent Need for Protection of Females

SERIOUS ALLEGATION AGAINST AUSTRALIA IN LONDON

Federal Control and Segregation Urged by Speakers

(Special to "The Daily News")

LONDON, June 16.

THE BRITISH Commonwealth League's conference this week fully discussed the position of Australian aborigines, and after a two days' debate, passed a resolution appealing to Australian women's societies to combine in directing the attention of their Governments to conditions akin to slavery under which detribalised aborigines and half-castes lived, including infant betrothal, natives lending wives in exchange for material gain, and the marriage of polygamous husbands to girls who were sometimes Christians.

The Federal Government was urged to provide a special department to deal with aboriginal offences.

POLICE AND NATIVES

Emphasising that he was dealing with the present time, the Rev. John Jones, of Melbourne, ex-chairman of the Australian Board of Missions, said the worst indictment of the whites in Western Australia and North Australia was the killing of natives by the police, whom it was almost impossible to convict because of the improbability of a white man's Court accepting a black man's evidence.

Mr. Jones quoted the Melbourne "Herald" of April 1 in regard to the establishment of native Courts, which he strongly endorsed in the Papuan system were followed. He added that despite the efforts of missions and State Governments, disintegration, corruption and disease continued among the natives.

Most murders of whites by blacks were due to the whites' appropriation of natives. Special attention should be given to white men's prostitution of native women and girls. The blackfellow who had a native wife, or was betrothed to a girl, knew she was merchandise that could be bartered for a stick of tobacco.

Mr. Jones averred the truth of the Australian messages to the London "Daily Herald," alleging the kidnapping of native women by Japanese. This long-standing custom was increasing because of the spread of Japanese indecente in the areas concerned. Aboriginal women were almost invariably the innocent cause of murders, similar to that reported in the "Kalgoorlie Miner" of March 20, in which a native was sentenced to death for the murder of a Japanese pearler, Nagaio, though no corpse was found, and though the trial was held 3000 miles from the scene of the alleged crime.

FEMALE SLAVES

A well-known station owner had told Mr. Jones that he was compelled to discharge an excellent stockman because the stockman seduced every native girl he encountered. Many aboriginal women and girls were virtually slaves; black men claimed them, and the whites used and abused them, evidence of which was the increasing number of half-castes whose mothers were black and the fathers were whites or Asiatics.

FEDERAL WORK

The chief obstacle to amelioration of the position was that aboriginal welfare was a State and not Federal responsibility, except in North Australia. The Federal Government reported to the League of Nations on the administration of the Papuan mandate; would it be willing to report on the administration of aborigines throughout Australia?

Mrs. Jones declared that with the cordially courageous exception of the Melbourne "Herald" few Australian papers would publish criticism of the administration of the aborigines.

NEW REGULATIONS

DARWIN, Saturday.

An amending aboriginal ordinance published in the "Government Gazette" for the protection of female aborigines and half-castes provides heavy penalties for breaches and aborigines are debarred from being on boat premises. Another ordinance abolishes trial by jury, except for offences punishable by death.

Used and Abused by All

(Special to "The Daily News")

LONDON, June 16.

The British Commonwealth League's conference this week fully discussed the position of Australian aborigines, and after a two days' debate, passed a resolution appealing to Australian women's societies to combine in directing the attention of their Governments to conditions akin to slavery under which detribalised aborigines and half-castes lived, including infant betrothal, natives lending wives in exchange for material gain, and the marriage of polygamous husbands to girls who were sometimes Christians.

The Federal Government was urged to provide a special department to deal with aboriginal offences.

W.A. WOMAN'S STORY

Miss Ruby Rich, of Sydney, read a letter from Mrs. W. W. Bennett, wife of a Western Australian missionary, urging the conference to combat the practice of placing native and half-caste females at the disposal of the police, some of whom were unfit, but others corrupt. Mrs. Bennett alleged that many white men kept black women in their camps, while the police hunted aboriginal mothers in order to remove their half-caste children to a remote Government settlement, causing the mothers agony. The whites encouraged any administration which protected polygamy. One official had ordered excepted native girls to return to their appropriators, and the girls had to submit to mutilation which, though discouraged by the mission authorities, increased wherever anthropological students and other copy-hunters commercialised such practices in order to supply their markets. Many startling confronted native women in civilised surroundings, and a wholesale prostitution prevailed in order that the women could obtain tobacco and flour for blackfellows. The remedy was to segregate the natives in an area where they could live naturally and grow their own food, unmolested by whites.

Examples of the press coverage of Bennett's allegations at the British Commonwealth League in the Western Australian Daily News, June 1933.

In drawing the Australian government's attention to 'conditions akin to slavery' in their territories, Bennett's claims constituted an unwanted and unwarranted intervention in an already volatile policy landscape. The humanitarian movement was beginning to make its presence felt, resuscitating the unnerving 'whisper' of discontent.[108] Bennett's claims and their very public national and international exposure added a sense of urgency at a critical time. The series of frontier clashes across the north from the late 1920s had already put the federal government on notice about the race problem in its midst. Bennett's slavery allegations coincided with the publicity around the Caledon Bay affair, which had focused the eyes of the world on Australian conditions and demonstrated how they were part of a broader empire-wide concern with the otherwise intractable and worrying problem of race.

It was in this context, too, that organisations like the BCL and the Anti-Slavery and Aborigines' Protection Society began corresponding with Australian governments concerning Aboriginal conditions and policies. Thanks to Bennett, Jones and Cooke, governments were now forced to confront the gendered implications of the policy setting, as sensational headlines concerning 'black slavery' in Australia were splashed across local and British newspapers, detailing the nature of Bennett's critique in full. As Haebich explains, Bennett's outpourings to an international audience, particularly her paper on the Aboriginal mother, created a furore in Western Australia and she was subjected to vitriolic attack.[109] While Neville fumed, federal authorities rejected the allegations as 'absurd and utterly untrue'.[110]

Thus, the focus on the status and condition of Aboriginal women added a particularly disturbing element to the already fraught politics around the Aboriginal problem in these years. Matters of a domestic nature were spilt, threatening to expose Australia's hypocrisy and isolation on this question. The position of Aboriginal women in Australia was one example of a broader empire-wide issue being forced under colonial governments' noses by a robust feminist movement. They were using the imperial humanitarian moment to call for the modernisation of indigenous domestic relations. By placing male sexual practice, prostitution and the position of Aboriginal mothers at the centre of the problem and its resolution, Bennett's critique threatened to destabilise a delicate balance between government propaganda, which focused on the ameliorative processes of protection, and administrative practice which increasingly focused on using Aboriginal women's (as well as white men's) sexuality as a conduit through which half-castes would be absorbed into the community.[111] In this way Australia could avoid the race problems manifesting elsewhere. In the face of threat, the bureaucracy responded by turning the problem on its head. Rather than a question of women's position in their own cultures or even caught between two cultures, the real issue, as the bureaucracy defined it, was the status of the Aboriginal problem within the domestic confines of the nation.

4

DOMESTIC RULES
Ignoring the Rights of Mothers

Mrs Bennett's assertions are somewhat sweeping. What she calls human rights would be rather hard to define. In this state natives and half-castes have very definite rights and protection provided by the Aborigines Act and other laws of the state. It is decidedly incorrect to say that slavery is in operation...[1]

Against the backdrop of the developing concern in Britain over the status of native women, Bennett's interventions forced the position of Aboriginal women onto the national agenda. The very public way in which she focused attention on the lives of Aboriginal women as mothers, in particular, was unprecedented. Yet, she wasn't alone. Feminists in Western Australia and elsewhere were very aware of the practice of Aboriginal child removal. Several raised concerns about it at the royal commission called as a result of Bennett's allegations. They also reiterated the central ideas around domestic slavery and marriage bondage emanating from the League of Nations, requesting its application to Aboriginal policy in Australia. Despite these synergies, there was not complete agreement between women reformers. This is perhaps best summed up in their participation in the royal commission and its aftermath. For the feminists, the royal commission represented a pivotal moment: a crowning achievement of their feminist input and symbol of their active citizenship. For Bennett it was the beginning of a bitter struggle with the administration, starting with her allegations of slavery and continuing long after the royal commission was over. In this context, feminist realignments occurred.

This story is bound up with the unanimous feminist demand that they have more power in native affairs, which I have explored elsewhere, but it is also bound up with changing interpretations of the nature of the problem itself.[2] As McGregor and others have shown, the debate became less and less about preserving a remnant people and more about what to do with a hybrid race.[3] Against the backdrop of the global colour problem, the international community was beginning to see that racial mixing was a likely outcome and the half-caste problem an inevitability which could no longer be ignored. The debate in Australia over what to do about the latter was symptomatic of this global concern, as was the national and international feminist community's growing anxiety over the fate and status of mixed-descent children.

For Bennett, the fate of the children remained intimately bound up with the fate of their mothers. For her it was about legal equality and citizenship for these women, which would ultimately ensure against the removal of the children in the first place. For feminists it was largely a maternalist desire to step in where fathers had failed and give these children, characterised as 'victims of the white man's depravity', a chance of 'fuller citizenship'.[4] The failure of the Australian Federation of Women Voters to endorse the principle of equal citizenship for Aborigines at its national conference in 1936 confirmed Bennett's sense that Australian women were as colour conscious as the administration itself.

Hence, white women's interventions around the position of Aboriginal women were enmeshed in a larger national and international story about the global colour problem. Just as debates over Indian marital practices in the interwar period were central to the reshaping of the empire, white women's attempts in interwar Australia to 'free' Aboriginal women were enmeshed in the reshaping and consolidation of a national Aboriginal agenda.[5] It was during these years that governments, consistently pressed by humanitarian demands, convened the first ever national Aboriginal welfare conference in 1937, which the all-male administrators responsible for Aboriginal affairs attended. It was there that they declared (biological) absorption of the half-castes as the 'destiny of the race'. As has been widely documented, conditions in Western Australia were something of a showpiece at the conference, along with Neville's administration. The feminists' relative silence on this momentous policy formula exposed a deep chasm in Bennett's understanding of the problem and its solution and theirs. The key feminist group in Western Australia, the Women's Service Guilds, with whom Bennett had worked closely, ultimately accepted the direction of policy, which Bennett saw as deeply problematic from the point of view of Aboriginal women's human rights.

This internal feminist strain was a microcosm of the larger struggle between Bennett and the Western Australian government over the Aboriginal problem. Both governments and 'others' – constituents, humanitarians, Aboriginal activists, missionaries, academics – battled between and among themselves for control and definition of the problem and its solution. This was a key moment in Australian history, not least because never before had the status and position of Aboriginal women been at the centre of discussions about the Aboriginal problem in Australia. In the contest which ensued, the body of the Aboriginal woman became a battleground over which the protagonists fought. As contentious as Bennett's slavery allegations were, they ultimately played into government hands. Emphasising the internal domestic nature of the problem, it rejected the allegations and simultaneously ignored the feminists' specific reforms for Aboriginal women. While the government declared victory, it was not without wounds. For her part Bennett raged over the defeat and what she saw as the 'evil' consequences for Aboriginal women. She also raged over what she saw as feminism's failure. Yet as she raged, new alliances were formed, particularly in feminist ranks, which were to have long-lasting implications for her ongoing crusade.

|

The response of the Western Australian Chief Protector, A.O. Neville, to Bennett's slavery allegations was to deny them and to argue that her assertions were mere generalisations. On the question of wages he said that payment in kind was 'no deprivation to a people unaccustomed to the use of money'. He spoke of vast well-watered reserves and refuted her claims of the traffic in women, denying that polygamy was permitted *to any extent* among civilised and half-caste Aborigines.[6] On Bennett's key request for the abolition of polygamy in the settled districts, he said:

> The evils attendant upon the plurality of wives have always been recognized by the Department…But it is doubtful whether a direct order forbidding the practice would be effective and extremely likely that such order might do more injury than good.[7]

By emphasising non-interference in Aboriginal domestic marital relations he was reiterating a widely held view among male administrators around the empire. His attempts to dampen Bennett's claims were also consistent with his 'letting sleeping dogs lie' approach.[8] Bennett's interventions came at a critical time in his administration when, in an effort to solve the half-caste problem, he was treading a difficult path between various vested interests in the west, including a 'squatter-dominated' Legislative Council which resisted his efforts to reform both Aboriginal labour and inter-racial sexuality.[9]

In order to counter this Neville had cultivated a relationship with the Women's Service Guilds. Together they were looking to amend section 43 of the Aborigines Act of 1905, which he claimed would give him greater power to act in cases of casual sexual intercourse between white men and Aboriginal women, a concern close to their reform agendas. This and this alone was the context in which he was prepared to intervene in Aboriginal domestic relations because he understood Aboriginal women's sexuality as the conduit for his reforms. By the early 1930s, this view appears to have been gathering pace. Australian officials in London and Canberra countered Bennett's allegations with the claims that they were improving the status of half-castes by encouraging marriages between half-caste women and white men.[10] The position of women *within* full-blood Aboriginal marriages was completely anathema to the policy agenda, as was the related question of their human rights.

Nevertheless, Bennett's allegations forced the government's hand, as the topic of Aboriginal conditions exploded both here and in Britain, largely on the back of her interjections. It was the Labor member for Kimberley, A. A. M. Coverley, who pushed for a royal commission, arguing that Bennett's sensational allegations of slavery cast a serious slur on Australian policies. He was particularly concerned that they cast a bad light on people in positions of authority and saw a royal commission as a means of allaying public fears.[11] As Biskup has shown, this was completely pragmatic as he was no defender of Aborigines, and certainly not of Aboriginal women. He had been a leading protagonist in the parliamentary defeat of Neville's reforms in the past.[12] It was for this reason that Neville also saw a royal commission as the solution, not only to settle the question but also to force a recalcitrant parliament to accept reform and change.

Furthermore, he had long seen Mary Bennett as problematic, disapproving of her book *The Australian Aboriginal as a Human Being* for dredging up the Gribble affair and Roth Report. Infuriated by the charges of slavery, he saw them as a usurpation of his authority. He admitted that while they contained a 'sub-stratum of truth', they were 'exaggerated', 'ill-defined', 'inconsistent' and 'inaccurate'.[13] In this way, he saw the royal commission as a means of restoring his power by refuting all charges of slavery and introducing legislative changes which would give him greater control and send missions like Mt Margaret into retreat. As he informed the Agent-General in London at the time, once the royal commission issued its report, 'emanations from Mrs Bennett would cease in the future'.[14]

For their part, the leading feminists in Western Australia saw this as a celebratory moment. Their endeavours had paid off and, for the first time in the state's history, women, including some Aboriginal women, would give evidence to a major government inquiry on Aboriginal affairs. This would be graphic illustration to the international feminist community of Australian women's commitment to, and responsibility towards, the 'less advanced races' in their borders. Paisley tells us that the leading feminist in the state, Bessie Rischbieth, lost no time in marshalling the support of a wide network of feminists for the appointment of a female commissioner. She justified this call on the basis that, as the Aboriginal woman was at the heart of the problem, only women could 'measure up the needs of the native women'.[15] This demand was symptomatic of the post-suffrage feminist push for a greater role for women in public life, on boards and commissions, and in prisons, the police service and the like to raise awareness of the welfare and specific needs of women and children.[16] Yet, as with other such demands at this time, the request failed, with Perth magistrate Henry Moseley being appointed to head the commission of inquiry in February 1934.

Feminist and Aboriginal evidence added a very important dimension to the inquiry, however. Looked at historically, this was a continuation of a long saga in Western Australian history where, following sensational charges of slavery, governments were forced to respond and act. Yet, the specific contributions of women had not been evident before. It was, as they declared, a rare moment when women's contributions were made to matter. As a consequence, the position of Aboriginal women and children was pushed before the government's nose. Aboriginal women's exploitation was raised, their demands were made and concern about the practice of child removal was front and centre. In the very least the commission demonstrated the extent of shared public knowledge about these questions. While a number of high-profile feminists in the state gave evidence, Bennett was asked to represent the Women's Service Guilds, with whom she had collaborated since the 1930s. The Aboriginal women who came forward had been encouraged by May Vallance and Ada Bromham, who were both active in the guilds and the Australian Aboriginal Amelioration Association (AAAA), the leading humanitarian group in the state with a particular interest in the position of Aboriginal women.[17] They were close friends of Bennett and had been in communication with Aboriginal communities in the southwest. Some of Bennett's women friends from Moore River government settlement in the southwest also came forward to complain of the oppressive Protection legislation as well as the over-crowding and prison-like conditions on the settlement.

Thus, the extensive evidence presented to the royal commission is a fascinating record of the consciousness and definition of the parameters of the problem as well as the humanitarian critique and feminist and reformist ideals leading up to World War II. In its pages humanitarian and Aboriginal voices are heard, as they are channelled and contained by chairman Moseley and Neville himself, who was a permanent fixture at the hearings.[18] Feminists were particularly concerned with the international aspects of the problem and while supporting the broader humanitarian demand for a national policy, specifically questioned the national status of all Aboriginal and mixed-descent people as British subjects. Representing the national feminist body, the Australian Federation of Women Voters (AFWV), Rischbieth alluded to the unacceptable 'smashing of family life' in the removal of children and, concentrating on the international arena, to the Australian government's hypocrisy in boasting of its trusteeship of mandated territories whilst ignoring Aborigines to whom it owed a debt of reparation.[19] Bromham highlighted the demand for education made by Aboriginal mothers for their children and critiqued the low position of Aboriginal women as being sanctioned by the state, commenting that there was a feeling that Aboriginal women had more or less provided a useful service to white settlement and development.[20]

As the state president of the Women's Service Guilds, Vallance reiterated the main planks of the feminist reform agenda of these years. These included the principle features of its honourable native policy, as enumerated at the BCL conference in 1932, and the five principles on

A Call to the Women of Australia to Demand an Honourable Native Policy

There is no more URGENT NATIONAL PROBLEM than that of the Native and Half-caste Population of our country, and delay in formulating and putting into effect a Consexvative National Policy makes the solution increasingly difficult. *Constructive*

Such a Policy is Practicable

if it provides:

1. Conditions which will help the Natives to free themselves from undesirable customs, while encouraging them to keep the many admirable elements in their own culture.

2. Adequate territories to the Natives which they can occupy and develop for their living (even where Natives are not at present able to develop territories they will become able before long).

3. Education without discrimination for the Native and Half-caste boys and girls growing up, for at present there are thousands of intelligent Native and Half-caste children without any education or training whatever.

4. Protectors of Aborigines to be married men living with their wives and a Doctor to be appointed as a Travelling Protector to treat Natives suffering from diseases which have been introduced among them.

5. And the most important fundamental reform of all, "the right of women to the sanctity of the person," for it is a deplorable fact that to-day Western Australian women Natives and Half-castes have neither human rights nor protection against irresponsible white men.

To Ensure This Protection

in our State, Section 43 of "The Aborigines' Act" must be amended (a) by deleting subsection (1), and inserting in lieu thereof a new subsection as follows:

"Any person other than an aboriginal or half-caste who habitually lives with aboriginals, and any male person other than an aboriginal or half-caste who cohabits with or has sexual intercourse with any female aboriginal or half-caste, not being his wife, shall be guilty of an offence against this Act.

Penalty: One hundred pounds or six months' imprisonment, or both.

Every male person, not being an aboriginal or half-caste, who travels accompanied by a female aboriginal or half-caste, shall be presumed, in the absence of proof to the contrary, to be cohabiting with her, and it shall be presumed, in the absence of proof to the contrary, that she is not his wife."

And (b) by adding a new subsection as follows:

"(3) Where a person who has been convicted of an offence against this section is the holder of a permit to employ aboriginals, the Court shall, in addition to inflicting a penalty for the offence, order that such permit be cancelled."

This legislation, if enacted and put into operation without delay, will **Reduce the Problem** which is becoming more serious year by year.

Further, Native and Half-caste girls and women who wish to free themselves from the polygamy and prostitution of the COMMERCIALISED PATRIARCHAL SYSTEM, shall be allowed to invoke and obtain the protection of the law of the land, and exercise their own free will in the choice of their husbands, and shall not be handed over to claimants as property.

A Well-informed Public Opinion is necessary to demand definite reforms and we APPEAL TO ALL WOMEN to help bring in definite Reforms, Justice and Protection for the Native race and Half-castes for whom we are responsible.

—*Reprinted from "The Dawn"*

Women's 'Honourable Native Policy', produced by the Australian Federation of Women Voters for presentation at the British Commonwealth League Conference in 1932 as a flyer and printed in The Dawn. Rischbieth Papers, NLA, MS2004/12/162.

Aboriginal welfare included in the AFWV's Charter of Human Rights, published in 1933: national responsibility for the problem, 'adequate reserves for outback tribes', education for those 'in touch with civilisation', the establishment of Aboriginal courts of justice (for intra-tribal cases) and the non-compellability of Aboriginal wives' evidence in all legal cases, and that women and girls have the right of sanctity to their own persons. Emphasising the status of Aboriginal women, Vallance also earmarked Jamieson-Williams' evidence from the League of Nations, arguing that the direction of native policy should be towards the gradual breakdown of 'domestic slavery', 'marriage bondage' and all customs which bordered on slavery. When asked by Neville whether this would conflict with tribal law, she argued that feminists believed that certain tribal laws should be modified gradually so as to give Aboriginal women 'sanctity of their persons'.[21]

While the feminists largely stuck to the script, Bennett's evidence spilled over into a carefully researched, evidence-infused dossier on historic state malpractice. It was as though the so-called slavery of Aboriginal women was the pretext for a much wider critique of 'the system analogous to slavery' which she had enumerated in *The Australian Aboriginal as a Human Being*. Unlike that of her feminist colleagues, Bennett's evidence was a critique of the whole edifice of native administration in the state. She identified four vital necessities for Aboriginal survival – land, family and community life, education and food.[22] Her remedy was the repeal of all protective legislation and the raising of Aboriginal camps into thriving, self-contained village communities throughout the country with medical and educational services. Her evidence was not only extensive but controversial. She informed the commissioner, for example, that 'conditions akin to slavery' had been perpetuated in Australia over the last century because colonial policy had ignored the illegality of white settlement.[23]

Divided broadly into the five main areas of her critique – women, labour, land, law and education, which largely mirrored the 1929 concerns of the East Africa Commission – it was a lengthy exposition, reiterating her main criticisms embellished with examples and statistics. Citing Jamieson-Williams' findings, Bennett emphasised from the start that the Aboriginal problem was the result of the victimisation of women and girls. Providing numerous examples of their exploitation by an 'oligarchy' of wealthy squatters, station managers and police on the one hand and a 'tribal patriarchal oligarchy' on the other, she called for the outlawing of their property status and the implementation of 'one law, the law of the land' for white and black in settled areas.

Part of her concern about the fate of the girls was their position as domestic servants under the system of child apprenticeship. She had witnessed Aboriginal girls' experience of this system at Moore River and was also in correspondence with Joan Kingsley-Strack, a white, middle-class woman in New South Wales who employed Aboriginal domestics. Strack had not only witnessed their vulnerability in city environments but also became embroiled in a bitter battle with the bureaucracy over their payment and treatment.[24] Bennett told the commission that

> what Australia's Aboriginal and half-caste daughters need is their own mothers who love them, and their own homes among their own people and teaching, until such time as they shall have attained legal and economic and political freedom, and meet white people on terms of equality.[25]

The problem of child apprenticeship for Bennett was wrapped in the whole system whereby 'white people cannot bring themselves to view their fellow creatures as human beings but only as profit-fodder and cheap labour to exploit'. She noted how in 1904 Commissioner Roth had recommended the cancellation of the indenture system of employment to no avail.[26] This meant, she said, that the advantage was entirely on the side of the employer, citing criminal code penalties embedded in the Aborigines Act for those who left their place of employment.[27] Referring to the Slavery and Forced Labour conventions, she argued that the Western Australian administration was implicitly guilty of breaking the latter. She identified the lack of a regulated wage or inspection system, no freedom of contract, poor conditions of employment, and the control of Aboriginal labour by station managers and police via a system of permit and/or indenture as evidence of this.[28] The poor and prejudicial treatment of Aboriginal prisoners was also of concern, particularly the holding of investigational arrests without warrant, the chaining of suspects and witnesses, and the lack of proper records of Aboriginal and 'mixed' trials, including criminal cases. Pointing to the unsuitability of police acting as prosecutor and protector, she called for the abolition of the 'police protectorate'.[29]

She argued that the disease problem was a direct consequence of Aboriginal women's prostitution, suggesting that the worst outcome of miscegenation was the lack of paternal responsibility, the result of which was the removal of the illegitimate child from its mother. She pointed to the discrimination in the Aborigines Act which expressly excluded the mother's evidence as to the father of the half-caste child and her rights to that child.[30] In detailing Aboriginal marriage customs and calling for them to be outlawed, she argued that monogamy would assure the

Aboriginal family against the department taking control of their otherwise illegitimate offspring. Some of her most moving evidence related to what she described as the victimisation of the Aboriginal mother, whose half-caste child was indiscriminately removed by the authorities because of her lack of legal rights:

> Many of these poor children are parted from their mothers, who are the only ones who do really love them, and their hearts are starved for want of love, but first for years they suffer the misery of hunted animals, always running away from the police in the hope of hiding in the country which they know, among their own people, but always in fear that any moment they may be torn away, never to see them again. They are captured at all ages, as infants in arms, perhaps not until they are grown up; they are not safe until they are dead. If they are not caught and deported as children, because their mothers have been victimised by white men, one day they will be caught and deported with their children because they have been victimised by white men, but the weary round will go on. From Moore River they may be sent out to service, and back to Moore River many of them will be sent again.[31]

Arguing that 'departmentalism was no substitute for mother love', she suggested that half-caste children be allowed to stay and marry in their own communities, rather than 'start promiscuous relationships with white people'.[32] She believed that there was nothing wrong with a half-caste girl marrying a full-blood man, suggesting that as we did not require white people to marry 'ethnologically', nor should we expect it of blacks.[33] In saying this, she was directly targeting Neville's policy of engineering particular inter-racial unions and identifying the practice as an exercise of racial discrimination which left the girls vulnerable to sexual exploitation and the subsequent removal of their children. When asked by Neville whether she would consider 'no case bad enough' to take the half-caste child away and put them into a settlement, she replied that Aborigines should be personally consulted about decisions affecting their lives and that they should be allowed to stay in their own country and communities.[34]

II

Bennett's was thus a powerful public indictment of 'the system' which brought together all the threads of discriminatory treatment as she saw it to demand rights and citizenship for Aboriginal people. As such it was closely aligned to Aboriginal people's own requests for freedom. Evidence from the Aboriginal people at Moore River in the south, most of whom were her friends, and from Broome in the north, concentrated on the oppression of living under the Aborigines Act, not only subject to its extensive surveillance and policing but also, on settlements like Moore River, with poor food and shelter, no education, cruelty and ill-treatment, an inability to control their own wages where paid, and a complete lack of freedom in marriage. This matched the broader Aboriginal quest for civil rights at this time which, born out of the late nineteenth-century context of land loss and removals, saw southern-based Aboriginal lobby groups demand freedom from all legislation and equal citizenship.[35] Bennett frequently cited the claims of Norman Harris, an educated part-Aboriginal activist from the southwest, who described living under the Act as being like 'a prisoner in his own country'.[36]

This was a profound moment in Aboriginal affairs. The level of humanitarian and Aboriginal protest was significant, international attention was focused on Australia and governments were confronted with a series of claims about their mismanagement of the problem, along with a list of potential solutions. The Aboriginal problem had become an extremely volatile arena of policy scrutiny. It was for all these reasons that the Moseley Royal Commission was important. Yet, like similar inquiries before it, it became yet another moment of humanitarian containment. Some of Moseley's recommendations, such as the abolition of police protectors, additional reserves, severe penalties for sex relationships between black and white, native courts, better education for half-castes and some medical reforms, would have pleased the humanitarians and feminists. Importantly, in what might be understood as the defence of Aboriginal women's human rights, Moseley recommended against the removal of children as potentially cruel and having a deleterious effect on the children. Disapproving of 'breeding out the colour' as policy, he argued for a policy that was not cruel to the mother but would benefit the half-caste child.[37] He recommended more settlements where entire families could be removed and trained, instead of children being removed on their own.[38]

However, while acknowledging the sexual dynamics of the problem, he categorically denied all charges of slavery or even 'conditions akin to slavery'.[39] Declaring that 'intercourse between black and white existed to a degree in the north that was as amazing as it [was] undesirable', he identified the social condition of women in the Kimberley as deplorable.[40] The impacts on the children were disastrous:

> These children…live in a hut worse by far than the kennel some people would provide for their dogs, whole families of nine or ten being huddled together in abject squalor, with no beds to lie on, all sleeping together in one hut…and intimate matters of sex relationship become, in the minds of the young, details of such minor importance that one is not surprised to find the girls at an early age having children of their own.[41]

He further maintained that despite the widespread knowledge of Aboriginal men's hostility for the white man who fraternised with their women, it was disregarded 'where the desire for sexual intercourse was uppermost'.[42] Yet, he repudiated all references to slavery and ill-treatment and, in a direct attack on Bennett, emphasised the impropriety of sending information to individuals and organisations overseas that had little or no knowledge of local conditions.[43] Notably, both he and Neville rejected the testimony of Aboriginal witnesses on the basis of Bennett's alleged interference.

As this suggests, another counter-attack which governments pursued was in emphasising the domestic nature of the problem. By the interwar years they were suspicious of feminist activity abroad on this question for that very reason. Paisley has shown how Constance Cooke's papers to forums such as the Pan Pacific conference on the Aboriginal woman in these years had been part of a confidential exchange between ministers, administrators and even some women, who regarded the matter as of internal import only.[44] In 1934, just before the royal commission, the federal Minister for Defence, Senator George Pearce, reminded Vallance and Rischbieth of the 'facts' when they quoted to him the covenant of the League of Nations and those sections which specified humane treatment of native inhabitants. He said:

> [The Covenant]…does not refer to the native races in the country by whom the mandate is held but to the native races in the country which is the subject of the mandate. The League of Nations and the Covenant have nothing whatever to do with the Australian Aboriginals…there can be no external responsibility in this matter.[45]

In referring to Australia's mandated territory of New Guinea he simultaneously rejected the appeal to international standards because it was an internal matter. Yet, as their evidence to the inquiry revealed, the feminists seemed unconvinced by this claim. They also seemed relatively pleased with the outcome of the commission and celebrated the moment as a feminist achievement, applauding Moseley's recommendations.

Bennett did not share the general feminist optimism, however. Indeed, the Moseley Royal Commission was a catalyst for exposing the differences between her and Rischbieth, in particular. To Rischbieth the commission was a showcase of feminist might and Australian progressivism. She appeared unconcerned by Moseley's denial of slavery and instead accused Bennett of manipulating her Aboriginal friends' evidence to fuel her personal feud with Neville. Certainly, while initially supported by Rischbieth, Bennett's approach at the commission appears to have alienated her. At its close Rischbieth informed Bennett that the appropriate forum for further study of the 'universal traffic in native women' was the League of Nations, rather than an international women's congress.[46] A further indication of the distance between her own view of the Aboriginal problem and Bennett's came in 1936 when the AFWV, of which she was president, flatly refused to agree to the principle of citizen rights for Aborigines which had been put to them at their triennial conference by Constance Cooke.

Up until the royal commission the pair had been useful to each other. Rischbieth had facilitated Bennett's entry to Perth's missionary and feminist community, and Bennett's considerable knowledge of the native question was relevant to a feminist community beginning to turn their attentions to it and anxious to prove themselves on the world stage. Bennett had long since identified Australian women as responsible for bringing about a humane native policy, particularly for Aboriginal women. Yet equal citizenship was at the heart of Bennett's demands, as it was for many Aboriginal people. Bennett was less interested in showcasing feminist might than in exposing the inhumane face of Aboriginal policy. Aside from her own practical experience she was working from a deep historical understanding of the problem. Part of her scepticism about the royal commission was that few in the past had managed to change either policy or practice. Unlike Rischbieth, she believed that the Moseley Royal Commission would deliver a 'squatter's verdict' in order to maintain the status quo, protect vested interests and provide Neville with greater power.[47]

She was right. As he had warned, Neville used the royal commission to steer policy in the direction he intended. With the passing of the *Native Administration Act* in 1936, the differences between Bennett and the broader feminist lobby became even more apparent. These were reforms which Neville spearheaded and which, apart from some notable exceptions, the feminists approved. The Act was the direct result of the Moseley Royal Commission but, far from implementing Moseley's recommendations, it widened the scope of Neville's control over all aspects of Aboriginal lives. In particular, it brought all half-castes under the Act and under his control and made all Aboriginal marriages subject to his consent, including full-blood marriages. His long-term plan was to exclude the full-blood from marrying anyone other than full-blood, disallowing marriage between half-castes and full-blood and between half-castes themselves, and encouraging marriages of half-castes and whites so as to elevate them 'to our own plane'.[48] Furthermore, section 8 of the Act made the Commissioner of Native Affairs the legal guardian of all Aboriginal children to the age of twenty-one. In 1937 his social engineering strategies influenced all policymakers to declare biological absorption as future policy at the inaugural national Aboriginal welfare conference in Canberra.

Looking back at the royal commission and its aftermath now, it is clear that Neville never intended to act on the feminist critique of Aboriginal child removal, despite the intensity and breadth of concern about this practice at the time. As subsequent chapters will show, he was out to prove his point and claw back control from the critics. As he said in his own evidence before the commission, 'the sore spot must be cut out for the good of the community as well as the patient, and probably against the will of the patient'. The 'sore spot' was the half-castes in the south who were 'rapidly increasing in number and constituting an incubus and danger to the community'.[49] Absorption of the half-castes and eradication of the colour problem had been on Neville's agenda since the 1920s. He had had a tremendously difficult task of steering this path through the conflict-ridden and poverty-stricken portfolio of Aboriginal affairs in the west and was not about to give up lightly. If the Moseley royal commission had given him critical momentum, science was validating his aims.

By the 1930s biological absorption had begun to leach into public discourse about the Aboriginal problem and its solution. The 'validating authority of science' produced a climate in which theories of race flourished.[50] In this context Neville was utilising some of the latest scientific evidence to back his claims and was supported by some leading scientific and even anthropological views of the day.[51] The discussion about 'racial intermixture' at the BCL in 1932 suggests a milieu in which it was possible to raise absorption as a viable solution. In this context Neville's argument that, despite the pain it might cause, it was for the good of the whole, either slipped through unnoticed or was more easily digested by many in the Australian community at the time. Indeed, the national feminist lobby approved it, despite the fact that absorption as Neville envisioned it necessarily rested on the breaking up of families, the removal of girls and, where necessary, the removal of their children, as well as their lack of choice in marriage and the continuation of tribal marital law where Neville consented.

Biskup notes that despite Neville's amending legislation being contentious and the cause of much parliamentary debate, its fate was never really in doubt.[52] He argues that there was general agreement about the need for reform and that the department required legislative authority to implement it. Interestingly, one of the more contentious parts of the new legislation, in terms of the politicians, related to those changes to section 43 of the old Aborigines Act which Neville and the feminists, including Bennett, had long been fighting for. As Neville's biographer, Pat Jacobs, describes it, placing tighter restrictions on inter-racial sex threatened to derail the two powerful forces by which the Legislative Council in Western Australia held the north: Aboriginal labour and Aboriginal female sexuality.[53] This was borne out in the lengthy parliamentary debate on the changes to section 43 in the new bill, which empowered the Commissioner of Native Affairs to intervene in cases of casual inter-racial sex, in addition to cohabitation, and to widen the net to include half-caste as well as full-blood women.

In introducing the bill, the Chief Secretary spoke of an Aboriginal problem, 90 per cent of which related to sex problems.[54] He alluded to the concerns of the women's organisations with the 'sanctity of the Aboriginal woman's person' and argued that greater protection was needed for the 'unfortunate coloured girl' sent into domestic service. He added that they were often the 'prey of unscrupulous white men' and that the state was left with the resultant problem of illegitimate half-caste and quarter-caste children, maintaining that the exposure of one or two offences in open court would help alleviate this problem. There was also unanimous concern about the spread of disease, one member suggesting the danger of the 'syphilisation' of white people.[55] All agreed that the word 'cohabit' in section 43 was insufficient and must be employed in connection with 'to have sexual intercourse with' to be effective. The bill also recommended that the penalty for cohabitation or sexual intercourse with a native should be a minimum 50 pound fine or six months imprisonment.

This was one of the most contentious parts of the bill, members resenting the criminalisation of what they argued was a natural act, two even suggesting the sterilisation of Aboriginal women as an alternative solution to the half-caste problem.[56] The member for the southwest argued that like brothels in the south, miscegenation in the north was a necessary evil where there was an absence of white women and where Aboriginal women enticed white men to their sides or sheltered under white men's blankets.[57] The Chief Secretary pointed out that in this area Western Australia lagged behind both the Northern Territory and Queensland, where laws had recently been tightened in order to act as a more effective deterrent.[58] In the Northern Territory amending legislation provided for imprisonment without the option of a fine. By contrast there had been several cases in the west where prosecutions were laid, convictions were obtained and small fines amounting to a few shillings were imposed.[59] He argued that an effective deterrent was necessary if only to save the state's reputation abroad.

Discussion in committee resulted in the reduction of the penalty from six to three months' gaol. Not all could agree, however, on the imposition of maximum and minimum fines. According to Mr Nicholson (Member for the Metropolitan), it was impossible to make men moral by act of parliament.[60] He suggested that members would regret the imposition of penalties if the 'stain of criminality were attached to one of their own family'.[61] He also maintained that there was a vast difference between a man who habitually cohabited with a black woman and one who occasionally satisfied a 'natural urge'.[62] Mr Hammersley (Member for the East) protested that restrictions should not be placed on the men of the 'back country', claiming that imprisonment would discourage young men from going there and would thus penalise employers.[63] The Member for the North, the Honourable J. J. Holmes, was most adamant that they were trying to achieve the impossible. He argued that white male frontiersmen were merely following the 'great men of Empire':

> Consider the great men of the British Empire, or of the world. One has to admit that they were fond of the opposite sex. Young men of brains in the South of this State, unable to get a job, go North. If they should chance to follow the example of the great men of the Empire, we are proposing to send them to gaol for three months. Consider the Biblical story of how scorn was pointed at a woman taken in adultery. To her persecutors it was said, 'Let him that is without sin cast the first stone' and there was not a stone thrown. I venture to suggest that if the same question were put to a good many people in and around Perth, there would not be too many stones thrown. We know this sort of thing is going on and that it will continue to go on, yet we ask that if a young man in the North slips he shall be fined or imprisoned.[64]

The Chief Secretary quelled the debate by reminding members that no complaint under this clause could be made in the first instance without the authority of the Commissioner, and that all offences under this section were to be tried and determined by a resident magistrate. He argued that if it were decided that a young man had 'inadvertently slipped', it was possible for a local protector not to authorise proceedings or for a magistrate to take a lenient view.[65] In the wording of the new Act, the penalty was imprisonment for a period *not exceeding* two years or a fine *not exceeding* 100 pounds, thereby giving the magistrate maximum leverage.

Humanitarians were outraged by the moral tone of this debate, a verbatim copy of which was published in the journal of the AAAA.[66] Bennett complained of how 'white men [had] tacitly arrogated and compounded legal immunity for the exploitation of Aboriginal women' and how the Act placed a premium on immorality and illegitimacy.[67] Edith Jones wanted to know why this was the only offence covered by the legislation which required the Commissioner's consent before a charge could be laid.[68] She complained that the debate revealed less a concern to protect the Aboriginal girl, than to minimise the consequence for the white man. In May 1936, in a paper to the British Commonwealth League, she stressed the urgency of women being included in the protectorship of detribalised Aborigines. The league resolved to urge upon enfranchised women in Australia to make a concerted effort to bring before their governments the 'long-standing omission' to appoint women as paid protectors. In the following year they urged that the Western Australian government appoint women travelling inspectors under clause 6 of the new Act.

Where Bennett and Jones found Neville's legislation profoundly disturbing as a violation of Aboriginal women's rights, particularly mothers, the leading feminist groups involved in this question during the interwar years did not. Both the Women's Non-Party Association (WNPA) in Adelaide and the Women's Service Guilds (WSG) in Western Australia, which had dominated feminist intervention on this question, were reasonably happy with the direction of policy, including the absorption proposal which not only underpinned the new legislation in the west but would become the basis of national policy the year after.

Part of the explanation for this might be that Neville's legislation, in fact, genuflected to many of the feminist demands including, importantly, those changes to section 43 of the old Act. Following the parliamentary debate this was redrafted to become section 46 of the new Act, with the words 'sexual intercourse', 'soliciting' and 'habitually living with' being added to 'cohabitation', thus extending the purview of surveillance and punishment around inter-racial sex in the manner the feminists had requested. Notwithstanding this, Neville subsequently admitted the limitations of this section, arguing that action had to be taken within six months of 'discovery' and that it was 'impossible to tell whether a child is the offspring of two natives until after it is born', rendering prosecution difficult.[69]

Feminists agreed that this section would require careful vigilance, particularly as modern systems of transport brought closer contact between Aborigines and white men. Nevertheless, in several other respects they had been placated. The new Native Administration Act brought half-castes under the legislation in the manner they had wanted. It legislated for native courts and for the non-compellability of Aboriginal wives' evidence, a theme I have addressed elsewhere.[70] But, more importantly under section 66, the Minister for Aboriginal Affairs could, upon the recommendation of the Native Commissioner, move to prohibit tribal practices in certain cases where they were found to be injurious to any Aboriginal. Included here were those 'cruel rites' which the feminists had requested be abolished. At the royal commission Neville had asked Bennett for details of these. She itemised introcision where, at the age of puberty, the girl's vagina was cut, and subincision, a process whereby the underside of the penis is incised, also at puberty. According to Bennett these processes not only caused human suffering, but the latter also prevented conception and thus impacted the population base.

There is little doubt that this was a pragmatic inclusion in the legislation by Neville, designed to placate the women reformers and quieten Bennett. There is no indication as to how, when and in what circumstances such an intervention might have taken place. Nevertheless, it did represent a changed administrative position in relation to Aboriginal custom which was directly related to Bennett's as well as the Schenks' and the feminist critique of these years. To that point Neville had adhered to the principle of non-interference in Aboriginal domestic relations. His determination, by the late 1930s, to interfere where and when he thought necessary was an indication that such critique had impacted on his thinking. It must be read as a direct counter-attack on Bennett's allegations and his attempt to reinstate his power and authority. But it was a double-edged sword: while he could now intervene in cases of so-called tribal cruelty, he could also move to prohibit Aboriginal marriages that contravened tribal custom. This was because, according to his marriage formula, full-blood people were to stay and marry among themselves whereas half-castes had to marry out. As Biskup puts it, in this way, Neville could prevent missionaries from marrying Aboriginal partners on the basis of romantic consideration alone.[71] Making these concessions while at the same time placating feminists about so-called cruel rites demonstrates the political opportunism involved here. This was about recognising tribal marriage as legally valid, and sacrosanct, within the confines of Aboriginal custom but it did not mean that they were legally valid according to the laws of the state. Rather, it was about arguing that tribal law mattered and that male elders' privileges must be preserved: both Aboriginal men's and his.

Where Neville wanted it to or thought it necessary, tribal marital law was to remain intact. Ironically, this was a concession to modernising anthropological discourses and to imperial male administrative practice. Neville's biographer describes him as an administrator who, in an effort to keep abreast of information, cast his net across a wide field from anthropology and sociology to an appreciation of what was happening in comparative administrative contexts, such as Canada and South Africa.[72] Haebich points to his anthropological interests and connections.[73] During the interwar years he was in communication with A. P. Elkin, the chair of anthropology at Sydney University, who had done fieldwork in the north of the state for his doctoral thesis on the strength of Neville's support. They had shared sojourns in the north, and Neville continued to facilitate Elkin's students undertaking fieldwork in the state, including in the south at places like Mt Margaret. Indeed, it appears that in response to Bennett's allegations concerning polygamy, Neville sought advice from Elkin on Aboriginal marriages. Biskup argues that Neville's recognition of Aboriginal marriage laws was consistent with his policy of 'preserving Aboriginal groups qua Aboriginal groups', which had been central to Elkin's thinking too. Targeted at the remaining full-bloods, it was the flipside of Neville's absorption of half-castes and it was endorsed at the national level at the conference of Aboriginal administrators in Canberra in 1937.

Thus, far from abolishing polygamy in the settled districts or allowing free choice in marriage, the new legislation put male privilege above any universalist conception of female rights. As Biskup suggests, Neville could now insist on adhering to proper tribal relationships in marriage and obtaining the elders' consent before marriage was celebrated. There would be no modernising of it in the way Bennett, the Schenks and the international feminist community had requested. In this way, the feminist and human rights appeal underpinning Bennett's critique was completely ignored. This is a fascinating moment where the appeal to a particular set of cultural rights is in contest with the emerging universalist discourses of human, including women's, rights. In this way, Neville's rhetoric resonated with the likes of Lugard, who had argued for non-interference on this question in Africa.

In any case, there was clearly little scope to hear or absorb Bennett's particular claims in the fractious politics of Aboriginal reform in the interwar years, particularly in Western Australia. Neville's attempts to point to inconsistencies in her argument at the royal commission demonstrated his inability to appreciate the complexity of her concerns or the feminism underlying them. Thus, at the royal commission he asked, 'Have you not been a little inconsistent? You spoke of the horrors of tribal rites and yet you infer that people who are subject to these rites should be left alone?' This put a subtle twist on Bennett's thesis.

Her answer went to the heart of the differences between her approach and his, as well as her approach and that of the two leading feminist groups. She said that she had not counselled non-interference. Rather, what she wanted to see was that all – both half-caste and full-blood Aboriginal people, particularly women – be assisted to stay in and establish viable communities of their own and that this was preferable to splitting families, deporting them or removing half-caste babies from Aboriginal mothers.[74] She had already questioned Neville's 'ethnographic' approach of arranging Aboriginal marriages according to caste and would later declare that some of the 'greatest servants of the human race' had come from mixed marriages. Furthermore, she argued that what Aboriginal girls needed was their own family and community life:

> What Australia's Aboriginal and half-caste daughters need is their own mothers who love them and their own homes and their own people and teaching, until such time as they shall have attained legal and economic and political freedom and [can] meet white people on terms of equality.[75]

In this way, unlike most others in these years, she did not distinguish between full-blood and half-caste people. Unlike the national feminist lobby she was not placated by Neville's legislative changes because, from her perspective, they merely entrenched discriminatory practice and, like administrative changes in the past, were not only subject to male whim but to male solidarity. Furthermore, her chief call throughout the interwar period was for legal equality for Aborigines and, in concert with many Aboriginal people themselves, the removal of all such legislation. For her, the extensive power now bequeathed to Neville represented a threat to Aboriginal human rights. She saw it as an irresponsible use of power.

Thus, while the feminists attempted to accommodate Neville's policy directives, Bennett was bitterly opposed to them, arguing that the worst part of them was the callousness of white men to their children.[76] Fuelling her distrust of Neville, she believed that it legitimised his plan to disperse, depopulate and ultimately destroy Aboriginal community life. She argued that we would be better able to evaluate it when the same kind of policy was applied to ourselves, 'as the absorption of the white race and the breeding out of white people!!!'[77] Styling the 1937 national absorption resolution as a 'gentlemen's agreement for condoning prostitution', she objected to it as a policy based on separating the half-caste men from the girls and sending the girls out among the whites so as to 'breed out the colour'.[78] While not objecting to the marriage of persons of mixed descent, she disagreed with the method by which this policy would be carried out. Quoting directly from Neville, Bennett argued that it placed a premium on illegitimacy and prostitution. At the 1937 Canberra conference Neville said:

> Our policy is to send them out into the white community, and if a girl comes back pregnant our rule is to keep her for two years. The child is then taken away from the mother and sometimes never sees her again…At the expiration of the period of two years the mother goes back into service so it really does not matter if she has half a dozen children…The Government institutions are simply clearing stations for the future members of the race.[79]

As one member of parliament subsequently argued, the idea was that if the Aboriginal or half-caste girl got 'into trouble' while in service, as it would be associated with white people it would be justifiable because it would help to 'breed out the dark colour'.[80]

What Bennett railed against, in this context, was the underlying assumption that it didn't hurt Aboriginal women to remove their half-caste children or to seek to biologically absorb them because they were 'non-moral', as she put it. She argued that there was a widespread view that concubinage was a natural condition for these women and that they were ultimately better off in white men's camps. Just as her work was littered with examples of women harassed under tribal law, it was also littered with tales of Aboriginal women's morality, also 'inculcated by their code'. She cited Wyma, the nursemaid of Lammermoor, as an example. Married to an old man of her tribe when young, she agreed to marriage with a young black stockman when he died and requested to be married 'like a white woman'.[81]

Edith Jones shared Bennett's abhorrence of the absorption decision. From her base in England, she supported Bennett's claims in a report to the BCL on Neville's legislation and the resolutions of the Canberra conference. In particular, she complained that the effectiveness of section 46 (the amended section 43) of Neville's Act was minimised by the proviso that a charge of cohabitation or sexual interference of Aboriginal women could only be laid by the consent of the Commissioner. However, like Bennett, she reserved most of her criticism for the absorption resolution in 1937, about which she was scathing.[82] She argued that the evidence provided by the administrators at the Canberra conference revealed the gross inequalities in policies between the states, highlighting the need for uniform legislation.[83] Like Bennett, she complained of the denial of basic human rights in Western Australia where, under the new Act, the Commissioner controlled the marriages of half-castes and could take any child from its mother, at any stage of its life, whether she was legally married or not.

In contrast to Bennett and Jones, the leading feminist groups – the AFWV and the WNPA – informed the BCL in the following year of their approval of absorption. The WNPA emphasised gradualism and free choice in the absorption process.[84] Similarly, the WSG emphasised a gradual process of absorption 'back into the white race' to be brought about by training and education on the one hand, and marriage between half-caste and white on the other. Citing Neville's views on atavism, they argued that it was a scientific fact that when Aboriginal blood mixed with white blood it did not throw back; rather, it gradually disappeared, never to come out more strongly. This was an explicit endorsement of Neville's view, which he had been advertising publicly since the early 1930s. Ignoring the fate of the full-blood remnant and the human rights of Aboriginal mothers, they suggested that being partly coloured was a temporary deviation from the 'norm'. Absorption of the half-castes into the majority was the way forward.[85]

III

If Bennett's position on the absorption decision seemed exceptional, it found more resonance in Britain. At the very same time administrators declared absorption official policy, the status of Aboriginal women in Australia was being raised as part of a broader submission on the status of native women throughout the empire by the St Joan's Social and Political Alliance at the League of Nations. The Woman's Christian Temperance Union (WCTU) of Australia also sent a submission on the status of Aboriginal women, informed by the work of Cooke, Jones and Bennett, to the league via the Pan Pacific conference. These groups believed that a survey on the status of women then being conducted by the league would be incomplete if it did not include native women. In their submissions, they rehearsed the old ideas about Aboriginal women's enslavement, calling for equality and guardianship of children:

> The only effective way of giving a better life to the detribalised native women of Australia, most oppressed of all women, is the gradual raising of the status of the coloured woman to that of the white woman amongst whom she lives. Coloured women living amongst whites should be allowed to appeal against conformity to native marriage customs…they should also have rights of guardianship over their children.[86]

In the following year, the BCL made representations to Dame Enid Lyons and her husband Joseph Lyons, the Australian Prime Minister, pointing to the work of the league's Native Races Committee and its desire to go into the question of native women's status in more detail in the future. As this suggests, the concern with the position of native women had reached a crescendo in Britain by the eve of World War II and Australian administrators, all the way to the Prime Minister, were aware of the issue. It is therefore remarkable that these entreaties were being made at the international level just as governments agreed on absorption and largely overlooked the specific feminist claims on behalf of Aboriginal women at the domestic level.

The interventions of the WCTU also signalled a shift in feminist mobilisations on this question. While for the St Joan's Alliance this issue represented a continuum, the WCTU entered the debates about the position of Aboriginal women relatively late. Its taking up of the cause of citizenship for Aborigines occurred at the same time as the AFWV rejected the principle of equality of status for Aborigines in 1936. In an issue of *White Ribbon Signal*, the official journal of the WCTU, in that year, they pledged to build a 'Bridge of Hope' from the shameful past to the 'glorious future' when, they hoped, the nation would no longer be ashamed of its ill-treatment of Aborigines. Reminiscent of Bennett, they drew comparisons between the women of India and Aboriginal women, reiterating the principle enunciated by the British feminist community in the early 1930s, that 'a woman was not a chattel to be sold by her father to a polygamist or anyone else' and that every woman must be a 'free agent to choose her own partner in life'.[87]

Other shifts were noticeable. Following the Moseley Royal Commission, Bennett's old allies, May Vallance and Ada Bromham, continued their work for Aboriginal rights through their affiliation with the union rather than the state feminist group, the Women's Service Guilds. Whether this was a reflection of their loyalty to Bennett can only be surmised but it does suggest that the WCTU became a more conducive space for continuing discussion and critique of Aboriginal conditions. Vallance became state president of the union in 1936. She also aligned herself more closely with the key humanitarian body in the state, the AAAA. She was already vice-president of the group and became editor of its journal, *The Ladder*, upon its launch in 1936. At the same time Bromham began publishing articles on this question in *White Ribbon Signal*. She also worked at the international level as an associate of the World's Woman's Christian Temperance Union (WWCTU) in the department known as Protection of Native Races between 1934 and 1937. As following chapters will show, these dynamics were to prove important to Bennett's continuing crusade until her death in 1961.

Once the royal commission was over Bennett ensconced herself in teaching at the Mt Margaret Mission and became embroiled in the deteriorating relationship between Neville and the missionaries. Her clash with Rischbieth after the royal commission left her very despondent about feminism's commitment to the cause. Indeed, it seems that Bennett's concerns about polygamy and Aboriginal women's marital status had either been rejected by the majority of Australian feminists or, more likely, had never been properly absorbed. This was reflected at the BCL conference in 1932 when the AFWV presented its recommendations for an honourable national policy based directly on Bennett's suggestions. Instead of the Aboriginal woman, her free choice in marriage and the ending of polygamy in the settled districts, which had been part of their honourable native policy, discussion centred around the rights and needs of the children of mixed unions. Furthermore, one of the underlying themes of the conference was the need for acceptance of inter-racial marriages. In this context, Neville's promotion of the welfare of half-caste children on the one hand and mixed-descent marriage on the other may have seemed progressive.

For Bennett, abolishing polygamy in the settled districts was part of a broader attempt to modernise Aboriginal domestic relations and reform black–white relations while advancing women's human rights as she and the international feminist community were increasingly defining them. As the quote at the beginning of this chapter reveals, Neville believed that, under his administration, Aboriginal women already had rights and protection and that entrenching them within the confines of tribal law, in the case of full-blood women, and state-based protective laws, in the case of those of mixed descent, would deliver further protection. Ultimately, Bennett was alone in advancing her slavery thesis. While she shared it with Jones and Cooke, they did not pursue it on the ground nor promote it in the same way as Bennett did. Cooke was pursuing her own battles on the mostly male South Australian Advisory Council on Aborigines to which she'd been appointed in 1929, while Jones had relocated to England and was pursuing the Aboriginal question through the BCL and the Anti-Slavery and Aborigines' Protection Society.

Bennett was looking for an Australian feminist-led anti-slavery campaign and was hoping that the liberation of Aboriginal women would be the pretext for a raft of other liberatory reforms. In confiding her disappointment with the 'majority of Australian women' to Olive Pink, an anthropologist working in central Australia who was also deeply concerned about the fate of Aboriginal women, she demonstrated how central slavery was to her vision of Australian conditions:

> When I was in Perth I read one of your articles in Oceania, and
> it made me long for a book from you, which would be the out-
> pouring of your experiences, unlimited by any merely scientific

requirements. Just as Harriet Beecher Stowe freed the South, don't you think you may, by your pen…free our tortured Innocents?[88]

In using the slavery motif Bennett was drawing on a long British tradition which, by the 1930s, dovetailed neatly with the campaign of the likes of Nina Boyle and Eleanor Rathbone in India, but ultimately less so with the concerns of Australian feminists, despite their demonstrable concern with the position of Aboriginal women.[89]

That the broader feminist community did not share the specificity of Bennett's concerns about the Aboriginal woman as mother at this point can be explained as a difference of perspective. There is no doubt that the interwar period represented a profound feminist intervention around the position of Aboriginal women, the likes of which was not seen again. There was even the view that white women's own protection was at the expense of Aboriginal women's. As Rischbieth explained, 'we know that white women are protected and it seems that the trouble is being thrown on to native women'.[90] However, on the whole, the feminist movement did not share Bennett's rage or vision either in relation to sexual or economic *slavery* at this point in time. Rather, looking to clean up after men and blinded by the racialist preoccupation with the danger and contamination of mixed-descent bodies, and utilising what was a progressivist vision of race unity, they turned their maternalist attentions to the half-caste children. Thus, along with many of their British counterparts, they shared a concern with the outcome of inter-racial unions rather than with the position of the native mother per se, her free choice or the security of her marital status and maternal rights.

This may have been because, by taking the focus off male sexual and domestic power and putting it onto vulnerable children, the feminists could ultimately be more effective. According to Pedersen this refocus is what accounted, in part, for the success of the campaign against *mui tsai* (child indenture or slavery) in Hong Kong. Feminist and humanitarian reframing of the issue as one of child welfare rather than sexual exploitation led to the reforms being carried because it 'offered officials a chance to respond to what had become an international cause célèbre without calling the entire principle of patriarchal authority into question'.[91] Similarly, in Australia, where Bennett's critique had spilled over into a full-scale attack on male sexual privilege, focusing on the vulnerable child enabled women's contribution to have traction and matter in the policy setting. Rather than being antagonistic and critical, it ultimately aligned with paternal instinct which, as Marilyn Lake has shown, emphasised the rights of the child over the rights of women as mothers at this time.[92]

Bennett had the same kind of racialist preoccupation with mixed-descent children as everyone else at this time. She called them 'the white man's burden borne by the hapless black woman to the destruction of the hapless black man' and their very existence was at the base of her critique of polygamy in 'the settled districts'.[93] Yet, she consistently saw in the half-caste the fate of the mother, who, under section 8 of Neville's Native Administration Act, lost all rights to her children. Given the changing dynamics of maternalist input in the empire, her uncompromising attack on male sexual power was both unprecedented and increasingly out of step, notwithstanding the demands by the international feminist community, by the mid-1930s, that native policy throughout the empire should be to free native women from domestic slavery and marriage bondage. By focusing on internal domestic relationships within Aboriginal culture, the international feminist reform agenda obscured the specificity of Bennett's simultaneous attack on unregulated white male sexuality and the way it impacted on Aboriginal women in forms of 'marriage bondage'. At the same time the national feminist acquiescence of the changed policy environment undercut the key arguments of Bennett's agenda for change and women's 'freedom'.

Bennett railed against Neville's absorption program as a race-based solution. As she saw it, Aboriginal advancement was to be achieved at the expense of the full-blood population. Furthermore, it discriminated against the half-caste man, in that the provision for 'bleaching out the Aboriginal strain' was only to apply to half-caste women, while the intermarriage of white women with half-caste men was not even contemplated. This was where their philosophies markedly differed. Bennett consistently resisted the sexual and racial imperatives of Neville's program, claiming that they perpetuated the double standard on which white settlement had been based and, despite his rhetoric, were premised on promiscuous relations rather than the promotion of marriage between consenting individuals. This was not entirely correct. As we shall see in chapter six, marriage was the linchpin of Neville's policy to breed out the half-castes and segregate the full-bloods. Yet, Bennett was promoting monogamous marriage as a defence against such intervention. Her championship of mixed marriages of whatever caste remained one of her most radical challenges to the absorption method of assimilation and to Neville's program of selective breeding.

The slavery moment in Western Australian race politics, spearheaded by Bennett, was explosive and should be interpreted as a pivotal moment in both Western Australian history and the broader national story. It was also part of the broader empire story. It represented an historic continuum. Bennett's plea on behalf of Aboriginal women resonated with and was part of a periodic humanitarian interjection regarding slavery in Western Australia. Yet, it was not confined to Bennett's charges of the enslavement of women. In fact, it can only properly be understood in the context of Bennett's time at Mt Margaret where, along with the missionaries, she was attempting to implement her own agenda for reform and where Aboriginal enslavement was also linked to their dispossession, starvation and lack of wages. It is important to note here that her specific charges about the enslavement of Aboriginal women were part of a much wider critique concerning the whole edifice of native administration in Australia, which Neville's administration exposed in stark relief. In this sense, her critique concerning the position of Aboriginal women was a digression made possible by a particular moment in the empire.

Furthermore, Bennett's specific claims about Aboriginal women made much more sense in interwar Britain than they did in interwar Australia. They were clearly shaped and influenced by developments in the empire which emboldened her to act and speak. In doing so, she rehearsed a particular empire story of emancipation which was being remembered and celebrated in these years. In this context the position of native women was being cast as part of the modernising project of empire. Bennett's efforts were part of a whole swathe of reforms being attempted by British feminists which centred around the liberation of non-western women from customs which were considered antithetical to women's freedom.

Yet, the native question had particular resonance for Australian women too. If, as Lake has suggested, the interwar years represented the golden age of the woman citizen, women's equal citizenship was far from assured.[94] As Rischbieth declared, civilisation stood at the crossroads between the patriarchal past, where men resorted to 'the law of force' and women were deprived of access to political life, and the present, where enfranchised women could help create new conditions of life.[95] Effecting a change in Aboriginal women's lives would be a test of white women's own freedom and citizenship. Thus it was that British and Australian women brought the sexual outcomes of colonial policy into debates about the native question. Concern coalesced around questions of women, custom, marriage, cohabitation, half-castes, disease, prostitution and male privilege. In the figure of the indigenous woman, feminists saw all the issues underpinning their own quest for freedom: consent and free choice, marriage, bodily sanctity, violence, abuse, alcoholism and protection.[96] They even saw their own gendered privilege and sought to exercise their maternal power for 'good'.

However, whereas in Britain white women's concern about native women became part of a maternal moment in the empire, the same cannot be said of Australian women's efforts. In *White Mother to a Dark Race*, Margaret Jacobs argues that white women's maternalism towards indigenous women ultimately reinforced government aims. She maintains that Cooke, Jones and Bennett were responsible for projecting an image of Aboriginal women which contributed to pathologising Aboriginal society and promoting child removal.[97] To be sure, the claims of Bennett and the feminists played into Neville's hands, as he hoped they would. Using Bennett's own logic he was able to declare that he wasn't prepared to leave half-caste women and girls vulnerable to polygamous men. He would have to remove them. This was political pragmatism, however. The flipside of his policy was to leave full-blood women and girls alone, that is, to entrench some Aboriginal women and girls *in* the very customary practices the white women had critiqued.

It is true that Cooke ultimately agreed with the removal of mixed-descent children but Bennett was implacably opposed to it from the start. Furthermore, as I've shown here, Australian governments were largely indifferent to the specific allegations of Bennett, Jones and Cooke in this period. Like their British counterparts, Australian administrators largely pursued a policy of non-interference when it came to Aboriginal domestic relations or, in Neville's case, interference to maintain the status quo. The notable feature of child removal policies was the lack of concern about how they might impact on Aboriginal mothers, which was at the core of Bennett's campaign and her maternalism.

Indeed, Neville positioned this process as being cruel to be kind. He and other administrators failed to engage with what women reformers had to say about the status of Aboriginal women. As much as she pathologised Aboriginal society, Bennett pathologised white society too, in particular, white men's sexuality. In the process she represented the women as the oppressed victims of men, white and black. Yet, this was not why administrators removed the children. Neville removed children because, in part, he wanted to prevent some Aboriginal women, notably those of mixed descent, living settled, monogamous, lives in their own communities.

On one level the desire to liberate Aboriginal women from customs which were defined as making them the property of their men and placing them on an equal footing with white women was a radical equalitarian aim. On another level, the assumption that white women's monogamous identities were the pinnacle of freedom and civilisation to which Aboriginal women aspired represented a profound form of cultural imperialism. Maternalism could be chauvinist, too. Furthermore, the labelling of Aboriginal customs as slavery and bondage skewed their domestic relations. Yet, Bennett insisted that this was true because of colonialism and dispossession. For her, as for like-minded humanitarians, this fact significantly complicated the issue, particularly for Aboriginal women. White contact put unprecedented pressure on Aboriginal societies, particularly women who were then caught in what Bennett referred to as a 'borderland of transition', the most vulnerable link between cultures.[98] For her, 'our' original interference justified an ongoing, albeit more humane, intervention. As she said to Commissioner Moseley:

> Missionaries do not ask that the way of living of the few wild uncontaminated tribes should be altered, nor that natives with several wives should be required to give them up. What they do ask is that these men shall not be allowed to appropriate any more wives, or claim property in the young women or girls whom they have bespoken in infancy.[99]

In Bennett's schema, elevating Aboriginal women's status and reforming marital practices was conceived as part of a process of gradual Aboriginal development and modernisation. It was about managing a transition and transformation which she and others thought inevitable if the Aboriginal people were to survive in the long term. What was radical about this and the wider debates about native women's status in the empire was that it was thought possible and desirable to alter parts of the culture without destroying the whole. As Jamieson-Williams reported, the League of Nations was pushing for nations to instil in the indigenous mind the importance of women's human rights. This investment in the historicity of native culture should be understood as part of the emergent human rights frame in the interwar period.[100] It demonstrated the breaking down of an old evolutionary paradigm which had long conceived culture as a bounded whole.

Susan Pedersen has shown how British women's attempts to remake domestic and sexual relations throughout the empire in these years resulted in very mixed outcomes. She argues that the eventual regulation of the *mui tsai* system, leading to its eradication, and the legislative implementation of a minimum age of marriage in India via the Child Marriage Restraint Act, demonstrates the extent to which reformers came to shape official views in England.[101] By contrast the campaign to stop clitoridectomies in east Africa became immobilised, fragmented and ultimately contained. Pedersen suggests a combination of factors behind its failure. While the reticence to deal with the question at the core of the issue – female sexual response and pleasure – was critical, so too was British male politicians' ridicule of feminist demands and their sex solidarity with African male leaders. Important, too, was British women's reluctance to jeopardise British national interests. As she argues, the failure of British feminists to construct reforms across cultural lines was significantly hampered by the imperialist context itself, as it was for interwar humanitarianism generally.[102]

We could say that Bennett's campaign to abolish polygamy 'in the settled districts' in Australia was similarly hampered by ridicule and male apathy towards feminist demands and even their sex solidarity with Aboriginal men. Equally important was Australian women's reluctance to jeopardise national interests. Whereas Bennett's understanding of Australian conditions was heavily influenced by the politics of colonial governance within the empire, she failed to appreciate the depth of nationalist sympathies in Australia. Indeed, she really only understood the Aboriginal problem as a problem of empire.[103] However, Australian feminists had dual loyalties to nation and to empire. Throughout the interwar years there were intermittent disagreements among women about the exposure of Australian conditions abroad. Bennett had described these in 1929 when she wrote to Mr Lees in Queensland describing how she had been advised that it was unpatriotic to criticise Australia's treatment of the Aborigines.[104] Lake suggests that Bennett's constant carping about the colour bar in Australia would have affronted the nationalistic loyalties of feminists like Rischbieth.[105]

Yet, it was these same loyalties that hampered maternalist interventions in Australia. Where maternalism became part of the apparatus of trusteeship in interwar Britain, the same cannot be said for maternalism in Australia. If, as I've argued here, the broader feminist community's focus on saving and absorbing the mixed-descent child aligned with paternal policy directives, on the related issue of their having more power to effect change in Aboriginal policy themselves, they failed dismally. As much as the national feminist lobby ended up agreeing to the racial parameters within which policy was framed, they disapproved of its gendered implications for themselves. As one feminist informed her male colleagues in 1929, following the Bleakley Report:

> We are looking to the men to help us in this matter. We feel that
> we are at a disadvantage in that at present we can only come and
> ask the men to do what we would like to be in a position to do if
> we had more power.[106]

In the national parameters of the debate, wherein it was firmly consigned, practical maternalism was curtailed.

Thus, Bennett's defence of Aboriginal women was part of a larger story of the interwar period concerning the gendered conflict within which debates about Aboriginal futures were realised.[107] Indeed, the story of Bennett's confrontation with the administration in Western Australia was underlined by this tension, as was her ability to make a change in the lives of Aboriginal women as mothers.

5

MT MARGARET
Promoting Adaptable Education

> I make for the Australian natives your claim for the African natives:
> that the whole race must enjoy the privilege of literate education,
> economic emancipation, robust physical health and that freedom
> and equality for which their character, culture and conduct fit
> them. The black man (in Australia as) in Africa has ever had a
> highly developed civilisation of his own, far more democratic than
> anything that Europe has known.[1]

Bennett's defence of Aboriginal women in general and the Aboriginal
mother in particular did not end with its containment by the Moseley
Royal Commission. Instead the commission represented a mere hiccup in
her crusade, which had always been more than a defence of Aboriginal
women. In fact, the period between the end of the royal commission
in 1935 and the eve of World War II saw Bennett wage an intense and
unrelenting campaign of protest against the administration in the west.
Her specific campaign for Aboriginal women's freedom and equality must
be understood as one part of her much wider critique of the whole edifice
of native administration in Australia, which she felt Western Australia
exposed in stark relief. Following her defeat after the Moseley Royal
Commission, she retreated to the Mt Margaret Mission where she carried on her education program, accumulated and distributed evidence to
various interested parties in Australia and England and continued to fire
shots at the administration. She also got caught up in the deteriorating
relationship between Neville and the Mt Margaret missionaries, which
culminated in Neville's attempts to close the mission down. Bennett's
tirades constituted a key part of this battle.

It is important to see this conflict as about fundamentally different
subject positions. Neville was a bureaucrat in an extremely difficult policy

portfolio. To the obfuscation, impoverishment, political maneuvering and outright indifference in Aboriginal affairs in Western Australia was added deeply engrained and historically conditioned racism. Neville's biographer tells the tale of a dutiful servant of empire, a reluctant recruit, who, once in a position to face the Aboriginal question first-hand, sought a humanitarian solution. Indeed, his desire for more reserves, national responsibility, education, training, employment and hospitals for Aboriginal people, along with his concern that they work out their own destiny, replicated the wider humanitarian voice. But his capacity to effect change, despite his position, was hampered at every turn. His power was consistently curtailed by lack of money, reductions in his status, derailment of his ideas, the doings of other officials – including the fragmentation of his own role by those who opposed him – mission intervention, the opinions of others, recalcitrant legislatures, hostile settlers and political whim. Indeed, Jacobs' account of Neville's life suggests that he was pitted against a bureaucratic and institutional framework which worked to undermine his attempts at truly protecting Aboriginal people.

In the face of these difficulties Neville pursued a program of quiet defiance which consisted of publicising conditions, harnessing the latest scientific knowledge and focusing on legislation as a means of maintaining his control, stamping his authority and defining the terms of a solution. The fact that he did so, rather than relinquish his position in the face of seemingly insurmountable difficulties, was also conditioned by his feeling that only he cared about and understood the issues, the Aboriginal people and their 'problems'. In this way, governmental neglect, ambivalence and interference, as well as settler hostility, helped shape what was seen by many as a form of dictatorship as he pursued his legislative agenda, including the control of the missions, with determination and at all costs. Although he saw himself as appreciating the circumstances of Aboriginal people as individuals, he ultimately saw them as problem populations. They were representatives of the colour or race problem not of dispossessed humanity, and he looked to a future where that problem would be eradicated. In this sense the solution was his firm but fatherly protection and control.

For their part, the missionaries at Mt Margaret were devoted servants of God – faith missionaries – for whom working among the Aborigines was accepting a call.[2] Beyond government permission, they required faith in God, self-righteousness, stoicism, Aboriginal cooperation and the support of the wider Christian community. Mary Bennett was among them. Once on the mission she gave very generously not only with her time but also in financial assistance, helping to fund a hospital and kindergarten and some of the mission workers. They also required departmental support. Neville initially did just that, advising Rod Schenk to keep the Aborigines away from the town and make them productive. In order to do this Schenk applied for and got 200 acres on the Mt Margaret Common where he established his mission in 1921. While combating animism was a key part of this endeavour, the Schenks saw the creation of independent Christian villages where Aboriginal people received education and wages for employment as a means of alleviating their poverty, starvation and so-called demoralisation, and ensuring their long-term survival.

In doing so they had to overcome many impediments, including local prejudice and apathy, particularly among the neighbouring landholders who scoffed at such efforts, police brutality, settler violence, other Christians who accused them of overstepping their reach, intra-tribal fighting, and the old men of the tribes, the 'law extremists' according to Mysie Schenk, who resisted their interventions. They also required the continuing goodwill of the government. The Schenks and Bennett explained the decline of this goodwill in the mid to late 1930s as a deliberate attack on them. However, it was also part of a much longer story of deep governmental suspicion and ambivalence about the usefulness of missions in Western Australia which dated back to the late nineteenth century.

Bennett identified 'good' missions in Western Australia – Kunmunya in the north and Mt Margaret in the south – as places of refuge where Aboriginal people were taught, fed and cared for in an environment where these things were widely denied them. They could be examples of indirect rule in practice where the good in Aboriginal culture was kept and celebrated and the bad was gradually eradicated by teaching and example. In this sense they could play an important role in the process of adaptation and transition to citizenship. Her self-righteousness derived from a blend of a firm Christian ethic and belief, imperial humanitarianism and her own history. Arguably it was her experience of the *humanity* of the Dalleburra on Lammermoor that underwrote her quest for justice for them. While guided by the example of her father's benevolent paternalism and her own construction of such, her exposure to late nineteenth- and early twentieth-century feminism in England persuaded her that women could be a considerable force for more humane governance. In this sense the solution was maternal care, guidance and protection.

As an advocate and a devotee to the cause, Bennett was a servant of empire. Her sense of the problem was shaped within the bounds of a vibrant interwar British culture for which the colonial question was a burning issue of the day. Bennett inherited the sense of British imperial mission and its humanitarian impulse. Her sense of the problem in Australia and its solution was founded on an appreciation of colonialism and its effects, particularly dispossession. While she saw the problem in world terms, from the vantage point of empire, Aboriginal Australians' predicament was similar to that of Africans and African Americans in terms of dispossession and its effects on conditions of labour. For her, the native question was less about reforming the Aboriginal people and eradicating a problem population than in reforming the *relationship* between whites and blacks, competitive societies and communal ones, 'immigrant invaders' and 'black subjects'. Her program of reform, once in Australia, was driven by a universalist, humanist conception of equality, rights and citizenship. In that sense, Neville's overarching legislation was part of the problem rather than the solution, and his control of missions was an infringement of both religious liberty and the liberty of the subject.

Given these different positions it is perhaps not surprising that Bennett and the missionaries came into conflict with Neville and his administration. But it was not inevitable. All were driven by a humanitarian sensibility, all nursed a sense of bitterness at Aboriginal exploitation, all were concerned to offer greater and more effective protection and futures for Aboriginal people. Furthermore, Mt Margaret Mission offered temporary release for Neville, an overburdened administrator in an overburdened portfolio covering an enormous geographical spread. With an eye on the full-bloods in the north and half-castes in the south, the eastern goldfields of Western Australia were initially outside Neville's immediate purview, although he had expressed interest in an Aboriginal settlement somewhere in the district.[3] Yet, it was the Schenks' very success that became a key problem for Neville's governance and control in the long term.

The conflict between Neville and the missionaries and Bennett, which resulted from the collision of their different perspectives and ideas about the way forward, demonstrates how the Aboriginal problem in the first half of the twentieth century was an intense battleground which

World War II went some way to contain. The historic 1937 Canberra conference of administrators, at which Neville dominated, was also an act of containment and it marginalised much of the humanitarian angst. While the history of Aboriginal policy and reform is punctuated by notable personality and ideological battles, that between Neville and Bennett was part of an historic continuum in Western Australia. But, unlike battles of old, particularly between missionaries and the state, this conflict occurred against the background of a globally recognised problem of colour and race on the one hand and an emerging human rights discourse on the other. Neville and Bennett were combatants on either side of this divide. In this context, Bennett felt that the extensive reach of Neville's power over Aboriginal lives represented a profound form of enslavement, dictatorship and inhumanity.

Bennett's time at Mt Margaret Mission and the breakdown of the relationship between Neville, the missionaries and herself is charted in this chapter and the one that follows. Bennett was at the mission from 1932 to 1941. It was her base and refuge while in Australia and an important backdrop to much of her activism and protest. It helped shape and con-solidate her vision. Many of the examples she provided to the Moseley Royal Commission came from the Aboriginal people with whom she was in contact on the mission. As Rod Schenk informed Neville, 'the natives and half-castes take all their troubles to her...she gives hours of her time hearing their troubles and...trying to help them'.[4] It was in her capacity as a teacher that she made some of the most strident claims about Aboriginal people's position at the same time as building a reliable databank of evidence about Aboriginal people's capacity for learning and citizenship. It was the work she most valued and was proud of and it gave her purpose. At the same time, she was among like-minded people. It was Rod Schenk who encouraged her to become a teacher at the mission. Like her, he saw education as the foundation of Aboriginal human rights and citizenship. Indeed, it was via his promotion of education, along with his missionising, that we see his own commitment to some of the core ideas of the imperial humanitarian ethos.

I

When Rod Schenk arrived in the northeastern goldfields of Western Australia in 1921, the once-thriving mining districts were long past their peak, having been replaced by pastoralists on huge leases of land paying peppercorn rents. Combined with severe drought, the eclipse of the gold boom brought a new level of vulnerability to the Aborigines of the district, reducing them to hangers-on on the edges of the towns surviving, in part, by begging and stealing. Schenk described communities in conflict and at the point of starvation. The local policeman – the Aboriginal Protector – warned Schenk not to bother with the Wongutha, as they were 'the wildest and laziest tribe in Western Australia'.[5] He executed his duty of keeping them away from the towns by using a stockwhip, a practice he undertook on a daily basis.

Neville's advice to Schenk was that he do something practical and keep the Aborigines out of the towns, a drive that was a key part of his administration. Working initially in an itinerant capacity, Schenk witnessed the intimidation of the Wongutha, including the violent, random deportation of some to the Moore River government settlement and the dispersal of others, who fled in fear. His witnessing of the latter led him to think of a settlement where the people could live, work and survive as a group. Despite local opposition and scorn, he successfully applied for and got the lease to the Mt Margaret Common for a reduced rent of a pound per annum. He bought 400 goats via the sale of his motorbike and, with donations from the Christian community, he fed the people and set about encouraging them to settle on the mission. From the outset he saw his mission as providing the Wongutha with an alternative. It would be their permanent home where they could be protected from being removed and dispersed.

His desire was to make it a self-sufficient community. One of the most important aspects of this would be meaningful employment and wages. Up until 1926 work was in sandalwood, of which there was plenty in the district. The Aboriginal men helped pull the wood, while the Aboriginal women stripped the bark. Schenk paid the workers on a piecework model. Aboriginal people did as much work as they wanted and were paid by the hour and by the work produced. Initially payment was in kind: flour, tea, sugar, jam, tinned meat or goat meat to the value of the work done. The first payment of a wage was in 1930. This was supported by donations of second-hand clothing and supplemented by the selling of dingo scalps to the Road Board for which the workers received 5 shillings per scalp. By 1936 men were receiving 3 and 4 shillings a day for their building work.[6] This vision of economic independence was further facilitated by Mysie Schenk, Rod's wife, who arrived on the mission from her home in Melbourne in 1923. Her task was to find a means of employing and paying the women as 'an alternative to obtaining their living in white men's camps'.[7] She established a raffia room attached to the Schenks' humble home where the women made items, the sale of which helped provide a small wage for them.[8]

Rod Schenk's early hope of the mission becoming a 'honey pot' for the Aborigines was not automatic. The local groups were not always convinced about its benefits. Rod noted the 'rigorously enforced tribal laws' as the basis of their indifference.[9] There were many early misunderstandings and miscommunications and there were rumours, circulated by Aborigines and some pastoralists, about Schenk's intentions. In addition, the older Aboriginal men resented the women going to the raffia room and the local pastoralists were constantly disgruntled about the mission's position, not only on viable land that they prized themselves but also in relation to Schenk's insistence that Aboriginal workers be paid wages for work off the mission.[10] According to Mysie Schenk, nothing was accomplished without harassment of some form or another. Furthermore, it became apparent to the Schenks that the mission was actually a buffer between two warring Aboriginal groups rather than a place of succour, relief and transformation, as they had intended.

Nevertheless, the period from the mid-1920s to the early 1930s, when Bennett arrived, was one of building and consolidation, particularly in the late 1920s as Neville not only praised the mission but also facilitated its growth, making Rod Schenk a Protector of Aborigines. In a piece published in *The West Australian* following a visit to the mission in 1927, Neville wrote:

These were a people where contact with civilisation had brought them low indeed in the social scale and yet today the young men and women seem to be avoiding the evil phases of their time honoured traditions and those acquired from whites and are accepting and practising the ethics of Christianity. Even the elders are inclined to renounce the 'Marbonjerry' or the witch doctor and are willing to resort to the white man's methods of healing the sick, cases being brought in from far and wide. Parents are leaving their children to be educated, industry is replacing idleness and the desire to work is growing...As one passes out into the star-spangled night, a line from a Kipling verse rushes to mind: 'You're a better man than I am, Gunga Din'. From mining camp to mission – time has wrought a change indeed.[11]

As this suggests, the mission's appeal was that it was self-propelled and self-funded. As part of the United Aborigines Mission, the missionaries were faith workers, which meant that they had no set income, depending on God for what they needed. This translated as donations from Christian friends. As Mysie noted, 'the Christian community around Australia underwrote everything'.[12] Initially, Mt Margaret was not financially subsidised by the government. The situation improved following Neville's visit when he closed down ration centres nearby, at Laverton, Linden and Morgans, and transferred those receiving rations to Mt Margaret. This swelled the population at the mission by 250, including between sixty and one hundred children, and brought weekly government rations (454 g sugar, 28 g tea, 8.8 kg flour and a plug of tobacco) to mission coffers. According to Bennett, 'friends' subsidised the cost of food for the children by contributing 52 shillings annually.[13]

It also led to a building boom as the missionaries needed to provide infrastructure to accommodate this rapid growth in numbers. This was a time of depression so the task was difficult. Buildings were bought at bargain prices or were made with second-hand materials, including from buildings in the once-thriving mining townships nearby. Among these was a school which Schenk relocated to the mission and remodelled to suit his purposes. With the donations they received, the Schenks were able to buy a truck to transport materials and rations. By the mid-1930s, so rapidly had the mission grown that it looked like a small town.[14] Buildings included girls' and boys' dormitories, a dining room, kitchen and pantries, a school, missionaries' houses, Aboriginal homes and stores.[15] In 1934 the Christison Memorial Hospital was added. Fulfilling a desire of her father's to build a hospital for the Dalleburra, Bennett provided the funds for such.[16] Another important part of the building program was the establishment of the Graham homes, purpose-built accommodation for the children to stay where food and education was provided. Stretcher beds were made of hessian and wood, clothing and quilts were made by friends around Australia, and Neville's department supplied blankets. The first of these homes was opened in 1928 and teaching began with sixteen children in the homes and thirty-two children from the local camp.

The Christison Memorial Hospital, added to the mission in 1934, State Library of Western Australia, 009893d.

It is likely that the Graham homes were modelled on the homes established by Reverend Dr John Anderson Graham in India at the turn of the century. It was during his time on a mission in northeast India that he wanted to 'do something' for the orphaned and abandoned Anglo-Indian children, mostly sons and daughters of British planters and local Indian women. With the help of the Governor of Bengal, he leased land from the government in the district and established a school in 1900. The idea behind the establishment of his home was a place of security for the children, a place where they would be educated to become independent citizens in the future and a place where they would be insulated from what he saw as their corrupt surroundings. The ideal was to create an environment of care and emotional support, like a family where the children would be provided with a 'home away from home'.[17]

Similarly, Rod Schenk placed much store in creating what he and Mysie conceived as a supportive and caring environment at the mission. Indeed, Rod saw environment as critical to his success, defining it as 'a home to live in and to which they belonged, to cater for physical and emotional needs'.[18] It is clear that the Schenks also established the homes as a place of refuge for the women and girls. As we saw in chapter three, one of the key concerns of the Schenks was what they perceived to be Aboriginal women's and girls' vulnerability in the polygamous tribal system made worse by dispossession. As Mysie noted, Rod discovered very early on that the drought exacerbated this as the men would sell their (mostly young) wives to white men as a means of obtaining basic necessities. Once Mysie arrived she also became concerned about the dearth of children among the family clusters who came to and from the mission. She later discovered that, due to the harsh conditions, infanticide was practised, one of her informants declaring 'can't walk with babies all the time'.[19] Another reason for the low birthrate was the rite of subincision which, Rod maintained, was still widely practised.

Rod argued that 'saving children from the evils of camp life' was one of the benefits of the homes. He believed that Neville would only accept mixed-descent children on the mission on the condition of their control in dormitories where they also had access to education. As in India, the Graham homes also accommodated the mixed-descent children who were either sent there by their parents or found their way to Mt Margaret as a way of escaping the government settlement at Moore River. Mysie's account of the mission provides several examples of children who escaped the latter and sought refuge at Mt Margaret. Indeed, some of the first children to arrive at the mission were among the group of people Rod had witnessed be deported some four months after his arrival in the district. The group of fifteen people escaped Moore River, taking 18 days to travel over 800 kilometres to return to their homes on the eastern goldfields. Some of the women who worked with Mysie in the raffia room also talked of hiding their children in various places at the mission to avoid them being snatched and deported by police. Some children were also deposited at the mission by police protectors and, on occasion, Neville sent children there.

In this way, the mission was caught up in the governmental policies relating to people who were part-Aboriginal and to the public unease and distaste about their presence, particularly in country towns. Neville was particularly preoccupied with the growth of a mixed-descent population in the south of the state, believing that without assistance and legislative control, their future was hopeless and tragic. He established Moore River settlement, three years into his chief protectorship in 1918, in order to deal with this growing problem. It soon became overcrowded, underfunded and under-resourced, and poorly equipped to deal with the numbers of part-Aboriginal people that swelled its ranks once Carrolup Aboriginal settlement in the south was closed and the people transferred there. The Schenks were aware that placing children in their homes without government consent was inappropriate, and they worried about Neville's response. However, Neville's position around mixed-descent children changed during the course of his protectorship. While of concern, the half-caste problem did not have quite the same kind of urgency for him at that point as it later would.

A. O. Neville opening the Graham home for girls, Mt Margaret, 1931, State Library of Western Australia, 009729d.

In fact, the Schenks' policy towards the children ran counter to his vision. At Mt Margaret the policy was that children would stay in the homes with the cooperation of the parents. Indeed, Rod Schenk complained about the fact that many native parents, 'from Coolgardie to Laverton' chose not to leave their children there.[20] While free choice was important, so too was allowing children and parents to stay in contact. The Schenks believed it was better for children to stay in their own country where parents had daily contact with them and knew that they were being 'properly fed'.[21] Mysie noted that Neville was undecided about the children at Mt Margaret at the time of his visit but indicated his preference that they be sent to Moore River and removed from camp influence altogether. He didn't know that Mt Margaret was developing a reputation

175

as an alternative to Moore River, as parents actively brought their children to the mission to avoid this fate.

Education was vital to Rod Schenk's vision at Mt Margaret. He believed that without it Aboriginal people 'would never have a voice in their own country'.[22] A school was first started among the camp children by one of the missionaries, Herbert Reichenbach, in 1926. This was fortified in 1928 when Beryl Kingston began teaching the children both in the camps and in the Graham homes. Like Reverend Graham, who saw his homes as critical to the education of the mixed-descent children in India, the Schenks represented their homes as a key part of their education program, believing they helped school improvement and attendance. They also represented the school as a culturally sensitive reform. While acknowledging the opposition of some of the old men of the tribes, they noticed that more and more parents sought to resist this pressure, deciding to leave their children in the homes because, unlike other government institutions, they could maintain contact:

> Returning from walkabout they made straight for the Children's Homes bringing special tidbits, sometimes a kangaroo tail, rabbit or goanna cooked in the tribal casserole style. They collected their full-blood children at Christmas, taking with them some food and a note. The note was carried around for the three-month holiday period – into the bush up to 320 kilometres east, up and down the line from Laverton to Kalgoorlie, and to station properties. After 'two moons' someone would read the note to them and tell them the school commencement date. Children were able to do that for themselves as they learned to read.[23]

This was a key part of Mt Margaret practice which Bennett highly approved of. Schenk argued that without education the Aborigines would always need others to speak for them.[24] She shared this sense of education as empowerment and it was one of the reasons she decided to stay on the mission. Their vision of education conformed to some of the central ideas of imperial humanitarianism, particularly those emanating from the Phelps-Stokes Commission, conducted in the early 1920s, which shaped thinking in the empire on native education in tropical Africa.

The new school at Mt Margaret, 1929, State Library of Western Australia, 009708d.

II

Bennett arrived on the mission in April 1932, following her year-long investigation along the northwest coast. Within months she had fired off her first allegation of slavery to the press, established weaving and spinning for the women and girls via the use of her own spinning wheels and looms, and decided to tackle the education of the children in the homes. At that time there was no education offered for the goldfields children nor any assistance in this direction from the state Aborigines Department or the Education Department. Bennett turned to the correspondence lessons Mysie Schenk gave to her own children as the basis of her curriculum, along with the instructions for outback mothers. She prepared aids and teaching materials for the start of the following year. As the mission received no assistance, she bought what she required – paper, pens and ink and pencils – to get started with her forty-five pupils in January 1933. Although she was assisted by two others, she devised a system of staggering the hours so that each class received one or two hours of concentrated teaching and when one class went out to play, another came in.

With Bennett's entry to the mission, the educational program changed from conversion and vocational skills to the latest methods and state school standards.[25] Believing that education was the foundation of equality and

Mary Bennett in the raffia room watching the Aboriginal women spin wool from two looms she imported from Sweden, 1932. The two women in front are 'carding' the wool, State Library of Western Australia, 009698d.

rights, Bennett set about ensuring that Aboriginal children learned what non-Aboriginal children learned. In two years, she raised the children to standard two examination level of the Western Australian Education Department Correspondence School. She obtained advice and up-to-date methods and standards from other qualified teachers and attracted the attention of progressive educationalists. Bennett attributed the success of her program, in part, to the student-centred learning which she promoted as a means of easing the load on the small staff. Rod Schenk identified her innovative practices in visual education and play.[26] With no training herself, her school nonetheless developed a reputation for the work she was doing and the results she was getting. People like Anton Vroland, the noted Victoria-based educator and Aboriginal rights activist, visited the mission to see her work and share his ideas. Teaching the children became Bennett's raison d'être. As she informed Bessie Rischbieth in 1934:

> it is such a privilege and a source of consolation to me to know that I am doing even the smallest bit to lift them up and set them on their feet, and help them to be what all are potentially, the most magnificent citizens that any country could desire.[27]

Furthermore, she saw in the mission the capacity to build data about her Aboriginal pupils to help advance the cause of Aboriginal education, intelligence and citizenship generally.

At this time Aboriginal education was not a priority anywhere in Australia, but least of all in Western Australia where the first properly trained teachers on government settlements appeared in 1945 and on missions in 1952.[28] Even where children were able to attend a school there was much discrimination, and a specific regulation in the Education Act allowed for white racism to prevail, precluding Aboriginal participation where non-Aboriginal parents requested it. Education on government settlements and missions was either non-existent or very poor. The Schenks believed that the state didn't care about the future of the people and Bennett saw the denial of education as the operation of the colour bar which, together with Aboriginal dispossession and starvation, constituted a grave dereliction of governmental responsibility. Her view was that the denial of education meant the denial of earning capacity and, thus, a cycle of impoverishment and the continued vulnerability and abuse of women as communities attempted to survive.

She also believed that not providing education was based on the insidious belief in low Aboriginal intelligence. Her mission occurred at a time when interest in Aboriginal intelligence and mentality was part of the scientific obsession with Aboriginal bodies. While Aboriginal capacity for education and assimilation was part of this process, the examination of Aboriginal physiology was also about expanding the frontiers of racial science.[29] As McGregor has shown, in these years the physical and psychological studies of Aborigines were entrenched within an evolutionary paradigm.[30] The major studies of Aboriginal mentality confirmed their alleged primitivity. Furthermore, as Warwick Anderson has suggested, the fascination with the primitive other was ultimately about European Australian anxiety about its own white racial purity and destiny.[31]

It was in an effort to combat the essentially negative view of Aboriginal intelligence that both Bennett and Rod Schenk compiled a photographic and discursive dossier of Aboriginal people's capacity. In her *Teaching the Aborigines: Data from the Mt Margaret Mission* (1935), Bennett had numerous full-page photographs of her classroom, her pupils active in their own education, with examples of the kind of exercises they did. She documents the age of the students and how much schooling they'd had against the state school standard to demonstrate the magnitude of their achievements and to underscore her view that they could learn like non-Aboriginal children. Queenie is pictured teaching the first infants' class. She is fourteen and her total time in school, 'reckoned in hours of a state school', was 12 months and 2 weeks. Seven-year-old Jean, pictured teaching the second infants' class, had only 5 months at state school hours, while 8-year-old Ngoonjie, writing on the board, had only 3 months and 3 weeks in state school hours. Particularly noteworthy was Vera, the daughter of married half-castes, who had been exempted from the provisions of the Aborigines Act but was denied education in the state system.

Such student-centred learning made a virtue out of a necessity but it was also way ahead of its time educationally, at least for the non-indigenous system. It is little wonder that Mt Margaret began to attract the attention of outsiders, for there was nothing else like it in Australia at the time. There had been model education institutions in the nineteenth century but they were long gone, and with their closure came the view of Aboriginal incapacity. There was no thought about education for Aborigines, no wider discussion or exchange of information about what Aboriginal education should be or look like. Bennett and the Schenks were unique in humanitarian circles in looking to ideas about native education emanating from the heart of empire. Indeed, it was in her arguments about Aboriginal education generally and Mt Margaret in particular that we have further evidence of the link, in her mind, between the fate of Africans and African Americans and that of the Australian Aborigines.

Particularly influential were the reports of the Phelps-Stokes commissions in Africa. Published in 1922 and 1925, the reports were the result of the African Education Commission, which grew out of missionary and philanthropic concern, both in England and the United States, to forge a link between black Africa and black America. It was funded by the Phelps-Stokes Fund, which had been established in 1911 by a wealthy philanthropist with the aim of connecting emerging leaders and organisations in Africa and the Americas for their social and economic development. It attracted the support of some powerful African American leaders such as Booker T. Washington, who argued that the situation of the two groups was analogous. According to Berman, the fund played a key role in reinforcing the belief that the educational methods which had been hammered out for the freed slaves in the postbellum period were relevant for black Africans in the twentieth century.[32]

Integral to this was the role of Thomas Jesse Jones, author of the reports. Before undertaking the African Education Commission in 1920 at the behest of the American Baptist Foreign Missionary Society, he had undertaken a survey of African American education. His ideas had been strongly influenced by Samuel Chapman Armstrong, the founder of the Hampton Institute in Virginia, where the thrust of education for African Americans was industrial and agricultural training. Berman argues that Jones' ideas for African American education provided something of a blueprint for his ideas on education in Africa. His African commission reports recommended four essentials of education-health, appreciation of environment, effective development of the home and recreation – to be built into the curricula at every stage, along with the overriding importance of agricultural and industrial training. He also emphasised the importance of cooperation between missions and governments for African education.

Following Jones' reports, the Phelps-Stokes Fund was considered an authority on education of so-called underdeveloped peoples. Indeed, by the early 1920s, as part of the imperial humanitarian focus on Africa, the British Colonial Office saw in the African Education Commission a means of creating a common educational policy for the region. This aim had been promoted in missionary circles in the 1910s and, although it did not initiate the African commission, the Colonial Office facilitated the venture and established a British Advisory Committee on Native Education in Tropical Africa in the early 1920s following it. Furthermore, the fundamental tenets of the reports in terms of agricultural and industrial training not only provided a palatable educational theory for British policymakers but also complemented the political philosophy of indirect rule.

That Rod Schenk saw the Phelps-Stokes African commission reports as providing an important theoretical basis for Mt Margaret is evidenced in his *The Educability of the Native* published in 1936, a year after Bennett's *Teaching*. Along with the Graham homes, this showed his deep connection not just with the United Aborigines Mission in Australia, but with the wider global network of imperial and Anglo-American Protestant evangelism and humanitarianism. His pamphlet sets out to establish the Wongutha's intelligence and capacity for education. It is a polemic about Australia's 'inglorious effort' in native education which should make us 'bow our heads in shame'.[33] Schenk uses Bennett's statistics, describes her methodology and makes extensive use of photographic evidence to illustrate the educative work of the mission under her leadership. Much of the publication is taken up with showcasing the work of one particular pupil, Toonda, who sat a test which was closely aligned to that of the Education Department, showing his great aptitude for English.

Toonda's Locality Map of Mt Margaret Mission

Toonda's Locality Map of Mt Margaret Mission. Toonda was one of Bennett's pupils in the 1930s. He drew a blue box around Bennett's house, centre left. This featured in Bennett's Teaching the Aborigines.

Schenk's pamphlet also showed his concern to instil the key principles of the African Education Commission at Mt Margaret, detailing the recreational, domestic and handicraft, as well as industrial, principles of training at the mission. In one year alone the women produced 1,376 items in the raffia room while the men were not only good builders and carpenters but had begun mining, including sinking shafts and managing a three-head battery. In 1936 they yielded 500 tons of ore, worth 600 pounds, providing them with 30 pounds each. He also cited other cases of achievement, industry and Aboriginal intelligence from across Australia, driving home Aboriginal capacity for education and development.

Ian Duckham interprets Schenk's efforts as assimilationist.[34] Of course, missions were at the heart of the civilising enterprise and assimilation via education had been a model solution for the native question elsewhere, notably in North America, as Schenk well knew. But this was also about Christian indoctrination and replacing one set of beliefs for another. At its roots Protestant evangelism is about conversion and the Schenks saw their primary task as replacing animism with Christianity. Despite Mysie's representation of their endeavour as non-dictatorial, education and food were primarily about 'shepherding' the children and the homes were a means of providing consistent training in the scripture. With Bennett, they promoted a non-Aboriginal curriculum, reflecting non-Aboriginal morality and values. English was the lingua franca. Mysie maintained that they upheld the moral law of the Aborigines in everything except where it conflicted with the Bible.[35] If they saw that their own moral law conflicted with that of the Aborigines they assumed that, in key areas, theirs was better. They saw themselves as part of enlightened Christianity while characterising the Wongutha as 'bound hand and foot by superstition'.[36]

Furthermore, there didn't seem to be much care for developing or maintaining certain aspects of Wongutha traditions and they were surprised to find that the people were not all as one. They attempted to refashion the family and community connections they sought to protect by discouraging polygamy and its associated practice of child marriage, and preventing infanticide and what they regarded as cruel rites associated with puberty and initiation into adulthood. This was classic missionary moralising about Aboriginal sexuality, the culture and meaning of which they did not understand. They also regarded aspects of the Wongutha's cultural practice, such as some corroborees and those associated with sorcery, as examples of a 'bloodless theology' to be discouraged. Indeed, the Schenks' firm belief about these issues led to serious conflict with notable anthropologists at the time like A. P. Elkin and his student Phyllis Kaberry, discussed in the next chapter.

Yet, while the Schenks' and Bennett's efforts can be understood within the context of the global Protestant assault on certain traditional customs at the time, their concerns cannot be explained solely as acts of assimilation. For example, they did not target only Aboriginal people. Just as Rod Schenk saw some corroborees as in direct conflict with the Bible, he also saw squatter opposition to what he was doing in the same light. To the argument that education made Aboriginal people conceited, Schenk retorted, 'not to the same extent as many whites'.[37] Furthermore, their desire to see the Aborigines of the region survive and prosper underpinned their concern with infanticide. According to Mysie Schenk, infanticide was a normal occurrence of Aboriginal life on the goldfields largely because of their impoverished condition.[38] She believed that, like the selling of women to white men, infanticide was exacerbated by their social, economic and environmental conditions and should be prevented as far as possible to ensure Aboriginal people's health and survival.

The language question further illustrates their concern with Aboriginal survival. At first Mysie Schenk saw the raffia room as a means of learning the language of the Wongutha. However, she soon discovered that there were several dialects in the room and that this made arriving at a consensus difficult. Suspecting that the Wongutha could be bilingual, the Schenks actively decided on English as the main language at the mission while they would attempt to get a working knowledge of the dialect most spoken. Bennett saw Aboriginal people as great linguists and the Schenks confessed that they were nowhere near as good at picking up Indigenous dialects as the Wongutha were at mastering English. But they also justi-fied English as the standard on the basis that it would enable the people to have a place of dignity in the white majority and a voice in their own concerns.[39]

The latter points to how the missionaries defined their task at Mt Margaret. This was not about instilling non-Aboriginal ways of being in the world and the eradication of Aboriginality. Rather it was about adaptation to new circumstances:

> For efficient education the natives need sufficient land in every tribal district to grow their own meat which is their main item of diet, then suitable industries provided. With education the natives can earn their own living in any district in any way that whites do, and herein lies the scope for adaptable education.[40]

Education would give Aboriginal people the chance to adapt and develop under changing conditions.[41]

This notion of education as an adaptive mechanism, and adapta-tion itself, was a novel idea in twentieth-century Aboriginal policy. *The*

Educability of the Native demonstrates how Schenk understood the mission as a necessary intervention in a wider context of dispossession and natal alienation. He critiqued the process of dispersing Aboriginal people to work for white men as antithetical to their education and long-term survival. In a section titled 'When Shall the Golden Rule be Applied to the Natives', Schenk uses evidence from the African Education Commission report to slam what he saw as Australia's and Britain's recalcitrance.[42] Australia not only lagged behind most other British territories in relation to native education, it also lagged behind Portuguese East Africa, which was condemned by the Phelps-Stokes report for placing commercial interests above native education.[43] He noted that, in many other British territories, native education was beginning to be prioritised by governors and administrators. He quoted 37,000 pounds spent annually on Africa's Gold Coast and 16,000 pounds in central Africa. In Tanganyika schools had been developed such that communication between governments and village headmen was in writing.

Bennett utilised the findings of the Phelp-Stokes Commission, too. Like Schenk, her ideas about education were bound up with the broader question of what a model native reservation should be. She argued that, without education, native reservations were simply places of impoverishment and imprisonment. At the time of the Moseley Royal Commission she critiqued the Moore River government settlement as such a place. In *Teaching* she argued that a reservation should be about social and material betterment. She provided the example of Toomberanno, a 'bush native' who, following a spear wound to the leg, consulted Mindie Nung'oo, the 'witchdoctor', instead of seeking skilled medical care at the mission. By the time the missionaries got word of his condition and got him to a hospital it was too late and the leg required amputation. He recovered at the mission and tried to regain independence off it but soon ran into problems hunting on crutches. When he speared a sheep rather than a kangaroo he was sentenced to six months' imprisonment in Fremantle gaol. In the meantime, his wife, who had fled the mission in fear of the police, lost her son who was born prematurely.

Throughout her publication of Mt Margaret's achievements, Bennett is at pains to point to the problems for Aboriginal people in the wake of dispossession. Toomberanno's story demonstrated the 'utter wastefulness of alienating all the natives' land for sheep walks', for 'it is time', she said, that 'white people realized that the main result of their occupation of other people's lands is the extinction of the food supplies of the native people':

> Parliament will have to raise vast sums for rations to avoid the frightful reproach of starving the natives to death in their own country or restore land, where, safe from molestation by whites, and safe from official deportations, for no fault, our natives can settle in homes and earn their own living and develop what is morally their country as well as ours.[44]

If starvation was one problem, the colour bar was another because she believed it underpinned the denial of education to the thousands of 'intelligent Aboriginal and half-caste children' in Western Australia. One of the insidious aspects of the colour bar, for Bennett, was that it sustained an inferiority complex among Aboriginal people which then made receptivity to education difficult. She argued that this not only went against trends in educational reform, but also acted like a brake on Aboriginal development. The example she frequently used to illustrate her point was the use of pidgin: 'The natives realize that in the white man's "pidgin" they are inarticulate but they can hardly free themselves from its shackles'.[45]

Education for Aboriginal people was therefore vital for overcoming the impediment of inferiority as well as raising Aboriginal leaders. Inspired by the cohort of educated African American leaders of the day, she went so far as to declare the purpose of Mt Margaret as finding Booker Washingtons, Dr Carvers and Aggreys in Australia. She also described Rod Schenk as 'another General Armstrong' and his mission 'another Hampton Institute in embryo'.[46] It is not surprising that she was inspired by the Hampton Institute and by Booker T. Washington. The latter had been born into slavery, a child of mixed descent who, once emancipated, received an education at the Hampton Normal Institute established by Armstrong under the auspices of the American Missionary Association in 1868 to provide education to former slaves. After teaching at Hampton, Washington eventually established Tuskegee, a training institute for black teachers, with Armstrong's tutelage and support. In fact, Armstrong and Washington were controversial figures both in their own time and subsequently because of their political machinations and because of their segregationist attitude to black education.[47] The emphasis in their institutions was on vocational training rather than academic aptitude and their adherence to segregation related to their view that African Americans' mixing and moving in white society was an impossibility.

As this suggests, in fact, the aims of the institute conflicted with those of Mt Margaret. With an emphasis on adaptable education the Schenks and Bennett were not advocates of segregation per se and, as their own results attested, they were as interested in academic aptitude as in vocational training. Indeed, Bennett never lost an opportunity to advertise Aboriginal children's capacity for learning and their intelligence. She pointed to an Aboriginal child who had won the prize for the best essay on the Sydney Harbour Bridge in the 1930s and how native children had won four prizes against white children in eight public schools in South Australia. Her own school pupils had won silver cups in the Batman All-Australia essay competition four years running. She constantly promoted the fact of the children's proficiency in her school, where they made up ground against the white standard in record time and where they excelled in mathematics. She subsequently noted how an Education Department representative had visited the mission and commented that she demanded high standards and got them.[48]

Bennett and the Schenks were also interested in vocational training and the mission establishment became a site of such as Aboriginal people were involved in every stage of its growth and development. In their publications Bennett and Schenk made extensive use of images of Aboriginal people in a variety of activities, from men roofing and cladding buildings, driving trucks, hauling equipment, building schools and homes, and purchasing items from the mission store, to children in the dining room, dormitories and schoolrooms.

As this suggests, Bennett's experience at Mt Margaret clearly influenced her thinking about the purpose and meaning of reservations and about the relationship between using them to segregate Aboriginal people and to educate them. On the front cover of *Teaching the Aborigines* was the following quote from Raphael Cilento, medical practitioner and public health administrator:

The outstanding problem of the native reservation may be said to be the establishment of a plan obvious to the native which makes for his social and material betterment. Without it, his detention in

187

a reservation becomes merely a period of imprisonment; with it he
may be encouraged towards development.[49]

In this sense, segregation was a means to an end. Education would enable
Aboriginal people to meet non-Aborigines on terms of equality. It was
about buying some time to bridge a gap, as Bennett wrote in 1930: 'The
solution is for each race to live as citizens in its own community until
such time as the disparity shall have been bridged, by one race giving
up its extreme competitiveness and the other race giving up its extreme
communalism and by educational advance'.[50]

Bennett admired the Hampton Institute for its tradition of building
strong, educated and articulate black leaders and teachers. She would also
have seen synergies between Washington's story of enslavement and mixed
descent with the Aboriginal people among whom she was living and
working. Yet, one of the many contradictions of her advocacy was the fact
that, in reality, her own theory and practice of Aboriginal education had
more in common with Du Bois, another prominent African-American
leader of the time, whom Bennett never mentions. Education had been at
the core of the disagreement between Du Bois and Washington, the former
explicitly rejecting the compromise of segregation for education which had
underpinned Washington's program for freed slaves. As a rights activist and
advocate of African-American equality and citizenship, Du Bois was deeply
critical of the philosophy of industrial and practical training at Hampton.

It is unlikely that Bennett absorbed the fractious politics of African-
American leadership at this time. For her, Washington and Hampton
Institute were symbols of black empowerment. Furthermore, her philosophy was informed less by American politics than by British colonial
policy, which promoted education as central to imperial trusteeship. Along
with economic equality, it was fundamental to the notion of gradual
development which underpinned the theory of indirect rule. The ideal
was education for citizenship. Bennett saw education as a right and as the
basis of all other rights. As she said, Aboriginal mothers endured slave
conditions not only because of loss of land but because they had been
deprived an education and the rights that were founded on it.[51]

Historian Cati Coe has shown how the romanticisation of African
culture was central to indirect rule.[52] We see this in Bennett's work. She
grafted the African and African-American experience onto that of the

Aborigines. The slavery motif was one such example, the demand for indirect rule another and the representation of Mt Margaret as a Hampton Institute in the making yet another. The irony of this from the point of her subsequent critique of assimilation was that Hampton was a key vehicle for assimilation in the United States, not just of African Americans but also native Americans. Nonetheless, underpinning her defence was a romanticisation of empire and an idealisation of the figure of the oppressed black man characteristic of imperial anti-slavery rhetoric and iconography.

This image, from Teaching the Aborigines, *shows Koonloon Jannoo comparing the work of the boy sitting next to him with the work in the book and then marking it,* State Library of Western Australia, 009750d.

Nowhere is this clearer than in her promotion of the figure of Dr Kwegyir Aggrey (1875–1927), a native from the Gold Coast (Ghana) who was selected to go to the United States to be trained as a missionary. He later returned to Africa, taking part in the Phelps-Stokes Commission and playing a pivotal role in the establishment of Achimota, a coeducational school for children, being appointed its first vice-principal in 1924. Formally opened in 1927, Achimota would raise an educated elite of African leaders who could create a bridge between the chiefs and their traditions and the educated elites and western civilisation.[53] It would produce a student who was intellectually western but remained African in 'sympathy and desirous of preserving and developing what is deserving of respect in tribal life, custom, rule and law'.[54]

189

A school day would begin with prayer, showing the importance of evangelisation to the mission, State Library of Western Australia, 009742d.

Aboriginal workers waiting for pay 'in kind', Mt Margaret, 1925. Payment was in food, cooked goat meat and clothes as required. Payment in cash commenced in 1926, State Library of Western Australia, 009686d.

Houses being built for the first 'families' married at Mt Margaret, 1932. In this image Rod Schenk is helping Bert Thomas build his house, State Library of Western Australia, 009812d.

Boys at school, Mt Margaret in the 1930s. Reggie Johnston, who Bennett cast as Aggrey in the school play, is first on the left. The other two boys are Wallace Blow (centre) and Frank Goongoonjanoo Grey, State Library of Western Australia, 009745d.

Arthur Stokes taking the class in reading at Mt Margaret, State Library of Western Australia, 009774d.

'Bullboard', the chief teaching tool for arithmetic at Mt Margaret in the 1930s and 1940s. At the 'go' the two with sticks hit any number and the first with the answer scores a point, State Library of Western Australia, 009776.

Building the three-head battery at Mt Margaret, so that the Wongutha could earn money from mining, 1935/6, State Library of Western Australia, 009820d.

That Bennett aspired to the same was demonstrated in a play she organised in 1935 called *Dr Aggrey of Africa*. The play told the story of the 'little boy from an African village who became the principal of Achimota College', and one of Bennett's pupils, Reggie Johnston, played Aggrey.[55] There were also images of Aggrey at the mission. It is not hard to see why someone like Aggrey inspired the people behind Mt Margaret. Aggrey represented the notion of adaptable education that they were promoting. He was also a representative of the ideals of interwar British imperial humanitarianism. His story epitomised the black hero who triumphed over adversity and racism to be a leader among his people. As Mysie Schenk noted, Bennett's play was a 'dramatization to inspire the children to visualize what they could become'.[56]

Without formal training herself Bennett initiated the education program at the mission on the basis of non-discrimination, fervently believing that education was the key to long-term Aboriginal survival. She modelled her lessons on the state school curriculum. This was a radical enough proposition at the time, as education for Aboriginal people was not at the forefront of the policy setting, certainly not in terms of creating leaders among their people or for the purposes of adaptation. Neville saw education as having a place in Aboriginal absorption. It was about fitness for inclusion in the general community. For this, he said, the three Rs were all that was necessary.[57] However, as Haebich has shown, access to education for Aboriginal children was significantly hampered by white racism in country towns.[58] It was also hampered by very poor standards in missions and on settlements across the country.

In a research project undertaken by P. W. Beckenham (which Bennett subsequently quoted from) under the auspices of the Australian Council for Educational Research about a decade after Bennett and the Schenks produced their record of Aboriginal achievement, it was found that not only was education reaching a relatively small number of Aboriginal children but there were also glaring deficiencies in the system. There were not enough trained teachers, buildings or proper equipment, with Beckenham declaring 'a nation which starves its white schools for equipment is unlikely to be generous to its helots'.[59] There was not enough unity between the states and between the state and mission schools, and there was insufficient Commonwealth Government intervention. His comments vindicated much of Bennett's theory and practice. Discrimination was a large part of the problem:

> The Black child's education is jeopardized by a colour consciousness that is unworthy of any democracy and that frustrates the best intentioned efforts of enlightened teachers, missionaries and government departments in their efforts to educate the Black child for useful living in a White continent.[60]

However, the research also criticised the white conception of education that was thought appropriate for Aboriginal children. Beckenham argued that there was no adaptation of the curriculum and that this was quite glaring in Western Australia, where it was said that education for Aboriginal children was on a high plane because white and black received identical education. Beckenham questioned this as a notion of equality:

> Is that not a false conception of educational equality? Identity of education is not equality of education. Black and White are as far apart as Kipling's famous East and West. To provide the same education for each is like prescribing penicillin for all diseases from septic sore to cancer.[61]

For Beckenham, then, the question was not the adaptability or otherwise of Aboriginal children to education but the capacity of the education system to adapt to meet the needs of Aboriginal children.

Clearly, this was not what the Schenks and Bennett were about. Seeing only discrimination and colour consciousness to blame for the deficiencies in education, they set about demonstrating Aboriginal children's capacity for learning: their educability. Bennett's efforts were particularly propelled by this notion of the 'colour bar', which led to her producing *Teaching the Aborigines*. At the back of the book was a discussion about intelligence and discrimination in which she quoted various authorities about Aboriginal intelligence, including the findings of the Adelaide Anthropological Expedition to the Musgrave Ranges in 1933 which found that the intelligence of the full-blood children was approximate to that of white children of the same age.

Given that the issue of curriculum-sensitive material has continued to dog Aboriginal education, the fact that Bennett imposed a non-Aboriginal curriculum on her pupils is not noteworthy. Indeed, in an article exploring the ways in which schooling has represented a form of internal colonialism, A. R. Welch argues that 'the myth of the ineducability of Aborigines has not only been pervasive but has licensed second rate education for Aboriginal people'.[62] In fact, Bennett was deeply approving of other mission experiments which she saw as being sympathetic to Aboriginal culture. Kunmunya, 'where pidgin was never heard', was one of these.[63] There, Aboriginal children were taught in English as well as their own language, Worrora, and the communities were kept intact. She would later also experience and praise Ernabella in the Musgrave Ranges, a mission established by her friend, fellow humanitarian Charles Duguid, where the pupils were taught in the vernacular, including the translation of the Gospels, and were encouraged to retain some of their tribal ways. Even Beckenham recommended it as a school deserving close study by the students of education among Aborigines.[64]

For Bennett, the question around retention of Aboriginal children was less about the content of what they were learning than an inferiority complex which handicapped their receptivity to education. She was very attuned to the psychological impacts of colonialism, arguing that learning things in a foreign language was a handicap which could be overcome. The problem with pidgin was that underpinning it was a 'lurking consciousness of inferiority' which, once transferred to the Aboriginal people, got right into their heart and spirit and then prevented them from 'feeling capable of wanting to fight'.[65] This, she said, went against the grain of modern educational reform:

> It is all in vain to talk of tests that may, or may not be tests, while we ignore the battle-ground that is every human soul. What we need are Intelligence Tests for the white people to discover how many of them have what Dante called, half a thousand years ago, 'INTELLIGENCE IN LOVE' [original emphasis].[66]

To be sure, Mt Margaret was first and foremost a mission and, in the Graham homes and in their missionising, the Schenks were clearly part of a global missionary assault which was, in turn, part of a broader Anglo-imperial modernist project that emerged in the first decades of the twentieth century. Instilling Christianity rather than education per se was the priority for the Schenks, and children were the target. This is what the Graham homes were all about. Holding children captive and close by was considered to be critical to success. However, Rod Schenk also facilitated Bennett's work and supported her approach, which necessarily refocused the education program from evangelism alone to vocational schooling. Like Beckenham after him, Schenk criticised what he saw as Australian recalcitrance on this matter. For both Bennett and the Schenks, education was part of a holistic approach, the goal of which was citizen-ship, independence and empowerment in white society. It sat alongside employment and wages, community support, food and self-sufficiency as integral components of mission aims. Indeed, while the photographic record of Mt Margaret documents classic missionary activity in terms of prayer, self-help and separation of girls and boys, it is also a strong and evocative record of education, community, family, activity, self-sufficiency and intergenerational connection. Assimilationist they may have been, but the aims of the Schenks and Bennett fitted demands for citizenship and progress being made by many Aboriginal leaders in the southeast and southwest at this time who were, in turn, part of a global indigenous movement seeking access, opportunity, education, paid work and equal civil rights.

AN INHUMANE DICTATORSHIP
Challenging Policy in Western Australia

It is time that Western Australia realised that the new Native Administration Act places all coloured people, thirty thousand native born Australians and some whites, at the disposal of a dictator, in this professing democracy of Western Australia, enabling him to take any coloured child from its mother at any stage of its life, no matter whether the mother be legally married or not; to refuse permission to any coloured people to marry; to take charge of the earnings of coloured people; to take charge of monies due to coloured people; to take charge of estates and dole out whatever he may please.[1]

The Departmental 'long range policy' is nothing but 'long range murder' with Bill Sykes in loco parentis.[2]

While Bennett would later claim the education program at Mt Margaret as one of the developments at the mission which Neville sought to destroy, in fact it was part of a suite of concerns by the mid to late 1930s when relations between him and the missionaries turned sour. Despite his own poor results on this front, the principle of training and education for Aboriginal people had been an underlying concern in his establishment of government settlements in the south. Indeed, education for mixed-descent children was compulsory in principle. Neville had approved Rod Schenk's initiatives in the 1920s. Yet, his early tolerance and promotion of the mission as a kind of model institution very rapidly turned to scepticism and mistrust in the following decade.

There were several issues at stake for Neville in his mounting unease with the mission. Just a week or so before Bennett's paper to the British Commonwealth League on the 'Aboriginal Mother' in 1933, he had warned Rod Schenk against the establishment of another mission further east in the Warburton Ranges. Establishing a mission in the interior had been a growing desire of Schenk's as it had come to his attention that there were many Wongutha between the mission and the ranges. He was particularly concerned about the activities of the white doggers around the area of the Central Aboriginal Reserve, hearing reports of the ill-treatment and murder of Aborigines inside the reserve itself. He informed Neville that missionaries from Mt Margaret could travel to the region and hold a small parcel of land until the Aborigines had capital and training to use it for themselves. He bought a team of camels with saddles, water cans and other accessories for 50 pounds and, despite Neville's instructions as well as his demand that the mission pay a bond before entering the reserve, pushed on with his plans and the expedition.

Between then and May 1935, when Neville finally agreed to a mission in the region on the proviso that Schenk not seek any government assistance for it, the relationship between the missionaries, Bennett and Neville deteriorated rapidly.[3] The obfuscation and disagreement over land for the mission at the Warburton Ranges was part of it, but the evidence of the Schenks and Bennett at the Moseley Royal Commission also demonstrated the gulf between their approach and his. The Schenks' evidence backed up Bennett's slavery thesis. Like her, Mysie Schenk focused on the position of Aboriginal women. She spoke against the sending of Aboriginal girls into domestic service and pointed out that Mt Margaret refused to cooperate with the policy on the basis of the girls' vulnerability while in service. Their policy was to keep the girls as close to their families as possible.

For his part, Rod Schenk spent much time focusing on the employment conditions of Aborigines in the eastern goldfields, providing examples of 'modern-day slavery' with Aborigines being in conditions of serfdom on pastoral stations in the district. He also critiqued the operation of the trust funds through which Aboriginal wages, where paid, were siphoned. He pointed out that wherever he went this was a source of grievance among Aboriginal workers. Related to this was his critique of the pastoralists and their 'Simon Legree tactics'.[4]

Pastoralist criticism had dogged the mission from the start. Mysie Schenk referred to constant attempts by pastoralists in the area to remove it. This was in part because they wanted the land but it was also because

Rod Schenk demanded wages for mission workers. According to Mysie, pastoralists only agreed to do so begrudgingly and were critical of the way the mission 'spoilt' the Aborigines, creating a condition of expectation for better conditions of work generally. Rod argued that the pastoralist view was that Aborigines could not be educated. He criticised them as wanting to continue the slave-like conditions of old. He also critiqued what he saw as their land monopoly, arguing that the mission and the Aborigines were locked in by vast sheep runs which limited the mission's capacity to establish self-sufficient communities. He wanted more land and suggested to Commissioner Moseley that the government resume half of the Mount Margaret Pastoral Company and give it to the mission stocked and fenced. He calculated that in five years the government would be spared the cost of Aboriginal relief as it would be a thriving township. Such an initiative would be further aided by increased land rental from the pastoralists.

Such criticism was not likely to get the Commissioner or Neville onside. Indeed, the pastoralist lobby, which included members of parliament, had always been problematic for Neville in the realisation of his reforms. Their resistance had led, in part, to his failure to make changes to the Aborigines Act in the late 1920s. They also made their claims felt before Moseley, who travelled to the Laverton district to hear the evidence of the pastoralists and townspeople before going to the mission where he combined a tour of inspection with listening to the Schenks' claims. According to Mysie, the testimony of the pastoralists was largely targeted at the mission. Complaints ranged from the spoilt nature of the mission boys and their uselessness, to Aborigines having too many dogs which killed the pastoralists' sheep. One station manager accused the Schenks of desiring equality for the Aborigines of the region and the general demand was that the mission be shifted 160 kilometres east of Laverton to 'useless spinifex country'.[5]

Commissioner Moseley supported the pastoralist view. Furthermore, his attack on the missions demonstrated a long-standing unease with missionary intervention and practice in that state which Neville increasingly shared. There was little reference to the condition of Aborigines on the goldfields in his report. Moseley dismissed claims of ill-treatment and cruelty as unsubstantiated and extravagant. He denied allegations of economic and sexual slavery and suggested that conditions on pastoral stations were good and that Aborigines suffered no hardship from non-payment of wages in money. He repudiated Rod Schenk's claim that the conditions of Aboriginal employment were 'modern slavery', inferring that the truth was probably more likely with the nearby pastoralists' contention that 'the boys trained on the mission [were] spoilt'. He dismissed Schenk's criticisms as the result of bad feelings between the mission and the pastoralists and supported the latter's suggestion that the mission be relocated.

This may very well have been what Neville wanted to hear. Missions had been part of his plans for the revision of policy for some time. At around the time of the Royal Commission, Neville had suggested that governments, rather than missions, should be the first point of contact with the Aboriginal people in order to avoid 'incidents which mean a constant reproach to Australia'.[6] His own marked preference was for government settlements like Moore River which he originally conceived as places of succour and uplift for the growing half-caste population living impoverished and despised lives on the edges of society. With food, accommodation and education, Aboriginal people need not die out.[7] However, as his ideas about how to solve the problem of the growing half-caste population evolved during the course of the 1930s, so too did his vision for government settlements. Rather than being productive communities, settlements would became holding zones or collection points, where mixed-descent children would be held for a short period of time and provided with some basic education to fit them for mergence in the community via work and marriage. The emphasis was on temporariness. In this way, settlements provided a short-term solution in the pursuit of a long-term goal, and missions would need firmer government control in order to effect it.

It was against this backdrop that Neville prevaricated over Schenk's mission in the Warburton Ranges. By the time he reluctantly approved it, three months after the Royal Commission, Schenk had been in communication with him over it for three years. It was during these years, when Neville remained silent or perfunctory to Schenk's letters, that Schenk began to sense Neville's mounting resistance. What appeared to tip Neville into bitter dispute with the missionaries, however, was Schenk's rejection of a proposed visit by Phyllis Kaberry, a student of anthropology under A. P. Elkin, Chair of Anthropology at Sydney University, to undertake fieldwork at the mission in 1935. Indeed, Schenk saw this episode as fuelling Neville's discomfort with the mission and his underlying aim to shut it down. In her account of this moment, Mysie Schenk claims that at this point Neville made a veiled threat that he could terminate the mission and strip Rod of his protectorship if he failed to cooperate.

It appeared to be a point of departure for Rod as well. Like many missionaries, Rod was suspicious of anthropologists, arguing that they treated Aboriginal people less as human beings and more as insects. He also saw them as disruptive, believing that they encouraged ceremonies and practices which the missionaries were trying to eradicate or change. He was already disgruntled with Elkin for 'reviving' old ceremonies and rituals on the mission during his fieldwork there in 1930. It was too much that Elkin's student now wanted to do the same. Yet, Kaberry had been given permission to do so by Neville himself. Despite Rod's objection she turned up at the mission, whereupon Rod refused her entry and sent off a rather angry note to Neville protesting her intrusion.

This episode of missionary recalcitrance came at a critical time in Neville's tenure. He was gathering momentum in terms of his reform agenda. The Moseley Royal Commission was over. The report was in and he was on track to deliver his revised legislation, empowering him to take control of the half-caste problem. In a fraught policy environment, with criticisms of his department and without allies, an appeal to science was his means of maintaining control and steering policy in the direction he had long sought. It was an appeal to rationality in the face of the overly emotive and extravagant claims of his detractors. Science would provide a rational way to fix the problem, and missions, while still envisaged as having a role, would be put in their place.

He had worked hard to develop a good working relationship with Elkin for this very reason and Schenk's refusal not only overstepped his reach but was a slight on Neville's professional standing. Neville had often been overshadowed by Elkin's success, public profile and esteem, including in Western Australia where his research in the north had led to critical acclaim.[8] Extending permission to one of Elkin's students was a means of addressing this imbalance and reasserting his importance and control. Furthermore, Kaberry's visit was a way of establishing normalcy in the context of Bennett's claims about Aboriginal women on the one hand, and the critiques of the northwest by anthropologist Ralph Piddington in the early 1930s on the other. The latter were particularly harmful as they concurred with many of Bennett's allegations. At the time Elkin had written approvingly of aspects of the Western Australian administration of Aborigines and, in the changing policy environment of the 1930s, his continued support and friendship was needed.[9]

Like the Schenks, Bennett was hostile to the intrusions of anthropologists. In her paper, 'The Aboriginal Mother', she had complained of their 'seeking copy' and, in the process, reviving ceremonies and practices of tribal law. She was also annoyed at how their intervention disrupted the education program at the mission, particularly for the full-blood children. While the full weight of Neville's policy agenda took some time to reveal itself to the Schenks, she had expected little from the Moseley Royal Commission and was not surprised by Neville's mounting attack. It was partly why she threw herself into the education program in the first place, to build reliable evidence and defence.

In 1935 she told fellow activist Olive Pink that Commissioner Moseley would deliver a 'squatter's verdict' in order to maintain the slavery status of Aboriginal people and placate vested interests. She had begun to feel that only an appeal to an external judiciary would expose the corruption and cruelty of Australia's colonial legacy.[10] Several months after Moseley's report a letter of hers was published in *The West Australian* in which she called on the League of Nations and the British Empire to investigate conditions in Australia which were 'a blot on humanity', arguing that Aborigines were robbed of their land and their women and that slavery existed in substance.

Certainly, her view of native freedom and emancipation was not what Neville had in mind. Indeed, he saw the Royal Commission as a conduit for the legislative changes he had long been wanting to implement. After years of parliamentary intransigence his new Native Administration Act was passed relatively easily in 1936. This was a pivotal moment for him as, via the legislation, he secured that which had eluded him for the previous 20 years of his protectorship. In seventy-four sections the Act gave him power over all aspects of Aboriginal people's lives: their domicile, their conditions of employment and pay, their children, their marriages and sexual relationships, their movements, even their deceased estates. He also became the legal guardian, acting *in loco parentis*, to all Aboriginal children until 21 years of age, and he was empowered to control their marriages. These changes were designed both to biologically absorb the mixed-descent people and leave the full-blood people to themselves. His eugenic solution would direct half-castes towards marriage in the white community, while full-bloods would continue to marry full-bloods according to tribal law.

His desire to control Aboriginal marriages highlights yet another source of contention between himself and the missionaries which would have sat uncomfortably with his long-term objectives. As we saw in chapter four, Bennett explicitly rejected Neville's so-called ethnological prescription, arguing that half-caste children needed to stay in their own communities. She saw Neville's solution of channelling girls into domestic service and then into the community as putting a premium on prostitution and denying children the right to their parents' love – father's as well as mother's. For her, choice in marriage was a fundamental human right and a right of citizenship. She lobbied for Christian monogamous marriages of whatever caste so that Aboriginal women could have the same rights of citizenship as white women, ensuring custody of their children. Furthermore, freedom of choice in marriage was part of a range of reforms being demanded by Aboriginal people at this time. In fact, Bennett and her feminist friend, May Vallance, had been expressly asked to promote this at the Royal Commission by Aboriginal women from Broome in the north and Collie in the south.

In an environment where he sought total control, the mission policy of encouraging marriages, irrespective of caste, was deeply problematic to Neville. It was problematic from the point of view of his long-term objective to 'breed out the colour' but it was also problematic because such marriages formed the basis of segregated, self-perpetuating Aboriginal communities, which were completely antithetical to his goal of eradicating the colour problem altogether. As he would subsequently advertise, settlements would be revolving doors, taking children in and spitting them back out into the community. Mt Margaret was an affront to this agenda, as he noted at the historic 1937 Canberra conference of Aboriginal administrators:

> At the mission stations, the natives are encouraged to multiply by marriage, with a consequent increase in population. The missions are thus able to claim that they are doing valuable work for the natives. Undoubtedly they are doing good work but they keep an increasing number of natives on their properties, whereas the departmental institutions, whilst approving marriages, encourage

the natives to mix with the general community and earn their own living...As a matter of fact, for some years now I have not been able to supply sufficient youngsters of both sexes to meet the demand for their labour.[12]

Mt Margaret's policy of refusing to send Aboriginal girls into domestic service in the towns was also an aggravation. As the work of Victoria Haskins has shown, the domestic service of Aboriginal women was critical to modernising settler societies like Australia.[13] Domestic service became a transitional point for Indigenous girls, a 'liminal space' into which the girls were inserted by the state in order to be absorbed by the majority.[14] As Neville's interjections show, siphoning Aboriginal girls into domestic service would solve at least two issues: the problem of the mixed-descent girl herself, and provision of a much needed cheap and reliable source of labour for white settlers.

Quite apart from his complaint with the missionaries and Bennett, Mt Margaret was worrying to Neville precisely because it represented an alternative to government settlements, particularly to Moore River. Of most concern was the rise of the mission population. By the 1920s Moore River was overcrowded and conditions very poor. There was insufficient food, little education or employment and punitive systems of discipline. Aboriginal people constantly sought to escape or took measures to evade being sent there at all.[15] At around the same time the numbers increased at Mt Margaret, particularly of girls. In just three years their numbers more than doubled from sixteen in 1928 to forty in 1931.[16] Mysie Schenk told Commissioner Moseley that the mission's policy of keeping families intact accounted for the increase:

> Mt Margaret policy was that children should stay in the homes only with the willing co-operation of the parents; that it was better for children to stay in their own country where parents had daily contact with them to nurse, cuddle and talk to them, and where they knew that they were being fed properly.[17]

She argued that this was the reason why Aboriginal parents preferred it to Moore River, a feared and hated place primarily because of the way Aboriginal children were often forcibly removed to it. It was so feared,

Bennett told the Royal Commissioner, that mothers would blacken their part-white children with charcoal to avoid that fate.[18] The Schenks argued that some of the girls who had escaped the settlement were among the first children in their mission homes and among the first to marry monogamously.

For Bennett, the Schenks' policy of not sending girls into domestic service was admirable. In service, she maintained, they suffered great loneliness and 'fell ready victims to those who offered them companion-ship but were out merely to serve their own base ends'.[19] As she had told the Commissioner, their own family and community life was central to Aboriginal people's long-term survival. She argued that half-caste children should be allowed to stay and marry in their own communities, rather than 'starting promiscuous relationships with white people, so that they belong to no-one and have no family ties'.[20] She saw government settlements like Moore River as part of a vicious cycle in the victimisation of Aboriginal women and girls. In this context, and in direct contrast to Neville, Bennett promoted mission settlements as the ideal haven for women and girls living in what she described as a 'borderland of transition'.

Thus, where Neville saw marriage as a way *out* of the Aboriginal community, Bennett and the Schenks saw it as a way *in*, a means of maintaining and ensuring community. Where Neville saw government settlements as the best administrative mechanism in the short term, Bennett promoted missions and village settlements for the long term: 'Our aim', she told Commissioner Moseley, 'should be to raise the native camps into thriving self-respecting village communities, rather than break them down materially by knocking their homes down and spiritually by taking their children and women from them'.[21] The missionaries could work with the Aboriginal people to gradually eradicate the 'bad' in their cultures, while promoting the 'good'. She stressed the way in which missions like Mt Margaret tried to counteract the practices of polygamy, infanticide and witchcraft by showing an alternative, rather than meeting violence with violence. She suggested that the missionaries might also provide role models, particularly missionary wives who could assist the women in childbirth and, with food and security, encourage them in child rearing. By training their charges in the domestic arts and other industries and paying them in cash for all work carried out on the missions, they could promote Aboriginal women's economic independence, the lack of which she identified as another cause of the half-caste problem.

Clearly, the Moseley Royal Commission exposed the divergent solutions of the missionaries and Bennett on the one hand and Neville on the other. Even before the royal commission, Neville had defended his removal of half-caste children to government settlements. The half-caste problem had dominated his concern from the moment he took office. On taking up the position of Chief Protector, he'd been appalled by the laissez-faire approach to Aboriginal affairs in the state, where no one seemed to care and the administration was in disarray. Furthermore, there was little thought about long-term solutions, and even his own attempts to improve conditions were consistently frustrated and side-lined. In response to Bennett's paper on the Aboriginal mother, he said removal was a necessity for so many reasons it was 'futile to mention them'. Describing half-castes as 'wards' and using Bennett's own logic he said that the department was not prepared to see them 'assigned to native husbands already in possession of a wife'.[22] Clearly, Bennett's impassioned defence of the Aboriginal mother did little to move him. The royal commission was a piece in Neville's jigsaw puzzle wherein he would give a range of interlocutors space but would ultimately take the reins and shape policy in the direction he had long wanted it to go.

The missions, and particularly Mt Margaret, represented a further stumbling block to the realisation of his plans. He had made mutterings about his desire to curb them throughout his administration. This was, in part, because he had been specially appointed to get rid of the missions, as Rufus Underwood, the Minister for Aborigines before him, saw them as a drain on Treasury coffers. Clearly, it was also because of Neville's own policy objectives and because, like the problem itself, they required firm control if his plans were to come to fruition. Just before the royal commission, he had publicly suggested the issuing of permits to missions and the submission of standardised teaching programs for government approval. In 1937, following the Canberra conference, he visited Mt Margaret and suggested that if they progressed any further they would be a source of embarrassment to the government.[23]

Once the report of the Canberra conference was released, the Schenks and Bennett characterised the national approach as the 'breed out, die out' policy: letting the full-bloods die out while, at the same time, breeding out the half-castes.[24] They began to comprehend what Neville had meant about the mission being an embarrassment. It also enabled them to contextualise the history of Neville's obfuscation since the early 1930s. For example, he had rejected the intake of full-blood children into the Graham homes and had attempted to withhold his permission for mission-arranged marriages. Furthermore, since the passing of the new Act, the missionaries experienced many bureaucratic impediments to their numerous attempts to commence work in different parts of the state, particularly in the north in the area of the Warburton Ranges. Neville also stripped Rod Schenk of his protectorship.

By 1938 Neville issued his trump card, with the publication of an additional 156 regulations to be administered alongside the Native Administration Act. These included the necessity for missions to obtain a licence from the Native Commissioner (himself) to operate. The licence was conditional on the mission abiding by government directives and could be revoked at any time without the right of appeal. In this way, the missions would lose their independence in much the same way as the Aboriginal people themselves. What followed was an extremely acrimonious battle between church and state, in which Neville attempted to bury Bennett and her charges of slavery once and for all.

II

The vociferous debate which ensued on the matter of the licencing of missions did more to put the Western Australian administration in the spotlight than the revised legislation itself. It brought a variety of concerns to the surface and widened the scope of discussion, with a range of interlocutors from politicians to humanitarians debating the legitimacy and acceptability of such a move. In particular, it precipitated pages and pages of parliamentary debate as politicians understood the move as representing a fundamental breach with the past. Yet, in many ways, it might be understood as unfinished business in Western Australia.

The conflict between Neville and the Mt Margaret missionaries was the latest in a series of crises between the administration and missions which stretched back to the nineteenth century. Indeed, Bennett's and the Schenks' charges of slavery echoed those of Gribble's some 50 years previous which saw him run out of town. However, in the context of the late 1930s, the conflict brought a range of other voices and concerns to the fore as new alliances were formed and battle lines drawn. For Bennett the licencing of missionaries was symbolic of the dictatorial nature of policy in the state. The denouement of her battle with Neville was largely propelled by her critique of him as a departmental dictator who was engineering total control of Aboriginal lives.

Friends and relatives from the camp visiting their children at the Mt Margaret Mission, 1930s, State Library of Western Australia, 009886d.

By the late 1930s she was also able to draw on a stronger support base to press her claims. From the passing of the Native Administration Act in 1936 until her departure from Australia in 1941, Bennett drew strength from an ongoing Aboriginal critique of the system on the one hand and an emerging Labor critique in the eastern states on the other. She also found support from Western Australia's humanitarian community. Particularly important was the Australian Aboriginal Amelioration Association (AAAA), which had been formed in 1932 as an offshoot of the Association for the Protection of Native Races (APNR), and of which Bennett's feminist ally May Vallance was vice-president. They took a pro-missionary stance and were antagonistic to Neville's legislation and the 1937 national absorption decision. Like Bennett, they called for a government-appointed Board of Commissioners to administer the Act to replace Neville's sole power.

In the wake of the Act being passed in 1936, the AAAA launched a journal, *The Ladder,* which became a vehicle for anti-government propaganda. They were particularly perturbed by the low level of par-liamentary discussion on the tightening of restrictions around inter-racial sex, canvassed in chapter four. The reasons given by many members of parliament for resisting this change was the ready availability of Aboriginal women to those who would pioneer the north. It was for this very reason that, under the editorship of Vallance, Bennett contributed a three-part series to the journal between 1936 and 1938 titled 'Native Women as Chattels', in which she repeated all of her previous claims and honed her argument about the victimisation of Aboriginal women. Venting her spleen on the Western Australian administration, she argued that 'Australian Native Policy' worked towards the extermination of the race. She concluded that under the new Act, Aborigines had lost the last vestiges of liberty and that they were virtually held hostage by the dictates of one man. She insisted that the way to liberate Aboriginal people was to eliminate all such legislation. Echoing the words of Aboriginal activist Norman Harris, she called for 'freedom, justice and one law for white and black'.[25]

As this suggests, Bennett was energised by the growing Aboriginal critique which was making itself felt in the southern states at this time. She had encouraged some of her Aboriginal friends from Moore River government settlement to give evidence to the Moseley Royal Commission in 1934. This was novel as very few Aboriginal people had been given this opportunity in the past. At the time, both Neville and Commissioner Moseley, and even her feminist ally Bessie Rischbieth, rejected their testimony as Bennett-inspired. Yet, by the late 1930s, most of her criticisms of living under restrictive government legislation in bleak and poverty-stricken circumstances were being echoed around the country as Aboriginal groups emerged to take up the political struggle. Increasing controls under revised oppressive protection laws were impacting on Aborigines around the country. Indeed, changes to the New South Wales laws precipitated the formation of a new political group, the Aborigines' Progressive Association (APA), with which Bennett was in communication.

She was also in communication with the Australian Aborigines' League (AAL), a Victorian-based Aboriginal organisation under the leadership of William Cooper, of which she was one of the few non-Aboriginal life members. In June 1937, a letter from Cooper was printed in *The Ladder* in which he emphasised his people's disapproval of the policy of absorption as expressed at the Canberra conference. In particular, he rejected the distinction being made between half-castes and full-bloods:

The supposed superiority of the half-castes is not admitted and, in fact, all thought of breeding the half-caste white, and the desire that that be accomplished, is a creature of the white mind. The coloured person has no feeling of repugnance toward the full-blood, and in fact, he feels more in common with the full-blood than with the white…We know that a dark person can do anything he is shown…as well as the white man. Our plea and aim is merely…full equality in every way with the white race.[26]

In November 1937, just after the Canberra conference, Cooper's league sent a petition to the Commonwealth for presentation to the King, imploring the prevention of Aboriginal racial extinction and the need for land, proper food, medical provision, funds, properly trained administrators and education.[27] Just a few months later, Cooper and Aboriginal activist William Ferguson, who was active in the APA in NSW, organised an Aboriginal Day of Mourning in Sydney. This coincided with the Australia Day celebrations associated with the sesquicentenary in 1938. Promoted as a demand for citizen rights, the Day of Mourning was an explicit critique of non-Aboriginal history and practice. It was a demand that non-Aboriginal Australians recognise 150 years of 'misery and degradation' imposed on Aboriginal people by 'white invaders'. Above all it was a critique of the system of protection and its associated legislative edifice, which they described as a system which had their extermination as its end goal: 'your modern day policy of "protection" (so-called) is killing us off just as surely as the pioneer policy of giving us poisoned damper and shooting us down like dingoes!'[28] Their overwhelming demand was for justice, decency and fair play, and equality in education, wages and rights.

The Day of Mourning occurred just months before Neville published his regulations. Bennett travelled to Sydney to participate and, while there, she met members of the Sydney Labor Council who were also supporting the Aborigines' claims. The council had produced a policy statement calling for justice for Aborigines in 1937, which she applauded. In the key areas of land, labour and law, as well as its insistence on parental rights, free compulsory education, and the abolition of slavery and the present administrative set-up, it was remarkably aligned to Bennett's critique. Referring to the white man's 'perversion of history', it spoke of Australia's treatment of the Aborigines as a social crime and called for the publication of the correct view of the historical treatment of the Aborigines. It spoke of the Aborigines' struggle against Australian imperialism and invited white and black workers to unite to prevent 'capitalism exterminating the race'.

It also spoke of defending Aborigines' freedom and building a 'New Australia where the national minorities here and in New Guinea would share in the privileges of society in a parallel manner to the USSR'.[29] By 1938, the council backed Bennett's view that absorption was impractical and undesirable, emphasising the need to respect Aboriginal people's 'pride of culture and race'.[30] One way that they argued this might be achieved was via the setting aside of large tracts of fertile land for the exclusive use of the Aborigines. It was believed that with adequate funds and government assistance for the establishment of farms, these inviolable reserves could become thriving self-governed Aboriginal communities.[31]

Encouraged by these political developments and alliances, Bennett launched the second phase of her campaign. During her visits east, she had developed important connections with people like Jean Devanny, communist stalwart and prominent campaigner for Aboriginal rights. This alliance prompted her to return to the economic dimensions of her thesis. In particular, she began to use the eastern Labor press to publicise slavery in the west. An article in *Workers' Weekly* allegedly authored by Devanny, titled 'Your Dark Brother Needs Your Aid', accused Western Australian 'squatters' of extracting approximately 60,000 pounds annually in Aboriginal 'slave labour'.[32] Heavily influenced by Bennett, if not written by her, it pointed to the lack of education and political and human rights of Aborigines, accusing the police of being some of the most prominent 'slavers'. A week later the contents of an interview between Devanny and Bennett was written up which complained of white feminist complacency and chauvinism:

> That women have not raised Cain throughout the length and breadth of Australia over this matter can only be due to the horrible idea that the Aborigines are different in some way, in their humanity, to whites.[33]

In defending Aboriginal women's rights, Devanny urged white women not to tolerate the removal of their babies.

Heading back home, Bennett stopped off in South Australia to visit Constance Cooke, and published material in the local press concerning the dictatorial nature of Western Australian Aboriginal legislation. She accused Neville of making colour, rather than civilisation, the basis of Aboriginal citizenship and of being a dictator, able to 'arrogate practically irresponsible control'.[34] Neville demanded that she provide evidence for her claims. In a lengthy response, she concentrated on the withholding of Aboriginal wages and interference in their personal lives. She went back to the Moseley Royal Commission, using the evidence of her Aboriginal friends and the personal representations of Aboriginal people who had complained of living 'under the Act'. She provided nine specific cases she was familiar with detailing Neville's interference in the marriage rights of Aboriginal people, going so far as to accuse him of causing the suicide of a young Aboriginal man who was unable to marry the girl of his choice.[35] Her examples included cases of Neville's arbitrary refusal to allow marriages between half-caste women and white men, half-caste couples and between full-blood girls and men of their choosing.

Back in Western Australia she wrote letters to the press and the Anti-Slavery Society criticising the authoritarian nature of Western Australian legislation. She also became embroiled in a full-scale fight with the Department of Native Affairs over the licencing of the missions. After the initial gazettal of the regulations in April 1938, the department shelved them in the face of their widespread unpopularity. They were understood to be a personal attack on Bennett and the Schenks, with various humanitarian groups, including the APNR and the AAAA, arguing that the regulations were also an attack on religious liberty and the rights of British citizenship. The APNR's chairman, Reverend William Morley, questioned their legality.[36] When the government reintroduced them six months later in slightly amended form, a furore erupted as, in an attempt to have the regulations passed and avert the criticisms of certain parliamentarians who were calling for their disallowance, the Minister for Native Affairs and Chief Secretary, William Henry Kitson, delivered a full-scale attack on the missions in parliament. In a very lengthy speech he unleashed a litany of claims about missions and missionaries, detailing stories of abuse, sexual and otherwise, dysfunctional management, and autocratic, immoral and abusive environments.

There were two main reasons for this onslaught. One was to demonstrate why the licencing of missionaries was necessary and the other was to expose the difficulties which the government had had to face in its administration of Aborigines over the years. It was, in effect, a defence of the government and of Neville against a barrage of criticism which the minister argued was the result of exaggerated propaganda both within Australia and around the world. He constructed his defence as the breaking of a silence the government was no longer prepared to maintain. Underpinning both was a statement about the pre-eminence of governmental control in managing the problem and administering policy for 'the native was first and last a charge upon the state'.[37] As he reminded his audience, under the terms of the new legislation all Aborigines under twenty-one were wards of the state. Furthermore, he argued that the licencing of missions was an accepted part of modern governmental practice within the empire. He cited policies in Kenya and South Africa where governments had oversight of missionary activity, and in Canada where the consent of the department was required before any church or mission could be erected on an Indian reserve.

In terms of policy in Western Australia, Kitson identified three key reasons why missions now required a permit to undertake their work. First, the government needed to be able to control the location of the proposed mission. He suggested that this was important to avoid the costly mistakes of the past, citing one of these mistakes as the Forrest River mission in the Kimberley. This had been the site of the Onmalmeri massacre in 1926 which had so energised the humanitarian lobby. Kitson suggested that the site was 'bad' without giving specific reasons.[38] Another mistake was the Mt Margaret Mission. He referred to the criticisms of the mission's location by the pastoralists and argued that, had the government had oversight of its establishment, it would never have been located where it was, as it was wholly unsuitable. The second reason for licencing was because some missionaries encouraged Aboriginal marriages irrespective of tribal law or the result of such unions from the tribal point of view. This was clearly a reference to the practices of the Mt Margaret missionaries and is further indication of the way in which protection of tribal law for full-bloods was as much part of government policy as absorption of the half-castes. It was also why the government needed firmer control of missionaries because, by allowing such marriages, they were contravening government policy. The third reason for licencing missions had to do with a changed dynamic between the governments and missions wherein the former now conceived of missions as government departments and thus formal instruments of policy. Kitson pointed out that under the revised legislation, missions could now be declared institutions with the same kind of power as the Child Welfare Department and that, as a result, they required the same kind of bureaucratic oversight and regulation.[39]

Kitson's unprecedented attack on the missions was therefore about demonstrating why the government needed to take control. In the process he unleashed a catalogue of missionary recalcitrance from the worst excesses of authoritarianism, including examples of brutality and cruelty, to sexual immorality and impropriety, exploitation, incarceration and the appointment of inappropriate personnel. Furthermore, the examples he used, he said, were representative of thousands of departmental files relating to the same. He justified doing this as a defence of the department with which he had been associated for a long time, as well as a defence of Neville, to demonstrate the difficulties faced by the department and particularly the Commissioner, who had to make decisions in an extremely fraught policy environment and who had to bear the brunt of criticism. He also reminded the parliament that the regulations were not new but had been part of departmental thinking for at least a decade.

As this suggests, Kitson's parliamentary speech was extensive and unprecedented. Several members of parliament were stunned by what one described as a barrage of accusations the likes of which had never before been heard in the state.[40] It was, in itself, an example of the fractious and highly tense environment of Aboriginal policy leading up to World War II. Kitson argued that he and the department had had to deal with a huge amount of correspondence and publicity as a result of exaggerated propaganda over the years. This was no longer generated internally. It was now coming from organisations and individuals around the world. In this context, there is little doubt that his attack was about trying to address an imbalance and claw back governmental control. It also demonstrates how the humanitarian critique had begun to take hold and have effect.

Bennett, the Schenks and their supporters saw Kitson's attack as targeting Mt Margaret. Yet, while the mission was mentioned, so were many others. In fact, Kitson singled out Mt Margaret as the only mission that had carried out its work in anything like a reasonably efficient manner.[41]

The bigger problem was the stranglehold that the missions had in the state and particularly the United Aborigines Mission, of which Mt Margaret was a part. It represented half of all missions in the state. More importantly, government officers were outweighed by missionaries with only fifty-five in paid government employment, as opposed to seventy-five missionaries. Apart from the numerical imbalance the problem was the fact that missions were completely unregulated, unsupervised and lacking in proper facilities. Importantly, very few missionaries were properly qualified, lacking any sort of anthropological training.

While this criticism squares with Neville's interest in anthropologically informed government policy and with an attempt to modernise and professionalise practice both in Australia and around the empire, the real problem for the government was mission independence. Mt Margaret was singled out for its lack of cooperation. It was cited as problematic for providing rations to Aborigines who were in paid employment and in not conforming to government policy in relation to the employment of men and boys in pastoralism and girls in domestic service. Where one politician questioned the fact that the government was not cooperating with the Mt Margaret missionaries, Kitson replied that the problem was the reverse: that the missionaries were not cooperating with the government. He pointed to the findings of the Canberra conference in 1937 where the following resolution was agreed to:

> Governmental oversight of mission natives is desirable. To that end suitable regulations should be imposed covering such matters as inspection, housing, hygiene, feeding, medical attention and hospitalisation and education and training of inmates, with which missions should be compelled to conform.[42]

Kitson was thus referring to a whole-of-government agreement on this matter and arguing that, for it to work, missionaries must cooperate with the department rather than contravene policy, particularly where they were expecting continued government financial support.[43]

Clearly, cooperation was the nub of the problem for Bennett and the Schenks as they did not approve of government policy. As Bennett would later write:

THE MISSION POLICY IS IN DIRECT CONTRAST TO
THE DEPARTMENT'S POLICY. The long-range policy of the
department DISPERSES AND DESTROYS. The policy of the
Missions GATHERS IN SETTLEMENTS AND BUILDS UP,
and the family is the unit. In 12 places in Western Australia Mr
Neville has prevented or tried to prevent settled mission work.
THE MISSION POLICY IS IN DIRECT CONTRAST TO
THE DEPARTMENT'S POLICY [original emphasis].[44]

Not surprisingly, Kitson's charges against the missions precipitated a
huge outcry. Of particular concern was his claim that, in the face of such
malpractice, the government had been powerless to act. As Reverend
William Morley suggested to Bennett, if offences had been committed
why had not Neville exposed them and used the common law to prosecute them? Several politicians were demanding a royal commission to sift
through Kitson's charges but the department established a departmental
conference instead. This was essentially a showdown between Bennett,
the Schenks and the administration, although several other missionaries
and church leaders were present. The issues at stake went far beyond the
licencing of missionaries. It became the final scene in the battle between
Neville, Bennett and the missionaries as they launched a counter-attack
on the whole edifice of native administration in the state.

In a lengthy letter to Morley in February 1939, Bennett gave a
detailed account of what had transpired. In the midst of much hostility
and accusation, Bennett and the Schenks provided specific examples of
how the legislation and regulations impacted on Aboriginal lives – proof,
so Rod Schenk claimed, of Neville's dictatorial intentions. They focused,
in particular, on the breakup of families and the removal of children
from mothers, with Bennett declaring: 'Mother love and filial love
alike come under the ban of Departmental disapproval'. Referring to
Neville's promotion of his long-range plan at the 1937 Canberra conference, she described it as long-range murder with 'Bill Sykes in loco
parentis', adding:

This power of splitting up families has been so terribly abused
and has caused so much anguish and terror that I believe the
only safeguard is the application of the same law to natives as

to whites, and meanwhile cases that are difficult – where the children are neglected – ought to be dealt with by a sympathetic *board* on which are women of the highest character…I refer not only to the mental anguish of the mother but to the stunting effect on the child of having been hunted for removal in early years…a mother's love and a father's love are part of the best of God's gifts, and parents should have the right to have their children educated in their own country and keep them with them as long as they look after them properly, *all* the fathers are not white men who deny their children. There are no more affectionate parents than our native people, full-blood *and* coloured too.[45]

These comments related to section 8 of the Native Administration Act which, Bennett said, should be altered to prevent the Commissioner from splitting up families and intimidating natives with the fear of having their children removed.

In the remainder of the letter, she went through other sections of the Act, providing specific examples to show how 'departmental tyranny' affected Aboriginal people's lives. She focused on marriages, conditions of labour, loss of property, the position of women, the lack of education and various legal injustices, singling out police, magistrates and the Crown Law Department as among the 'worst law-breakers'. Conditions of labour was one of her key concerns and the new Act did little to allay this. She described section 18, which provided for the issuing of permits to employ Aboriginal workers, as 'slavery by another name'. Section 64 provided for the payment of wages to a departmental officer or police officer rather than to the worker, with the result that 'many, many natives complain that they cannot get monies due to them by the Commissioner, nor any statement' regarding the same. Particularly concerning was the fact that under this section the department could absorb any monies which had been unclaimed for three years. Related to this was the vulnerable position of Aboriginal girls sent into service. She described them as 'hardly more than children' who often ended up with an illegitimate child as a result of their being trapped in conditions of great loneliness. This was part of a cycle of victimisation and resulted in the removal of their children.

Bennett's letter to Morley was, thus, a detailed indictment of the administration of Aboriginal affairs which she claimed amounted to racial persecution and a violation of human rights. Furthermore, it was thoroughly racially discriminatory. She pointed to section 2 of the Act, which widened the definition of 'native' to include all people with any degree of Aboriginal blood, to demonstrate that the basis of citizenship for Aboriginal people was denial of their Aboriginality, as 'no native associating with other natives may exercise citizen rights, no matter how well educated, competent and worthy he or she may be'. She concluded that her experience was that native and coloured children were as good as white in intelligence, character and appearance, and that they were intrinsically the 'finest material for citizenship to be found anywhere'. She described how most of Neville's Act required either reworking or abolition. Indeed, she argued for a royal commission to review the many cases of injustice it sanctioned.

As well as writing to Morley, Bennett simultaneously penned a memorandum to the Australian High Commissioner, titled 'Justice for our Minority', in which she drew his attention to the 'dictatorship' of the Western Australian native affairs administration and focused on a number of concerns in the administration of justice.[46] A large part of the memo was dedicated to the theme of the compellability of Aboriginal wives in courts of law. This issue was a broader humanitarian concern in the interwar years and is notable as being one of the few, along with the related demand for courts of native justice, to be explicitly addressed at the 1937 Canberra conference of native affairs bureaucrats.

It had largely come to Bennett's attention in the early 1930s in the context of the sensational frontier clashes of the day, involving key Aboriginal male resistors in the north, including Tuckier (Dhakiyarr) and Nemarluk.[47] Both men were charged with murder on the strength of their wives' evidence, a practice Bennett claimed was not only discriminatory, as white women were not forced to give evidence in such cases against their spouses, but open to abuse as the women often had to travel long distances to court under the custody of police. Furthermore, it was hypocritical. While there were few prosecutions of white men for cohabiting with, or having casual sex with, Aboriginal women, there were many examples of wronged Aboriginal men who had been sentenced to life imprisonment or death for killing white men under this provocation and from the evidence of their wives.

Bennett had raised her concern about the position of Aboriginal men and their provocation as husbands in *The Australian Aboriginal as a Human Being* and, as we've seen, her deep concern about the operation of the law was at the core of her critique. The compellability issue related to her, and the wider humanitarian, concern about the dual role of police as protectors and prosecutors. Her particular concern following the eruption with Neville was that, despite a determination at the 1937 administrators' conference that made the compelling of Aboriginal wives' evidence illegal in Western Australia and the Northern Territory, in 1936 and 1937 respectively, subsequent cases were being tried which did not apply the ruling. She wanted the High Commissioner's support in lobbying the Western Australian and federal governments for the review of legal cases involving Aboriginal men who had been sentenced for murder on the strength of their wives' evidence and the release of all Aboriginal men convicted on such both before and after these legal changes.

In her study of native courts of justice in Western Australia, Kate Auty argues that Neville agreed to establish them, as well as recognise the principle of non-compellability, as a way of silencing Bennett and other humanitarian critics.[48] She suggests it was a rather cynical exercise as the principle of non-compellability was only to apply in the native courts and not in all other courts where the majority of inter-racial cases were heard and where the ordinary laws of evidence still applied. Arguably, these developments fitted his desire to preserve tribal law among the full-bloods. It also fitted his sense of himself as a progressive, scientifically informed, administrator as his recommendation for them was influenced by similar courts in South Africa and Kenya which made use of a headman to 'bring in the offender'.[49] However, Auty points out that the courts were anything but just and that in their relatively short life, the ruling on non-compellability was never applied.[50]

Bennett's letters to Morley and the High Commissioner on the eve of the war were pleas for intervention. So critical was she of the system of protection, the corruption it veiled and the practices it legitimised that she argued for international scrutiny of Australia. The only solution, she said, was the exposure of injustice at an international forum like the Hague Tribunal. Calling for a code of international justice in relation to inter-racial relations, she suggested that through this means the names of states judged to fail in administering justice could be listed publicly for the discipline of public opinion.[51] She rejected Neville's 'veiled threats against missionaries who expose injustice', arguing that she had written or said nothing that she would not 'gladly maintain on every possible occasion in the hope and with the prayer that Australia will wake up to their stupid wickedness and reverse their policy and do justice'.[52]

Providing these accounts to external interlocutors was a critical part of her own defence. Morley, in particular, had become an uncompromising crusader for Aboriginal justice in the 1930s and was in regular communication with her, particularly at this time.[53] At the conclusion of the departmental conference in 1939 she also lobbied her other supporters, sending information regarding the Act and Regulations to the Anti-Slavery Society in London, which wrote to the Premier of Western Australia in June 1939 complaining about the far-reaching powers conferred on the Native Commissioner.[54] They argued that the regulations put a different complexion on the Act, stipulating that while section 8 represented a grave interference on family life, the power to control all or forbid any marriages between natives, whether among themselves or with anyone outside, was, as far as they were aware, without precedent under any British government.[55] They urged the suspension of the Act, pending its reconsideration.

Their requests had little effect. While being extremely acrimonious, the departmental conference achieved little. Instead, Neville pursued a campaign to close Mt Margaret, reducing rations, opening Cosmo Newbery as an alternative ration depot, refusing permission for mission-arranged marriages and thwarting the United Aborigines Mission from any further attempts to establish missions in the state. In the midst of a severe drought in 1940 he ordered all 'indigents' and all full-blood children off the mission altogether, leaving it to function as a half-caste home.[56] According to Mysie Schenk, this included people who had been at the mission for over 15 years. The result of this unrelenting pressure, according to historian Anna Haebich, was that Mt Margaret never regained its former position.[57]

Haebich's point is certainly true for the short term, but Neville's regulations did not spell the end of the mission in the long term. According to Mysie, the period at the end of the 1930s and early 1940s was quite productive. In 1939 Rod Schenk built a new five-head battery to replace the inefficient three-head battery built three years earlier for the Aboriginal men to make money from mining. So successful was the enterprise that some of the mission men were able to buy trucks and pay back their debt to the mission store. Others bought houses. At the same time several escapees from Cosmo Newbery found their way back to the mission. Furthermore, the war had increased the demand for Aboriginal labour in the district and the school continued to progress. By 1949 the Education Department supplied the mission with its first full-time, trained teacher. Four years later Rod and Mysie retired, but Rod's son bought some land and established a training farm – the Wongutha Mission Training Farm – under an independent council. In 1982 a new educational venture was established in the goldfields – the Christian Aboriginal Parent-Directed School – where, influenced by their own educational experiences at Mt Margaret, parents developed a network of schools in the region to deliver Christian education to their children.[58]

No doubt Bennett would have been pleasantly surprised and pleased by this outcome, primarily because she thought conditions were so bad on the eve of the war in terms of Aboriginal education. By the end of 1939, Neville's regulations were finally passed retaining the provision for the licencing of missionaries. In March 1940 he retired and by the end of the following year Bennett had gone to London for the war effort. Her distrust of the bureaucracy continued unabated, while she and Neville remained bitter enemies. In the years to come she would warn her comrades to beware of him, for 'he was a real white-ant, whose enmity [was] safer than his friendship'.[59] For his part, Neville blamed Bennett for the straining of relations between the missions and the department, and simply decided not to respond to her criticisms at all. He claimed that they were so one-sided, untrue and fanatical that any counter-claims would fall on deaf ears. He even suggested that to reply to the Anti-Slavery Society, a body which had 'obviously been primed', would be 'beating the air'.[60] In a subsequent account of his absorptionist objectives, he wrote the campaigns of Bennett and other women reformers out of the historical record altogether.[61]

Thus ended one of the most vociferous conflicts in Aboriginal affairs of the interwar years. The story of the rise and fall of the Mt Margaret Mission and Bennett's role in it tells us much about the politics of Aboriginal reform in these years. It reveals a battleground in which Aboriginal lives and futures were fought over with great intensity and passion. A diabetic, Bennett had periods of ill-health during these years and Neville came close to being defeated by his critics.[62] In many ways theirs was a battle of wills. Both had a sense of imperial mission. Both were tenacious, pragmatic and blinded by their own zeal. Bennett's dogged critique and sensational public utterances complicated an already difficult portfolio. Pat Jacobs argues that part of Neville's problem was a squatter-dominated Legislative Council which 'resisted attempts to break the two powerful forces which held the north in its crude organic unity – Aboriginal labour and Aboriginal female sexuality'.[63]

In this sense Bennett's and the missionaries' hostile relationship with the pastoralists of the eastern goldfields did not help their cause or Neville's. His frustration at being unable to act had been one of the most difficult burdens of office.[64] He had first attempted legislative reform in 1929. It took just under a decade to achieve and the Moseley Royal Commission was a critical step in this direction. Ironically, then, Bennett and the Schenks helped to mould his increasingly dictatorial vision and hold of Aboriginal affairs. The law became the primary means of enacting his control and he wielded it like a weapon.

The conflict reveals much about the layers of power in colonial governance and the ways in which they underwrote the problem. It was a fraught landscape. Government administrators, missionaries, employers and land-holders, scientists, academics and concerned citizens shared investment in the problem and its solution. At the formal level governance of Aboriginal people was increasingly ensconced in a tripartite relationship between governments, missionaries and anthropologists, each with their own ideas and practices and each with their own theories of the Aboriginal position and future. Humanitarians added yet another layer. In this context Neville's 1936 legislation and subsequent regulations, and the 1937 Canberra conference at which he and his administrative agenda starred, were as much acts of political containment of these disparate forces as containment of the problem itself. It is notable that neither Elkin, Neville's scientific mentor, nor the missionaries were included in the discussions between Aboriginal Affairs bureaucrats in Canberra in 1937. This was a statement of the power of the state. Science and religion would be made to serve it.

In his study of governance in the Northern Territory, Andrew Markus has argued that the efforts of governments to place tighter restrictions on the missions in the 1920s and '30s was an attempt to rein in the worst excesses of missionary authoritarianism.[65] Certainly, this was the government's defence in Western Australia. The minister justified his convulsive attack on the missions as the breaking of a difficult-to-maintain silence about the way missions did their business. The charges of dysfunction and sexual abuse and impropriety were certainly a tactic to redirect the critique. If the Aborigines needed more paternal oversight so, too, did the missionaries.

The conflict with the Mt Margaret missionaries suggests a more complex story, however, particularly where it seems that the mission was not necessarily the target of the critique in parliament. There is no doubt that Neville's licencing of the missions represented a changed relationship between the two. The truth was that missions had always been useful to the state. In an environment where Aboriginal bureaucracies were consistently underfunded and under-resourced and yet were responsible for protecting Aboriginal populations in remote locations, missions filled important gaps in the administrative oversight of their Aboriginal charges. As Mt Margaret showed, theirs was a reciprocal relationship. The missions were given land and various forms of subsidy, including rations. They took in children and provided local communities with a cheap source of labour. Contrary to Kitson's claims, Neville had sanctioned the establishment of Mt Margaret. In recognition of his compromised position he even tried to keep Schenk and Bennett apart. Yet, he was explicit about where the mission should be and what it should do. What Mt Margaret did became the nub of the problem.

This was largely because of the nature of the problem itself. Like bureaucrats the world over at this time, Neville utilised his administrative power to impose controls and restrictions on people's lives in order to eliminate the colour problem in his midst. This had been identified as one of the most disturbing problems of the new century and, in the figure of what he defined as the despairing, purposeless and inferior half-caste, interwar Western Australia encapsulated it.[66] Neville's burden was to solve it. If science would provide the route, he would mark out the journey and point to the destination.

According to Pat Jacobs, for the pragmatic overburdened administrator in an extremely impoverished bureaucratic framework, who had to deal with growing part-Aboriginal communities on the fringes of settlement in states of acute crisis, biological assimilation became a means of taking active control, a means to an end.[67] However, it was reserved for half-castes alone. As we've seen, Neville increasingly made very clear distinctions between half-castes and full-bloods. His legislation forged and enacted a sexual divide between the two, looking to promote monogamous marriage in the white community for the former and the recognition and maintenance of tribal law in marriage for the latter.

This was completely antithetical to what Bennett and the Schenks were demanding. For them, tribal marriage could sanction forms of violence and repression toward Aboriginal women. This possibility was made worse by their dispossession. The recognition of the human rights of Aboriginal women and girls therefore demanded the reform of tribal marriages. Christian monogamous marriage, sanctioned by the state, would ultimately ensure the long-term survival of the Aboriginal people, providing wives for young men, custody of children and community survival. Of course, it would also mean the state's intervention in Aboriginal domestic arrangements. The Schenks and Bennett justified this as humane intervention for communities in crisis. For Bennett it was also about the latest international thinking on this question. Here was a moment when it was possible to throw the spotlight on the ways in which contact between cultures had impacted Aboriginal women's lives and to demand their advancement along with Indigenous men. Neville's controlled marriage schema was not about the protection and advancement of women or the rights of mothers. Rather it was about the protection of white society at the expense of the black.

At the crux of the different approaches of Neville and the missionaries and Bennett, then, was a different way of defining the problem and its solution. Where Neville saw the issue in terms of race and colour, Bennett and the Schenks saw it in terms of human rights as they defined them. It was about social and cultural change and modernisation. For Bennett, Neville's law was a form of direct rule and was therefore antithetical to the central aims of benevolent trusteeship. But it was also deeply racist. Although there was a growing mixed-descent community at the mission, there were also full-blood communities either on the mission or camped nearby. The experience of the Mt Margaret community was that if they were despairing, purposeless and inferior it was because the colonisers had caused it and current policies were exacerbating it. The education program at Mt Margaret was an explicit rejection of their supposed inferiority. Both Rod Schenk and Bennett saw the full-blood children as talented and as capable of education as those of mixed descent. Indeed, like many humanitarians of their day, they saw in the full-bloods even greater promise than the half-castes, as they were 'uncontaminated' by whites. Rejecting Neville's racial categories, they argued that all Aborigines, whether full-blood or half-caste, were vulnerable and needed education, employment, land, food and their own communities if they were to survive in the long term.

From the beginning of her crusade Bennett had defined the colour problem as the most important of the twentieth century. From the outset she described the solution as the founding of a just relationship between black and white. As she said in the midst of her battle with Neville, this was about justice, freedom and one law. Fundamentally, then, it was about non–discrimination and racial equality. For Neville, it was increasingly about two laws and about discrimination. Neville's distinction between half-castes and full-bloods was as important to his long-term solution as the biological absorption of the former. Recognising tribal law in marriage was not just a policy solution, it was a means of taking back control and re-establishing his paternal authority. A key part of this was projecting himself as an informed, professional Aboriginal affairs adminis-trator applying modernist, scientifically grounded, principles to a difficult and delicate task.

In this context, the showdown with the missionaries signalled the increasing intrusion of the state in the control of the problem. It was not that missions were no longer needed. Indeed, as Kitson intimated, in the postwar world they would be relied on even more as conduits of policy. Mt Margaret – and Mary Bennett – had taught the state a lesson, however. For the new policy of absorption to work, missions needed to become modernised and professionalised. They needed to be brought under state control to work effectively as an arm of government, as a new, disciplined and more tightly controlled apparatus of the state. Yet, the battle over

Aboriginal affairs was far from over. The contest in the west would go some way to fuelling a postwar humanitarian critique which saw both dictatorial government control and the postwar administrative and legislative framework as part of the ongoing problem.

7

HUNT AND DIE
Saving the Race from Extinction

Why should the Aborigines not be taught to earn their living in the more profitable ways – herding, gardening and other industries – and hunt only of their own volition, not because they are starved into it? To persist in the laissez-faire policy and force the Aborigines back to the hunting stage from which they are emerging is to become guilty of race extermination by starvation and infanticide.[1]

In 1950 the Anti-Slavery and Aborigines' Protection Society published a pamphlet penned by Bennett called 'Hunt and Die: the Prospects of the Aborigines of Australia'. The crux of her argument was that, if left to hunt as their only means of survival, the full-blood remnant would surely die. For her, this question of imminent Aboriginal extinction was wrapped up in anxiety over Aboriginal education, particularly for the full-bloods. The future looked grim without food and without education or training. She had returned to Australia briefly, in 1947, to witness the opening of a school at the Roelands Mission in Western Australia. One of her ex-pupils, Gladys Vincent, was the teacher–missionary in charge. Bennett paid three subsequent visits to the mission that year and wrote a glowing reference of the work being done and the achievements of Vincent to the Roelands Mission Council. While there, she supported another of her ex-pupils, Dora Quinn, as she worked towards becoming an accredited missionary. When Dora's examinations were over, in late 1948, Bennett organised a visit to Ernabella mission in central Australia which had been established by her good friend, Charles Duguid, a decade earlier.

Her return coincided with a heightened discourse around the Aboriginal problem precipitated by British rocket testing at Woomera in central Australia. Humanitarians were concerned about the impact of this on the Aboriginal people of the region, including those occupying the

Central Aboriginal Reserve. Leading the charge were the Duguids. Like Bennett, they were deeply worried about the demoralised condition of Aborigines in the centre and north and shared Bennett's concern about the long-term viability of the full-blood remnant. Both believed that the war had exacerbated their vulnerability. In notes that she sent to Duguid before leaving Australia in 1941, Bennett argued that what Aborigines needed was 'education and sustenance to tide them over the transition from communal stone-age conditions to our competitive industrialism'.[2] After the war this message seemed even more pertinent and saving the Aborigines from extinction even more pressing.

Gladys Vincent, about to board the train after being accepted at the Roelands Mission Farm, State Library of Western Australia, 010013d.

Concerned by what she saw and learned of the ongoing threats to Aboriginal survival, Bennett wrote 'Hunt and Die' with a sense of urgency. At the heart of it was a critique of the 1937 Aboriginal welfare conference and its resolutions. Revisiting them, she sought to expose governmental neglect, accusing them of race extermination via a laissez-faire approach to the full-bloods. She argued that, in their straightened circumstances, including drought, to leave the Aborigines to their own devices would lead to their death through starvation and infanticide, a practice which she maintained went hand-in-hand with a hunting life. She quoted extensively from the conference report to demonstrate that the bureaucrats involved were well aware of this. The only way to alleviate the condition of the full-bloods, she said, was for intervention in the form of a large vote of money for training to rebuild 'their shattered hunting economy'.

By 1950 her critique of the conference and her concern with the future of the still numerically strong full-blood remnant in the north resonated with similar concerns by a small but growing clutch of humanitarians similarly disaffected by the decisions of 1937. The Duguids were part of this but so, too, were people like Olive Pink and Tom Wright of the NSW Labor Council and Donald Thomson, a leading anthropologist with extensive fieldwork in the north. Like Bennett, this group saw the postwar Aboriginal problem as about the transition, adaptation and survival of the remnant full-bloods in the north as much as equality and citizenship for the mixed-descent people. A key part of this was a concern with the viability of Aboriginal economies and the need to both preserve and respect tribal culture while encouraging development.

In part this was a discourse of decolonisation. The very idea of *rehabilitation* for Aboriginal people, which surfaced in the war and immediate postwar years, signified a conceptualisation of the Aboriginal predicament as similar to the conditions of people in war-torn Europe or colonial territories in need of recovery and rebuilding. It was also an incipient model of development. The immediate context for 'Hunt and Die' was the growing drift of Aborigines from reserves in Arnhem Land and the western and central deserts after the war. The principal reason for this migration, Bennett supposed, was food as well as the material goods of white men's stations and settlements. She argued that it was conditioned by dispossession in the first place and the disruption of the tribes by the war, which caused the concentration of whites on tribal territory and the 'impressment' of Aboriginal labour in the Australian Native Labour Corps.

As this suggests, war once again entrenched the deep concern with non-Aboriginal civilisation's contaminating influence. In fact, the experience of the holocaust and Hiroshima propelled a discussion about how the 'tribal past' could meet the 'technological present' sympathetically. It was in this context that Bennett's earlier concerns about the clash between two different civilisations – communal and competitive – and how to effect change in the former justly and humanely came to the fore. Bennett's former ideas about the need to both preserve and develop

Aboriginal societies resurfaced in arguments about a policy that would ensure Aboriginal futures. Her relationship with the Duguids and her experience of Ernabella was critical to this second phase of her critique.

I

Bennett's departure from Australia in 1941 was clouded by the intense battle between herself, the missionaries and the bureaucracy. She left Australia, railing against conditions, and used the time back in London to shore up her defences for the Aboriginal cause. At the point of her departure the humanitarian landscape was changing, new alliances were forming and the critique was deepening. Bennett was an active participant in this process, having made contact with a burgeoning Aboriginal and Labor critique emerging in the eastern states by the late 1930s. While she was embroiled in her battle with Neville a significant group of people, including some anthropologists, missionaries and feminists, as well as parts of the Labor movement, were deeply troubled by the resolutions regarding the future direction of Aboriginal policy by administrators in 1937. Furthermore, conditions in Western Australia were becoming more widely known, due largely to Bennett's protestations and the furore over licencing the missions. When John McEwen in the federal government announced a New Deal for the Northern Territory on the eve of the war, there remained an unease about government policy. It was from this group of disaffected people, including Bennett, that the postwar advancement movement was built.

The 1937 Canberra conference and the 1939 New Deal represented governments' collective response to over three decades of humanitarian critique and agitation. As we've seen, the interwar humanitarians had focused on the north. There was a desire to see a completely reformed administration and federal control for what was regarded as a national problem. Both government responses were evidence of the dent that the critique had made before the war. Governments had to respond, they had to claw back control and they had to define the terms of an Aboriginal future. While sidelining most of the humanitarian concerns, the major recommendation of the 1937 conference was that the mixed-descent community would be absorbed (biologically) into the Australian community. This represented a profound contraction of Aboriginal and humanitarian demands and concerns.

Two years later, the New Deal genuflected to citizenship for Aboriginal people, suggesting that training was the key and reserving this goal for the half-castes and 'fully detribalised' in the Northern Territory. The latter was defined as in contact with European civilisation, on pastoral stations and/or living around the towns. The New Deal left the myalls or 'natives living in a tribal state', of which there was still a significant number in the Northern Territory, out of the equation at least for generations to come.[3] If they were to get citizenship they must become detribalised first, and this was projected as a long way off. In the meantime they would be subjected to district stations, styled 'centres of hope', which would provide 'intensive control and administration' in outback regions, via district and patrol officers and native constabulary.[4] The employment conditions of Aboriginal people in the north were largely to remain the same. In particular, missions and stations would continue to act as employment reservoirs for non-Aboriginal industry. Like the 1937 resolutions, there was no mention of land for Aboriginal people, either then or in the future, and there were no details about how the projected inclusion of Aboriginal people in the north would eventuate.

However, one of the ways the New Deal resonated with the continuing humanitarian critique was its concern with transition. The aim of policy in the north was to turn a nomadic people into individual citizens living settled lives. By the end of the 1930s most people who were engaged in the politics and discourse around the Aboriginal problem believed that the Aboriginal future lay in their integration or sympathetic adaptation to the broader Australian community. The question was how could or should this be achieved and for what ends. The answer depended on definitions of the problem in the first place. At the heart of the humanitarian critique had been a concern that if the system of protection was to stay in place, the future looked grim for Aboriginal people. All were driven by an appreciation of the fact of dispossession and all believed that detribalisation led to demoralisation. Rejecting the notion of their inevitable demise, humanitarians were on a salvation mission, an attempt to prevent the extinction of the race while there was still time. While most groups recognised reserves as important, it was only the members of the Aborigines' Protection League (APL) in South Australia, along with Mary Bennett, who saw land and some form of self-determination as vital to an Aboriginal future there.[5]

As we've seen, the views of Bennett and the APL reflected the central dictates of imperial humanitarianism. Indeed, Bennett's 'Native Policy for Australia', which she took from the findings of the 1929 East Africa Commission report, helped shape the ideas of the APL. The Commission addressed native policy under six core principles: land, economic development, labour, education, and political and administrative institutions. Reserving adequate areas of land for native use was regarded as the first charge on the government because, in part, such reserves would help to protect natives from economic exploitation:

> If the native peoples are left in indefeasible possession of sufficient land, not merely to afford them the bare possibility of existence but to provide them with an adequate opportunity to improve their standard of living according to their capacity...For the government can then say to the natives 'you are not to be deprived of the opportunity to gain an adequate living on your land'...If you wish to continue living according to your own traditions in a native community you can do so and if you leave your land to work for wages elsewhere, it will be of your own free will and not because you are forced to do so as your only means of earning a living.[6]

Furthermore, land and labour were intimately connected to the notion of native advancement which the Commission argued should be considered an end in itself. Indeed, the paramountcy of native interests was defined as 'the creation and preservation of a field for the full development of native life'.[7] The concepts of development and advancement were thus built into the notion of responsible trusteeship, for the alternative, in the eyes of the commissioners, was 'a policy of consistent and perpetual repression'.[8] Under the influence of the functionalist anthropologist Bronislaw Malinowski, particularly his concern with the effects of culture contact, the emphasis moved from preservation for its own sake to an acceptance of cultural change and the progressive adaptation of natives to new conditions. As Porter puts it: 'Indirect rule was not a policy of static non-interference, but a way of breaking the African in, slowly and gently, to modern civilisation'.[9]

Theoretically at least, land was understood as the 'indispensable foundation of native advancement' because it would be the means of both preserving culture and providing a resource for economic development.[10] According to the East Africa commissioners, the government was required not merely to set aside adequate reserves for native use but to provide resources and assist them to learn new methods of agriculture and stock-raising. This would give the natives protection from economic exploitation by immigrants and provide them with a measure of choice. But advancement was not to be at the expense of native institutions. The principle was preservation and development on their own lines and the ideal was to preserve 'all that is good in the arts and customs, the social and political organization and the moral code which they already possess and to build up from that foundation'.[11]

As this suggests, the recommendations of the East Africa Commission were based on the *a priori* assumption that the land was African territory. The colonisers were immigrants and the ideal was a dual policy involving the complementary development of native and non-native communities. Government regulation of relations between the two was at the heart of the issue. Yet, governments in Australia were not preoccupied with these kind of questions when it came to determining Aboriginal policy. Despite humanitarian protestations, governments didn't talk about or accept the responsibility of a trust. Nowhere were native interests considered paramount. The connection between questions of land and labour went largely unremarked and, apart from the New Deal, the concept of native advancement as an end in itself was anathema, at least till after the war. When it was recognised, as in the New Deal, it was a long-term objective which was apparently never intended for the full-blood remnant. While mentioned, education was not a priority and an appreciation of the importance of culture was minimal. Nowhere was there a sense that governments paused to ask themselves what some critics and humanitarians had, both here and in England. In Porter's terms the question was how should the empire govern its colonies in the interests of *both* native peoples and immigrant communities?[12]

One of the key reasons for this was because, in Australia, governments were not operating from the recognition that the land was Aboriginal territory. Unlike many of the humanitarians, governments did not see dispossession as the *a priori* issue. The Aboriginal problem was not a problem of colonial governance or of dispossession as such. It was about the management of a problem population with limited resources. By focusing on absorbing the half-castes and leaving the full-blood remnant alone, as the 1937 resolutions did, and by focusing on the detribalised and aiming to further that process of detribalisation while leaving the full-blood remnant alone, as the New Deal did, the governments of the day were totally ignoring what for people like Bennett was the principal focus. Full-bloods could have citizenship, too, so the bureaucrats said, but only once they became detribalised, and the governments were hoping to stall this process for as long as possible.

For Bennett and a handful of others the government was therefore doing little about a viable long-term future for Aboriginal people which avoided the detribalisation of old. In openly repudiating the New Deal, Olive Pink and her Labor activist colleague Tom Wright encapsulated this concern:

> The problem of coping scientifically with the tribalised and semi-tribalised natives can never be solved on the basis of repeating past methods used on the present detribalised natives. We must envisage a policy whereby there will be no demoralisation at any stage. This can be accomplished only by very gradual internal changes brought about by the aborigines themselves over a long period; the gradual development of their tribal life to a new social organisation, under the control of the members of the tribe and their own leaders and in step with their gradual assimilation of new ideas conveyed to and discussed with them by special 'advisers', not 'converters', or 'dictators' and with benevolent aid from the Government of the Commonwealth.[13]

As vice-president of the New South Wales Labor Council, Wright had led the Labor campaign for justice for Aborigines in the late 1930s described in the previous chapter. Six months after the federal government released its New Deal, he published his own 'New Deal for the Aborigines'. In it he argued that leaving full-blood people out of the equation without some program for their gradual development was consigning them to no future at all. Indeed, there was even the view that the 'inclination of those in authority was to aim at the elimination of the race by means of a gradual but planned "vanishing" and the physical absorption of the remnants into the white population'.[14]

As we've seen, Bennett shared this view. In correspondence with Pink following the Moseley Royal Commission she applauded her use of the phrase 'Commonwealth-wide camouflage' to describe Aboriginal affairs.[15] Pink used it when raging against the widely popularised concept of a 'vanishing race', the view that Aboriginal extinction was an inevitability. She believed that notions of race suicide were camouflage explanations for the real conditions causing depopulation of the full-bloods, and that venereal infection of women and poor government rations for the old and infirm were more reasonable explanations.[16] She was, in turn, impressed with Bennett's notion of a 'conspiracy of silence' about the real conditions in which Aboriginal people lived and worked, and in which policy was enacted. Both Bennett and Pink likened the situation of the Aborigines to that of the Jews, Bennett referring to a Nazi complex in Australia.[17]

Certainly, the general tenor of discussion regarding the full-bloods at the 1937 conference was an acceptance of the theory of their inevitable demise, if not through natural decrease or detribalisation, through eventual physical absorption. Professor J. B. Cleland pushed for resolutions for half-castes only, adding, 'any suggestion of a deliberate attempt on the part of the Conference to hurry up the detribalisation of the full-bloods would offend scientific and sentimental sensibilities'.[18] For the disaffected this was profoundly concerning as they saw detribalisation as part of the problem rather than the solution. Their determination to save the race represented a sort of inverted eugenicism where what mattered most was not protecting the purity of the white but that of the black. However, embedded in the latter was a relativist appreciation that culture, or what Constance Cooke referred to as 'racial respect and initiative', mattered to the survival of a people.[19] The experience of the holocaust pushed this notion further. This was why concepts of preservation and development appealed as, theoretically, the latter did not have to be at the expense of culture.

Furthermore, as Aboriginal culture was bound up in land, the provision of land or inviolable reserves was fundamental to their advancement and development. While emphasising land as the foundation of advancement, the East Africa Commission argued that territorial segregation might be needed for a time in the interests of native paramountcy. It was this principle which propelled the Model Aboriginal State in 1927. However, J. C. Genders did not see segregation as the ultimate goal of the state. As I argued in chapter one, following the Canberra conference in 1937, he retrospectively justified his proposal as following the principles of indirect rule. As he said at the time, the Model Aboriginal State represented his attempt at an alternative form of administration to direct rule where native interests were subservient to the dominant European population. That he retrospectively reiterated his original intentions indicates his angst over the direction of policy in 1937.

Governments were aware of British colonial policy, too. Indeed, just months before the Canberra conference they were sent a copy of the Anti-Slavery and Aborigines' Protection Society's land trust proposal which was a model statement of the core ideals of imperial humanitarianism. It argued that the way forward on the Aboriginal question depended on the right solution to the land question. Citing the indigenous people of South America, Bechuanaland, Canada and South Africa and the nomadic tribes of Kenya and Tanganyika, the society believed that the prospects of the Australian Aborigines were not significantly different to these groups. It argued that in all these territories the indigenous population was emerging from their 'backward' stage of history, learning modern methods of rearing stock and showing an interest in agriculture. According to the secretary of the society, the land trust proposal was built on the work of Dr Herbert Basedow, who had previously recommended the return of territories to Aborigines in order that they 'work out their own destiny'.[20]

On this basis, the society suggested that governments develop reserves by means of Aboriginal labour under white trusteeship. They envisaged a chain of self-supporting cattle stations right across the northern half of the continent. For the more settled regions they suggested smaller blocks of good farming land provided by the state in a number of localities, placed in the hands of trustees on behalf of the Aborigines and provided with schools and other communal amenities. Central to the principles of the land trust system was that the area of land set aside should be able to provide sustenance for the indigenous people and so be capable of development. They argued that title to the reserved lands should be securely vested and placed in the hands of a Board of Trustees, consisting of knowledgeable and sympathetic men and women who would protect the inhabitants from intrusion and secure the delimitation of boundaries.

At the 1937 conference J. W. Bleakley, Chief Protector of Aboriginals for Queensland, was the only administrator to genuflect to the ideas of the society, even suggesting that its proposal stemmed from the example of the mission reserve system in his state.[21] He described at length Aboriginal reserves in northern Queensland vested in trustees representing the department, where self-governing communities lived in well laid out villages and maintained themselves by gardening, fishing and gathering bush foods. He cited the native settlement at Cowal Creek in the Cape York region where some 20 years previously, the 'remnants' of the Seven Rivers and Red Island tribes had formed their own settlement with cottages, a teacher and self-government via their own councillors and police. Bleakley described this as a thriving, self-governed, self-sufficient village settlement.

Indeed, the Queensland government had been the only one to put the matter of the 'protection of nomadic tribes, their gradual development to self-dependence and restoration of racial pride' on their list of items to be discussed at the Canberra conference.[22] Bennett applauded Bleakley's appeal and argued that the idea of promoting village communities provided the only alternative to the policy of 'breeding out the colour'.[23] She had advocated such a scheme in her evidence to the Moseley Royal Commission, arguing that localised village communities on good arable land in the Aborigines' 'home districts' were far preferable to removing Aborigines and dispersing families to government settlements. She suggested that at least fifty such territories were needed in Western Australia alone, equitably spaced throughout the state. Similarly, the Association for the Protection of Native Races had long argued that Aboriginal labour should be utilised as far as possible to improve, and make self-supporting, Aboriginal reserves.[24] It saw the Cowal Creek settlement as a disavowal of the governments' oft-repeated objection that Aborigines could not be made cultivators.[25]

However, the federal government maintained that this could not be done. It dismissed the society's proposal by insisting on the peculiarity of the Aboriginal problem in Australia, the failure of past experiments based on a similar model, the impossibility of Aborigines living in permanent settlements on account of their nomadic lifestyle and the improbability of them becoming cultivators.[26] Yet, there had historically been examples of thriving Aboriginal farming communities, particularly in the southeast. Indeed, at this very moment Aboriginal representatives from these very communities were appealing to the federal government to rethink the decisions of the 1937 conference. The petition from the Australian

Aborigines' League to the King requested his intervention to prevent the extinction of the race.[27]

This petition was taken up by a small fraternity of people in London, who were also concerned with the direction of policy on the eve of the war. A letter was sent from the Committee on Applied Anthropology of the Royal Anthropological Institute in London to the federal government detailing their reservations.[28] This critique was led by W. E. H. Stanner, Alfred Radcliffe-Brown, Reverend A. Capell, Phyllis Kaberry and Donald Thomson, all of whom had scientific knowledge and experience of Australian conditions. They pointed to the lack of adequate funds and properly trained administrators.[29] They suggested that poor diet and insufficient health and medical supervision were central to the problem. Arguing that the provision of inviolable reserves should be a cardinal point in all Australian policies, they criticised the violation of largely unpatrolled Aboriginal reserves by agricultural, maritime and commercial interests. They believed that all of these things were exacerbated by lack of reliable information and European attitudes to Aborigines. Stanner even went so far as to suggest that most of the resolutions of the 1937 conference were 'tragically irrelevant to the main problems'.[30]

Donald Thomson was by far the most passionate critic of the government's New Deal. He had been given the task to investigate Aboriginal conditions in Arnhem Land following the inter-racial unrest associated with the Caledon Bay affair in 1933.[31] Afterwards, as patrol officer and anthropologist, he was to discover the causes of unrest and depopulation and obtain scientific data on the cultural and social organisation of the people which could then form the basis of policy. His subsequent report, presented to the government in 1937, outlined recommendations for future policy in the Northern Territory.[32] These were based on the imperative of saving the remnant Aboriginal population in the north. In particular he argued that if the government really meant to 'save these people', steps must be taken to ensure their segregation on inviolable reserves, as well as the preservation of their culture. Citing the East Africa Commission Report, he argued that all native reserves be administered solely in the interests of the Aborigines themselves and that their culture and institutions be retained as *integrating* forces.[33]

In correspondence to a feminist friend in Australia between 1939 and 1940 he detailed his bitterness at the direction taken by the government of the day, as well as its attitude and treatment of him. He described how he saw his peace mission in 1935 as a means of 'proving the case' for the Aborigines, demonstrating that there were other approaches to solving the Aboriginal problem than police dispersals and settler might.[34] He believed that his work in the region would open the way for him to become the new administrator of native affairs and to completely reorganise the administration. He felt profoundly betrayed when the department appointed E. W. P. Chinnery instead, arguing that he had been used for press propaganda and to save them from embarrassment, but that they had turned a deaf ear to his chief recommendations.[35] He maintained that this was demonstrated by the government's shafting of his report and singling out of his policy of segregation for attack and distortion, as well as its claim that he had been unable to advance any definite policy at all.[36]

II

Bennett's relationship with the Duguids solidified at this moment, too, as they shared a deep concern with the direction of policy and the long-term survival of the remaining full-bloods. Bennett had been writing to Duguid, on and off, since the early 1930s, but in the context of her bitter feud with Neville their alliance strengthened, as she sent him regular detailed updates about Neville's law and administration. He shared her concern over the decisions taken at the 1937 conference. It, along with the conditions in the west, formed part of the backdrop to his establishment of Ernabella, a mission in central Australia under the auspices of the Presbyterian church which was strongly influenced by the central planks of the imperial humanitarian ethos.

His interest in the Aboriginal question had been stimulated when, as a young doctor, he examined a female missionary who had contracted leprosy in the north from the Aborigines in her care and told him of their deplorable condition. After a survey of the region he was convinced of the need for a mission to act as a 'buffer zone' between white and black, to prevent the spread of disease and the further demoralisation of the Aboriginal population. A precipitating factor was the need to check the breeding of mixed-descent children and what he subsequently described as the 'inhuman' and 'irresponsible' attitude of many white men in the area.[37]

As this suggests, the Duguids shared Bennett's angst about the status of Aboriginal women, which became more acute in the context of the military build-up of the north in preparation for war. These concerns were exacerbated by the tenor of debate in the Western Australian Parliament about the changes to section 43 of the new Act dealing with the regulation of and punishment for inter-racial sex, as canvassed in chapter four. By the time of the Canberra conference in 1937 there was also much concern over reports of the traffic in native women along the northern coastlines, the so-called black slave trade from Cairns to Broome.[38] In the light of this, the fact that the administrators made no new resolutions about the protection of Aboriginal women in 1937 was deeply worrying.

The position of Aboriginal women was on the agenda of the conference but it occasioned very little discussion. Administrators generally congratulated themselves on the stringency and effectiveness of protective laws, while nevertheless noting the difficulties of conviction in cases of inter-racial sex and cohabitation. Carrodus, secretary for the Department of the Interior, thought that it was satisfactory merely to have on record that the subject was discussed at the conference and no resolution was passed.[39] The issue of Aboriginal women's legal compellability as spouses was resolved satisfactorily, at least superficially. However, the equally long-running feminist campaign for the appointment of white women protectors in the north did not fare so well.[40]

This had been the signature feminist campaign of the interwar years, which was supported by an international feminist demand for women to have greater roles in the welfare and protection of vulnerable women and children worldwide. From the humanitarian perspective this was about reforming the whole edifice of protection. Not only should the positions of police and protector be separated but Aboriginal women needed the assistance and care of white women. The feminist demand in Australia was also part of an empire-wide demand for women to have greater responsibilities in administrative and governance roles within native administration. This was an extension of the widespread concern about adequate protections for women during World War I, an experience which precipitated the demand for women police. Indeed, feminists in Australia cited developments in women policing as a template for women protectors in the north.

The demand for women protectors was echoed across the interwar years as white women attempted to make a difference in the lives of Aboriginal women. It demonstrated how critical the position of Aboriginal women was to white women's conceptualisation of the problem and its solution, and it was the subtext of many notable battles between men in positions of power and women seeking access to it within native administrations. It is what linked Bennett's story with several other women including Daisy Bates, Olive Pink and Annie Lock, as well as others on the periphery of the administration in these years. They generally found a wall of opposition from male bureaucrats. Neville's experience of Bennett underpinned his implacable opposition to women having greater protective roles within the administration. After a short debate at which the very idea of women protectors was ridiculed, the administrators at the Canberra conference agreed that they would 'serve no good purpose'.[41] On the eve of the war, there were fewer women than ever within the policy environment and their views on the greater protection of Aboriginal women were completely marginalised.

It was in this context that Phyllis Duguid (Charles' wife) decided to investigate conditions first-hand and, following an exploratory trip to the north with several other feminist friends, she established a new organisation, the League for the Protection and Advancement of Aboriginal and Half-Caste Women, in 1938. On one level this was symptomatic of the recalibration of feminist input on this question following the Moseley Royal Commission. Duguid was state president of the Woman's Christian Temperance Union, which took up this question with much gusto in the late 1930s. It was also symptomatic of the leading roles of Charles and Phyllis Duguid in the cause of Aboriginal reform at this time and through the war and postwar years.

Not only did the league become the home of a developing rights discourse for Aborigines, but also Phyllis took a lead in feminist circles in promoting Aboriginal advancement. Indeed, in the context of the times her league was a ground-breaking development. It was the first humanitarian group in Australia to include the word 'advancement' in its title and it was an important bridge from the pre-war to the postwar advancement model of reform. Indeed, the first national humanitarian lobby group to emerge, the Federal Council for Aboriginal Advancement, was built on the template of Duguid's original league.

As the Duguids and Bennett promoted it, advancement was an antidote to the view of inevitable Aboriginal loss and decline which they felt underscored policy decisions in 1937. It was also primarily targeted to the full-blood community. Just as Daisy Bates promoted her vision of a futureless Aboriginal race in her bestseller *The Passing of the Aborigines* in 1938, Bennett, the Duguids and others argued that this needn't be their fate. They critiqued the government notion of detribalisation as, if not obliteration, on the road to it. As Phyllis declared, Aborigines were not dying where they were not being exploited or mistreated.[42] Through the league the Duguids promoted alternative solutions.

League for the Protection and Advancement of Aboriginal and Half-Caste Women

PUBLIC MEETING

Thursday, November 23rd
at 8 p.m.

at the

Institute, North Terrace

Lady Muriel Barclay-Harvey has graciously consented to be present

An Illustrated Lecture

will be given by

PROFESSOR HARVEY JOHNSTON

"The Aboriginal Woman of Australia"

VOCAL ITEMS BY ABORIGINAL GIRLS

Chair to be taken by Mrs. Chas. Duguid, B.A.

COLLECTION

The Future of the Aboriginal Women Concerns Every Australian Citizen

League for Protection and Advancement of Aboriginal and Half-caste Women

Illustrated Lecture

Native Peoples in the Post War World

with films showing the NEW DEAL FOR RED INDIANS and its importance to AUSTRALIAN ABORIGINES

by

Dr. A. GRENFELL PRICE

Chairman Dr. C. DUGUID

Tuesday, October 9th, 1945
at 8 p.m.

The Institute, North Terrace

Collection in aid of work for Aborigines

The Aborigines are our responsibility
Come and hear about them

Hon. Secretary A. F. Hollidge, 24 Westall Street, Hyde Park

Flyers advertising events hosted by Phyllis Duguid's League for the Protection and Advancement of Aboriginal and Half-Caste Women.

Indeed, while an explicit response to the failure of the women protectors campaign, in advancing the cause of full-descent as well as half-caste women, Duguid's league cut straight across the 1937 governmental resolutions. The administrators were not concerned to do anything proactive for the 'myalls', nor were they concerned about the position of women. In founding the league, she identified 'salvation of the race by compensating them for the loss of their means of subsistence' as the driving force. This was really important because critical to the Duguids' concerns was that it was not sufficiently appreciated just what the loss of their own means of subsistence entailed for Aboriginal survival.

The loss of a means of subsistence had been a critical part of Bennett's understanding of the problem, too. The loss of land meant the loss of an economy – and of food. This not only made Aboriginal people vulnerable to starvation but to a host of other problems in its wake, including disease, infertility, migration to stations and towns, economic dependence, including the prostitution of women, and social and political vulnerability. Drought further exacerbated the problem. The Duguids and Bennett shared the view that, because of these conditions, nomadism and hunting alone were not viable in the long term. Leaving them alone for generations to come was therefore an inhumane and unjust policy. As Charles Duguid declared following a patrol to the Petermann Ranges in 1939, wherein he surmised that the fate of a few hundred Aborigines had been death by starvation, nobody on that patrol advocated 'that the natives are best left entirely alone'.[43]

The Duguids' particular concern was the Pitjantjatjara community in the northwest of South Australia with whom Charles had made contact following a trip to the region in 1935. He found the people the 'finest and largest group of unspoilt natives in the whole of the Interior'.[44] It was for them that he established Ernabella mission in the Musgrave Ranges. The mission was intended to provide the Aborigines with a chance to survive in their own country and to act as a buffer between them and the 'encroaching' white man, to 'stop the native coming in to the South–North line, and the East–West line, and to stop the white man going further into tribal territory'.[45] The purpose of such buffers was to 'ensure that the inevitable interchange between the two cultures would be as slow and gradual as possible'.[46] Duguid saw land and security of tenure for the traditional owners as key in this process because, as he put it, 'all the principal features' of their 'father's country' are related to their life and well-being.[47]

This insistence on land was what linked Ernabella to the Model Aboriginal State concept. In taking up the presidency of the APL in 1935, Charles Duguid remained true to its foundation ideals of self-government and land for Aborigines. In this way, the philosophy of Ernabella had a strong lineage to the ideas of Wood-Jones and Basedow in the late 1920s and the Anti-Slavery Society in the 1930s. Yet, as Duguid's biographer, Rani Kerin, has shown, this adherence to the principle of land as a means of stemming detribalisation, as it played out at Ernabella, was problematic.

The fact was that Ernabella did not prevent the migration of the Pitjantjatjara to stations and urban centres for white man's goods. Worse still, from the point of view of Duguid's strong condemnation of the 'sub-nutrition' of Aborigines, Ernabella was dogged by claims of uncleanliness and malnutrition and there were disagreements between missionaries and superintendents, the mission board and the South Australian government about who was at fault for the deficient diet. Part of the problem, as Duguid and Bennett both saw it, was the lack of government support. For Bennett, the missionaries who educated Aborigines should be supported primarily because they were filling a deficit in government responsibility. Duguid was of the same opinion, arguing that the churches needed the support of governments, particularly in terms of finance and in advancing the interests of Aborigines as human beings rather than passing 'legal sanctions to increase the control of the white race over them'.[48]

The important point was that the Duguids and others like them believed it was possible and desirable to engineer and control the processes of contact. Ernabella was, in part, a response to what Duguid perceived as governmental neglect. Described as the 'biggest scheme yet devised for assisting the Aborigines, Duguid saw it as an alternative to the direction of policy promoted by administrators in 1937.[49] The Duguids believed that the decisions of the Canberra conference had revealed the governments' collective desire to wash their hands of their responsibilities. Empathising with Bennett's crusade, Charles Duguid criticised A. O. Neville's Regulations as inhumane, seeking to deny Aboriginal 'racial purity'.[50]

In *The Ladder*, Duguid argued that a mission to the Aborigines must be run on similar lines to Christian missions in the mandated territory of New Guinea, where missionaries learned the language of the indigenes and tried to develop an understanding of culture clash from their perspective.[51] Rather than 'ruin them spiritually and socially' by policies of absorption, he advocated respect for native custom, keeping families intact, and cooperation between tribal elders and missionaries.[52] Central to the constitution of the Aborigines' Advancement League was the encouragement of Aboriginal people in an appreciation of and pride in their cultural heritage.

Hence, evident in the Duguids' promotion of Ernabella was the same concern with detribalisation, gradualism and 'development on their own lines' in the formulations of Bennett, Wright, Pink, Thomson and the Anti-Slavery Society. The major difference was that it was mission controlled, and Wright and Pink repudiated all missionary activity in favour of an entirely secular, scientifically informed administration.[53] In that sense, it conformed more closely to the British model. But it also conformed to Thomson's ideal of a buffer station, established by missionaries on the outskirts of reserves to prevent the entry of outside influence.[54] Like Thomson, the Duguids stipulated an intelligent and sympathetic approach. Ernabella was to protect the Pitjantjatjara from further intrusion by white men. But it was also to provide a conducive environment for their 'inevitable transition' by protecting the 'myall native' from too sudden an introduction to twentieth-century 'competitive civilisation'.

As this suggests, the Duguids were also strongly influenced by Mary Bennett's considerable writings and ideas, particularly *The Australian Aboriginal as a Human Being*.[55] It was Bennett who had informed Charles about the misappropriated bequest to the Presbyterian church that was intended for a mission to the Aborigines but was spent on the Australian Inland Mission for the white settlers. Such knowledge was a significant spur in the establishment of Ernabella in the first place. Their relationship solidified at the time of the Moseley Royal Commission when Bennett sent Charles copies of her own and Aboriginal people's testimony, at around the same time that he was investigating conditions in the north. Their relationship was further strengthened during Neville's attack of her and the missionaries. She continued to send him her notes, archives and evidence right up to her death.

During her battle with Neville, Bennett sent Duguid detailed notes on the 1936 Western Australian Native Administration Act and how it discriminated against Aborigines. This caused him to write to the Chief Secretary in Western Australia in his capacity as president of the APL. He argued that Neville seemed 'unsympathetic to the native', that he was 'strangely unmoved by the human appeal of the family' and that 'breeding the dark colour of the native out of the state population' seemed his 'guiding motive'.[56] That he was deeply concerned about conditions in the state and what they demonstrated about the direction of policy was evident in his 1941 publication, *The Future of the Aborigines of Australia*, where, in a section headed 'Western Australia's Reputation', he focused almost exclusively on the lack of education for both mixed-descent and full-blood children and cited Bennett's work at Mt Margaret as the standard for teachers to Aborigines elsewhere, including Ernabella.

In the late 1920s Bennett had been the APL's London representative and her ongoing friendship with the Duguids was part of this historic connection. Furthermore, the Duguids belonged to the same transnational circuit of imperial humanitarian reform as Bennett. They were both deeply religious, of Protestant faith, and moved in the same missionary and humanitarian circles. Indeed, in 1937 Charles was in London presenting papers on Ernabella and the role of the church in solving the Aboriginal problem at the Royal Empire Society and a conference on church and state at Oxford University. He was a corresponding member of the Anti-Slavery Society and the APNR, occasionally presenting papers to the former. During the war and postwar years the Duguids and Bennett constituted part of the subterranean politics of Aboriginal reform. Their friendship and allegiance continued to be conditioned by their sense of themselves as moving against the grain. Charles once referred to defending the Aboriginal cause as a form of warfare.[57] Similarly, on more than one occasion, Bennett referred to the hostile influences one must persevere against in defending Aborigines.[58] Both defined Aboriginal rights as fundamental human rights and both advocated advancement via economic security, including land and paid work, education, employment, medical care, adequate food and citizenship.

By the late 1930s Bennett and Duguid also shared a particular view about segregation. A decade earlier, and still from her base in England, Bennett promoted segregation as the only solution for the Aborigines in the north. It was why she supported the Model Aboriginal State and it matched a wider humanitarian appeal for the same. In this context segregation meant segregation pending transition to social and legal equality with whites.[59] For her it also meant the necessity to keep a communally based culture away from a competitive one until such time as they had the resources to meet the latter on terms of equality. Yet, segregation did not preclude development. As we've seen, Bennett had long been a promoter of Aboriginal advancement. Furthermore, as Genders argued, the Model Aboriginal State had always had a component of development in its aims.

However, following the 1937 Canberra conference, segregation in government hands was seen as part of the problem because it meant preservation of full-blood tribal people or supervision of so-called semi-civilised people *without* any prospect of development or advancement. It was not the Thomsonesque idea of segregation pending future, sympathetic develop-ment and it was not the model of advancement promoted by the Duguids. Nor did it conform to Bennett's idea of land, food and education for all.

She had great admiration for what the Duguids were attempting at Ernabella. Following the East Africa Commission, she had long since argued for more reserves and territories for Aboriginal people to develop for themselves. In one of her first papers to the feminist community in Western Australia, she earmarked Kunmunya, a Presbyterian mission in northwest Western Australia, as a first-class native administration precisely because Reverend Love conserved all that was 'good in native culture while enabling the natives to acquire what they needed from ours'.[60] She had visited the mission on her fact-finding trip along the Western Australian coast in 1930 and even compared it with Lugard's administra-tion in Nigeria. She said that Love consulted the 'chiefs' and the children lived with their parents, often going bush for holidays. In this way, they did not lose their English but gained 'their own language, their tribal history and traditions and knowledge of tracking and hunting'. Love encouraged the naming of children with their own 'expressive' names and encouraged their own songs and dances. She compared this administration with contemporary practice:

> Compare with this clean happy life of freedom of expression the disruptive effects of a dormitory system which I have seen else-where, little native girls taken away from their parents and herded together, growing up without root and with a coarseness which appears in endless fights and recriminations. Yet the girls are intrinsically as good as one could find anywhere. The initial evil is in the criminal presumptuousness which substitutes for family life a dead system of segregation of the sexes, morbid inhibitions which do not fail to produce a crop of morbid reactions.[61]

Despite her glowing account of Kunmunya, the fact was that Love did not share Bennett's commitment to education. It was partly because of his reputation as a sound and humane administrator that he was eventually appointed to Ernabella in 1941. However, as Kerin shows, his time there

was not the resounding triumph hoped for, in part because of his intransigence about preserving tribalism at all costs.[62] Love resisted attempts at
education and training for the Pitjantjatjara because he saw them as agents
of detribalisation. Whereas Charles Duguid not only characterised the
school at Ernabella as one of its greatest successes, he came to understand
the value of a bilingual education. Indeed, in *The Future of the Aborigines
of Australia* he itemised land, respect for their own culture, medicine and
first-class education as crucial to the future of the 'myalls'.[63]

For Bennett, education was a vital tool for Aborigines' long-term
survival. Despite the issues and problems at Ernabella she saw it as an
ideal reservation, an example of sympathetic adaptation, where full-blood
people learned to blend the old with the new.

> Ernabella mission runs sheep to provide instruction, employment
> and meat for the Pitjantjatjara tribe who would otherwise starve
> in time of drought. One industry leads to others: thus the new
> herding industry, which complements the old hunting industry,
> does not end with its main employments – shepherding for the old
> people and shearing for the young man – but by providing wool to
> spin, it is preserving the ancient handicraft of the women.[64]

Indeed, she had a hand in this process herself, having helped initiate the
craft industry there while on a visit to the mission in 1949. During her
stay she taught the older Aboriginal women to spin wool by adapting their
traditional spinning methods and the younger ones to weave it into rugs,
mats, cosies and the like. She subsequently praised the policy of cultural
maintenance and development of the Pitjantjatjara at Ernabella as in stark
contrast to that of laissez-faire adopted by Aboriginal administrations
in 1937.

III

That Bennett nursed a deep unease about the position of the full-bloods
was evident in her extensive publicising of the removal of full-blood
children from Mt Margaret just before she left Australia. This episode
appears to have had a galvanising effect on her as she disseminated a
detailed account of it through her humanitarian networks, including

Charles Duguid, the Anti-Slavery and Aborigines' Protection Society, the National Council of Civil Liberties and the League of Coloured Peoples in London, who subsequently wrote to the Agent-General in Western Australia as well as the Save the Children Fund. When Rod Schenk subsequently wrote about it, he intimated that it had had a profound impact on Bennett, devastating her.[65] Indeed, it might well have been what precipitated her return to England.

What concerned her most about this particular episode was not just the denial of education to these children but how, in the face of drought and consequent dearth of food, it revealed the government's lack of concern for their very survival. In her detailed account of the event she countered each of the departmental justifications for removing the children from Mt Margaret: that they were being separated from their parents; that their parents were being attracted away from the departmental ration depot; that being nomads, the children were disqualified from receiving the Child Endowment payment requested by the mission on their behalf; and that education was not desirable for 'tribal natives' or necessary for those classified as 'semi-civilised'. She believed these justifications camouflaged the facts and her extensive notes on the affair were an attempt to set the record straight.

As she told it, at the end of 1940, there was a large camp of bush natives about a mile and a half from Mt Margaret who had been in touch with white civilisation for 50 years:

> The parents and grandparents of these children have been detribalised for fifty years, and if these children are not educated and cared for, they become easy prey for whites, as the number of first-generation mixed race children proves. Illiteracy and nomadism do not constitute tribal life. Many white people on the goldfields are fully as nomadic as many Natives.[66]

Furthermore, it was a time of drought and they were starving. She argued that far from the children being separated from their parents, the parents wanted to leave their children in the mission homes to be fed and educated. She maintained that the parents voluntarily left the children at the mission and, being camped nearby, were in constant touch with them. They were able to remove them at any time and take them away on holidays:

the parents came and went as they moved around the country and they saw their children and always took them with them during their holidays. The children were not separated from their parents any more than a white child in a boarding school is separated from its parents.[67]

In a letter Schenk wrote to the editor of *The West Australian* newspaper some years later, he reiterated that they had taken the children into the mission 'on the desire of the parents', saying that Bennett and all the missionaries could 'bear witness that the parents begged us to take these children'.[68] He also wrote that 'we have never taken children by force from any parents'.[69]

Bennett maintained that when the children came into the homes and school there was no breach of the Native Act or Regulations. Schenk was merely observing a practice that had always been followed and he informed the department in writing of the new admissions. However, after several months, wherein the children had begun to respond positively to education, the Commissioner of Native Affairs ordered the children away from the mission citing the objections listed earlier. She argued the fact that they did not immediately go to the ration depot at Cosmo Newbery, established by Neville as a means of attracting them away from Mt Margaret, demonstrated that the 'starvation ration' was not worth staying for.

The objection to the mission obtaining Child Endowment, according to Bennett, further demonstrated the government's strategic definition of these children as nomadic. She argued that the objection did not apply while ever they were at the mission. However, under the terms of the legislation Child Endowment was not to be paid to tribal and nomadic people. As Bennett said, 'the only way to disqualify these poor children was to make them nomads again by ordering them to be put off the mission and sent to the departmental ration depot where there is neither school nor hospital'. She maintained that the fact the department ordered their transferral as it simultaneously transferred some half-caste children from Cosmo Newbery back to Mt Margaret was proof, not of their impartiality as the government implied, but of the plan to isolate full-blood Aborigines and prevent their education 'even when they have become detribalised'.

In the story of these children and their parents were all the issues Bennett had long since raised about dispossession and its consequences

and about the departmental obstacles to Aboriginal survival. It demonstrated how critical economics was to her understanding of Aboriginal
vulnerability. The loss of land meant loss of an economic base but the
denial of education meant the loss of a future earning capacity. When the
department declared that education was not needed for semi-civilised or
tribal natives, Bennett countered that this contradicted the Declaration
of Geneva which stated that 'the child must be put into a position to
earn a livelihood', adding, 'to refuse, or to stop or to hinder education of
full-blooded Aboriginal children who are in touch with civilisation is to
condemn them to die of starvation'.[70]

After her experience at Ernabella in 1949 she developed her economic thesis still further, adding another key demand for postwar justice:
the prevention of the extermination of the full-bloods by 'rebuilding
their shattered hunting economy' and 'giving them a new interest in life
through work'.[71] At a picnic in the Musgrave Ranges with about twenty
children she witnessed the difficulty of their obtaining food by hunting.
The children travelled many miles and returned with five or six small
lizards. This experience fuelled her publication, 'Hunt and Die'. In it she
argued that the problem for the remaining full-bloods in the central and
western deserts and in the north was that because of dispossession and
environmental conditions, their hunting economies were shattered. Not
only was there no food, nor was there any determination on the part of
the government to reverse this process. Instead the desire was to 'keep the
Aborigines in the hunting stage' and so compass their death.

She quoted Charles Duguid on the connection between poor diet and
disease. Duguid referred to the fact that, even in good seasons, the people
were not getting enough to eat and the lack of fat in their diet contributed
to yaws and a form of blindness.[72] Bennett also quoted a medical inspector
of Aborigines in Western Australia who argued that the decreased resistance to disease and considerable mortality rate of Aboriginal people in
epidemics of what were mild diseases, was due to a seriously deficient
native diet. To this Bennett added the fact of infanticide. Quoting from the
anthropologist A. P. Elkin, she argued that hunting depended on a balance
between numbers and food resources and this was why infanticide was part
of the hunting life.[73]

Her characterisation of infanticide as a 'fact' of hunting life was
devoid of moral sentiment or censure. Indeed, she was quick to decry

any critique of Aboriginal women, adding, 'they love their children as much as white women love theirs'.[74] As we've seen, Bennett also had first-hand knowledge of the practice at Mt Margaret Mission. In drawing attention to it, her purpose was two-fold. Firstly, she wanted to emphasise how hunting in such difficult environmental constraints put pressure on the population base and particularly the women, and secondly, that this was something that governments well knew. She went back to the 1937 Canberra conference report for her evidence, stating 'that hunting is not equal to maintaining life – because hunting depends on restricting the native population by infanticide – is the clear evidence of Mr Bleakley, Mr Neville, Dr Cook and Professor Cleland'.[75] Selecting key quotes from the report by the administrators, she argued that Aboriginal people's position was exacerbated by the policy of laissez-faire adopted by administrators before the war. She also earmarked some of Bleakley's evidence, arguing that he understood the fact that encroachment of white civilisation on the natives' hunting grounds made a purely nomadic life impossible.

Indeed, in 1937, Neville, Cleland and Cook all agreed that, if left to themselves, the 'problem' of the full-bloods would solve itself. Neville singled out starvation and their own tribal practices, including infanticide and abortion, which left the women sterile, as the cause of their decimation.[76] He argued that these tribal practices were the direct result of a lack of food, adding, 'in a bad season in the north practically no children are reared, while in a good season the number may be fairly considerable…if there is food, the children are fed and looked after'.[77] Cleland cited low numbers among the Aborigines of the Musgrave Ranges, suggesting that it would be more economical to leave them alone than to improve them socially.[78] Cook argued that if a policy of laissez-faire was adopted the full-bloods would be extinct within 50 years through disease, including the sterilisation of the women through gonorrhoea, as well as starvation. Bleakley alone argued for a form of benevolent intervention because contact with whites was already occurring. He argued that while 'we' had no right to destroy their national life, nor could they be left entirely alone, particularly because of the precariousness of their means of subsistence.[79]

For some time Bennett had referred to the extermination of the Aborigines, the long-range policy of murder and the Nazi-style administration in the west. In 'Hunt and Die' she explicitly charged the administrators with race extermination. The fact that she could characterise Australian

Aboriginal affairs policy as genocidal in 1950 is partly symptomatic of the times. The United Nations (UN) Declaration of Human Rights had been ratified in 1945 and its convention on genocide had been ratified in 1948. Her book, *Human Rights for Australian Aborigines*, published in 1957, went on to detail at least seven principles of the UN Declaration of Human Rights that did not apply to the full-bloods, starting with the right to life, liberty and the security of the person. Yet, in 1950 when 'Hunt and Die' was published, she was basing her view on a policy document which was dated some 13 years earlier. Given the slow pace of reform in Aboriginal affairs this was reasonable. The Canberra conference was described as an 'epoch-making event' at the time and subsequently.[80] However, it occurred just before the outbreak of war, before the New Deal and before the rise of an explicitly human rights agenda for Aborigines.

On one level, by 1950, her comments were rehearsing an old refrain. It is fair to say that they were a product of her Western Australian experience where she had claimed that the policy of the department was the 'disappearance of the native race'. She found Neville's evidence in the 1937 Canberra report some of the most disturbing. Not only did he use the occasion to criticise the missions once again, he openly advertised all the features of policy which she had so long campaigned against in terms of his custody and removal of children, his control of Aboriginal marriages, the lack of wages and his policy of absorption. Yet it was his comments regarding the full-bloods that she singled out in 'Hunt and Die'.

So the question remains: was it laissez-faire and did he intend race extermination in the way Bennett was inferring? If anything, his statements revealed an underlying thread in the report which might be summed up as commission by omission. The problem, he said, would solve itself. Full-bloods would die out through natural decrease and where they didn't, they would eventually be absorbed. They posed little threat which he represented as a good thing because ultimately the problem as he defined it was one of cost. The state could not afford to keep them, particularly as all resources were required to solve the problem of the half-castes first and foremost. The administration in Western Australia, he said, was ridiculously underfunded.[81]

In fact, Bennett's and the Schenks' old epithet 'breed out and die out' is a good summation of the key resolution of the Canberra report. The administrators defined their task as the eradication of the colour problem in

Australia but the full-bloods were not the pre-eminent problem of colour in the way the half-caste and detribalised were. Whereas all administrators at the conference agreed that the full-blood population was either in stasis or going backwards, the half-caste and detribalised, by contrast, was understood to be increasing at alarming rates. In his opening comments at the conference Cleland summed up the anxiety felt by all:

> The number of half-castes in certain parts of Australia is increasing, not as a result of additional influx of white blood, but following on inter-marriage amongst themselves, where they are living under protected conditions…This may be the beginning of a possible problem of the future. A very unfortunate situation would arise if a large half-caste population breeding within themselves eventually arose in any of the Australian States.[82]

It was also Cleland who pushed for some sort of special resolution on behalf of the full-bloods. In fact, he advised inviolable reserves for them so as to *prevent* their detribalisation precisely because, if they became detribalised via the 'admixture of white blood', they would constitute yet another problem population and increase the expenditure on the state.[83] Like Neville, Cleland was deeply concerned about cost. The special clauses for the full-bloods in the Canberra report demonstrate that the policy was to separate them from half-castes and try and leave them alone. There was little intention of doing anything about or for them. The entire focus was on the detribalised, and the longer the tribal people could remain tribal and, thus, not constitute a financial burden, the better. Yet, as Cook pointed out, this model of supervision was problematic. While he characterised a laissez-faire approach to the full-bloods as 'repugnant', he promoted absorption as the middle ground between the extremes of laissez-faire and protection, the latter merely resulting in an Aboriginal population that was likely to swamp the white.[84]

The point is that all who attended the conference knew that the result of their policy towards the full-bloods would mean either their eradication or their detribalisation. While the end or elimination of the full-blood was the desired result, the fate of the full-bloods was a source of anxiety because the administrators were aware that they walked a fine line. On the one hand they didn't want to upset 'sentimental or scientific sensibilities' and, on the other, they didn't have the money to commit to detribalisation. At the same time, the possibility that they might survive and grow, as Cook thought might happen in the north, was even more worrying. 'If we meddle', said Cook, 'we shall be raising another colour problem'.[85]

Thus, the best that can be said is that the full-bloods fell through the gaps in 1937. The problem was almost too hard and there was a sense that it was left unresolved despite a detailed listing of the expected movement of the full-bloods from uncivilised to semi-civilised to detribalised in the report. There was never a sense that this journey would be for adult and elderly natives so classified, however. The final end, if it were to be achieved, was for children of the detribalised who lived near the white community to be educated to become workers in low-level jobs which would not bring them into conflict with white workers. This was evident in a coded census of full-bloods undertaken in 1961, the year of Bennett's death, which was an enumeration based on their distribution in industry. At that stage, the national full-blood figure was 36,137.[86]

In this sense the key resolution of the conference revolved around the half-castes because they were considered easier to address. This was also more pressing because it was about race and colour, whereas the full-blood problem was about the tribe. In any case it was felt that working on the former would help solve the latter in time. As Cleland observed, 'we would achieve exactly the same object in the ultimate if we dealt first with natives of less than full-blood.'[87] But the whole premise on which the administrators' objectives rested, for either the full-blood or half-caste, was Commonwealth financial assistance to the states which, 'unless extended', would 'bring discredit upon the whole of Australia'.[88] When the New Deal was published two years later, as a statement of Commonwealth responsibility, it targeted the Northern Territory only. It did little to change the status quo while funding arrangements in the states largely remained unchanged. Furthermore, despite the rhetoric of assimilation, it did little to change the edifice of protection which had been in place since the turn of the century.

To that extent Bennett's subsequent characterisation of policy in the Northern Territory as 'between laissez-faire and protection' was quite right. The one thing she agreed with the administrators on was money. To enable the full-bloods to survive, she said, required 'a large vote of money'.[89] I wrote at the start of this chapter that the alternative solutions for the full-blood remnant put forward by the likes of Bennett, the Duguids, Wright, Pink and Thomson represented an incipient debate about humane intervention in relation to the Aboriginal problem. While the emphasis varied between each, they were all propelled by a desire to save the Aborigines rather than see them die out. All presupposed some form of intervention at some point, even Thomson's model. All justified it on the basis of dispossession and colonialism. As Bennett said, 'since, humanly speaking, help can come to the Aborigines from the white people only, the attitudes of the white people have to be faced as well as the needs of the tribes and their drift in search of satisfaction'.[90] If they were completely at odds with governments, their efforts were nevertheless absorbed into and underwrote the growing demand for Aboriginal human rights in the postwar period.

Humane intervention was what Bennett had been calling for ever since she penned 'A Native Policy for Australia' and *The Australian Aboriginal as a Human Being* in 1930. To her particular concern for intervention in the lives of Aboriginal women the governments insisted on non-interference in Aboriginal domestic relationships where those relationships were still classified tribal. At the time of Bennett's slavery allegations, Neville argued that there was little 'we' could do for full-blood women in respect of their subjection to their husbands, as 'we' were not responsible.[91]

Yet, the whole premise of absorption was intervention in the lives of those classified detribalised and half-caste. Indeed, the freedom Neville was extending to full-bloods, including preservation of tribal law, sat rather oddly with the stretch of his controls over the lives of half-caste people. Presumably the right to such intervention was because 'we' were implicated in the majority of cases. In some respects the decision to leave full-blood Aboriginal people to their own devices in 1937 worked along the same trajectory: non-interference in tribal ways which were so different to our own, non-interference in the domestic concerns of others. Was this a tacit acknowledgement of Aboriginal sovereignty and 'domestic' jurisdiction? Non-interference in the domestic affairs of another nation or nations was an entrenched practice in international law and one that the Australian state jealously guarded for itself, particularly in relation to race. It is still a critical issue in debates about humanitarian intervention around the world.[92]

Acknowledgement of Aboriginal sovereignty was not what propelled governments in 1937 , however. Bennett argued that the principal attraction of leaving full-bloods alone was that they would be the cause of their own undoing. If this was the case, it was an incredibly pragmatic, even opportunistic, policy and the justifications crude indeed: we couldn't afford them. The discussion of the administrators in 1937 suggested we couldn't afford them either in the financial sense or in the social, cultural and demographic sense.

It is worth noting that, at the time Bennett wrote 'Hunt and Die', the federal government was aware of the accuracy of her claims. A 1946 report detailed the appalling working conditions, squalor, poverty, endemic malnutrition and poor health, low birth rates and high infant mortality rates of Aborigines on cattle stations and army settlements across the north. It also documented high rates of cohabitation between white men and Aboriginal women and a gradual but continual migration of bush Aborigines to centres of European life. Commissioned by Vesteys, a large pastoral company employing Aboriginal labour, the concern was to stop the marked decline in numbers to ensure a future labour supply in the north.[93]

Interestingly, the recommendations made by the Berndts, the anthropologists who undertook the survey and penned the report, resonated with the alternative humanitarian solutions represented in this chapter, particularly the core ideas of preservation and development. The Berndts suggested economic security via the gradual introduction of a wage economy, and a measure of independence via the maintenance of community structures, education and training, diet and 'an interest and faith in life and living'. In this sense they were drawing a vital connection between population increase and well-being, where the latter was bound up with prospects for a viable future. That future, according to the Berndts, would not necessarily occur under an assimilationist framework alone. Rejecting the idea of inevitable decline in the face of European contact, they recommended the welding of introduced ideas and actions onto the traditional Aboriginal background.[94] The funding for such a scheme would come from the company itself (Vesteys), as it 'controlled such a large portion of north Australia' and was thus in a financial position to underwrite these changes, but it would be developed in cooperation with the administration.[95]

At the time of researching and writing the report, the Berndts complained of handicaps and difficulties, not only in terms of the company's own interests but from settler suspicion and hostility. Indeed, it was largely because of these that they terminated the survey and decided to postpone the report's publication. When they finally got around to publishing in its entirety, nearly 40 years later, they titled the book, *End of an Era*, taking up C. D. Rowley's view of the war as representing a new phase in Aboriginal relationships with other Australians.[96] As he, and they, recognised, it was the question of Aboriginal labour that would largely underwrite this change. In this sense, Bennett's long quest for economic justice became much more relevant to a developing postwar reform agenda. Indeed, she used an abbreviated copy of the Berndts' report, published by Archibald Grenfell Price in 1949, to return to her slavery thesis in *Human Rights for Australian Aborigines*, her next and final publication.[97]

It was the advent of an internationally sanctioned discourse around human rights which also signalled the end of an era. Whereas, in 1937, Cleland characterised entreaties like Bennett's as sentimental, this was a little harder to sustain after the war in the context of the formulation of global human rights standards, wherein her claims seemed disturbingly serious. This she readily understood and exploited, writing to Duguid from England asking how the denial of education to Western Australian full-bloods squared with the 'Declaration of Geneva concerning the rights of the child to be put into a position to earn a livelihood' and that the 'child must be brought up in the consciousness that its talents must be devoted to the service of its fellowmen'.[98]

Indeed, as the Canberra conference demonstrated, human rights were anathema when it came to the full-blood Aborigines on the eve of the war. Were they even considered fully human? In the conference report they were variously described as 'one of the wonders of the world', 'a neglected race' and an 'untouchable population'.[99] While there was agreement, in 1937, that there was little possibility they would survive as such for the long term, whether or not they would survive as detribalised permutations rested on the Commonwealth's shoulders – and depended on money. As the following chapter will show, the human rights of Aborigines and the quest for national responsibility would become interwoven in the postwar years and Bennett would continue to play a pivotal role.

8

DEFENDING FATHERS AND SONS
Human Rights for Australian Aborigines

The Aborigines were not a dying race till white people made them die by refusing them the most elementary human rights.[1]

Broken hearts of Rachels, of fathers who have been dispossessed of their families strew the whole way of Aboriginal life.[2]

When Bennett came back to Australia for good in 1951, she returned to a landscape which was both familiar and new. On the one hand, the administration of Aboriginal affairs had changed little despite the new postwar rhetoric of assimilation. On the other, the humanitarian landscape had changed and new influences and alliances continued to shape Aboriginal rights discourse. The ideas which emerged during the war years, explored in the previous chapter, were emblematic of this changing terrain. Indeed, it is impossible to tell the story of the final stages of Bennett's life without recognising it as part of a shifting landscape of rights-based reform and activism. Critical to this was the discourse of human rights. Where the League of Nations had put the condition of native races around the empire on the international agenda in the interwar period, the United Nations (UN) carried it further, becoming the new hope for postwar justice for racial minorities around the globe.

If, as Don Watson has argued, a campaign for Aboriginal human rights emerged on the national scene in 1946, Bennett's role had been crucial to its development.[3] Human rights had always underpinned her critique but the more conducive environment of the postwar years saw it become the central and explicit focus of her continued efforts. While, in the decade leading up to her death, she recapitulated her central ideas her efforts were now being more widely recognised and applauded. Her well-worn defence of Aboriginal human rights was part of the reason for this, as was the economic dimension of her critique which dovetailed with a developing postwar humanitarian agenda. In detailing the last decade of Bennett's life, this and the following chapter demonstrate not only her continued influence after the war and the focus of her final years, but also how her work informed a heterogeneous group of advocates who were committed, in varying degrees, to peace, civil and human rights and social justice.

I

Bennett's last trip to Australia was an interesting time to be in the country in general and Western Australia in particular. The rocket range affair had sparked an impressive groundswell of humanitarian anxiety. The joint British/Australian defence project would see the firing of rockets from Mt Eba in South Australia across the northern portion of the Central Aboriginal Reserve to 80-mile beach on the northwest coast of Western Australia, between Broome and Port Hedland. Humanitarians criticised the project as inimical to the approximately 1,800 nomadic Aborigines of the Central Reserve. Here was a full-blood community whose reserve was being violated. While the Duguids were concerned about the 'sudden and rough' contact between the white workers of the military settlements and the Aborigines who still inhabited the region, they also worried that the rocket range would set a precedent for further incursions on Aboriginal land.[4]

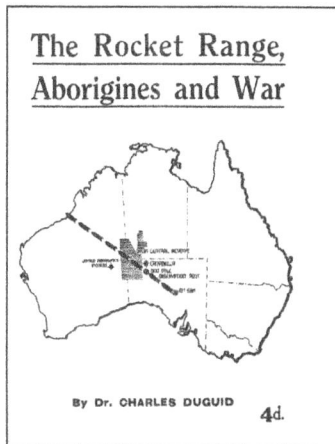

One of Charles Duguid's pamphlets protesting the rocket range, showing the impact on the Central Aboriginal Reserve.

The anxiety over the rocket range might well have been exacerbated by the dramatic events in the northwest where a group of Aboriginal workers in the Pilbara region had gone on strike just months before. This was part of a groundswell of Aboriginal opposition to unequal economic conditions and wage injustice after the war which saw strike activity right across the northern half of the continent in the 1940s and 1950s from the Pilbara in the west to Darwin in the north and Palm Island in the east. This was exactly the region which had been earmarked by the Anti-Slavery and Aborigines' Protection Society, at the turn of the century, as the 'slave zones of modern Australia'.[5] The strikers were requesting a minimum wage of 30 shillings a week, as well as better living and working conditions and the abolition of the Native Administration Act (1936). They were also requesting the right to elect their own advisers and representatives, which related to the charging of Don McLeod, the white miner, unionist and friend of the Aborigines who they had chosen to represent their demands to the administration. For associating with them, McLeod was charged with breaching the Act. He was fined and two of the Aboriginal leaders, Clancy McKenna and Dooley Bin Bin, were arrested and jailed for allegedly enticing Aborigines from their employment.

This was a very significant moment in the history of Aboriginal rights. It was very important to Bennett because it vindicated so much of what she'd been concerned with for so long, not only in terms of her critique of the legislation but also her critique of Aboriginal working conditions. It also demonstrated that the labour movement was finally getting on side. As we've seen, the economic position of Aboriginal workers had been a key concern of Bennett's from the start and it was those sections of the Native Administration Act which dealt with Aboriginal employment about which she was most scathing before leaving Australia in 1941. She styled section 18 of the Act as legalising and disguising slavery by indenture.[6] Aboriginal people could be imprisoned for leaving service and they could be forced back to work. Many of her Aboriginal friends had complained to her that the permit system of employment also prevented them from getting work on their own terms and that they were constantly hounded by police for the same.

That this issue had not left her upon her departure from Western Australia in 1941 was evident in her continued efforts on this front once back in England. In 1943 she delivered a memorandum to the

Anti-Slavery Society titled 'Australian Aboriginal Workers in the Federal Territory and the States of Queensland and Western Australia'. In it she called for postwar justice for Aborigines, warning that the work of the reformer was complicated by differing state laws. She pointed to the non-enfranchisement of Aborigines, their inability to own land and the state guardianship of Aboriginal children as some of the worst forms of discrimination and abuse. However, it was the 'wages scandal' which she believed was the most crippling of all. Concentrating on the characteristic slave zones of the north and northwest – as those areas contained the majority of full-blood Aborigines – Bennett's memorandum described two phases of Aboriginal employment. The first was what she described as the exclusion of the Aborigines from their way of life by 'our' expropriation of their hunting grounds and the second was their exclusion from 'our' way of life by 'our' expropriation of their wages.[7]

She described the labour legislation in each state and territory, singling out the withholding of Aboriginal wages in trust fund accounts and the permit/licence system for criticism. She complained that conditions of Aboriginal labour were not subject to a disinterested inspectorate and that Aboriginal workers were excluded from the Northern Territory Workers' Compensation Ordinance. Furthermore, Aboriginal men and women were ineligible for unemployment benefits. In Queensland, where Aboriginal wages were fixed by the Arbitration Court, she complained that they were still subject to large deductions, resulting in several thousand pounds being invested in government funds and Aboriginal workers complaining of the difficulty of obtaining their earnings:

> They live and die in poverty while the Department collects the larger part of their slender wages which eventually accrue to the Department as 'estates of deceased natives' and 'unclaimed bank balances' amounting to several tens of thousands of pounds.[8]

For a general permit in Western Australia costing 2 pounds, a white employer could employ any number of Aborigines and was required to feed, clothe and provide reasonable medical aid to workers in return. Under the Native Administration Act and Regulations (1938), Bennett maintained, the Commissioner of Native Affairs could collect and control all Aboriginal wages where specified, whether of full-blood or mixed-descent workers. She concluded that the two minimum resolutions for postwar justice for Aborigines must be education and full payment of 'just' wages for all Aboriginal workers.

Her memorandum came at a critical time in the program of the Anti-Slavery Society. By the 1940s it had taken a lead in articulating the parameters of postwar British colonial policy, and questions of indigenous labour were at the fore. As members of the National Peace Council in Britain, the society endorsed its demands for the ending of exploitation and monopoly over indigenous people in the postwar world. Central to this was self-government for dependent peoples and the safeguarding of their freedom of expression and association. Capitalising on the imminent transferral of 'Aboriginal welfare' in Australia to Commonwealth control for five years of postwar reconstruction, the Society took the opportunity to circulate Bennett's memorandum to some thirty humanitarian organisations in Australia, enclosing a copy of their own International Colonial Convention. A set of principles for the governance of colonial peoples and the best means of applying them, the convention promoted a partnership between colonial and other peoples on the basis of equality and the promotion of self-government.[9]

Given its emphasis on co-operative enterprises, the society was deeply interested in developments in Australia's northwest. Following a series of court battles, Don McLeod finally won the right to associate with the Aboriginal workers and assisted them to take out a number of mining leases and start a co-operative mining venture of their own. At the time of his arrest, a Perth-based lobby group emerged – the Committee for the Defence of Native Rights (CDNR) – to provide financial and legal support to the Aboriginal workers' cause. McLeod became the vice-president of the group and it received nationwide backing from a variety of organisations. Key among these was the Woman's Christian Temperance Union (WCTU), whom McLeod maintained was one of the few groups prepared to back him at the time. Bennett's old ally, May Vallance, was on the CDNR and was clearly energised by developments at the UN, requesting that the Minister for Native Affairs in the west free Aboriginal people caught in outmoded systems:

> Dictatorships are outmoded and administrative dictatorships are being laid low all round us. Will the writing on the wall be seen

in time and constructive policies replace destructive ones – to the everlasting benefit of everyone, of whatever race, creed or colour?[10]

As this demonstrates, the new rights-based discourse and the international environment was critical to advocates' sense of the Aboriginal problem after the war. The slavery theme emerged quite strongly in the protests in Western Australia. The CDNR saw the struggle of the northwest station hands as symptomatic of a larger problem. It sought the support of the Anti-Slavery Society in its appeal to the UN and the World Federation of Trade Unions, requesting the application of international standards of trusteeship to the Aborigines. It called on the federal government to apply the Atlantic Charter and the Australian–New Zealand Pact in its administration, with the aim of making the Aborigines an economically and culturally independent people.[11] A further action was the committee's appointment of lawyer Fred Curran to lodge appeals on behalf of McLeod and the Aboriginal men who had been convicted of breaching the Act. Curran quoted the British Slavery Abolition Act of 1833 and concentrated on those sections of the legislation which demonstrated the coercive and restrictive nature of the contract system and the 'serf-like' status of Aboriginal workers.[12]

Bennett was also deeply encouraged by these developments. Writing to McLeod from her base in London, she congratulated the Aboriginal workers' efforts, subsequently arguing that the co-operative would enable them to live independently of the 'offal and harness economic of most squatters'.[13] At the time of receiving news of the strike she had just finished working on a booklet called *Black Chattels: The Story of Australian Aborigines* with Geoffrey Parsons of the National Council of Civil Liberties in London. Published by the council in 1946, the book contained large slabs of her critique and was primarily concerned with the full-blood Aborigines. Much of it was either written by her or taken from her notes, copies of which she had sent to Charles Duguid. After a short chapter on the past situation, the chapter 'The Aborigine Today' was divided into her two key themes: expropriation and exploitation, in which she focused on dispossession and conditions of work. The third chapter, titled 'The Young Aborigine', covered three topics: education, the state as parent and young Aborigines in employment. The 'education' section was taken up with Bennett's story about the removal of full-blood children from Mt Margaret in 1941 which, as the previous chapter revealed, influenced her critique about the long-term implications of the 1937 Canberra resolutions. 'The state as parent' was about the separation and institutionalisation of Aboriginal children, and the last section of the chapter described the limited range of opportunities for young Aboriginal people in education and employment. A fourth chapter, 'The Aborigine and Civil Liberty', explicitly focused on the human rights violations in the system of protection. The focus was Bennett's – on the legislation in Western Australia, Queensland and the Northern Territory – and its multiple restrictions on Aboriginal people, including the operation of a police state and the corruption of such a system, including the criminalisation of Aboriginal people, the actual killing of Aborigines by police and their collusion with settlers, and the power to remove and detain Aborigines at will. The booklet contained many examples from Bennett's first-hand experience and recounted many of the stories of individual cases she had collected in the past, including the testimony of her Aboriginal friends at the Moseley Royal Commission.

Black Chattels started with a quote from Dr Evatt, then Commonwealth Minister of State for External Affairs and a leader in the Australian delegation to the UN, about respect for, as well as observance of, human rights, and ended with a 'stop press' chapter titled 'The Aborigine Fights Back'. It detailed two cases of Aboriginal resistance, one by a group of Aboriginal workers in the north of South Australia that had run away from an employer who had refused to pay them and were subsequently tracked down, brought back, beaten and chained. The employer was eventually charged with ill-treatment, due to missionary intervention, the special magistrate declaring: 'I am firmly of opinion that whatever display of force was shown by the Aborigines was in the nature of resistance to a completely unlawful and unjustified intrusion on their rights as humans'.[14] The second case was that of the Aboriginal station-hand strike in the Pilbara. Providing quite a detailed account of the affair, Parsons argued that it could be the start of a fight to obtain justice for all 'remaining Aborigines' but recognised that it would not be a short one.

Indeed, the strike of the northwest station hands had a profound and prolonged impact in Western Australia, not just for the Aboriginal workers and their supporters but for the administration. Historian Peter Biskup describes it as the most important single event in the history of Aboriginal affairs in Western Australia to that date.[15] Part of the challenge, from an administrative perspective, was the changed climate of the postwar years. The strike, as well as the workers' refusal to go back to prewar conditions on the pastoral stations and the support they marshalled, signified that the department would need to approach Aboriginal policy differently despite having done very little during the war. One of the immediate problems was a replacement for Francis Illingworth Bray, who had taken office on Neville's retirement in 1941 and who was now looking to retire himself. In response the government appointed the Perth magistrate F. E. A. Bateman to undertake a survey of the Aboriginal problem and make recommendations for change and reform.

Bennett gave evidence at the inquiry while in Australia on her 1947–49 trip and a synopsis of it was printed up in *White Ribbon Signal*, the journal of the WCTU, in October 1948. Much briefer than her evidence to the Moseley Royal Commission some 14 years earlier, it rehearsed the essentials of her reform agenda. She reiterated her desire for one law for black and white, free compulsory education and teachers to be found from among the Aboriginal people themselves, adequate food, parental rights and the repeal of all 'undemocratic' legislation. She held up Ernabella as an example of how cultural maintenance and development could work, while criticising the rocket testing over the Central Aboriginal Reserve in 1946 as indicative of the laissez-faire policy adopted by administrations.

Biskup argues that one of the most important outcomes of Bateman's inquiry was the appointment of S. G. Middleton as the new Commissioner of Native Affairs. Recruited from the Papua New Guinea Department of Native Affairs, he was the first outside appointment to the position in Western Australia. This was an important development for Bennett's continued work largely because Middleton pursued a Papuan welfare-style administration which emphasised a positive role for missions. Just as Neville had focused on building up the government settlements and limiting the role of the missions, Middleton focused on closing down the settlements and working closely with the missions, which he saw as the administrative adjuncts of the department, following the precedent of Sir Hubert Murray in Papua New Guinea. There, missions were given a free hand with the education and welfare of the indigenous population. Ironically, then, Bennett returned to Western Australia just as the administration was facilitating and consolidating missionary efforts in the state. Part of this process was the closure of government settlements, including Moore River, which had been the site of much angst from many of the Aboriginal residents and, in turn, the Schenks and Bennett in the interwar period. It is indeed ironic that, following Bateman's critique of the institution, it was eventually transferred to mission control in 1951.

II

Bennett may very well have returned to Western Australia to take up a teaching post at Cundeelee, a mission created out of Middleton's reforms. It had originally been established as a ration depot in the desert to segregate the Aborigines from the Trans-Australian Railway line and Kalgoorlie. On Bateman's recommendation, it had been abandoned. However, when a representative of the Australian Aborigines' Evangelical Mission, a splinter group of the United Aborigines Mission (UAM), was looking to establish a mission, Middleton suggested reoccupying Cundeelee. In 1949 he sent the missionary and about 150 full-blood Aborigines, with rations and medical supplies, back to the abandoned ration station near the Trans-Australian Railway, north of Zanthus.

Perhaps Bennett had been offered the position before leaving Australia in 1949 and had gone back to London, briefly, to settle her affairs prior to taking up the post. She moved in missionary circles and Mt Margaret had been sponsored by the UAM too. She had also spent some time in the intervening years shoring up her teaching credentials, having matriculated from the University of London in 1944 in English literature and history, elementary mathematics, French and geography.[16] She taught at Cundeelee between 1951 and 1953 before resigning and moving to nearby Kalgoorlie, where she lived till her death in October 1961. She would subsequently write about Cundeelee as a perfect example of the determination of governments to segregate full-blood Aborigines and leave them untaught and unfed.[17] She quoted from departmental reports in which the Commissioner made reference to the department's specific approach to the full-bloods. In 1950 Middleton had referred to the fact that they required little assistance from the department, despite recognising the absence of young children in their camps. In 1954 he described their limited share in the national prosperity and their poor working conditions as 'traditional' and 'time-honoured', noting that there was little his department could do to bring about change.[18]

Cundeelee came into existence much like Mt Margaret: to remove impoverished Aborigines from view. Middleton had shut down the original ration depot but, according to Bennett, had made no provision for the 'untaught, unsheltered' and 'starving' Aborigines who had congregated there.[19] As a result, they gravitated to Kalgoorlie for work, food and employment. Bennett wrote that this translated to occasional entertaining and begging as they tried to survive in the bush. However, Kalgoorlie soon became the site of a large congregation of Aborigines as some came over from Ooldea in central Australia to join the group and participate in ceremonial activity. With the onset of autumn and cold weather came an epidemic of influenza, which resulted in an emergency situation as there was much sickness and death in the camps. One departmental officer, with the help of two local missionaries, tried to treat and feed the sick, and many others were taken to Kalgoorlie hospital. With Aboriginal people coming and going from the town to the bush and into the hospital, some of the nursing staff also became ill.

This state of affairs created a huge public outcry. The white people of the town criticised the Native Affairs Department and sent a resolution to the Commissioner requesting an area of a 10-mile radius from Kalgoorlie be prohibited for the Aborigines. Bennett wrote: 'The main concern is still to keep them out of sight of Kalgoorlie and the Trans line lest their serious malnutrition and their untaught efforts to earn should appal the tourists' conscience and embarrass the Native Department'.[20] It was in this context that a Canadian missionary, representative of the evangelical mission, approached the department with a view to establishing a mission. Middleton suggested Cundeelee despite its inappropriateness as a site, and transferred the people there. As Bennett mused, this 'broke up the big crowd at Kalgoorlie and the Department escaped odium'.[21]

For Bennett there were many problems with the site, the lack of a permanent water supply being the chief one. This meant that the communities could not be self-sufficient as they couldn't keep cattle or sheep, they couldn't garden and there was no continuous work. Hygiene was also impossible in such circumstances. The department provided some work with the Australasian Sandalwood Company, cutting and dressing sandalwood. Despite the fact that this was not continuous work and the Aborigines received little remuneration, the department saw it as a step towards self-reliance. But Bennett railed:

> On the contrary, this useless, unskilled and unprofitable drudgery reduces the Aborigines to disorganised remnants with no rights, no proper economic bearings, no horizon before them, no honourable ambition to fulfil and their capacities are arrested…How else shall they maintain their families in a good state?…Casual work makes casual men and the men know it. It defeats, embitters and degrades. It forces them back to nomadism against their will…How can these untaught segregated people be assimilated culturally?[22]

Given this background it is hardly surprising she agreed to go to the mission in the first place. The Cundeelee community had all the hallmarks of the problem as she articulated it. Here was a predominantly full-blood community comprising adults and children who were bush people but because of current conditions, including dispossession and drought, were deprived of sustenance and a livelihood. They were then deprived by an administration and a policy framework which deliberately excluded them from 'national prosperity' despite the fact that such prosperity was built on their land. While starvation was a big problem so, too, was education. She was needed there.

She began her educational program on the mission pretty much as she had left off at Mt Margaret: trying to get children through an equivalent state school curriculum and make up time for the lack of state-supported education for them. Starting the school in July 1951 with students straight from the bush and without any European education, she used the Western Australian Education Department's correspondence papers and tests, so that the work of this cross-section of full-blood Aboriginal children could be compared with that of white children.[23] She later reported that their total time at school was 2.5 years and 3 weeks, in which they completed a 3-year correspondence course, all starting 'with the handicap of having to learn English – a foreign language to them'.[24] Despite her hard work and early success, Bennett left the mission within two years. Ironically, given Neville's and Kitson's earlier critique of the problematic nature of some missions, part of the reason for her leaving related to intimacies between some of the missionaries. The other, far more profound, reason related to the removal of one of her students from his parents and the inability of the family to be reunited because of government and missionary collusion.

*A newpaper story about the Cundeelee school lauding its
educational achievements in The West Australian, 28 February 1953.*

Bennett resigned from the mission in August 1953, along with two of the missionaries, over 'familiarities' between the staff which they felt compromised the work they were doing in the school and the children's dormitories. They felt that the affair between the wife of a missionary and another worker was destabilising, particularly as it was carried on in full view of the Aboriginal children and the other workers. Bennett was particularly concerned that this created a double standard, making it difficult to chastise Aboriginal men, for example, for doing the same and making it difficult to protect the women and girls. In leaving the mission she was particularly concerned about the fate of the children and sought assurance from the mission director that the Education Department would bus the children from Cundeelee to Zanthus each day so that they could attend the Zanthus state school.

She was particularly anxious about the fate of one of her pupils, Peter Pontara, a full-blood boy whom she had earmarked as particularly bright. Her concern related to the mission superintendent's desire to take him back to Canada with him. When she sought assurance from the Mission

Board that this would not happen, she was accused of plotting against the missionary, particularly as he denied ever making such a claim. It was in this context that she sent a worried letter to Shirley Andrews in the Council for Aboriginal Rights (CAR), a Melbourne-based group established in 1951, with which she made immediate contact on returning to Australia. The council was receptive to Bennett's accusations around the abuse of Aboriginal human rights which the case revealed. By the early 1950s there was also a greater appreciation of the impact of removals on Aboriginal families and communities.

The Council had been launched by Charles Duguid in response to the jailing and deportation of Fred Waters, the leader of a strike of Darwin-based Aboriginal workers. Like the Pilbara workers, they were demanding better wages and working conditions. Waters' deportation to Haast Bluff, some 1,000 miles from his home country in Darwin, was sanctioned by section 16 of the Northern Territory Aboriginals Ordinance. For the members of the council the legislation, along with the banishment of Waters, demonstrated the administration's wide-ranging powers over the personal lives and liberties of Aboriginal people. Bringing together a heterogeneous mix of concerned advocates, including communist, pacifist, union, feminist, academic and Christian reformers, the group formed initially to protest the government's action and to support the workers' claims. It was principally concerned with legislative change on a nationwide level and based its reform agenda on the UN Declaration of Human Rights.[25]

In every other way its program aligned with Bennett's critique, particularly her concern about assimilation. As we saw in the last chapter, she had reiterated her concerns with government policy in her pamphlet 'Hunt and Die', namely the need for improved diet and health, education, work, wages and inviolable territories as critical to Aboriginal futures in the region. These were the same planks on which the council developed its own program for Aboriginal futures. It formed almost simultaneously with governments announcing assimilation as the foundation of postwar Aboriginal policy. The council published a program which explicitly rejected this policy and reiterated, instead, four key reforms around the abolition of discriminatory legislation; the inviolability of Aboriginal reserves and assistance for development of the same; the provision of health surveys and medical facilities, wages and social services; and free compulsory education with teaching in both the vernacular and English.

RIGHTS COUNCIL PROGRAMME ON ABORIGINES' FUTURE

With interest heightened in the formulation of a policy towards Australia's aborigines following a Commonwealth-States conference this week the programme below is worthy of study and discussion.

Drawn up by the Council for Aboriginal Rights (Victoria), it is opposed to the "assimilation" proposals of the Canberra Conference.

RESPONSIBILITY-LEGISLATION

All aboriginal matters to be placed in hands of Commonwealth Government. Full citizenship rights to non-nomadic aborigines. All Acts, etc., which discriminate against aborigines to be repealed and discrimination on the ground of color to be an offence.

RESERVATIONS

■ All existing reservations for tribal natives to be rendered inviolable, and in marginal areas where tribal organisation still exists, adequate areas to be resumed for the tribes concerned. Admission to such reserves to be confined to approved persons solely engaged in activities concerned with the welfare of the natives.

■ Every encouragement and assistance to be given to natives on reserves to develop their own cultural and economic life.

■ Reservations not to be established in areas where no tribal structure exists.

HEALTH AND AWARDS

A complete medical survey to be carried out to determine special needs of aborigines. Federal and State medical services to be extended to cover them and each tribal area to have its own medical facilities.

All relevant awards to apply to aborigines in employment and the full benefits of the Commonwealth Social Services to be received by aborigines.

EDUCATION

The programme seeks free, compulsory education for all non-nomadic aboriginal children, to the same standards as those prevailing for whites. Similar facilities, but non-compulsory, are sought for nomad children on reserves.

Asking for non-segregation of aboriginal children in schools the programme also desires governmental supervision over non-governmental schools on standards and curricula. Teaching in both the vernacular and English is sought.

Advertisement for the newly formed Council for Aboriginal Rights,
Northern Standard, *7 September 1951.*

It was, therefore, no accident that Bennett joined the council on her return to Australia and looked to them for support. In many ways she had never really left. When she heard of what happened to Fred Waters, for example, she immediately sent a subscription to the North Australian Workers' Union, which was rallying support for his cause. In notes she sent to Duguid, she detailed how section 16 of the Northern Territory Ordinance, which sanctioned Waters' deportation, allowed for

271

the arbitrary removal of Aboriginal people without appeal to a court.[26] It therefore contravened their human rights and, she argued, should immediately be repealed. In her correspondence with CAR she detailed what she considered to be the essential reforms for Aboriginal survival – an improved diet, free compulsory education and the abolition of all discriminatory legislation, including the arbitrary deportation and removal of Aborigines (workers and children) without due legal process. By the time she would fight Pontara's case three years later, there was a more receptive rights-based humanitarian community for whom the issue of Aboriginal family breakup and removal of children had much more traction as part of a deepening awareness of the violation of human rights embedded in the practice.

Indeed, there were various ways that this issue, and Bennett's influence, surfaced in the context of the late 1940s and 1950s. By then her critique of Aboriginal child removal was well worn and widely known. She raised state guardianship of children in both her 1943 memorandum to the Anti-Slavery Society and in *Black Chattels*, both of which were widely circulated in the humanitarian fraternity in Australia. As early as 1946 an explicit feminist rejection of the process was included in the agenda of the Women's Charter conference that year, largely through the influence of Phyllis Duguid and Ada Bromham, who were familiar with and connected to Bennett's long-term campaign on this front. In what amounted to the first explicitly feminist reform agenda on this question, the conference urged that the laws controlling guardianship of Aboriginal people be the same as those controlling guardianship of other races, that Aboriginal parents be given the same opportunity as other races to appear before a court to offer evidence about their suitability as parents and that these be legally impartial proceedings. Furthermore, the forced removal of people, either as children or adults, from their communities was critiqued, it being urged that Aboriginal people not be removed to, held in or returned to institutions, except by a magistrate's order after they had appeared before a court.[27]

This was clearly part of what Watson sees as the emergence of a wider campaign for Aboriginal human rights at this time. Certainly, by the 1950s, concern about the issue of child removal could no longer be contained. Following a trip to the Northern Territory in 1951 Charles Duguid criticised the policy of forcible removal of half-caste babies from their full-blood mothers as cruel.[28] Furthermore, by the time Bennett was exposing Pontara's story in the mid-1950s, there was a community of feminists in Victoria, in the WCTU and the Women's International League for Peace and Freedom, which were working with Aboriginal communities for whom the process of family dispersal and removals, as well as loss or closure of reserves and forced relocations, had wrought significant dislocation over a long period of time.

One of these was Helen Baillie, who was a close friend of Bennett, having been inspired to take up the Aboriginal cause after reading *The Australian Aboriginal as a Human Being*. Another was Anna Vroland, a Christian socialist and ardent pacifist who had been interested in Aboriginal issues since the 1930s.[29] She was a very close friend and supporter of Aboriginal activist Margaret Tucker, who had approached Vroland to help her tell her story of removal, institutionalisation and family dislocation. Vroland was also in close contact with many others in the Victorian Aboriginal community, particularly the itinerant and semi-itinerant communities around east Gippsland which sprang up after the war, partly in response to policies of the Victorian Protection Board.

Along with her husband, Anton, Vroland was an educationist and human rights advocate. They shared Bennett's passion for Aboriginal education, Anton sending samples of his school lessons and other teaching aids to Bennett and visiting Mt Margaret in the 1930s. It was in the social ferment of the war and postwar years that Anna threw herself into the Aboriginal cause, being particularly interested in the work and ideas of Donald Thomson as an alternative to government policies and looking to publicise his views. Her commitment became stronger when she became secretary of the Women's International League for Peace and Freedom in 1951.

Following two years' research and work with Aboriginal women and their communities between 1951 and 1953, the Women's International League produced a statement of aims and recommendations on Aboriginal policy. Based on the ideas of Thomson, it called for a continuous review of state policies and the recognition of the human rights of Aborigines, including land, cultural and economic rights. While the education of Aboriginal people was fundamental so, too, was the education of white Australians to an awareness of their responsibility. Importantly, it called for the reversal of the policy of breaking down family and social ties via assimilation, and the substitution of a 'mother and child' welfare system for the practice of forcibly separating mother and child.[30] Vroland sent a copy to the Minister for Territories, Paul Hasluck, and several to Gertrude Baer, the league's UN representative, for transmission to UNESCO and the Human Rights Commission of the UN.

With black arm bursting out of Australia to the UN Charter of Human Rights, this illustration reflects the optimism inside Australia concerning the potential of the charter for the recognition of Aboriginal rights, The Guardian, October 1958.

Thus, processes of assimilation and the removal of children in its name began to provide an important backdrop to a developing rights-based discourse such that when Bennett sounded the alarm over the case of Peter Pontara she found a receptive audience. Indeed, her old allies at the WCTU responded to the call by putting the issue of child removal on their national agenda. Under the direction of Ada Bromham, they drafted a new set of resolutions at their national convention in 1954 which included one on racial discrimination and another on Aboriginal child removal. Following the resolutions of the Australian Women's Charter, they recommended parity in guardianship laws for Aboriginal children with all other Australian children, subsequently requesting state unions to actively protest against the practice of Aboriginal child removal. Included was the specific resolution that the Western Australian administration enable the full-blood Aboriginal boy at Cundeelee to obtain an education which would not necessitate his separation from his parents.[31]

III

The case of Peter Pontara had all the features of discrimination and injustice that Bennett had been railing against for many years, in terms of parental rights and the rights of children. It had been some 20 years since she had sought a specifically feminist response to the particular question of Aboriginal child removal. Whether or not she was aware of these contemporary developments, she had nevertheless played an important part in them through her endless outspoken critiques of the policy and practice. Her work was intricately woven through this new postwar humanitarian agenda. As the Women's International League was sending off its recommendations to the UN, Bennett was turning her back on the 'rotten missionaries' for their collusion with governments in the 'dismemberment of Aboriginal families'. Her anxiety was initially caused by her imagining Peter in Canada, as she confided to Shirley Andrews:

> I suffered two years of misery imagining this desert child developing tuberculosis in the raw climate of western Canada or the arctic cold of eastern Canada in a ghastly loneliness, and mocked at whenever he went out because he was different.[32]

A core part of this anxiety was the fact that a departmental representative would be allowed to deport another man's son, effectively denying Peter and his parents their familial rights. It might have been the case that her imagination of Peter's loss was amplified by the memories of Jane Gordon, the Aboriginal child taken back to England by her mother at the turn of the century, only to be sent back to Australia to be institutionalised on Fraser Island. As I pointed out in chapter two, Jane had allegedly been 'bought' by Bennett's mother before her moving back to England to settle. There is some suggestion that this was an act of rescue.[33] However, as I pointed out in chapter two, Mary's mother could not cope with the child and the child could not cope with the northern hemisphere climate. In the negotiations which transpired, Canada was cited as a potential destination for the child.

It was Peter's potential fate as an exile in Canada which caused Bennett great anxiety and she implored Shirley Andrews to protect children 'against deportation, to an alien climate just to gratify somebody's greed or vanity and "property" in another [soul], which I regard as too sacred for "property" rights'.[34]

Peter, or Pontara, which was his tribal name, arrived at Cundeelee with his mother, father and brother in 1951, the same year as Bennett herself. They came after a severe drought, when Pontara was about nine, from the desert northeast of the Warburton Ranges where he'd been born. The family were starving and Tjantjika, Pontara's father, made the decision to move them to Cundeelee. The missionaries immediately renamed the family: Tjantjika became John, his wife, Baninya, became Fanny and Pontara became Peter. Bennett subsequently maintained that Tjantjika allowed his son to go to the Nissen house at the mission for food and shelter, not doubting that he could take him away again when he found better living conditions.[35] Due to inter-tribal differences and squabbles at the mission, Tjantjika was forced to seek a new home, which he found at Kurrawang, 10 miles from Kalgoorlie. When he attempted to get his son relocated to the mission hostel at Kurrawang – purpose-built accommodation for the children who attended school in Kalgoorlie – Tjantjika confronted departmental and missionary opposition. Despite their repeated efforts to have their son returned to them, Tjantjika and Baninya were consistently denied.

At issue, for Bennett, was the power of the state to strip Aboriginal parents and children of their rights. As she would later write, 'Peter was held at Cundeelee Mission not by any legal right or process but because he is an Aboriginal'.[36] Such an action was sanctioned by the Native Administration Act which, under section 8, made the Commissioner the guardian of Aborigines, whether or not the child had a parent, until they reached 21 years of age. The department also had the ability to delegate this power to another person and it had powers of removal and custody. As she noted there was another section of the Act, section 13, which empowered the Native Affairs Department to take neglected and delinquent Aboriginal children before a children's court. However, Pontara was neither neglected nor delinquent. It was therefore an indiscriminate action, a matter outside the courts, and purely an administrative decision on the whim of officials and missionaries.[37] For Bennett, the problem was exacerbated by the fact that the parents had little recourse to justice, particularly because his parents did not speak English and were not aware of their right to appeal or how to go about it. As she subsequently wrote, 'No-one explained to John that morally he was entitled to apply to a magistrate for a decision. No one helped him to make complaint and application'.[38]

Part of Bennett's appeal to Andrews was to rope the Council for Aboriginal Rights into the family's defence. She befriended Tjantjika and Baninya, who repeatedly returned to Cundeelee to see their boy and seek his return. Baninya had also sought help from the missionaries at Kurrawang to support their claims and they also appealed to the Mission Board. At the same time, Bennett fired off letters to the department, to the Mission Board, to the Anti-Slavery Society and even to Paul Hasluck, the new federal minister responsible for the Northern Territory, hoping for their effective intervention. Supporting Bennett, Andrews also wrote letters to the department seeking justice for the family. However, each appeal met with a wall of resistance.

For Bennett this case was disturbing from the vantage point of the Aboriginal family but it was also concerning from the point of view of Aboriginal education. From the start Bennett recognised in Pontara a very bright boy with much aptitude – he had 'the finest brain in the neighbourhood'.[39] In her school report for 1952, she noted that Pontara passed all his subjects for the half-yearly test with credit. He was particularly good at arithmetic, 'giving the hundred and five answers to tables correctly in three and a half minutes, maintaining a rate of two seconds per answer'.[40] Furthermore, he had an independence of spirit and self-discipline, he tested 'arithmetical principles for himself' and eschewed Bennett's assistance.[41]

Clearly, in Bennett's mind Pontara was an Aggrey in the making. As she wrote to Andrews, his fine brain was God's 'good gift to his own tribe, broken though they be by starvation and the hard desert life'.[42] The notion of producing teachers from among their own people had been critical to Bennett from the Mt Margaret days. It was why she personally supported Gladys Vincent and Dora Quinn, as well as a host of others, in their efforts to gain educational qualifications. As she would later write, 'before it is too late may the Aborigines have their own Aggreys'.[43] As we saw in the previous chapter, one of her chief criticisms after the war was the segregation of full-blood children from receiving the benefits of education. She had earmarked the administrators' decisions in 1937, showing how education was considered necessary for the half-caste children in the process of absorption and assimilation but not for the full-bloods. Middleton's approach of attempting to enforce school participation for the mixed-descent children of the state appeared to confirm her fear. Bennett railed against this discrimination. She saw education as a defence. It was not only the means of the people earning a livelihood, it was also the means of bridging the divide between white and black – it would allow Aboriginal people to meet non-Aboriginal people on terms of equality. Furthermore, along with food, it would prevent non-Aboriginal people being charged with their destruction, there being 'no worse condemnation of ourselves'.[44]

Yet, the story of Pontara went from bad to worse. By the end of 1954 Bennett was visiting Tjantjika in Kalgoorlie hospital where he was recovering from a burn to his back. In a long letter to Andrews she tells how it was when trying to locate Baninya, who had gone with another man, that Tjantjika rolled onto his camp fire one night and burned the whole of his back. He was found by two officers of the Kalgoorlie police and taken to the hospital. Bennett visited him regularly and spoke about his loneliness and solitude, referring to a 'deep depression that does not lift'.[45] Despite difficulties of language she mentions his constant pleading for Pontara and his sadness at hearing anyone mention his name. She tells how in each of her visits he would ask about his son and 'the longing for his own people – the Wongkai – and his language'. In a letter to Andrews in 1955 about the family, she quotes Peter Abrahams, the African activist who wrote extensively about the trials of his people, writing, 'to live without roots is hell', to which Bennett added, 'To sever a sensible son from a devoted father is to make them "men in hell".[46] She worried that Tjantjika would fret to death.[47]

Andrews suggested that one recourse might be to take habeas corpus action on behalf of Tjantjika. Bennett thought this a wonderful idea and mentioned that she had some money set aside for Pontara's education which she could use for the purpose. She wondered whether a 'hard fighter' like Dr Evatt could be persuaded to take up the case.[48] However, five months later she advises Andrews that she has decided against bringing legal action against the department as the guardianship section of the Native Administration Act gave total power to the officials. Claiming insufficient funds she said that it was better to withdraw because, 'if they win it rivets chains on the Aborigines'.[49] In March 1957, she writes to update Andrews about Pontara. He was then at Norseman state secondary school and living in a Church of Christ home and hostel for Aboriginal children. He was sixteen and had passed his stage six exam. Bennett claimed that she was constantly being told that he was an average student, to which she replied:

I am not surprised and I could see him going off while I was there. He was very lonely, desperately lonely and the local natives were hostile. With nobody interested in him he seemed to be losing interest, drifting about without caring much where he drifted next. Then he has become alienated from his parents.[50]

She didn't want to raise any further concerns, despite having the opportunity to do so in the context of widespread publicity about the people of the Warburton Ranges then taking place. To draw further attention to Pontara's predicament, she said, might potentially give the department an opportunity to 'smash up his chances and send him out to casual labour [and] to segregation'.[51]

The case of Peter Pontara had a profound effect on Bennett. Although she decided to pull back, the story of familial loss and dismemberment which it symbolised continued to fuel her antagonism to government policy and her own efforts to seek redress. She also continued to hope for some form of legal intervention to prevent the unwarranted separation of children from parents. She remained friends with Pontara's father and mother until her death. They became part of the itinerant Aboriginal community on the fringes of Kalgoorlie who would visit her for assistance. She often fed them and took them to the local doctor who kindly treated their ailments. She maintained that Pontara's mother would not have 'gone to pieces' if she had been able to maintain contact with her son, 'after all plenty of white women go to pieces when a child is taken'. Writing to London for more money she suggested to Ada Bromham the use of a lawyer:

to put such a strong case for all removals of children to be by a competent and merciful magistrate who understands that young children never feel safe away from their parents and would not unreasonably break up any home.[52]

This did not happen. However, the money that she had saved on Pontara's education and legal expenses went towards the establishment of a trust fund to be spent on the Aboriginal cause. Variously described as an educational or political fund, a publications fund and a travelling scholarship,

Bennett determined that what happened to the money would ultimately be left in Bromham's capable hands. This was partly because she wanted someone else's name, other than her own, attached to the trust. As she commented to Bromham,

> You see most of the people I have worked with regard me as a 't'other sider' and if my name does not appear they will have nothing to quarrel with, and they know I will not placate them.[53]

It was also because she wanted to facilitate Bromham's campaign for Aboriginal rights, particularly in the state of Queensland where Bromham was living, by the mid-1950s, trying to drum up support from within women's and labour ranks for the cause of Aboriginal advancement. This spoke volumes for her very close bond with Bromham, which was to become even closer in the final four years of Bennett's life.

IV

One of the first tasks of the fund was to help in the publication of a 'statement' Bennett set about writing in the wake of Pontara's story. It was initially intended to publicise the violation of human rights evident in his case. However, it became a much bigger exploration of the violation of Aboriginal human rights more generally. Pontara's story became one chapter in a book titled *Human Rights for Australian Aborigines: How Can They Learn Without a Teacher?* As the title suggests, this book was fuelled by Bennett's concern with the education of both half-caste and full-blood Aborigines. It drew on her experiences of the same at Mt Margaret and Cundeelee. This concern had been evident in 'Hunt and Die' too, and everything she read and experienced afterwards confirmed her sense that the failure to educate full-blood children, in particular, indicated that native administrations did not have a future for them in mind at all. Her concern was that policy imposed a vicious cycle on Aboriginal lives. Without education Aboriginal people could not earn a decent living, which rendered them poverty stricken, as did their lack of adequate wages, rations and access to social welfare benefits. It also left the parents without the means to voice their claims. Their impoverished lives then made it easier for the children to be removed to institutions in the name of assimilation as 'one evil prepared another'.[54]

Pontara's case exposed this quite dramatically. When she sought assurances that his education would not be impeded by her resignation, she was told that both the mission and the government would see to the education of the children. However, not long after her departure she was alerted to the fact that the superintendent of the mission was seeking, instead, to have Pontara and a couple of other school students employed in the mines. At the time Bennett calculated Pontara's age as approximately thirteen. She immediately wrote to Andrews arguing that his case demonstrated not one, but two, grave injustices: destruction of family and child labour.[55] As such she maintained that it constituted a clear violation of the UN Declaration of Human Rights, principally article 12, which stated that 'no-one shall be subjected to arbitrary interference with his privacy, family, home'.[56]

While the question of Aboriginal education dominated the book, it also rehearsed the key features of her critique, including questions of land and labour. As well as article 12, Bennett identified several other principles of the UN Declaration which did not apply to Aborigines and organised her chapters around them. These included the right to life, liberty and the security of the person, the right to a standard of living adequate for health and well-being of self and family, the right to education, the right to work, the right to own property, the right to family and the need for education to strengthen respect for human rights and fundamental freedoms.

She was greatly assisted in bringing the book to fruition by Bromham, who came and stayed with her for a short time and took the manuscript away to tidy it up. Born in Victoria in 1880, Bromham had lived in Western Australia since 1893. She was a leading Australian feminist involved in such groups as the Australian Federation of Women Voters and the Women's Service Guilds in Perth. However, from the 1930s she was most active in the WCTU at the national and international levels. She gave evidence at the Moseley Royal Commission, backing many of Bennett's claims, and afterwards, in the midst of Bennett's battle with Neville, she became a member of the Australian Aboriginal Amelioration Association in Perth.[57]

Having moved to Adelaide in 1936 to take up the post of general secretary of the South Australian branch of the WCTU, Bromham became a member of Phyllis Duguid's League for Aboriginal Women in 1938 and was active in the campaign for women protectors. Her interest in

Aboriginal issues was part of her broader Christian socialist disposition. She had long been interested in a range of social issues, from the position of women and temperance to penal reform and peace, to conditions of labour and union activity and, after the war, Sino–Australian relations. She was also interested in how questions of social welfare and justice were tackled elsewhere and, while overseas attending the WWCTU convention in Stockholm in 1935 with her friend and colleague Isabel McCorkindale, she travelled through Italy, Germany, Russia and China. Both women were impressed with what they saw as the more progressive social welfare policies of places like Sweden and Russia.

The promotion of universal human rights at the end of World War II greatly stimulated Bromham's commitment to the Aboriginal cause. By the late 1940s she was living and working for the WCTU in Melbourne and was thus exposed to the vibrant humanitarian and feminist network there. In the federal elections of 1949 she stood as an independent 'Human Rights' candidate for the Senate. Like her feminist friend and colleague in the WCTU, Doris Blackburn, who sought re-election in the Labor government that year, she was unsuccessful. Like Blackburn, she threw herself into the Aboriginal cause with much determination after this defeat, drawing on her peace and feminist affiliations.

She became a key player in the Aboriginal advancement movement, particularly as it grew into a national organisation in the late 1950s from the roots of Phyllis Duguid's league. Bromham's commitment to the WCTU saw her move to and live for periods of time in most Australian states. She had pursued work on Aboriginal welfare in South Australia, Western Australia and Victoria. In the early 1950s she was living with McCorkindale in Brisbane, undertaking work in the national WCTU, and from that base able to marshal support for the cause of Aboriginal advancement in Queensland.

As Bromham's efforts and her collaboration with Bennett attests, the UN Declaration of Human Rights provided an important template with which to assess Aboriginal people's predicament. It came about at a critical moment in the Aboriginal rights cause. It was a powerful corrective for rights activists and it fuelled much of the postwar advancement movement. Charles Duguid began documenting the ways in which the treatment of Aborigines contravened the declaration, on which the Council explicitly based its campaign. Bennett's book was thus characteristic of the times in matching the Aboriginal position against the principles of the UN Declaration. While this was an important international intervention there was also a key development in Western Australia in the mid-1950s, as Bennett's book was coming into being, which provided a valuable local fillip to the cause of Aboriginal human rights and to the finishing of her book.

V

All of Bennett's concerns, along with her focus on the remaining full-bloods, were magnified in December 1956 when a report was presented in the Western Australian Parliament publicising the extremely poor condition of the Aboriginal people of the Warburton Ranges in the Central Aboriginal Reserve. Tabled by Liberal MLA William Grayden, it exposed conditions of malnutrition and disease among the Aborigines of the region. The report dealt with the problem of tribal people on the reserve as well as those on the eastern goldfields who were found to be eking out a 'hand-to-mouth' existence. A direct link was made between their poor condition and the forced exodus of the Aborigines from the area of the weapons establishment at Woomera and, subsequently, Maralinga, which had forced them into less productive country. The most pressing needs were food, water and medical attention.[58]

Bennett had been warning of this for some time and she made use of Grayden's findings in her book. The starvation of the people of the Central and Western reserves, their consequent drift to white settlement and their decline in numbers had been the key message of her pamphlet, 'Hunt and Die'. In *Human Rights* she reiterated and embellished this theme, arguing that the opening of portions of the reserves after the war to mining and weapons testing had exacerbated the problem. Part of her criticism was that governments were well aware of the conditions and not only did nothing about it but actively facilitated it. In *Human Rights* she pointed to the work of anthropologist Norman Tindale who, in 1953, published an article in *The West Australian* titled 'Blacks Struggle for Life in the Western Desert'. In it he talked about the lack of game in the deserts and the consequent drift of the people onto the pastoral stations where they stopped bearing children. Tindale noted how, 'In most of Western Australia the birthrate of full Aboriginal children is sufficient to replace only five per cent of the present population'. He predicted that within

25 years, unless the trend were reversed, the Aborigines 'in touch with civilisation' would be reduced to a handful.[59]

Following rocket testing at Woomera, large portions of the Central and Western reserves had increasingly been set aside for mining investigation and operations. This included roads and infrastructure as weather stations were constructed, all of which impacted on tribal affinities, water supply, game population and even travel freedom. Bennett had already raised the issue of inter-tribal conflict as a result of encroachment on one another's tribal grounds as each group looked further afield for game. She pointed to increased vulnerability as a result of reductions in the 1956/57 departmental budget.[60] On the basis of approximately 21,362 Aborigines, each would receive 4 pence per year of the budget, much of which would be taken up by departmental salaries. Although Aboriginal people were able to make use of seasonal employment, they were vulnerable to a lack of unemployment pay, no rations and little natural food to live on when out of work.

The Grayden Report confirmed her fears as well as her critique. It reported on the violation of the reserves for the construction of a Commonwealth weather station and the excise of a large portion to a mining company that was prospecting for nickel. This was around the portion of the reserve most favourable to the Aboriginal people, of which there were approximately 1,200. Grayden's committee drew a picture of an Aboriginal community suffering not only from lack of food but also fear of these intrusions, with a desire to cling onto their way of life and group identity in incredibly straightened circumstances and despite some contact with whites. The report was a strident and urgent call for the state to take responsibility for the problem. It was argued that given the interference with the natives' natural way of life, intervention was needed to prevent the further demoralisation of the people:

> Members of the Committee find it hard to visualise that any people, anywhere in the world, could be more in need of such assistance than the natives in the inland area of Western Australia... Subsequent welfare work must be carried out on a strictly scientific basis since the society, language and customs of these people are too complex to admit of a fumbling uninformed approach to their problems.[61]

While the report clearly echoed the concerns of the growing humani-tarian lobby about the increased violation of reserves and the need for a more empathetic approach to the problem, it also made some very forceful statements about the need for education and the removal of children which validated Bennett's arguments. Coming just after her decision not to pursue Peter Pontara's case, it had particular relevance for her as Peter and his family were refugees from this area. The report singled out the Warburton and Mt Margaret missions, both of which had been initiated by the UAM's Rod Schenk, as those which had done 'excellent work' for the Aborigines of the region over a long period of time. It also pointed out the deficiencies in the current standard of education, noting that many children did not start their education until around 10 years of age and that they only reached grade four standard upon completion. Not only was there a need for post-primary education, there was no industry in the region for their profitable employment.[62]

The report's comments concerning the removal of children consti-tuted a strident criticism of the practice at an official level which was then canvassed in parliament. It came at a time when Commissioner of Native Affairs, Middleton, had mooted the idea of removing 400 children of school age from the Warburton Ranges, without the consent of the par-ents, to Cosmo Newbery, some 400 miles away. In its recommendations the Grayden Report disagreed 'unequivocally and unanimously' with this idea, providing a detailed explanation in the body of the report. Discussing the fate of these still-nomadic groups, the commissioners raised the ques-tion of whether the children should be removed in the name of their welfare. They pointed to the practice at Mt Margaret and the Warburton Ranges where children were separated from parents for religion, food and, in some cases basic education, but where the parents were free to maintain contact. While the commissioners argued the need to monitor this process, they also pointed out why the permanent or semi-permanent removal of children was unthinkable from a humane point of view.[63]

Arguing that native women had the same bond of affection to their children as white women, the commissioners pointed to four key factors which made this issue 'abominable'. Firstly, there was the impracticality of obtaining consent from the parents in terms of language difficulties. Secondly, Aboriginal parents had often left their children at missions only because of a lack of food, and removing the children and abandoning the parents in such circumstances would constitute a form of duress. Thirdly, it was stated that given the environmental constraints of the area where even birds and animals found it hard to survive, to take the children away from mothers who had reared them in these difficult circumstances, sometimes never to be seen again, would be an 'unpardonable violation of human rights'. The last reason was the 'intolerable' impact of this separation on the children. Echoing Bennett's comments to the Moseley Royal Commission some 20 years before, the report commented:

> The children, coming into the mission from outlying portions of the reserve may make contact with the missionaries only when of school age. Very few…would be able to speak even a smattering of English or would have absorbed any of the Western way of life. Children of that kind, separated from the parents and transported long distances away from their parents and from their tribal country would be lost souls indeed. They would be perplexed to the extreme and would be without a single stabilising influence on which to orient themselves to the new way of life thrust so inhumanely upon them.[64]

While the report spoke of the gradual assimilation of the bush children, its main thrust was to argue for the capacity of the people of the Warburton ranges to continue to live in their country, in their family groups, and to contribute to the community in viable ways. Nowhere had such a notion been accepted as part of the policy framework. Rather, assimilation was premised on the detribalisation of people and the breaking down of their family and community ties. While employment was important, this was understood as Aboriginal people working in the white community. Instead, Grayden's committee put forward a proposal for economic self-sufficiency for the community via the creation of a pastoral co-operative in the Warburton Reserve based on the successful running of sheep and cattle by the mission. This would provide food and employment as well as stock for sale in the outside market.[65]

By suggesting an alternative solution to the problem of the Warburton communities, the Grayden Report gave the rights movement critical momentum. It was in the midst of this moment that the Victorian-based Aborigines' Advancement League emerged out of Doris Blackburn's Save the Aborigines Committee, which not only called for the immediate provision of water and food for the Warburton people but for the abandonment of military testing and for full human rights to the Aboriginal people of the area, including ownership of their land.

Equally important, though, was a notion of development, and the Grayden committee's suggestion for economic self-sufficiency in the form of a co-operative enterprise echoed ideas percolating in the humanitarian community after the war about the importance of such to avoid further indigenous exploitation and economic disadvantage. In its International Colonial Convention, for example, the Anti-Slavery Society stressed the economic and racial equality of minorities and the encouragement of co-operative enterprises. These would protect indigenous minorities from the economic monopoly and domination of commercial activities and organisations during the decolonisation process. Co-operatives would ensure that colonial peoples would retain economic viability during the transition to self-government.[66] This was why they were interested in events in the Pilbara.

As a white adviser and supporter of Aboriginal people developing forms of economic independence, Don McLeod fitted the society's notion of an ideal trustee. This went right back to conceptions of trusteeship being worked out in the 1920s. Bennett had referred to these and, in telling the story of her father, she emphasised how important these positions were in the colonial enterprise. Just as she had defined it, the society argued that an ideal trustee was someone who would assist in the improvement of relations between the immigrant and indigenous races by building trust and mutual respect and by genuine interest, competence and commitment.

The society maintained an interest in the progress and fortunes of the Pilbara community from the strike in 1946. The co-operative mining venture which McLeod assisted the Aboriginal workers to form was initially known as the Northern Development and Mining Company. The group achieved considerable economic success, basing itself largely on prospecting for minerals. At the height of its operation, it had bought four stations with the profits and attracted up to 600 station workers. When financial difficulties set in, in 1953, the decision to liquidate the company was largely taken by the government nominees on the co-operative's board. In addition, the Native Welfare Department took control of the company's station assets, including Yandeyarra station, which had been the base of its enterprise. In an effort to retain some of these, McLeod formed Pindan Pty Ltd in which, apart from himself and one other white person who signed the original articles, only Aborigines were shareholders. For the next six years Pindan operated as a co-operative mining venture. It employed a significant number of workers, built houses, started a school, developed a kibbutz-style camp for children and had communal washing, dining and kitchen facilities.[67]

This was not only a phenomenal achievement, but it also appeared to provide tangible proof that, given the right circumstances and with some technical assistance, the Aborigines could develop independent industries. For many advocates of Aboriginal reform, co-operative enterprises were favoured because they were understood to provide an empathetic platform for Aboriginal development. It was felt that they were a form of economic activity which would suit the communal nature of Aboriginal culture. Furthermore, they appealed to a wide range of humanitarians, from those like Olive Pink, who preferred a secular approach, to the Christian co-operative movement sponsored by the Australian Board of Missions (ABM) in places like Cape York in the mid-1950s.

While Pink attempted to establish a communal mining venture for the Warlpiri in central Australia, Reverend Alf Clint of the ABM established a cattle, farming and trochus fishing co-operative among the Lockhart River community in the Cape York region.[68] This was about introducing Papua New Guinean missionary techniques into missionary enterprise in Australia, as Clint had previously taught the New Guineans to form their own co-operatives and work their own plantations as a means of economic independence via land ownership and resource management. Clint believed that the communal basis of Aboriginal society would translate well into co-operative development. According to him, the Lockhart River experiment would demonstrate a practical way in which Aborigines could bridge the gap between tribal society and western civilisation.

The idea of Aborigines needing to bridge a gap between one lifestyle and another was threaded through much of the humanitarian discourse of the 1950s and 1960s. It reflected a preoccupation with the fate of a remnant tribal population not only threatened by continuing excisions of reserves and revocation of lands for mining in the postwar period, but also by the exigencies of a new atomic age. As a representative of the Anti-Slavery Society put it in 1944, the transition from a 'tribal past to a technological present' needed very careful handling in this context.[69] This was understood as a fundamental difference of culture and economy, between a hunting people and a modern, competitive, industrial and scientifically advanced society. Such a view had been central to Bennett's thinking from the start. She understood this to be at the heart of the clash of cultures and argued that any developmental or ameliorative work for Aborigines must preserve and build upon the co-operative base of their societies.

For Bennett, then, co-operatives provided a model of economic adjustment for Aboriginal people. As we saw in the previous chapter, she believed that the need for sympathetic developmental schemes were even more necessary in the postwar environment as the war had accelerated the migration of Aborigines from reserves to white men's stations and settlements. In 'Hunt and Die' she had argued that Aborigines needed to develop settled community lives if they were to survive and increase. Governments needed to supply funds to provide training and thus help to rebuild their 'shattered' hunting economy. While work was important, so too was the development of industries such as pastoralism, herding and gardening on their own land and for themselves. She saw the Grayden committee's recommendations as a standard for Australia to allow Aboriginal people to become self-supporting in their own country.[70]

Bennett's investment in the case of Peter Pontara resonated with the concern of the Duguids for the many Aboriginal people they knew. As Kerin's work has shown, the Duguids were not only personally acquainted with many South Australian Aboriginal people, they employed some in their home and in Duguid's surgery, and adopted two full-blood Aboriginal children.[71] Kerin shows how Charles Duguid's investment in one of these children in particular, Sydney Cook, became a personal crusade. Cook had been in the Duguids' care since he was a baby. They raised and educated him along with their own children. However, on reaching adolescence and following some disruption at school, in which Cook had been charged with sexual impropriety, Duguid had him relocated to a mission in the Northern Territory. This was not an easy decision but it conformed with Duguid's firm belief in the vital and living force of Aboriginal culture and tribal integrity. Cook's removal to an Aboriginal community in the north was justified by the Duguids as allowing the boy to reconnect with his

Aboriginality, rather than have his identity completely unravel in white society.[72]

Of course, these investments ultimately tell us more about the white advocates than about Aboriginal people or their predicament. Like a handful of other humanitarians, Bennett and Duguid were particularly focused on the remaining full-blood people at this time often because the condition of many mixed-descent communities among whom they were moving threw into relief the cost of cultural loss. Yet, as this book has shown, this concern was very much against the grain in twentieth-century Australia, which was preoccupied with the rising half-caste population. This was a eugenic concern to preserve the purity of the white race against the rising tide of colour.

While both the Duguids and Bennett wanted to see equality and rights for the half-castes, the intensity with which they cared about the full-bloods like Cook and Pontara demonstrates how invested they were in seeing a viable future for them, too. Yet their desire was certainly not matched by the politicians and bureaucrats. In fact, in the assimilationist framework of the day, Cook's removal back to a full-blood community was anathema to policy directives which were to point Aboriginal people in the opposite direction. As Kerin notes, it precipitated an intense, anxious and ongoing surveillance of the boy by the bureaucracy.[73] On the other hand, Pontara's case demonstrated the ways in which church and state worked together to achieve assimilation, in violation of the human rights of Aboriginal parents and children.

The Duguids' and Bennett's concern, and their heightened anxiety after the war, was tied up with ideas about the ideal transition of full-blood people into white society, which was not necessarily one and the same as assimilation as governments promulgated it. At all times it was premised on a vision of their long-term survival which privileged their adaptation as Aboriginal people, rather than as clones of non-Aborigines or as necessarily detribalised. In this sense, cultural identity was understood as important. This included family but it also included land. Even for those advocates who came to this question via their contact with mixed-descent communities in the south, the remaining full-blood population became a focus. Half-caste communities struggling to survive on the periphery of white society demonstrated the problems with a loss of identity and roots which were now threatening the few remaining full-blood people in the centre, the north and the northwest.

The discussion around co-operatives and the enthusiasm for them was therefore part of this concern with Aboriginal transition and survival. More than that, it was part of a developing conception of Aboriginal people as minorities who had *rights* to culture, land and self-determination. For Bennett such rights were grounded in the *a priori* recognition of Aboriginal human rights. This became even more urgent as the postwar policy of assimilation took shape in policies and practices which, as in the case of Peter Pontara, continued to discriminate and circumscribe human rights. By the 1950s Bennett had been defending Aboriginal human rights for decades. Arguably she remained the most bitter, and outspoken, critic of assimilation in the late 1950s. Part of her singularity in this sense related to the Cold War context within which she and other rights activists of the time worked. On the one hand, this context exposed differences and distances between activists. However, it also produced very close bonds between individuals and within groups, as the following chapter shows.

DEMANDING JUSTICE AND FREEDOM
Critiquing Assimilation

Hasluck (with his ideas of Assimilation and NO co-operatives but only exploitation)…it is a difficult policy to fight against with words only. It will need a revolution [original emphasis].[1]

Rachel will weep for her children, but Mr Middleton says this is better for their assimilation, and the people generally are taken by this sacred word assimilation and forget the parents and the disruption of the family…The question is are we going to stick to our allegiance to Human Rights…?[2]

The Grayden Report was vital to Bennett because it provided an official critique of policies and practices which echoed her own. She had been bitterly opposed to absorption in the interwar years as a policy premised on the removal, institutionalisation and exploitation of Aboriginal children and the violation of mothers' and children's rights. Pontara's case further exposed the impact of such a policy on Aboriginal fathers. Despite the promise of citizenship which the postwar assimilation policy promoted, she remained implacably opposed to it as 'perfect to the destruction of the Aborigines', believing that this was what was intended.[3] She saw assimilation as the means of denying Aboriginal people freedom and independence and ultimately survival. Coinciding as it did with her writing of *Human Rights for Aborigines*, in the aftermath of Pontara's case, the Grayden Report reinforced her mission.

Despite being part of a broader humanitarian network at this time, she remained quite singular in her approach after her return to Australia. Part of this was due to her age and ailing health, part of it was because she was focused on working very closely with her Aboriginal friends in and around Kalgoorlie in these last years, and part of it was because not everyone shared the particularity of her commitment or her views. Of the small clutch of people who did, they shared her commitment to an economic critique of dispossession and they were mostly women. She took much solace from this, musing to Jessie Street a year or so before her death, 'there are some fine men, too, but it is an encouragement when women fight'.[4]

This and the following chapter chart Bennett's final years and her collaborations in the late 1950s Aboriginal affairs landscape. Her friendship with Ada Bromham, Shirley Andrews and Jessie Street, in particular, was critical to her ongoing efforts. There were several things which brought them together, apart from their commitment to Aboriginal rights. While their feminism and pacifism was important, so, too, was their politics. All saw in the cause of Labor and the left the means of improvement in Aboriginal lives – at least initially. All were deeply critical of the system in place and looked for alternatives to assimilation. All promoted human and/ or minority rights for Aborigines and all sought improvement and redress in the international setting. Most importantly, all were earmarked by the state for critique and surveillance because of their political allegiances and activities, including their espousal of Aboriginal rights.

I

The clearest example of Bennett's intention to counter government propaganda and publicise the lived experiences of Aboriginal people under what she considered to be totalitarian policies was the establishment of a trust fund – 650 pounds – in Ada Bromham's name. A not insignificant sum, the fund was intended to be for the education of the public and the promotion of Aboriginal human rights.[5] Indeed, she originally wanted it to be called 'The Australian Aborigine: Fundamental Human Rights Trust Fund'. This was about spreading enlightenment, both in Australia and abroad, and it was designed to lighten Bromham's load.

This spoke volumes for Bennett's admiration and trust of Bromham, 'her dearest and kindest friend' and 'most devoted worker in the cause'. Their friendship was built on shared political views, strong Christian faith and feminist and humanitarian commitments. By the 1950s Bromham had been contributing to the cause of Aboriginal rights for some 20 years. While her interests and concerns were wide-ranging, the Aboriginal cause was increasingly occupying more of her time. Symptomatic of this was her giving up a salaried position as an office bearer in the Woman's Christian Temperance Union (WCTU) to take up the Aboriginal cause in earnest in 1950. In this context, Bennett's subsidy was invaluable. It was also a very good investment as Bromham became her right-hand person in the cause, at a time when she was less able to get around.

Ada Bromham and an advertisement showing Bromham standing as an independent 'human rights' candidate in the federal elections of 1949.

The first charge on the fund was the publication cost of *Human Rights for Australian Aborigines*. As we've seen, what started out as a report on Pontara's case became a treatise on the violation of Aboriginal human rights in policies, practices and laws. Pontara's case was important in this regard because it demonstrated the range of violations involved from the denial of parental rights to the rights of the child, to legal rights and inequality. The fact that his parents were denied access to their son and the fact that the missionary in charge had decided to work him in the mines, at age thirteen, lent veracity to Bennett's critique. More importantly, with the subtitle *How Can They Learn Without a Teacher?*, it demonstrated the singular importance of education to her sense of the realisation of Aboriginal people's rights.

Bennett was worried about assimilation, too, precisely because she saw it as further violation of Aboriginal rights. It was the embodiment of a particular kind of ideology about Aborigines and race which had

underpinned her critique all along. Her chief gripe was that it was premised on the separation of the full-bloods from the half-castes, 'like Caesar
"Divide and rule"'.[6] She believed it cast the former adrift, ultimately to die.
She therefore interpreted it as building on the template which the native
affairs administrators had laid down before the war:

> I feel I ought to write to the Department again asking them
> questions which will bring out the livid truth behind all these
> cryptic reasons that are devised to disguise their evil thought
> which is the same as the 1937 Canberra infamies. Coddle the
> half-castes for 'token justice' and let the full-bloods die out. And
> abstain from Aboriginal vital statistics so that Government can
> write them off as ineligible – age not known! – Why not known?
> Because of Government default…meanwhile advise full-bloods to
> ask for exemption: that will retain them as underpaid casuals for
> the squatters![7]

There was also the removal of the children which continued apace in
assimilation's name. This was demonstrated in Middleton's removal of
the Warburton children to Cosmo Newbery in the wash-up of the crisis
caused by the Grayden Report. To his critics he claimed that the process
was necessary for their assimilation, to which Bennett opined 'and the
people generally are taken by this sacred word assimilation and forget the
parents and the disruption of the family'.[8]

Indeed, it was the new policy environment of the postwar years and
the politicians who were involved in it that made her re-arm herself for
battle. She was suspicious of the new laws being promulgated and felt
that 'the enemy' had become more astute. Of Paul Hasluck, Minister for
Territories, she said:

> he is undoubtedly clever and skillfully clouds thefts of mines
> in reserves and thefts of children with noble sentiments. So it
> behoves us to be very discriminating…our strength will be in not
> defending ourselves, but in keeping meticulously to the letter of
> the law and demanding justice only for the Aborigines – for justice
> is so much more costly than charity.[9]

This notion of sticking to the facts and the letter of the law was a key part of Bennett's weaponry in these years. In the midst of writing her book she referred to being anxious to collate facts, 'however small' that would put the native case fairly, 'sledgehammer facts that are perfectly incontrovertible so that the enemy cannot twist them or charge us with saying anything that we do not prove true'.[10]

Indeed, governments were being very careful about how they framed assimilation. In fact, Hasluck confirmed Bennett's suspicions concerning the link between the agendas of 1937 and the 1950s. By then, the resolutions of the 1937 conference had been on the books for 13 years, seven of which had been during the war. In practice this meant very little change. While McEwen's 1939 New Deal for Aborigines in the Northern Territory stalled and was never implemented, the 1937 solution to the Aboriginal problem, to biologically absorb the half-castes into the majority, remained the most succinct statement of government aims. However, the war heralded a recalibration of Aboriginal affairs. When the Aboriginal affairs bureaucrats and administrators got together again, in 1951, the notion of biological absorption so celebrated in 1937 was absent. Instead, the unanimous decision of the conference was that assimilation was the objective of all postwar Aboriginal administrations. Hasluck saw the 1951 conference as building on the resolutions of 1937, arguing that assimilation was 'wider in range and more definite in purpose' than at that time.[11]

This rhetorical switch, from absorption to assimilation, seemed to matter. Hasluck was determined to counter criticism of the position of Aborigines in Australia in the 'global climate of concern over race following the second world war'.[12] The clearest example of this was his insistence that assimilation policy was an exercise in social, rather than race, relations. His secretary defined his approach:

> He wants a new approach in which we do not legally distinguish these people as a race, but start off on the basis that they are by birth citizens of Australia, and will only be deprived of that citizenship where and because we do not feel that they are capable of fulfilling the obligations of citizenship and being self-dependent and, consequently, are in need of special guardianship, guidance and help.[13]

Hasluck's innovation, after the war, was in freeing all people declared half-castes in the Northern Territory, some 2,000 in all, from the constraints of specifically defined Aboriginal legislation. According to his new approach, they were no longer defined as in need of special protection. However, no other administration followed Hasluck's example in this regard. By and large, the old edifice of protection stayed in place despite all agreeing that the goal was assimilation and inclusion in the Australian way of life.

As this suggests, the policy framework was different after the war, if not in real terms, at least at the level of discourse and aspiration. The bureaucratic framework and language was altered so that, instead of protection, administrations defined their task as welfare. The Minister for Native Affairs in Western Australia had presaged this change when justifying Neville's legislative changes in 1936. Missions would need to tow the government line and become more professional in their role as child welfare operators. At the same time legislation was now styled welfare legislation and in a couple of jurisdictions chief protectors became native or welfare commissioners or directors of welfare. In this way there was a more explicit articulation of the Aboriginal problem as a social problem and the measures taken as welfare reforms.

Assimilation and welfare spoke to a new postwar rhetoric of citizen-ship and inclusion for all, against the backdrop of global human rights, without being about human rights. Indeed, it might be argued that it was explicitly formulated to contain such claims. Importantly, welfare consolidated the principle of the state's guardianship of children which had also underwritten protection and absorption. Because of the so-called welfare provisions of the legislation there was increased capacity to remove children from families to institutions, citing neglect, poor nutrition and dysfunction. There was also, at this time, an increased level of financial support, in all jurisdictions, for settlements and missions for the same.

Nowhere was this clearer than in the Northern Territory, where Hasluck specifically defined Christian mission stations as the agents of native welfare. In addition, he established a new Directorate of Welfare which would provide care and welfare for all people in the community who were in need of special care and assistance, in addition to Aborigines. The new Welfare Ordinance (1953) repealed the old Aboriginals Ordinance and was specifically targeted to the remaining, mostly full-blood, Aborigines – some 15,700 – whom it was felt were in need of continued guardianship.

These people would be declared 'wards', explicitly defined as in the same category as state orphans, neglected children, the 'feeble-minded' or other persons whom it was thought needed special care.[14] Importantly, they would lose their ward status, as well as their Aboriginality, once they demonstrated that they could live in the general community as all other (white) Australians.

In keeping with the creation of the postwar welfare society, Hasluck believed that labour, or 'useful avenues of work and endeavour', would be the quickest way to Aboriginal advancement and assimilation. Of course, work was not new for Aborigines, particularly in the north where they constituted approximately 80 per cent of the labour on pastoral stations. But Hasluck emphasised training in his Wards' Employment Ordinance (1953) via a new wards-in-training category and he stipulated a ward's wage (well below the award rate). He was also clear that the policy of assimilation was specifically designed to change the life of Aborigines, noting that government policy in the past was less extensive in this regard.

Much has been made of the liberalism underpinning Hasluck's vision of assimilation. Tim Rowse has shown how Hasluck believed that Aboriginal group ties constituted a break on their progress and that they must emerge from their pasts as individuals free of the tribe.[15] Certainly a hallmark of the postwar governmental agenda was the promotion of cultural homogeneity through commitment to the 'Australian way of life'. This was very much tied to the Cold War context where differences of culture and allegiance were understood as disloyalty. However, the policy of assimilation for Aborigines was also explicitly tied to the wider policy framework within which Hasluck and his government were operating, which had particular relevance for the north.[16]

Nowhere was this clearer than in relation to land. Hasluck tied his notion of cultural change in Aborigines to changes in policies with regard to Aboriginal reserves. Indeed, he admitted that current Aboriginal policy was being worked out in the context of the postwar need to develop Australia's national resources and hence the need to open Aboriginal reserves for mineral exploration, previously prohibited under the terms of the Aboriginals Ordinance. In parliament he noted how this represented a 'clash of interest' between the Aboriginal and non-Aboriginal inhabitants of the Northern Territory.[17] Yet, he saw this as less of a problem as fewer and fewer Aboriginal people were residing on reserves. They were either moving to the missions or to government settlements. He made this clear in a parliamentary speech:

> I mention these facts to honourable members, not to suggest that reserves are no longer needed, but to indicate the tendency towards change in the use of reserves and to suggest that, as this breaking down of primitive native life continues over the years, we, – both the Government and the Missions – are tending to reduce the need either for extensive hunting grounds or for tribal ceremonial sites. A policy of assimilation and the measures taken for the education and care of natives mean that less dependence is placed on reserves as an instrument of policy than in the days when it was considered that the interests of the natives could only be served by keeping them away from white settlement.[18]

Hasluck argued that reserves had been created several decades earlier when policy was 'less hopeful' than it was in the 1950s and when 'governmental and church activity designed to change the life of the natives was less extensive than it is today'.[19] Hence, as promoted by Hasluck, assimilation rested on four key assumptions: it was the implementation of a solution first formulated at the 1937 Canberra conference, and it was premised on labour as an assimilatory mechanism, the gradual resumption/diminution of Aboriginal reserves, and engineering social and cultural change.

In some ways, Hasluck's definition of assimilation sounded similar to the views of Bennett and the other advocates of Aboriginal rights canvassed in this book. He talked about increased education and training, hygiene, better medical facilities and housing. He talked about guarding against sudden change and assisting Aborigines to make the transition from one stage to another. Most importantly, he referred to the abolition of racial discrimination. Yet, while he and other administrators used the term 'advancement' interchangeably with 'assimilation', assimilation in government hands was quite different to the model of advancement being promoted by Bennett and others clustered around the Council for Aboriginal Rights. For a start, opposition to assimilation was a foundational platform of the group.

Hasluck's sentiments around land and reserves was another glaring example of their different emphases. The alternative policy suggestion to emerge after the war – preservation and development – saw land and the *inviolability* of reserves as key. Such reserves were understood as important to the preservation of culture, the maintenance of which was thought to be important in the process of adapting to change. This was not about being less hopeful. Indeed, for these humanitarians, inviolable reserves were the key hope for Aboriginal futures. One of the best examples of this thinking was presented in *Black Chattels*:

> The function of the reserves therefore should be to enable the tribes to pass from the Neolithic age to the atomic age, as a community, without suffering disintegration or demoralisation at any stage. This is a progress that can only be accomplished by the Aborigines themselves over a long period and under their own control, aided by white advisers and teachers who will not seek to impose upon them an alien way of life, but provide knowledge and give practical training...The assimilation of these new ideas and techniques by the Aborigines will lead to a gradual development of their tribal life, and in accordance with their long established tradition of sharing, will almost certainly result in a co-operative form of society that will preserve on a higher stage, the existing organisation of tribes and clans.[20]

Another way in which the humanitarian advancement model differed from the government version of advancement was in the emphasis on human rights as a more desirable policy framework. More importantly, the key sticking point between the two models of advancement related to what the acknowledgement of human rights stood for, which amounted to international intervention in domestic affairs.

Hasluck's rejection of this constituted a fifth arm of his policy framework. Certainly, some of the critique around human rights had begun to have traction. Hasluck's Welfare Ordinance forbade the power of removal of children under 14 years where this meant removal from a parent. Yet in every other way, wardship was as repressive as protection had been and children, particularly half-caste children long classified as 'parentless', were still routinely removed to institutions, as they were in other jurisdictions across Australia, even if, by 1950, consent had to be obtained before removal in the Northern Territory.[21] As Stephen Gray observes, this concession was hardly an assurance that human rights were being observed.[22]

Hasluck's objection to international intervention was clearly demonstrated in his response to the Anti-Slavery Society's efforts to have the position of the Aborigines raised at the United Nations in 1955. This was partly symptomatic of the society taking a lead in articulating justice for colonised peoples after the war, but was also generated by the ongoing concerns with Australian conditions which had been facilitated by Bennett, who had continued to write to the society since her return to Australia, as well as by people like Don McLeod and Charles Duguid. In 1954 Duguid presented a paper to the society in which he spoke of the reluctance of governments to extend citizenship to Aborigines and the various discriminations they suffered as a result of special Aboriginal laws.

The society believed that legislation targeting Aboriginal people infringed their basic human rights and its secretary, Charles Wilton Wood Greenidge, was hoping that the more conducive environment generated by the United Nations, with which the society had consultative status, would enable exposure of their condition and treatment before the Human Rights Commission. While the drafting of covenants – on Civil and Political Rights, and Economic, Social and Cultural Rights – were helpful, Greenidge was also encouraged by the establishment of the Sub-Commission for the Prevention of Discrimination and the Protection of Minorities (hereafter, Sub-Commission for Minorities) in 1948. It had explicitly encouraged non-governmental organisations to bring matters of concern and opinion before it and it published a definition of minorities in 1949 which Greenidge believed applied to Aborigines in Australia. Its work would be in protecting groups it defined as those who shared a common ethnic origin, language, culture or religion and/or who were interested in preserving either their existence as a national community or their particular distinguishing characteristics as minorities.

Encouraged by this development and the requests for assistance and intervention by Bennett, the Duguids and the Council for Aboriginal Rights in particular, the Anti-Slavery Society decided to bring the plight of the Australian Aborigines before the UN. In order to do so it invited the prominent Australian feminist Jessie Street to become a member of its executive committee in November 1954. By then, Street had been on the periphery of the Aboriginal rights movement since the late 1930s, but she had also had experience at the UN, having been in the Australian delegation to the conference which established the UN in 1945. She had helped found the Status of Women Commission within the Economic and Social Council and was Australia's representative on the commission in 1947–48. She had also attended meetings of the Sub-Commission for Minorities as a member of the British section of the Women's International League for Peace and Freedom. The league had played a role in the formation of the sub-commission, and her exposure to the politics of decolonisation in the UN, particularly the emerging claims of colonised groups in African and Asian nations, made her genuinely interested in the prospects of international exposure of the Aboriginal question.

This was quite a bold move by the society because, on becoming the new Minister for Territories in the Menzies Liberal government in 1951, Hasluck specifically referred to his new native welfare policy as 'distinctively Australian'. While claiming it was based on equality of opportunity and egalitarianism, he spelt out his frustration with the burgeoning Aboriginal rights movement of the day:

> Some persons who advocate the cause of the natives will quote any source except an Australian source when they tell us about human rights. We do not have to learn these things in a strange accent. More that is fundamentally true in principle and well-established in practice concerning human rights and liberties and humanitarian reform, can be found in our national institutions and our heritage of English law than in any of the wordy qualifications and vague aspirations of the various documents or pamphlets which are so freely quoted today. In placing before this House proposals for the advancement of native welfare I…[am] offering an Australian policy based on an Australian view that was shaped in freedom in this land.[23]

This amounted to a critique of the international human rights framework and a simultaneous denunciation of the notion of minority rights. As Hasluck declared in 1951, 'we in Australia want to build a society in which there shall be no minorities or special classes and in which the benefits yielded by society shall be accessible to all'.[24] As Rowse argues, for Hasluck, cultural difference challenged national unity.[25] In this context the Anti-Slavery Society's push to have the Aboriginal question raised before the UN was fraught. Indeed, it was rebuked by Hasluck in 1955 after commentary appeared in the *Melbourne Herald*, attributed to Greenidge, that a form of slavery existed in the Northern Territory and suggesting that once Australia signed the new Slavery Convention, the Aborigines would finally get the new deal they'd been promised.[26] In order to avoid further alienating Hasluck, the society decided to canvas opinion in Australia about its plan, including that of Hasluck himself.

They sent a draft copy of a letter, which they intended to send to the sub-commission for minorities, to their humanitarian contacts in Australia. This stated that it was their view that the Aborigines constituted a minority as defined by the sub-commission and requested that it consider the study of their treatment as urgent. Under article 2(7) of the UN Charter member states were precluded from intervening in other states' domestic concerns. However, the society argued that if members abrogated their responsibilities under articles 55 and 56, to 'work for universal respect for and observance of human rights and freedoms irrespective of race', they were not entitled to plead protection under 2(7). Attached to the letter was an annexure, which was hoped would form the basis of a memorandum written by Street. It was to that end that the society asked all participants to provide as much information as possible on the condition of Aborigines in their respective states.

Here Bennett's extensive research and knowledge was utilised, as key individuals set to work on gathering information about Aboriginal conditions around Australia. Bennett was not terribly hopeful, however. In warning Bromham about his cleverness, she argued that Hasluck was too patriotic 'to do justice' and when the Anti-Slavery Society wrote to tell her about those sections in the UN Charter which would make it difficult for the Australian government to claim protection from outside critique, she said that this would uncover Hasluck's 'true practice' and would make governments fight. And they did. To his earlier rebuke he now rejected the society's UN move, arguing that the federal government held the principle of domestic jurisdiction 'quite unyieldingly'.[27]

Fearing it was in danger of antagonising Australian public opinion, the society sent a confidential letter to Bennett, the Council for Aboriginal Rights and the Duguids informing them of its decision to cancel its plans. Instead, the society decided to send Street to Australia to canvas opinion and investigate conditions first-hand before taking further action. The decision to do so was also influenced by the advice of McLeod, the white associate of the Aboriginal strikers in the Pilbara. H. G. Clements, a member of the Australian Peace Council in Western Australia, had sent the society two tape-recordings made by McLeod which detailed the historic mistreatment of Aborigines in the state and had been important in the society's decision to take the issue to the UN. However, McLeod advised both Street and the society that they make their own independent investigations before proceeding.

To build a watertight case with sound evidence they prepared a lengthy questionnaire to be sent to all Australian correspondents. The aim was to gather information on all points where the treatment of Aborigines did not conform with the UN Declaration of Human Rights, divided into nine special categories including administration, civil rights, living conditions, marriage, education, land and employment. Once complete, it would provide an exhaustive and detailed balance-sheet from which the society could assess the legal, economic and social status of Aborigines as well as their cultural rights, such as retention of language, and broader questions around land ownership and compensation.

II

Street returned to Australia to undertake this mission in December 1956 at a pivotal moment in Aboriginal affairs and humanitarian momentum. The Grayden Report had sparked heated debate and publicity, fuelled by government inertia, and injected fresh energy into the advancement movement. The formation of a national humanitarian body was understood by most reformers, both Aboriginal and non-Aboriginal, as vital to their effectiveness. The desire for such had been around for a decade or more. Street's visit provided the catalyst. Once here she rallied the troops – the Duguids in South Australia, Bromham in Queensland, Faith Bandler and others in New South Wales, and Doris Blackburn, Andrews, Stan Davey and others in Victoria – to bring their respective humanitarian organisations together in a national lobby group. She believed that the Anti-Slavery Society's hand would be strengthened by the creation of such a body and set about renewing her contacts in the feminist and peace communities whose work on the Aboriginal question she had facilitated during the 1940s via the Women's Charter conferences.

It was no accident that the Federal Council for Aboriginal Advancement (FCAA) was born in South Australia in 1958. While there was a Victorian Aborigines' Advancement League by then, it had only been established the year before in response to the Warburton crisis. By contrast the advancement movement in South Australia had been going strong for 20 years, having begun as Phyllis Duguid's League for the Protection and Advancement of Aboriginal and Half-Caste Women in 1938. The league became an important forum for discussion about the Aboriginal problem during the war years and afterwards the work of the Aborigines' Protection League, begun initially by J. C. Genders in 1925, was absorbed into it. By 1946 Charles Duguid had become its president and it became the first Aborigines' Advancement League.

By then the Duguids had been articulating advancement for some time. As we've seen, their campaign and ideas were very closely aligned with and influenced by Bennett's work and ideas. Like her, they promoted equal citizenship for Aboriginal people and based their ideas for reform on the principles of preservation and development. They also actively promoted Bennett's work. In the pages of *White Ribbon Signal* the WCTU advertised her educational work and that of Mt Margaret Mission. They suggested members read her book, *The Australian Aboriginal as a Human Being*, as well as Schenk's 'The Educability of the Native'. Photographs of Aborigines from Mt Margaret Mission, demonstrating their capacity for citizenship, were printed. Editorials spoke of the freedom and development of Aboriginal people as important considerations of peace and reconstruction.

Phyllis Duguid took these ideas on Aboriginal advancement to the postwar Women's Charter conferences. Organised by Street, the conferences were an expression of her sense that feminism needed to devise a political response to social questions rather than maintain the traditional non-party stance of the movement. Largely through the input of Duguid and other leading WCTU representatives, between 1943 and 1957, the charter developed an impressive set of resolutions on 'Aborigines and Coloured People' which remain the most detailed feminist program of reform on this question in the twentieth century. Indeed, as we saw in the previous chapter, the charter's resolution against Aboriginal child removal in 1946 constituted the first specifically feminist resolution on the subject.

At the first charter conference in 1943 Duguid dominated with the main thrust of reform promoted by her league. At her instigation, the conference adopted proposals to 'save the Aborigines from extinction' via inviolable reserves for tribal Aborigines with full property rights in the land and natural resources. All reserves were to be protected, contact being restricted to qualified people and/or members of the medical services. Adequate health and medical surveys, complemented by scientific research on problems of diet, were recommended as compensatory measures. The charter also called for the abolition of the licencing system of employment, a 'system worse than slavery', as well as the trust-fund system, and for full payment of wages to Aborigines to be enshrined in law.

Duguid's ideas were also to the fore at the second Women's Charter conference in 1946. Bromham was on the organising committee, while May Vallance and Isabel McCorkindale co-chaired the conference with Street. While the resolutions were similar, there was a noticeable shift of register, with considerations of Aboriginal cultural and economic rights to the fore. The Pilbara workers' strike had occurred just three months before the conference and so it, along with the co-operative established in its wake, became central to the discussions and resolutions on Aborigines. The charter immediately endorsed the aims of the Aboriginal strikers' Defence Committee, while questions of Aboriginal labour came to the forefront of the discussions and resolutions. Demonstrating the influence of Bennett and groups like the Anti-Slavery Society, the charter resolved that Aborigines were part of the world's colonised peoples whose rights and independence as indigenous minorities must be recognised.

Furthermore, the resolutions called for the participation of Aboriginal people in the spiritual, cultural, political and economic life of the country on the basis of laws in keeping with the fundamental principle of preservation and development. Reserves were to be inviolable, and the land and other natural resources were to be the property of the Aboriginal owners. As well as the abolition of the licencing and trust-fund systems, they called for payment in cash of total wages earned and the right of those earnings to be secured in law. The charter stipulated that in the struggle for adequate wages and better working conditions, governments acknowledge Aborigines' right to organise and appoint representatives of their own choosing, and that these representatives have the right of entry to all places where Aborigines and 'coloured' people were employed. They suggested that governments provide opportunities for young Aboriginal men and women to be trained in a range of professions in order to use these benefits for the betterment of their own people. They also suggested a closer study of the co-operative movement, nationally and internationally.

With this background, Street was very quickly incorporated into the broad social movement desiring reform and change in Aboriginal policy, and the FCAA was born very quickly. It was immediately subject to government surveillance. This was partly because of Street's involvement, as her feminist agenda in the war and postwar years had seen her branded a communist by the more conservative feminist establishment. Her left-wing allegiances, including friendship with the Soviet Union, had earned her the title of 'red' Jessie.[28] However, it was also a climate where the mere mention of rights was treated with suspicion, and membership of the FCAA ensured ASIO surveillance.

This context also gave the Anti-Slavery Society's mission a sense of covertness, particularly where it had been challenged for its interventions in the past. In the letter it distributed to accompany Street's visit, the society stipulated that its decision to bring the Australian Aborigines' case before the Economic and Social Council of the UN was the result of representations of Australian members of the society over many years. It emphasised that it was acting in a de facto capacity, until such time as a home-grown organisation could take the Aboriginal question to the UN directly.

As this suggests, by the late 1950s, Aboriginal affairs in Australia was volatile. The FCAA and the CAR set to work on gathering the information about Aboriginal conditions for the Anti-Slavery Society's questionnaire against the backdrop of the Woomera and Warburton affairs and the ongoing struggles of the Aboriginal strikers in the northwest. In May 1955 Middleton had issued an ultimatum to the Pindan group that it either toss McLeod out and listen to him or face starvation. By March 1956, in the context of the Anti-Slavery Society's intervention, McLeod informed Brian Fitzpatrick, Street's colleague in the Council for Civil Liberties, of endless litigation and persecution of the Pindan group and the denial of the Aborigines' independent struggle or initiative by the portrayal of him as a communist infiltrator.[29] There was a general sense that Pindan and McLeod were being persecuted by a hostile government anxious to counteract such efforts toward Aboriginal autonomy. As Street commented to Fitzpatrick at the time, McLeod seemed 'to be the victim of the very powerful interests that have exploited and almost exterminated the Aboriginals in the past and evidently wish to continue to do so'.[30]

She would no doubt have had this confirmed when she visited Bennett as part of her mission. What was happening to the group was threaded through Bennett's correspondence in her final years. The efforts of the administration to prevent the Pindan co-operative from being a success was a perfect example of the core features of her argument. This case was proof to her that the exploiters – the squatters – did not want to give up their slave labour and that governments and squatters colluded to jealously guard their own power and the latter's wealth. Keeping the Aborigines down and at a disadvantage was part of this and it was demonstrated to her every day as she sheltered and fed the many itinerant goldfields Aboriginal workers, the Wongkai, who came to her for help.

By the time Street caught up with Bennett there was a more widespread recognition of the economic and legal discriminations which Aboriginal people faced under the new laws. Street visited and stayed overnight with Bennett as part of her 10-week tour of reserves, government stations and missions in Western Australia, South Australia and the Northern Territory on behalf of the society. At the time, Bromham was working very closely with Bennett as they finalised *Human Rights* with the help of Shirley Andrews who, at Bennett's request, agreed to write an addendum for the book. Bennett's relationship with all three was very important to her but she described Street's visit as inspirational.

They certainly had much in common. Like Bennett, Street had inherited a respect for Aboriginal people from her family's pioneering in northern New South Wales. She spoke of her maternal grandfather, Edward Ogilvie, who established a pastoral run on Bundjalung land in the nineteenth century where over 200 Aborigines camped on his property, Yulgilbar, on the Clarence River. Like Christison, he established a close working rapport with the group, clothing, housing, feeding and employing them. Like Christison, he learned their language and captured a young boy, Pundoon, forming a compact with him: while he wanted the grass for his stock, the Bundjalung could have the kangaroo, fish, honey and small game.[31] Street maintained that he respected their customs and would allow no fraternisation or abuse by surrounding settlers. His benevolent attitude was maintained by Street's mother, who provided clothing and blankets for the surrounding camps, and her Aunt Mary, who established a school for Aboriginal children on the property.[32]

If a shared familial tradition of benevolent paternalism is what spawned their later campaigns for racial justice, it was their relationships with Aboriginal people that spawned a deep-seated hatred of racial discrimination. Both women had a strong memory and affection for Aboriginal people. Both were deeply critical of an administration which was antithetical to the example set by their paternal forefathers while, at the same time, recognising the role of the patriarchy in the dispossession of Aborigines and the racially discriminatory policies which dominated their lives. Bennett called the administrators and politicians 'cardboard lions in their dens' while Street maintained that Hasluck's critique of international intervention as domestic interference was exactly the argument used when the right of a man to beat his wife was first questioned.[33]

Bennett took Street to the local Aboriginal camp – the New Dam Camp – on the outskirts of Kalgoorlie. Visiting these places had become a feature of Bennett's final years. She wrote scathingly of them as concentration-style camps and was appalled at the deprivation, neglect and hunger they epitomised. She spoke of rubbish, broken tin mia mias and rusty sheets of iron, and she wrote of feeling ashamed when she visited these 'horrible camps not fit for kennels'.[34] She was particularly pleased that Street took many photographs of this 'infamous place', hoping that they would get a wider audience. Indeed, this visit became part of the evidence Street collected for her report to the Anti-Slavery Society. While with Bennett only fleetingly, the friendship between the two would last for the remaining four years of Bennett's life. The pair stayed in regular communication. Street would even send Bennett copies of responses from government ministers, such as Hasluck, to her questions while Bennett sent her regular updates on what was happening in Australia, as well as copies of relevant Hansards, newspaper clippings and the like. She saw Street as 'our hope for bringing in better things'.[35]

While Street continued her investigations in other states, armed with Bennett's insights and critiques, Bennett worked with Bromham and Andrews to complete her manuscript. When it was eventually published in 1957 she admitted to almost being defeated by it, declaring, 'it is an exacting and exhausting business bringing out a book on Aborigines because there are so many considerations to be worked out'.[36] While her own ailing health was part of the problem so, too, was the work she was doing helping Aboriginal people in and around Kalgoorlie. She would provide a meal and sometimes a bed. She would give them odd jobs such as wood chopping and weeding. She would take them to the doctor when needed and she would listen to their stories of struggle and complaint, jotting down the details to take their claims to government officials and departments. While Bromham came and took the manuscript away to clean it up, Andrews got to work on the conclusion.

III

The fact that Bennett agreed to Andrews undertaking this task spoke volumes about her admiration of her. At this very time Bennett felt more isolated than ever and more surrounded by people she felt she could not trust. While politicians and native welfare officials were part of this land-scape, so, too, were many missionaries, including even the Schenks with whom she maintained only peripheral contact once leaving Mt Margaret in 1941. This was not because of any falling out with them at the time. She later commented to Bromham that, once she had left a mission, she never returned but nor did she continue assisting them through financial aid, and she had been very generous to Mt Margaret. By the 1950s, however, she was deeply critical of the churches generally, and of missionaries, and seemed to think that the Mt Margaret missionaries were tarred with the same brush. The case of Peter Pontara had demonstrated to her the mis-sions' collusion with governments. By the mid-1950s she complained that, in a policy framework where they were doing much of the government's work, and where governments were siphoning funds their way, the system was open to much corruption. At the very least missions were less likely to be critical.

Nor was she particularly trusting of other humanitarians, telling Bromham that she regarded most 'champions' of Aborigines as 'time-wasters'.[37] She had recognised in Andrews a hard worker and a courageous one. Their relationship developed over the Pontara case, Andrews taking up both Pontara's and Bennett's defence. At the time, Bennett com-plimented her writing: 'you are a very brave girl to take up the cause of defenceless Aborigines and give them your articulateness'.[38] It was Andrews' rage over the discrimination practised against full-bloods, in particular, as Pontara's case amply demonstrated, that gave Bennett much heart. In the midst of this case she wrote to Bennett describing her abject disgust of the new Ordinance of the Northern Territory, arguing that 'as far as the full-bloods are concerned, things are just as bad as ever'. She identified policy as attempting to drive a wedge between half-castes and full-bloods, just as Bennett had been railing, concluding:

> all these conceptions about white and Aboriginal blood make me inarticulate with rage; I don't like even using the expression full-blood…I was disgusted to read in the Western Australian report you sent me that they classified people there in 64ths of Aboriginal blood. I can't see any difference between that and Hitler's records of 'Aryan Blood'.[39]

It was because of her championship of human rights that Bennett asked her to be a trustee, along with Bromham, of the trust fund she established.

At one stage Bennett had said that she wanted the book to end on the controversial subject of child removal. At another point she thought a petition on human rights drawn up by a good lawyer, like T. J. Hughes, the lawyer defending McLeod and the Pindan group, would be good. In Andrews' hands the conclusion became, instead, a summary of the key features of Bennett's ideas. Her addendum in *Human Rights* was titled 'The Future'. Pointing to the fact that Aborigines in Australia were excluded from nineteen of the thirty articles of the UN Declaration, Andrews argued that this was reprehensible in a prosperous country like Australia. While political and legal rights were important, so, too, were economic rights, in particular equal wages. Singling out the pastoral industry for attack she wrote:

> It is an extraordinary situation in a country like Australia that one industry should be singled out for special privileges and permitted to underpay the bulk of its employees. Imagine the outcry there would be among white workers if one particular industry was authorised to pay its main workers less than 10% of the wage paid to workers doing similar jobs in other industries. This is the situation for Aboriginal workers in the pastoral industry and the situation has actually deteriorated in modern times.[40]

Echoing Bennett, Andrews pointed to education, for both children and adults, as critical. While education would enable the children to earn a living in the modern technological world around them, it would provide similar opportunities for adults, many of whom had grown up in twentieth-century Australia without education, opportunities or a real place in society. For this purpose a large-scale scheme of training facilities would be needed which would involve proper planning, organisation and finance.

The key message of Andrews' piece was that Australia had a responsibility to provide opportunities long denied to Aborigines, whose country it leased, and that formal legal equality meant nothing without immediate practical benefit. As much as this was necessary for the mixed-descent communities, the handling of the remaining full-bloods was critical. She cited 6,000 tribal people in 'inhospitable country' in Western Australia and about 600 in Arnhem Land. These people had not suffered the same kind of discrimination and degradation, they still had social status within their own communities and had a closely knit family and tribal life. However, it was wrong to assume they should stay that way. Not only was a tribal life hard, particularly on women and children, the lack of medical attention, the extreme climate, and the shortage of water and food meant that leaving them alone almost certainly spelled their end.

Picking up on Bennett's key postwar theme as encapsulated in 'Hunt and Die', Andrews argued that, in an era of constantly improving communications and expansion, full-blood Aborigines should not be left alone indefinitely. Instead, immediate practical schemes were needed to help tribal people make the transition from tribal life to a modern industrial society should they wish to do so. She argued that some means must be put in place that would allow these people to come and go freely in the new environment so that they could observe and judge for themselves the advantages of a new way and prevent the demoralisation that accompanied contact in the past. While she acknowledged that research was needed to understand what might work best, she argued that co-operatives were an ideal solution for people used to operating in groups and could provide the means whereby Aborigines maintained economic self-sufficiency. Citing developments in the Pilbara and at Lockhart, she noted how they had been established by the Aborigines themselves.

If economic self-sufficiency was important so, too, was self-determination. The most important factor in any developmental scheme was the ideal of Aborigines controlling their own affairs, with whites being restricted to providing technological assistance, education and finance. Citing policies of minority rehabilitation elsewhere, Andrews noted how the maintenance of cultural ties and an area that they could regard as their own and develop for themselves was important. Critiquing the current policy of assimilation as swallowing them up in the majority, she advocated integration instead:

> Any group of human beings with a culture and history that go back for hundreds of years is surely entitled to be proud of such a heritage and keep this heritage for present and future members of the group. We do not want a policy that would destroy this heritage by assimilating all the Aborigines in such a way that they would disappear into the general population and lose all connection with their past.[41]

The notion of rehabilitation undergirded Andrews' message. She argued that it rested on the rehabilitation of those elements in non-Aboriginal society, too, who continued to hold prejudicial views about Aboriginal inferiority. She maintained that this ingrained sense of Aboriginal inferiority related to the way in which pre-agricultural societies were regarded as 'primitive' in the European sense.

This was an interesting claim for the time. World historians have shown how the development of agriculture was an important threshold in human history. David Christian argues that it represented an accumulation of knowledge and resource use on which rested further historical development.[42] Other historians have shown the connection between agriculture and concepts of civilisation within the imperial imaginary.[43] The fact that Aboriginal communities had not developed agriculture had been used to relegate them to primitivity ever since. According to this thinking, Aboriginal people had wasted the opportunity that was the Australian continent. The arrival of British agricultural civilisation was therefore necessary and justifiable in order to bring the continent into productive use for humankind.

Bennett had pointed out the fallacy of this thinking as early as 1930 in *The Australian Aboriginal as a Human Being*. Andrews used this work to pick holes in the argument regarding Aboriginal development which she believed had justified a racist heritage in Australia. Quoting directly from the opening section of Bennett's book, she noted what world historians have since pointed out: that humans made the transition from a nomadic hunting life to settled agriculture in conditions where suitable plants could be cultivated or animals domesticated. As Australia had neither, Aboriginal nomadism was simply an important adaptation to circumstance.

Andrews' message was, as Bennett's had always been, that discriminatory practice rested on discriminatory views. Reiterating Bennett's argument about the need for justice rather than charity, she wrote that 'doing good' and 'uplifting the Aborigines' would be more harmful than good and that we had a responsibility because 'our national prosperity is entirely based on the natural resources in the land that our ancestors stole from these people'. For Andrews, as for Bennett, it was merely about paying a 'long overdue debt'. It was also about saving Australia's reputation in the eyes of the world. She wrote that millions of people elsewhere were assuming control of their affairs and that Australia was itself looking backward as a country that allowed discrimination to continue unchecked. She believed that this left 'us' open to the contempt of other nations and that the remedy lay in the federal government taking steps to abolish racial discrimination. All legal barriers must be removed.

IV

A strong part of Bennett's conception of human rights for Aborigines was their economic independence. In *Human Rights* she argued that by questioning the government's policy of assimilation and emphasising independent industry on their own land, Grayden's report had demonstrated the need for a new economic base for the people which did not imply their dispersal in the white community or the destruction of their cultural base. She applauded developments like the Pindan co-operative as showing the way forward for Aborigines, who were in what she described as a transitional phase, by which she meant full-blood people who could no longer live a fully tribal life and needed to adjust to the new. She argued that the ideal was the provision of training schools on reserves to enable the people to develop the land's resources for themselves and to make an equal contribution to Australia's development. Quoting E. D. Morel, she maintained that the policy should not be in converting black labour into 'a dividend-producing force for the individual white', but in encouraging forms of enterprise in which the Aborigine figured as a cooperator and partner.[44]

Much of this argument was replicated in Street's report, which was completed at around the same time as Bennett's book and demonstrated the influence of her ideas. Indeed, Street criticised the removal of half-caste children from mothers as the cause of immense maternal grief, family breakdown, drunkenness and anti-social habits. She also spoke at length on the Pindan co-operative, arguing that it offered a model of economic and cultural independence to the people and was one of the few examples she had visited where Aborigines appeared to have independence and some objective they wanted to achieve. After discussions with the people of Pindan, Street took their grievances to leading businessmen in the area arguing that not only did they resent their discriminatory treatment in wages and living and working conditions, but they also grieved the loss of Yandeyarra station, which was the biggest and had been the base of their enterprise prior to Pindan's formation.[45] They believed that the department had deliberately deprived them of the station to prevent their development of the land for themselves and to force them back to their old employers. Street suggested that as a new approach was needed, Yandeyarra should be returned to the people with sufficient resources to get it started again.

Like Bennett, she argued that the problem of Aborigines as workers was inseparable to the larger problem of Aborigines as second-class citizens, whose subject status increased their colonial dependency. Equating citizenship with self-government and economic independence, she argued that governments needed to devise labour schemes that would heal Aboriginal economies demoralised by policies aimed at breaking tribal organisation. Like Bennett, Street argued that work should be understood as compensation for dispossession:

> No aborigines should be left without employment. We took the land from them and should hold ourselves responsible for providing occupation which will enable them to earn enough to live on.[46]

This sounded very similar to Hasluck's view that labour was the means of assimilating Aborigines. However, Street was adamant that labour schemes needed to recognise the differences between Aboriginal and non-Aboriginal culture. She argued that all attempts to impose white civilisation on Aboriginal people had failed because concepts of white racial superiority had blinded us to the fact that Aborigines were just as attached to their way of life as we were to ours.[47] She argued that Aboriginal civilisation was very different to non-Aboriginal civilisation. It was communally oriented whereas white civilisation was the culmination of many centuries of development and was individualistic, competitive and acquisitive.

Street advocated co-operatives as the way forward because they not only conformed to the basic idea of tribal life but also resembled what she termed 'the historical way of life' of the Aborigines. She argued that they would provide equality by bridging the gap between a sedentary life on a mission, reserve or station run on paternalistic principles and an active, participatory one as independent citizens. She suggested that native welfare departments and missions should plan co-operative enterprises on their stations, such as poultry or pig-farming, dairying or cattle raising, which the Aborigines could live on and learn to manage. Co-operatives not only conformed more closely to their 'hereditary way of life' but would restore their self-confidence by guiding their 'age-long instincts and patterns of thought and behaviour into channels which would fit them to the modern Australian way of life'.

Co-operatives were also an *alternative* to government policy. Defining assimilation as an ambiguous policy objective, she maintained that it would only work if it retained the communal essence of Aboriginal culture and was based on group adaptation rather than individual assimilation. The question, she maintained, was how to help Aborigines adjust to a different economic system to their own without being exploited. This was critical to Bennett's support of co-operatives, too. Both Street and Bennett referred to the Rochdale pioneers, who established co-operatives for the workers in Manchester whose lives had been impacted by the socio-economic changes of the industrial revolution – 'poor men who saved a starving nation', said Bennett.[48] She argued that this was necessary in Australia because the native affairs legislation denied them access to labour awards. She cited the Northern Territory Welfare Ordinance, arguing that the problem with making 15,000 Aborigines 'wards' was that they were workers. She railed that, according to Hasluck's definition, this would render 'first-class horsebreakers' and 'indispensible pastoral workers' children and, thus, unable to access wages and awards.[49] She complained that the new Welfare Ordinance was similar to the old Aboriginals Ordinance in protecting by restriction.

Street agreed, earmarking policy in the Northern Territory as among the most subtly discriminatory in the country. She argued that while purporting to deliver citizenship to Aborigines in the territory, it actually rendered all but six of the 15,700 full-blood Aborigines 'wards' and subject to the guardianship and tutelage of the Native Welfare Department. She complained that, in effect, this did not change their status at all, the only difference being that those so declared could appeal to a tribunal presided over by a judge of the Supreme Court. She argued that this accounted for little as most Aborigines were unaware of the provisions of the Ordinance or their rights therein. As a result of Street's report, the Anti-Slavery Society also questioned the credibility of the law, citing the Eskimo[50] minority in Canada and Greenland who were less developed than the majority population but nonetheless had unqualified citizenship 'without untoward consequences for the majority'.[51]

The other problem with the legislation, as Street saw it, was that to obtain freedom from it, and citizenship, full-blood Aborigines in the territory had to lose their Aboriginality. They could appeal against their wardship and request exemption from the special legislation governing their lives but once they were declared exempt they could no longer be declared Aboriginal. One of the key conditions of their being granted exemption was that they no longer associate with their kith and kin. She criticised this model of family separation underpinning Aboriginal citizenship, pointing to the resentment of the Pindan Aborigines at the government's assimilationist objectives. She argued that they were unwilling to be separated from their own people and therefore refused to apply for exemption. She also pointed out that many Aborigines who did apply for exemption suffered loneliness and unhappiness which resulted in their surrender of these rights.[52]

When the Anti-Slavery Society submitted Street's report to Hasluck, it supported her position on co-operatives. Ever since its land trust proposal in 1937, the society had occasionally lobbied Australian governments for the establishment of co-operatives, suggesting that a possible source of revenue for such enterprises could be the accumulated capital in Aboriginal trust fund accounts. It now argued that as co-operatives had 'solved the problem' of the American Indians in Mexico and were then being successfully applied to the same problem in Guatemala and Bolivia, they may also solve the Aboriginal problem in Australia.[53] Yet, the official response was to refute these claims on the basis that the Aboriginal problem was a unique domestic issue, that there was insufficient information about the viability of co-operatives and that Aborigines were apathetic to any venture which required their initiative. Community settlements were dismissed on the basis that they impeded assimilation. Yandeyarra was not returned to the people of Pindan, and Street's report was dismissed as biased.[54]

Street sent Bennett a copy of Hasluck's response to her suggestion of co-operatives, about which Bennett was scathing. She said that they threw much light on 'white infamy'. In a letter to Bromham she pointed to his 'effrontery' to say of co-operatives that they were not the key to the problem of providing worthwhile employment for Aborigines and that Aborigines were apathetic to any venture in which they must use initiative. In typically colourful prose she declared: 'anything more Satanic I cannot imagine', arguing that his 'shameful ignorance and/or falsehood should be met and defeated'.[55] She wrote a letter to the Anti-Slavery Society to respond to 'his assaults on freedom' under the banner of assimilation but acknowledged that the policy was difficult to fight against with words only, arguing that 'it will need a revolution'.[56]

Rather than revolution, the Anti-Slavery Society seemed to become more cautious in its approach to Australian governments, largely because of Hasluck's implacable resistance. Shortly after its correspondence with him concerning Street's report, the society decided not to push ahead with its questionnaire or UN approach. Beaten back by Hasluck, Street's report was also denied a hearing in the British Parliament, despite the society's efforts, on the basis of respecting the principle of Australia's domestic jurisdiction in the matter.

Placated by the formation of the FCAA under the presidency of Charles Duguid, whose efforts were in large part directed to challenging discriminatory laws, the society retreated. Yet, its fact-finding mission had been a very important development. It came at a time when, despite the changing dynamics and a developing consciousness, there was still wide-spread ignorance of Aboriginal conditions. As Andrews had taken charge of gathering the information for the Anti-Slavery Society's questionnaire, the Council for Aboriginal Rights became the data engine room and Bennett's considerable, long-term and ongoing efforts on this front were critical.

From 1957 until Bennett's death in 1961, the divergence of views, charted in this chapter, between the governments with their policy of assimilation and the advocates of advancement with their promotion of Aboriginal rights, widened. This was in the context of the latter's slow realisation of the impact of assimilation on Aboriginal people's lives. By the late 1950s Bennett was firmly of the view that 'the system' was against the recognition of Aboriginal human rights and that she, along with her few close confidantes, were engaged in warfare. During this period, she spoke of the powers of evil active against them and that they were in a big fight and needing all the help they could get. She also felt that the attitude of Australians generally was very bad when it came to the Aboriginal problem, commenting on how they needed to suffer from stricken consciences and that the country, as a whole, needed training in just ideas.[57] In this context she felt that very few people were fighting for the things that mattered. She argued that while McLeod was hounded by 'vested interests', it was the 'solitary Namatjira, Tjantjika in his loneliness, the few co-operatives here and there' who were standing for Aboriginal liberty and the things which mattered.[58]

AT WAR WITH EVIL
Dying in the Fight

Anybody who takes up the cause of the Aborigines will have a tough fight with the most astute enemies.[1]

The Departmental attitude is swim and if you can't swim – sink. And this is the attitude that unfailingly takes the heart out of them. The old people have borne the burden of the day and by their faithfulness and grand work have established the white man in their country. Shame to allow a Departmental officialdom to implement genocide.[2]

From 1957 and the publication of *Human Rights for Australian Aborigines* to her death on 6 October 1961, Bennett's mission became something more than a critique of the violation of human rights in Australian Aboriginal policies. It was a campaign to defeat the enemy: governments and their policies, politicians, bureaucrats, missionaries, welfare officials and the exploiters – the squatters – embroiled in the edifice of native affairs. She literally died in that battle believing, until the very end, that she and some of her closest allies were on the winning side. Less able to get around, suffering bouts of ill health largely conditioned by her diabetes, she nonetheless focused on gathering and spreading information both in Australia and overseas, monitoring and critiquing government policies and statements, amassing evidence and documenting the concerns of the many Aboriginal people who sat on her verandah in Kalgoorlie and shared their stories in their 'heroic and desperate effort to survive'.[3]

The last stages of Bennett's crusade must be understood in the Cold War context in which it played out. That context not only shaped her final efforts, it helped draw Jessie Street, Ada Bromham and Shirley Andrews together as they facilitated Bennett's subterranean ideological war. Bennett's target – and theirs – was the governments of the day, particularly those in Western Australia and the Northern Territory, 'the most retrograde of all the states', which had long been the focus of Bennett's campaign.[4] To Bennett's compilation of facts they contributed their own, building a case 'against Australian governments' as Bromham put it.[5]

Bennett characterised policy in these states and the politicians who administered it – Middleton and Hasluck – as evil and saw her task as attempting to combat it and them. Indeed, one way of understanding Bennett's final years is to see them as an effort in counter-surveillance. She accrued evidence, collected and policed parliamentary debate, studied laws, made notes on actions, policies and people, collected newspaper coverage and statistics, monitored government pronouncements, published her own propaganda, produced case histories and wrote letter after letter after letter setting out her angst and her ideas for the way forward.

This collaboration brings Bennett's life story, the story of her active role in Australian Aboriginal affairs, full circle. At the very start of her intervention she had wanted to see women take up the cause. In the 1950s and early 1960s, Bromham, Andrews and Street did just that, if not literally at least at the level of research. But they also shared another building block of her vision, which was its internationalism. It was largely the pursuit of this vision that brought these women together. It was also Bennett herself, for whom they had a great deal of affection and admiration.

I

Bennett's inclusion of Namatjira as among the people fighting for the 'things that mattered' demonstrated how his story acted as a lightning rod to the developing rights discourse in the late 1950s. In many ways it was symptomatic of the war Bennett was engaged in. For a long time she had been railing against what she saw as the artificial separation between half-castes and full-bloods under assimilation. As if to counter this critique the federal government conferred citizenship on Albert Namatjira, the first full-blood Aboriginal man to obtain citizenship in the Northern Territory, in 1957.[6] By that stage Namatjira had won fame in Australian society via his watercolour paintings, mostly depicting his own country but also bringing the centre and north into the households of ordinary middle-class Australians.[7] If conferring citizenship on him was an act of political pragmatism, it was also propaganda. The case of Namatjira would demonstrate the federal government's commitment to its assimilationist objectives. Assimilation was a possibility for all. However, a year after becoming a citizen Namatjira was charged under the Northern Territory Welfare Ordinance for supplying liquor to an 'unexempted' man, his tribal brother, near his home at Hermannsburg mission, and was sentenced to 6 months' imprisonment with hard labour.

This occurred as the Federal Council for Aboriginal Advancement (FCAA) came into being, and when Namatjira declared his intention to appeal the conviction and sentence, the humanitarians in the south rallied in support. In particular, the Victorian Aborigines' Advancement League in collaboration with the Council for Aboriginal Rights set up a defence fund and provided legal counsel. At the time the humanitarians believed this would be a test case, not just for Namatjira, but for the legislation itself. Namatjira's story revealed how discriminatory the Northern Territory Ordinance was, particularly where a condition of citizenship was the severing of familial links which were part of Namatjira's downfall.

A prominent fellow civil libertarian, M. J. Ashkanasy, appeared on Namatjira's behalf in the Northern Territory Supreme Court, declaring the Ordinance invalid and appealing against the harshness of the sentence. In dismissing his claims, Justice Kriewaldt referred to the serious social consequences of Aborigines consuming alcohol and reduced the sentence to 3 months. Although Namatjira appealed to the High Court and was supported by the rights community, the court confirmed Kriewaldt's earlier findings. While Namatjira served his time at Papanya Native Reserve in Aranda territory, the Victorian Aborigines' Advancement League condemned the Northern Territory administration through the pages of its journal, *Smoke Signals*, claiming that it had consigned Northern Territory full-bloods to years of discrimination, exploitation and degradation.

This case threw into relief the considerable legal, political and institutional barriers that were against the realisation of Aboriginal equality. It demonstrated how fraught citizenship was, as embodied in government directives and hands. Bennett told Street that Hasluck should be impeached for 'conspiracy against the freedom of the Aborigines'.[8] At the same time, Andrews complained to Street of the ignorance and prejudice of the judge in Namatjira's High Court appeal.[9] The case confirmed, for Bennett, the perils of assimilation and its many contradictions. As she said to Bromham, 'why object to Namatjira's drinking like a white man! Isn't this complete assimilation?'[10]

The discriminations and contradictions embedded in Namatjira's story became more obvious across the policy landscape. By the late 1950s, the Native Affairs Commissioner in Western Australia, S. G. Middleton, sought to legislate to take control of Aboriginal property. This would allow him to take control of developments like the Pindan co-operative. Because of this Bennett's critique now extended to totalitarian regimes that would deny Aborigines any freedom or independence. Native Affairs opposed co-operatives because they would make the natives free, she said.[11] Namatjira's case demonstrated this, too, as did claims by government representatives, notably J. J. Brady, the Minister for Native Welfare and Police in the Western Australian government, that Aborigines were better off without citizenship rights. She had long seen Australian conditions mirroring those of South Africa and railed against apartheid in Australia.

Since her promotion of indirect rule in the 1930s Bennett had been promoting alternatives to government policy which she considered forms of direct rule. At that time she promoted the Model Aboriginal State. In the postwar context she was pushing for co-operatives as an economic model that would help to heal the 'shattered hunting economy' of the Aborigines, particularly in the centre, north and northwest.[12] Like Street and Bromham she saw models of good governance elsewhere. At the time of the Warburton crisis, for example, she praised the post-revolution rehabilitation of Eskimos and Russian methods of relocating families to the city and providing them with both adult and child education which they then took back to their tribes. This was in direct response to Middleton's proposal to separate the children of the area and send them south for schooling.[13]

In the midst of the Warburton crisis and its aftermath Bennett ordered a copy of the recently published International Labour Organization (ILO) Convention 107 – Concerning the Protection and Integration of Indigenous and Other Tribal and Semi-Tribal Populations in Independent Countries – from the United Nations and was deeply impressed with its potential for Australia. Indeed, it would help to 'rehumanise our dealings with minorities at our mercy', she said.[14] One of the single most important parts of the convention for Australian conditions, according to Bennett, was its promotion of integration as against 'artificial assimilation'. She sent a copy to Andrews with the suggestion that the FCAA adopt it as a set of working principles for reform, which it did in 1959.

Convention 107 was adopted by the ILO in June 1957. It recommended measures to promote the social, economic and cultural development of indigenous people, creating possibilities for their 'national integration' and excluding measures which tended towards their 'artificial assimilation' in the community. The primary purpose of integration was to foster individual dignity and community initiative. It called for the recognition of equal pay and industrial protections, the right of association and the extension of social security schemes. The basic principle regarding land tenure was that the right of ownership be recognised. That Bennett was aware of this and was advocating its use in Australia, six months after its release by the ILO, demonstrates how attuned she was to developments in the field. Using it in the domestic setting was not only to demonstrate a better model for Aboriginal rights than assimilation but to demonstrate Australia's backwardness.

She felt that integration was a much better representation of the policies she and her colleagues were wanting to see. In fact, her characterisation of it suggests that she saw it very much like indirect rule. This was about letting them 'keep all the good, all the skill they possess and develop it and add to it and become one with us in all that is good, but losing nothing of their own'.[15] It was thus about preservation and development. In fact, she wasn't opposed to assimilation in and of itself, if we take it to mean convergence of the Aborigines with the majority. She actually agreed that the Aboriginal future was in their advancement. Yet she rejected the methods and vision of assimilation in government hands. She felt that this was not about encouraging the development of an indigenous minority and fostering their dignity and initiative as a people. It was not about respecting them as human beings. Rather, it was continuing processes of exploitation and dependence and, ultimately, obliteration by the majority.

She felt confirmed in this when Hasluck critiqued the FCAA's promotion of integration. He understood the term to mean the preservation of the separate cultural identity of the two races and rejected it on the basis of probable, and eventual, biological absorption and the inevitable loss of a distinctive culture. At the Australian and New Zealand Association for the Advancement of Science conference in August 1958 he said: 'There is need for them to escape shame over their racial origins but this does not necessarily mean that they have to retain their distinctiveness as aborigines'.[16] For her part, Bennett never lost sight of the fact that, in assimilation's name, children were separated from parents, families were dispersed and broken, and people were denied economic independence.

Her first use of the ILO convention was in the evidence she tended, one last time, to the Western Australian Committee of Inquiry on Native Matters in March 1958. This was the last governmental inquiry Bennett attended in an effort to make the state recognise the impact of their policies on Aboriginal lives. It was her last formal attempt to provide a detailed and factual statement of the need for an alternative. The committee came about partly as a result of the Warburton crisis, the publishing of Grayden's report and the consequent widespread concern about the people of the Warburton region. Bennett's contributions were made against the backdrop of her befriending many local Aboriginal people. As she commented to Street, 'to live in Kalgoorlie is like watching people drown and being pushed under. I think some of us must be condemned hereafter for just that'.[17]

Since her return to Australia she had consistently expressed concern about the position of Aboriginal workers on the goldfields who were unable to access either union support, as they were specifically excluded from the Federal Pastoral Industry Award, or social security as a safety net when their otherwise seasonal and casual work dried up. Worse still was the fact that the Native Welfare Department in Western Australia, in its 1956/57 budget, decided to save money by cutting out rations to unemployed Aborigines altogether. This meant that Aboriginal people on the goldfields had only casual employment at below-award rates and in menial jobs due to lack of education, no unemployment benefit when the shearing season ended and no old-age pension for those people who had helped build the wealth of the country but could no longer work.

Bennett described a cycle of grinding poverty which often ended in the removal of children from destitute parents. Worse still was the department's attitude about native begging which was the result of their starvation. The department reminded Aboriginal people that this was an offence for which they were liable to a term of imprisonment for up to 6 months. The government argued that after a period of work on the stations around the goldfields the Aboriginal men had money and could go on holidays. Bennett railed:

> There are no holidays. Unemployment is no holiday. Butchers have been asked not to give them scraps, bakers not to give them stale bread, railwaymen not to let them travel in empty trucks and now railway stations are policed! The Native Department says that to deal effectively with the natives it must have the co-operation of the public – in refusing food![18]

Her evidence to the committee on native matters was characteristically detailed. She focused primarily on the full-blood community of the eastern goldfields, drawing from her first-hand experience of their conditions. At the start she tabled the ILO Convention and wove her evidence around its key principles. Focusing first on work and pay, she argued that recurring destitution was the lot of the goldfields Aborigines because they had casual labour in the pastoral industry, with wages that were too small to save and that stopped between jobs. While the federal government denied them access to social services, the state government denied them rations.

Another key concern was the Aboriginal family. Here, as usual, she was scathing. Utilising a very old refrain, she argued that 'our dereliction' of duty to help Aboriginal parents to adjust to new conditions, as well as their poverty, was the cause of the removal and institutionalisation of their children, a practice she described as 'retrograde, contrary to reason and justice'. It was also invidious:

> It should be noted that when removing neglected and delinquent native children from their parents the Native Department used the Child Welfare Act in a magistrate's court, but to take and hold well-behaved Aboriginal children from devoted parents it has used the guardianship section 8 of the enslaving Native Welfare Act.[19]

Citing articles on child health from the World Health Organization she emphasised the impact of child removal on families. Such a process led to enormous suffering and to maladjusted individuals. She argued that this was the cause of many young natives being in prison. Citing the eighty-nine in Fremantle prison at that time she complained: 'They are not criminals, but maladjusted persons, many deprived in childhood of father and mother through poverty or casualty'.[20]

She concluded by claiming that Aboriginal people needed what 'we' needed: equal citizenship rights; equal remuneration for work of equal value and the same industrial protections; children not to be taken from parents or natural guardians (except in accord with existing child welfare legislation); and improvements in the condition of the family and educa-tion, including for adults, 'for vocations to earn a living'. She finished by reiterating her old argument about finance. To the view that there was not enough money to implement such reforms, she reminded the committee that Australia had spent a total of 66.5 million pounds to help 'backward peoples of other countries', to June 1957, and that it had covered the cost of educating Asian students via the Colombo Plan.[21]

While federal economic support for the states was important, Bennett also argued that, where funds could not be found, an approach to Great Britain should be made. This was largely on the basis of their part in dislocating the lives of the Aborigines through rocket testing at Woomera and, subsequently, at Maralinga in central Australia. To Grayden's recom-mendation that immediate action be taken for the tribesmen so disrupted, the Minister for Native Welfare in Western Australia argued it would need 100,000 pounds to carry out all the recommendations. Bennett suggested that while the federal government should provide half, she also questioned the responsibility of Great Britain given that it was providing the funds for the experiments and carrying out a large part of the work.

She tabled evidence of a debate in the British Parliament on this very question, which had been precipitated by Fenner Brockway, a con-troversial and outspoken left-wing British parliamentarian and member of the British Labour Party. In fact, his questions in parliament were largely the result of her own lobbying of the Anti-Slavery Society. Despite Brockway's repeated questions regarding Great Britain's responsibility to do something for the 1,000 Aborigines 'beset by hunger and disease and living in the worst conditions in the world', the response by the Under-Secretary of State, Cuthbert James McCall Alport, was that no approach had been made to the British government on this issue and nor should it. He dismissed the issue as a domestic responsibility: 'These are not our bomb-testing grounds. The area in question is a part of Australia, under the sovereignty of Australia, and the problems therein must be dealt with by the Australian government'.[22] That Bennett had access to this material is further evidence of how closely embroiled she was in all these debates and the network of humanitarians worldwide who were connected to them. In tabling it, along with ILO Convention 107, she was demanding that Australia recognise the Aboriginal situation as part of a worldwide one demanding redress. She was showing how intimately connected the race problem was to the broader global problem of peace, asking 'why should we worry about the slow death of 1000 primitive aborigines in the desert wastes when we are considering how best to bring about the sudden death of millions in the great cities of the civilised world?'[23]

If the large scale was important to Bennett's philosophy it had long been shaped by the small scale, and she spent the final years of her life working with the goldfields Aborigines to help them survive and bring their case to the wider community. The core issues she raised before the committee, particularly economic security and the health of the people, remained uppermost in her list of concerns until her death. She also spent many hours feeding and listening to the Aborigines around Kalgoorlie, providing a regular count of the numbers who visited her in search of work and/or food:

> I find the best way to come to grips with people who seek me is to provide a meal. Then they discuss the matter for which they have sought me...More than 30 people visited me between Monday March 16th and Sunday March 22nd 1959.[24]

It was these thirty or so people that she worked very closely with in documenting their lives and their personal conditions in the final years of her life. She spent many hours writing letters for them, often simply writing out what they dictated, and helping to facilitate their various requests for relief to government ministers. This was mostly connected with their need for access to social security, particularly the age pension and unemployment benefits. She was often seen helping Aboriginal people at the local courthouse and she would regularly leave food out at night for them so that they would avoid being charged with begging. She also commissioned a series of photographs to be taken of the people which she would annotate with their details along the bottom of the photograph and then send to groups like CAR and the FCAA, which were campaigning on the issue of access to a variety of social welfare benefits. Like the photographs of the Dalleburra that she donated to the British Museum in 1927, these were images which bore witness not only to the humanity of the people but to their conditions and struggle to live within the system – they were the first-hand evidence and incontrovertible facts she had long seen as necessary to the cause.

While justice and equality for these people were her key demands, she suggested a couple of possible measures which would help to relieve their plight in the meantime. The first and most important was connected to the ration they received. She consistently railed against the poor quality and quantity of the ration Western Australian Aborigines received, maintaining that it was the basis of their poor health and malnutrition. Just months before her death she was lobbying the Native Welfare Department to increase the Aborigines' ration to match that of the Commonwealth Department of Health's Ration Scale for Feeding of Aborigines. Of particular concern was the meat ration, which in Western Australia, by 1961, was 4 pounds compared to 5 pounds for women and 7 pounds for working men, youth and children in the Northern Territory. She argued that Aboriginal men should be assisted by the department to find employment and that the department should also encourage the establishment of co-operatives wherever possible.

II

While Bennett was giving evidence to the Western Australian committee, Bromham and Street were also busy searching for and promoting alternative solutions. Street travelled to Russia and China to investigate what steps had been taken to develop people who were illiterate and nomadic. Following her tour in 1958 she argued that the more sympathetic policies of minority rehabilitation in these countries demonstrated the 'absurdity' of Australia's treatment of Aborigines. She reported that, in both cases, previously illiterate and subject minorities, who were without civil or political rights, had been rehabilitated by policies of health and education, land and self-government. She argued that after the defeat of Chiang Kai Chek in China in 1949, minority groups had been encouraged to elect their own representatives to the national and provincial parliaments and that institutes of minorities had been established to train the people in the application of new policies and developmental schemes. Citing Nehru's integration policy in India, she stressed the importance of preserving tribal culture while advancing economic, educational and welfare developmental schemes.[25]

Bromham had also long been an admirer of post-revolution Russian policy for its minorities, having presented a paper to Phyllis Duguid's league in 1942 on the ways in which the Kalmyk minority of Soviet Asia had been rehabilitated after the revolution.[26] Describing the Kalmyks as low in cultural development, she showed how the Soviet government created settled autonomous communities out of a previously nomadic, pre-literate people. Education was provided to train the people in health and welfare work, as well as collective methods of farming, and those trained went back to teach their communities new skills. Within 25 years they had their own schools and books in their language and, by the 1940s, they were governed by an autonomous republic which had representatives on the central Soviet government.

Along with Bennett and Street, Bromham championed co-operative enterprises as providing a key to the desired policy of 'integration and the ultimate goal of the abolition of racial discrimination'. At the age of eighty, as superintendent of native races for the WA branch of the Woman's Christian Temperance Union and with the financial backing of Bennett's trust fund, she formulated and costed a plan to turn the Warburton Aboriginal community into a self-sufficient farming settlement to 'save' the Aborigines of those regions 'from extinction'.[27] She argued that her chief reason for doing so was to provide the able-bodied Aborigines in the district with work. Of approximately 400 Aborigines in the area, about thirty had permanent work while the remainder relied on seasonal employment. Being classified 'nomadic' meant that they could not access social service benefits. She envisaged a settlement under the management of a European, whose salary could be offset by profits from a general store, which might trade in things like kangaroo and dingo scalps. The settlement could have a handful of buildings, with work activity being confined to the growing of vegetables for consumption by the settlement. In October 1960 she led a deputation of women's, union and church groups to the Western Australian Minister for Native Welfare to request that her plan be implemented.

Her scheme was dismissed as 'fantastic' and 'idealistic'.[28] The Western Australian Native Commissioner informed Bennett that they opposed co-operatives on the basis that they were contrary to the department's policy of assimilation. As a result Bennett complained to the director of the International Federation of Free Trade Unions in Brussels that rather than being 'free to choose their co-operative way of life', Aborigines would be 'dragooned into serfdom and disintegration which are the means of assimilation', for, 'as they are only serfs, uneducated, undervalued and underpaid they *die* and as they disappear Australia will forget that they ever had a native race to ruin'.[29]

This was an eerie echo of the claim of her old adversary A. O. Neville who, at the time of the 1937 Canberra conference of Aboriginal adminis-trators, said that, eventually, following mergence of the Aborigines into the white community we could 'forget that there ever were any Aborigines in Australia'.[30] Their different interpretations of this notion of forgetting had been at the core of their disagreement at the time and remained at the core of Bennett's disagreement with governments ever since. For Neville, this was about clearing away all signs of colour. For Bennett it was about willed race extermination.

This sense that what was being promoted was government-backed genocide continued to solidify in Bennett's mind. In the late 1950s her angst over this and over the way in which she thought departments and departmental officials were promoting it led her to a bitter hatred of the policy framework and a sense that politicians, on both sides, were treacherous. For Hasluck to reject integration as antithetical to assimilation because it aimed to preserve the separate cultural identity of Aborigines was one thing. The Liberal Party was among her long-term enemies. However, when Labor colluded and facilitated the 'liquidation' of the Aborigines, as she saw it, she became deeply despondent and critical. It was a Labor ministry in Western Australia that had Brady as Minister for Native Welfare and Middleton as Native Affairs Commissioner.

She was particularly scathing of the legislative changes which were supposedly designed to give citizenship to Aborigines in the west. On the one hand, these changes were illustrative of the impact that the humani-tarian critique was having in these years. In 1944 and 1958, with small amendments in between, the Western Australian government brought in legislation designed to give effect to citizenship for Aborigines in that state. The Natives (Citizenship Rights Act) of 1944 and the Amendment Act of 1958 enabled an Aboriginal person to apply for citizenship to a stipendiary magistrate or government resident in their district on the condition that they had dissolved tribal and native associations (except for lineal descendants of the first degree) for two years prior to the date of application or were deemed to be a 'fit and proper person' to obtain a certificate of citizenship. Two written references from 'reputable citizens' were required certifying the 'good character and industrious habits of the applicant'.

Amendments to the first Act in 1951 provided for Native (Citizenship Rights) Boards which would supplement the sole authority of the determining magistrate. Where there was disagreement between the board members, the application was refused or the complaint dismissed. The 1958 amendment removed the requirement for two years prior dissolution of tribal contacts and allowed the nomination of children under 21 years. Not surprisingly, Bennett labelled this legislation 'atrocious' and 'monstrous', arguing that, like the Northern Territory Welfare Ordinance, it gave with one hand and took away with another. She argued that Brady was doing in Western Australia what Hasluck was doing in the Northern Territory.

She saw the legislation as an assault on Aboriginal communities for whom extended family was key and railed against the department's abuse of power over Aboriginal lives. The determination of the Western Australian Labor government to 'dismember' Aboriginal families, according to her, was illustrated by a government proposal to establish a mission at Roebourne, about 200 kilometres from Port Hedland. Bennett was scathing, seeing it as a direct response to the Pilbara co-operative, writing to Street:

> The proposed 'Roebourne' institution you can see is aimed against Don McLeod. Saddest of all is the default of an otherwise good Labor member, Mr Lapham, who demands the disruption of Aboriginal families 'in the interests of the Australian way of life'. Could anything be more horrible than this 'glory to white man in the highest!!!!!!!'[31]

The comment about Lapham related to his evidence before the committee inquiring into native matters in 1958. He argued that the Aboriginal problem would be solved in 20 years if native children were separated from their parents and taught the white man's way of life in mission institutions. Bennett wrote to Street complaining about the legislation and about Lapham saying that although she had voted Labor all her life, she would no longer do so if 'Brady manoeuvres his betrayal'.[32]

The idea that assimilation constituted a betrayal of Labor policy is interesting. As Markus has shown, the labour movement did not have a terribly strong record on the question of Aboriginal rights by the 1950s. There was no Labor policy specifically on assimilation. Rather assimilation was an ideal all subscribed to. Bennett singled out the right to property and the sanctity of the family, but Labor didn't have a distinct policy on that either. While the alternative policy agenda which some of the humanitarians espoused, of preservation and development, had been included in the campaigns of the New South Wales Labor Council under Tom Wright, the Labor Party and union movement was slow to develop an alternative policy response in the 1950s. It was two years after Bennett's death, in 1963, that the Australian Council of Trade Unions adopted, for the first time, a policy statement on Aborigines which mostly revolved around the relevant labour awards and social services. This was largely due to the pressure exerted on it by the FCAA's wages and employment sub-committee headed by Shirley Andrews.[33]

By the 1950s there were certainly some Labor politicians who Bennett identified as taking a valuable lead on this question. She earmarked Don Dunstan in South Australia and Gordon Bryant and Kim Beazley (senior) at the federal level. As the long-term president of the Victorian Aborigines' Advancement League, Bryant was particularly noteworthy and she developed a close friendship with him in her final years. Yet, despite these men, the policies of Labor were still in their infancy strongly enmeshed in the developing politics of the FCAA and CAR. It might be that, in referring to a Labor betrayal, Bennett was thinking of the Labour Party in Britain, which had a much stronger record on this question than Australian Labor. Certainly, her own ideas on justice for Aborigines had solidified in interwar Britain where the Labour Party had played an important role in shaping a progressive program of reform for the 'native races' of empire.

Indeed, apart from the co-operative movement itself and the strikes of the Aboriginal workers, which forced a realisation of wage injustice on the labour movement, it was Labor women, including Bennett herself, who helped shape a postwar Labor response to this question in Australia. From Phyllis Duguid's League for Aboriginal Women to the Australian

Women's Charter conferences, the rocket range and Warburton protests, to the burgeoning interest of the Council of Civil Liberties in the
question, it was women such as Street, Doris Blackburn, Bromham and
Andrews who facilitated and helped define a specifically Labor response.
Bennett consistently lobbied the unions on behalf of the goldfields workers
while much of the work Bromham undertook in Queensland, supported
by Bennett's trust fund, was among the unions and labour movement,
including Labor women.

Bennett's frustration with the Labor ministry in Western Australia
went beyond a sense of betrayal, however. Her disquiet was with the
whole 'system', but particularly politicians whom she felt simply abused
and 'played about with' their power. Rather than doing good and setting
things right, politicians and their deputies – the civil service – worked to
undermine and destroy:

> We ought not to allow our civil service to debate how few they
> can spend on. They ought to be seeing how much they can do for
> how many. Social service should be a right bought by contribu-
> tion, and claimed by those who earn it. Otherwise starvation and
> malnutrition of unemployed Aborigines will go on apace. We
> need to see that our departments do the work they are paid to
> do and that all perversions that have been introduced are cleared
> away.[34]

This was the result of her own confrontation with the civil service. In
an environment where welfare was the catchphrase, somewhat ironically,
Bennett became a voluntary welfare worker, writing to and meeting many
politicians and officials as she represented the Aborigines' claims to the
department. She didn't hold back, writing directly to people like Hasluck
and Middleton for confirmation of policies, personally interviewing the
local native welfare officials and confronting various workers in the field.
By 1958 she had seen enough to feel confirmed in her suspicions. She
constantly referred to being in battle, writing to Bromham that life was
a 'battle-field strewn with casualties'.[35] The battle with native affairs, as
she defined it, was in wading through a jungle, 'facing the conspiracy of
silence in order to tell the truth'.[36] It was a complex maze – deliberately
so – and, based on half-truths and half-lies, difficult to sift fact from

fiction. Bennett felt that the business of native affairs and the policy of assimilation, particularly in Western Australia and the Northern Territory, was a sham, a disguise used to cover all sorts of contumely and brutality, and was built on lies. She frequently referred to its totalitarian grip and saw it as an abuse of power.

Nowhere was this clearer than in her depiction of the leading politicians involved in the administration about whom she penned some excoriating comments in the final years of her life. Although she had little time for Middleton, 'a mischievous and conceited fool' whose bubble needed bursting, and Brady, the 'renegade Laborite', it was Hasluck for whom she reserved some of her more colourful critique.[37] Her sense of him was that he was too patriotic and polite to do justice for Aborigines and that he was ultimately constrained by his office:

> Poor Hasluck! I am sorry for him. He is a 'prisoner of office' and wriggles like a worm on a hook in his efforts to justify the unjustifiable and blame it on to the Aborigines that they are not what we are without our advantages.[38]

This syndrome of blaming their alleged failures on the Aborigines themselves made her livid. In a letter to Bromham she complained that Australians had no right to blame them for having no idea of the value of money since we denied them the opportunity to learn its value by 'robbing' them of the money they earned:

> I believe the Queensland government still subsidises missions by several thousands of pounds every year MISAPPROPRIATED from Aborigines wages which the Government has invested in Government stock and these thousands of pounds are the dividends of these investments and rightly belong to the Aborigines who earned them [original emphasis].[39]

There is a sense at this time that some of her closest colleagues and friends with whom she was working felt this, too. Bennett was at the centre of a circuit of information, data collection and critique which was an important part of coming to terms with the new postwar policy agenda as it was unfolding. Indeed, this was an intense part of Bennett's life at a time when she constantly talked about not working hard any more. This was for good reason. As she aged she suffered from bouts of giddiness, blood-shot eyes and rheumatism. Her head and eyes ached.[40] She spent periods of time hospitalised, including for a broken arm. Despite her exhaustion and her claim to be slowing down, she was working harder than ever, channelling her crusade through Bromham.

Reading the correspondence between the two in these last years is like listening in on a private conversation. They were in touch just about every week via letter and this was interspersed with visits to one another. Bennett travelled to the eastern states to visit Bromham and, in the course of her extensive travels around the country in the cause of Aborigines and her many other political commitments, Bromham would stop in on Bennett. Much of the correspondence reveals the amount of work they engaged in to advance Aboriginal human rights as they saw them. This was about sharing information, publicising conditions and rallying others to the cause. But it was also a critical discourse as they thrashed out what was wrong with native affairs. Some of it was gossip which revealed just how hollow and hypocritical Bennett thought some in positions of power were – 'everything these dishonest men touch is equally deadly'.[41] In talking about Hasluck she revealed her complete lack of respect for him. He was full of 'puff' as he attempted to 'snuff out' the Aborigines.[42] She wrote to Bromham, 'I would rather have a kindly workman for a judge than these self-idolaters'.[43]

This was more than a feminist critique. Bennett had close male friends and colleagues, some of whom were politicians. She was railing against native affairs and those who administered it because she felt that it was built on and continued to propagate a lie that was at the heart of the policy framework in Australia. At the centre of this was the 'golden image' of the pastoralists whom she saw as the chief exploiters and whose interests were being protected by the politicians. Hasluck was a 'stooge of the squatters' while Middleton had a 'squatter clientele'.[44] As this suggests, she firmly believed that native affairs legislation helped to maintain the slave labour of Aboriginal workers. The problem with the golden image was that it denied the fundamental truth that via their labour, Aborigines had established the pastoral (as well as the mining and pearling) wealth of Australia without sharing in it. More than that, the entire continent had been explored and occupied by the white man with their aid, for 'without them it would be impossible for squatters in the Never-Never to work their cattle and sheep stations'.[45]

This fact rendered their poverty, neglect and starvation unconscionable. Many of the old people were 'grand citizen-workers' who had spent their lives doing all the hard work, 'importing their own gifts into it and building fortunes for others by their faithfulness'.[46] She earmarked a particularly difficult period for Aboriginal station workers as between Christmas and March when they were laid off. She wrote that just as pastoralists rested and saved wages, Aborigines were unemployed and starving. When she put this to the native welfare officer in Kalgoorlie in June 1960, he said that the pastoralists couldn't be blamed because they needed to make a living. She described her response to Bromham 'I wasn't sharp enough to say at him *who* are to blame for abandoning Aboriginal labour, neglecting their protection and throwing the souls of men to the wolves'.[47] The problems that the Pindan co-operative suffered, and the way in which the department put obstacles in the way of the workers and McLeod, merely confirmed her view that the squatters would resist any attempts to enable the Aborigines – 'their station serfs' – to develop independently.

The same applied to the Northern Territory with its history of exploitation. This was a region she had earmarked in 1930 where it was still possible, at that time, to have an honourable settlement with the Aborigines. To that extent native affairs represented a massive failure for Bennett. She was bitter and very angry at what she saw as the Australian state's dereliction of duty and violation of human rights. She wanted to break down what she saw as the 'iron curtain' around Aboriginal affairs and expose the lies and injustices. The lies she identified as being propagated by 'the enemy' were that 'Aborigines were declared wards only when they needed protection, that they lost more than they gained by being given citizen rights and that they could not be helped because they will not help themselves'.[48] Her other core argument, threaded throughout her work, was the way in which racist persecution in Australia underpinned a governmental attempt to extinguish them:

> The destruction of the Aborigines is heart-breaking. I suppose
> it has all come about in my lifetime or most of it. And I am
> afraid I do entirely agree with you that it has been brought about

– deliberately – by persecutionary legislation such as would wipe us out if we had to endure it.[49]

Worse still, the conditions of Aboriginal people's lives facilitated an ongoing persecution which manifested as a self-fulfilling prophecy by the state and justified ongoing policing and dependence. Relegated to casual labour, their nomadism was then used to refuse them pensions and benefits. Their inexperience in the use of money was used to argue their irresponsibility and deny their economic independence. Their lack of education was used to blame them for hopelessness and unreliability.

III

It was no accident, then, that Bennett complained to Street about Labor's betrayal. Like Bennett, Street was an old left-wing warrior and shared all of her concerns, including her despondency about Labor. Just a few months before Bennett died, Street decided to retire temporarily from the cause to concentrate on writing her autobiography. This was as much conditioned by her experience of racism in Australia as it was by her long feminist struggles. Before doing so she wrote to Bennett thanking her for all the information and pamphlets she had sent her and explaining her decision to concentrate on the autobiography. Part of this was because, like Bennett she was disillusioned with politics, but she was comforted to know that 'good people' like Mary herself, Bromham, Andrews and others were doing all they could to improve Aboriginal conditions. She thanked Bennett for her efforts, writing,

> My dear love, dear Mary and keep on with what you are doing. 'Constant dripping wears away a stone' and none can assess the amount you have really achieved by your constant endeavours in the past.[50]

Indeed, Bennett was wearing away the stone right up to her death, visiting her Wongkai friends in Kalgoorlie hospital only a month before she died in the same. She wrote and fought, read and lobbied until she literally could do these things no more. Interestingly, just months before she died, she returned to her old refrain: the position of Aboriginal women. In the lead-up to International Women's Day she wrote to tell Bromham about

'Harriet', an Aboriginal girl who, having been trained to become a nurse in Leonora hospital, was 'enticed' away by an old man of her tribe who took her to work for him and his other wives. Bennett said that despite her not wanting this fate and despite a native affairs officer being informed, Harriet was told that it was not departmental policy to interfere with native customs. Echoing her argument of old, Bennett wrote:

> This is riveting slavery by Departmental ukase on a woman against her will: it proves the complete incapacity of the Native Department to assume or be allowed to order or arrange other people's lives: it is chattel slavery...The victims of tribal and departmental misrule should not be hunted or frightened or beaten back, for Aboriginal women recognise the better way that every woman should have the right to dispose of her own person.[51]

Too frail to attend in person, she also prepared a detailed statement for the fourth annual conference of the FCAA in 1961. While it rehearsed all her old arguments and made use of particular case studies, it concentrated on the role of the police and the position of Aboriginal prisoners. Harking back to a very old refrain, she complained of the dual and contradictory role of the police 'protector' who both prosecuted and was supposed to defend Aboriginal people. She provided examples of police brutality and discrimination and argued that Kalgoorlie gaol had a reputation for starving the prisoners, many of whom were Aboriginal.

Despite the gains being slowly made, Bennett found that their delivery to Aboriginal people were still subject to departmental obfuscation. By 1959, largely as a result of the lobbying of the FCAA, Bennett and the CAR, the federal government conferred social services on Aborigines. Yet, while Aborigines had won entitlement to these services, they were still being denied them and obstacles were put in their way when they tried to obtain them. Bennett spent hours assisting applicants for these services who required proof of age. She wrote many letters dictating their circumstances and represented their claims to departmental officials.

By 1960 she was complaining that just as they were still not receiving equal pay, many of the goldfields Aborigines were still not receiving their pensions in hand. Instead, the delivery of social services were used to further control, police and belittle the communities. She saw the position of the so-called guarantor as demonstrative of this. Rather than be allowed to handle the pension themselves, they got access to it via the guarantor, who would spend the money on their behalf. She railed:

> You see the natives (a few of the old ones) get the age pension but not the right to spend it, they are assumed to be so silly, so ignorant, so drunk, so wasteful – all of them – and *idle*, I was forgetting idle – that they must have a guarantor to spend their money for them. You see MONEY is precious and some must be kept to build houses that not all will live to occupy, but HUMAN BEINGS are only waste material – this is the way of the world – OUR way of LIFE [original emphasis].[52]

Bennett argued that a further impediment was when the guarantor was away and the Aboriginal pensioners were forced to starve on the state ration.

It was against this backdrop and context that she received the news that Aboriginal co-operative enterprises would finally get some much-needed backing. In September 1961, one month before she died, she heard from Bromham that Alf Clint, the promoter of Aboriginal co-operatives for the Australian Board of Missions, had secured the backing of the British Co-operative Movement and Trade Union Council for Aboriginal co-operatives in Australia. Bennett was overjoyed with this news, declaring: 'I seem to have been waiting for it all my life'.[53]

There is no doubt that this news helped her to die peacefully, as she reflected to Bromham on hearing the news, 'it has brought me such peace of mind…it is such peace I find I am not fooled in everything'.[54] It brought her long crusade full circle. It connected the Australian and British strands of her life story and it helped lift the burden of her guilt which had propelled her crusade. Underpinning this was her sense that she had been fooled, that as she grew up, she had been shielded from the brutalities and vulgarities of imperialism. Co-operatives – their success and her promotion of them – made her feel that she had not been completely fooled, she had not been so 'shocking as to accept their [the imperialists'] blasphemies'.[55] One of the core blasphemies of imperialism had been race prejudice and the denial of humanity to indigenous peoples that went with it. She saw co-operatives as part of the solution because they fundamentally denied the force of that ethos.

IV

Before her death Bennett was classifying her considerable personal archive to assist the CAR in its publication of another book. *The Struggle for Dignity* was the result. This was a combination of the council's own work on building a picture of state-by-state laws for Aborigines which the Anti-Slavery Society's mission and questionnaire had precipitated. It was also based on Bennett's considerable knowledge and contributions. She had been compiling notes and information about state Aboriginal policies, earmarking specific clauses in the legislation, since the 1930s. She had sent these notes and jottings to friends and supporters in Australia and in England and CAR benefited greatly from her knowledge.

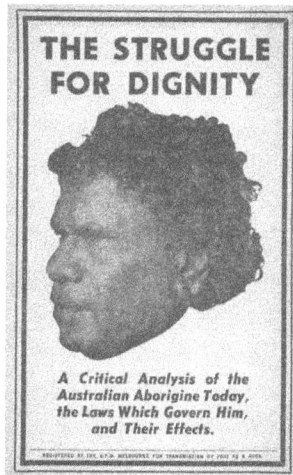

The Struggle for Dignity, *produced by the Council for Aboriginal Rights in 1962, 6 months after Bennett's death.*

The chapter on Western Australia in *Struggle for Dignity* was authored by Bennett and Barry Christophers, the council's president and a correspondent of hers. He had been a long-time admirer of Bennett, particularly of her argument concerning Aboriginal development that opened her book, *The Australian Aboriginal as Human Being*. This appeared to have been something of a revelation to him. It demonstrated for him, as for Andrews, how nomadism had been an economic necessity for Aboriginal people, rather than symptomatic of a presumed backwardness. He later claimed that Bennett was the first person to explain Aboriginal lifestyle

341

in a way Europeans could understand and that her work had influenced Professor Frederic Wood Jones, whom Christophers also greatly admired and had studied at some length.[56] He believed that they were the two most advanced thinkers on the Aboriginal question for the first half of the twentieth century and reprinted Bennett's argument on the back page of *Struggle for Dignity*, under the heading 'The Myth Exploded'.[57]

Bennett died before the book was completed. Christophers and Andrews dedicated it to 'our friend Mary M. Bennett', and started by quoting her key argument in *The Australian Aboriginal as a Human Being* regarding the founding of a just relation between 'white and dark' races as a world problem and the most important one of the twentieth century. The introduction provided a potted history of Bennett's life and work and a bibliography of her publications. This was a very fitting end to Bennett's life and her efforts, for it demonstrated, some 40 years after she had begun her campaign, that her message had, at last, sunk in.

Symptomatic of this was the CAR's involvement, with Bromham, in rescuing her papers when, within the hour of her death, the state barged into her home and confiscated them. Following a year-long battle Bromham finally retrieved them. While the Institute of Aboriginal Studies in Canberra had shown an interest in them, Bromham was determined to send them to Christophers and the council on the basis of their being outside the establishment. Writing to Christophers, she said:

> We secured the right to the papers and documents after a big struggle and I feel sure that you can publicise the importance of Mrs Bennett's thinking and experience in the right way much more so than a State or Government Department can and in arguments that can arise where vested interests also come into the picture, confuse the public and the real principles at stake are lost sight of.[58]

A couple of months later she wrote to Christophers reiterating that he and the council would deal with Bennett's work in a way that would make it 'live as the most important contribution to the rights and future of the First Australians that has ever been made'.[59]

Once the battle was over and the papers were lodged with the CAR in October 1962, Bromham continued in her educational work and picked up where Bennett had left off in assisting her many Wongkai friends in their encounter with the bureaucracy until she, too, died just three years after Bennett. She had remained faithful to Bennett's trust, as Bennett knew she would. In the annals of the collaborative efforts of the activists involved in the Aboriginal cause, theirs would have to have been one of the closest. As they corresponded with each other the two formed a very close and loving bond. To Bennett, Bromham was 'Valiant-before-Truth'.[60] She never failed to praise her, endlessly thanking her for her support, her 'toleration and unselfish and essential help in bringing my efforts for the natives into shape', and her political vision.[61] Concerned about how hard Bromham was working and about how the disappointments they confronted impacted on her, she sent Bromham a prayer:

> Heaven ye, all…
> Thus saith the Lord unto you.
> Be not afraid nor dismayed by
> Reason of this great multitude
> For the battle is not yours, but God's
> Ye shall not need to fight in this
> Battle, stand ye still and see the
> Salvation of the Lord with you.[62]

Comforting words, indeed, for a friend who shared Bennett's deep Christian faith.

If Bromham's support and friendship helped to prolong Bennett's life, Street and Andrews worked to build on Bennett's legacy. Not long after her death they made one last attempt to have the Aboriginal position raised at the UN. This was sparked by Street reading a newspaper account of continued Aboriginal discrimination in Queensland regarding retention of wages and confiscation of a portion of the Aboriginal reserve at Cape York Peninsula. Believing this to be arbitrary and without legal basis, Street suggested one more attempt at raising Aboriginal discrimination before the Trusteeship Council of the UN.[63] Her justification was that on occasions when she had attended sessions of the council black African representatives from various African colonies had given revealing evidence about their treatment and that the subsequent criticism of delegates had helped to bring about reforms.

Left: Shirley Andrews, 1947, Papers of Shirley Andrews,
National Library of Australia, MS6000.
Right: Jessie Street, 1945, National Archives of Australia.

She turned to her old ally, the Anti-Slavery Society, for counsel despite the fact that previous efforts in this direction had collapsed. She had heard of a 'special committee on colonialism' set up at the UN in the early 1960s to hear complaints about the treatment of people as though they were subordinate to a colonial power.[64] She argued that some of the cases presented before this committee resembled the position of the Australian Aborigines. However, she now met with some ambivalence on the part of the society, which would only assist Street on the condition the plan was approved by the Federal Council for Aboriginal Advancement. Notably, it refrained from affiliating with the council, emphasising 'mutual trust' instead.[65]

Street got advice from Reverend Michael Scott, experienced and respected campaigner for African reform in the UN and someone Bennett had been in communication with, too. Street had probably met him via her connection with the Women's International League for Peace and Freedom, which had supported his efforts to obtain a hearing at the Trusteeship Council for the Herero people of southwest Africa.[66] His championship of them had become a symbol of hope for black minorities throughout the world. He informed Andrews of a new organisation being launched under UN auspices known as the International Committee for the Study of Group Rights which was designed to 'fill the gap' as there were no provisions, under the UN Charter or in international law, whereby small groups within sovereign states had an opportunity of impartial examination by an international authority. He maintained that the idea of a sub-committee on the Aboriginal problem had been raised but lack of information and funds prevented further action. He suggested further investigation was required before representations could be made.[67]

In the meantime, the Anti-Slavery Society's hesitancy seemed to be matched at the local level. Despite initial support for the plan, primarily from trade unions, the FCAA began to question the propriety of such a move. In July 1963 Andrews informed Street of caution creeping into council circles. She added that even those people who approved of UN intervention were unwilling that it be raised by an external organisation. She concluded that it would be best if Street made personal inquiries as to what was possible on her return to England late in the year and that she would supply her with material for the visit. She suggested that an alternative course of action might be to raise the question of Aboriginal wages at the ILO.

By November, just before Street's return to England, the FCAA had gone completely cold on the idea of UN representation. Andrews informed Street that the issue had become so volatile that it had nearly caused a split in the executive. This led Andrews to comment:

> I was quite surprised to find out how many people are opposed to having the matter raised outside Australia. It seems to touch on a question of national pride and all sorts of people who are quite progressive in their attitude on the Aboriginal question seem to have this weak spot.[68]

For its part, the Anti-Slavery Society resorted to its traditional methods of raising concern by sending letters to the ILO and the Australian High Commissioner dealing with the need for constitutional reform, the under-payment of Aborigines and the need to discontinue the trust-fund system. The information it used was based entirely on the collective research of Bennett and Andrews. Andrews recommended that the Australian Council of Trade Unions approach the ILO in support of the society's submission. In the meantime, Street went to New York to make further inquiries about ways in which the Aboriginal cause could be further advanced at the UN.

Plate 2

A station hand's wife and young family. 1960
Tapukari with Bernadette and Roderick
(Joya Maher) (13 yrs) (3 mths) 56
The eldest son Raymond, aged 14 works on a station.
The second son died at Norseman Mission. The low wages
for Aborigines enables institutions to remove their children.

Daisy Imari and Angel
are a grand Aborigine couple who have always worked faithfully as station hands
wherever work was to be found. Now that they are ageing it is difficult to get
station work, so they take work in the bush and Angel cuts wood. It happens that
they are not always paid and there is no redress.

Samples of the kinds of photographs Mary Bennett commissioned in Kalgoorlie of her many Wongkai friends, showing her handwritten notes providing their names and the details of their conditions. Boxes 12/5-6, Council for Aboriginal Rights (Vic), Papers, MS 12913, State Library of Victoria.

Bennett died without a solution having been found for the Aboriginal problem. As the work of Street and Andrews showed, nor had the international dimensions been understood, much less accepted. Yet, the revolution Bennett had hoped for was just beginning to break through. She was not there to witness the significant changes in Aboriginal politics wrought by the period of social and political change of the 1960s, yet much of them bore the imprint of her legacy. Nowhere was this more obvious than in the influence of international standards on local conditions that was a hallmark of the 1960s phenomenon.[69] Some 100 years after her birth the notion of Aboriginal *rights* forced its way into the national consciousness. Australians were showing signs of the 'stricken conscience' she had hoped for.

A key part of the 1960s revolution was the reappraisal of Australian history which recuperated the Aboriginal people and their historic relations with the settlers. Instead of a 'melancholy footnote', Aboriginal history became a vibrant field of research and inquiry which resuscitated the Australian story. It also demonstrated the veracity of many of Bennett's claims, from the fact of dispossession, the significant exploitation of Aboriginal labour, the collision between Aboriginal people and the law, the deeply problematic nature of protection – and assimilation – as well as the possibilities of interaction and cooperation which her own story revealed. The 1996 Human Rights and Equal Opportunity Commission's report, *Bringing Them Home*, put her 30-year long struggle to stop the removal of Aboriginal children from their families into historical perspective.[70] The recent campaign to 'close the gap' reverberates with her long campaign to promote better educational and health outcomes for Aboriginal people. At a time when Aboriginal human rights continue to cause concern, Bennett's considerable legacy is a timely reminder of the cost of their non-recognition and worse, their violation.

CONCLUSION

COMMISSIONER MOSELEY: You are something of an idealist, and wish to bring about an ideal system all at once?

MARY BENNETT: I wish to treat other people like human beings. I do not put it higher than that.

COMMISSIONER MOSELEY: In your view there is no case bad enough to take out of the bush and put into a settlement?

MARY BENNETT: A native's own will should be consulted. His desire to improve his own position should be studied. His co-operation ought to be sought for the improvement of his own life…He is not a nut to put under a screw and given an extra twist to. He is a human being and his co-operation must be sought and encouraged in any welfare scheme.[1]

This conversation between Commissioner Moseley and Mary Bennett in 1934 neatly sums up Bennett's vision of Aboriginal rights. From the moment of her own discovery of Aboriginal people's humanity to her death, her primary claim was that, as human beings, Aboriginal people deserved respect and some form of self-determination. In the very least, their humanity required that they be consulted about policies and practices which impacted their lives. For her, there was simply no case bad enough for the state to override their wishes and take children away. The fact that Bennett was framed an idealist suggests that the notion that mixed-descent children should remain with a parent or parents was anathema to the state at that time, even in the face of Bennett's extensive evidence of the trauma, terror and violations involved.[2] Moseley described her as 'well-intentioned but extravagant' in her views of what was possible for 'the native'.[3] Although not entirely alone in her criticism of child removal then, she was virtually alone three years later when the state implemented its absorption decision which would escalate and systematise the process of child removal. Her defence of the rights of Aboriginal mothers, fathers, children and communities remained a hallmark of her long crusade.

Aboriginal child removal was but one part of her larger critique of the system in Australia, however. She described the system as premised on the denial of Aborigines' legal rights to their lands. Instead, land had been constituted Crown Land and, via legislation, leased or sold by the government to the white settlers. Protection, as it evolved in the Australian setting, had been recognised as early as the 1840s to be a failure not only because it denied legal rights, but also because Aborigines continued to be injured and exploited 'with impunity'.[4] In the battle over land, the Aborigines defended their country but it had been an unequal war – wooden spears and bushcraft against firearms. In losing their lands, they lost their means of survival in economic and spiritual terms. They were 'let in' to the townships 'to become a prey to the vices of the whites and die off like rotten sheep'.[5] To make matters worse these conditions prevailed even as Australia was explored and settled with Aborigines' help through their clever hunting, superb tracking abilities, skilful inter-tribal negotiations and knowledge of the land and its resources.

Bennett's defence of Aboriginal human rights rested on an appreciation of their dispossession. As she wrote in *The Australian Aboriginal as a Human Being*, 'recognised, or, not recognised, the principle stands: that dispossession and control of one race by another are opposed to freedom and justice and perpetuate all the evils of slavery'.[6] The importance of this fact was that it rendered Aboriginal people completely at the colonisers' mercy and thus strengthened the 'temptation to abuse our power'.[7] On the other hand an appreciation of the centrality of land to Aboriginal culture was, for her, the first principle of a sounder administration.[8] Schooled in the hothouse politics around colonial governance in interwar Britain, Bennett saw the central tenets of indirect rule as a means of delivering that administration. It was an alternative to the 'fatal course of domination' which she maintained Australia had, to that point, pursued in the Northern Territory in particular. Bennett's belief in this core idea can be traced from her promotion of it in 1930 to her commitment to the principles of preservation and development which emerged in the war years, and her support of integration after them.

On one level her devotion to indirect rule as a model of reform proved Moseley right. This was an ideal to aspire to and it demonstrated her and her fellow humanitarians' idealism. As it played out, indirect rule was as open to the abuse of power as direct rule had been. While an attempt to develop a new approach to the moral dilemma the British had in Africa, it was chiefly a pragmatic colonial policy – in Porter's words, an alternative imperialism.[9] However, for the humanitarian concerned about the long-term viability of indigenous societies under colonial rule, and operating outside government and administration, it provided a powerful antidote to historical practices of subjugation, denial and extermination. As Bennett said at the time, indirect rule was understood as a form of scientific humanism because, in theory, it rested on the notion of maintaining and building on indigenous institutions as they adapted to change. Rather than domination and obliteration it respected the form and content of many aspects of their cultures.

Indeed, to read the Hilton Young Report, on which Bennett placed so many of her ideas for reform, is like reading a wish list for colonial best practice. Targeting the problem of British rule in east Africa, it spoke to the concern of how to rule a colony justly and humanely. Native interests would be paramount. They should have land, education, a voice in their own concerns, conditions for developing their cultures and forms of economic independence, including assistance to develop their own territories. Native policy should rest on the need to discover and apply principles of a just relationship between a white, immigrant and invading race and a subject Aboriginal race. It was about legal justice and citizenship and it was a moral issue to remove abuse and the disparity in status which bred abuse. The three core issues for resolving the Aboriginal problem were land, labour and a voice in their own concerns. Immigrant communities were to claim partnership rather than control.

As it unravelled, Bennett's crusade represented the Australian chapter of this British story. Yet her attempts to fit this model onto Australian conditions would prove deeply problematic. Her sense that conditions in Africa had a '*pianissimo*' counterpart in Australia was not shared by administrators.[10] Indeed, native policy in Australia was largely an attempt to avoid the problems of colour and race being played out there. Nor did administrators consider themselves immigrants, colonisers or partners. Aboriginal people were 'primitives' who had underutilised the land and wasted their opportunity.[11]

The task of the governors and administrators was neither recognising native interests nor creating opportunities for Aboriginal development and independence. They were protectors, and protection evolved in the nineteenth century against the backdrop of Aboriginal claims for land and independence without recognition of them. It was ambivalent and ultimately reflected contemporary ideas around race, class and respectability, the rural–urban divide and philanthropy.[12] Protection meant rations and blankets. It might mean attempts to civilise, or segregation and protection from the ill-effects of contact. Most importantly, however, at the time that indirect rule was being theorised in Britain, Aboriginal people were widely regarded as inevitably doomed. Protection was about smoothing their 'dying pillow'.

At the heart of the nascent humanitarianism of the interwar years, of which Bennett was a key protagonist, was the rejection of this idea. This was a radical proposition. There was nothing inevitable about Aborigines' alleged doom. Rather it was the accumulated result of their dispossession, injustice and ill-treatment. In Bennett's terms it was about the perpetuation of an old evil system and her central purpose was to reverse this process and save the Aborigines from extinction. Indeed, she saw the salvation or extinction of Aborigines as the central question for native administrators, acknowledging not long before she died that it was a question which had not yet been seriously faced.

Salvation rested on humane intervention to arrest population decline, to prevent disease, to stop the abuse of women, to put an end to the exploitation and near slavery of Aboriginal workers, to provide education and land and to stop the pauperisation and demoralisation of the people. Importantly, intervention was needed to stop the breakup of Aboriginal families. Furthermore, these conditions and reforms must be available to all, irrespective of class or caste. Tracing Bennett's crusade has recovered an alternative discourse concerning the Aboriginal problem threaded across the middle years of the twentieth century. Where the state was primarily concerned with solving the problem of those of mixed descent, Bennett and some of her allies were interested in preserving and developing those classified full-blood who were the majority Aboriginal population for much of the twentieth century. It was their fate which underpinned the quest for advancement in the immediate postwar years. It was mostly in relation to them that Bennett laid the charge of genocide against the Australian state.

On one level, Bennett's commitment to the salvation of the Aborigines was very similar to that of Helen Hunt Jackson's on the American frontier. Ironically, Jackson's quest for the reform of Indian policy in the US began in the year Bennett was born, 1881, with the publication of her book, *A Century of Dishonor*. Like Bennett, she came to the cause late in her life. Just as Bennett had been concerned about dispossession, Jackson became committed to the native cause in the context of the forced removals of the Poncas from their home territory in the 1870s. Like Bennett's publications, *Century of Dishonor* was intended to arouse the national conscience to the wrongs perpetrated on the Indians, particularly in relation to their title to land. The parallel histories of these two women are suggestive of the parallel histories of Australia and America as settler-colonial states.

Bennett's own heroine was Harriet Beecher Stowe, the novelist made famous by her classic tale, *Uncle Tom's Cabin*. Her admiration of Stowe reflected the impact that novel had on British society as the best-selling book of the nineteenth century.[13] Whether or not Bennett styled herself on Stowe, it is clear that she saw Stowe's work as central to the cause of slave freedom. She saw that a powerful work of literature was a means of exposing slave conditions and creating a wave of sympathy both for the slave cause and for abolition. Bennett longed to see such a work in the Australian setting, declaring, 'We want an Australian Maeterlinck, an Australian Masefield, an Australian Harriet Beecher Stowe'.[14] She wanted Olive Pink to write a work based on her experiences in order to free Aboriginal people, as Stowe had done for southern America.[15]

Many years later, Bennett was relieved to find that such a book had finally been produced. When Donald Stuart wrote *Yandy*, which was the story of the Aboriginal workers' strike in the Pilbara and their attempts to establish a co-operative, she publicised it to her friends and supporters as the Australian *Uncle Tom's Cabin*, writing to Commander Fox-Pitt of the Anti-Slavery Society,

> You will realise how devastating this book of Don Stuart's is, but its writer has a real appreciation of the soul and music of words and so I hope this book will achieve for Australia's robbed

and trampled Aboriginal station hands what Uncle Tom's Cabin achieved for the slaves.[16]

It might be tempting to say that Bennett was, in fact, Australia's Stowe. We might see the culmination of her life's work as an anti-slavery crusade. She used her pen in an effort to free the Aborigines from conditions approximating slavery in the Australian setting. Her stories and case studies of individuals, from the Dalleburra to the Wongutha and Wongkai, might be considered akin to Stowe's slave narratives. Like Stowe, she was a writer, an extremely hard-working and prolific one at that. She spent her days and nights writing, mostly letters but also notes, reports, case studies and anecdotes. She was writing about the Aborigines right up to her death. Yet, Bennett was no novelist. While such stories were needed, she would stick to the facts. Her writings were those of a political activist, more in the style of a columnist and a polemicist than a novelist. She was more a Morel than a Stowe, using her pen as a weapon against wrongdoing, exposing injustice on as wide a scale as possible and utilising images as testimony.[17] As she wrote following the showdown between the missions and Neville in 1939:

I have written nothing that I will not gladly maintain on every possible occasion in the hope and with the prayer that Australia will wake up to their stupid wickedness and reverse their policy and do justice.[18]

The sense of justice and injustice defined her humanitarian crusade. Thinking about her as a humanitarian *worker* allows us to understand what drove her to make the Aboriginal cause her life-long work. According to Michael Barnett, the three forces of destruction (violence), production (economy) and compassion are critical to understanding humanitarianism.[19] We can see these forces at work in the context of Bennett's endeavours. The first decades of the twentieth century saw the alignment of these in the form of World War I and the violence it unleashed, as well as the new conceptions of international order it presaged. At the same time the expansion of imperial rule on the one hand and global depression on the other had profound economic implications, while the growth of the welfare state helped to reconfigure the relationship between the state and individuals. Collectively, these forces helped to produce a crisis of faith which had been growing since the end of the nineteenth century and which the war did much to cement. The importance of these forces, according to Barnett, is that they spawned an ethical awakening and a corresponding desire for atonement. At the core of this process was the recognition that a sin had been committed which demanded a response.

This template is a useful way of understanding the cause of Aboriginal reform and the nascent humanitarian movement in the first decades of the twentieth century, the existence of which propelled Bennett to return to Australia. In this case, the original sin was dispossession and, after the war, the belief in inevitable Aboriginal demise. Saving the race was an act of atonement for a society deeply implicated in that process and characterised by profound indifference to the Aboriginal plight in the past. For Bennett, the daughter of one of Australia's most successful pastoralists, the forces Barnett describes were a potent mix, shaping her ideas, feelings and inter-ventions. They impacted on her in a profound and deeply personal way, for as Barnett notes, outbursts of compassion and corresponding ethical awakenings are most acute when we feel implicated in the suffering. They give rise to the emotionally wrenching process of critical self-reflection.[20] As he notes, humanitarianism is sustained by a particular story we tell ourselves but some encounters force individuals to re-examine everything that they thought they knew about themselves.

There is no doubt that Bennett had such a moment. Her meeting with Anthony Martin Fernando during his trial in the Old Bailey in 1928 was an important part of this process. He did not want to engage with her. He saw her as part of the system he despised. He had no faith in the humanitarian set among whom she moved, considering them to be part of the problem. Yet, as important as this meeting was, it is more likely that her crisis of faith occurred a little earlier, in the early to mid-1920s, while she was collating her father's papers and writing his biography. It was there that she read about the humanity of Aboriginal people and learned of her father's defence of the same. Her father's papers were full of anecdotes which demonstrated this. One anecdote which she took from his notes and subsequently retold in *The Australian Aboriginal* was about the Aborigines on Flinders Island, the settlement the remnant Tasmanian Aborigines were sent to at the end of the Black War in that colony. It was told to Christison by a Mr Gardiner, who lived on the island. The

Aboriginal people would perch themselves on the top of Mount Arthur in the early morning and, as the sunrise exposed the mountains of their native land, exclaim, 'Country belonging to me!'.[21] In her book Bennett also used the many tales of nineteenth-century exploration, including her father's, which demonstrated the help the European explorers were given by the various tribes.

In this way, Bennett came to see what she had been blind to, which was that the Dalleburra – particularly Barney, her father's right-hand man, and Wyma, her nursemaid – were among the most faithful of all. The collection of photographs and objects she donated to the British Museum before returning to Australia in 1930 demonstrated how profound her awakening was. They are a beautiful and very moving inventory of people and place which she asked to be added to her father's collection, deposited at the turn of the century. Hers would complete the collection. To her mother's many photographs of individuals and working groups, Bennett inserted her own annotations, including names as well as tribal names and marriage sections where she knew them. Writing to the keeper of the ethnographic department, she described the collection as unique and suggested how the photographs should be displayed:

> For completeness' sake, & to make a mass of information readily assimilable by the public, I would suggest that the photographs should be shown in a stand (like the leaves of a book) showing first a map of the Dalleburra country – on tower Hill Creek at the head of the Thomson (between Hughenden and Muttaburra in Queensland) with the native names, where ascertainable, placed alongside of the European names, secondly, pictures of their favourite fishing holes – Mattnundukka, Narkool, etc..., thirdly, the pictures of aboriginals of the Dalleburra Tribe...[22]

The realisation of Aboriginal people's humanity and the fact that they had been wronged was the epiphany which largely underpinned her crusade. As Barnett notes, such moments can lead to acts of atonement, including sacrifice. It certainly did cause Bennett to re-examine everything she thought she knew about herself, including her own family and her society. She had been selfish, dismissive, rude and racist to Wyma. She had benefited from Wyma's largesse without recognising it as such at the time. Where her mother was flighty and inconsistent, Wyma was steadfast and loyal. Her awakening also came at a particularly poignant time in her life when, alienated from her family, she lost her husband. Her decision to go slumming in London's east end was indicative of her and many others' crises of faith at this time. Her meeting with Fernando was a critical moment because it spoke directly to her own story of loss and grief. It was a catalyst, deciding her future course of action to ameliorate the burden of her privilege and make amends for the past.

As this suggests, her awakening was not a cursory appreciation of colonialism's worst effects. Rather it was a profound enlightenment, a life-changing revelation. A veil was lifted exposing what she saw as a fundamental truth (and lie) underpinning Australian settlement and, by implication, her own story. It was as though she had shed a layer of her own identity, its imperial and colonial crust, and, looking back, saw the arbitrary and constructed nature of imperial power. As her own exposure had revealed such power was coated in defence and self-justification which, in turn, protected it from its own excesses, savagery and lies. Once alive to it she remained forever attuned to the use and abuse of power, ever alive to the 'faults of the rulers' as she put it.[23]

Furthermore the dawning awareness that, far from being primitive and backward, Aboriginal people and cultures were representative of a complex and fascinating civilisation of their own was powerful. The idea that the very success of her own vaunted civilisation rested on Aboriginal ingenuity, labour, resilience, generosity and patience saw her devote herself to what she saw as their restitution. This fact made the exploitation of Aboriginal labour and its lack of remuneration abominable in her eyes. White prosperity – her own prosperity – had been at the expense of the Aborigines and it rested on their land. They were robbed of it and the freedom and independence that went with it. Her – our – debt was significant and there was no turning back. She would not abandon the Aborigines as they had not abandoned her father.

There was a certain amount of anger about this. She felt that her life and her upbringing had shielded her from the world, had made her immune from the worst excesses of imperialism. 'Why did I grow up and live so ignorant in a world of desperate need?', she asked Ada Bromham towards the end of her life.[24] Clearly, the Aboriginal problem became a way of Bennett critiquing herself, her own society and even her own family who, according to her sister, became part of the world she wished to renounce.[25] Indeed, Bennett had no further contact with them from the early 1920s when her sister took her mother to Australia to live after her marriage. So wide was the gap between them that, as the struggle raged over her papers, there was no sense that she had family in Australia. This was despite her sister's attempts to make contact and it was despite the many aspects of their lives which they shared. The fact was that her sister, Helen (Lily) Roberts, shared Mary's deep interest in Aboriginal culture. From her base in northern New South Wales she maintained contact with people who had connections to the Dalleburra, including those who had been relocated to Cherbourg Aboriginal settlement in Queensland. Like Mary, she corresponded with and assisted them.

This distance speaks volumes for some kind of family rift which we will never know from Bennett's own perspective. However, it is also suggestive of her renunciation of the life she knew for her life of atonement on the Australian frontier. Both reflected her own profound disenchantment with her world. Her engagement in the Aboriginal problem was an outlet for her own alienation, self-imposed and otherwise. As she reflected to Maxwell Brown towards the end of her life, whereas white society talks of the importance of family, Aboriginal people lived it.[26] Where Aboriginal societies were communal and co-operative, her own civilisation was competitive, nasty and cut-throat.[27] She spoke of the 'gross prosperity' of the white people, as against the poverty and starvation of the Aborigines. She contrasted the 'Australian way of life' – the catchphrase of assimilation – with the 'Wongkai way of life' and questioned why the former was considered better or more civilised.[28] She never lost the sense that we had a lot to learn from Aboriginal people and her deep appreciation of co-operative enterprises was not just emblematic of her faith in Labor to bring about justice. It was about what her own story told her: at the core of the relationship between her father and the Dalleburra was cooperation, or so the story went.

This demonstrates how commitment to the Aboriginal cause was part of a larger political vision which was shaped by her Christianity on the one hand and the ideals of Labor on the other. Her hands-on engagement fed her critique. She started out by saying that her quarrel was not with individual settlers or police but with 'the system'. The more she saw, the more she experienced with Aboriginal people as they attempted to live within it, the more disenchanted she became. More importantly she came to believe that governments were actively perpetuating a lie about Australian settlement. They were in cahoots with the squatters and together they discouraged and disadvantaged the Aborigines and browbeat them into submission. She never denied that there were some officials who truly tried to protect their Aboriginal charges but believed that they were ultimately defeated by pastoralists and industrialists on the frontiers who made profits from their unpaid services. Furthermore, she argued that the latter were supported by the respective governments, as she noted a year before her death:

> God can deliver us and our Aborigines from the fiery furnace of their burnt earth policy – but if not, be it known to the adversary we will NOT bow down to his ugly idol the golden image of these exploiters [original emphasis].[29]

This was before many of the gains of the later 1960s in terms of the slow recognition of Aboriginal rights, including access to equal wages. As it suggests, she became very hostile to 'the system' in her final years. Part of this was because she believed that dispossession bred persecution: 'the mass of white Australians have always objected to any kind of justice or protection for the unhappy people whom they are dispossessing'.[30] Yet she satisfied herself that she, Bromham and a handful of others were on the winning side. This was not just stubborn bloody-mindedness and self-righteousness, it was because they were doing God's work:

> But we are 'on the Lord's side' and I feel now I must put the burden on him and acknowledge to HIM my own ineptness. He will work and use us and we must trust HIM to perform His justice which is perfect [original emphasis].[31]

Defining herself as God's worker also spoke to her sense of being an outsider and alone in the cause, as did her reliance on Bromham towards the end. Having lost faith in both sides of the political spectrum, most missionaries and most others, she and Bromham could appeal to the ultimate higher authority, the being that, hovering above all, could see all. Faith was not just about Bennett's deep Christian commitment. It was critical to her life's work and self-definition. Indeed, her constant companion in the final years of her life was her little black dog, Faith. Faithful the Dalleburra had been. Faithful she was to her father's legacy and wishes, and faithful she had been to the Aboriginal cause in general and the cause of Fernando in particular. It was little wonder that she would remember him in the final stages of her life as an important catalyst for her life's work. His resentful accusation in 1928 that, 'if you are not working for the Aborigines, you are working against them', had stuck.[32] As she said at the time, although he would not cooperate with her and other humanitarians in working for more humane conditions for his people, 'we must not relax our efforts, but try not to deserve his judgement of ineptitude. He must follow his star and we must work as faithfully as we can in our way too'.[33]

Nonetheless, her evangelicalism, self-righteousness and anti-slavery rhetoric are symptomatic of tensions and contradictions in her crusade. Her humanitarianism both affirmed and critiqued claims of British justice and was emancipatory and dominating.[34] As a classic anti-slavery crusader Bennett had inherited over 100 years of moral certainty and evangelical zeal characteristic of the cause. On one reading of her we can say that she was part of the empire's civilising mission, particularly her attempt to reform Indigenous domestic relations, her education program at Mt Margaret and her slavery critique. Her crusade was the romantic embodiment of an idealised humane empire, her defence of Aboriginal people simultaneously embedded in and given definition by the very empire which had underpinned Aboriginal dispossession. Just as she had cordoned her father from the worst excesses of colonialism, her life-long crusade had the effect of doing the same for herself. Furthermore, her defence of Aboriginal humanity often rested on and rehearsed a trope of noble savagery, long since deployed in British anti-slavery rhetoric.

Barnett argues that any act of intervention, no matter how well intended, is also an act of control. He argues that nowhere is this clearer than in the paternalism which often underpins humanitarian endeavour. Bennett's crusade is certainly laced with a heavy dose of paternalism. Indeed, ironically, in Christison, we see the twin imperatives of benevolence and autocracy which Pedersen argues underwrote the trusteeship system.[35] The construction of the Dalleburra as his 'faithfuls' was a powerful representation of his power and paternalism. Faithful they may have been but they had few alternatives. In this light, Christison might very well have been their 'faithful'. They sought refuge in his benevolence and there is certainly a sense of his faithfulness to them in return. However, the construction of the 'faithful Dalleburra' is more about him than about them. It is a semantic rendering of his colonising project, his heroic stoicism. It thus obscures the Dalleburra's own heroic struggle – and his autocracy.

Of course, the 'faithful Dalleburra' is also about Bennett as dutiful daughter and redeemed crusader. Bennett's story is also laced with maternalism. There is no doubt that she acted in the role of mother at times, which included thinking that she knew best. She saw herself as a mediator, worrying about Aboriginal well-being, advancing their cause and acting as their confidante. She characterised Aboriginal people as victims and, despite believing in justice above charity, clearly engaged in charitable acts of her own. When she spoke for the Wongutha or Wongkai or represented their claims it was because, as she put it, they had no voice in their own concerns or weren't listened to. Her sense of them as 'civilisation's casualties' obscured their agency, including in their interactions with her.[36] While she listened long and attentively, she also had a clear vision of what she thought their future should be. Education as she promoted it was about introducing non-Indigenous systems of thought and being in the world, and when it came to implementing indirect rule she was quite clear about which aspects of their society constituted the good and should be kept and which were the bad and should go. Indeed, her battle with Neville before the war should, at least partially, be understood as a battle between paternal and maternal ideas about the way forward.

The duality in her work between imperial crusader and human rights advocate is also revealed in her insistence on co-operatives and agrarianism as solutions to the problem. In one view, her thinking betrayed the long-held British view that Aboriginal people should become cultivators of the soil. This related to the ways in which agriculture was deeply tied to notions of civilisation and progress in imperial ideology. The Anti-Slavery Society frequently cited various success stories in this regard. It was a model which undergirded the Model State and the society's own land trust submission. Yet, Bennett's insistence on co-operatives and growing their own food was fundamentally about a model of economic development. It was not capitalism which 'robbed the poor and kept them poor' and it was not socialism which 'did things *for* people'. Rather, co-operatives were about Aboriginal people doing things for themselves.[37] Furthermore, cooperation was the opposite of competiveness which had been the basis of the white settlers' treatment of Aboriginal people. Cooperation with Aboriginal people could promote their self-determination as well as race justice and peace for, 'if instead of cooperating with our natives we persist in competing against them, then assuredly they will go down before our competitiveness'.[38]

Hence, Bennett's maternalism and Christian chauvinism must be tempered by an appreciation of how radical she was in terms of thinking about this question in ways which were only beginning to be under-stood and uncovered by the 1990s in the context of a widely revised and revitalised Australian story. I said at the start of this book that it was the resonances between then and now that propelled my desire to recover the contours of the biography of one of Australia's leading twentieth-century human rights advocates. The cacophony of claims and counter-claims at the end of the twentieth and beginning of the twenty-first centuries about past wrongs and Aboriginal futures echoed those of 100 years earlier. The focus on the Northern Territory resonated with the same about 80 years earlier when the nascent humanitarian movement called for a royal commission into the Aborigines of these regions said to be dying out as a result of white civilisation.

This book is about one woman's attempts to make the Australian state realise its historic mistreatment, its debt and its responsibilities to Aboriginal people as she defined them. Yet, it is not her story alone. Focusing on her humanitarian ideas and activism the story told here reveals that, while distinctive and tireless, Bennett's crusade was part of a larger humanitarian story in Australian history not yet fully told. It demonstrates that Aboriginal affairs has been a battle-ground over which heated and passionate debates have been had. In this sense, the recent history wars are part of a continuum which have some resonance with Bennett's efforts as they were discursive wars where the word, the text and the story itself were the source of conflict. What her story reveals is that while historians may have facilitated a 'cult of forgetfulness' concerning Aboriginal people for much of the twentieth century, this was not matched on the ground where there had been a constant, often vociferous, discourse about the condition of Aboriginal people, its relationship to the history and about the need for reform.[39] There has long been a *politics* of reform.

In the very least, Bennett's story demonstrates the impossibility of 'not knowing'. Nowhere is this clearer than in relation to the question of child removal. She wrote about it in 1930. She and others raised it, in sensational circumstances which she had largely created, in 1933. She raised it again in 1937 at the time of the first conference of Aboriginal welfare officials and in 1943 to the Anti-Slavery Society. In 1946 opposition to the practice was embedded in a key resolution of the Women's Charter conference and in 1951, just as the practice was stepped up by the administrators and politicians, concern became more widespread still. The case of Peter Pontara demonstrated to her and others that the policy was not necessarily about child welfare alone. It involved considerable violation of human rights. As she said at the time, if Peter's welfare had been a leading consideration, the boy would have been reunited with his family, which was critical to Aboriginal well-being and 'the first university where learning was apprenticeship to life'.[40]

On this and other questions Bennett was an early contributor to the debate concerning the relationship between genocide and colonisation, which has been stimulated in more recent times by the findings of the 1996 Royal Commission into the removal of Aboriginal children and the history wars. She focused, initially, on the question of Indigenous labour. Using the 1837 Report of the House of Commons Select Committee on Aborigines she argued that questions of land and labour went hand in hand. Conditions analogous to slavery were the result of the demand for native labour which arose from white colonisation and ownership of native lands. This view underpinned her implacable opposition to the impoverishment of Aboriginal workers, particularly in the pastoral industry. After the war, she also focused on the dictatorial nature of Aboriginal policy, frequently referring to it as a form of totalitarian rule. As she said to Shirley Andrews in the midst of the Pontara affair:

> Of course what makes this case so difficult is that the WA Native Administration Act – which the late Neville compiled – places the officials of the Department above the law (as in section 8) and this authority is delegated by the Commissioner to junior officials and of course missionaries can wield terrific power. But the quickest way to corrupt the human being is to give him total power... Hence we are engaged in the most unpopular fight of all, the fight against – not injustice but total power which is corruption. It is not the slightest use pretending it is anything else.[41]

Along with others she drew connections between the situation of the Jews in Nazi Germany and that of the Aborigines in Australia.

Whether the wider public knew or didn't know was not, for Bennett, the issue, despite her own efforts in publicising the same. According to the historian Anna Haebich, racism accounts, in part, for the general public apparently 'not knowing'.[42] They knew but they didn't necessarily see anything wrong, as the historic appalling conditions of Aboriginal people and discriminatory treatment had become normalised. They were immune to it. Bennett was concerned about the racism of ordinary Australian folk, too, but her target was the people in positions of power. Her key point was that administrators, welfare officials and politicians *did* know.

This notion of governmental responsibility was echoed by Donald Thomson in 1937 when he noted in his report to government on conditions in Arnhem Land that, as an anthropologist, he could advise governments about policy but that ultimate responsibility 'for action or failure of action' rested with the government.[43] Bennett reserved her critique for 'the system' and targeted it directly at governments. Not only were they negligent and wilful, they 'propagated ignorance' about the Aboriginal people and policy. Nowhere was this more apparent than in the concept of assimilation which she believed developed an almost sacred aura after the war. Her concern was that as everyone was apparently taken in by it, the breakup of families continued apace.[44]

Just as her critique of assimilation after the war resonates with contemporary debates about the legacies and meaning of it, her focus before World War II was particularly resonant in the context of the so-called crisis in Aboriginal communities which surfaced in the 2000s. For at least a decade around the turn of the century there were murmurings of things not right in the north. The high level of child sexual abuse and violence against women as well as the so-called domestic dysfunction of Aboriginal communities saw them imploding. Drug and alcohol abuse were accompanied by unprecedented violence, targeted mostly at women. Reports were commissioned, allegations aired and debate raged about the causes of alleged Aboriginal dysfunction. Emergency intervention was justified for communities in crisis and to avert disaster. A space was provided in the public domain whereby the most intimate aspects of Aboriginal people's lives were laid bare. The consensus seemed to be that Aboriginal people were, at least partly, the cause of their own undoing and the reasons ranged from their passive welfare dependency to inherent flaws in their own cultures, including the violence and cultural chauvinism of Aboriginal men.

Inasmuch as the situation has been understood or interpreted, the blame has rested on the last 30 years of the policy setting.[45] The period from the 1970s and the advent of self-determination as government policy is understood to have created the contemporary social deterioration of the people in the north. Importantly, the era of so-called rights-based policy and discourse which followed in Bennett's wake is understood to have delivered, in the words of Noel Pearson, the right to misery, mass incarceration and early death. In what could be seen as a radical critique of Bennett's position, Pearson pinpointed the nub of the problem as he saw it:

> Why has a social breakdown accompanied the advancement in the formal rights of our people?...The irony of our newly won citizenship in 1967 was that after we became citizens with equal rights and the theoretical right to equal pay, we lost the meagre foothold that we had in the real economy and we became almost comprehensively dependent upon passive welfare for our livelihood. So in one sense we gained citizenship and in another sense we lost it at the same time. Because we find thirty years later that life in the safety net for three decades and two generations has produced a social disaster.[46]

This is a searing critique of that which Bennett had long campaigned for – Aboriginal advancement and citizenship, equal pay and rights – and there were others who agreed. She was not around in 1967 and nor was she around to see that which she had long hoped for, the award of equal pay in the pastoral industry. Yet there is little doubt that she would have felt much of Pearson's angst by the 2000s. Her writing, research and monitoring of government policy stopped in 1961. At that point Aboriginal people had only just been awarded access to social service benefits and, as she saw, this was far from satisfactory in terms of implementation. To be granted citizenship in Western Australia, they still had to apply for exemption with its requirement for the dissolution of family ties. Children were still being removed and there was not even a glimmer of land rights. There was much poverty, starvation and ill-health in the communities as well as extremely low levels of educational attainment and high levels of incarceration. People existed under the shadow of an inferiority complex, and alcohol and drug abuse was, as it had always been, widespread.

It is very likely that Bennett would have agreed that the policy framework of the last 30 years had hindered rather than advanced Aboriginal well-being. It was built on the edifice of the old and she would have shared Pearson's despondency about a political solution to the problem. She had long said that governments gave with one hand while they took away with another. She would not have been surprised that equal wages in the pastoral industry resulted in Aboriginal workers losing their jobs. As she said, squatters would 'resist and fight hard against any attempt to enable the Aborigines to develop'.[47] It is for this reason that she shared Pearson's sense of the importance of a viable economic base and a place in the real economy as vital to Aboriginal well-being and survival, including co-operative partnerships. Like him she fought for education for the communities. Yet she would not have equated the delivery of rights and self-determination with social deterioration. She would not have accepted his sense of a paradox. Rather, she would be more likely to notice continuities between the new policy framework and the old. She had long been railing against misery, incarceration and early death.

She almost certainly would not have agreed with his critique of 'symptom theory' which locates the cause of the so-called social disaster in Aboriginal communities in the contemporary setting as the result of history – trauma, intergenerational grief, racism, dispossession, unemployment and poverty. Her years of advocacy were all about emphasising the salience of these issues to understanding the problem and finding a solution. Indeed, the longevity of her claims about social deterioration in the communities including, most importantly and centrally, the vulnerability of women and children, suggests that history is far more central than Pearson allows. While Aboriginal deterioration certainly spiralled and became very acute by the end of the twentieth century, her own crusade across the middle years of the century demonstrates something of the inevitability of this outcome, in the event that these issues were not dealt with earlier.

In fact, far from the acknowledgement of a rights agenda, it might be said that the acute level of the social deterioration in the communities in the north in contemporary times demonstrates the failure of a rights-based agenda to take hold. Bennett might have interpreted the crisis of recent years as, at least in part, the failure to heed hers and the humanitarians' warnings before the war. All of the issues which were raised at the end of the twentieth century had been raised at the beginning of it. This included concerns around land, citizenship, the vulnerability of Aboriginal women and children, Aboriginal health, mortality and education, the high rates of incarceration, Aboriginal economies, Aboriginal futures and discrimination.

Indeed, some of the issues have a much longer trajectory still. Alcohol, drugs and sex have been the means of doing business with Aboriginal people from 1788. Sex, in particular, has been the primary currency. It is possible to trace a discourse about the same, in official and unofficial circles, through 200 years of white settlement: from the concerned comments of Saxe Bannister, the Attorney-General of New South Wales, and Justice Burton of the NSW Supreme Court in the 1830s, to the allegations of sexual abuse by Reverend Gribble at the end of the nineteenth century, Bleakley's allegations of sexual violence and immorality in the north in the 1920s, to the *Little Children are Sacred* Report of recent times and many instances in between. As we saw in chapter four, even Commissioner Moseley had some rather pointed comments to make, in 1934, about the exposure of young Aboriginal children to sexual activity at an early age.

Arguably, one of the clearest examples of the lineage between then and now and the failure of a rights agenda to take hold is in relation to the position of Aboriginal women. Bennett's arguments about the human rights of Aboriginal women in the 1930s have surfaced in more recent times. In 2004 Joan Kimm even referred to the 'fatal conjunction' in which Aboriginal women's lives were caught, between traditional Aboriginal law and Australian law, thus echoing Bennett's notion of a 'double-bondage'.[48] Today's debates about Aboriginal women's human rights, and the rights of women in developing nations, resonate with some of the issues and ideas promoted just before World War II about Aboriginal women's freedom which, once silenced and contained, took some time to reappear, even in feminist activism and theorising.[49] Of particular concern then were issues around what feminists styled 'marriage bondage' and 'domestic slavery'. The targets were cultural practices such as polygamy and infant betrothal that were understood to impact on Aboriginal women's freedom, including freedom of choice, and were sometimes accompanied by varying degrees of violence.

In the interwar period Bennett provided numerous examples of girls and women subjected to violence and argued that many used the mission at Mt Margaret as a source of protection from such. She detailed the complications with wife barter to white men in terms of the low survival rates of first-born babies and argued that 'the great need which would quickly effect reform was a sound public opinion founded on the Christian teaching of the intrinsic value of every human being'.[50] This was an approach which equated women's rights with universal human rights and recognised that violence towards women was one of the 'bad' aspects of the culture requiring change.

It is really only in the last decade or two that some discussion has ensued again, in similarly sensational circumstances, around the issues raised by Bennett in the interwar period.[51] Notably, it has been spearheaded by Aboriginal women themselves. Following the controversial claims about Aboriginal 'domestic dysfunction' in the 2000s and the unprecedented intervention of the federal government into the Northern Territory in 2007, there has been a spate of works by Aboriginal female activists, lawyers, historians and commentators who argue that, where in conflict with women's human rights, cultural rights should go.[52] One of the recommendations of the *Little Children are Sacred* Report was that:

> traditional marriage practices as they once existed cannot continue
> in the modern world, especially where they conflict with modern
> international human rights. Practices such as accepting goods in
> exchange for a 'wife' are not consistent with wider international
> human rights.[53]

This resonates with an international demand by indigenous women that indigenous laws, customs and traditions which discriminate against women be eradicated.[54]

As this suggests, while building on a long tradition of Aboriginal women's activism, a key part of the contemporary Aboriginal women's political agenda is an explicit focus on human rights, utilising the framework of international human rights law. Some of the central building blocks of this agenda are that any discussion of violence must be located in a historical context, that sexual violence needs to be addressed in a human rights framework, that the sex and race discrimination endured by

Indigenous women must be acknowledged, and that the principle of equality before the law must be recognised. This Indigenous women's agenda is best summed up in the words of Aboriginal lawyer Hannah McGlade:

> Any future law reforms should also be accompanied by comprehensive human rights education and awareness raising strategy within both the criminal justice system and Aboriginal communities that aims at promoting the right of Aboriginal women and girls to freedom and protection from sexual violence. More specifically there should be a concerted campaign that recognizes that Aboriginal society and culture and the tradition of promised bride has changed such that it should not be accepted anymore.[55]

The demand for education in the recognition of women's human rights, which was also a recommendation of the *Little Children are Sacred* Report, as well as McGlade's argument that customary practice be eliminated where it conflicts with women's rights, resonates with Bennett's campaign in the interwar years.

The importance of that campaign was that it demonstrated how women and children were often the most vulnerable link between the two cultures. In her opening comments to the Moseley Royal Commission, she summed up how critical she saw the position of Aboriginal women to the problem and the solution overall: 'The deplorable social and economic position of Aborigines and people of Aboriginal origin is caused and conditioned by the victimisation of Aboriginal women'.[56] This victimisation was not only about violence in their own communities. Rather, and more importantly, it was about the violence, intimidation and victimisation of Aboriginal women by white men and their collusion with, and abuse of, Aboriginal men. Yet, the tendency in more recent times has been to focus attention on the apparently inherent violence of Aboriginal societies, particularly men, often as a means of critiquing and questioning the so-called legacies of rights and self-determination.[57] The comment that 'if violence is endemic, self-determination emerges as an error of tragic proportions' sums up this view.[58] As with Pearson's critique, much of this literature problematises as indulgent those who would pinpoint the cause of Aboriginal 'dysfunction' in the legacies of colonialism.

Bennett's view was that violence to women was no more endemic to Aboriginal societies than it was to non-Aboriginal societies. She simply saw violence to women in the communities and railed against it. At the heart of her demand for the outlawing of polygamy in the 'settled districts' was to put a stop to the violence which she and others claimed was integral to settlement but not, necessarily, to the unsettled districts, the Aboriginal domain. But it was also to protect the communities from the incursions of white settlers whose exploitation of the women exacerbated their vulnerability.

Indeed, she thought it was far preferable that the women stay and marry in their own communities, railing against the idea that they were better off out of them:

> Yet I read or heard in one week statements by a feminist, a China Inland Mission man, and a Protector of Aboriginals, to the effect that Aboriginal women are better off, 'socially and morally', living with white men than with their own Aboriginal husbands.[59]

On the contrary, she argued that white men, including officials and police, capitalised on women's property status for personal gain. She saw colonialism and its historical legacies as intricately woven into the problem because it sanctioned dispossession, which robbed the communities of an economic base and then forced the women into prostitution as a means of survival. This process of exchange across the frontier, between men, was frequently occasioned by violence both intra- and inter-racial. The very reason she targeted the settled districts was because she argued that this process was continuing in conditions where Aboriginal people had long been in contact with white society, rather than in 'traditional' settings.

There was a moment in the interwar period where western feminists did attempt to raise human rights issues around what they saw as cultural practices which harmed Aboriginal women. This happened in the heart of empire where issues such as indenture, clitoridectomy and indigenous marital practices were targeted for reform. As I argued in chapter three, we must understand Bennett's and the interwar feminists' campaigns on behalf of Aboriginal women as part of this project. These were attempts to modernise indigenous domestic practices in an effort to elevate women's status and they went all the way to the League of Nations.

Part of this work was in educating Aboriginal men about women's freedom and rights. These campaigns had very mixed results at the time. They were totally ignored in Australia, as male administrators pursued policies which Bennett argued further exacerbated Aboriginal women's position. A key part of this was a declared policy *not* to interfere with tribal custom. Bennett argued that this effectively preserved men's rights – Aboriginal and non-Aboriginal. Critiquing the limited legal provisions around cohabitation in the Western Australian legislation, she said: 'White men had tacitly arrogated and compounded legal immunity for the exploitation of Aboriginal women'.[60]

This suggests that Bennett's story raises some important questions about the nature of humanitarian critique and its relationship to governance. It also puts Pearson's despondency about the capacity of rights and advancement to deliver any real benefits for Aboriginal people into a broader frame. In the very least it calls for an investigation into the relationship between rights and self-determination. Arguably, there has not been, one historic moment when Aboriginal people 'got' citizenship rights, and Bennett's 40-year campaign showed that human rights had been violated rather than acknowledged. Until relatively recently, the 1967 referendum was thought of as an historic turning point in the acknowledgement of rights but, as the work of Attwood and Markus has shown, it did not deliver citizenship in the way people have supposed or in the way Aboriginal people wanted.[61] Instead, access to rights associated with citizenship, such as social security, equal pay and the vote, trickled in. Their lack of celebration or commemoration obscures the significance of the struggle by Aboriginal and non-Aboriginal activists which underpinned these gains, as well as the significance of international pressure.[62] It also obscures the fact that the old edifice of protection and assimilation slowly, and quietly, crumbled or morphed into other programs.

It is true that self-determination was a radically different policy agenda. It had never been tried before. Introduced under the prime ministership of Gough Whitlam, it should be seen as part of Labor's push to end the practices and policies of racial discrimination in Australia. It also genuflected to international rights-based standards and generated some important developments, such as land rights, homelands and the rise of an 'Indigenous sector'.[63] Although implemented a decade earlier, access to social welfare was an extremely important development, the result of a long campaign by Aboriginal people themselves. As Bennett observed at the time, it helped to alleviate considerable individual and community hardship for people with little or no employment and little or no education, starving and living below the poverty line. It would provide the kind of safety net Aboriginal people had long needed.

Yet, Bennett never saw welfare as an end in itself. Rather, it was part of a suite of reforms that were needed. Land, food and medical assistance were required, as was education. The latter was a means to independence and equality.[64] It was also needed to assist individuals and communities whose lives had long been conditioned by forms of passive dependency in systems that denied them these things. Indeed, in the context of welfare payments, education was needed more than ever. As Bennett said about the guarantor who doled out pensions and benefits to the goldfields Aborigines, once social welfare benefits became available, we could not blame them if they did not know how to handle money – they had historically been denied being able to do so, either receiving no wages at all or having their earnings siphoned off for other purposes. The guarantor demonstrated a perpetuation of these practices, and the problem was not the irresponsibility of the Aborigines, but the irresponsibility of white governments and their deputies.

The guarantor was symbolic of the problem for Bennett because it demonstrated a refusal to hand responsibility to the Aboriginal people themselves, as she said to Bromham:

> I feel the men who are good enough to run the Northern Territory cattle industry should be allowed a fair wage and settle their own interests. I hate all this pretending they are babies to be minded by the Trustee white people who can't even keep sober.[65]

As the quote at the beginning of this chapter suggests, one of her key recommendations was that Aboriginal people be consulted about issues, policies and reforms which affected their lives. This was not only a sign of respect. It was a basic human right denied them for so long. This was why she valued cooperation above all. Non-Aboriginal people needed to cooperate with Aboriginal people, rather than dictate to them, compete with them or ignore their wishes. They needed to provide assistance, financial and otherwise, and help where required and when wanted or needed. This suggested that some form of adviser was necessary in the transition to self-determination. This had been recognised as a vital part of the founding of a just relationship between an 'immigrant, invading community' and a 'subject Aboriginal one' in the East Africa Commission report. The recurring complaints of Aboriginal people about the managers and advisers who oversaw their lives under various government policies suggests that this had historically been an issue for Aboriginal people, too. Yet evidence suggests that, despite Labor's intention to restore to the Aboriginal people 'their lost power of self-determination in economic, social and political affairs', ongoing forms of paternalism have been a characteristic part of the implementation of self-determination and, according to some, part of the reason for its failure.[66] Rights and consultation have had little to do with it.[67]

With Pearson's poignant warning that, if not checked, passive welfare dependency and alcohol and drug addiction would cause the final breakdown of traditional social relations and values in his communities, Bennett would have concurred. As far back as the Moseley Royal Commission she declared that 'the surest way to destroy a race is to destroy its communities'.[68] At that time she said that their own family and community life was one of four essentials for their survival.[69] Instead of passive welfare dependency to describe their condition she would probably have used the phrase 'slave mortality', as she did in *The Australian Aboriginal as a Human Being*. That book's plea that the founding of a just relationship between black and white was the most important business of the twentieth century hung heavily over the fractious politics around Aboriginal affairs in the last quarter of the century. At her most cynical and despondent Bennett would have claimed that the breakdown Pearson feared would be the end result for his people was actually the desired outcome. This was not just about extermination or genocide, it was about the failure to accord Aboriginal people humanity and human rights.

EPILOGUE

> Knowing Mrs Bennett as well as I did, my *personal* feeling is that the authorities would even go to the length of destroying the papers, rather than that their contents be made public [original emphasis].[1]

> I have always found WA hostile and unreliable. I ought really to say I can always rely on them to thwart me if they can, especially under offers of help.[2]

There could be no better way for the state of Western Australia to thwart Mary Bennett than in the confiscation of her personal papers. She believed that publicity was the strongest weapon there was against wrongdoing.[3] In her battle with the state her pen had been her principal weapon, her papers the embodiment of her life's work. Her crusade for Aboriginal human rights was based on the collection of evidence and collation of facts. As Ada Bromham reflected, 'from her reference library Mrs Bennett continually supplies facts and information which helps inquirers in Australia and elsewhere to understand the problems of our Aboriginal population'.[4] Bennett had been classifying this library just before being taken to hospital where, following a diabetic coma, she died. Within the hour of her death, two Crown Law officers, representing the office of the Public Trustee, walked into her house and scooped the papers up into their suitcases. When Bromham complained that some of the papers were, in fact, her own, she was told to 'put a claim in'.[5]

Bennett's papers became yet another site of conflict between the state and its representatives and Bennett, via her supporters, at the end of her life. The state maintained that it was merely following established procedure where it believed a person died intestate and with no known relatives and no local executor of a will.[6] However, her closest allies believed that the Crown Law Officers were acting for the Native Welfare Department, which was 'not always in agreement with Mrs Bennett's work'.[7] According to Bromham, the department was 'unscrupulous in their treatment of the natives' and, by implication, Bennett.[8] What was at stake, so they said, was the legacy of her years of work. Taking the lead in the struggle to get the papers back, Bromham wrote to Bennett's friends and supporters, including Jessie Street, Gordon Bryant and even some very old and dear friends in England. Labor MP Kim Beazley (senior) advised writing to the state Attorney-General's department.

Bromham also worked in concert with Shirley Andrews and the Council for Aboriginal Rights. It was Andrews who, on being alerted by a mutual friend that Bennett was ill and receiving hospital treatment, had contacted Bromham to see if she could go to Kalgoorlie to help Bennett sort out her papers. The CAR believed that Bennett's work demonstrated the great need for a forward program for Aboriginal people. It felt that a book based on her material would be suitable recognition of her 'outstanding service' to Aboriginal people over many years and a means of securing public support for Aboriginal advancement. The book would contain much of her own material and the CAR would meet the cost of printing. When Bromham reached Kalgoorlie, Bennett was too ill to be consulted. Between daily visits to the hospital, Bromham sorted through her papers, selecting large amounts of typed script for the projected publication. In an affidavit she wrote on the day after their removal, she explained how detailed Bennett's work was:

> It took several long working days to get even the foundations of the various sections laid down but in doing so I realized what a splendid contribution the book would make to the knowledge of present day Australians on the rights and needs of the first Australians and decided to forward the material to Melbourne as soon as possible.[9]

A year later and after a lengthy and tiring battle, Bromham took custody of the papers from the Western Australian state trust department and sent them by rail to Barry Christophers in Melbourne, where he stored them in the garage of his surgery. He later claimed that a few days after receiving them they were stolen. Although he reported it to the police, nothing happened.[10] Thus, in the end and despite Bromham's efforts, Bennett's papers were lost to history and the cause.

This is an amazing story and a fascinating end to Mary Bennett's life. It demonstrates the impact she had both during her life and after it and the investment in it by various parties. Had she been privy to the conflict she would almost certainly have seen it as symptomatic of her status as a trouble-maker. It was also symptomatic of the state's attempts to thwart her. She constantly referred to the fact that the Aboriginal cause was enough to 'set all authorities' against one and worried how her outspokenness impacted the Aboriginal people she defended.[11] Ironically, one of the issues she had been railing against until her death was the attempts by the department to take control of Aboriginal people's property, sanctioned by section 35 of the native welfare legislation. Citing article 17 of the UN Declaration of Human rights, which stipulates that no one will be arbitrarily deprived of their property, she argued that this was yet another violation of their human rights. Was the removal of her papers yet another example of such? While the state acted in a 'business-as-usual' way, Bennett's supporters felt sure that they were attempting to silence her once and for all. Andrews felt that both the removal of the papers and its timing was unusual, stating: 'I think the authorities realized the papers would have contained much criticism of official actions and much confidential information about the ill-treatment of Aborigines'.[12] For this reason the Council for Aboriginal Rights engaged a firm of solicitors in Perth who made representations to the Public Trustee seeking the release of the papers.

Given the eventual recovery of the papers, to what extent were the council's concerns valid? Was the state attempting, at best, to keep Bennett's considerable archive from public view or, at worst, to destroy it? Was it attempting to silence her once and for all? There certainly were some anomalies, including the fact that these claims were not resuscitated once Bennett's papers were stolen from Christophers' garage. Was he not suspicious? Was it just a coincidence? Certainly, Bennett had felt that her activities and those of the various groups she interacted with were the subject of surveillance in these years. In correspondence with Bromham in July 1959 she relayed a story about a prospective visit to her from Gordon Bryant, a member of the Federal Council for Aboriginal Advancement and a Labor parliamentarian. An officer of the Native Welfare Department had visited her on the advice of Cyril Gare just prior and drilled her about Bryant's political allegiance. Gare was the president of the Native Welfare Council in Western Australia, an umbrella organisation established by the Western Australian government in the 1950s to contain the various activist groups in that state. Notably, it refrained from affiliating with the FCAA. Although Bennett participated in and corresponded with the council and counted friends among them, she identified Gare as a 'facing both ways man, devoted to frustrating them'.[13]

Intriguing, too, was the position of Wilfred Henry Douglas, a close friend of Bennett. Douglas and his wife had been named as the benefactors of her personal chattels, including her papers, in a codicil to her will in 1959. He worked in the language department of the United Aborigines Mission and had a great love of Indigenous languages and a close knowledge of the desert people. Bennett and he became firm friends at the time of the Pontara case as he was able to translate aspects of his biography. He had also been a great friend to Bennett in her final years and was one of the few missionaries she earmarked as trustworthy because, she said, he treated Aboriginal people as human beings.

When Bromham sought advice about her papers from the Attorney-General he replied that Bennett's estate had been reported to the Public Trustee and that the bulk of her papers were held by the Clerk of Courts at Kalgoorlie, on Douglas' behalf. Bennett's will had been found among her papers and named Sir William Trower of Trower, Still and Keeling in London as the executor of her will. The Attorney-General said that while the Douglas' would deal with the papers as Bennett would have wished, it was not known what their intentions were. The letter concluded with a remonstrance to Bromham concerning her claims that the Public Trustee was acting as the agent of the Native Welfare Department. He rejected this firmly, stating that the Crown Law officers were acting in the normal course of their duties after the matter was reported to the Clerk of Courts by Douglas.[14]

What was 'the matter' and why did Douglas report it to the Clerk of Courts? Douglas relayed what happened to Bennett's papers in a private memoir. He referred to his and his wife's very close bond with Bennett, which had developed in the latter days of her life in Kalgoorlie, where they also lived. Concerned about her health and her living alone, they visited her regularly. On one occasion when he went to visit her he found 'another woman there going through Mrs Bennett's papers' and 'felt it necessary to inform the Clerk of Courts about the stranger in the house'. When Bennett died, the woman was expelled from the house and Bennett's papers officially removed. He concluded by saying that while he became involved in the conflict, he managed to avoid a court case by 'cooperating with the Public Trustees in Perth'.[15]

This is an intriguing account. The 'other woman' was clearly Bromham but she maintained that she had been in contact with Douglas before Bennett's death. They certainly knew of one another and how closely regarded they both were by Bennett. As Douglas mentioned to Bromham at the time, her name was often on Bennett's lips. The reason Bromham had contacted him was that she knew he was another of Bennett's friends in Kalgoorlie and she wanted to know whether he thought her and the CAR's use of Bennett's papers in a book was in order. Douglas was away at the time but, once he returned, he came to visit Bromham and confirmed that he could see no legal barrier to their use in the manner suggested. It was therefore a surprise to Bromham to learn, via the press in the reportage of the subsequent affair, that Bennett had left all her effects to him. When the papers were taken she contacted him again to ask his opinion as to the possibility of Bennett's papers being available to her for the book, which would be a memorial to Bennett and include some of her latest writings.

Douglas' account of the affair is therefore at odds with Bromham's version, including her alleged expulsion from the house. Nowhere is this detail recorded by Bromham and she was very careful to document the whole affair. If they had met previously, as Bromham suggested, and he was privy to what she was doing and had agreed with it, it is hard to understand why he acted in the way he did. It is also hard to understand why he went to the Clerk of Courts, agents of the Public Trustee, rather than the police if he believed that there was a strange person in Bennett's house, rifling through her possessions. And why did he have to cooperate with the Public Trustee if Bennett's papers were to go to him? In subsequent communication with Bromham, Douglas confirmed that he had, in fact, met up with her over the matter but said that her request came as Bennett was still alive. While she had instructed him what to do with the disposal of her property 'in favour of certain people', he could do nothing, so he said, while she was still alive and, once she had died, until her will was found. In a letter dated 27 November 1961 he confirmed that they must wait until word came from the London executors of the will.[16]

The role of the Public Trustee is also intriguing. Why did Douglas have to cooperate with them? Given that the state trust department eventually released the papers to Bromham and the CAR, and not to Douglas himself, they had obviously assumed control of them and wanted them to be sent to the CAR. On the one hand, this suggests the bureaucracy overstepping its reach. The papers were not the state's to dispense and they were not the CAR's to have, until Douglas agreed to renounce his claims to them. On 10 September 1962, the Public Trustee wrote to Andrews informing her of Douglas' decision to do just that. As long as the CAR produced a document indemnifying the papers from further claims, they could have them. The fact that Douglas styled this 'cooperation' suggests that he may have been persuaded to renounce his claims and that the Western Australian government wanted to be seen to be acceding to the CAR's wishes. This was certainly how Andrews interpreted it at the time:

> I suspect that he has been acting as a tool for the Native Welfare Dept. in this matter and that as they have now had an opportunity to look at Mrs Bennett's papers, they may be prepared to let them go to try and make it look as if everything is above board.[17]

The question remains, then, whether the state had a role in the subsequent theft of her private papers from Christophers' garage?

This is not beyond the realms of possibility. It would seem to put the state's request that the CAR indemnify them against other claimants into perspective. It is also conceivable that the state and/or the Australian Security Intelligence Organisation had an officer track the box of papers as they were sent by rail from Perth to Melbourne. A key part of ASIO activities was in surveillance work which included taking photographs, closely monitoring people and tracking their movements, and watching and listening to individuals' private affairs and undertakings.[18] There was also the fact of Christophers' and Andrews' communist allegiance. ASIO had been formed to counter communist influence and many people and organisations were caught up in its net.[19] Certainly, Aboriginal activists and pro-Aboriginal activists were targeted. Christophers, Andrews, Street, Bromham and Bennett all had ASIO files and Bennett frequently complained that 'native affairs' was behind an iron curtain, writing that, if someone raised a concern about their conditions, the view was taken that communists were behind the trouble.[20] It was for this very reason that the federal government refused to deal with the FCAA until the late 1960s when it considered its political character more appropriate.[21]

Christophers' relative silence on the theft of Bennett's papers once he got them is interesting but not remarkable. Perhaps he didn't want to draw further attention to the issue or fan the flames. Perhaps he didn't want to break the news to Bromham who had worked so hard to recover the papers. Perhaps he was simply too busy as a medical practitioner and as an avid campaigner for Aboriginal rights, particularly when the campaign escalated in the 1960s. Indeed, he informed Bromham that he had been unable to go through the papers at the outset because of the heavy demands of the petition campaign, which was the FCAA's 10-year effort for constitutional changes to give effect to Aboriginal rights.

Bennett's legacy clearly lived on. Christophers, along with Andrews, had managed to produce *The Struggle for Dignity,* which was a memorial to Bennett's work, just 6 months after her death and before the papers had been released to them. Furthermore, the CAR already had a significant collection of Bennett's letters in its own archive, and a characteristic feature of Bennett's work was that she wrote out her letters in duplicate and triplicate as she repeated her concerns and information to all friends and colleagues. In this sense, if there was a battle over her papers between herself and the state, she ultimately won because, if not in her own collection, her considerable documentation could be found in someone else's.

It is fair to say that the swift removal of Bennett's papers, whether intended as a means of silencing her or not, must be seen as part of the fabric of the times. There is no doubt that Bennett had caused the state concern during her long crusade. According to Geoffrey Bolton, she was widely regarded as a 'gadfly of the official conscience'.[22] By the late 1950s her reputation as such was widely known but her explicit defence of Aboriginal human rights in these years was deeply problematic as Australia was beginning to face serious questioning and criticism abroad on this very issue. This interest had been noticeable since the conclusion of World War II when the External Affairs Department began fielding state premiers for data in order to respond to these questions, and there is evidence that the administration was trying to build its own story of reform and success to counter what it saw as negative propaganda around human rights by the likes of Bennett.[23] In this context, her documentation of human rights violations was deeply concerning to the state.

Clearly, the state and Bennett were bitter enemies locked in an ideological battle. She frequently referred to being at war with the politicians and bureaucracy, reflecting 'honest criticism is most necessary but it is seldom forgiven'.[24] The state's reaction to her might very well have been magnified because she was an insider, born and raised in the establishment. She was also a trouble-maker, declaring to Andrews that there was a time to avoid trouble and a time to seek it out.[25] She described Western Australia as 'unreliable' and as 'the beam' in her 'conscience that prevented it from working properly'.[26]

The state, and its representatives, were as wary of her. In 1932 A. O. Neville warned Rod Schenk to be careful of her as she would 'look under the beds, behind the doors and all sorts of things'.[27] At the time of the Moseley Royal Commission in 1934, he stated in a letter to the Secretary of the Premier's Department that once the royal commission issued its report 'emanations from Mrs Bennett would cease in the future'.[28] Similarly, Paul Hasluck, who was born and raised in Western Australia and had even penned a history of native policy in that state, saw her work at that time as counter-productive and later denied that her papers had ever been confiscated.[29]

Whether or not the state consciously sought to thwart Bennett at the moment of her death as she maintained they had during her life, the dramatic moment of the seizure of her papers threatened to obliterate not only her own story but the stories her archive contained: the evidence of Aboriginal people's struggles and her attempts, across four decades, to publicise them. As she said in *Human Rights for Australian Aborigines*, departments are concerned with a mass and carry out in the mass things arranged elsewhere for the whole Aboriginal community:

> to consider individual persons upsets their routine. But a person
> is not a mass, and Aborigines suffer as persons. They suffer the
> injustices of unlawful laws which infringe more than one human
> right and they suffer their personal tragedies.[30]

In defending Aboriginal human rights she jeopardised her own for, if nothing else, the removal of her papers was a violent act. The state swooped and, within the hour of her death, took her life's work away in front of her nearest and dearest friend, even confiscating that which she had left aside for herself, remnants and mementos of their years of collaboration in the cause and of their love and friendship.

Their removal was a profound personal violation because her papers were inextricably connected to Bennett's spirit and self-definition. They were deeply rooted in her own past and family story as they documented those of others, and they were critical to her crusade because, above all else, she was a writer. She understood the importance of words for social change and transformation and saw herself as building in the tradition of William Blake. Her letter to Olive Pink in 1935, following the personal defeat that was the Moseley Royal Commission, gives this away: 'don't you think you may, by your pen – Blake's sword with which he is still building – free our tortured Innocents?'.[31] One of England's leading eighteenth-century poets and artists, Blake stressed the importance of people taking responsibility for change and building a better society. Through his literary and artistic outputs, Blake was the social commentator of his times, critiquing poverty and oppression and explicitly using language to invoke political action in the present.[32] Nowhere is this clearer than in the preface to his poem, *Milton,* wherein he writes:

> I will not cease from mental fight,
> Nor shall my sword sleep in my hand,
> Till we have built Jerusalem
> In England's green and pleasant land.

There is no doubt that Bennett's crusade was a mental fight and her pen her sword which never slept. She saw her task as the pursuit of truth and the evidence she collated as a means of countering what she saw as the lies of the department as it (ab)used its power to defeat Aboriginal lives. She also compiled the evidence for posterity, informing Andrews at the time of the Pontara affair that she was giving her all the facts of the case, for the issue of child removal would come up for justice some day, when she was no longer around to provide the facts.[33] Come up for justice it did. As did many of her other concerns and claims.

The question which hovers over the dramatic removal of Bennett's papers is why, if it was an act of political sabotage, and particularly when most of her activist life the state had shrugged off her critique as exaggerations, half-truths and 'manifest absurdities'.[34] Neville even went so far as to say that 'the wrongs of the natives' were her obsession.[35] Her claims about child removal were less contentious by the 1950s, when they were being supported by a number of other voices of discontent. They had been dramatically aired at the inquiry into the Warburton affair. Yet they could be rebuffed by claims to welfare and assimilation, part of the widely endorsed and implemented western progressivist postwar ethos.

Yet, her trenchant opposition to child removal became more acute as she recognised it as part of a wider assault on Aboriginal survival after the war. Above all, it was grounded in economics for, 'the unjust destitution of the parents has been the excuse throughout the years for disrupting Aboriginal families and drafting their children in institutions'.[36] Furthermore, in the postwar climate her exposure of human rights violations in Aboriginal policy was arguably the most contentious of her advocacy, particularly as it related to her assertions about genocide of the full-bloods. Governments certainly needed to hose down any claims of human rights violations at this time. Bennett's death, in 1961, occurred at a critical juncture in diplomatic affairs. In the wake of the Sharpeville massacre and Freedom Rides in the US, the government was working overtime to duck international scrutiny on the race question and maintain its hardline commitment to the principle of domestic jurisdiction.[37]

Either way, her accumulation of data, statistics, reports, photographs and case studies and her extensive notes were unsettling to say the least. More than criticism of official actions, as Andrews had framed them, they were a dossier of state malpractice and neglect on a significant scale. They certainly represented documentary evidence of human rights abuses. Indeed, in creating her archive Bennett was undertaking very important work in the recognition of human rights, for it is now understood that the collection and analysis of data is fundamental to the implementation and monitoring of human rights standards.[38] Her long crusade demonstrated the poor appreciation of human rights – documented or otherwise – in twentieth-century Australia.

NOTES

Abbreviations:

ACC   Accession
AIATSIS   Australian Institute for Aboriginal and Torres Strait Islander Studies
ML   Mitchell Library
MN   Manuscript
MS   Manuscript
NAA   National Archives of Australia
NLA   National Library of Australia
SASA   South Australian State Archives
SAWA   State Archives of Western Australia
MLSA   Mortlock Library South Australia
SLV   State Library of Victoria
SLWA   State Library of Western Australia
UQ   University of Queensland
USA   The University of Sydney Archives

Note on Terminology

1   M. Lewis, Gary F. Paul, G. Simons, and Charles D. Fennig (eds), *Ethnologue: Languages of the World, Seventeenth edition,* SIL International, Dallas, 2013, http://www.ethnologue.com.

2   M. Bennett, *Christison of Lammermoor,* Alston Rivers, London, 1927, p. 58.

3   L. Aberdeen, 'Australian Scientific Research, "Aboriginal Blood" and the Racial Imaginary', M. Crotty, J. Gernov and G. Rodwell. (eds), *'A Race for a Place': Eugenics, Darwinism and Social Thought and Practice in Australia,* Proceedings of the History and Sociology of Eugenics Conference, University of Newcastle, April, 2000, pp. 101–11.

4   Online Etymology Dictionary, http://www.etymonline.com/index.php?term=native.

5   D. McNab, 'Herman Merivale and the Native Question, 1837–1861', *Albion: A Quarterly Journal Concerned with British Studies,* vol. 9, no. 4, Winter, 1977, p. 361.

Prologue

1   *Kalgoorlie Miner,* 7 October 1961.

Introduction

1   'Book Which Charged Australia With Slavery', *The Register News-Pictorial,* Adelaide, 28 July 1930.

2   M. Bennett, *The Australian Aboriginal as a Human Being*, Alston Rivers, London, 1927, p. 33.

3   Ibid., p. 11.

4   *The Stock and Station Journal*, 22 December 1908.

5   At the time of the sale of Lammermoor in 1908 the estate was described as 800,000 acres, with 21,000 head of cattle and 600 horses.

6   M. Bennett to A. Bromham, 3 September 1961, Mary Montgomerie Bennett and Ada Bromham, Private Archives, State Library of Western Australia, MN2958; ACC 8303A/2.

7   M. Bennett to A. Bromham, 13 September 1958, Mary Montgomerie Bennett and Ada Bromham, Private Archives, SLWA, MN2958; ACC 8303A/13.

8   Bennett, *The Australian Aboriginal*, p. 75.

9   Ibid., p. 52.

10 P. Grimshaw and J. Evans, 'Colonial Women on Intercultural Frontiers: Rosa Campbell Praed, Mary Bundock and Katie Langloh Parker', *Australian Historical Studies*, no. 106, 1996, pp. 79–95; M. McGuire, 'The Legend of the Good Fella Missus', *Aboriginal History*, vol. 14, nos 1–2, 1990, pp. 124–151.

11 Bennett, *The Australian Aboriginal*, p. 11.

12 M. Brown, 'Fernando. The Story of an Aboriginal Prophet', *Aborigine Welfare Bulletin*, vol. 4, no. 1 1964, pp. 9–11.

13 R. McGregor, *Imagined Destinies. Aboriginal Australians and the Doomed Race Theory, 1880–1939*, Melbourne University Press, Melbourne, 1997.

14 Bennett, *The Australian Aboriginal*, p. 135.

15 M. Bennett, *The Condition of the Aborigines of Australia Under the Federal Government*. A Paper Read Before the British Commonwealth League, June 1929.

16 B. Buchan, *Empire of Political Thought: Indigenous Australians and the Language of Colonial Government*, Pickering and Chatto, London, 2008; P. McHugh, *Aboriginal Societies and the Common Law: A History of Sovereignty, Status and Self-Determination*, Oxford University Press, Oxford, 2004; P. Havemann (ed.), *Indigenous People's Rights: in Australia, Canada and New Zealand*, Oxford University Press, Auckland, 1999.

17 With the exception of the Batman Treaty, see B. Attwood with H. Doyle, *Possession. Batman's Treaty and the Matter of History*, Miegunyah Press, Carlton, Victoria, 2009.

18 D. M. Schreuder and S. Ward, *Australia's Empire. The Oxford History of the British Empire*, Oxford University Press, Oxford, 2008, pp. 13, 33–53.

19 M. Lake and H. Reynolds, *Drawing the Global Colour Line. White Men's Countries and the Question of Racial Equality*, Melbourne University Press, Melbourne, 2008; McGregor, *Imagined Destinies*.

20 D. McNab, 'Herman Merivale and the Native Question, 1837–1861', *Albion: A Quarterly Journal Concerned with British Studies*, vol. 9, no. 4, winter 1977, p. 361.

21 Ibid., p. 363.

22 Ibid., p. 368.

23 M. Bennett, *Christison of Lammermoor*, Alston Rivers, London, 1927, p. 81.

24 P. Biskup, *Not Slaves Not Citizens. The Aboriginal Problem in Western Australia*, University of Queensland Press, Brisbane, 1973; A. Haebich, *For Their Own Good. Aborigines and Government in the South-West of Western Australia*, University of Western Australia Press, Perth, 1988; C. Brown, *The Blackfellow's Friend*, Access Press, 1999; C. Halse, *A Terribly Wild Man*, Allen & Unwin, Sydney, 2002.

25 G. Reid, *That Unhappy Race. Queensland and the Aboriginal Problem, 1838–1901*, Australian Scholarly Publishing, Melbourne, 2006; R. Kidd, *The Way We Civilise. Aboriginal Affairs – the Untold Story*, University of Queensland Press, Brisbane, 1997; A. Haebich, *Broken Circles. Fragmenting Indigenous Families, 1800–2000*, Fremantle Arts Centre Press, Fremantle, 2000.

26 A. Markus, *Governing Savages*, Allen & Unwin, Sydney, 1990; F. Paisley, *Loving Protection? Australian Feminism and Aboriginal Women's Rights 1919–1939*, Melbourne University Press, Melbourne, 2000; R. McGregor, *Imagined Destinies*.

27 Bennett, *The Australian Aboriginal*, p. 10.

28 R. Kerin, *Doctor Do-Good. Charles Duguid and Aboriginal Advancement, 1930–1970s*, Australian Scholarly Publishing, Melbourne, 2011, p. 4.

29 Ibid., pp. 24, 39, 42–3, 97.

30 A. Holland, '"Saving the Aborigines": The White Woman's Crusade. A Study of Gender, Race and the Australian Frontier, 1920s–1960s', PhD thesis, University of New South Wales, 1998, pp. 136–7, 142–4, 220–6.

31 S. Taffe, *Black and White Together. FCAATSI: The Federal Council for the Advancement of Aborigines and Torres Strait Islanders, 1958–1973*, University of Queensland Press, Brisbane, 2005, p. 9.

32 B. Porter, *Critics of Empire. British Radicals and the Imperial Challenge*, I. B. Tauris, London, 2008, p. 2.

33 J. W. Cell, 'Colonial Rule', in J. Brown & W. M. Roger Louis. (eds), *The Oxford History of the British Empire: Volume IV: The Twentieth Century*, Oxford Scholarship Online, 2011, http://dx.doi.org/10.1093/acprof:oso/9780198205647.001.0001.

34 Porter, *Critics of Empire*, p. 154; S. Pedersen, 'Metaphors of the Schoolroom: Women Working the Mandates System of the League of Nations', *History Workshop Journal*, vol. 66, no. 1, 2008, p. 195; J. C. Myers, *Indirect Rule in South Africa. Tradition, Modernity and the Costuming of Political Power*, The University of Rochester Press, 2008; Porter, *Critics of Empire*, especially chapter 9, pp. 291–329; B. Bush, *Imperialism, Race and Resistance: Africa and Britain*, 1919-1945, Taylor and Francis, Abingdon, 2002.

35 R. McGregor, 'Develop the North: Aborigines, Environment and Australian Nationhood', *Journal of Australian Studies*, vol. 28, no. 81, 2004, pp. 33–45.

36 Porter, *Critics of Empire*, p. 2.

37 Ibid., p. 182.

38 Ibid., p. 3.

39 A. Hochschild, *King Leopold's Ghost. A Story of Greed, Terror and Heroism in Colonial Africa*, Mariner Books, Houghton Miffler Company, New York, 1999.

40 N. Pearson, 'On the Human Right to Misery, Mass Incarceration and Early Death', *Up From The Mission. Selected Writings*, Black Inc, Melbourne, 2009, pp. 172–80; P. Sutton, 'The Politics of Suffering: Indigenous Policy in Australia Since the 1970s', *Anthropological Forum*, vol. 11, 2001, pp. 125–73; J. Howard, '2009 Menzies Lecture', *The Australian*, 27 August 2009; D. Kennedy, 'The International Human Rights Movement: Part of the Problem?', *Harvard Human Rights Journal*, vol. 15, 2002, pp. 101–125.

41 Bush, *Imperialism, Race and Resistance*, p. 182.

42 F. Cooper, 'Modernizing Colonialism and the Limits of Empire', in C. Calhoun, F. Cooper and K. Moore. (eds), *Lessons of Empire: Imperial Histories and American Power*, New Press, New York, 2006, pp. 65–7; A. Stoler and F. Cooper (eds), 'Between Metropole and Colony: Rethinking a Research Agenda', *Tensions of Empire: Colonial*

Cultures in a Bourgeois World, University of California Press, Berkeley, 1997, pp. 1–57.

43   M. Barnett and T. G. Weiss (eds), *Humanitarianism in Question. Politics, Power, Ethics*, Cornell University Press, London, 2008, p. 22.

44   M. Barnett, *Empire of Humanity*. A History of Humanitarianism, Cornell University Press, London, 2011, p. 10.

45   J. Heartfield, *The Aborigines Protection Society. Humanitarian Imperialism in Australia, New Zealand, Fiji, Canada, South Africa and the Congo, 1836–1909*, Columbia University Press, New York, 2011; E. Elbourne, 'The Sin of the Settler: The 1835–36 Select Committee on Aborigines and Debates over Virtue and Conquest in the Early Nineteenth Century British White Settler Empire', *Journal of Colonialism and Colonial History*, vol. 4, no. 3, 2003; C. McLisky, '"Due Observance of Justice, and the Protection of Their Rights": Philanthropy, Humanitarianism, and Moral Purpose in the Aborigines Protection Society circa 1837 and its Portrayal in Australian Historiography, 1883–2003', *Limina*, vol. 11, 2005, pp. 57–66; Z. Laidlaw, 'Integrating Metropolitan, Colonial and Imperial Histories – the Aborigines Select Committee of 1835–37', T. Banivanua Mar & J. Evans, *Writing Colonial Histories: Comparative Perspectives*, University of Melbourne, 2002, pp. 75–91; A. Lester, 'Colonial Networks, Australian Humanitarianism and the History Wars', *Geographical Research*, vol. 44, no. 3, 2006, pp. 229–41; J. Mitchell, *In Good Faith? Governing Indigenous Australia Through God, Charity and Empire, 1825–1855*, ANU E Press, 2011; A. O'Brien, 'Humanitarianism and Reparation in Colonial Australia', *Journal of Colonialism and Colonial History*, vol. 12, no. 2, 2011; P. Edmonds, 'Collecting Looerryminer's "Testimony": Aboriginal Women, Sealers and Quaker Humanitarian Anti-Slavery Thought and Action in the Bass Strait Islands', *Australian Historical Studies*, vol. 45, no. 1, 2014, pp. 13–33; A. Lester & F. Dussart, *Colonization and the Origins of Humanitarian Governance. Protecting Aborigines across the Nineteenth Century British Empire*, Cambridge University Press, Cambridge, 2014.

46   F. Paisley and J. Lydon, 'Special Issue: Anti-Slavery and its Legacies', *Australian Historical Studies*, vol. 45, no. 1, 2014.

47   Paisley, 'An Echo of Black Slavery: Emancipation, Forced Labour and Australia in 1933', *Australian Historical Studies*, vol. 45, no. 1, 2014, pp. 103–25.

48   Census of Aboriginals, 30 June 1939 and 30 June 1944, NAA: Prime Minister's Department: A 461, Correspondence files, multiple number series; items, A 46, A300/1 Part 3.

49   Barnett, *Empire of Humanity*, p. 16.

50   K. Cmiel, 'The Recent History of Human Rights', *American Historical Review*, vol. 109, no. 1, 2004, p. 127.

51   Barnett, Empire of Humanity, p. 7.

52   M. Bennett, Notes on the Native Administration Act of Western Australia, Duguid Papers, NLA MS5068, series 11.

53   *Declaration of the Rights of Indigenous Peoples*, Allen & Unwin, Sydney, 2009.

54   See, for example, H. McGlade, *Our Greatest Challenge. Aboriginal Children and Human Rights*, Aboriginal Studies Press, Canberra, 2012; L. Behrendt, 'As Good As It Gets Or As Good As It Could Be? Benchmarking Human Rights in Australia', *Balayi: Culture, Law and Colonialism*, vol. 10, 2009 pp. 3–13; K. Cripps, 'Understanding Indigenous Family Violence in the Context of a Human Rights Agenda', *Human Rights Defender*,

vol. 15, no. 3, 2006, pp. 3–5.

55   Marilyn Lake, *Faith. Faith Bandler, Gentle Activist*, Allen & Unwin, St Leonards, Sydney, 2002. H. Reynolds, *This Whispering in Our Hearts*, Allen & Unwin, Sydney, 1998; Kerin, *Dr Do-Good*; T. Rowse, *Nugget Coombs: A Reforming Life*, Cambridge University Press, Cambridge, 2002; J. Marcus, *The Indomitable Miss Pink. A Life in Anthropology*, University of New South Wales Press, Sydney, 2001; V. Haskins, *One Bright Spot*, Palgrave Macmillan, 2005; F. Paisley, *The Lone Protestor. AM Fernando in Australia and Europe*, Aboriginal Studies Press, Canberra, 2012.

56   United Nations, Human Rights Council, *Draft report of the Working Group on the Universal Periodic Review—Australia*, February 2011, http://www.upr-info.org-en/ review/Australia/Session-10---January-2011/Review-in-the-Working-Group#top; T. Calma, 'Essentials for Social Justice', http://222.hreoc.gov.au/social_justice/ essentials/index.html; T. Calma, 'A Human Rights Agenda for the Northern Territory', November 2008, http://www.hreoc.gov.au/aboutmedia/speeches/ social_justice/2008/2008111; T. Calma, '"Still Riding For Freedom" – An Australian Aboriginal and Torres Strait Islander Agreement for the Twenty-First Century', *The Charles Perkins Memorial Lecture*, October 2007; M. Gooda, 'The Practical Power of Human Rights', *Queensland University of Technology Faculty of Law Public Lecture*, May 2010; M. Gooda, 'Recognising opportunity for all of us: a rights approach', 26 May 2011, www.hreoc.gov.au/about/media/speeches/social_justice/2011/20110526_ bringing_together.html; Behrendt, 'As Good As It Gets Or As Good As It Could Be? Benchmarking Human Rights in Australia'; Cripps, 'Understanding Indigenous Family Violence in the Context of a Human Rights Agenda'.

57   Australian Government, Attorney-General's Department, Australia's Human Rights Framework, http://www.ag.gov.au/humanrightsframework.

Chapter 1 – Contextualising Dissent

1   F. Wood Jones, 'The Claims of the Australian Aborigine', *Reports of the Australasian Association for the Advancement of Science*, vol. 18, 1926, p. 497.

2   D. Jackson, 'Aborigines of Australia', Commonwealth Parliamentary Papers, 13 October 1927, pp. 507–11.

3   F. Wood Jones, *Australia's Vanishing Race*, Angus & Robertson, Sydney, 1934, p. 6.

4   M. Bennett, *The Australian Aboriginal as a Human Being*, Alston Rivers, London, 1930, p. 142.

5   F. Paisley, *Loving Protection? Australian Feminism and Aboriginal Women's Rights, 1919– 1939*, Melbourne University Press, Melbourne, 2000; A. Woollacott, *To Try Her Fortune in London: Australian Women, Colonialism and Modernity*, Oxford University Press, Oxford, 2001.

6   C. Cooke, 'Paper to the British Commonwealth League Conference', British Commonwealth League, *A Report of Conference*, June 1927, p. 29.

7   Notes on Deputation from the Anti-Slavery Society to the Australian High Commissioner at Australia House, 2 December 1927, NAA: A431/1, 1948/273, Part 1.

8   R. McGregor, *Imagined Destinies. Aboriginal Australians and the Doomed Race Theory, 1880–1939*, Melbourne University Press, Melbourne, 1997.

9   M. Bennett to O. Pink, 16 March 1935, Olive Pink Papers.

10   R. McGregor, 'The Doomed Race: A Scientific Axiom of the Late Nineteenth

Century', *Australian Journal of Politics and History*, vol. 39, no. 1, 1993, pp. 14–22.

11   Wood Jones, *Australia's Vanishing Race*, p. 6.

12   Professor Radcliffe-Brown quoted in Bennett, *The Australian Aboriginal*, p. 130; see also McGregor, *Imagined Destinies*, pp. 102–13.

13   A. P. Elkin, 'Australian Aboriginal and White Relations. A Personal Record', *Journal of the Royal Australian Historical Society*, vol. 48, part 3, 1963, p. 220.

14   M. Barnett, *Empire of Humanity. A History of Humanitarianism*, Cornell University Press, Ithaca, NY, 2011, p. 27.

15   G. H. Lane-Fox Pitt-Rivers, *The Clash of Culture and the Contact of Races. Anthropological and Psychological Study of the Laws of Racial Adaptability with Special Reference to Depopulation of the Pacific and the Government of Subject Races*, George Routledge and Sons, London, 1927, p. xii

16   Ibid., p. 27.

17   G. Sweet, 'Women and International Relationships', Second Pan Pacific Conference, Honolulu, 1930, p. 336.

18   S. Garton, 'Sound Minds and Healthy Bodies: Reconsidering Eugenics in Australia, 1914–1940', *Australian Historical Studies*, no. 103, 1994, p. 176.

19   McGregor, *Imagined Destinies* and 'The Doomed Race'.

20   Wood Jones, 'The Claims of the Australian Aborigine', p. 516.

21   Wood Jones, *Australia's Vanishing Race*, p. 39.

22   Ibid., p. 32.

23   G. Bolton, *Spoils and Spoilers: A History of Australians Shaping their Environment,* Allen & Unwin, Sydney, 1992.

24   M. MacCallum, 'Jones, Frederic Wood (1879–1954)', Australian Dictionary of Biography, National Centre of Biography, Australian National University, http://adb. anu.edu.au/biography/jones-frederic-wood-6872/text11907, accessed 12 March 2012.

25   D. Hutton and L. Connors, *A History of the Australian Environmental Movement*, Cambridge University Press, Cambridge, 1999, p. 25.

26   D. J. Mulvaney, 'Spencer, Sir Walter Baldwin (1860–1929)', Australian Dictionary of Biography, National Centre of Biography, Australian National University, http://adb. anu.edu.au/biography/spencer-sir-walter-baldwin-8606/text15031, accessed 12 March 2012.

27   Hutton and Connors, *A History of the Australian Environmental Movement*, pp. 20–23.

28   Ibid., pp. 24–59.

29   Association for the Protection of Native Races in Australasia and Polynesia, Aims and Objects, NAA: CRS A1, 1915/6691 Protection of Aborigines.

30   Australasian Association for the Advancement of Science, 'The Future of the Australian Aborigines', NAA:, CRS A1, 1915/6691 Protection of Aborigines.

31   Ibid.

32   J. McCorquodale, *Aborigines and the Law: A Digest*, Aboriginal Studies Press, Canberra, 1987.

33   M. F. Christie, *Aborigines in Colonial Victoria, 1835–86*, Sydney University Press, Sydney, 1979.

34   Christie, *Aborigines in Colonial Victoria*; E. J. B. Foxcroft, *Australian Native Policy: Its History, Especially in Victoria,* Melbourne University Press, Melbourne, 1941.

35   R. Kidd, *The Way We Civilise: Aboriginal Affairs – the Untold Story*, University of

Queensland Press, St Lucia, 1997; J. Richards, *The Secret War: A True History of Queensland's Native Police*, University of Queensland Press, St Lucia, 2008; R. Evans & K. Saunders, *Exclusion, Exploitation and Extermination: Race Relations in Colonial Queensland*, Australia and New Zealand Book Co, Sydney, 1975.

36 P. Biskup, *Not Slaves Not Citizens: The Aboriginal Problem in Western Australia*, University of Queensland Press, St Lucia, 1973; A. Haebich, *For Their Own Good: Aborigines and Government in the South-West of Western Australia*, University of Western Australia Press, Perth, 1988; A. Haebich, *Broken Circles, Fragmenting Indigenous Families 1800–2000*, Fremantle Arts Centre Press, Fremantle, 2000.

37 J. R. Gribble, *Dark Deeds in a Sunny Land, or Blacks and Whites in North-West Australia*, Stirling Bros, Perth, 1886.

38 Biskup, *Not Slaves Not Citizens*, p. 57.

39 S.-J. Hunt, *Spinifex and Hessian: Women's Lives in North-Western Australia 1860–1900*, University of Western Australia Press, Nedlands, 1986.

40 *The Aboriginals Protection and Restriction of the Sale of Opium Act*, 1897

41 Biskup, *Not Slaves Not Citizens*, pp. 55–9.

42 B. Porter, *Critics of Empire. British Radicals and the Imperial Challenge*, IB Tauris & Co, London, 2004, p. 51.

43 Ibid.

44 A. Markus, 'Morley, William (1854–1939)', Australian Dictionary of Biography, National Centre of Biography, Australian National University, http://adb.anu.edu.au/biography/morley-william-7656/text13391, accessed 13 March 2012.

45 Porter, *Critics of Empire*, pp. 295–6.

46 Articles 22 and 23 League of Nation's Covenant, http://www.firstworldwar.com/source/leagueofnations.htm

47 J. Heartfield, *The Aborigines' Protection Society: Humanitarian Imperialism in Australia, New Zealand, Fiji, Canada, South Africa and the Congo, 1836–1909*, Columbia University Press, New York, 2011, p. 49.

48 Porter, *Critics of Empire*.

49 Ibid., p. 182.

50 Ibid., pp. 151–4.

51 Barnett, *Empire of Humanity*, p. 74.

52 Porter, *Critics of Empire*, p. 300.

53 Ibid., pp. 262–87.

54 Ibid., p. 266.

55 Ibid., p. 324.

56 R. Maxon, *Struggle For Kenya: The Loss and Reassertion of Imperial Initiative, 1912–1923*, Cambridge University Press, Cambridge, 1997.

57 R. Hyam, 'Bureaucracy and "Trusteeship" in the Colonial Empire', J. M. Brown & W. R. Louis (eds), *The Oxford History of the British Empire: The Twentieth Century*, Oxford University Press, Oxford, 1999, p. 269.

58 L. J. Butler, *Britain and Empire: Adjusting to a Post-Imperial World*, IB Tauris & Co, London, 2002, p. 20.

59 J. W. Cell, 'Colonial Rule', *The Oxford History of the British Empire*, p. 241.

60 'Indirect Rule', *Anti-Slavery Reporter and Aborigines' Friend*, series V, vol. 23, no. 1, 1933, p. 3.

61   Cell, 'Colonial Rule', p. 233.

62   L. P. Mair, *Native Policies in Africa*, George Routledge & Sons, London, 1936, p. 12.

63   Porter, *Critics of Empire*, p. 324.

64   McGregor, *Imagined Destinies*, pp. 102–3.

65   Porter, *Critics of Empire*, p. 323.

66   B. Bush, *Imperialism, Race and Resistance: Africa and Britain*, Routledge, London, 1999.

67   Cell, 'Colonial Rule', p. 250.

68   F. Paisley, *The Lone Protestor: AM Fernando in Australia and Europe*, Aboriginal Studies Press, Canberra, 2012.

69   W. Anderson, *The Cultivation of Whiteness: Science, Health and Racial Destiny in Australia*, Melbourne University Press, Carlton, 2002.

70   F. Wood Jones, 'The Claims of the Australian Aborigine', p. 498.

71   Mrs John Jones, 'A Plea For a Co-operative National Policy for Australian Aborigines', British Commonwealth League, *Report of Conference*, 1932, p. 34. See also, F. Paisley, '"Don't Tell England!": Women of Empire Campaign to Change Aboriginal Policy in Australia Between the Wars', *Lilith*, no. 8, Summer 1993, pp. 139–52.

72   Woollacott, *To Try Her Fortune in London* Oxford University Press, Oxford, 2001; R. Pesman, *Duty Free: Australian Women Abroad*, Oxford University Press, Melbourne, 1996.

73   See J. Arnold, P. Spearritt & D. Walker (eds), *Out of Empire. The British Dominion of Australia*, Mandarin, Melbourne, 1993; W. R. Brock, *Britain and the Dominions*, Cambridge University Press, Cambridge, 1951.

74   Paisley, *The Lone Protestor*.

75   Jackson, 'Aborigines of Australia', p. 509.

76   Wood Jones, 'The Claims of the Australian Aborigine', pp. 510–14.

77   H. H. Finlayson, *The Red Centre. Man and Beast in the Heart of Australia*, Angus & Robertson, Sydney, 1935, p. 73.

78   T. Austin, 'False Start in Capricornia: Herbert Basedow, Northern Territory Chief Protector of Aborigines', *Journal of the Historical Society of South Australia,* vol. 17, 1989, pp. 112–23.

79   Ibid., p. 118.

80   H. Zogbaum, 'Herbert Basedow and the Removal of Aboriginal Children of Mixed Descent from their Families', *Australian Historical Studies*, no. 121, 2003, p. 126.

81   Porter, *Critics of Empire*, p. 304.

82   B. M. Harris to J. A. Lyons, 10/8/1937, NAA: A431, 194848/273, Part 1.

83   K. Blackburn, 'White Agitation for an Aboriginal State in Australia, 1925–1929', *Australian Journal of Politics and History*, vol. 45, no. 2, 1999, pp. 157–80.

84   M. Roe, 'A Model Aboriginal State', *Aboriginal History*, vol. 10, no. 1, 1986, p. 40–4.

85   McGregor, *Imagined Destinies*, p. 119.

86   J. C. Genders, 'The Australian Aborigines', *The NSW Honorary Magistrate,* 15/12/1937; Feminist Club Papers, ML MSS 1703, Box K21801.

87   Roe, 'A Model Aboriginal State', p. 42.

88   H. K. Fry, 'The Problem of the Aborigines: Australian Policy, In Retrospect and Prospect', *The Australian Rhodes Review*, Melbourne University Press, no. 2, 1936, p. 36.

89   Genders, 'The Australian Aborigines'.

90   Mair, *Native Policies in Africa*.

91   Genders, 'The Australian Aborigines', p. 7.
92   M. Bennett, 'A Native Policy for Australia', NAA: A461, A 300/ Part 3, Aboriginals –
      Policy, 1937–1943.
93   Ibid.
94   Roe, 'A Model Aboriginal State', p. 44.
95   Blackburn, 'White Agitation for an Aboriginal State', p. 170.
96   P. Read, 'Northern Territory', in A. McGrath (ed.), *Contested Ground: Australian
      Aborigines Under the British Crown*, Allen & Unwin, Sydney, 1995, p. 280.
97   N. Stepan, '*The Hour of Eugenics': Race, Gender and Nation in Latin America*, Cornell
      University Press, Ithaca, 1991.
98   See, for example, Haebich, *Broken Circles*; H. Reynolds, *Nowhere People*, Penguin,
      Victoria, 2005; T. Austin, 'Cecil Cook, Scientific Thought and "Half-Castes" in
      the Northern Territory, 1927–1937', *Aboriginal History*, vol. 14, 1990, pp. 104–122;
      P. Bartrop, 'The Holocaust, the Aborigines and the Bureaucracy of Destruction: An
      Australian Dimension of Genocide', *Journal of Genocide Research*, vol. 3, no. 1, 2001,
      pp. 75–87; R. McGregor, '"Breed out the Colour" or the Importance of Being White',
      Australian Historical Studies, no. 120, 2002, pp. 282–302.
99   Wood Jones, *Australia's Vanishing Race*.
100   Cell, 'Colonial Rule', p. 243.

Chapter 2 – Defining a Reform Agenda

1   M. Bennett, *Christison of Lammermoor*, Alston Rivers, London, 1927, p. 99.
2   M. Bennett to Mr Lees, 18 June 1929, in Bennett, *The Condition of the Aborigines of
     Australia Under the Federal Government,* a paper read before the British Commonwealth
     League Conference, London, 5 June 1929, pp. 10–22.
3   M. Sinha, *Specters of Mother India: The Global Restructuring of an Empire*, Duke University
     Press, Durham, 2006.
4   B. Porter, *Critics of Empire: British Radicals and the Imperial Challenge*, IB Taurus, London,
     2008, pp. 295–6.
5   Ibid., p. 304.
6   A. Woollacott, *To Try Her Fortune in London. Australian Women, Colonialism and Modernity*,
     Oxford University Press, Oxford, 2001; F. Paisley, *Loving Protection? Australian Feminism
     and Aboriginal Women's Rights, 1919–1939*, Melbourne University Press, Carlton,
     2000; B. Bush, '"Britain's Conscience on Africa": White Women, Race and Imperial
     Politics in Inter–war Britain', in C. Midgley (ed.), *Gender and Imperialism,* Manchester
     University Press, Manchester, 1998, pp. 200–23.
7   'Slave Conditions in Australia. Allegations at Women's Conference', *The Manchester
     Guardian*, 20 June, 1930, Rischbieth Papers, NLA, MS2004/12/304.
8   M. Bennett, 'Notes on the Dalleburra Tribe of Northern Queensland', *Journal of the
     Royal Anthropological Institute of Great Britain and Ireland,* vol. 57, 1927, pp. 399–415.
9   A. Holland & F. Paisley, 'Fernando, Anthony Martin (1864–1949)', *Australian Dictionary
     of Biography,* National Centre of Biography, Australian National University, http://
     adb.anu.edu.au/biography/fernando-anthony-martin-12918/text23339, accessed 22
     March 2012.
10   F. Paisley, *The Lone Protestor: AM Fernando in Australia and Europe*, Aboriginal Studies
     Press, Canberra, 2012; F. Paisley, 'Australian Aboriginal Activism in Interwar Britain and

Europe: Anthony Martin Fernando', *History Compass*, vol. 7, no. 3, 2009, pp. 701–718.

11   Ibid.

12   M. Bennett, *The Australian Aboriginal as a Human Being*, Alston Rivers, London, 1930, p. 112.

13   Bennett to Lees, 18 June 1929, in Bennett, *The Condition of the Aborigines of Australia Under the Federal Government*.

14   Bennett, *Christison*, p. 87.

15   M. Bennett, 'A Native Policy for Australia', Rischbieth Papers, NLA MS2004/12/217; *The Australian Aboriginal as a Human Being*, p. 11.

16   R. Hyam, 'Bureaucracy and "Trusteeship" in the Colonial Empire', in J. M. Brown & W. R. Louis (eds), *The Oxford History of the British Empire: The Twentieth Century*, Oxford University Press, Oxford, 1999, pp. 256–78.

17   Lord Olivier, 'Imperial Trusteeship', *Fabian Tract*, no. 230, The Fabian Society, London, October 1929, p. 15.

18   Report of the Commission on Closer Union of the Dependencies in Eastern and Central Africa, HM Stationery Office, London, 1929.

19   Ibid., p. 40.

20   Ibid., p. 41.

21   Hyam, 'Bureaucracy and "Trusteeship"', p. 269.

22   Eastern and Central Africa, House of Lords Debate on the Report of the Commission on Closer Union, *African Affairs*, vol. xxviii, no. cxi, London, 1929, p. 253.

23   B. Malinowski, 'Review of Report of the Commission on Closer Union of the Dependencies in Eastern and Central Africa', *Africa: Journal of the International African Institute*, vol. 2, no. 3, 1929, pp. 317–20.

24   A. Beck, 'Some Observations on Jomo Kenyatta in Britain, 1929–1930', *Cahiers d'Études Africaines*, vol. 6, no. 22, 1966, p. 309.

25   A. McGrath, *Born in the Cattle: Aborigines in Cattle Country*, Allen & Unwin, Sydney, 1987; H. Reynolds, *North of Capricornia: The Untold Story of Australia's North*, Allen & Unwin, Sydney, 2003.

26   W. Anderson, *The Cultivation of Whiteness: Science, Health and Racial Destiny in Australia*, Melbourne University Press, Carlton, 2002.

27   M. Bennett, A Native Policy For Australia, Rischbieth Papers, NLA 2004/12/217

28   Report of the Commission on Closer Union, p. 53.

29   E. Scott, 'William Harrison Moore – An Appreciation', *The Argus*, 6 July 1935, p. 4.

30   In Robert Christison's 'Notes on the Dalleburra' in the University of Queensland Library the tribe is recorded as 500 in 1865. For further information, see Beddoe, 'On the Aborigines of Central Queensland', *The Journal of the Anthropological Institute of Great Britain and Ireland,* vol. 7, 1878, pp. 145–48.

31   J. Richards, *The Secret War: A True History of Queensland's Native Police*, University of Queensland Press, St Lucia, 2008; A. Palmer, *Colonial Genocide*, Crawford House Publishing, Hindmarsh, South Australia, 2000; A. Nettlebeck & R. Foster, *In the Name of the Law: William Willshire and the Policing of the Australian Frontier*, Wakefield Press, South Australia, 2007.

32   Bennett, 'Notes on the Dalleburra', p. 402.

33   Bennett, *Christison*, p. 68.

34   S. Robinson, *Something Like Slavery? Queensland Aboriginal Child Workers, 1842–1954*,

Australian Scholarly Publishing, Victoria, 2008.

35 Bennett, *Christison,* p. 83.

36 For context see D. Carment, 'The Wills Massacre of 1861: Aboriginal-European Conflict on the Colonial Australian Frontier', *Journal of Australian Studies,* no. 6, 1980, pp. 49–55.

37 Bennett, *Christison,* p. 246.

38 Ibid., pp. 259–60.

39 In *Christison of Lammermoor,* which she was writing at the same time as her dedication to Wyma, this word appears in the Dalleburra dictionary as 'Kobiberry' and it meant 'wise man', 'elder'.

40 M. Cryle, 'A "Fantastic Adventure": Reading Christison of Lammermoor', in F. McKenzie (ed.), *Journeys Through Queensland History: Landscape, Place and Society: Proceedings of the Professional Historians Association (Queensland) Conference, Marking the Sesquicentenary of Queensland 1859–2009,* Professional Historians Association (Queensland), St Lucia, 2009, pp. 223–34. I thank Shirleene Robinson for passing this reference onto me.

41 Lammermoor was described as extending to 1,161 square miles in 1909.

42 *Dalgety's Review* was the periodical of the Southern Sheepbreeders Association.

43 E. M. Allingham, 'Christison, Robert (1837–1915)', Australian Dictionary of Biography, National Centre of Biography, Australian National University, http://adb.anu.edu.au/biography/christison-robert-222/text4823, accessed 10 December 2013.

44 Bennett, *Christison,* p. 155.

45 Bennett, *Christison,* p. 157.

46 S. Sleight, 'Reading the British Australasian Community in London, 1884–1924', in C. Bridge, R. Crawford & D. Dunstan. (eds), *Australians in Britain: The Twentieth Century Experience,* Monash University ePress, Melbourne, 2009, pp. 7.1–7.14.

47 Bennett, *Christison,* p. 159.

48 M. Brown, 'Fernando. The Story of an Aboriginal Prophet', *Aborigine Welfare Bulletin,* vol. 4, no. 1, 1964, pp. 9–11.

49 H. Cameron Roberts to Reverend F. H. Griffiths, 21 November 1961, Noel Butlin Archives Centre and University Archives, Australian National University.

50 J. S. Cameron, 'Sir Robert Christison (1797–1882): The Man, his Times and his Contributions to Nephrology', *Journal of the Royal College of Physicians of Edinburgh,* vol. 37, no. 2, 2007, pp. 155–72.

51 S. Koven, *Slumming: Sexual and Social Politics in Victorian London,* Princeton University Press, Princeton, New Jersey, 2006.

52 Paisley, *The Lone Protestor,* p. 128.

53 Koven, *Slumming,* p. 8.

54 Brown, 'Fernando', pp. 9–11.

55 Bennett, *Christison,* p. 267.

56 M. Bennett to B. Rischbieth, 19 December 1931, Rischbieth Papers, NLA, MS2004/12/22.

57 M. Bennett, 'Wyma', *Townsville Daily Bulletin,* Queensland, 19 May 1928.

58 Ibid.

59 State Archives of Western Australia, An 537, Royal Commissions, Acc2922, *Royal Commission Appointed to Investigate, Report and Advise upon Matters in Relation to the*

Condition and Treatment of Aborigines, 1935, Acc 1934/2, Transcripts of Evidence, 264.

60 Cryle, 'A Fantastic Adventure', p. 231–33.

61 Raymond Evans, 'Kings in Brass Crescents: Defining Aboriginal Labour Patterns in Colonial Queensland', in Evans, *Fighting Words. Writing About Race*, University of Queensland Press, St Lucia, 1999, pp. 180–200.

62 Bennett, *Christison*, p. 259.

63 This is a fascinating snippet told to me in passing by Bennett's elderly niece.

64 Records Collected by Mary Bennett and Presented to the University of Queensland, University of Queensland Library, UQFL 202, Mary Bennett, Box 1.

65 Bennett, *Christison*, p. 86.

66 Ibid., p. 99.

67 Bennett, *The Condition of the Aborigines of Australia Under the Federal Government*, p. 9. Interestingly, Bennett's version of what happened at the time corresponds, in crucial particulars, with a revision of the incident by Bill Wilson and Justin O'Brien published in 2003. See Wilson and O'Brien, "To Infuse an Universal Terror": A Reappraisal of the Coniston Killings', *Aboriginal History*, vol. 27, 2003, pp. 59–78.

68 Bennett, *The Australian Aboriginal*, p. 80. According to Rani Kerin, the South Australian government had introduced legislation in 1912 providing a bounty of 7 shillings and 6 pence per dingo scalp. This had been provided earlier in other states. See R. Kerin, 'Dogging For a Living. Aborigines and "Undesirables" in South Australia', in B. Attwood & T. Griffiths (eds), *Frontier, Race, Nation. Henry Reynolds and Australian History*, Australian Scholarly Publishing, Victoria, 2009, pp. 136–156.

69 Bennett, The Australian Aboriginal, pp. 79–80.

70 C. Bishop, '"She has the Native Interests Too Much at Heart": Annie Lock's Experiences as a Single, White, Female Missionary to Aborigines, 1903–1937', in A. Barry, J. Cruickshank, A. Brown-May & P. Grimshaw. (eds), *Evangelists of Empire? Missionaries in Colonial History*, University of Melbourne eScholarship Research Centre, 2008.

71 Bennett, *The Australian Aboriginal*, p. 84.

72 A. Lock to M. Bennett, August 1929, Papers of Mrs CM Ternent Cooke Relating to Aboriginal Affairs, 1927–1967, South Australian Archives, GRG 52/32/31.

73 Ibid.

74 Bennett to T. Buxton, 30 January 1929, Papers of Mrs CM Ternent Cooke Relating to Aboriginal Affairs, 1927–1967, South Australian Archives, GRG 52/32/23.

75 ibid.

76 M. Bennett, *The Condition of the Aborigines of Australia Under the Federal Government*, p. 22.

77 Ibid., p. 18.

78 Ibid., pp. 18–19.

79 Bennett, *The Australian Aboriginal*, p. 15.

80 S. Pedersen, 'National Bodies, Unspeakable Acts: The Sexual Politics of Colonial Policy-Making', *The Journal of Modern History*, vol. 63, no. 4, 1991, p. 655.

81 Bennett, *The Australian Aboriginal*, p. 138.

82 Ibid., pp. 140–41.

83 Australia Parliament, *The Aboriginals and Half-Castes of Central and North Australia*, Report by J. W. Bleakley, 1929, p. 7.

84 A. Holland, 'Feminism, Colonialism and Aboriginal Workers. An Anti-Slavery Crusade',

Labour History, no. 69, 1995, pp. 52–64.

85 M. Bennett, 'Whites and Natives: Allegations of Slavery', *The West Australian*, 17 May 1932.

86 Bennett, *The Australian Aboriginal*, p. 97.

87 Ibid., p. 100.

88 Ibid., p. 122.

89 Ibid.

90 Ibid., p. 137.

91 Ibid., p. 135.

92 M. Bennett, *The Condition of the Aborigines of Australia Under the Federal Government*, p. 22.

93 M. Barnett, *Empire of Humanity. A History of Humanitarianism*, Cornell University, Ithaca, 2011, p. 74.

94 Porter, *Critics of Empire*, p. 254–60.

95 Bennett, *The Australian Aboriginal*, pp. 13–14.

96 M. Bennett to B. Rischbieth, 9 November 1930, *Rischbieth Papers*, NLA, MS2004/12/112–161.

97 Bennett, *The Australian Aboriginal*, p. 75.

98 Ibid., p. 141.

99 M. Bennett, 'A Native Policy for Australia', Rischbieth Papers, NLA MS2004/12/217.

100 Ibid.

101 Bennett, *The Condition of the Aborigines of Australia Under the Federal Government*, p. 19.

102 Bennett to Rischbieth, 9 November 1930, Rischbieth Papers.

103 M. Bennett to C. Duguid, 7 October 1934, Duguid Papers, NLA, MS5068, series 11.

104 M. Bennett, Lecture to the Women's Service Guilds, 11 December 1932, Rischbieth Papers, NLA, MS2004/12/235–303.

105 M. Bennett to B. Rischbieth, 19 December 1931, Rischbieth Papers, NLA, MS2004/72/22.

106 M. Sinha has since shown how the Child Marriage Restraint Act was ultimately a victory for Indian feminists and nationalists who exploited it in their refashioning of Indian national identity. For a full exploration of this moment see M. Sinha, *Specters of Mother India* and 'Reforming Mother India: Feminism and Nationalism in Late Colonial India', *Feminist Studies*, vol. 26, no. 3, 2000, pp. 623–44.

107 Bennett, *The Australian Aboriginal*, p. 127.

108 A. Burton, *Burdens of History: British Feminists, Indian Women and Imperial Culture, 1965–1915*, University of North Carolina Press, Chapel Hill, 1994.

109 C. Midgley, *Women Against Slavery. The British Campaigns, 1780–1870,* Routledge, London, 1992.

110 Papers of the Anti-Slavery and Aborigines' Protection Society, Rhodes House, Oxford, Mss British Empire, S22 G379. See also, F. Paisley, *Loving Protection?* pp. 18–22.

111 Brown, *Fernando*, p. 7.

Chapter 3 – Freeing Women

1 E. Jones, 'Australia. Aborigines', British Commonwealth League, *Report of Conference*, June 1936, p. 27.

2 B. Bush, 'Gender and Empire: The Twentieth Century', in P. Levine (ed.), *Gender and Empire*, Oxford University Press, New York, 2004, p. 80.

3   Mrs Jamieson-Williams, 'The League of Nations and a Problem for the Future – The Native Woman', Rischbieth Papers, NLA, MS2004/12/215–234. Jamieson-Williams attended the Assembly as the Alternate Delegate of the Australian Federation of Women Voters.

4   British Commonwealth League, 'Resolutions', *Report of Annual Conference*, June 1935, p. 7; Report of the Twelfth Congress of the International Alliance of Women, Resolution on Polygamy, 1935, Papers of the Australian Federation of Women Voters, NLA, MS2818, Box 15.

5   Records of the Association for the Protection of Native Races, Sydney University Archives, series 9.

6   Feminist Club of New South Wales, Records, ML MSS 1703, K21801.

7   P. Grimshaw, 'Settler Anxieties, Indigenous Peoples and Women's Suffrage in the Colonies of Australia, New Zealand and Hawai'i 1888–1902', *Pacific Historical Review*, vol. 69, no. 4, 2000, pp. 553–73.

8   F. Paisley, *Loving Protection? Australian Feminism and Aboriginal Women's Rights, 1919–1939*, Melbourne University Press, Melbourne, 2000; A. Whittick, *Woman into Citizen*, Athenaeum and Frederick Muller, London, 1979.

9   *The Anti-Slavery Reporter and Aborigines' Friend*, vol. 23, no. 2, July 1933, p. 83.

10   C. Cooke, 'Australian Aboriginal Women', British Commonwealth League, *Report of Conference*, June 1927, p. 30.

11   V. Haskins, 'Domestic Service and Frontier Feminism. The Call for a Woman Visitor to "Half-Caste" Girls and Women in Domestic Service, Adelaide, 1925-1928', *Frontiers*, vol. 28, nos. 1 & 2, 2007, pp. 124–64.

12   Ibid.

13   Cooke, 'Australian Aboriginal Women', p. 30.

14   M. Bennett, *Christison of Lammermoor*, Alston Rivers, London, 1927, p. 29.

15   Ibid., p. 227.

16   Ibid., p. 228.

17   A. Lock to M. Bennett, August 1929, Papers of Mrs C. M. Ternent Cooke Relating to Aboriginal Affairs, 1927–1967, South Australian Archives, GRG 52/32/31.

18   Australia, Parliament 1928, *The Aboriginal and Half-Castes of Central and North Australia*, Report by J. W. Bleakley.

19   Ibid., pp. 9, 27.

20   R. Wild & P. Anderson, *Ampe Akelyernemane Meke Mekarle, Little Children are Sacred*, Report of the Northern Territory Board of Inquiry into the Protection of Aboriginal Children from Sexual Abuse, Government Printer of the Northern Territory, Darwin, 2007, pp. 57–61.

21   S. Bannister, Evidence before the Select Committee on Aborigines (British Settlements), Report of the Select Committee on Aborigines (British Settlements), vol. 1, Part II, 1837 (British Parliamentary Papers), p. 20.

22   S.-J. Hunt, *Spinifex and Hessian: Women's Lives in North-Western Australia 1860–1900*, University of Western Australia Press, Nedlands, 1986.

23   See, for example, R. Hyam, *Empire and Sexuality. The British Experience*, Manchester University Press, Manchester, 1990; G. Smithers, *Science, Sexuality and Race in the US and Australia, 1780s–1890s*, Routledge, London, 2011; A. McGrath, '*Born in the Cattle*'. *Aborigines in Cattle Country*, Allen & Unwin, Sydney, 1987; A. McGrath, 'Sex, Violence

and Theft 1830–1910', in P. Grimshaw et al. (eds), *Creating a Nation, 1788–1990*, McPhee Gribble Publishers, 1994; K. Ellinghaus, *Taking Assimilation to Heart. Marriages of White Women and Indigenous Men in the US and Australia, 1887–1937*, University of Nebraska Press, Lincoln, 2006; A. Stoler, *Carnal Knowledge and Imperial Power: Race and the Intimate in Colonial Rule*, University of California Press, Berkeley, 2010; A. McClintock, *Imperial Leather. Race, Gender and Sexuality in the Colonial Conquest*, Routledge, New York, 1995; R. Ganter, 'Living an Immoral Life—"coloured" women and the Paternalistic State', *Hecate*, vol. 24, no. 1, 1998, pp. 13–41.

24 'No Mission at Jay River. Mixed Alliances a Live Problem', *Sydney Sun*, 1 April 1935.

25 R. Frances, *Selling Sex. A Hidden History of Prostitution*, UNSW Press, Sydney, 2007; McGrath, *'Born in the Cattle'*.

26 Frances, *Selling Sex*, p. 86.

27 British Commonwealth League, *Report of Conference*, June 1926, p. 4.

28 C. Cooke, 'The Status of Aboriginal Women in Australia', *Second Pan Pacific Conference*, 1930, p. 130.

29 J. Harris, 'Some Servitudes of Women', British Commonwealth League, *Report of Conference*, June 1927, p. 23.

30 S. Pedersen, 'The Maternalist Moment in British Colonial Policy: The Controversy over "Child Slavery" in Hong Kong 1917–1941', *Past and Present*, no. 171, 2001, pp. 161–202; 'National Bodies, Unspeakable Acts: The Sexual Politics of Colonial Policy-Making', *The Journal of Modern History*, vol. 63, no. 4, 1991, pp. 647–80. See also S. Paddle, 'The Limits of Sympathy: International Feminists and the Chinese "Slave Girl" Campaigns of the 1920s and 1930s', *Journal of Colonialism and Colonial History*, vol. 4, no. 3, 2003.

31 M. Sinha, *Specters of Mother India. The Global Restructuring of an Empire*, Duke University Press, Durham, 2006.

32 Cooke, 'The Status of Aboriginal Women', p. 130.

33 E. Jones, 'The Case for the Australian Aboriginals in Central and Northern Australia', British Commonwealth League, *Report of Conference*, June 1934, p. 34.

34 M. Bennett, Speech to the British Commonwealth League, British Commonwealth League, *Report of Conference*, June 1930, pp. 38–9.

35 N. Boyle, 'Speech to the British Commonwealth League', British Commonwealth League, *Report of Conference*, June 1930, p. 40.

36 Ibid., p. 41.

37 J. Harris, 'Some Servitudes of Women', p. 21.

38 Pedersen, 'The Maternalist Moment', p. 189.

39 H. F. Morris & J. S. Read, *Indirect Rule and the Search for Justice: Essays in East African Legal History*, Clarendon Press, Oxford, pp. 214–15.

40 N. Boyle, 'Slavery', British Commonwealth League, *Report of Conference*, 1932, p. 38.

41 Ibid.

42 'Position of Women Under Colonial Administration', Records of the United Associations of Women, c.1930–1970, ML MSS 2160, Box Y789.

43 E. Jones to Women's Non-Party Association, 19 August 1931, State Library of South Australia, Papers of the League of Women Voters (Formerly WNPA), SRG 116/2/2.

44 Bennett, *Christison*, p. 29.

45 R. Foster & M. Paul, 'Married to the Land: Land Grants to Aboriginal Women

in South Australia, 1848–1911', *Australian Historical Studies*, vol. 34, no. 121, 2003, pp. 48–68.

46   See, for example, J. Chesterman & B. Galligan, *Citizens Without Rights. Aborigines and Australian Citizenship*, Cambridge University Press, Cambridge 1997, pp. 46–50.

47   'Slave Horror of the North', *Smith's Weekly*, 9 January 9 1937.

48   Frances, *Selling Sex,* pp. 90–1.

49   Chesterman & Galligan, *Citizens Without Rights*, p. 48. See also K. Ellinghaus, 'Absorbing the "Aboriginal Problem": Controlling Interracial Marriage in Australia in the Late 19th and early 20th Centuries', *Aboriginal History*, vol. 27, 2003, pp. 183–207.

50   P. Pascoe, *What Comes Naturally. Miscegenation Law and the Making of Race in America,* Oxford University Press, New York, 2009; K. Ellinghaus, *Taking Assimilation to Heart.*

51   V. Haskins, 'A Better Chance? Sexual Abuse and the Apprenticeship of Aboriginal Girls under the NSW Aborigines Protection Board', *Aboriginal History*, vol. 28, 2004, pp. 33–58.

52   'New Laws for Protection of Aborigines', *Adelaide Advertiser*, 2 June 1933.

53   F. Probyn-Rapsey, *Made to Matter: White Fathers, Stolen Generations*, University of Sydney Publishing, Sydney, 2013.

54   Chesterman & Galligan, *Citizens Without Rights*, p. 48.

55   M. Bennett to B. Rischbieth, 20 September 1933, Rischbieth Papers, NLA, MS2004/12/1–81.

56   Pascoe, *What Comes Naturally.*

57   T. Austin, '"A Chance to be Decent": Northern Territory "Half-Caste" Girls in Service in South Australia', *Labour History*, no. 60, 1991, pp. 51–65; P. Edmonds, 'Mixed Metaphors: Other Mothers, Dangerous Daughters and the Rhetoric of Child Removal in Burma, Australia and Indo-China', *Balayi: Culture, Law and Colonialism*, vol. 6, 2004, pp. 41–61; R. Ganter, 'Living an Immoral Life: "Coloured" Women and the Paternalistic State', *Hecate*, vol. 24, no. 1, 1998, pp. 13–40; A. Stoler, 'Making Empire Respectable: the Politics of Race and Sexual Morality in Twentieth Century Colonial Cultures', *American Ethnologist*, vol. 16, no. 4, 1989, p. 647.

58   A. Holland, 'Wives and Mothers Like Ourselves? Exploring White Women's Intervention in the Politics of Race, 1920s–1940s', *Australian Historical Studies*, vol. 32, no. 117, 2001, p. 303.

59   Ibid., pp. 292–310.

60   Cooke, 'Australian Aboriginal Women', p. 29.

61   P. Jacobs, 'Science and Veiled Assumptions: Miscegenation in Western Australia, 1930–1937', *Australian Aboriginal Studies*, No. 2, 1986, pp. 15–22.

62   H. Zogbaum, 'Herbert Basedow and the Removal of Aboriginal Children of Mixed Descent from their Families', *Australian Historical Studies*, vol. 34, no. 121, 2003, pp. 122–38.

63   C. Cooke, Letter to the Editor, 6 October 1924, Newspaper Clipping, South Australian Archives, Papers of Constance Cooke, GRG 52/32/15.

64   Australian Federation of Women Voters, Interim Report, June 1933 – May 1934, Papers of the United Associations of Women, ML Mss 2160, Box Y789.

65   A. O. Neville to the Women's Service Guilds, 15 June 1933, Rischbieth Papers, NLA, MS2004/12/42.

66   M. Bennett, 'White and Natives. Allegations of Slavery', *The West Australian,* 19 May 1932, p. 19.

Notes

67　Ibid.
68　M. Wyllie, 'A Study of Polygynous Marriage with Special Reference to North Australia and Papua New Guinea and the Attitude thereto of Administration and Christian Missions', MA, University of Sydney, 1951, pp. 22–46.
69　M. Morgan, *A Drop in a Bucket. The Mount Margaret Story*, United Aborigines' Mission, Victoria, 1986, p. 10.
70　M. Bennett, *The Australian Aboriginal as a Human Being*, Alston Rivers, London, 1930, pp. 20–1; see also B. Spencer, *Wanderings in Wild Australia*, Volume 1, Macmillan and Co, London, 1928, pp. 192–202.
71　Bennett, *The Australian Aboriginal*, p. 22.
72　Morgan, *A Drop in a Bucket*, pp. 58–60.
73　M. Jacobs, *White Mother to a Dark Race. Settler Colonialism, Maternalism and the Removal of Indigenous Children in the American West and Australia, 1880–1940*, University of Nebraska Press, Lincoln, 2009.
74　Ibid., pp. 119–20.
75　M. Bennett to B. Rischbeith, 6 March 1932, Rischbieth Papers, NLA, MS2004/12/1–81.
76　Ibid.
77　M. Bennett, *Teaching the Aborigines. Data from the Mt Margaret Mission*, City and Suburban Print, Perth, 1935, p. 29.
78　See, for example, P. Pepper, *You are What You Make Yourself to be: The Story of a Victorian Aboriginal Family, 1842–1980*, Hyland House, Melbourne, 1980; P. Brock, *Outback Ghettos: A History of Aboriginal Institutionalisation and Survival*, Cambridge University Press, Melbourne, 1993; C. Choo, *Mission Girls: Aboriginal Women on Catholic Missions in the Kimberley, Western Australia, 1900–1950*, University of Western Australia Press, Perth, 2001; M. Morgan, *Mt Margaret: A Drop in a Bucket*, Mission Publication of Australia, 1991.
79　Diane Bell, 'Choose Your Mission Wisely: Christian Colonials and Aboriginal Marital Arrangements on the Northern Frontier', Tony Swain and Deborah Bird Rose (eds), *Aboriginal Australians and Christian Missions*, Australian Association for the Study of Religions, Adelaide, 1988, pp. 338-53; Tony Scanlon, '"Pure and Clean and True to Christ": Black Women and White Missionaries in the North', *Hecate*, vol.7, nos.1-2, 1986, pp.83-105; Catherine and Ronald Berndt, 'An Oenpelli Monologue: Culture Contact', *Oceania*, vol.22, no.1, September, 1951, pp.24-52; Peggy Brock, *Outback Ghettos: A History of Aboriginal Institutionalisation and Survival*, Cambridge University Press, Melbourne, 1993, pp.150-51.
80　Choo, *Mission Girls*, p. 219.
81　Western Australia, Parliament 1935, Report of the Royal Commissioner Appointed to Investigate, Report and Advise upon matters in relation to the Condition and Treatment of Aborigines, Perth (hereafter, Moseley Royal Commission Report), p. 220.
82　Choo, *Mission Girls*, pp. 186–243.
83　Morgan, *Drop in a Bucket*, p. 54.
84　Bennett, *Teaching the Aborigines*, pp. 28–9.
85　M. Bennett, Lecture to the Women's Service Guilds, 11 December 1932, Rischbieth Papers, NLA, MS2004/12/235–303.
86　*Allegations by Mrs Mary Bennett in regard to native slavery, inadequate reserves and traffic in native women* SLWA, AN 1/7, Department of Native Affairs and Native Welfare, ACC

993, 116/1932, (hereafter, Bennett, Allegations of slavery, SLWA)

87 Ibid.

88 In the 1920s Indian political activists saw that reforming the practice of child marriage would not only eradicate a social evil but demonstrate to the wider world the capacity of Indians for self-rule. What for Katherine Mayo was a discourse about the sexual depravity of Hindu society and, therefore, an argument against self-rule, became an attack on the colonial state as an obstacle to progressive social reform in India. Sinha, Specters of Mother India, p. 6.

89 Bennett, Notes, Duguid Papers, NLA MS5068, series 11.

90 Bennett, *Teaching the Aborigines*, pp. 28–29.

91 'Natives and Polygamy', Letter to the Editor, *The West Australian*, 30 June 1932, Bennett, *Allegations of Slavery, etc.*

92 Bennett, 'Whites and Natives. Allegations of Slavery', *The West Australian*.

93 Bennett, *The Australian Aboriginal as a Human Being*, p. 82.

94 Frances, *Selling Sex*, p. 99.

95 A. O. Neville, Response to Bennett's Allegations, in Bennett, 'Allegations of slavery', SLWA.

96 A. O. Neville to Mr Kitson, 19/6/1933, in Bennett, 'Allegations of slavery', SLWA.

97 R. Piddington, 'Aborigines on Cattle Stations are in Slavery', *The World*, 14 January 1932; *Anti-Slavery Reporter and Aborigines' Friend,* vol. 22, no. 2, 1932, pp. 82-84. For a helpful analysis of Piddington's critique see G., '"Piddington's Indiscretion": Ralph Piddington, The Australian National Research Council and Academic Freedom', *Oceania*, vol. 64, no. 3, 1994, pp. 217–45.

98 Mrs Sawdon to Women's Service Guilds, 29 April 1932, Rischbieth Papers, NLA, MS2004/12/39.

99 Frances, *Selling Sex*, pp. 88–94.

100 'A Call to the Women of Australia to Demand an Honourable Native Policy', Australian Federation of Women Voters, Rischbieth Papers, NLA, MS2004/12/162.

101 Mrs Jamieson-Williams, 'The League of Nations and a Problem for the Future – The Native Woman', Rischbieth Papers, NLA, MS2004/12/215-234.

102 Ibid.

103 Ibid.

104 E. Jones, 'The Australian Aborigine Woman: Is She a Slave?', Rischbieth Papers, NLA, MS2004/12/314.

105 M. Bennett, 'The Aboriginal Mother', 1933, Elkin Papers, University of Sydney Archives, Box 23, Item 8.

106 Ibid.

107 Newspaper clipping, Bennett, 'Allegations of Slavery', SLWA.

108 H. Reynolds, *This Whispering in Our Hearts*, Allen & Unwin, St Leonards, 1998.

109 A. Haebich, *For Their Own Good. Aborigines and Government in the South West of Western Australia, 1900–1940*, University of Western Australian Press, Perth, 1992, pp. 324–25.

110 Newspaper clipping, Department of Home Affairs, Correspondence Files, NAA: A1, 1935/1388, Allegations of Slavery in the Northern Territory, 1933–1935.

111 P. Jacobs, 'Science and Veiled Assumptions: Miscegenation in Western Australia, 1930–1937', *Australian Aboriginal Studies*, no. 2, 1986, pp. 15–22.

Chapter 4 – Domestic Rules

1   A. O. Neville, Response to Mary Bennett's allegations, SAWA, AN 1/7, Department of Native Affairs and Native Welfare, ACC 993, 116/1932, (hereafter Bennett, Allegations of slavery, SLWA.

2   A. Holland, 'The Campaign for Women Protectors: Gender, Race and Frontier between the Wars', *Australian Feminist Studies* , vol. 16, no. 34, 2001, pp. 27–42.

3   See, for example, R. McGregor, *Imagined Destinies. Aboriginal Australians and the Doomed Race Theory, 1880–1939*, Melbourne University Press, Carlton, 1997; R. McGregor, 'Representations of the "Half-Caste" in the Australian Scientific Literature of the 1930s', *Journal of Australian Studies*, vol. 17, no. 36, 1993, pp. 51–64.

4   C. Cooke, 'Australian Aboriginal Women', British Commonwealth League, *Report of Conference, 1927*, p. 30.

5   M. Sinha, *Specters of Mother India. The Global Restructuring of an Empire*, Duke University Press, Durham, 2006.

6   Neville, Response to allegations, Bennett, Allegations of slavery, SLWA.

7   Holland, 'The Campaign for Women Protectors'.

8   F. Paisley, *Loving Protection? Australian Feminism and Aboriginal Women's Rights, 1919–1939*, Melbourne University Press, Carlton, 2000, p. 114.

9   P. Jacobs, *Mister Neville: A Biography*, Fremantle Arts Centre Press, Fremantle, 1990, p. 185.

10 Paisley, *Loving Protection?*, p. 114.

11 Ibid., p. 116.

12 P. Biskup, *Not Slaves Not Citizens. The Aboriginal Problem in Western Australia, 1898–1954*, University of Queensland Press, St Lucia, 1973, p. 86.

13 A. O. Neville to Minister Kitson, June 1933, Bennett, Allegations of slavery, SLWA.

14 A. O. Neville to the Secretary of the Premier's Department, 24 November 1934, Bennett, Allegations of slavery, SLWA.

15 Paisley, *Loving Protection?*, p. 118.

16 M. Lake, 'Feminist History as National History: Writing the Political History of Women', *Australian Historical Studies*, vol. 27, no. 106, 1996, p. 162.

17 Paisley, *Loving Protection?*, p. 112.

18 A. Haebich, *Broken Circles. Fragmenting Indigenous Families 1800–2000*, Fremantle Arts Centre Press, Fremantle, 2000, p. 276.

19 B. Rischbieth, Transcripts of Evidence, SAWA, AN 537, Royal Commissions, Acc 2922, Royal Commission appointed to investigate, report and advise upon matters in relation to the condition and treatment of Aborigines, 1935, Acc 1934/2, Transcripts of Evidence, pp. 537–544. (Hereafter Moseley Royal Commission, Transcripts of Evidence, SAWA).

20 A. Bromham, Moseley Royal Commission, Transcripts of Evidence, p. 557.

21 Women's Service Guilds, 'Women and the Royal Commission', SAWA, MN 393, Women's Service Guilds, Welfare of Aborigines, February–November 1937.

22 On the issue of food, Bennett maintained that the existing adult weekly ration resulted in the starvation of Aboriginal people in their own land. The ration consisted of 10 pounds of flour, 1.5 pounds of sugar and 0.25 pound of tea. Her criticism of diet had been part of her overall public attack on the government. While she admitted that occasionally meat was added to the ration, she pointed to the wide variation

in practice. She also pointed to the fact that only children over the age of 3 years received half this overall ration. Those under 3 years were not catered for at all.

23   Moseley Royal Commission, Transcripts of Evidence, p. 270.

24   V. K. Haskins, *One Bright Spot*, Palgrave Macmillan, New York, 2005.

25   M. Bennett, Moseley Royal Commission, Transcripts of Evidence, p. 267.

26   Ibid.

27   The relevant sections of the act were Section 25: 'Any Aboriginal who, without reasonable cause, shall neglect or refuse to enter upon or commence his service, or shall refuse or neglect to work in the capacity in which he has been engaged, or shall desert or quit his work without the consent of his employer, or shall commit any other breach of his agreement, shall be guilty of an offence against this Act'; and Section 58: 'Every person convicted of an offence against this Act shall, except as is herein otherwise provided, be liable to imprisonment with or without hard labour, for not exceeding six months or to a fine not exceeding fifty pounds'.

28   She cited a government report for 1932 which showed that 3,856 Aborigines were assigned under 577 general permits, concluding that large numbers of people must have been worked under some permits.

29   Moseley Royal Commission, Transcripts of Evidence, p. 286.

30   Section 34 of the Aborigines Act 1905 (WA) read: '(1) Whenever a half-caste child whose age does not exceed fourteen years is being maintained in an Aboriginal institution or at the cost of the Government, a protector may, with the approval of the Minister, apply to a justice of the peace for a summons to be served on the alleged father of such child for the purpose of obtaining contribution to the support of the child. (2) On the return of such summons, any two justices of the peace shall proceed to hear the matter of the complaint, and if the paternity of the defendant and his ability to contribute to the support of such child are proved to the satisfaction of the justices, they may order the defendant to pay such weekly sum (not exceeding ten shillings) for the maintenance of the child as such justices think fit: Provided that *no man shall be taken to be the father of any such child upon the oath of the mother only* [emphasis added]'.

31   Moseley Royal Commission, Transcripts of Evidence, p. 228.

32   Ibid., pp. 229–301.

33   Ibid., p. 301.

34   Ibid., pp. 301–3.

35   See, for example, H. Goodall, *Invasion to Embassy. Land in Aboriginal Politics in New South Wales, 1770–1972*, Allen & Unwin/Black Books, Sydney, 1996; B. Attwood & A. Markus, *The Struggle for Aboriginal Rights. A Documentary History*, Allen & Unwin, Sydney, 1999; B. Attwood, *Rights For Aborigines*, Allen & Unwin, Sydney, 2003; B. Attwood & A. Markus (eds), *Thinking Black. William Cooper and the Australian Aborigines' League*, Aboriginal Studies Press, Canberra, 2004.

36   Bennett, Moseley Royal Commission, *Transcripts of Evidence*, p. 225. Norman Harris was the nephew of prominent Aboriginal activist in the southwest William Harris, who was the driving force behind the formation of the Native Union and had been campaigning for Aboriginal rights since the turn of the century.

37   Paisley, *Loving Protection?*, p. 128.

38   Biskup, *Not Slaves*, p. 168.

39   Western Australia, Parliament 1935, Report of the Royal Commissioner Appointed to Investigate, Report and Advise upon matters in relation to the Condition and Treatment of Aborigines, Perth.

40   Ibid., p. 5.

41   Ibid., p. 10.

42   Ibid.

43   Ibid., p. 22.

44   F. Paisley, '"For a Brighter Day": Constance Ternent Cooke', in A. Cole, V. Haskins & F. Paisley. (eds), *Uncommon Ground. White Women in Aboriginal History*, Aboriginal Studies Press, Canberra, 2005, pp. 172–93.

45   Report of Deputation to Senator Sir G. F. Pearce, Minister for Defence, 20 January 1934, NAA: A1, 1938/12974, Australian Aborigines Amelioration Association. Re Aboriginal Affairs, 1932–1938.

46   Bessie Rischbieth to Mary Bennett, 5 December 1934, Rischbieth Papers, NLA, MS2004/12/1–81.

47   Mary Bennett to Olive Pink, 6 March 1935, Olive Pink Papers, Australian Institute of Aboriginal and Torres Strait Islander Studies, MS2368.

48   Australia, Parliament, *Aboriginal Welfare: Initial Conference of Commonwealth and State Aboriginal Authorities*, L. F. Johnston, Commonwealth Government Printer, Canberra, 1937, pp. 10–12 (hereafter Canberra, *Aboriginal Welfare Conference*, 1937); A. O. Neville, *Australia's Coloured Minority. Its Place in the Community*, Currawong Publishing Co, Sydney, 1948, pp. 54–63.

49   A. O. Neville, Moseley Royal Commission, *Transcripts of Evidence*, p. 3.

50   Jacobs, *Mister Neville*, p. 192.

51   McGregor, 'Representations of the "Half–Caste" pp. 51–64; A. Haebich, *For Their Own Good. Aborigines and Government in the South West of Western Australia, 1900–1940*, University of Western Australian Press, Perth, 1992, pp. 316–18.

52   Biskup, *Not Slaves*, p. 169.

53   Jacobs, *Mister Neville*, p. 185.

54   Western Australia, Legislative Council 1936, *Debates*, vol. 97, p. 715.

55   Ibid., p. 826.

56   Ibid., p. 1068.

57   Ibid., p. 823. Su-Jane Hunt makes the point that this justification was frequently resorted to in relation to the widespread miscegenation in northern Western Australia and that it was also a common theme in the literature dealing with contact between black women and European men in the southern states of America; see S.-J. Hunt, *Spinifex and Hessian: Women's Lives in North-Western Australia 1860–1900*, University of Western Australia Press, Nedlands, 1986, pp. 104–6.

58   WA Legislative Council, *Debates*, p. 985.

59   Ibid., p. 1065.

60   Ibid., p. 1068.

61   Ibid.

62   This was a common refrain. Moseley pointed to the difficulty of policing men's 'natural urges' and Cecil Cook, Chief Protector of the Northern Territory, maintained that it was not possible to regulate morality by acts of parliament.

63   WA Legislative Council, *Debates*, p. 1069.

64   Ibid., p. 1109.
65   Ibid., pp. 1107–08.
66   Association for the Amelioration of Australian Aborigines, *The Ladder*, vol. 1, no. 3, 1937.
67   M. Bennett, 'Native Women as Chattels. Playthings of Men', *The Ladder*, vol. 1, no. 2, 1936, p. 7.
68   E. Jones, 'Comments on Native Administration Act for Western Australia', SAWA, MN 393, Women's Service Guilds of WA, Acc 1949A/62, *Welfare of Aborigines, February – November, 1937*.
69   Canberra, *Aboriginal Welfare Conference*, 1937, p. 36.
70   A. Holland, 'Compelling Evidence. Marriage, Colonialism and the Question of Indigenous Rights', *Women's History Review*, vol. 18, no. 1, 2009, pp. 121–36.
71   Biskup, *Not Slaves*, p. 184.
72   Jacobs, *Mister Neville*, p. 190.
73   Haebich, *For Their Own Good*, p. 154.
74   M. Bennett, Moseley Royal Commission, *Transcripts of Evidence*, p. 307.
75   Ibid., pp. 301–3.
76   Bennett, 'Native Women as Chattels', p. 9.
77   M. Bennett, 'Notes on Aboriginal Policy', *Duguid Papers*, NLA, MS5068, series 11.
78   Mary Bennett to William Morley, 26 December 1937, Papers of the Association for the Protection of Native Races, Sydney University Archives, series 7.
79   Mary Bennett to the Commissioner of Native Affairs, 14 February 1938, Bennett, Allegations of Slavery, SAWA. Note that Bennett is quoting directly from Neville's statement to the Conference of Commonwealth and State Authorities in Canberra in April 1937, pp. 11, 12 and 17 of that report.
80   WA Legislative Council 1936, *Debates*, p. 823.
81   M. Bennett, 'The Condition of the Aborigines of Australia Under the Federal Government', a paper read before the British Commonwealth League Conference, June 1929, pp. 14.
82   Comments by Mrs John Jones on Native Administration Act for WA, 1936, SAWA, MN 393, WSG, Welfare of Aborigines, February–November, 1937.
83   E. Jones, 'Remarks on the Resolutions passed at the First Federal Conference on Aboriginal Welfare', 25 November 1937, Papers of Donald Thomson, Private Collection, loaned to author by Dorita Thomson.
84   Australian Federation of Women Voters, Annual Report (June 1937 – May 1938), 'Welfare of the Aborigines and Race Culture', Papers of the United Associations of Women, ML Mss 2160, Box Y789.
85   Women's Service Guilds to Miss Todhunter, 28 January 1938, SAWA, MN 393, Women's Service Guilds, *Welfare of Aborigines*, February–November, 1937.
86   St Joan's Social and Political Alliance, 'Native and Half-Caste Women in Australia', League of Nations, Status of Women, Geneva, 24 August 1937, A14.
87   Woman's Christian Temperance Union, 'A Bridge of Hope. Our Native Races', *The White Ribbon Signal*, 2 March 1936.
88   Bennett to Pink, 6 March 1935, *Olive Pink Papers*.
89   S. Pedersen, 'The Maternalist Moment in British Colonial Policy: The Controversy over "Child Slavery" in Hong Kong 1917–1941', *Past and Present*, no. 171, 2001, pp. 161–202; S. Pedersen, 'National Bodies, Unspeakable Acts: The Sexual Politics of Colonial Policy-Making', *The Journal of Modern History*, vol. 63, no. 4, 1991,

pp. 647–680; S. Pedersen, *Eleanor Rathbone and the Politics of Conscience,* Yale University Press, New Haven, 2004.

90 Report of a Deputation to Senator George Pearce, Minister for Defence, Perth, 20 January 1934, NAA: A1, 1938/12974.

91 Pedersen, 'The Maternalist Moment', p. 195.

92 M. Lake, 'Childbearers as Rights-Bearers: Feminist Discourse on the Rights of Aboriginal and non-Aboriginal Mothers in Australia, 1920–50', *Women's History Review*, vol. 8, no. 2, 1999, p. 352.

93 M. Bennett, 'Wyma', *Townsville Daily Bulletin*, 19 May 1928.

94 M. Lake, 'Feminist History as National History: Writing the Political History of Women', *Australian Historical Studies*, no. 106, 1999, p. 166.

95 B. Rischbieth, 'The Influence of Women in Government', *Pan Pacific Conference*, 1928, p. 179.

96 For a helpful discussion of Australian feminists' conception of citizenship see M. Lake, 'Personality, Individuality, Nationality: Feminist Conceptions of Citizenship, 1902–1940', *Australian Feminist Studies*, no. 19, 1994, pp. 25–38.

97 M. Jacobs, *White Mother to a Dark Race. Settler Colonialism, Maternalism and the Removal of Indigenous Children in the American West and Australia, 1880–1940*, University of Nebraska Press, Lincoln, 2009, pp. 93, 107, 118.

98 Mary Bennett to Bessie Rischbieth, 6 March 1932, Rischbieth Papers, NLA, MS200/12/1–81.

99 Bennett, Moseley Royal Commission, *Transcripts of Evidence*, p. 219.

100 M. Barnett, *Empire of Humanity. A History of Humanitarianism*, Cornell University Press, Ithaca, 2011.

101 Pedersen, 'The Maternalist Moment', p. 164.

102 Pedersen, 'National Bodies', p. 679.

103 'Treatment of Aborigines. League Intervention Sought', *The West Australian*, 17 August 1935, Bennett, Allegations of Slavery.

104 M. Bennett to Mr Lees, 18 June 1929, in M. Bennett', The Condition of the Aborigines of Australia Under the Federal Government', a paper read before the British Commonwealth League Conference, London, 5 June 1929, pp. 10–22.

105 M. Lake, 'Feminism and the Gendered Politics of Antiracism, Australia 1927–1957: From Maternal Protectionism to Leftist Assimilationism', *Australian Historical Studies*, no. 110, 1998, p. 96.

106 Mrs B. James, 'Conference of Representatives of Missions, Societies and Associations interested in the Welfare of Aborigines to consider the Report and Recommendations submitted to the Government by JW Bleakley', Rischbieth Papers, NLA, MS2004/12/506–511.

107 Holland, 'The Campaign for Women Protectors'.

Chapter 5 – Mt Margaret

1 Excerpt of letter from Mary Bennett to Harold Moody, League of Coloured Peoples, reprinted in *The West Australian*, 17 February 1935, p. 9.

2 Mt Margaret was non-denominational. Faith missionaries differed from denominational missions in requiring their missionaries to raise their own support instead of relying on money from the mission society. See I. Duckham, 'Visionary,

Vassal or Vandal? Rod Schenk – Missionary: A Case Study in Western Desert Missions',
Limina, vol. 6, 2000, pp. 41–56.

3   Ibid., p. 46.

4   R. S. Schenk to A. O. Neville, 27 January 1937, SAWA, AN 1/7, Department of Native
     Affairs and Native Welfare, ACC 993, 116/1932, Allegations by Mrs Mary Bennett
     in regard to native slavery, inadequate reserves and traffic in native women (hereafter
     Bennett, Allegations of slavery, SLWA)

5   M. Morgan, *Drop in a Bucket. The Mount Margaret Story*, United Aborigines' Mission,
     Victoria, 1986, p. 5.

6   R. S. Schenk, 'The Educability of the Native', United Aborigines' Mission, Perth, 1936,
     p.34. In that year, the Schenks paid out 160 pounds for work done at the mission.

7   Ibid., p. 57.

8   Bennett recorded that, in 1934, 1,251 raffia articles and 169 woven articles were made
     and sold, with the money going to the workers. See M. Bennett, *Teaching the Aborigines:
     Data from the Mt Margaret Mission,* City and Suburban Print, Perth, 1935, p. 5.

9   Ibid., p. 18.

10   Schenk haggled the local pastoralists for a minimum of 1 pound a week and keep.

11   A. O. Neville, 'Old Mining Scenes. Foundations of a Native's Home', *The West
     Australian*, 6 January 1931.

12   Morgan, *Drop in a Bucket*, p. 96.

13   Bennett, *Teaching the Aborigines*, p. 5.

14   Morgan, *Drop in a Bucket*, p. 151.

15   Bennett, *Teaching the Aborigines,* p. 5.

16   'Caring for Aborigines', *The West Australian*, 3 October 1934, p. 27.

17   Dr. Graham's Homes, History of the homes, http://drgrahamshomes.net/history-of-
     homes.php, accessed 7 February 2013.

18   Morgan, *Drop in a Bucket*, p. 102.

19   Ibid., p. 66.

20   Schenk, 'Educability', p. 28.

21   Morgan, *Drop in a Bucket*, p. 107.

22   Ibid., p. 102.

23   Ibid., pp. 107–8.

24   Ibid., p. 138.

25   A. Haebich, *For Their Own Good: Aborigines and Government in the South-West of Western
     Australia 1900–1940,* University of Western Australia Publishing, Perth, p. 266.

26   Schenk, The Educability of the Native, p. 24.

27   M. Bennett to B. Rischbieth, 16 November 1934, *Rischbieth Papers*, NLA,
     MS2004/12/1–81, Box 30.

28   P. Biskup, *Not Slaves Not Citizens: The Aboriginal Problem in Western Australia, 1898–
     1954*, University of Queensland Press, St Lucia, 1973, p. 133; P. W. Beckenham, *The
     Education of the Australian Aborigine,* Australian Council for Educational Research, 1948.

29   See, for example, H. K. Fry & R. H. Pulleine, 'The Mentality of the Australian
     Aborigine', *The Australian Journal of Biology and Medical Science*, vol. 8, 1931, pp. 153–67.

30   R. McGregor, *Imagined Destinies: Aboriginal Australians and the Doomed Race Theory*,
     Melbourne University Press, Melbourne, 1997, p. 106.

31   W. Anderson, *The Cultivation of Whiteness: Science, Health and Racial Destiny in Australia*,

Duke University Press, Durham, 2006, p. 193.

32 E. H. Berman, 'American Influence on African Education: The Role of the Phelps-Stokes Fund's Education Commissions', *Comparative Education Review*, vol. 15, no. 1, 1971, pp. 132–45.

33 Schenk, The Educability of the Native, p. 31.

34 I. Duckham, 'Visionary, Vassal or Vandal? Rod Schenk—Missionary: A Case Study in Western Desert Missions', Limina, vol. 6, 2000, pp. 41–56.

35 Morgan, *Drop in a Bucket*, p. 110.

36 Ibid., p. 18.

37 Schenk, Educability, p. 31.

38 Morgan, *Drop in a Bucket*, pp. 66, 91.

39 Ibid.

40 Schenk, Educability, p. 31.

41 Ibid.

42 Ibid.

43 Ibid., p. 28.

44 Bennett, *Teaching the Aborigines*, p. 36.

45 Ibid., p. 66.

46 M. Bennett to W. Morley, 26 February 1939, Papers of the Association for the Protection of Native Races, Sydney University Archives, series 7.

47 D. Johnson, 'W. E. B. DuBois, Thomas Jesse Jones and the Struggle for Social Education, 1900–1930', *Journal of Negro History*, vol. 85, no. 3, 2000, pp. 71–95.

48 M. Bennett to E. Nulsen, 28 May 1942, Duguid Papers, MS NLA, MS5068, series 11.

49 Bennett, *Teaching the Aborigines*.

50 M. Bennett, 'A Native Policy for Australia', NAA: A461, A 300/ Part 3, Aboriginals – Policy, 1937–1943.

51 Bennett, 'The Aboriginal Mother'.

52 C. Coe, 'Educating an African Leadership: Achimota and the Teaching of African Culture in the Gold Coast', *Africa Today*, vol. 49, no. 3, 2002, pp. 23–44.

53 Ibid., p. 28.

54 Ibid., p. 29.

55 Morgan, *Drop in a Bucket*, p. 201.

56 Ibid.

57 Australia, Parliament, *Aboriginal Welfare. Initial Conference of Commonwealth and State Aboriginal Authorities*, L. F. Johnson, Commonwealth Government Printer, Canberra, 1937, pp. 10–12.

58 A. Haebich, *For Their Own Good*; A. Haebich, *Broken Circles. Fragmenting Indigenous Families 1800–2000*, Fremantle Arts Centre Press, Fremantle, 2009, p. 182.

59 Beckenham, *The Education of the Australian Aborigine*, p. 46.

60 Ibid.

61 Ibid., pp. 37–8.

62 A. R. Welch, 'Aboriginal Education as Internal Colonialism: The Schooling of an Indigenous Minority', *Comparative Education*, vol. 24, no. 2, 1988, p. 210.

63 M. Bennett, Lecture to the Women's Service Guilds, 11 December 1932, Rischbieth Papers, NLA, MS2004/12/235-303.

64 Beckenham, *The Education of the Australian Aborigine*, p. 17.

65 Bennett, *Teaching the Aborigines*, pp. 66–7.

66 Ibid., p. 67.

Chapter 6 – An Inhumane Dictatorship

1   M. Bennett to A. O. Neville, 14 February 1938, SAWA, AN 1/7, Department of Native Affairs and Native Welfare, ACC 993, 116/1932, Allegations by Mrs Mary Bennett in regard to native slavery, inadequate reserves and traffic in native women (hereafter Bennett, Allegations of Slavery, SLWA).

2   M. Bennett to W. Morley, 26 February 1939, Papers of the Association for the Protection of Native Races, Sydney University Archives, series 7.

3   M. Morgan, *A Drop in a Bucket. The Mount Margaret Story*, United Aborigines' Mission, Victoria, 1986, p. 195.

4   Ibid., p. 163. Legree refers to the cruel slave owner Simon Legree in Harriet Beecher Stowe's novel Uncle Tom's Cabin. Schenk is using it here to refer to the slave-like conditions in which Aboriginal people were employed in the pastoral industry.

5   Ibid., p. 161.

6   Morgan, *Drop in a Bucket*, p. 161.

7   P. Jacobs, *Mister Neville. A Biography*, Fremantle Arts Centre Press, Fremantle, 1990, p. 66.

8   Ibid., p. 168.

9   G. Gray, *A Cautious Silence: The Politics of Australian Anthropology*, Aboriginal Studies Press, Canberra, 2007, p. 96.

10 M. Bennett to C. Duguid, 3 January 1935, Duguid Papers, NLA 5068, series 11.

11 Bennett to Morley, 26 February 1939.

12 Australia, Parliament 1937, *Aboriginal Welfare. Initial Conference of Commonwealth and State Aboriginal Authorities*, Commonwealth Government, Canberra, p. 11.

13 V. Haskins & C. Lowrie (eds), *Colonization and Domestic Service: Historical and Contemporary Perspectives*, Routledge, New York, 2015.

14 V. Haskins, 'Domestic Service and Frontier Feminism: The Case for a Woman Visitor to "Half-Castes" Girls and Women in Domestic Service, Adelaide, 1925–1928', *Frontiers*, vol. 28 no. 1, 2007, pp. 124–164.

15 A. Haebich, *Broken Circles. Fragmenting Indigenous Families 1800–2000*, Fremantle Arts Centre Press, Fremantle, 2009; Haebich, *For Their Own Good. Aborigines and Government in the South-West of Western Australia, 1900–1940*, University of Western Australia Press, Nedlands, 1988.

16 Morgan, *Drop in a Bucket*, pp. 106, 124.

17 Ibid., p. 107.

18 M. Bennett, Moseley Royal Commission, *Transcripts of Evidence*, p. 227.

19 'Treatment of Aborigines', newspaper clipping, Rischbieth Papers, NLA, MS2004/12/162.

20 Moseley Royal Commission, *Transcripts of Evidence*, p. 301.

21 Ibid., p. 229.

22 A. O. Neville to Mr Kitson, 19 March 1933, Bennett, Allegations of Slavery, SLWA.

23 Morgan, *Drop in a Bucket*, p. 216.

24 Ibid., p. 213.

25 Moseley Royal Commission, *Transcripts of Evidence*, p. 225.

26 W. Cooper, 'An Aboriginal Plea', *The Ladder*, vol. 1, no. 4, 1937, pp. 23–4.

27 A. Markus, 'William Cooper and the 1937 Petition to the King', *Aboriginal History*, vol. 7, 1983, pp. 46–60.

28 B. Attwood & A. Markus, *The Struggle for Aboriginal Rights. A Documentary History*, Allen & Unwin, St Leonards, 1999, p. 82.

29 'Redeem Cruel Past', *Workers' Weekly*, 9 November 1937, p. 3.

30 *Workers' Weekly*, 14 January 1938, p. 1.

31 The Communist Party had argued for the Aborigines' right to retain and develop native culture and for the handing over of large tracts of fertile country in central, north and northwest Australia as independent states or republics, as part of their 'Struggle Against Slavery' in 1930, see *Workers' Weekly*, 24 September 1931, p. 2.

32 J. Devanny, 'Your Dark Brother Needs Your Aid', *Workers' Weekly*, 15 February 1938, p. 3.

33 J. Devanny, 'Voice of Our Native Women. A Call To Women Readers', *Workers' Weekly*, 25 February 1938, p. 4.

34 A. Holland, 'Colour not Civilisation: Contesting Boundaries of Citizenship and Rights in Inter-War Australia', in L. Boucher, J. Carey & K. Ellinghaus. (eds) *Historicizing Whiteness: Transnational Perspectives on the Construction of Identity*, RMIT Press, Melbourne, 2007, pp. 89–97.

35 Bennett to Neville, 14 February 1938, Bennett, Allegations of Slavery, SAWA.

36 W. Morley to M. Bennett, 30 June 1938 and 10 August 1938, Duguid Papers, NLA MA 5068, series 11.

37 Western Australia, *Parliamentary Debates*, August-October 1938, 1939, vol. 1, part 1.

38 Ibid., p. 2330.

39 Ibid., p. 2328.

40 Ibid., p. 2493.

41 Ibid., p. 2350.

42 Canberra, *Aboriginal Welfare Conference*, 1937, p. 4.

43 WA, *Parliamentary Debates*, p. 2340.

44 Bennett to Morley, 26 February 1939.

45 Ibid.

46 M. Bennett, Memorandum for submission to H. M. High Commissioner for Australia, Justice for our Minority', NAA, Administrator Northern Territory, Central Registry, F1, Correspondence Files, 38/536 (hereafter referred to as NAA Correspondence Files F1/38/536).

47 B. Shaw, 'Nemarluk (1911–1940)', *Australian Dictionary of Biography*, National Centre of Biography, Australian National University, http://adb.anu.edu.au/biography/nemarluk-11222/text20009, 2000, accessed 13 February 2015.

48 K. Auty, *Black Glass. Western Australian Courts of Native Affairs 1936–54*, Fremantle Arts Centre Press, Fremantle, 2005.

49 K. Auty, 'Western Australian Courts of Native Affairs 1936–1954 – One of "Our" Little Secrets in the Administration of "Justice" for Aboriginal People', *University of New South Wales Law Journal*, vol. 23, no. 1, 2000, p. 151.

50 Auty, *Black Glass*, p. 11.

51 Bennett to Morley, 26 February 1939.

52 A. Holland, 'Compelling Evidence. Marriage, Colonialism and the Question of

Indigenous Rights', *Women's History Review*, vol. 18, no. 1, 2009, pp. 121–136. See also M. Finnane & F. Paisley, 'Police Violence and the Limits of Law on a Late Colonial Frontier: The "Borroloola Case" in 1930s Australia', *Law and History Review*, vol. 28, no. 1, 2010, pp. 141–171.

53 A. Markus, 'Morley, William (1854–1939)', *Australian Dictionary of Biography*, National Centre of Biography, Australian National University, http://adb.anu.edu.au/biography/morley-william-7656/text13391, accessed 21 June 2013.

54 J. Harris to the Premier of Western Australia, 12 June 1939, SAWA, AN1/7, Departments of Native Affairs and Native Welfare, Acc 993, 218/1946, The Anti-Slavery and Aborigines Protection Society – general correspondence.

55 Section 8 made the Commissioner the legal guardian of every native child regardless of the fact of a parent or relative, until the child was 21 years old. Under this section he could therefore do whatever he thought fit, which usually meant the removal of children to institutions.

56 A. Haebich, *Broken Circles*, pp. 267–8.

57 Ibid., p. 268.

58 Aboriginal Independent Community Schools, http://aics.wa.edu.au/schools/caps-coolgardie#field-field-showcase.

59 M. Bennett to H. Wardlaw, 1 December 1951, MS12913, Papers of the Council for Aboriginal Rights, La Trobe Manuscript Collection, State Library of Victoria, Box 4.

60 A. O. Neville to the Minister for the North-West, 21 December 1939, SAWA, AN1/7, Departments of Native Affairs and Native Welfare, The Anti-Slavery and Aborigines' Protection Society – general correspondence.

61 A. O. Neville, *Australia's Coloured Minority. Its Place In the Community*, Currawong Publishing Co, Sydney, 1948, pp. 39–40.

62 Ibid., p. 263.

63 Jacobs, Mister Neville, p. 185.

64 A. Markus, *Governing Savages*, Allen & Unwin, Sydney, 1990, p. 74.

65 M. Lake & H. Reynolds, *Drawing the Global Colour Line. White Men's Countries and the Question of Racial Equality*, Melbourne University Press, Melbourne, 2008.

66 Jacobs, *Mister Neville*, p. 192.

Chapter 7 – Hunt and Die

1 M. Bennett, 'Hunt and Die'. 'The Prospects for the Aborigines of Australia', Anti-Slavery Society, London, 1950, p. 9.

2 M. Bennett, Notes on Aboriginal Policy, *Duguid Papers*, NLA, MS5068, series 11.

3 In 1928 the Commonwealth Year Book gave the estimate of full-descent Aborigines as 60,663, of which one third were in the Northern Territory.

4 NAA: Department of Territories (I), Central Office, A52, 572/994 AUS, Commonwealth Government's Policy with respect to Aboriginals, 1939.

5 Although not part of the broader humanitarian landscape at the time, the Communist Party of Australia also promoted land and self-determination which followed Comintern policy.

6 Report of the Commission on Closer Union of the Dependencies of Eastern and Central Africa, HM Stationery Office, London, 1929, p. 43.

7 Ibid., p. 40.

8   Ibid., p. 38.

9   B. Porter, *Critics of Empire. British Radicals and the Imperial Challenge*, I. B. Taurus, London, 2008, p. 324.

10 Report of Commission, p. 44.

11 Ibid., p. 46.

12 Porter, *Critics of Empire*, p. 233.

13 T. Wright, 'New Deal for the Aborigines', The Forward Press, Sydney, 1939, p. 19.

14 Ibid., p. 32.

15 M. Bennett to O. Pink, 16 March 1935, *Olive Pink Papers*, AIATSIS, MS2368.

16 R. McGregor, 'The Doomed Race: A Scientific Axiom of the Late Nineteenth Century', *Australian Journal of Politics and History*, vol. 39, no. 1, 1993, pp. 14–22.

17 O. Pink, 'Australian Aborigines. What is Their Future? Dictation or Freedom in Civilisation?', *Canberra Times*, December 1938; M. Bennett to E. Nulsen, 28 May 1942, Duguid Papers, NLA, MS5068, series 11.

18 Australia, Parliament, 1937, *Aboriginal Welfare. Initial Conference of Commonwealth and State Aboriginal Authorities*, Commonwealth Government, Canberra, p. 21.

19 '"Efforts To Revive a Dying Race". Vicious Whites', *Bristol Evening News*, 2 July 1927, GRG 52/32/15, State Archives of South Australia, Papers of CMT Cooke Relating to Aboriginal Affairs, 1927–1967.

20 Letter from B. M. Harris to J. A. Lyons, 10 August 1937 NAA: A431, 1948/273 Part 1, .

21 Australia, Parliament, *Aboriginal Welfare*, p. 7.

22 P. Pease to the Prime Minister of Australia, 25 March 1937, NAA: A461, A300/1, Part 3, Aboriginals Policy 1937–1943.

23 M. Bennett, Notes on Aboriginal Policy, *Duguid Papers*, NLA, MS5068, series 11.

24 The Association for the Protection of Native Races, *Policy on Native Labour*, 1912, *Papers of the Association for the Protection of Native Races*, The University of Sydney Archives, Series 7, 1911–1940.

25 'Review of the Chief Protectors Conference in Canberra', April 1937, *The Aborigines' Protector*, vol. 1, no. 5, 1938.

26 Letter from Cecil Cook to the Northern Territory Administrator, 6 December 1937 NAA: A431/1, 1948/273, Part 1.

27 A. Markus, 'William Cooper and the 1937 Petition To the King', *Aboriginal History*, vol. 7, 1983, pp. 46–60.

28 For context see W. E. H. Stanner & D. Barwick, 'Not By Eastern Windows Only: Anthropological Advice to Australian Governments in 1938', *Aboriginal History*, vol. 3, nos. 1–2, 1979, pp. 37–60.

29 'Australian Aborigines', *The Times*, 25 November 1937.

30 Stanner & Barwick, 'Not by Eastern Windows', p. 46; W. E. H. Stanner, 'The Aborigines', in J. C. G. Kevin (ed.) *Some Australians Take Stock*, Longmans, Green and Co, London, 1939, pp. 23–35.

31 For analysis and overview of the Caledon Bay murders see Reynolds, *This Whispering In Our Hearts*, Allen & Unwin, Sydney, 1998, pp. 201–215; M. Dewar, *The 'Black War' in Arnhem Land: Missionaries and the Yolngu 1908–1940*, North Australia Research Unit, 1995.

32 D. Thomson, Australia, Parliament, 1937, *Recommendations of Policy in Native Affairs in the Northern Territory of Australia*, Government Printer, Canberra.

33	D.Thomson, 'Justice for Aborigines'. Reprinted from *The Herald*, Melbourne, 28, 30, 31 December 1936, NAA: A431/1, 49/176, Part 1.

34	D.Thomson to Mrs Ransom, 10 February 1939, Private Papers, Mrs D.Thomson.

35	Thomson to Ransom, 7 January 1939.

36	Rosalind Kidd shows how Thomson's earlier work in Cape York was panned by the Queensland administration. She details a 'propensity to slander and ridicule Thomson's pro-Aboriginal observations' and that this had occurred to other workers in the field who criticised or reported adversely on any aspect of Aboriginal administration in that state. See R. Kidd, *The Way We Civilise*, University of Queensland Press, St Lucia, 1997, pp. 120–122.

37	C. Duguid, *Doctor and the Aborigines*, Rigby, Australia, 1972, p. 115.

38	'Slave Horror of the North. Intolerable Insensibility to Australia's Shame', *Smith's Weekly*, 9 January 1937.

39	Ibid., pp. 35–6.

40	A. Holland, 'The Campaign for Women Protectors: Gender, Race and Frontier between the Wars', *Australian Feminist Studies*, vol. 16, no. 34, 2001, pp. 27–42.

41	Ibid., p. 33.

42	P. Duguid, 'The Future of the Aboriginal', *The White Ribbon Signal*, March 1942, p. 24.

43	C. Duguid, *The Future of the Aborigines of Australia*. An Address to the National Missionary Council, Vardon and Sons, Adelaide, 1941, p. 11.

44	Ibid., p. 7.

45	Ibid., p. 8.

46	Ibid., p. 9.

47	Ibid.

48	Duguid, The Future of the Aborigines, p. 2.

49	'A Mission Established', *The Ladder*, vol. 1, no. 4, 1937, p. 19.

50	C. Duguid to W. H. Kitson, 19 September 1938, Duguid Papers, NLA, MS5068, Series 11.

51	C. Duguid, 'Natives of the Interior. A Doctor's Impression', *The Ladder*, vol. 1, no. 4, 1937, p. 17.

52	Duguid, *The Future*, p. 9.

53	Wright, 'New Deal for the Aborigines', pp. 24–32.

54	Commonwealth Parliament, *Recommendations of Policy in the Northern Territory of Australia*, Melbourne, December, 1937, p. 7.

55	R. Kerin, *Doctor Do-Good. Charles Duguid and Aboriginal Advancement, 1930s–1970s*, Australian Scholarly Publishing, Melbourne, 2011, p. 42.

56	C. Duguid to W. H. Kitson, 19 September 1938, Duguid Papers, NLA, MS5068, series 11.

57	Duguid, *The Future*, p. 2.

58	M. Bennett, *Teaching the Aborigines. Data From the Mt Margaret Mission*, City and Suburban Press, Perth, 1935, p. 67.

59	M. Bennett, *Christison of Lammermoor*, Alston Rivers, London, 1927, p. 99.

60	M. Bennett, Lecture to the Women's Service Guilds, 11 December 1932, *Rischbieth Papers*, NLA, MS2004/12/235–303.

61	Ibid.

62	Kerin, *Dr Do-Good*, p. 56.

63   Duguid, *The Future*, pp. 9–10.
64   M. Bennett, 'Spinners and Weavers On Ernabella Mission, South Australia', MS12913, The Papers of the Council for Aboriginal Rights, La Trobe Manuscript Collection, State Library of Victoria, Box 2/1.
65   R. S. Schenk, 'Aborigines' Mission, Departmental Attitude', *The West Australian*, 15 November 1944.
66   M. Bennett to C. Duguid, 15 February 1943, *Duguid Papers*, NLA, MS5068, series 11.
67   Copy of Bennett's letter to Emil Nulsen, MLA, 28 May 1942, *Duguid Papers*, NLA MS5068, Series 11.
68   Schenk, 'Aborigines' Mission'.
69   R. S. Schenk, Letter to the Editor, *The West Australian*, 8 November 1944.
70   Ibid.
71   M. Bennett, 'Hunt and Die', p. 8.
72   Ibid., p. 4.
73   Ibid., p. 6.
74   Ibid., p. 5.
75   Ibid., p. 6.
76   Canberra, *Aboriginal Welfare Conference*, 1937, p. 16.
77   Ibid.
78   Ibid., p. 18.
79   Ibid.
80   Ibid., p. 3 ; P. Hasluck, 'The Future of the Australian Aborigines', Paper read to Section F (Anthropology) at the Australian and New Zealand Association for the Advancement of Science, 22 August 1958, MS9377, Women's International League for Peace and Freedom, Papers, La Trobe Manuscript Collection, State Library of Victoria, Box 1747/5.
81   Ibid., p. 12.
82   Ibid., p. 10.
83   Ibid., p. 13.
84   Ibid., p. 14.
85   Ibid., p. 18.
86   Census Tabulation – NSW, Victoria, Queensland, South Australia, Western Australia, Northern Territory – Full-blood Aborigines, 1961, NAA: A9410, 11/87.
87   Canberra, *Aboriginal Welfare Conference*, p. 21.
88   Ibid., p. 2.
89   Bennett, 'Hunt and Die', p. 8.
90   Ibid., p. 6.
91   M. Bennett, Allegations of Slavery, SAWA, ACC 993 166/32.
92   T. G. Weiss, *Humanitarian Intervention*, Polity Press, Cambridge, 2012; M. Barnett & T. G. Weiss, *Humanitarianism in Question: Politics, Power, Ethics*, Cornell University Press, Ithaca, 2008; T. G. Weiss & C. Collins, *Humanitarian Challenges and Intervention: World Politics and the Dilemmas of Help*, Westview Press, Boulder, 2000.
93   R. M. Berndt & C. H. Berndt, *End of an Era. Aboriginal Labour in the Northern Territory*, Australian Institute of Aboriginal Studies, Canberra, 1987.
94   Ibid., pp. 248–9.
95   Ibid., pp. 32–3.

96 C. D. Rowley, *The Destruction of Aboriginal Society*, Australian National University Press, Canberra, 1970, p. 337.

97 A. G. Price, *White Settlers and Native Peoples. An Historical Study of Racial Contacts between English-speaking Whites and Aboriginal Peoples in the USA, Canada, Australia and New Zealand*, Georgian House, Melbourne, 1949, pp. 205–9.

98 Bennett to Duguid, 15 February 1943.

99 Canberra, *Aboriginal Welfare Conference*, 1937, pp. 14, 21.

Chapter 8 – Defending Fathers and Sons

1 M. Bennett, *Human Rights for Australian Aborigines. How Can They Learn Without a Teacher?*, Truth, Brisbane, 1957, p. 14.

2 Mary Bennett to Shirley Andrews, 16 April 1955, Council for Aboriginal Rights, Papers, MS12913, La Trobe Manuscript Collection, State Library of Victoria, Box 1.

3 D. Watson, *Brian Fitzpatrick. A Radical Life*, Hale & Iremonger, Sydney, 1979, p. 203.

4 C. Duguid, *The Rocket Range, Aborigines and War*, An Address at the Melbourne Town Hall, The Rocket Range Protest Committee, March 1947, Street Papers, NLA, MS2683, Box 29.

5 'Slave Map of Modern Australia', *Anti-Slavery Reporter and Aborigines' Friend*, September–October 1891.

6 Mary Bennett to William Morley, 26 February 1939, Papers of the Association for the Protection of Native Races, Sydney University Archives, Series 7. Section 18 of the Act related to the issuing of permits to employ Aboriginal labour.

7 M. Bennett, Australian Aboriginal Workers in Federal Territory and the States of Queensland and Western Australia, Anti-Slavery and Aborigines Protection Society – NT, 1939–1946, NAA: A431/1, 48/273, Part 2.

8 M. Bennett, 'Notes on Native Labour Conditions in Queensland', Duguid Papers, NLA, MS5068, Series 11.

9 Anti-Slavery and Aborigines' Protection Society, An International Colonial Convention, May 1943, Elkin Papers, Sydney University Archives, Box 176, Item 202.

10 M. Vallance, Letter to the Editor on Native Affairs, *The West Australian*, 27 July 1942.

11 Committee for the Defence of Native Rights, Resolutions carried at a Public Meeting, May 1946, Elkin Papers, Sydney University Archives, Box 76, Item 262.

12 For background information and discussion on this see M. Brown, *The Black Eureka*, Australasian Book Society, Sydney, 1976, p. 138 and *Tribune*, May–December 1946.

13 M. Bennett to S. Andrews, 12 July 1954, Council for Aboriginal Rights, Papers, MS12913, La Trobe Manuscript Collection, SLV, Box 1.

14 G. Parsons, *Black Chattels. The Story of the Australian Aborigines*, National Council for Civil Liberties, London, 1946, p. 15.

15 P. Biskup, *Not Slaves Not Citizens. The Aboriginal Problem in Western Australia*, University of Queensland Press, St Lucia, 1973, p. 219.

16 Mary Bennett to Jessie Street, 10 September 1957, *Street Papers*, NLA, MS2683, Box 10.

17 Australian National University Archives: Australian Dictionary of Biography, ANUA 312, Box 47, Mary Bennett.

18 Bennett, *Human Rights*, pp. 15–18.

19 ibid., p. 14.

20 Ibid., p. 15.

21 Ibid., p. 17.

22 Ibid.

23 Ibid., pp. 17–18.

24 M. Bennett, 'Peter. The Story of a Clever Aboriginal Boy', Mary Bennett and Ada Bromham, Private Archives, State Library of Western Australia, MN 2958; ACC 8303A/18.

25 Ibid.

26 Council for Aboriginal Rights, Policy, MS12913, Council for Aboriginal Rights, Papers, La Trobe Manuscript Collection, SLV, Box 5/6.

27 M. Bennett, Notes, Duguid Papers, NLA, MS5068, Series 11.

28 Second Women's Charter Conference, 'Resolutions on Aborigines', Blackburn Papers, MS11749, La Trobe Manuscript Collection, SLV, Box 85.

29 'Aborigines', *The White Ribbon Signal*, December 1951, p. 170.

30 R. Kerin, *An Attitude of Respect: Anna Vroland and Aboriginal Rights, 1947–1957*, Monash Publications in History, Melbourne, 1999.

31 Women's International League for Peace and Freedom (Australian Section), 'Policy regarding Australian Aborigines', NAA: B356, 97.

32 'Resolutions. Aborigines', NWCTU, *Reports and Mintues of the 21st National Convention*, 1954, pp. 22, 78.

33 M. Bennett to S. Andrews, 10 October 1953, Council for Aboriginal Rights, Papers, MS12913, La Trobe Manuscript Collection, SLV, Box 4.

34 M. Cryle, 'A "Fantastic Adventure": reading Christison of Lammermoor', in F. McKenzie (ed.), Journeys Through Queensland History: Landscape, Place and Society: Proceedings of the Professional Historians Association (Queensland) Conference, Marking the Sesquicentenary of Queensland 1859–2009, Professional Historians Association (Queensland), St Lucia, 2009, p. 232.

35 Bennett to Andrews, 10 October 1953.

36 M. Bennett, *Human Rights*, p. 35.

37 Ibid., p. 36.

38 Ibid., pp. 36–8.

39 Ibid., p. 37.

40 Bennett to Andrews, 10 October 1953.

41 Ibid.

42 Ibid.

43 M. Bennett to S. Andrews, 23 May 1954, Council for Aboriginal Rights, Papers, MS12913, La Trobe Manuscript Collection, SLV, Box 1.

44 Bennett to Andrews, 10 October 1953.

45 Bennett, *Human Rights*, p. 47.

46 M. Bennett to S. Andrews, 23 May 1955, Council for Aboriginal Rights, Papers, MS12913, La Trobe Manuscript Collection, SLV, Box 1.

47 M. Bennett to S. Andrews, 2 November 1954, Council for Aboriginal Rights, Papers, MS12913, La Trobe Manuscript Collection, SLV, Box 1.

48 M. Bennett to S. Andrews, 24 April 1955, Council for Aboriginal Rights, Papers, MS12913, La Trobe Manuscript Collection, SLV, Box 1.

49 Bennett to Andrews, 27 November 1954, Council for Aboriginal Rights, Papers, MS12913, La Trobe Manuscript Collection, SLV, Box 1.

50 Bennett to Andrews, 16 April 1955, Council for Aboriginal Rights, Papers, MS12913, La Trobe Manuscript Collection, SLV, Box 1.

51 M. Bennett to S. Andrews, 4 September 1955, Council for Aboriginal Rights, Papers, MS12913, La Trobe Manuscript Collection, SLV, Box 1.

52 M. Bennett to S. Andrews, 24 March 1957, Council for Aboriginal Rights, Papers, MS12913, La Trobe Manuscript Collection, SLV, Box 1.

53 Ibid.

54 Mary Bennett to Ada Bromham, 21 April 1957, Mary Bennett and Ada Bromham, Private Archives, State Library of Western Australia, MN 2958; ACC 8303A/10.

55 M. Bennett to A. Bromham, 1 November 1955, Mary Bennett and Ada Bromham, Private Archives, SLWA, MN 2958; ACC 8303A/13.

56 M. Bennett to S. Andrews, 16 May 1954, Council for Aboriginal Rights, Papers, MS12913, La Trobe Manuscript Collection, SLV, Box 1.

57 Bennett to Andrews, 23 May 1954.

58 M. Bennett to S. Andrews, 17 April 1954, Council for Aboriginal Rights, Papers, MS12913, La Trobe Manuscript Collection, SLV, Box 1.

59 W. Birman, 'Bromham, Ada (1880–1965)', Australian Dictionary of Biography, National Centre of Biography, Australian National University, http://adb.anu.edu.au/biography/bromham-ada-5368/text9081, accessed 11 March 2014.

60 W. L. Grayden, Western Australia, Parliament, *Report of the Select Committee Appointed to Inquire into Native Welfare Conditions in the Laverton–Warburton Range Area*, 12 December 1956 (hereafter, Grayden Report).

61 Bennett, *Human Rights*, p. 5.

62 Ibid., p. 7.

63 Grayden Report, p. 12.

64 Ibid., pp. 10–11.

65 Ibid., pp. 12–13.

66 Ibid., p. 13.

67 Ibid., p. 14.

68 Anti-Slavery and Aborigines' Protection Society, International Colonial Convention, May 1943, p. 7.

69 For an account of the co-operative see Don McLeod, *How the West was Lost. The Native Question in the Development of Western Australia,* Port Hedland, 1987; J. M. Wilson, 'Authority and Leadership in a "New Syle" Australian Aboriginal Community, Pindan, Western Australia', MA thesis, University of Western Australia, 1961.

70 N. Loos & R. Keast, 'The Radical Promise: The Aboriginal Christian Cooperative Movement', *Australian Historical Studies*, vol. 99, 1992, pp. 286–301.

71 The Earl of Listowel, 'The Australian Aborigines', *The Anti-Slavery Reporter and Aborigines' Friend*, April 1945, pp. 3–5.

72 Bennett, *Human Rights*, p. 9.

73 R. Kerin, *Doctor Do-Good. Charles Duguid and Aboriginal Advancement, 1930–1970s*, Australian Scholarly Publishing, Melbourne, 2011.

74 R. Kerin, 'Becoming Aboriginal in the Era of Assimilation', A. Holland & B. Brookes (eds), *Rethinking the Racial Moment: Essays on the Colonial Encounter,* Cambridge Scholars Publishing, 2011, pp. 205–28.

75 R. Kerin, 'Sydney James/Duguid and the Importance of "Being Aboriginal"', *Aboriginal History*, vol. 29, 2005, pp. 46–63.

Chapter 9 – Demanding Justice and Freedom

1 M. Bennett to A. Bromham, 24 October 1958, Mary Bennett and Ada Bromham, Private Archives, State Library of Western Australia, MN 2958; ACC 8303A/10.

2 M. Bennett to A. Bromham, no date, Mary Bennett and Ada Bromham, Private Archives, SLWA, MN 2958; ACC 8303A/13.

3 M. Bennett to J. Street, 10 September 1957, Street Papers, NLA MS2683, Box 10.

4 M. Bennett to J. Street, 26 March 1960, Street Papers, NLA, MS2683, Box 10.

5 650 pounds is approximately $24,000 in Australian dollars today.

6 M. Bennett, Notes on Aboriginal Policy, Duguid Papers, NLA, MS5068, Box 11.

7 M. Bennett to A. Bromham, 13 March 1956, Mary Bennett and Ada Bromham, Private Archives, SLWA, MN 2958; ACC 8303A/18.

8 M. Bennett to A. Bromham, Mary Bennett and Ada Bromham, Private Archives, SLWA, MN 2958; ACC 8303A/13.

9 M. Bennett to S. Andrews, 29, December 1954, MS12913, Papers of the Council for Aboriginal Rights, La Trobe Manuscript Collection, State Library of Victoria, Box 4.

10 M. Bennett to A. Bromham, 17 May 1956, Mary Bennett and Ada Bromham, Private Archives, SLWA, MN 2958; ACC 8303A/12.

11 Paul Hasluck, 'Statement on Native Welfare Conference, 1951, Elkin Papers, Sydney University Archives, Box 55, item 7.

12 A. Haebich, *Broken Circles. Fragmenting Indigenous Families 1800–2000*, Fremantle Arts Centre Press, Fremantle, 2000, p. 424.

13 Letter from C. R. Lambert to the Administrator of the Northern Territory, 4 September 1952, NAA: A452, 1952/162.

14 Letter from Hasluck to Wise, 28 July 1952, NAA: A452, 1952/162.

15 T. Rowse, *White Flour White Power. From Rations to Citizenship in Central Australia*, Cambridge University Press, Cambridge, 1998, p. 110.

16 A. Maccallum, 'The Compatibility of Hasluck's Assimilation Policy and Mining on Aboriginal Reserves in the Northern Territory: An Illusion?', *Melbourne Historical Journal*, vol. 38, 2010, pp. 89–111.

17 Australia, House of Representatives, 1952, *Debates*, vol. 218, p. 46.

18 Paul Hasluck, Statement by the Minister for Territories on Native Welfare in the Northern Territory, 6 August 1958, NAA, A452, 1952/162.

19 Ibid.

20 G. Parsons, *Black Chattels: The Story of the Australian Aborigines*, The National Council for Civil Liberties, Walthemstow Press, London, 1946, p. 44.

21 S. Gray, *The Protectors. A Journey through Whitefella Past*, Allen & Unwin, Sydney, 2011, pp. 152–3.

22 Ibid., pp. 159–71.

23 P. Hasluck, 'Statement on Native Welfare Conference, 1951', Elkin Papers, Sydney University Archives, Box 55, Item 7.

24 'Policy For Welfare of Natives', *Adelaide Advertiser*, 19 October 1951.

25 Rowse, *White Flour*, pp. 109–11.

26 Australia, House of Representatives, 1955, *Debates*, vol. s.6, pp. 1667–69.

27 Draft Letter from Paul Hasluck to the Anti-Slavery Society sent to the Administrator for the Northern Territory, July 1956, NAA: A452/1, 55/594.

28 L. Coltheart (ed.), *Jessie Street. A Revised Autobiography*, The Federation Press,

Sydney, 2004; P. Sekuless, *Jessie Street. A Rewarding but Unrewarded Life*, University of Queensland Press, St Lucia, 1978.

29   D. McLeod to B. Fitzpatrick, 28 March 1956, Street Papers, NLA MS2683/10/70.

30   J. Street to B. Fitzpatrick, 5 May 1956, Street Papers, NLA, MS2683, Box 10.

31   M. Rutledge, 'Ogilvie, Edward David Stewart (1814–1896)', Australian Dictionary of Biography, National Centre of Biography, Australian National University, http://adb.anu.edu.au/biography/ogilvie-edward-david-stewart-777/text7017, accessed 17 October 2014.

32   J. Street, *Truth or Repose*, Australasian Book Society, Sydney, 1966.

33   J. Street, *Report on the Aborigines in Australia*, May/June, 1957, p. 1. Mary Bennett to Charles Duguid, 28 June, 1961, Duguid Papers, MS 5068, series 1.

34   M. Bennett to A. Bromham, 25 May 1957, Mary Bennett and Ada Bromham, Private Archives, SLWA, MN 2958; ACC 8303A/10.

35   M. Bennett to J. Street, 23 January 1959, Street Papers, NLA MS2683, Box 10.

36   M. Bennett to A. Bromham, 9 May 1957, Mary Bennett and Ada Bromham, Private Archives, SLWA, MN 2958; ACC 8303A/10.

37   M. Bennett to A. Bromham, 8 November 1959, Mary Bennett and Ada Bromham, Private Archives, SLWA, MN 2958; ACC 8303A/2.

38   M. Bennett to S. Andrews, 10 October 1954, MS12913, Papers of the Council for Aboriginal Rights, La Trobe Manuscript Collection, SLV, Box 4.

39   M. Bennett to S. Andrews, 8 October 1954, MS12913, Papers of the Council for Aboriginal Rights, La Trobe Manuscript Collection, SLV, Box 4.

40   M. Bennett, *Human Rights for Australian Aborigines. How Can They Learn Without a Teacher?*, Truth, Brisbane, 1957, p. 52.

41   Ibid., p. 53.

42   D. Christian, *Maps of Time: An Introduction to Big History*, University of California Press, Oakland, 2004.

43   B. Buchan, 'Traffick of Empire: Trade, Treaty and Terra Nullius in Australia and North America', *History Compass*, vol. 5, no. 2, 2007, pp. 1–20; 'Subjects of Benevolence: Concepts of Society and Civilization in Early Colonial Indigenous Administration', *Journal of Australian Studies*, no. 85, 2005, pp. 37–48; 'Of "Social Ties" and "Savage Hordes": The Denial of Indigenous Sovereignty in Australia', Technical Report, Political Science Program, RSSS, Australian National University, Canberra, 2001, pp. 1–37.

44   Bennett, *Human Rights*, pp. 32–3, 63.

45   Street, *Report on Aborigines*, pp. 29–30.

46   Ibid., p. 5.

47   Ibid., p. 7.

48   M. Bennett to A. Bromham, 13 June 1958, Mary Bennett and Ada Bromham, Private Archives, SLWA, MN 2958; ACC 8303A/10.

49   Bennett, *Human Rights*, p. 26.

50   Eskimo was the term used for the Indigenous peoples of the northern circumpolar region including Russia, Alaska, Canada and Greenland. I reproduce it in the book as it was used at the time. However, I acknowledge that this is considered derogatory by many in the region who now use the term 'Inuit'.

51   Letter from C. W. W. Greenidge to P. Hasluck, 17 December 1957, NAA: F1, 58/77.

52   Street, *Report on Aborigines*, p. 2.
53   Greenidge to Hasluck, 17 December 1957.
54   Paul Hasluck to C. W. W. Greenidge, 5 March 1958, NAA: F1, 58/77.
55   M. Bennett to A. Bromham, 27 March 1961, Mary Bennett and Ada Bromham,
       Private Archives, SLWA, MN 2958; ACC 8303A/15.
56   Bennett to Bromham, 24 October 1958.
57   These ideas were contained in a range of letters between Mary and Ada Bromham
       between 1956 and 1961 held in the Battye library at Mary Bennett and Ada Bromham,
       Private Archives, SLWA, MN 2958; ACC 8303A.
58   Bennett to Andrews, 29 December 1954.

Chapter 10 – At War with Evil

1   M. Bennett to A. Bromham, 4 April 1957, Mary Bennett and Ada Bromham, Private
       Archives, State Library of Western Australia, MN 2958; ACC 8303A/10.
2   M. Bennett to A. Bromham, 7 May 1960, Mary Bennett and Ada Bromham, Private
       Archives, SLWA, MN 2958; ACC 8303A/19.
3   M. Bennett to C. Duguid, 28 June 1961, Duguid Papers, NLA, MS5068, Series 11.
4   M. Bennett to A. Bromham, 31 May 1958, Mary Bennett and Ada Bromham, Private
       Archives, SLWA, MN 2958; ACC 8303A/15.
5   A. Bromham to M. Bennett, 7 June 1957, Mary Bennett and Ada Bromham, Private
       Archives, SLWA, MN 2958; ACC 8303A/22.
6   J. T. Wells & M. F. Christie, 'Namatjira and the Burden of Citizenship', *Australian
       Historical Studies,* vol. 114, 2000, pp. 110–30.
7   R. McGregor, *Indifferent Inclusion. Aboriginal People and the Australian Nation,* Aboriginal
       Studies Press, Canberra, 2011.
8   M. Bennett to J. Street, 25 December 1958, Street Papers, NLA, MS2683, Box 10.
9   S. Andrews to J. Street, 28 April 1959, Street Papers, NLA, MS2683, Box 10.
10   M. Bennett to A. Bromham, n.d., Mary Bennett and Ada Bromham, Private Archives,
       SLWA, MN 2958; ACC 8303A/13.
11   M. Bennett to A. Bromham, 14 March 1960, Mary Bennett and Ada Bromham,
       Private Archives, SLWA, MN 2958; ACC 8303A/18.
12   M. Bennett, 'Hunt and Die: The Prospects of the Aborigines of Australia', The Anti-
       Slavery Society, London, 1950.
13   M. Bennett to S. Andrews, 28 July 1957, MS12913, Papers of the Council for
       Aboriginal Rights, La Trobe Manuscript Collection, State Library of Victoria, Box 4.
14   M. Bennett to W. Grayden, 23 April 1959, Mary Bennett and Ada Bromham, Private
       Archives, SLWA, MN 2958; ACC 8303A/6.
15   M. Bennett to A. Bromham, 9 May 1957, Mary Bennett and Ada Bromham, Private
       Archives, SLWA, MN 2958; ACC 8303A/10.
16   P. Hasluck, 'The Future of the Australian Aborigines', Paper read to Section F
       (Anthropology) at the Australian and New Zealand Association for the Advancement
       of Science, 22 August 1958, MS9377, Women's International League for Peace and
       Freedom, Papers, La Trobe Manuscript Collection, SLV, Box 1747/5.
17   M. Bennett to J. Street, 8 September 1960, Street Papers, NLA MS2683, Box 10.
18   M. Bennett to J. Brady, 3 November 1957, MS12913, Council for Aboriginal Rights,
       Papers, La Trobe Manuscript Collection, SLV, Box 4.

19 M. Bennett, Evidence to the Inquiry on Native Matters, SAWA, MN1176, Western Australian Aboriginal Advancement Council, ACC 3869 A/2, 4.

20 Ibid., p. 5.

21 Ibid., p. 2.

22 Ibid.

23 M. Bennett, Evidence before Special Committee on Native Matters, 25 March 1958, SAWA, MN1176 Western Australian Aboriginal Advancement Council, ACC 3869A/2, Copies of Submissions to Parliamentary Committee on Citizen Rights to Aborigines 1958.

24 M. Bennett to The Secretary of the Western Australian Native Welfare Council, 14 April 1959, Street Papers, NLA, MS2683, Box 10.

25 J. Street to S. G. Middleton, 23 June 1958, MS12913, Council for Aboriginal Rights, Papers, La Trobe Manuscript Collection, SLV, Box 2.

26 A. Bromham, Proposal for Aboriginal Cooperative in the Laverton District, 11 July 1960, State Archives of Western Australia, MN585, Women's Service Guilds of WA, Acc 2350A/56, Native Question 1934–1961.

27 Minister for Native Welfare to Ada Bromham, 7 November 1960, SAWA, MN585, Native Question, 1934–1961.

28 A. Bromham, Proposal for Aboriginal Co-Operatives in the Laverton District, 11 July 1960, SAWA, MN85, Women's Service Guilds of WA, ACC 2530A/56, Native Question 1934–1961.

29 M. Bennett to Mr Millard, 29 July 1960, MS12913, Council for Aboriginal Rights, Papers, La Trobe Manuscript Collection, SLV, Box 4.

30 Australia, Parliament 1937, Aboriginal Welfare. Initial Conference of Commonwealth and State Aboriginal Authorities, Commonwealth Government, Canberra, p. 11.

31 M. Bennett to Lady Street, 27 April 1958, Street Papers, NLA, MS2683, Box 10.

32 M. Bennett to J. Street, 6 October 1958, Street Papers, NLA, MS2683, Box 10.

33 A. Markus, 'Talka Longa Mouth', in A. Markus & A. Curthoys (eds), *Who Are Our Enemies? Racism and the Working Class in Australia,* Hale & Iremonger, Sydney, 1978, pp. 154–5.

34 M. Bennett to A. Bromham, 13 July 1959, Mary Bennett and Ada Bromham, Private Archives, SLWA, MN 2958; ACC 8303A/18.

35 M. Bennett to A. Bromham, 9 December 1953, Mary Bennett and Ada Bromham, Private Archives, SLWA, MN 2958; ACC 8303 A/18

36 M. Bennett to A. Bromham, 13 April 1955, Mary Bennett and Ada Bromham, Private Archives, SLWA, MN 2958; ACC 8303 A/18

37 For her comments on Middleton see M. Bennett to A. Bromham, 12 October 1959, Mary Bennett and Ada Bromham, Private Archives, SLWA, MN 2958; ACC 8303A/19. For her comments on Brady see M. Bennett to A. Bromham, 6 October 1958, Mary Bennett and Ada Bromham, Private Archives, SLWA, MN 2958; ACC 8303A/13.

38 M. Bennett to A. Bromham, 9 September 1955, Mary Bennett and Ada Bromham, Private Archives, SLWA, MN 2958; ACC 8303A/18.

39 M. Bennett to A. Bromham, 17 May 1956, Mary Bennett and Ada Bromham, Private Archives, SLWA, MN 2958; ACC 8303A/12.

40 M. Bennett to A. Bromham, 18 April 1960, Mary Bennett and Ada Bromham, Private Archives, SLWA, MN 2958; ACC 8303A/19.

41   M. Bennett to A. Bromham, 27 September 1958, Mary Bennett and Ada Bromham, Private Archives, SLWA, MN 2958; ACC 8303A/13.

42   M. Bennett to A. Bromham, 13 September 1958, Mary Bennett and Ada Bromham, Private Archives, SLWA, MN 2958; ACC 8303 A/13

43   M. Bennett to A. Bromham, 26 March 1956, Mary Bennett and Ada Bromham, Private Archives, SLWA, MN 2958; ACC 8303A/18.

44   M. Bennett to A. Bromham, 2 February 1960, Mary Bennett and Ada Bromham, Private Archives, SLWA, MN 2958; ACC 8303 A/22

45   M. Bennett, *The Australian Aboriginal as a Human Being*, Alston Rivers, London, 1930, p. 47.

46   M. Bennett, Western Australia: Native Policy and Practice 1961, Papers of Anna Vroland, SLV, MS10301 1/2.

47   M. Bennett to A. Bromham, 17 June 1960, Mary Bennett and Ada Bromham, Private Archives, SLWA, MN 2958; ACC 8303A/11.

48   M. Bennett to A. Bromham, n.d.

49   M. Bennett to A. Bromham, 13 April 1955, Mary Bennett and Ada Bromham, Private Archives, SLWA, MN 2958; ACC 8303A/18.

50   J. Street to M. Bennett, 1 August 1961, Street Papers, NLA, MS2683, Box 10.

51   M. Bennett to A. Bromham, 9 March 1961, Mary Bennett and Ada Bromham, Private Archives, SLWA, MN 2958; ACC 8303A/15.

52   M. Bennett to A. Bromham, 27 March 1961, Mary Bennett and Ada Bromham, Private Archives, SLWA, MN 2958; ACC 8303A/15.

53   M. Bennett to S. Andrews, 31 August 1961, MS12913, Papers of the Council for Aboriginal Rights, La Trobe Manuscript Collection, SLV, Box 4.

54   M. Bennett to A. Bromham, 3 September 1961, Mary Bennett and Ada Bromham, Private Archives, SLWA, MN 2958; ACC 8303A/2.

55   Ibid.

56   B. Christophers, *Collaborating for Indigenous Rights*, National Museum of Australia, http://indigenousrights.net.au/person.asp?pID=995.

57   W. M. Murray (ed.), *The Struggle For Dignity: a critical analysis of the Australian Aborigine today, the laws which govern him and their effects*, The Council For Aboriginal Rights, 1962.

58   A. Bromham to B. Christophers, 25 October 1962, Mary Bennett and Ada Bromham, Private Archives, SLWA, MN 2958; ACC 8303A/5.

59   A. Bromham to B. Christophers, 31 December 1962, Mary Bennett and Ada Bromham, Private Archives, SLWA, MN 2958; ACC 8303A/5.

60   M. Bennett to A. Bromham, 25 May 1959, Mary Bennett and Ada Bromham, Private Archives, SLWA, MN 2958; ACC 8303 A/12

61   M. Bennett to A. Bromham, 28 March 1957, Mary Bennett and Ada Bromham, Private Archives, SLWA, MN 2958; ACC 8303A/10.

62   ibid.

63   J. Street to S. Andrews, 'The Question of Discriminations Against Aborigines and the Unite Nations', 7 January 1963, Street Papers, NLA, MS2683, Box 10.

64   J. Street to Commander Fox-Pitt, 29 March 1963, Street Papers, NLA, MS2683, Box 10.

65   Commander Fox-Pitt to J. Street, 29 March 1963, MS12913, Council for Aboriginal Rights, Papers, La Trobe Manuscript Collection, SLV, Box 8.

66   G. Bussey & M. Tims, *Women's International League For Peace and Freedom, 1915–1965*.

A Record of Fifty Years' Work, George Allen and Unwin, London, 1965.

67   M. Scott to S. Andrews, 9 August 1963, MS12913, Council for Aboriginal Rights, Papers, La Trobe Manuscript Collection, SLV, Box 8.

68   S. Andrews to J. Street, 13 November 1963, MS12913, Council for Aboriginal Rights, Papers, La Trobe Manuscript Collection, SLV, Box 9.

69   J. Clark, *Aborigines and Activism. Race, Aborigines and the Coming of the Sixties to Australia*, University of Western Australia Press, Nedlands, 2008.

70   Report of the National Inquiry into the Separation of Aboriginal and Torres Strait Islander Children from Their Families, April 1997, https://www.humanrights.gov.au/publications/bringing-them-home-report-1997.

Conclusion
1   Moseley Royal Commission, *Transcripts of Evidence*, pp. 299–303.

2   Ibid., pp. 225–229.

3   Moseley, H.D., Report of the Special Commissioner appointed to Investigate, Report, Advise upon matters in relation to the Condition and Treatment of Aborigines, Government Printer, Perth 1935, p. 22.

4   Mary Bennett, *Christison of Lammermoor*, Alston Rivers, London, p. 86.

5   Ibid., p. 97.

6   Mary Bennett, *The Australian Aboriginal As A Human Being*, Alston Rivers, London, p. 141.

7   Ibid., p. 142.

8   Ibid., p, 15.

9   Andrew Porter, *Critics of Empire. British Radicals and the Imperial Challenge*, I. B. Tauris, London, p. 317.

10   Mary Bennett to Shirley Andrews, 29/12/1954, MS12913, Council for Aboriginal Rights, Papers, La Trobe Manuscript collection, State Library of Victoria, Box 4.

11   Bruce Buchan, 'Traffick of Empire: Trade, Treaty and Terra Nullius in Australia and North America', *History Compass*, 5 (2), 2007, pp. 1–20; Buchan, 'The Empire of Political Thought: The Language of Civilization and Perceptions of Indigenous Government', *History of the Human Sciences*, 18 (2), 2005, pp. 1–22; Buchan, 'Subjecting the Natives: Aborigines, Property and Possession Under Early Colonial Rule', *Social Analysis*, 45 (2), 2001, pp. 143–62.

12   Anna Doukakis, *The Aboriginal People, 'Parliament and Protection' in New South Wales 1856–1916*, The Federation Press, 2006.

13   Bernard Porter, *The Absent-Minded Imperialists: Empire, Society and Culture in Britain*, Oxford University Press, 2006, p. 162.

14   Bennett, *The Australian Aboriginal*, p. 50.

15   Mary Bennett to Olive Pink, 6/3/1935, *Olive Pink Papers*, Australian Institute of Aboriginal and Torres Strait Islander Studies, MS2368.

16   Mary Bennett to Commander Fox–Pitt, 14.3.1960, *Street Papers*, National Library of Australia, MS2683, Box 10.

17   Adam Hochschild, *King Leopold's Ghost. A Story of Greed, Terror and Heroism in Colonial Africa*, Houghton Mifflin Company, New York, 1998.

18   Mary Bennett to William Morley, 26/2/1939, *Papers of the Association for the Protection of Native Races*, Sydney University Archives, series 7.

19   Michael Barnett, *Empire of Humanity. A History of Humanitarianism*, Cornell University

Press, USA, 2011, pp. 22–5.

20   Ibid., p. 26.

21   Bennett, *The Australian Aboriginal*, p. 39.

22   Mary Bennett to the Keeper of the Ethnographic Department of the British Museum, 21/3/1927, British Museum, http://www.britishmuseum.org/research/collection_online/.

23   M. Bennett to Mr Knight, 17 April 1959, Mary Bennett and Ada Bromham, Private Archives, SLWA, MN 2958; ACC 8303 A/6

24   Mary Bennett to Ada Bromham, 7 August 1960, Mary Bennett and Ada Bromham, Private Archives, State Library of Western Australia, MN 2958; ACC 8303A/13

25   Helen Cameron Roberts to Reverend F.H. Griffiths, 21.11.61, Australian National University Archives: Australian Dictionary of Biography, ANUA 312, Box 47, Mary Bennett.

26   Maxwell Brown, 'Fernando. The Story of an Aboriginal Prophet', *Aborigine Welfare Bulletin*, 4 (1), 1964, pp. 9–11.

27   M. Bennett to A. Bromham, 13 September 1958, Mary Bennett and Ada Bromham, Private Archives, SLWA, MN 2958; ACC 8303 A/13

28   M. Bennett to A. Bromham, 27 March 1961, Mary Bennett and Ada Bromham, Private Archives, SLWA, MN 2958; ACC 8303 A/15

29   Mary Bennett to Ada Bromham, 9 November 1960, Mary Bennett and Ada Bromham, Private Archives, State Library of Western Australia, MN 2958, ACC 8303A/7

30   Mary Bennett, *Christison*, p. 29.

31   Mary Bennett to Ada Bromham, Mary Bennett and Ada Bromham, Private Archives, State Library of Western Australia, MN 2958, ACC 8303A/2.

32   Fiona Paisley, *The Lone Protestor. AM Fernando in Australia and Europe*, Aboriginal Studies Press, Canberra, 2012, p. 128.

33   Ibid., pp. 126–7.

34   Barnett, *Empire*, p. 11.

35   Mary Bennett to Shirley Andrews, 8/4/1954, Council of Aboriginal Rights, Papers, MS12913, La Trobe Manuscript Collection, State Library of Victoria, MS12913, Box 4.

36   Mary Bennett to Ada Bromham, 9 November 1960, Mary Bennett and Ada Bromham, Private Archives, State Library of Western Australia, MN 2958, ACC 8303A/7

37   Mary Bennett, *The Australian Aboriginal As A Human Being*, Alston Rivers, London, 1930, p. 75.

38   W.E.H. Stanner, 'The Great Australian Silence', *The Dreaming and Other Essays* with an introduction by Robert Manne, Black Inc., Victoria, 2009, pp. 182–193.

39   Mary Bennett, *Human Rights For Australian Aborigines. How Can They Learn Without a Teacher?*, Truth, Brisbane, 1957, p. 34.

40   Mary Bennett to Shirley Andrews, 4/5/1954, Council for Aboriginal Rights, Papers, MS12913, La Trobe Manuscript Collection, State Library of Victoria, Box 1.

41   Anna Haebich, '"Between knowing and not knowing": Public knowledge of the Stolen Generations', *Aboriginal History*, vol. 25, 2001, pp. 70–90.

42   Australia, Parliament, 1937, *Recommendations of Policy in Native Affairs in the Northern Territory of Australia* by Dr Donald Thomson, Government Printer, Canberra, p. 4.

43   Mary Bennett to Shirley Andrews, 10/11/1954, Council for Aboriginal Rights, Papers,

MS12913, La Trobe Manuscript Collection, State Library of Victoria, Box 4.

44 M. Bennett to A. Bromham, Mary Bennett and Ada Bromham, Private Archives SLWA, MN 2958; ACC 8303A/13.

45 Peter Sutton, *The Politics of Suffering. Indigenous Australia and the End of the Liberal Consensus*, Melbourne University Press, Melbourne, 2009.

46 Noel Pearson, 'On the Human Right to Misery, Mass Incarceration and Early Death', Inaugural Charles Perkins Memorial Lecture, 25 October 2001, Sydney.edu.au/koori/ news/pearson.pdf.

47 Mary Bennett to Ada Bromham, Mary Bennett and Ada Bromham, Private Archives, State Library of Western Australia, MN 2958, ACC 8303A/12.

48 Kimm, J., *A Fatal Conjunction. Two Laws. Two Cultures*, The Federation Press, Sydney, 2004.

49 Jennifer Koshan, 'Sounds of Silence: The Public/Private Dichotomy, Violence and Aboriginal Women', Susan Boyd (ed.), *Challenging the Public/Private Divide. Feminism, Law and Public Policy,* University of Toronto Press, Canada, 1997, pp. 87–101.

50 Moseley Royal Commission, *Transcripts of Evidence*, pp. 220.

51 See, for example, Kimm, *A Fatal Conjunction*; 'Crown Prosecutor Speaks Out About Abuse in Central Australia', http://www.abc.net.au/lateline/content/2006/s1639127. htm

52 Larissa Behrendt, 'As Good As It Gets Or As Good As It Could Be? Benchmarking Human Rights in Australia', *Balayi: Culture, Law and Colonialism*, vol. 10, 2009, pp. 3–13 ; Megan Davis, 'The Recognition of Aboriginal Customary Law and International Law Developments', Human Rights and Equal Opportunity Commission, Indigenous Peoples: Issues in International and Australian Law', http:// www.hreoc.gov.au/social_justice/publications/International; K. Cripps and S. C. Taylor, 'White Man's Law, Traditional Law and Bullshit Law: Customary Marriage Revisited, *Balayi: Culture, Law and Colonialism*, vol. 10, 2009: pp. 481–5; K. Cripps, 'Understanding Indigenous Family Violence in the Context of a Human Rights Agenda', *Human Rights Defender*, 15 (3), 2006, pp. 3–5; Boni Robertson, *The Aboriginal and Torres Strait Islander Women's Task Force on Violence Report*.

53 *Ampe Akelyernemane Meke Mekarle* 'Little Children Are Sacred', p. 69.

54 Megan Davis, 'The Recognition of Aboriginal Customary Law and International Law Developments', Human Rights and Equal Opportunity Commission, Indigenous Peoples: Issues in International and Australian Law', http://www.hreoc.gov.au/ social_justice/publications/International.

54 Hannah McGlade, 'Aboriginal Women, Girls and Sexual Assault', *Australian Centre for the Study of Sexual Assault Newsletter,* 12, September 2006, p. 12.

55 Moseley Royal Commission, *Transcripts of Evidence*, p. 213.

57 Sutton, *The Politics of Suffering*; Louis Nowra, *Bad Dreaming. Aboriginal Men's Violence Against Aboriginal Women and Children,* Pluto Press, Sydney, 2007; Nicholas Rothwell, *Another Country*, Black Inc, Melbourne, 2007; Stephanie Jarrett, Connor Court Publishing, Ballarat, 2013.

58 Elizabeth Farrelly, 'Protecting a Cultural Right to Abuse', *Sydney Morning Herald*, 11/4/2013.

59 Bennett, *The Australian Aboriginal*, p. 38.

60 Mary Bennett, 'Native Women as Chattels. Playthings of Men', *The Ladder*, vol. 1, 2, October 1936, p. 7.

61 B. Attwood and A. Markus, *The 1967 Referendum. Race, Power and the Australian Constitution*, Aboriginal Studies Press, Canberra, 2007.

62 J. Chesterman, *Civil Rights. How Indigenous Australians Won Formal Equality*, University of Queensland Press, St Lucia, 2005.

63 T. Calma Appointed next University of Canberra Vice-Chancellor, http://www. healthinfonet.ecu.edu.au/about/news/1904.

64 M. Bennett to A. Bromham, 8 November 1959, Mary Bennett and Ada Bromham, Private Archives, State Library of Western Australia, MN 2958; ACC 8303A/2.

65 T. Rowse, 'The Indigenous Sector', in D. Austin-Broos and G. Macdonald (eds), *Culture, Economy and Governance in Aboriginal Australia*, Academy of the Social Sciences and the Department of Anthropology, University of Sydney Press, Sydney, 2005, pp. 207–223.

66 L. Lippmann, *Generations of Resistance. Mabo and Justice*, Longman, 1991, 55; G. Cowlishaw, 'Erasing Culture and Race: Practicing "Self-Determination"', *Oceania*, vol. 68 (3), March, 1998, pp. 145–169.

67 S. Maddison, 'Indigenous autonomy matters: what's wrong with the Australian government's "intervention" in Aboriginal communities', *Australian Journal of Human Rights,* vol. 14 (1), 2008, pp. 41–61.

68 Moseley Royal Commission, *Transcripts of Evidence*, p. 248.

69 Ibid., pp. 231–2.

Epilogue

1 J. Street to Mr D. Collard, 26 January 1962, Street Papers, NLA, MS2683, Box 10.

2 M. Bennett to S. Andrews, 15 October 1957, MS12913, Papers of the Council for Aboriginal Rights, La Trobe Manuscript Collection, State Library of Victoria, Box 1.

3 M. Bennett to S. Andrews, 17 April 1954, MS12913, Papers of the Council for Aboriginal Rights, La Trobe Manuscript Collection, SLV, Box 1.

4 A. Bromham, 'Forward', in M. Bennett, *Human Rights for Australian Aborigines. How Can They Learn Without a Teacher?*, Truth, Brisbane, 1957, p. 1.

5 A. Bromham to J. Street, 19 November 1961, Mary Bennett and Ada Bromham, Private Archives, State Library of Western Australia, MN 2958; ACC 8303A/5.

6 'Allegations are Denied', *Daily News*, Perth, 21 October 1961.

7 'Welfare Chief: Papers Charge is Nonsense', *The West Australian*, 1 November 1961.

8 'Kalgoorlie Papers Charge', *Daily News*, Perth, 21 October 1961.

9 A. Bromham, Affidavit, 7 October 1962, M. Bennett to A. Bromham, Mary Bennett and Ada Bromham, Private Archives, SLWA, MN 2958; ACC 8303A/4.

10 Letter from B. Christophers to author, October 2013.

11 M. Bennett to J. Street, 24 February 1957, Street Papers, NLA, MS2683, Box 10.

12 'Kalgoorlie Papers Charge', *Daily News*, Perth, 21 October 1962, Mary Bennett and Ada Bromham, Private Archives, SLWA, MN 2958; ACC 8303A/2.

13 M. Bennett to A. Bromham, 13 July 1959, Mary Bennett and Ada Bromham, Private Archives, SLWA, MN 2958; ACC 8303A/18.

14 A. F. Watts to A. Bromham, 3 November 1961, Mary Bennett and Ada Bromham, Private Archives, SLWA, MN 2958; ACC 8303A/18.

15 Unpublished private memoirs of Wilfred Henry Douglas. I thank his son, Rob, for sharing this information with me.

16 A. Bromham to J. Street, 29 November 1961, Mary Bennett and Ada Bromham,

Private Archives, SLWA, MN 2958; ACC 8303A/5.

17 S. Andrews to A. Bromham, 10 September 1962, Mary Bennett and Ada Bromham, Private Archives, SLWA, MN 2958; ACC 8303A/19.

18 H. Keenan (Director), *Persons of Interest: The Asio Files*, SBS, 2014, http:// smartstreetfilms.com.au.

19 'Many people were caught up in the intelligence dragnet. Persons of interest caught in ASIO's net', *The Australian*, 4 January 2014.

20 M. Bennett to A. Bromham, 13 April 1960, Mary Bennett and Ada Bromham, Private Archives, SLWA, MN 2958; ACC 8303A/10.

21 L. Clohesy, 'Fighting the Enemy Within. Anti–Communism and Aboriginal Affairs', *History Australia*, vol. 8, no. 2, 2011, p. 151.

22 G. C. Bolton, Mary Montgomerie Bennett, Draft of Australian Dictionary of Biography entry, Australian National University Archives: Australian Dictionary of Biography, ANUA 312, Box 47, Mary Bennett.

23 M. Bennett to Mr Knight, 17 April 1959, Mary Bennett and Ada Bromham, Private Archives, SLWA, MN 2958; ACC 8303 A/6

24 United Nations. Human Rights – Australian Natives and Other Minorities, 1946– 1963, NAA: A1838, 929/5/3 Part 1.

25 M. Bennett to A. Bromham, 13 October 1956, Mary Bennett and Ada Bromham, Private Archives, SLWA, MN 2958; ACC 8303A/13.

26 M. Bennett to S. Andrews, 10 October 1953, Council for Aboriginal Rights, Papers, MS12913, La Trobe Manuscript Collection, SLV, Box 4.

27 M. Bennett to A. Bromham, 30 August 1958, Mary Bennett and Ada Bromham, Private Archives, SLWA, MN 2958; ACC 8303A/13.

28 M. Morgan, *A Drop in a Bucket*, United Aborigines' Mission, Victoria, 1986, p. 136.

29 A. O. Neville to the Secretary of the Premier's Department, 24 November 1934, Mary Bennett, *Allegations by Mrs Mary Bennett in regard to native slavery, inadequate reserves and traffic in native women*, State Archives of Western Australia. AN 1/7, Department of Native Affairs and Native Welfare, ACC 993, 116/1932.

30 Australian National University Archives: Australian Dictionary of Biography, ANUA 312, Box 47, Mary Bennett.

31 M. Bennett, *Human Rights for Australian Aborigines,* p. 38.

32 M. Bennett to O. Pink, 6 March 1935, Olive Pink Papers, Australian Institute of Aboriginal and Torres Strait Islander Studies, MS2368.

33 C. Rowland, 'William Blake: A Visionary for our Time', https://www.opendemocracy. net/article/william_blake_a_visionary_for_our_time; C. Rowland, *Blake and the Bible*, Yale University Press, New Haven, 2011.

34 Bennett to Andrews, 10 October 1953.

35 See, for example, A. O. Neville, Response to Mary Bennett's allegations, *Allegations of slavery,* SLWA.

36 M. Bennett to Commander Fox-Pitt, 14 March 1960, Street Papers, NLA MS2683, Box 10.

37 A. O. Neville to the Chief Secretary, 21 February 1938, Allegations of slavery, SLWA.

38 Commonwealth of Australia, Australia's National Human Rights Action Plan, Canberra, 2012, p. 83; Law Council of Australia, Australia's National Human Rights Action Plan, Canberra, February 2012.

39 J. Clark, *Aborigines and Activism. Race, Aborigines and the Coming of the Sixties to Australia,*

UWA Press, Nedlands, 2008, pp. 25-40.

BIBLIOGRAPHY

Primary Sources

Published

The Anti-Slavery Reporter and Aborigines' Friend, July 1912 – October 1941

Anna Haebich, *Broken Circles. Fragmenting Indigenous Families 1800-2000*, Fremantle Arts Centre Press, Fremantle, 2000.

Anna Haebich, *Spinning the Dream. Assimilation in Australia 1950-1970*, Fremantle Press, Fremantle, 2008.

Annual Report of the Anti-Slavery and Aborigines' Protection Society, 1943–68.

'Australia's Burden', *Nature*, 18 December 1937.

Baillie, H., *The Call of the Aboriginal*, Fraser and Morphet, Melbourne, 1933.

Basedow, H., *The Australian Aboriginal*, F. W. Preece and Sons, Adelaide, 1925.

Bates, D., *The Passing of the Aborigines. A Lifetime Spent Among the Natives of Australia,* John Murray, London, 1938.

Beckenham, P. W. *The Education of the Australian Aboriginal*, Australian Council for Educational Research, 1948.

Bennett, M., *Christison of Lammermoor*, Alston Rivers, London, 1927.

Bennett, M., *The Australian Aboriginal As A Human Being*, Alston Rivers, London, 1930.

Bennett, Mary, *The Condition of the Aborigines of Australia under the Federal Government*. A Paper Read before the British Commonwealth League, June 1929.

Bennett, M., 'Notes on the Dalleburra Tribe of Northern Queensland', *Journal of the Royal Anthropological Institute of Great Britain and Ireland*, vol. 57, 1927, pp. 399–415.

Bennett, M., 'The Aboriginal Mother in Western Australia'. A Paper read at the British Commonwealth League Conference, June 1933, Elkin Papers, Sydney University Archives, box 23, item 8.

Bennett, M., *Teaching the Aborigines. Data From the Mt Margaret Mission*, City and Suburban Print, Perth, 1935.

Bennett, M., *Human Rights for Australian Aborigines. How Can They Learn Without a Teacher?*, Truth, Brisbane, 1957.

Bennett, M., *Hunt or Die. The Prospect For the Aborigines of Australia*, The Anti-Slavery Society, London, 1950.

Bennett, M., 'Australian Aboriginal Workers in Federal Territory and the States of Queensland and Western Australia', 1943.

British Commonwealth League, *Reports of Conference* 1926–29; 1932, 1934–37.

Bromham, A., *The First Australians and the New Australians*, Port Printing Works, Fremantle, August, 1959.

Bush, B., Imperialism, Race and Resistance: Africa and Britain, 1919-1945, Taylor and Francis, Abingdon, 2002.

Central Women's Department Communist Party of Australia, *The Working Woman*, August 1930 – July 1936.

The Dawn, 1927–45.

Duguid, C., *The Future of the Aborigines. An Address to the Nationary Missionary Council*, Vardon and Sons, Ltd, Adelaide, 1941.

Duguid, C., *The Aborigines of Darwin and the Tropic North*, July, 1951.

Duguid C., *The Aborigines of Australia*. An Address by Dr Charles Duguid to the Annual Meeting of eh Anti-Slavery Society, 15 June 1954.

Duguid, C., *No Dying Race*, Rigby, Ltd, Adelaide, 1963.

Duguid, C., *Doctor and the Aborigines*, Rigby, Ltd, Adelaide, 1972.

Elkin, A. P., *Citizenship For The Aborigines. A National Aboriginal Policy*, Australasian Publishing Co Pty Ltd, Sydney, 1945.

Fry, H. K., 'The Problem of the Aborigines. Australian Policy, in Retrospect and Prospect', *The Australian Rhodes Review*, Melbourne University Press, no. 2, 1936.

Fry, H. K and Pulleine, R. H., 'The Mentality of the Australian Aborigines', *Australian Journal of Experimental Biology and Medical Research*, vol. 8, no. 3, 1931, pp. 153–65.

Gribble, Reverend E. R. B., *The Problem of the Australian Aboriginal*, Angus and Robertson, Ltd, Australia, 1932.

Gribble, Reverend E. R. B., *A Despised Race. The Vanishing Aboriginals of Australia*, Australian Board of Missions, Sydney, 1933.

The Ladder. Official Organ of the Association for the Amelioration of the Australian Aborigines., vol. 1, no. 1, May 1936 – vol. 1, no. 10, July 1939.

Lefroy, Reverend C. E. C. 'The Aborigines of Australia. A Plea for the Remnant', Reprinted from *The Manchester Guardian*, October 3, 1932.

Justice for the Aborigines, Sydney Labour Council's Policy, 6/11/1937, *Papers of Donald Thomson*, Private Collection, loaded to author by Dorita Thomson.

Love, J. R. B, *Stone-Age Bushmen of Today. Life and Adventure Among A Tribe of Savages in North-Westerns Australia*, Blackie and Sons Ltd, London, 1936.

Man: A Monthly Record of Anthropological Science, 1927–1939.

McCorkindale, I. (ed.), *Pioneer Pathways Sixty Years of Citizenship 1887–1947*, Morris and Walker, Pty, Ltd, Melbourne, 1948.

Murray, W. M. (ed.), *The Struggle For Dignity: a critical analysis of the Australian Aborigine today, the laws which govern him and their effects*, The Council For Aboriginal Rights, 1962.

National Woman's Christian Temperance Union, *Reports of Convention*, 1936, 1939, 1945, 1948, 1951, 1954, 1957, 1960, 1963, 1969.

Nicholls, Y., *Not Slaves Not Citizens. Conditions of the Australian Aborigines in the Northern Territory*, Australian Council for Civil Liberties, Melbourne, 1952.

Neville, A. O., *Australia's Coloured Minority. Its Place in the Community*, Currawang Publishing Co, Pty, Ltd, Sydney, 1948.

Oceania, vol. 1, no. 1, April 1930 – vol. 37, no. 1, September 1966.

Parsons, G., *Black Chattels. The Story of the Australian Aborigines*, National Council of Civil Liberties, London, 1946.

Pink, O., 'Camouflage'. Summary of a lecture on culture contact delivered by Olive Pink,

3/12/1935, *Mankind,* vol. 2, no. 1, April 1936, p. 20.

Pink, O., 'Australian Aborigines. What is their Future? Dictation of Freedom in Civilisation?', *Canberra Times,* December 1938.

Pink, O., 'Is Social Science and Social Anthropological Research – or is Emotionalism – to Decide the Fate of the Wailbri-Speaking Tribe in the Northern Territory of Australia?, Paper Read to Section F (Anthopology), at 1946 Adelaide Science Congress.

Pink, O., 'An Open Letter to Defenders of the Tribes People Anywhere in Australia, *Communist Review,* no. 102, February 1950, pp. 444–7.

Powell, R., *The First Ten Years at Mt Margaret, Western Australia,* Spectator Publishing Company, Melbourne, 1933

Price, A. G., *White Settlers and Native Peoples. An Historical Study of Racial Contacts between English-Speaking Whites and Aboriginal Peoples in the United States, Canada, Australia and New Zealand,* Georgian House, Melbourne, 1950.

Schenk, R., *The Educability of the Native, United Aborigines Mission,* Perth, 1936.

'Some Aspects of the Aboriginal Problem in Australia', *The Australian Geographer,* vol. 1, part 1, August 1928, pp. 67–9.

Smith, H. P. (ed), *The First Ten Years at Mt Margaret, WA: as given in a letter following a visit to Mt Margaret by Mr Robert Powell and extracts from prayer-letters, written during the years by Rod Schenk,* Keswick Book Depot, Melbourne, 1933.

Smoke Signals, Journal of the Aborigines' Advancement League, 1957–60.

Stuart, D., *Yandy,* Georgian House, Melbourne, 1959.

Wright, T., *New Deal For The Aborigines,* The Forward Press, Sydney, 1939.

Declaration on the Rights of Indigenous Peoples, illustrated by Michel Streich, Allen & Unwin, Sydney.

Turner, V. E., The 'Good Fella Missus', Hunken, Ellis and King, Ltd, Adelaide, 1929.

United Aborigines Messenger, 1929–1967.

UNESCO, *The Race Question in Modern Science,* 1956.

Vroland, A., 'Creativeness Needed in Education of the Aborigines', *New Horizons in Education,* no. 9 winter 1952.

Woman's Christian Temperance Union, *The White Ribbon Signal,* March 2, 1936 – January 1962.

Women's International League for Peace and Freedom, Report of the Work on this League with the United Nations at Geneva from the 12th and 13th International Congress of the Women's International League for Peace and Freedom, July 1953 and July 1956.

Wood Jones, F., *Australia's Vanishing Race,* Angus and Robertson, Ltd, Australia, 1934.

Workers Weekly, 1937, 1938.

Worsley, P., 'The Aborigines: Their Present Situation', *Outlook,* vol. 1, no. 3, October 1957, pp. 20–2.

Unpublished
Duguid, P., Brief History of Aborigines Advancement League, South Australia, 1969, personal papers of Nancy Barnes.

Private Papers
Papers of Donald Thomson reproduced with the permission of Mrs D. M. Thomson.

Letters from Donald Thomson to Mrs Edith Ransom.

Statutes
Aboriginals Ordinance 1933 (NT)
Aborigines Protection Act 1905 (WA)
Aborigines Act 1928 (VIC)
Aborigines Act Amendment Act 1936 (WA)
Native Administration Act Amendment Act 1940 (WA)
Native Administration Amendment Act 1942 (WA)
Native Administration Act Amendment Act 1954 (WA)
Native Administration Ordinance 1940 (NT)
Native (Citizenship Rights) Act 1944 (WA)
Police Offences Act 1953 (SA)
Police Offences Act Amendment Act 1957 (SA)

Parliamentary Papers
Australia Parliament, The Aboriginal and Half-Castes of Central and North Australia, Report by J. W. Bleakley, Parl. Paper 21, Melbourne, 1929.

Western Australia, Parliament 1935, Report of the Royal Commissioner Appointed to Investigate, Report and Advise upon matters in relation to the condition and treatment of Aborigines, Perth.

Australia Parliament 1937, Aboriginal Welfare. Initial Conference of Commonwealth and State Aboriginal Authorities, Canberra.

Australia Parliament 1937–38, Recommendations of Policy in Native Affairs in the Northern Territory of Australia, Donald Thomson, Canberra.

Australia Parliament 1951, Native Welfare Meeting of Commonwealth and State Ministers, Canberra.

Western Australia Parliament 1956, Report of the Select Committee Appointed to Inquire into Native Welfare Conditions in the Laverton-Warburton Range Area, Perth.

Manuscripts
OM 79–21, Robert Christison Papers; M. M. Bennett Collection, John Oxley Library, State Library of Queensland, Australia.

Records Collected by Mrs Bennett and Presented to Queensland University, UQ FL 202.

The Papers of the Anti-Slavery Society, MSS British Empire, S22, Rhodes House, Bodleian Library, Oxford.

Bennett, Mary Montgomerie and Bromham, Ada, Private Archives, SLWA, MN 2958; ACC 8303A.

Elkin, A .P. Papers, USA, P130.

Papers of Jessie Street, NLA, MS2683.

Papers of Bessie Rischbieth, NLA, MS2004.

Papers of Charles Duguid, NLA, MS5068.

Papers of Barry Christophers, NLA, MS7992.

Papers of the Australian Federation of Women Voters, NLA, MS2818.

Papers of the Australian Women's Charter Movement, NLA, MS2303.

Papers of Mrs Ternent Cooke Relating to Aborignal Affairs, 1927–67, SASA, GRG52/32.

Bibliography

Olive Pink Papers, AIATSIS, MS2368.

Papers of the Council For Aboriginal Rights, SLV, MS12913

Records of the Aborigines Advancement League, MLSA, SRG250, series 1–4 and 10.

Records of the Woman's Christian Temperance Union, MLSA, SRG186, series 144 and 157, 381, Yurtookee Club.

Records of the League of Women Voters, MLSA, SRG116, series 1–2.

Records of the Association For The Protection of Native Races, series 1–15.

NAA: Department of Interior (II), Central Office; A431, Correspondence Files, annual single number series, 1946; items.

1949/176, Conference of Aboriginal Welfare Authorities, February 1948, Part 1.

1946/1999, Donald F. Thomson, Articles in press re Aboriginal Affairs, 1943–47.

1949/1047, Appointment of Protectors of Aboriginals, 1911–51.

1947/2492, Women's Service Guilds of Western Australia re Aboriginal Affairs, 1934–1947.

1948/1551, Association for the Protection of Native Races, Aboriginal Matters, 1936–46.

1948/273 Part 1, Anti-Slavery and Aborigines' Protection Society, Aboriginal Matters, 1928–39.

1948/273 Part 2, Anti-Slavery and Aborigines Protection Society, Aboriginal Matters, Northern Territory, 1939–46.

1948/273 Part 3, Anti-Slavery and Aborigines Protection Society, Aboriginal Matters, Northern Territory, 1938–48.

NAA: Department of Territories (I), Central Office; A452, Correspondence files, annual single number series, 1951–75; items.

1952/541, Government Police re Aborigines in the Northern Territory, Part 2, 1938–53.

1952/162, Northern Territory, Local Conference on Aboriginal Welfare, Darwin, Native Affairs Policy matters arising out of the First meeting of the Native Welfare Council.

1955/694, Anti-Slavery and Aborigines' Protection Society, Aboriginal Welfare, Northern Territory, 1949–56.

1960/2086, General representations by Miss O. M. Pink re Northern Territory Matters, 1953–63.

NAA: Department of Home Affairs (II), Central Office and Department of Interior (I), Central Administration; A1, Correspondence files, annual single number series, 1903–38; items.

1936/9595, Association for the Protection of Native Races, Aboriginal Matters, file no. 1, 1929–35.

1932/4262, Proposed Model Aboriginal State, 1925–33.

1938/12974, Australian Aborigines' Amelioration Association re Aboriginal Affairs, 1932–38.

1935/1388, Alleged Slavery in the Northern Territory, 1933–35.

NAA: Prime Minister's Department: A461, Correspondence files, multiple number series; items.

A300/1 Part 1, Aboriginal Policy, 1933–35.

A300/1 Part 2, Aboriginal Policy, 1933–41.

A300/1 Part 3, Aboriginal Policy, 1937–43.

A300/1 Part 4, Aboriginal Policy, 1943–49.

A300/1 Part 5, Aboriginal Policy, 1949–50.

B326/1/2, International Conventions. Slavery and Servitude. Slavery Convention, 1926

(League of Nations), 1926–50.

NAA: Department of Home and Territories, Central Office and Department of Interior (I), Central Administration, 1925–33; A659, Correspondence files, class 1 (general, passports), 1939–50; items.

1942/1/4450, Compellability of Aboriginal Witnesses, 1934–42.

1945/1/676, League for the Protection and Advancement of Aboriginal and Half-Caste Women, Proposed Federal Commission, re Native Affairs, 1945.

NAA: Department of External Affairs; A1067, Correspondence files, multiple number series with year and letter prefixes, 1945–46; IC46/117/3, Recommendations and Resolutions. Resolutions passed by WCTU Convention re uplift of Aborigine Race and Peace Terms, 1946.

NAA: Department of External Affairs (II), Central Office; A989, Correspondence files, multiple number series with year prefix, 1942–1945; 1943/735/1036, Post-War Reconstruction, Colonies, General, British Empire Anti-Slavery and Aborigines' Protection Society. An International Colonial Convention, 1943.

NAA: Australian Security Intelligence Organisation, Central Office; A6126/XMO, Microfilm copies of personal and subject files, 1960; items.

19, Miss Olive Pink, 1946–55.

112, Doris Blackburn, 1949–60.

156, Communist Party of Australia, Activities among Aborigines in Australia, 1939–54.

NAA: Attorney-General's Department, Central Office; A432, Correspondence files, annual single and number series, 1929; items.

1934/691, Compellability of Aboriginal witnesses, 1934–37.

NAA: Administrator Northern Territory (II), Central Registry; F1, Correspondence files, annual single number series, 1915–78; items.

38/536, Aboriginal prisoners, wives as compellable witnesses.

58/77, Welfare branch, Anti-Slavery Society. Representations re welfare of Aborigines, 1957–61.

1937/600, Pearling vessels in Northern Territory waters, interference with lubras, watering places, etc, 1936–37.

NAA: Central Board for the Protection of Aborigines and Aborigines Welfare Board; B356, 97 Lake Tyers, Outside unofficial reports and complaints—Miss Ann Vroland (WILPF) 1937–57.

NAA: Administrator Northern Territory, Central Registry, F1, Correspondence Files, 38/536, Memorandum for submission to H.M. High Commissioner for Australia, Justice For Our Minority.

NAA: Department of Territories (I), Central Office, A52, 572/994 AUS, Commonwealth Government's Policy with respect to Aboriginals, 1939.

NAA: A1838, Correspondence files, multiple number series; item 929/5/3 Part 1, United Nations. Human Rights – Australian Natives and Other Minorities, 1946–1963).

SAWA, AN 1/7, Departments of Native Affairs and Native Welfare:

–ACC 993, 116/1932, Allegations by Mrs Mary Bennett in regard to native slavery, inadequate reserves and traffic in native women;

–ACC 993, 384/1957, Warburton Ranges and Surrounding Districts – Living Conditions of Natives in Area Investigations and Reports of;

–ACC 993, 344/1957, Women's Parliament, Perth—Request for information re native matters;

–ACC 993, 842/1951, Labour Women's Central Executive – Correspondence re native matters;

–ACC 993, 565/1957, Aboriginal Welfare Society – General Correspondence;

–ACC 993, 218/1946, The Anti-Slavery and Aborigines Protection Society – general correspondence;

–ACC 993, 866/1942, League of Coloured Peoples – Questionnaire.

SAWA, MN393, Women's Service Guilds of Western Australia:

–ACC 1949A/62, Welfare of Aborigines, February–November, 1937;

–ACC 1949A/38, British Commonwealth League, 1937;

–ACC 1949A/37, British Commonwealth League, January 1929 – June 1937;

–ACC 1949A/59, Native Affairs, 1950;

–ACC 1949A/60, Native Affairs, 1951;

–ACC 1949A/58, Native Affairs, 1949–50;

–ACC 1949A/63, Native Welfare, 1958–59

SAWA, MN1176, Western Australian Aboriginal Advancement Council:

–ACC 3869A/1, Copies of Submission to Parliamentary Committee re Citizenship Right to Aborigines 1958;

–ACC 3869A/2, Copies of Submissions to Parliamentary Committee on Citizen Rights to Aborigines 1958.

SAWA, MN 585, Women's Service Guilds of Western Australia:

–ACC 2350A/76, Correspondence with other Western Australian Organisations 1953–1968;

–ACC 2530A/90, Correspondence with other Western Australian Organisations, 1961–65;

–ACC 2530A/66, Native Welfare and Strike by Aborigines in the Pilbara 1946;

–ACC 2530 A/56, Native Question 1934–61.

SAWA, AN 537, Royal Commissions:

ACC 2922, Royal Commission Appointed to Investigate, Report and Advise Upon Matters in Relation to the Condition and Treatment of Aborigines, 1935, ACC 1934/2, Transcripts of Evidence.

Secondary Sources

Anderson, W., *The Cultivation of Whiteness. Science, Health and Racial Destiny in Australia*, Melbourne University Press, Victoria, 2002.

Archer, L. J. (ed.), *Slavery and Other Forms of Unfree Labour*, Routledge, USA, 1988.

Attwood, B., *Rights For Aborigines*, Allen & Unwin, Sydney, 2003.

Attwood, B. and Markus, A., *The 1967 Referendum. Pace, Power and the Australian Constitution*, Aboriginal Studies Press, Canberra, 2007.

Attwood, B. and Markus, A., *The Struggle For Aboriginal Rights. A Documentary History*, Allen & Unwin, St Leonards, 1999.

Auty, K., *Black Glass. Western Australian Courts of Native Affairs 1936–54*, Fremantle Arts Centre Press, Fremantle, 2005.

Babre, J. W., *et al, Interpreting Women's Lives. Feminist Theory and Personal Narratives*, Indiana University Press, USA, 1989.

Bandler, F. and Fox, L. (eds), *The Time Was Ripe. A History of the Aboriginal–Australian Fellowship, 1956–1969,* Alternative Publishing Co–Op Ltd, New South Walews, 1983.

Barnett, M., *Empire of Humanity. A History of Humanitarianism*, Cornell University Press,

Ithaca, 2011.

Barnett, M. and Weiss, T. G., *Humanitarianism in Question: Politics, Power, Ethics*, Cornell University Press, USA, 2008.

Barnett, M., 'Humanitarianism Transformed', *Perspectives on Politics*, vol. 3, no. 4, December, 2005, pp. 723–40.

Bartrop, 'The Holocaust, the Aborigines, and the bureaucracy of destruction: an Australian dimension of genocide', *Journal of Genocide Research*, 3:1, 2001, pp. 75–87.

Barwick, D. and Stanner, W. E. H., 'Not By Eastern Windows Only: Anthropological Advise to Australian Governments in 1938', *Aboriginal History*, vol. 3, 1–2, 1979, pp. 37–53.

Behrendt, L., 'Consent in a (Neo) Colonial Society: Aboriginal Women as Sexual and Legal 'Other', *Australian Feminist Studies*, vol. 15, no. 33, 2000, pp. 353–67.

Behrendt, L., 'Aboriginal Women and the White Lies of the Feminist Movement: Implications For Aboriginal Women in Rights Discourse', *Australian Feminist Law Journal*, vol. 1, 1993, pp. 27–44.

Behrendt, L., 'As Good As It Gets or As Good As It Could Be? Benchmarking Human Rights in Australia', *Balayi: Culture, Law and Colonialism*, vol. 10, 2009, p. 313.

Berman, E. H., 'American Influence on African Education: The Role of the Phelps-Stokes Fund's Education Commissions', *Comparative Education Review*, 15, 1, June 1971, pp. 132–45.

Berndt, R. M. and C. H., *End of an Era. Aboriginal Labour in the Northern Territory*, Australian Institute of Aboriginal Studies, Canberra, 1987.

Berting, J. *et al.* (eds), Human Rights in a Pluralist World. Individuals and Collectivities, Meckler, Ltd, London, 1988.

Bishop, C., 'She Has the Native Interests Too Much At Heart': Annie Lock's Experiences As A Single, White, Female Missionary to Aborigines, 1903–1937', Barry, A. (ed.), *Evangelists of Empire?: Missionaries in Colonial History*, University of Melbourne eScholarship Research Centre, 2008.

Biskup, P., *Not Slaves Not Citizens: the Aboriginal Problem in Western Australia, 1898–1954*, University of Queensland Press, St Lucia, 1973.

Blackburn, K., 'White Agitation For An Aboriginal State In Australia, 1925–1929', *Australian Journal of Politics and History*, vol. 45, 2, 1999, pp. 157–80.

Brock, P., 'Aboriginal Families and the Law in the Era of Segregation and Assimilation, 1890s–1950s', Kirby, D. (ed.), *Sex Power and Justice Historical Perspectives of Law in Australia*, Oxford University Press, Melbourne, 1995, pp. 133–49.

Brown, M., *The Black Eureka*, Australasian Book Society, Sydney, 1976.

Brown, M., 'Fernando. The Story of an Aboriginal Prophet', *Aborigine Welfare Bulletin*, 4 (1), 1964.

Burton, A., *Burdens of History. British Feminists, Indian Women and Imperial Culture, 1965–1915*, The University of North Carolina Press, USA, 1994.

Bush, B., '"Britain's Conscience on Africa": white women, race and imperial politics in interwar Britain', Midgley, C. (ed.), *Gender and Imperialism*, UK, 1998, Manchester University Press, Manchester, pp. 200–23.

Bussey, G. and Tims, M., *Women's International League for Peace and Freedom, 1915–1965. A Record of Fifty Years' Work*, George Allen and Unwin Ltd, London, 1965.

Callaway, H., *Gender, Culture and Empire. European Women in Colonial Nigeria*, The

Macmillan Press, Ltd, London, 1987.

Carter, A., *Peace Movements. International Protest and World Politics Since 1945*, Longman, London, 1992.

Cell, J., 'Colonial Rule', Brown, J. *et al.* (eds), The Oxford History of the British Empire: Volume IV, The Twentieth Century, Oxford Scholarship Online, pp. 233–54.

Chappell, L. *et al.*, *The Politics of Human Rights in Australia*, Cambridge University Press, Cambridge, 2009.

Charlton, A., 'Racial Essentialism: A Mercurial Concept at the 1937 Canberra Conference of Commonwealth and State Aboriginal Authorities', *Journal of Australian Studies*, 26:75, pp. 33–41.

Chaudhuri, N. and Stroebel, M. (eds), *Western Women and Imperialism. Complicity and Resistance,* Indiana University Press, USA, 1992.

Cheater, C., 'Olive Pink and The Native Problem', *Bulletin of the Olive Pink Society*, 1 (2), 1989, pp. 4–8.

Chesterman, J. and Galligan, B., *Citizens Without Rights. Aborigines and Australian Citizenship*, Cambridge University Press, United Kingdom, 1997.

Chesterman, J., *Civil Rights. How Indigenous Australians Won Formal Equality*, University of Queensland Press, 2005.

Chesterman, J., 'Taking Civil Rights Seriously', *Australian Journal of Politics and History*, vol. 46, no. 4, 2000, pp. 497–509.

Chesterman, J., 'Defending Australia's Reputation. How Indigenous Australians Won Civil Rights. Part One', *Australian Historical Studies*, 116, 2001, pp. 20–39.

Chesterman, J., 'Defending Australia's Reputation. How Indigenous Australians Won Civil Rights. Part Two', *Australian Historical Studies*, vol. 32, 117, 2001, pp. 201–21.

Choo, C., *Mission Girls: Aboriginal Women on Catholic Missions in the Kimberley, Western Australia, 1900–1950*, University of Western Australia Press, Perth, 2001.

Claeys, G., *Imperial Sceptics: British Critics of Empire*, Cambridge University Press, Cambridge, 2010.

Clark, J., *Aborigines and Activism. Race, Aborigines and the Coming of the Sixties to Australia*, University of Western Australia Press, Western Australia, 2008.

Clohesy, L., 'Fighting the enemy within. Anti-communism and Aboriginal Affairs', *History Australia*, vol. 8, (2), 2011, pp. 128–52.

Cmiel, K., 'The Recent History of Human Rights', *American Historical Review*, vol. 109 (1), February 2004, pp. 117–35.

Coe, C., 'Educating an African Leadership: Achimota and the Teaching of African Culture in the Gold Coast', *Africa Today*, vol. 49, no. 3, fall 2002, pp. 23–44.

Cole, A., V. Haskins & F. Paisley (eds), *Uncommon Ground. White Women in Aboriginal History*, Aboriginal Studies Press, Canberra, 2005.

Coltheart, L., 'Citizens of the World: Jessie Street and International Feminism', *Hecate,* vol. 31 (1), 2005, pp. 182–94.

Coltheart, L. (ed.), *Jessie Street. A Revised Autobiography*, The Federation Press, Annandale, 2004.

Cowlishaw, G., 'Erasing Culture and Race: Practising 'self-determination'', *Oceania*, vol. 68, no. 3, March 1998, pp. 145–69.

Cripps, K., 'Understanding Indigenous Family Violence in the Context of a Human Rights Agenda', *Human Rights Defender*, 15 (3), 2006, pp. 3–5.

Cryle, M., 'A "Fantastic Adventure": Reading Christison of Lammermoor', McKenzie, F., 'Journeys Through Queensland History: Landscape, Place and Society', *Proceedings of the Professional Historians Association (Queensland) Conference*, Marking the Sesquicentenary of Queensland 1859–2009, Brisbane 3–4 September 2009, pp. 223–34.

Curthoys, A. and Markus, A. (eds), *Who Are Our Enemies? Racism and the Working Class in Australia*, Hale & Iremonger, Pty, Ltd, Sydney, 1978.

Curthoys, A. and Merritt, J. (eds), *Australia's First Cold War, 1945–1953, Society Communism and Culture*, George, Allen and Unwin, Sydney, 1984.

Curthoys, A. and Merritt, J. (eds), *Australia's First Cold War, 1945–1959. Better Dead Than Red*, Allen and Unwin, Sydney, 1986.

Dallas, K. M., Slavery in Australia, Convicts, Emigrants Aborigines', *Tasmanian Historical Research Association, Papers and Proceedings*, vol. 16, no. 2, 1968, pp. 61–76.

Davis, M., 'How Do Aboriginal Women Fare in Australian Democracy?', *Indigenous Law Bulletin*, 27, 2007.

Devereux, A., *Australia and the Birth of the International Bill of Human Rights 1946–1966*, The Federation Press, Annandale, 2005.

Dippie, B., *The Vanishing American. White Attitudes and US Policy*, University Press of Kansas, USA, 1982.

Duckham, I., 'Visionary, Vassal or Vandal? Rod Schenk—Missionary: A Case Study in Western Desert Missions', *Limina*, vol. 6, 2000, pp. 41–56.

Edwards, P., 'Mixed Metaphors: Other Mothers, Dangerous Daughters and the Rhetoric of Child Removal in Burma, Australia and IndoChina', *Balayi: Culture, Law and Colonialism*, vol. 6, 2004, pp. 41–61.

Elkins, C. and Pedersen, S. (eds), *Settler Colonialism in the Twentieth Century. Projects, Practices and Legacies*, Routledge, London, 2005.

Ellinghaus, K., *Taking Assimilation to Heart: Marriages of White Women and Indigenous Men in the US and Australia, 1887–1937*, University of Nebraska Press, Lincoln, 2006.

Ellinghaus, K., 'Absorbing the "Aboriginal problem": controlling interracial marriage in Australia in the late 19th and early 20th centuries', *Aboriginal History*, vol. 27, 2003, pp. 183–207.

Evans, R., 'Kings in Brass Crescents. Defining Aboriginal Labour Patterns in Colonial Queensland', Saunders, K. (ed.), *Indentured Labour in the British Empire, 1834–1920*, Croom Helm, Ltd, 1984, pp. 183–212.

Frances, R., *Selling Sex. A Hidden History of Prostitution*, University of New South Wales, Sydney, 2007.

Ganter, R., 'Living an Immoral Life: "coloured" women and the paternalistic state, *Hecate*, vol. 24, issue 1, 1998.

Garton, S., 'Sound Minds and Healthy Bodies: Re-Considering Eugenics in Australia, 1914–1940', *Australian Historical Studies*, vol. 26, no. 103, October, 1994, pp. 163–81.

Goodall, H., *Invasion to Embassy. Land in Aboriginal Politics in New South Wales, 1770–1992*, Allen and Unwin/Black Books, Sydney, 1996.

Gray, G., *A Cautious Silence: The Politics of Australian Anthropology*, Aboriginal Studies Press, Canberra, 2007.

Gray, G., '"You are...my anthropological children": AP Elkin, Ronald Berndt and Catherine Berndt, 1940–1956', *Aboriginal History*, vol. 29, 2005, pp. 77–106.

Bibliography

Gray, G., '"Piddington's Indiscretion": Ralph Piddington, The Australian National Research Council and Academic Freedom', *Oceania*, 64:3, 1994, pp. 217–245.

Gray, G., 'Dislocating the Self, anthropological fieldwork in the Kimberley, Western Australia, 1934–1936', *Aboriginal History*, vol. 26, 2002, pp. 23–50.

Gray, G., 'Abrogating Responsibility?: Applied anthropology, Vesteys, Aboriginal labour, 1944–1946', *Australian Aboriginal Studies*, no. 2, 2001, pp. 27–39.

Gray, G., 'From Nomadism to Citizenship: A.P. Elkin and Aboriginal Advancement', Nicolas Peterson and Will Sanders (eds), *Citizenship and Indigenous Australians: Changing Conceptions and Possibilities*, Cambridge University Press, United Kingdom, 1998, pp. 55–76.

Gray, S., *The Protectors. A Journey through Whitefella Past*, Allen & Unwin, Sydney, 2011.

Grimhsaw, P. and Evans, J., 'Colonial Women on Intercultural Frontiers: Rosa Campbell Praed, Mary Bundock and Katie Langloh Parker', *Australian Historical Studies*, no.106, April, 1996, pp. 79–95.

Haebich, A., *For Their Own Good. Aborigines and Government in the South West of Western Australia, 1900–1940*, University of Western Australian Press, Perth, 1992.

Haebich, A., *Broken Circles. Fragmenting Indigenous Families, 1800–2000*, Fremantle Arts Centre Press, Fremantle, 2000.

Haebich, A., *Spinning the Dream. Assimilation in Australia, 1950–1970*, Fremantle Arts Centre Press, Fremantle, 2008.

Haebich, A., '"Between knowing and not knowing": Public knowledge of the Stolen Generations', *Aboriginal History*, vol. 25, 2001, pp. 70–90.

Haggis, J., 'Gendering Colonialism or Colonising Gender? Recent Women's Studies Approaches to White Women and the History of British Colonialism', *Women's Studies International Forum*, vol. 13, nos. 1–2, 1990, pp. 105–15.

Harper, N. and Sissons, D., *Australia and the United Nations*, Manhattan Publishing Co, New York, 1959.

Harris, J., *One Blood. 200 Years of Aboriginal Encounter with Christianity: A Story of Hope*, Albatross Books, Pty Ltd, Australia, 1990.

Haskins, V. K., *One Bright Spot*, Palgrave Macmillan, New York, 2005.

Haskins, V., '"Lovable Natives" and "Tribal Sisters": Feminism, Maternalism, and the Campaign for Aboriginal Citizenship in New South Wales in Late 1930s', *Hecate*, vol. 24 (2), 1998, pp. 8–21.

Haskins, V. K., 'Domestic Service and Frontier Feminism. The Call for a Woman Visitor to "Half-Caste" Girls and Women in Domestic Service, Adelaide, 1925–1928, *Frontiers*, vol. 28, nos. 1 & 2, 2007, pp. 124–64.

Haskins, V. K, '"A Better Chance?" Sexual Abuse and the Apprenticeship of Aboriginal Girls under the NSW Aborigines Protection Board', *Aboriginal History*, vol. 28, 2004, pp. 33–58.

Hasluck, P., *Black Chattels: A Survey of Native Policy in Western Australia, 1829–1897*, Melbourne University Press, Victoria, 1942.

Hasluck, P., *Shades of Darkness. Aboriginal Affairs, 1925–1965*, Melbourne University Press, Victoria, 1988.

Holland, A., 'Wives and Mothers Like Ourselves? Exploring White Women's Intervention in the Politics of Race, 1920s–1940s', *Australian Historical Studies*, 32, 117, 2001, pp. 292–310.

Holland, A., 'The Campaign for Women Protectors: Gender, Race and Frontier between the Wars', *Australian Feminist Studies*, vol. 16, no. 34, 2001, pp. 27–42

Holland, A. and Brooks, B., *Rethinking the Racial Moment. Essays on the Colonial Encounter*, Cambridge Scholars Publishing, Newcastle upon Tyne, 2011.

Holland, A., 'To Eliminate Colour Prejudice: The WCTU and Decolonisation in Australia', *Journal of Religious History*, vol. 32, no. 2, 2008, pp. 256–76.

Holland, A., 'Compelling Evidence. Marriage, Colonialism and the Question of Indigenous Rights'; *Women's History Review* , vol. 18 , (1), November 2009, pp. 121–36.

Holland, A., 'Colour not Civilisation: Contesting Boundaries of Citizenship and Rights in Inter-War Australia', in L. Boucher, J. Carey & K. Ellinghaus (eds), *Historicizing Whiteness: Transnational Perspectives on the Construction of Identity*, RMIT Press, Melbourne, 2007, pp. 89–97.

Holland, A., 'Feminism, Colonialism and Aboriginal Workers: an Anti-Slavery Crusade', Aboriginal Workers, *Labour History*, no. 69, November, 1995, pp. 52–64.

Horton, J., 'The Case of Elsie Barrett: Aboriginal Women, sexuality and the Victorian Board for the Protection of Aborigines', *Journal of Australian Studies*, vol. 34, no. 1, March 2010, pp. 1–18.

Hochschild, A., *King Leopold's Ghost. A Story of Greed, Terror and Heroism in Colonial Africa*, Houghton Mifflin Company, New York, 1998.

Hunt, S.-J., *Spinifex and Hessian: Women's Lives in North–Western Australia 1860–1900*, University of Western Australia Press, Nedlands, 1986.

Hyam, R., 'Bureaucracy and Trusteeship in the Colonial Empire', Brown, J. *et al.* (eds), *The Oxford History of the British Empire: The Twentieth Century*, Oxford Scholarship Online, pp. 256–79.

Jackson, M. (ed.), *Infanticide: historical perspectives on child murder and concealment, 1550–2000*, Ashgate, Aldershot, 2002.

Jacobs, M., *White Mother to A Dark Race. Settler Colonialism, Maternalism and the Removal of Indigenous Children in the American West and Australia, 1880–1940*, University of Nebraska Press, Lincoln, 2009.

Jacobs, P., *Mister Neville A Biography*, Fremantle Arts Centre Press, Fremantle, 1990.

Jacobs, P., 'Science and Veiled Assumptions: Miscegenation in Western Australia, 1930–1937', *Australian Aboriginal Studies*, no. 2, 1986, pp. 15–22.

Kerin, R., *Doctor Do-Good. Charles Duguid and Aboriginal Advancement, 1930s–1970s*, Australian Scholarly Publishing, Melbourne, 2011.

Kerin, R., 'Sydney James Cook/Duguid and the importance of "being Aboriginal"', *Aboriginal History*, vol. 29, 2005, pp. 46–63.

Kim, J., *A Fatal Conjunction. Two Laws Two Cultures*, The Federation Press, Annandale, 2004.

Koven, S. and Michel, S. (eds), *Mothers of a New World. Maternalist Politics and The Origins of the Welfare State*, Routledge, London, 1993.

Koven, S., *Slumming: Sexual and Social Politics in Victorian London*, Princeton University Press, Princeton, 2004.

Lake, M., 'The Politics of Respectability: Identifying the Masculinist Context', *Historical Studies*, 22, no. 86, April 1986, pp. 116–131.

Lake, M., 'Feminism and the Gendered Politics of Anti-Racism, Australia 1927–1957:

From Maternal Protectionism to Leftist Assimilationism', *Australian Historical Studies*, 110, 1998, pp. 91–108.

Lake, M., 'Citizenship as Non-Discrimination: Acceptance or Assimilationism? Political Logic and Emotional Investment in Campaigns for Aboriginal Rights in Australia, 1940 to 1970', *Gender and History*, vol. 13, no. 3, November 2001, pp. 566–92.

Lake, M., 'Childbearers as Rights-Bearers: Feminist Discourse on the Rights of Aboriginal and non-Aboriginal Mothers in Australia, 1920–50', *Women's History Review*, 8:2, 1999, pp. 347–63.

Lake, M. and Reynolds, H., *Drawing the Global Colour Line. White Men's Countries and the Question of Racial Equality*, Melbourne University Press, Melbourne, 2008.

Lester, A., 'Colonial Networks, Australian Humanitarianism and the History Wars', *Geographical Research*, 44 (3), 2006, pp. 229–41.

Lester, A. and Dussart, F., *Colonization and the Origins of Humanitarian Governance: Protecting Aborigines Across the Nineteenth Century British Empire*, Cambridge University Press, Cambridge, 2014.

Lester, A. and Skinner, R., 'Humanitarianism and Empire: New Research Agendas', *The Journal of Imperial and Commonwealth History*, 40 (5), 2012, pp. 729–747.

Levine, P. (ed.), *Gender and Empire*, Oxford University Press, New York, 2004.

Lewis, G. K., *Slavery, Imperialism and Freedom. Studies in English Radical Thought*, Monthly Review Press, London, 1978.

Loos, N. and Keast, R., 'The Radical Promise: The Aboriginal Christian Co-operative Movement', *Australian Historical Studies*, no. 99, October, 1992, pp. 286–301.

Maccallum, A., 'The compatibility of Hasluck's assimilation policy and mining on aboriginal reserves in the northern territory: an illusion?', *Melbourne Historical Journal*, vol. 38, 2010, pp. 89–111.

Maddison, S., 'Indigenous autonomy matters: what's wrong with the Australian government's "intervention" in Aboriginal communities', *Australian Journal of Human Rights*, vol. 14 (1), 2008, pp. 41–61.

Marcus, J. (ed.), *First In Their Field. Women and Australian Anthropology*, Melbourne University Press, Victoria, 1993.

Marcus, J., *The Indomitable Miss Pink. A Life in Anthropology*, UNSW Press, Sydney, 2001.

Markus, A., 'Talka Longa Mouth', Curthoys, Ann and Markus, Andrew (eds), *Who Are Our Enemies? Racism and the Australian Working Class*, Hale and Iremonger, Sydney, 1978, pp. 138–60.

Markus, A., 'William Cooper and the 1937 Petition to the King', *Aboriginal History*, vol. 7, 1983, pp. 46–60.

Markus, A., *Governing Savages*, Allen & Unwin, Sydney, 1990.

McClintock, A., *Imperial Leather. Race, Gender and Sexuality in the Colonial Contest*, Routledge, Great Britain, 1995.

McLisky, C., '"Due Observance of Justice, and the Protection of their Rights": Philanthropy, Humanitarianism and Moral Purpose in the Aborigines Protection Society circa 1837 and its portrayal in Australian Historiography, 1883–2003', *Limina*, vol. 11, 2005, pp. 57–66.

McGlade, H., *Our Greatest Challenge. Aboriginal Children and Human Rights*, Aboriginal Studies Press, Canberra, 2012.

McCorkindale, I., *Forward in Faith. An historical Record of the Woman's Christian Temperance*

Union, 1947–1973, Woman's Christian Temperance Union, Melbourne, 1975.

McCorquodale, J., *Aborigines and The Law: A Digest,* Aboriginal Studies Press, Canberra, 1987.

McGrath, A., *'Born in the Cattle'.* Aborigines in Cattle Country, Allen & Unwin, Sydney, 1987.

McGrath, A., 'Consent, Marriage and Colonialism: Indigenous Australian Women and Colonizer Marriages, *Journal of Colonialism and Colonial History*, 6:3, 2005.

McGrath, P. F. and Brooks, D., 'Their Darkest Hour: the films and photographs of William Grayden and the history of the 'Warburton Range Controvesy' of 1957', *Aboriginal History*, vol. 34, 2010, pp. 115–141.

McGregor, R., *Indifferent Inclusion. Aboriginal People and the Australian Nation*, Aboriginal Studies Press, Canberra, 2011.

McGregor, R., *Imagined Destinies. Aboriginal Australians and the Doomed Race Theory, 1880–1939*, Melbourne University Press, Victoria, 1997.

McGregor, R., 'Assimilationists Contest Assimilation: T. G. H. Strehlow and A. P. Elkin on Aboriginal Policy', *Journal of Australian Studies*, 75, 2002, pp. 43–50.

McGregor, R., 'The Clear Categories of Olive Pink', *Oceania* 65, 1994, pp. 4–17.

McGregor, R., 'Representations of the Half-Caste in the Australian Scientific Literature of the 1930s, *Journal of Australian Studies*, no. 36, 1993, pp. 51–64.

McGregor, R., 'Avoiding Aborigines: Paul Hasluck and the Northern Territory Welfare Ordinance, 1953', *Australian Journal of Politics and History*, vol. 51, no. 4, December 2005, pp. 513–529.

McGregor, Russell, 'Wards, words and citizens: A.P. Elkin and Paul Hasluck on assimilation', *Oceania*, vol. 69, no. 4, June 1999, pp. 243–59.

McNab, D., 'Herman Merivale and the Native Question, 1837–1861', *Albion: A Quarterly Journal Concerned with British Studies*, vol. 9, no. 4, Winter, 1977, pp. 359–84.

Midgley, C., *Women Against Slavery. The British Campaigns, 1780–1870,* Routledge, London, 1992.

Midgley, C. (ed.), *Gender and Imperialism*, Manchester University Press, Manchester, 1998.

Morgan, M., *A Drop In A Bucket. The Mount Margaret Story*, United Aborigines' Mission, Victoria, 1986.

Mukherjee, S., 'Using the Legislative Assembly For Social Reform: The Sarda Act of 1929', *South Asia Research*, vol. 26 (3), 2008, pp. 219–33.

O'Brien, A., *God's Willing Workers: Women and Religion in Australia*, UNSW Press, Sydney, 2005.

Paddle, S., 'The Limits of Sympathy: International Feminists and the Chinese "Slave Girl" Campaigns of the 1920s and 1930s', *Journal of Colonialism and Colonial History*, 4:3, 2003.

Paisley, F., *The Lone Protestor. AM Fernando in Australia and Europe*, Aboriginal Studies Press, Canberra, 2012.

Paisley, F., 'An Echo of Black Slavery: Emancipation, Forced Labour and Australia in 1933', Australian Historical Studies, 45:1, pp. 103–25.

Paisley, F., '"Don't Tell England!": Women of Empire Campaign to Change Aboriginal Policy in Australia Between the Wars', *Lilith*, no. 8, Summer, 1993, pp. 139–52.

Paisley, F., *Loving Protection? Australian Feminism and Aboriginal Women's Rights, 1919–1939*, Melbourne University Press, Carlton, 2000.

Paisley, F., 'Australian Aboriginal: Activism in Interwar Britain and Europe: Anthony Martin Fernando', *History Compass*, 7/3, 2009, pp. 701–18.

Pascoe, Peggy, *Relations of Rescue: The Search for Female Moral Authority in the American West, 1874–1939*, Oxford University Press, Oxford, 1990.

Pascoe, P., *What Comes Naturally. Miscegenation Law and the Making of Race in America*, Oxford University Press, Oxford, 2010.

Pearson, N., *Up From the Mission. Selected Writings*, Black Inc, Melbourne, 2009.

Pedersen, S., *Eleanor Rathbone and the Politics of Conscience*, Yale University Press, New Haven 2004.

Pedersen, S., 'Metaphors of the Schoolroom: Women Working the Mandates System of the League of Nations', *History Workshop Journal*, 66, 2008, pp. 189–207.

Pedersen, S., 'The Maternalist Moment in British Colonial Policy: The Controversy over "Child Slavery" in Hong Jong, 1917–1941', *Past and Present*, 171, May 2001, pp. 161–202.

Pedersen, S., 'National Bodies, Unspeakable Acts: The Sexual Politics of Colonial Policy-Making', *The Journal of Modern History*, vol. 63, no. 4, December 1991, pp. 647–80.

Petersen, N. (compiler), *Donald Thomson in Arnhem Land*, Currey O'Neil Ross Pty Ltd, 1983.

Porter, B., *Critics of Empire. British Radicals and the Imperial Challenge*, I. B. Taurus, London, 2008.

Porter, B., *The Absent-Minded Imperialists: Empire, Society and Culture in Britain*, Oxford University Press, 2006.

Raynes, C., *The Last Protector. The Illegal Removal of Aboriginal Children from their Parents in South Australia*, Wakefield Press, South Australia, 2009.

Reynolds, H., *This Whispering in Our Heart*, Allen and Unwin, Sydney, 1998.

Reynolds, W., 'Rethinking the Joint Project: Australia's Bid For Nuclear Weapons, 1945–1960', *The Historical Journal*, vol. 41, no. 3, September 1998, pp. 853–73.

Robinson, S, *Something Like Slavery – Queensland's Aboriginal Child Workers, 1842–1945*, Australian Scholarly Publishing, 2008.

Robinson, S., '"We Do Not Want One Who Is Too Old': Aboriginal Child Domestic Servants in Late 19th and Early 20th Century Queensland", *Aboriginal History*, vol. 27, 2003, pp. 162–182.

Roe, M., 'A Model Aboriginal State', *Aboriginal History*, 10, (1), 1986, pp. 40–4

Rowley, C. D., *Recovery: The Politics of Aboriginal Reform*, Penguin Books, Australia, 1986.

Rowse, T., 'The Indigenous Sector', in D. Austin-Broos and G. Macdonald (eds), *Culture, Economy and Governance in Aboriginal Australia*, Academy of the Social Sciences and the Department of Anthropology, University of Sydney Press, Sydney, 2005, pp. 207–223.

Rowse, T., *White Flour, White Power. From Rations to Citizenship in Central Australia*, Cambridge University Press, Cambridge, 1998.

Rowse, T., *Contesting Assimilation*, API Network, Western Australia, 2005.

Silverstein, Ben, 'Indirect Rule in Australia: A Case Study of Settler-Colonial Difference', Fiona Bateman and Lionel Pilkington (eds), *Studies in Settler Colonialism. Politics, Identity and Culture*, Palgrave Macmillan, United Kingdom, 2011, pp. 90-105.

Sinha, M., *Specters of Mother India. The Global Restructuring of an Empire*, Duke University Press, Durham, 2006.

Spencer, P. and Wollman, H., 'Nationalism and the problem of humanitarian interven-tion', *Australian Journal of Human Rights*, vol. 13, (1), 2007, pp. 79–111.

Stanner, W. E. H. and Barwick, D., 'Not By Eastern Windows Only: Anthropological Advice to Australian Governments in 1938, *Aboriginal History*, vol. 3, nos 1–2, 1979, pp. 37–60.

Stepan, N., *The Idea of Race in Science. Great Britain 1800–1960*, Macmillan Press, Ltd, London, 1982.

Stepan, N., *'The Hour of Eugenics'. Race, Gender and Nation in Latin America*, Cornell University Press, London, 1991.

Stoler, A. L., 'Making Empire Respectable: the Politics of Race and Sexual Morality in 20th-Century Colonial Cultures', *American Ethnologist*, vol. 16, no. 4, 1989, pp. 634–60.

Street, J., *Truth or Repose*. Australasian Book Society, Sydney, 1966.

Sutton, P., *The Politics of Aboriginal Suffering. Indigenous Australia and the end of the Liberal Consensus*, Melbourne University Press, Melbourne, 2009.

Taffe, S., *Black and White Together. FCAATSI: The Federal Council for the Advancement of Aborigines and Torres Strait Islanders, 1958–1973*, University of Queensland Press, 2005.

Taffe, S., 'Shirley Andrews. An Architect of the national Aboriginal civil rights move-ment, 1952–1968', *History Australia*, vol. 8, (2), 2011, pp. 153–76.

Tay, A. E.–S., *Human Rights for Australia. A Survey of Literature and Developments and a Select Annotated Bibliography of Recent Literature in Australia and Abroad*, Australian Government Publishing Service, Canberra, 1986.

Torvognick, M., *Gone Primitive. Savage Intellects, Modern Lives*, The University of Chicago Press, Chicago, 1990.

Tyrrell, I., *Woman's World Woman's Empire. The Woman's Christian Temperance Union in International Perspective, 1880–1930*, The University of North Carolina Press, United States, 1991.

Victorian Aborigines Advancement League, *Victims or Victors? The Story of the Victorian Aborigines Advancement League,* Hyland House Publishing Ltd, Victoria, 1985.

Ware, V., *Beyond the Pale. White Women, Racism and History*, Verso, London, 1992.

Watson, D., *Brian Fitzpatrick. A Radical Life*, Hale and Iremonger, Sydney, 1979.

Weiss, T., G., *Humanitarian Intervention*, Polity Press, Cambridge, 2012.

Welch, A. R., 'Aboriginal Education as Internal Colonialism: The Schooling of an Indigenous Minority in Australia', *Comparative Education*, vol. 24 (2), 1988, pp. 203–15.

Whitlam, G., *The Whitlam Government, 1972–1975*, Viking, 1986.

Whittall, D., 'Creating Black Places in Imperial London: The League of Coloured Peoples and Aggrey House, 1931–1943', *The London Journal*, vol. 36, no. 3, November 2011, pp. 225–46.

Wilson, B. and O'Brien, J., '"To infuse an universal terror": a reappraisal of the Coniston killings', *Aboriginal History*, vol. 27, 2003, pp. 59–78.

Wilson, R. A. and Brown, R. D., *Humanitarianism and Suffering. The Mobilisation of Empathy*, Cambridge University Press, Cambridge, 2009.

Woollacott, A., *To Try Her Fortune in London: Australian Women, Colonialism and Modernity*, Oxford University Press, Oxford, 2001.

Wright, H., 'Protecting the National Interest: The Labor Government and the Reform of Australia's Colonial Policy, 1942–45', *Labour History*, no. 82, May 2002, pp. 65–79.

Newspapers

The Adelaide Advertiser
The Australian Abo Call
The Bulletin
Communist Review
Smiths Weekly
Sydney Morning Herald
The Age
The Illustrated London News
The Melbourne Herald
The Northern Standard
The West Australian
The Times
Worker's Weekly
Tribune

Theses

Cole, A., The Institutionalisation of Aboriginal Children in Western Australia During the 1930s: Some Feminist Questions, BA Honours, University of Western Australia, September 1992.

Cheater, C., Argonauts of the Primitive World. A Social History of Angl-Australian Anthropology 1850–1950, PhD, University of New South Wales, 1993.

Jordan, D., Conflict in the unions: The Communist Party of Australia, Politics and the Trade Union Movement, 1945–1960, PhD, School of Social Sciences and Psychology, Faculty of Arts, Education and Human Development, Victoria University, 2011.

Tamura, K., The Craft Industry and Women in Ernabella, MA, Australian National University, 1985.

Wanken, H. M., 'Women's Sphere' and Indian Reform: The Women's National Indian Association, 1879–1901, PhD, Marquette University, Wisconsin, 1981.

INDEX

www.ingramcontent.com/pod-product-compliance
Lightning Source LLC
Chambersburg PA
CBHW020330270326
41926CB00007B/121